D0057359

Tuscany & Umbria

Alex Leviton, Josephine Quintero,
Rachel Suddart, Richard Watkins

Contents

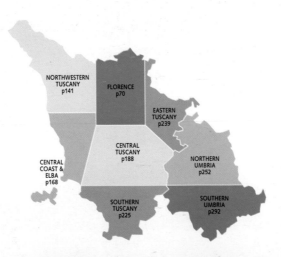

NORTHWESTERN TUSCANY p141

FLORENCE p70

EASTERN TUSCANY p239

CENTRAL TUSCANY p188

NORTHERN UMBRIA p252

CENTRAL COAST & ELBA p168

SOUTHERN TUSCANY p225

SOUTHERN UMBRIA p292

Lonely Planet books provide independent advice. Lonely Planet does not accept advertising in guidebooks, nor do we accept payment in exchange for listing or endorsing any place or business. Lonely Planet writers do not accept discounts or payments in exchange for positive coverage of any sort.

Le pubblicazioni Lonely Planet provvedono consigli indipendenti. Lonely Planet non accetta nelle sue guide né inserzioni pubblicitarie né compensi per aver elencato o approvato qualsiasi luogo o impresa. Gli autori delle guide Lonely Planet non accettano sconti o pagamenti in cambio di recensioni favorevoli di qualsiasi tipo.

Destination: Tuscany & Umbria

Tuscany and Umbria offer the quintessential Italian experience, from rolling green hills bedecked with fertile vineyards and olive groves to majestic Renaissance cities overflowing with some of the world's greatest art treasures. Florence, with its peerless array of museums, galleries and churches is the highlight for most visitors, while cities such as Pisa, home of the famous Leaning Tower, Orvieto with its spectacular Duomo, and Arezzo with its sublime frescoes, are not to be missed.

The land of Dante, Da Vinci, Michelangelo and Botticelli, ancient homeland of the Etruscans, and essential port of call for 19th-century Grand Tourists, Tuscany has never lost its unique charm for foreign visitors. Its countryside is legendary, and Il Chianti especially entices a constant stream of tourists to sample its fine wines and explore its picturesque hill towns. Elsewhere, colourful festivals and contests spring up throughout the year, many exercising the age-old neighbourhood rivalries of the once fiercely independent city-states, and giving the locals a chance to parade in fancy dress.

Though not widely regarded as a beach-holiday destination, Tuscany does have a long coastline; elegant Viareggio remains popular with Italians, while the island of Elba, with its clean waters and white sands, has exploded in popularity in recent years.

Umbria, known as the 'Green Heart of Italy', is a walker's and cyclist's paradise, with large swathes of verdant countryside, still largely untouched by the commercialism apparent in parts of its more famous neighbour. For those looking to get off the beaten track, the wild Valnerina region is hard to beat. You could also choose to pay your respects to St Francis and Giotto with a visit to the renowned Basilica in Assisi.

JON DAVISON

Both Tuscany and Umbria have rich traditions of feasts and festivals, and there always seems to be something going on somewhere. High points include Arezzo's **Giostra del Saracino** (p244), a flamboyant medieval joust, Cortona's annual crossbow competition, the **Giostra dell'Archidado** (p250) and the **Festa di San Francesco** (p284), a major religious holiday taking place in Assisi in October.

The regions also host a wide range of music festivals, including Spoleto's month-long **Festival dei Due Mondi** (p297), attracting artists from around the world, the free **Arezzo Wave festival** (p244) and Perugia's **Sagra Musicale Umbra** (p260), an important classical music festival.

DALLAS STRIBLEY

Children on the confetti-strewn street at Viareggio's colourful **carnevale** (p160)

Masks on sale for the **carnevale** festivities in Florence (p112)

RUSSELL MOUNTFORD

Historical procession in Siena's spectacular **Il Palio** horse race (p198)

DAVID TOMLIN

MARTIN HUGHES

Contemporary dining in Florence (p117)

Interior of a Norcineria, **Norcia** (p299)

ALAN BENSON

DOUG MCKINLAY

Bottles of locally produced,
world-famous **Chianti** (p135)

HIGHLIGHTS Food & Wine

Tuscans and Umbrians love to cook; from a simple *bruschetta* (grilled bread) to dishes using the rare and elusive *tartufo nero* (black truffle), the allure of food draws Italians and foreigners alike. For a truly unique gastronomic adventure, visit during festival time when you'll experience the broad repertoire of Tuscan and Umbrian fare (p56). The regions' wines are well known outside Italy for their consistent exceptional quality. Visit **Montalcino** (p214), near Siena, for a taste of its esteemed Brunello wine or **Montepulciano** (p219) for its distinctive Vino Nobile, and **Orvieto's** (p313) white Classico is a must try.

Tuscany and Umbria have an embarrassment of riches when it comes to art. Tuscany, after all, is the region that gave rise to the Renaissance, while Umbria has a distinctive artistic heritage of its own. Florence is the place to begin; from the unconventional and much-traversed **Ponte Vecchio** (p104) to the grand **Palazzo del Bargello** (p90), the city is a veritable treasure-trove. Masaccio's glorious frescoes in the **Cappella Brancacci** (p107) are also not to be missed. No art-lover should bypass Piero della Francesca's wonderful fresco cycle in **Arezzo** (p241), **Orvieto's** elaborate cathedral (p315) or Giotto's frescoes in the Basilica at **Assisi** (p281).

BETHUNE CARMICHAEL

The unrivalled collections of the **Uffizi gallery**, Florence (p94)

Detail of ceiling fresco in the **Basilica di San Lorenzo** in Florence (p98)

HANNAH LEVY

The **Duomo**, Florence (p86)

JON DA

JULIET COOMBE.

The **Giardino di Boboli** (Boboli Garden; p105) was created in the mid-16th century around
Palazzo Pitti in Florence (p104)

MARTIN HUGHES

Statue in the **Palazzo del
Bargello**, Florence (p90)

Detail from the **Battistero door** on Piazza di
San Giovanni in Florence (p89)

HANNAH LEVY

These regions are very ancient lands, once ruled over by the Etruscan civilisation (p20) and the Roman Empire, and much still remains to be seen and discovered. Just north of Florence, you can see Etruscan tombs, and Volterra was one of the largest of the Etruscan settlements, today hosting the vast **Museo Etrusco Guarnacci** (p212), as well as an Etruscan necropolis. More Etruscan tombs can be visited in the countryside around **Cortona** (p249), while the Museo dell'Accademia Etrusca in that town holds an impressive collection of Etruscan finds.

Arezzo's Roman amphitheatre (p243) is worth a quick visit, while **Lago di Trasimeno** (p266), the site of one of history's most famous battles between the Romans and Hannibal, is still an evocative place to soak up the past.

BETHUNE CARMICHAEL

The Roman theatre in **Volterra**, which also includes a Roman bath (p213)

Ancient Etruscan tombs at the **Necropolis of San Rocco** (p237)

DIANA MAYF

The **Zona Archeologica** in Fiesole includes a theatre, Etruscan temple and baths (p133)

JULIA WILKIN

Getting Started

Tuscany and Umbria offer some of the most diverse and rewarding landscapes in Italy. Tuscany has been on the international tourist trail since the days of the Grand Tour in the 18th century, while its neighbour, largely rural Umbria, has only been 'discovered' by foreign visitors in recent years and still sees only a fraction of the numbers that swarm around Tuscany.

Florence is one of the main entry points, and this treasure house of art should not be missed. The Chianti region, world-famous for its wines, is also high on most visitors' lists, while cities such as Pisa, with its breathtaking Campo dei Miracoli, Siena and Orvieto are all hugely popular. Having said that, there are plenty of places to get off the beaten track, such as the little-explored Casentino region in eastern Tuscany, the spectacular Garfagnana in the northwest, or southern Umbria.

As you would expect, Florence is, by far, the busiest and most expensive place to stay, though there are still economical options around if you look hard enough. Other places on the well-trodden tourist-trail tend to be relatively pricey too; Chianti, for example, has a paucity of budget accommodation. The smaller towns and less-visited rural areas tend to be significantly cheaper.

All main towns are easily reached by train or bus, but to explore the countryside in any depth you will need your own transport.

DID YOU KNOW?
More than 70% of tourists visiting Umbria are from other parts of Italy.

WHEN TO GO

Tuscany and Umbria attract visitors throughout the year, though the busiest time is between May and September when you will certainly need to book accommodation in advance, at least in the main tourist centres. August is best avoided; the weather tends to be humid and clammy, especially inland, and many Italians take their holidays at this time, closing up their businesses and adding to the already lengthy queues for tourist

DON'T LEAVE HOME WITHOUT...

- A small backpack with a lock
- Mosquito repellent
- A small pair of binoculars
- Sturdy walking shoes
- An Italian phrasebook
- A Swiss Army knife (including corkscrew)
- An adaptor plug for electrical appliances
- Waterproof and thermal clothing for hiking
- A portable clothesline and travel iron
- At least one set of smart casual clothes; Italians like to dress up when they go out, and jeans and T-shirts just won't do in many restaurants, clubs or other nightspots. Note that churches will often refuse admittance to the skimpily dressed.
- A valid visa; although EU citizens are free to stay as long as they wish, citizens of the USA, Canada, Australia and New Zealand are limited to 90-day visits. Other nationals should contact the Italian embassy in their countries for details of visa requirements.

See Climate Charts (p324) for more information.

attractions. The coastal resorts in particular are often filled to capacity. The best time to visit is in the low season, from March to early May and late September to October, when the weather is usually pleasantly warm, prices are lower and there are fewer tourists. Be aware, though, that definitions of 'low' and 'high' season are mutable and vary from hotel to hotel.

The Vallombrosa and Camaldoli forests and especially the Apuane Alps can be a real relief from the heat – although even here you can easily strike very hot weather. The Alps also happen to be the wettest zone in Tuscany, receiving up to 3000mm of rainfall a year.

Temperatures can reach a sweltering 35°C at the height of summer, and rarely dip below 12°C in spring and autumn. Winter temperatures average at around 6°C to 10°C, slightly higher on the coast, but snowfalls are common in inland hilly areas.

You may prefer to organise your trip or itinerary to coincide with one or more of the many festivals that bedeck the Tuscan and Umbrian calendars, including such unmissable events as the Palio in Siena, the Giostra del Saracino in Arezzo or the Sagra Musicale Umbra in Perugia. To help start planning around such events, see Top Tens later in this chapter and relevant sections in the main text.

COSTS

Tuscany's popularity makes it expensive, especially in the cities, while Umbria's growing international profile has also pushed up prices. As you might expect, Florence is the place that will empty your pockets the quickest. A double room in a three-star hotel will cost anything from around €90 upwards while you'll pay around €16 for a dorm bed. In smaller towns you can expect a decent standard of accommodation from about €60. A three-course meal with wine will likely set you back roughly €30 per person, but of course, cheaper options are always available, whether they be pizzas, which cost as little as €4, light pasta dishes or a variety of filling rolls and sandwiches.

Public transport in the region is very economical; one way from Florence to Arezzo by train, for example, will cost only €4.85. Museums cost between €3 and €9.

Ways to Save

If possible, avoid paying for breakfast at your hotel; you'll get much better value at a local café. Stand at the bar to drink your coffee or eat your croissant, as prices can double, or even triple, if you sit down and are served at a table.

Read the fine print on menus (usually posted outside eating establishments) to check the *coperto* (cover charge) and *servizio* (service fee).

Check museums for free or discounted entrance fees; EU citizens under 18 or over 65 often get in free, while showing a student card can get you a discount. Look out too for free days – ask at the tourist office.

If you're staying for a while, consider purchasing weekly or monthly bus passes.

TRAVEL LITERATURE

Tuscany has been a favourite subject for writers for centuries, and whether you're looking for history, literature or populist travelogue, you'll be spoilt for choice. Umbria, on the other hand, is only beginning to attract international attention, although some titles are appearing. We recommend:

The Decameron (Giovanni Boccaccio) Medieval Florentine society comes vividly to life in these humorous and bawdy tales, a classic of European literature, set during the Black Death of 1348.

LONELY PLANET INDEX

Litre of gas/petrol
€1.10

Litre of water
€0.60

Bottle of Peroni beer
€1.50

Souvenir T-shirt
€15

Pizza
€6

HOW MUCH?

Cappuccino
€1.10

Gelato
€2

One night in a hostel
€20

One night at a 3-star hotel
€60

Local phone-call
€0.20

A Room with a View (EM Forster) A comedy of manners exploring the emotional awakening of a prim young English lady as she encounters the vitality, beauty and passion of Florence.
Where Angels Fear to Tread (EM Forster) Another 'clash-of-cultures' tale, telling the tragic story of Lilia, who defies family and class convention to marry a young Italian gigolo in 'Monteriano', a fictionalised version of San Gimignano.
Under the Tuscan Sun (Frances Mayes) A leading example of the popular expat-literature genre, following Mayes' experience of restoring an old villa in the Tuscan countryside, and her musings on local life, cuisine and history.

TOP TENS

FESTIVALS & EVENTS

- Carnevale (Viareggio) February/March (p160)
- Scoppio del Carro (Florence) Easter Sunday (p112)
- Corsa dei Ceri (Gubbio) 15 May (p273)
- Giostra dell'Archidado (Cortona) June (p250)
- Festival dei due Mondi (Spoleto) June/July (p297)

- Estate Fiesolana (Fiesole) June–August (p133)
- Il Palio (Siena) late June/early July (p198)
- Giostra del Saracino (Arezzo) June & September (p244)
- Sagra Musicale Umbra (Perugia) September (p260)
- Festa di San Francesco (Assisi) 3–4 October (p284)

FILMS

- *A Room With A View* (1986) Director: James Ivory
- *Romeo & Juliet* (1968) Director: Franco Zeffirelli
- *Life is Beautiful* (1998) Director: Roberto Benigni
- *Tea With Mussolini* (1999) Director: Franco Zeffirelli
- *Stealing Beauty* (1996) Director: Bernardo Bertolucci

- *The English Patient* (1996) Director: Anthony Minghella
- *The Talented Mr Ripley* (1999) Director: Anthony Minghella
- *Hannibal* (2001) Director: Ridley Scott
- *Much Ado About Nothing* (1993) Director: Kenneth Branagh
- *Gladiator* (2000) Director: Ridley Scott

LITERATURE

- *The Divine Comedy* Dante
- *The Decameron* Giovanni Boccaccio
- *La Vita Nuova* Dante
- *Canzoniere* Petrarch
- *The Lives of the Artists* Giorgio Vasari

- *Orlando Furioso* Ludovico Ariosto
- *Autobiography* Benvenuto Cellini
- *The Prince* Machiavelli
- *Notebooks* Leonardo da Vinci
- *On Painting* Leon Alberti

Sketches of Etruscan Places (DH Lawrence) An evocative collection of Lawrence's typically colourful observations on the Etruscan civilization of central Italy.

Vanilla Beans & Brodo (Isabella Dusi) An enjoyable account of the author's efforts to join in the close-knit community of Montalcino in southern Tuscany, with all its daily dramas and vibrant characters.

The Rise and Fall of the House of Medici (Christopher Hibbert) A fascinating, highly readable account of Florentine society during the centuries of Medici rule.

Brunelleschi's Dome (Ross King) Examines the social and cultural background to the construction of Florence's Duomo, one of the most awe-inspiring architectural feats of the Renaissance.

INTERNET RESOURCES

One of the best places to start your web explorations is the **Lonely Planet** site (www.lonelyplanet.com). Here you'll find concise information, postcards from other travellers and the Thorn Tree bulletin board, where you can ask questions before you go or dispense advice when you return. Other useful sites include:

www.greatdante.net explains all you wanted to know about the great poet, his life and works.

Bella Umbria (www.bellaumbria.net) A comprehensive guide to the region, with online hotel-booking facility and email newsletter.

Chianti (www.chianti.it - Italian only) A useful portal for the popular wine region.

Turismo in Toscana (www.turismo.toscana.it) The official Tuscany tourism website with extensive information on accommodation, restaurants and the like.

Tuscany Life (www.tuscanylife.it) Slightly offbeat information on a range of topics, from wine routes and festivals to where to find 'aged trees'.

Umbria Tourism (www.umbriatourism.com) General information with links to other sites, including various towns.

Itineraries
CLASSIC ROUTES

TUSCAN HILL TOWNS   2 days / 85km

Start early in **Monteriggioni** (p205) – you can see the whole place in half
an hour and still have time for an espresso fix. From here it's 9km north
to **Colle di Val d'Elsa** (p205). Go to the *alta* (high) part of town for a stroll
and end up at the leafy piazza. It's a pretty run due west of here to **Volterra**
(p211), where you can check out the region's oldest town hall and have
a late lunch, then head northeast to **San Gimignano** (p206). Walk quickly
around town before climbing up the Torre Grossa for an eye-popping
panoramic view. The next morning, leave town and head north to the
charming **Certaldo** (p138) where you can hop on the *funicolare* (cable car)
to the old part of town. Dip into the Palazzo Pretorio for a quick peek at
the frescoes and stay for lunch before setting off 11km south to Poggibonsi.
Put your foot on the pedal and hit the road south to **Siena** (p190) or north
to **Florence** (p71); either city is easily reachable within an hour.

While we recommended travelling by car, this trip is possible by public
transport, but with a bit of forward planning – public transport can be fairly
light on weekends and public holidays (see p343).

This itinerary is a
good introduction
to Tuscany. You
can cover all these
towns in a couple
of days, although if
you opt for the bus,
it'll take double the
time. The drive is
almost as good as
the arrival, with
plenty of breathtak-
ing scenery.

FIVE CITIES IN SIX DAYS

6 days / 250km

This blockbuster trip kicks off with 24 hours in **Siena** (p190). Spend the morning 'doing' the Duomo group clustered around the cathedral. After lunch lose yourself in the backstreets for a couple of hours, finishing up with a spot of retail therapy on Via di Città, before winding up at the magnificent Il Campo piazza. Hit a couple of museums before bedding down. Next day it's north to another heavy – **Florence** (p71) for a minimum of two days. Don't miss *David* and yet another Duomo, the Palazzo Pitti or the Uffizi. Next day hit the E35 to **Arezzo,** (p241) making a quick detour to Reggello, 8km east of Sanmezzano, a sumptuous medieval town set amid olive groves. You will be in Arezzo in plenty of time for lunch, or to buy picnic goodies at the market on Piazza Sant'Agostino. Wander around the medieval centre, stopping for a cold beer at the Piazza Grande overlooking the Romanesque Pieve di Santa Maria. Either stay overnight here or head south for **Perugia** (p254) in Umbria, dipping into the quintessential Tuscan hill town of **Cortona** (p248) with its medieval alleys, Renaissance art and stunning views. The road to Perugia passes the north end of Lago di Trasimeno where you should stop for refreshment (ice cream?) on the banks at Passignano. Once you hit **Perugia** keep the blinkers on and aim straight for the medieval centre where, after doing a little shopping on Corso Vannuci, you can enjoy yet more cultural overload at the 19th-century ensemble around Piazza IV Novembre. From Perugia it's a mere 14km east to lovely, pink-stoned **Assisi** (p279).

This journey is easily accomplished in six days by car, but could take longer if you do it by train and bus.

It's possible, promise! The only problem is that you won't quite be able to do any place justice – but you can always come back. At least this itinerary will give you a taste of the big-city scene. You'll be surprised at how different they all are.

BEST OF THE REGION

2 weeks to 2 months / about 800km

Starting in **Florence** (p71) move westwards to take in the towns of **Prato** (p130), **Pistoia** (p127), **Lucca** (p143) and **Pisa** (p152), making one of the last two an overnight stop. From Pisa you might want to pop along to one of the beaches around nearby **Viareggio** (p159). The centre of Tuscany's white-marble industry, **Carrara** (p163), is a worthwhile stop and in the northwestern corner of the region you could easily lose yourself for several days. The main attraction is the walking in the **Garfagnana** (p150), the **Apuane Alps** (p167) and in the still less visited **Lunigiana** (p165).

Return to Pisa via **Barga** (p151) and **Bagni de Lucca** (p150) and travel along the coast, stopping at **Castiglioncello** (p175). Head inland from the coast then south towards **Piombino** (p178), visiting towns such as **Suvereto** (p176) and **Massa Marittima** (p229). Unless it's August, hop on the ferry for Elba from Piombino and spend a couple of days touring. Back on the mainland, head northeast to **Siena** (p190) where you should base yourself to take in surrounding hill-top villages. Cross into Umbria and continue east to Assisi, stopping next at **Spello** (p286) for a quick fix of small-town Umbria. Next stop is **Spoleto** (p294), an unbeatable base for hiking. Carry on to the hill-top town of **Narni** (p309) where you can catch the highway back to **Perugia** (p254) and return to Florence, having a quick look at **Arezzo** (p241) en route.

This trip can be speedy or luxuriously slow, depending on how much time you have. The total number of kilometres you clock up depends entirely on how adventurous you are when exploring the Apuane Alps, Lunigiana and Elba (but you will probably manage at least 800km). Public transport is an option, but only if you haven't got a plane to catch.

Few will have time to complete this monster trip. But if you have the time and a sense of adventure, this route will provide you with a few more poetic superlatives to describe the region, as well as improve your map-reading skills.

TAILORED TRIPS

TUSCANY & UMBRIA FOR KIDS   5 days / 300km

Start your kiddie trip with Collodi's **Parco di Pinocchio** (p149), followed by a paddle at the bucket-and-spade resort of **Viareggio** (p159). Hightail it to **Pisa** (p152) for a shot of the tower for the family album. From here, head for the fairytale city of **San Gimignano** (p206) and (the not so fairytale, but the little horrors will love it) **Torture Museum** (p209). Next stop: Siena. Jump on the **Treno Natura** (p199) steam engine for a family-fun trip, then check out the activities at the **Museo d'Arte per Bambini** (Via dei Pispini 164), where programmes for kids include painting and pottery. Carry on to the **Museo della Mezzadria**

Senese (Via Tinaia del Taja) in Buonconvento with its multimedia presentation about what life was like living on the land. If this sounds a bit heavy going for your two-year- old, swing east for the natural reserve at **Lago di Montepulciano** where feathered friends like the purple heron make a change from feeding the ducks back home. Finally, dip into Umbria for a boat trip or swim at **Lago di Trasimeno**.

By car is usually the only real option when travelling with children (although you may want to be in one automobile and the kids in another). With approximately 300km spread over five days, this is quite manageable.

TIPPLER'S TOUR   7 to 8 days / 375km

Kick-start this trip in Chianti country at **Rùfina's** (p136) wine museum, followed by a tour of the nearby **Castello di Brolio vineyard** (☎ 057 77 301). Take the E76 to **Montecarlo**, the main wine-producing town in the foothills of the Appenines. Try the local drop, *Montecarlo*, at Piccola Enoteca (Via Roma 26). The region south of Pisa is famous for its dry whites. Head for **Crespina** and try the light, crisp *Novello* at Enoteca Alisi Cristiana (Località Cenaia) in town. Next, sample the wines of the Etruschi Costa. Take Hwy 1 to Grosseto, stopping off at **Bolgheri** at the centre of this wine region. Enjoy a glug of the complex *Sassicaia di Bolgheri* cabernet at Enoteca Tognoni (Piazza Teresa 2). Weave your way southeast to lovely **Massa**

Marrittima (p229) surrounded by vineyards and treat your wine cellar to a couple of bottles of *Vino Monteregio*. It's a short hop from here to the Enoteca at **Montalcino's** (p214) Fortezza and a taste of the velvety *Brunello*. Next stop is **Montepulciano** (p219), home of the deliciously snooty *Vino Nobile*, which you can try at several wine cellars in town. Southeast of here is Umbria's main wine-producing area of **Torgiano** (south of Perugia). Look for the aromatic *Rubesco Riserva*, one of Italy's finest wines.

This trip is recommended by car and, as it involves countless hectolitres of vino, with a designated driver.

WORLD HERITAGE SITES   10 to 11 days / 325km

This is the kind of itinerary you take pics of to *really* impress the folks back home! Start off with a serious slug of religious culture at the Duomo group in the **Historic Centre of Florence** (p71). After a couple of days, hit the road to **Pisa** (p152). The easiest route is via **Lucca** (p143) – have a quick dip into the old centre. Pisa is just down the road and its **Piazza del Duomo** (with the Leaning Tower; p155) is unforgettable. Backtrack towards Florence, turn south on the SS429, taking a quicky detour to **Certaldo** (p138). A short jig south of here is the **Historic Centre of San Gimignano** (p206) where you can easily hang out for a few hours, before hightailing it to the **Historic Centre of Siena** (via Monteriggioni – another treat). You can't do this place justice in less than two days. Then it's an easy run south on the SS2 to Pienza. Turn left at San Quirico d'Orca (signposted) to the **Historic Centre of Pienza** (p218). You should be able to walk from one end of town to the other in 20 minutes (or less). It's pretty much a straight line due east from here to your final destination: **Assisi** (p279). Look for the following towns en route: Montepulciano (put the brakes on here), Castiglione del Lago and Perugia. Stay a night in Assisi: it's especially magical at dusk after the coach tours have left.

This Grand Tour of itineraries is a modest 325km in distance but can be spread over a stately 10 to 11 days. While motoring is considered the best option, it is still possible by public transport.

The Authors

ALEX LEVITON

Alex has visited Italy five times in the past five years (four of those times were spent falling in love with Umbria) and wrote the Umbria chapters and the Arts chapter for this guide. After university, a deep urge to try every form of public transportation and ice cream available led her to visit 46 countries on six continents. After getting her masters in journalism from UC Berkeley, she moved to Durham, North Carolina, where she is a freelance writer, editor, journalist, restaurant critic, travel columnist and Scrabble fanatic.

JOSEPHINE QUINTERO

Josephine updated the Northwest, Central and Southern Tuscany, Central Coast and Elba, Itineraries and Outdoors chapters. She is a freelance writer specialising in travel, and has lived and worked in both California and Kuwait. She has written for a food and wine magazine, been a ghostwriter for several biographies, come up with snappy slogans for international ad campaigns and been held hostage in Iraq. Josephine now lives in Andalucía and contributes to various magazines and travel guides. To Josephine's delight, her daughter lives in northern Italy.

RACHEL SUDDART

Originally from the Lake District and a graduate of Manchester University, Rachel spent several years trying to work out how to combine her love for words with her love for travel (apart from just talking about it). She had her first taste of LP authorship when she took part in a BBC documentary about travel writing, and after getting her foot stuck firmly in the door she took on a full-time role in Lonely Planet's London office. The pull of her northern roots and a certain cricket enthusiast proved too much for her to resist and she now lives in Newcastle. Rachel wrote the Environment, Directory and Transport chapters.

RICHARD WATKINS

Richard was born in south Wales and studied ancient history at Cardiff University, before continuing his interest in all things ancient and Roman at Oxford University. He put academic life on hold and went travelling, during which time he realised his preference for writing, and has since written for a number of guidebooks. For this book, Richard wrote the chapters on Florence and Eastern Tuscany, as well as Destination Tuscany & Umbria, Getting Started, Snapshot, Highlights and the chapters on history and culture.

Snapshot

Tuscany and Umbria are among Italy's most prosperous and productive regions. Both have significant agricultural and manufacturing bases, although tourism is an increasingly important sector of the local economies, particularly in Tuscany, which is also one of the country's more industrialised regions. Politically, both regions have traditionally favoured the left; in the 2000 regional elections, the centre-left Ulivo Alliance won the biggest share of the vote in both Tuscany and Umbria.

As elsewhere in Italy, Prime Minister Silvio Berlusconi, with his political and judicial problems, is a hot topic of conversation. Ever distrustful of central government and politicians in general, Tuscans and Umbrians aren't shy in expressing their feelings about their government in Rome. As well as holding the highest political office in the land, Berlusconi owns newspapers, television stations and a publishing company, conflicts of interest that would not be tolerated in most other Western countries, but it's his legal wranglings that stir up most interest. In 2003 one of his closest friends, Cesare Previti, was found guilty of bribing judges and sentenced to 11 years in prison. Berlusconi had similar charges quashed in 2001 and as prime minister has enacted legislation to help him avoid such prosecution. His support for the war led by the USA and the UK against Iraq in 2003 also proved unpopular with many Tuscans and Umbrians, and a large-scale peace movement grew up across both regions to oppose it. Both Tuscany and Umbria are keen to be granted more autonomy from the central government.

One of the greatest ecological headaches in Tuscany is the question of marble extraction in the Apuane Alps. The quarries here have been worked since Roman times, but the rate of extraction today is gathering pace, disfiguring part of an area being considered for national park status. The waste produced is creating disposal problems and the heavy truck traffic is itself an ecological disaster. However, Carrara marble is one of Tuscany's prestige exports, and with more than 2000 jobs at stake it seems unlikely anything will be done in the near future to placate the environmentalists and long-suffering local residents. Meanwhile, noise pollution, heavy road traffic and poor air quality are the bane of residents living in suburban Florence and the heavily populated Prato-Pistoia area.

In Umbria, concerned environmentalists are campaigning to save the wild Monti Sibillini region; although officially designated a national park, there are no laws stopping Umbrians following one of their favourite pursuits, hunting, while building development also poses a threat to this remote and unspoilt corner of the country.

Italy has one of the lowest birth rates in Europe, and Tuscany and Umbria are no exception. In fact, both have seen their population drop over recent years, which has caused some concern. Immigration, legal or otherwise, has failed to reverse the trend.

FAST FACTS

Population: 4.38 million

Annual population growth: -3.5%

GDP per head: US$25,000

Inflation: 2.5%

Unemployment: 7%

Land area: 31,430 sq km

Vineyard area: 108,000 hectares

Annual wine production: 4.7 million hectolitres

History

ETRUSCANS & ROMANS

By the 8th century BC, the Etruscan civilisation had established itself across central Italy and within 200 years it had become the dominant power in what are today known as Tuscany and Umbria, overcoming the native Umbrians, as well as parts of Lazio. The Etruscan settlements, though, were largely independent of one another, held together in a loose confederation of 12 main cities, including Fiesole, Cortona, Volterra, Arezzo and Perugia. Remnants of this fascinating culture may still be seen, from extensive museum collections of bronzes and pottery to once richly adorned tombs scattered around the countryside.

The precise origins of these ancient people remains something of a mystery. The Greek historian Herodotus suggested that they migrated in waves from Asia Minor in the wake of the Trojan Wars, while others have claimed they were an indigenous tribe. Work still continues today on translating their archaic language, which may throw some more light on the matter, but in the meantime what we know of them comes mostly from the archaeological record.

The rise of Rome spelled the end for the Etruscans; in 309 BC the Romans took Perusia (modern Perugia), a major Etruscan stronghold. This marked the start of a campaign of conquest that would eventually bring the whole of Etruria under Roman influence, firmly bound to the Eternal City through a system of compulsory alliances. The independent culture of the Etruscans was slowly eroded, and gradually the language was lost. However, things didn't always go the Romans' way. In the late 3rd century, they faced their most dangerous foe, the Carthaginian leader Hannibal, who famously invaded the Italian peninsula with his army of elephants. In 217 BC the two forces met on the shores of Lago di Trasimeno, in what is now northern Umbria, and the Romans suffered a monumental defeat, losing as many as 16,000 men.

The 1st century BC saw a rapid expansion of Romanisation in Tuscany, with the founding of cities such as Florentia (Florence), Saena Julia (Siena) and Pistoria (Pistoia), while Umbria too thrived under Roman administration, with the foundation of towns such as Hispellum (Spello), which grew wealthy on the passing trade of the Via Flaminia, one of Rome's most important roadways. From the 1st century AD onwards, Christianity spread rapidly through the two regions, and Umbria especially played an important role in the growth of monasticism; St Benedict, born in Norcia in 480, was one of the early pioneers.

THE EARLY MIDDLE AGES

The Western Roman Empire was disintegrating in the 5th century AD, and Tuscany and Umbria succumbed to the might of the Gothic armies led by Totila. The Eastern Roman Empire, otherwise known as Byzantium, was still very much alive and well, however, and its emperor, Justinian, was keen to recapture Italy. His eunuch general, Narses, was sent to face the Barbarian horde, and in 552 he defeated and killed Totila near the modern

In *Daily Life of the Etrus-cans*, Jacques Heurgon's up-to-date research attempts to unravel the mysteries of this archaic culture, investigating the origins of their language and religion.

www.mysterious etruscans.com has inter-esting and comprehen-sive information on this ancient and still poorly understood civilisation.

DID YOU KNOW?

The Carrara marble quarry, first exploited by the Romans, is still the world's largest producer of marble.

TIMELINE
c800–600 BC	309 BC
Etruscan civilisation is established across central Italy and reaches its peak of power and wealth.	Rome takes Perugia, signalling the decline of the Etruscans and the rise of the Roman Empire.

town of Gualdo Tadino. Within 20 years, though, the invading Lombards wrested control of Tuscany and most of Umbria from Byzantine forces and established powerful dukedoms based around Lucca and Spoleto. They in turn were driven out by the Franks in the late 8th century, who also favoured Lucca as their power-base. In 800 Charlemagne formed an uneasy alliance with the papacy to create the Holy Roman Empire, and installed margraves to rule the various districts on his behalf. In 978 Willa, the widow of Margrave Uberto, established the Badia in Florence, and in 1000 her son, Ugo, transferred his capital to the city.

This was an unstable period, fraught with provincial squabbles and regional rivalries. Umbria had passed into the nominal control of the Papal States and saw a spate of castle-building and neighbourhood feuds, while 11th-century Tuscany saw the beginnings of the disastrous Imperial-Papal divisions that were to dominate the Middle Ages in central Italy. Under the rule of Countess Matilda Canossa, the County of Tuscia (Tuscany) had achieved considerable independence from the Empire, and when hostilities broke out between Emperor Henry IV and Pope Gregory VII, Matilda allied herself with the pope, setting a precedent that would long resonate through Florentine history. Henry tried to have the pope deposed in 1077, but instead found himself at Matilda's castle at Canossa, in Emilia, imploring him to lift an order of excommunication.

Influential as the state may have been under Matilda, her death in 1115 spelled the end of Tuscany as a political unit as disputes over the ownership of her lands led to the cities of Florence, Siena and Lucca declaring independence and the other lands coming under papal rule.

Florence: The Biography of a City by Christopher Hibbert is a fascinating and scholarly account of the great city's history and art.

Medieval Tuscany comes vividly to life in Iris Origo's *The Merchant of Prato*, a tale of domestic and business affairs based on the extensive correspondence of a 14th-century entrepreneur.

GUELPHS & GHIBELLINES

In the 13th century, the city-states of Pisa, Siena, Perugia and especially Florence, grew fat on the proceeds of trade, most notably textiles and banking. In fact, Florence was now one of the largest and richest cities in Europe, with 100,000 inhabitants by 1300. Political machinations brought increasing instability in the 14th century, and many cities divided into the opposing factions of the pro-empire Ghibellines and the pro-pope Guelphs. In reality, though, the divisions were as often based on family feuds, personal promotion and class antagonism as any lofty political ideology. This rumbling conflict broke out into open and bloody warfare, with Guelph Florence gaining the upper hand over Pisa, Siena and Arezzo.

Umbrian cities, developing into independent republics, also used the factional rivalries as an excuse for mercenary wars, land-grabbing and violent vendettas, but none had the resources of the great Tuscan cities and they came close to destroying themselves. The papacy, keen to exploit this weakness, began to pick them off, starting with Spoleto in 1354. Only Perugia managed to hold out against the papal forces, and Umbria gradually passed into the background of Italian power-politics.

Besides the warmongering, though, this was also the age of St Francis of Assisi (see the boxed text, p22), and of Dante, Boccaccio, Cimabue and Giotto, whose revolutionary artistic style laid the groundwork for the masters of the Renaissance.

59 BC	AD 568
Julius Caesar founds the colony of Florentia.	Lombards invade, turning Tuscany and Umbria into dukedoms controlled from Lucca and Spoleto.

ST FRANCIS OF ASSISI

St Francis is one of the best known and most loved of the Catholic saints. Born in Assisi in 1182, the son of a wealthy cloth merchant, Francis was a boisterous and reckless youth who showed little aptitude for study, preferring to hang out with the other young men of Assisi, carousing and squandering his father's money.

During a skirmish with the rival city of Perugia, the 20-year-old Francis was captured and held prisoner for a year. He became very ill and started to regret his idle youth. On his return to Assisi, he adopted an eccentric and nomadic lifestyle, embracing lepers, talking to crucifixes and once, during a pilgrimage to Rome, swapping clothes with a beggar. However, when he sold a large stock of his father's merchandise to raise money to rebuild a church, the old man's patience snapped. Francis fled his father's wrath, hiding in a cave. When he emerged a month later, dirty and emaciated, he was the laughing stock of Assisi and his father disinherited him. Francis renounced all worldly goods and headed for the hills behind Assisi, engaging in charitable works and preaching. His message was to discard the materialistic trappings of life and embrace a simple philosophy of poverty, chastity and obedience. He also preached of the need to see the presence of God in all the beauty of nature, a tenet of the new humanism, and an idea that soon won him adherents.

Francis eventually obtained permission from the pope to found a new religious order, although he was never himself ordained. He also helped create an order for women, the Poor Clares, and continued with his teachings, travelling as far as the Holy Land.

In 1224 he received the stigmata at La Verna, but by now he was a sick and ailing man and died on the mud floor of his hovel in Assisi in 1226, aged 44. Four years later he was made a saint, and a great basilica was erected in his honour in an attempt by the Church to bring the popular movement under its control, and diminishing Francis' message of poverty in the process.

The Civilization of the Renaissance in Italy by Jacob Burckhardt is a classic 19th-century work on this vital period.

The Black Death of 1348 ravaged the towns and countryside, decimating the population. Florence was badly affected, especially after the collapse of two of its largest banks, but soon bounced back, capturing Prato just three years later and simply buying Arezzo in 1384. By this time, the old Guelph-Ghibelline allegiances had been consigned to the dustbin of history. Florence continued its expansionist policy into the next century, taking Pisa in 1406.

THE RENAISSANCE

In 1434, Cosimo de' Medici (Il Vecchio), head of a wealthy banking family, took effective control of the Florentine lands, initiating the lengthy and influential rule of the Medici dynasty. Though extinct for some 250 years, the Medici remain a powerful presence in Tuscany to this day and there are few towns that don't boast at least one Medici-commissioned structure or other, while their heraldic shield with its six balls is a common sight.

www.franciscanfriars
tor.com has information on the life and teachings of St Francis and the work of the modern Franciscans.

It was under Cosimo, a passionate patron of the arts, that the humanist revolution in thinking and the accompanying *Rinascimento* (Renaissance) in the visual arts took off. The process had been under way since the previous century, as witnessed by the work of artists such as Giotto, but the generous patronage of the Medici family was a catalyst that would turn Florence into the most innovative centre of the arts in all of Europe. The growing number of universities in the 14th and 15th centuries had encouraged the serious study of a range of subjects, not just theology, as many important ancient Greek and Latin texts were rediscovered. The process was also aided by the contact with the decaying Byzantine Empire, that last vestige of the old Roman world and repository of ancient learning and culture on the fringe of Europe. The Church Council of Florence in 1439 brought many Byzantine scholars to the city, while many others, seeing the rapidly approaching end of Constantinople as the Turks advanced, were flowing into western Europe at this time. The rediscovery of classical learning soon became a rediscovery of classical art-form, while the study of science blossomed, led by that most famous of polymaths, Leonardo da Vinci.

Da Vinci, who considered himself first and foremost an artist, began to explore everything from astronomy to zoology, and had a particular interest in human anatomy. He is best known, though, as a visionary engineer, producing detailed diagrams of his far-sighted inventions. He never got round to actually constructing his flying machines, armoured cars or cranes, but you can see accurate models of many of them in his home town of Vinci today.

Lorenzo il Magnifico (the Magnificent) continued his grandfather's work, expanding the city's power and maintaining its primacy in the artistic realm. See the boxed text (following) for more details.

Lorenzo's death and his succession by his charmless son Piero in 1492 spelled the temporary end of Medici rule and the start of heated times for Florence.

Umbria, meanwhile, had declined into something of an agricultural backwater, disputed by petty princes and the papacy. Orvieto in particular became a favoured papal residence.

DID YOU KNOW?
St Clare, a friend of St Francis and founder of the Poor Clares, became the patron saint of television in 1958.

Browse some of the fascinating documents of the Medici archives at www.medici.org

THE LATER MEDICIS
In 1494 Piero was obliged to hand Florence over to the invading French king Charles VIII, before fleeing from an increasingly hostile population. The people had turned against the opulence and excess of the Medici

THE MAGNIFICENT MEDICI
At a time when freedom of expression was not always encouraged by the ruling elite, Lorenzo the Magnificent created a climate of tolerance in which the great Renaissance artists and scholars could flourish. Among others, he gave patronage and protection to Michelangelo, Luca della Robbia, Botticelli and Leon Battista Alberti. Lorenzo was a poet and is credited by some as saying 'Whoever wants to be happy, let him be so: about tomorrow there's no knowing'.

But his wisdom didn't stop at art and literature. Lorenzo's diplomatic skills brought a much-needed period of peace to the region when, soon after taking power, he managed to negotiate with the king of Naples, averting war and earning himself the respect of the Florentines into the bargain. A papal-inspired assassination attempt in 1478 – the Pazzi Conspiracy – only served to boost his popularity further. For the rest of his rule, he slowly reinforced, through peaceful means, the position of Florence as a great city-state.

Just as his popularity was coming under fire from the doom-laden Savonarola (see p24), Lorenzo died. The outpouring of grief in Florence marked the beginning of a new era as relative peace and prosperity gave way to political uncertainty, economic gloom and an artistic downturn. No wonder they called him magnificent.

1434	1469–1737
Cosimo de' Medici establishes Medici rule in Florence and encourages the birth of the Renaissance.	Tuscany's fortunes rise and fall as the later Medicis continue to rule.

court and found a new champion in the dour Dominican monk, Girolamo Savonarola, who instituted a puritanical republic.

Savonarola's austere rule soon lost its attraction though and he was burned as a heretic in 1498. A brief republican interlude ensued, but in 1512 the Medicis, headed by Giuliano, returned to power backed by a Spanish-led army. He and his vicious successors never gained popular affection and the family was once again sent packing in 1527, only to return once more in 1530, courtesy of a papal-imperial siege (see p73).

Cosimo I assumed power in 1537. Although in many respects Florence and its Tuscan dominions had by now been eclipsed on the European stage by the emergence of more powerful nation states, Cosimo was determined to keep a key role for Florence in the affairs of a still-fractured Italy.

A crucial moment came in 1555 when at long last Florence captured its old rival, Siena, after a year-long siege. Apart from Lucca and its modest possessions, Florence was now in control of the whole of Tuscany, and in 1569 Pope Pius V conferred upon Cosimo the title of Grand Duke of Tuscany.

Though clearly a ruthless despot, Cosimo did sort out the city's finances, build a fleet (which participated in the crushing defeat of the Turkish navy in the Battle of Lepanto in 1571) and promote economic growth across Tuscany with irrigation programmes for agriculture and mining. He was a patron of the arts and sciences, and also reformed the civil service, building the Uffizi in Florence to house all government departments in a single, more easily controlled building. He and his family also acquired and moved into the Palazzo Pitti.

THE MEDICIS OF THE GRAND DUCHY

From the death of Cosimo I until that of the dissolute lout Gian Gastone de' Medici in 1737, the once glorious family continued to rule over Tuscany though a long period of decline was setting in. Umbria at this time was a forgotten, rural corner of Italy with poor communications to the outside world, whose agricultural-based economy was suffering badly under the poor management of the papacy.

Cosimo I's two immediate successors, Francesco and Ferdinando I, between them managed to keep Tuscany out of trouble and go some way to stimulating the local economy and promoting agriculture, building hospitals and bringing some relief to the poor. Cosimo II invited Galileo Galilei to Florence, where the scientist could continue his research under Tuscan protection (see the boxed text opposite).

The lengthy reign of the humourless, anti-Semitic, anti-intellectual Cosimo III was a real low-point in Tuscan history. The population was in decline, the economy was a mess and taxes were skyrocketing. The pathetic figure of Gian Gastone signalled a sad end indeed to the Medici dynasty, and when he died in 1737, Francis, Duke of Lorraine and husband of the Austrian empress Maria Theresa, was appointed grand duke of Tuscany.

The last significant act of the Medicis was six years after the death of Gian Gastone. His sister Anna Maria, who died in 1743, bequeathed all the Medici property and art collections to the grand duchy of Tuscany, on condition that they never leave Florence.

VIVE TDVX ALEXANDER
MED SECVL.APEROMNIA

MEDICI TIMELINE

Giovanni di Bicci
(1360–1429)

Cosimo il Vecchio
(1389–1464)

Piero il Gottoso
(1416–69)

Lorenzo il Magnifico
(1449–92)

Piero di Lorenzo
(1471–1503)

Giuliano Duke of Nemours
(1478–1516)

Lorenzo Duke of Urbino
(1492–1519)

Giovanni, Pope Leo X
(1475–1521)

Giulio, Pope Clement VII
(1478–1534)

Alessandro
(1511–37)

Cosimo I
(1519–74)

Francesco I
(1541–87)

Ferdinando I
(1549–1609)

Cosimo II
(1590–1621)

Ferdinando II
(1610–70)

Cosimo III
(1642–1723)

Gian Gastone
(1671–1737)

ILLUSTRATION BY JANE SMITH

1799	1860
Napoleon marches on Florence.	Tuscany and Umbria join the Kingdom of Piedmont on the way to Italian unification.

THE WORLD TURNS

'Eppur si muove', Galileo is said to have muttered after being compelled to recant his teachings on astronomy before the Inquisition in Rome in 1633. 'And yet it does move'. He was referring to the Earth, whose prime position at the centre of the universe he had questioned. The Earth rotated around the Sun with the other planets, just as Copernicus had said.

Born in Pisa in 1564, Galileo studied at the monastery of Vallombrosa before pursuing his study of medicine at the university of Pisa. His fascination with mathematics and the study of motion led him to astronomy, and in 1610 he moved to Florence, where the Grand Duke offered him permanent residence to continue his research.

As early as 1616 Galileo had been warned by conservative church authorities not to proceed with his wild claims, which they felt threatened the Christian view of the world and of creation itself, not to mention the position of the Catholic Church. His works were placed on the index of banned books and declared blasphemous.

The mood changed somewhat in 1624 and he was given permission to write an 'objective study', a triumph of argumentation in favour of his own theory. However, he was summoned before the Inquisition in Rome in 1632 in order to explain himself, and was confined to internal exile in Florence until his death 10 years later, although he continued to study, experiment, write books and correspond with other scientists across Europe.

He lies buried in the Basilica di Santa Croce.

AUSTRIA & FRANCE IN CHARGE

The imperial Austrian couple paid a brief visit to Florence, but from then until 1765 the grand duchy was to be ruled by the *Reggenza* (regents).

The regents brought a period of peace and order, enacting much-needed reforms and streamlining the civil administration, while Pietro Leopoldo, who took over in 1765, proved to be an enlightened ruler, abolishing torture and the death penalty, suppressing the Inquisition, and embarking on a number of plans of civic improvement. This was the Golden Age of the Grand Tour, when wealthy young men from across Europe would travel through Italy to finish their education and find inspiration in the landscape, art and architecture.

Austrian rule was ended in 1799 when Napoleon marched into Florence. The following year he made it capital of the new 'Kingdom of Etruria' under Louis de Bourbon. The French reorganised Umbria in an attempt to stimulate the economy, and succeeded in bringing a new vigour to this moribund corner of the peninsula. In 1809 Tuscany was handed over to Napoleon's sister Elisa, who reigned as Grand Duchess for the next five years, before the Lorraine dynasty was reinstated.

TOWARDS ITALIAN UNITY

Grand Duke Ferdinando III proved to be one of the more popular of the Tuscan overlords. He pushed through a raft of reforms at every level of city and grand-ducal administration, and Tuscany became an ever-bigger draw for foreign artists and writers such as Byron and Shelly.

Under the rule of his son Leopoldo II, the first long-distance rail line (Florence–Pisa–Livorno) and the first telegraphic link (Florence–Pisa) were both opened in the 1840s. In 1847, he saw Lucca transferred to the control of the grand duchy, ending centuries of Luccan independence.

DID YOU KNOW?

It was only in 1992 that a Catholic Church commission acknowledged that the ecclesiastical judges who condemned Galileo's scientific theories as blasphemy made an error.

www.pierodella francesca.it will teach you about Piero della Francesca and his masterpieces, including his fresco cycle in Arezzo.

1865–70	1915–18
Florence is the temporary capital of the newly independent Italy.	Italy joins the Allies against Germany and Austria in WWI, beginning three years' heavy combat.

The progressive political movements that were sweeping through Europe also found supporters in Italy. In 1848, when the whole continent seemed to be up in arms, there were insurrections in Pisa and Livorno, calling for a Tuscan constitution. Very soon, there were calls for a united Italian state, and after mass demonstrations Leopold was forced out in 1859. The following year Tuscany and Umbria joined the Kingdom of Piedmont, and in 1865 Florence became the temporary capital of the newly independent Italy until Rome was freed from papal rule and given the honour in 1870.

WWI & FASCISM

Tuscany and Umbria at the beginning of the 20th century were, like much of Italy, poor and economically weak. Social discontent led to the growth of socialist and anarchist movements, while conditions in Umbria were worse still, with mass emigration adding to the problems. Florence, meanwhile, had never been more popular with foreign visitors, especially the British, and a thriving tourist industry quickly grew up. EM Forster, DH Lawrence and Oscar Wilde were just some of the writers and artists who fell in love with the city of the Medicis.

Italy's decision to enter WWI in 1915 initially had little direct impact on Tuscany and Umbria, tucked far away from the front lines in the north. Like the rest of the country, however, they paid a high price in the lives of their young men sacrificed as cannon fodder.

By 1917 the situation on Italy's home front had become grim too. All basic products were strictly rationed and that winter, a harsh one, brought intense hardship as heating fuel was virtually unavailable.

Political turmoil following the end of hostilities was inevitable. By 1920 Benito Mussolini's Blackshirts had established branches in Florence, which in less than two years would become one of the Fascists' key strongholds. Tuscany became one of the single biggest sources of card-carrying Fascist members, and Fascist violence in Florence became so alarming that Mussolini sent people in to shake out the local organisation and put a brake on the bloodshed.

DID YOU KNOW?

The world's first officially designated wine-producing area was created in Chianti in 1716. Modern Chianti Classico wine was created by Baron Ricasoli in the 1860s.

WWII

Mussolini's decision to enter the war on the side of Germany meant disaster for Italy. Resistance groups began to operate in Tuscany almost immediately and the mountainous and hilly countryside was frequently the stage for partisan assaults and German reprisal. Allied bombers meanwhile caused heavy damage to coastal cities such as Piombino and Livorno. Pisa too was badly bombed; the Camposanto is a tragic monument to the conflict, while raids on Florence were comparatively light.

By July 1944, Free French troops occupied the island of Elba. At the same time, Allied forces approached the German lines near Florence. At this point, the German high command decided to blow the city's bridges, sparing only the Ponte Vecchio (some say it was Hitler who ordered it be spared). Allied troops moved into the city later that day, and Pisa and Lucca both fell to the Allies in the first days of September.

The Allies did not finally break through to the Po valley and force the Germans north until April 1945.

1940	1946
Fascist Italy enters WWII on Nazi Germany's side.	Italians vote in national referendum to abolish the monarchy and create a republic.

TO THE PRESENT

In the 1946 referendum on whether to institute a republic or a monarchy, Tuscans and Umbrians voted overwhelmingly, along with most of Italy, for a republic. Since then they have watched the comings and goings of national governments (59 since WWII) from a distance, concerned primarily with what's happening in their regions. The incumbent at the time of writing, Silvio Berlusconi, is a controversial and sometimes tactless media-magnate, who is either loved or loathed by Italians, though he has managed to keep his right-of-centre coalition in power for longer than many of his predecessors.

Until the 1950s, Tuscany's economy remained largely based on agriculture, and was suffering with problems of rural depopulation. The advent of light industry saved the region from becoming an economic backwater and by the 1970s, tourism, fashion and banking had become important factors. Umbria, meanwhile, experienced little of the success of its bigger neighbour, and remained a quiet rural corner of Italy best known for its wines and truffles, though in recent years tourism has made inroads into the local economy and the region is beginning to enjoy increasing prosperity.

Both Tuscany and Umbria have limited autonomy and, with their strong regional loyalties and distrust of the central state, believe that more power should be devolved to the regions. Since the 1990s the regions, along with others, have been campaigning to this effect and with some success. It is now envisaged that more powers, including the crucial ability to raise revenue, will be slowly and quietly handed over to the regions.

Read *The Renaissance* by Walter Pater for an idiosyncratic account of Italian art, much favoured by louche Victorian aesthetes.

The British Abroad: The Grand Tour in the Eighteenth Century by Jeremy Black is a witty and well-researched book covering the pleasures and pitfalls of the nascent tourism industry in continental Europe, with quotes from early tourists.

2001

Silvio Berlusconi's right-wing Casa delle Libertà (Liberties House) coalition wins absolute majority in national polls.

2003

Italy takes up the six-month presidency of the European Union.

The Culture

REGIONAL IDENTITY

Tuscany and Umbria are at the geographic heart of Italy, and to many foreigners represent the essence of the country. In many ways their people are the archetypal Italians, passionate, family-oriented, fond of food and wine and fanatical about clothes and appearance. Tuscans especially are hard-working, proud of their long history of innovation and entrepreneurial spirit. Small-scale, family-run industry thrives in both regions, with tradition and quality still favoured over quantity. These regions are among the richest in Italy and are still largely rural. These are mostly the lands of small towns of close-knit, ancient communities, where local matters and local gossip are of great concern and national politics are of secondary interest at best.

Italy as a modern nation state is a comparatively new creation, dating only from 1870, and Tuscans and Umbrians, like most Italians, identify themselves first and foremost with their town and their region. Unless there's an international football match in the offing, you won't see many Italian tricolours flying here, but you may well see streets festooned with the pennants of rival *quatiere*, or quarters, the age-old division of cities such as Arezzo, Siena and Cortona. Here neighbourhood loyalty is strong, and events such as the Palio and the Giostra del Saracino boost community spirit and give everyone an opportunity to indulge in the typical Italian passion for dressing up, as they strut about in coloured tights, felt hats and the like.

Sport, of course, is a major passion, dominated by football, while rugby is also gaining ground as the Italian team receives more international exposure and success. Food, too, is a popular topic of conversation, while the wines of Tuscany and Umbria are a source of much local pride and a subject upon which many express expertise.

Politically, both regions are left-leaning and the centre-left Ulivo Alliance, formed in 1995, has especially strong support in Umbria. As elsewhere in Italy, support for both the Communists and the parties of the far-right has fallen off in recent years, and, like other Italians, the citizens of these two regions distrust central government.

LIFESTYLE

Tuscans and Umbrians are particularly attached to their home ground and family. These ties continue to influence how people do things in this part of the world. Many businesses are relatively small, family enterprises. From the great names in wine, such as the Antinori, through to the flower-producing industry of Pescia and the small-scale farms of Umbria, most are run by families who pass on the business from generation to generation. In some respects this has contributed to a degree of immobility in these parts.

The family remains the cornerstone of Tuscan and Umbrian society. Although the big extended families of the past are in most cases little more than a distant memory, family ties remain tightly knit. Children still typically remain at home with their parents until they reach their 30s, often only leaving when they get married.

Women – at least young women – are shaking off old stereotypes and are active in all departments of work and society. However, chauvinistic attitudes do remain, particularly in rural areas. Tuscans and Umbrians of both sexes are increasingly choosing to concentrate on studies or careers before getting married, and tend to have smaller families than in previous generations, as much through economic necessity as anything.

For those tiring of the expat villa-fixers, Dario Castagno's *Too Much Tuscan Sun*, giving a local's views on his home and the foreign incomers, offers some light relief. However, you may have difficulty finding it outside Tuscany.

Italy and its Discontents: Family, Civil Society, State: 1980-2001 by Paul Ginsborg is a thorough study of this recent period of Italian history, with an emphasis on the role of the family in society, and the decline of Catholicism and communism.

William Trevor's *My House in Umbria* is a tender novel about the relationships between the survivors of a terrorist bomb attack as they recuperate in the Umbrian countryside. In 2003 it was made into a film starring Dame Maggie Smith.

DID YOU KNOW?

85% of Tuscany's wine production is red, while in Umbria the position is reversed; 80% of its wine is white.

MUMMY'S BOYS

Although it's a well-worn stereotype, Tuscan and Umbrian men, like other Italians, have always loved mamma, and in an age of rising house prices and job insecurity, increasing numbers are choosing to stay at home. In fact, recent statistics suggest that up to 70% of single, unmarried men under 35 either still live with their parents or have moved back at some stage. Those who do leave the nest rarely go far, most remaining in their home town, and if marriage fails, a quarter of men return to their parents' abode.

For Luigi Barzini, whose 1964 book *The Italians* remains a classic, the family represented a 'stronghold in a hostile land'. That hostile land is a state that places no value on the provision of unemployment benefits and other aid that makes it easier for youths in other countries to fly the nest – and stay out.

The age of consent for homosexuals in Italy is 16 and Tuscany and Umbria are usually very tolerant of gay and lesbian communities, although outside Florence and Viareggio, there is little 'scene' as such, and overt public displays of affection could meet with a negative response.

The stereotypical perceptions foreigners tend to have of Italians, while they inevitably contain a grain of truth, do not tell much of the story. The image of an animated, gesticulating people seemingly with plenty of time to kill is some distance from the truth.

Thrifty and hard-working, the Tuscans can also be a fairly reserved lot. To be swept up into Tuscan social life (as opposed to circles of resident Italians from other parts of the country) is no mean feat and a sign of considerable success. Umbrian society is also very close-knit and provincial in outlook, and outside the cities, not an easy one for foreigners to penetrate.

POPULATION

Tuscany's population of just over 3.5 million includes some 80,000 foreigners who have made Tuscany their home. Most people live in the northwest in an area bounded by Florence, Livorno, Massa and Pistoia. Prato province is the most crowded, with 614 people per square kilometre.

Umbria, with a population of just 840,000, is one of Italy's smaller regions, with 70% of the people living in the northern province of Perugia. Though a largely rural region, these days only 7% of Umbrians work in agriculture. Industries such as electronics in Terni or textiles in Perugia now draw a larger number of workers.

The make-up of the family unit is perhaps surprising in view of the traditional child-friendliness associated with Italians in general. In line with a national trend, approximately a third of Tuscan families are childless (Italy's birth rate is one of the lowest in Europe).

In recent years Italy has become popular with immigrants from North Africa, Albania and Kosovo, and Tuscany, Florence particularly, is no exception, with a relatively small multiethnic community. Prato, meanwhile, is home to Tuscany's largest Chinese community, while Chianti is a favourite with British, German and Swiss expats. Internal migration also takes place. Although migrants from the south traditionally favour northern cities such as Milan and Turin, Florence is also a popular spot.

Charles Richards' *The New Italians* gives an in-depth look at the paradoxical world of modern Italy and how Italians battle bureaucracy to make their country work.

The expat author Matthew Spender muses on the history of the region he has called home for 20 years, and shares his observations on contemporary Tuscan culture in *Within Tuscany: Reflections on a Time and Place.*

Zygmunt Baranski and Rebecca West (Eds) *The Cambridge Companion to Modern Italian Culture* is a comprehensive and invaluable collection of essays on all aspects of modern Italian culture, such as regionalism, mass media, feminism and religion, with suggestions for further reading.

SPORT
Football (Soccer)

Il calcio excites Italian souls more than politics, religion and good food all put together, and this fanatical devotion can be bewildering to outsiders. There was much consternation, therefore, when once high-flying AC Fiorentina, Tuscany's only Serie A (premier league) club, collapsed amid mounting debts and managerial scandal and was relegated to the bottom division.

DOS & DON'TS

Tuscans, and to a slightly lesser extent, Umbrians, take particular pride in their dress and appearance. To many outsiders such concerns can seem a trifle overdone, but no self-respecting local would dream of just throwing any old thing on to go out. A sense of style is important!

Your average Tuscan or Umbrian in the more touristed areas such as Florence or Perugia may have grown accustomed to the scruffy, dress down foreigners, but in restaurants, cafés, clubs and bars, baggy shorts, flip-flops and tacky T-shirts are definite no-no's. Away from the main tourist trail such an appearance will certainly attract stares.

Many churches will not allow you entry if you are deemed to be inadequately attired (generally shorts or skirts above the knees and sleeveless tops are out). No-one's suggesting you bring your Sunday best along but a little common sense and sensitivity go a long way, and you'll feel a lot more comfortable if you can at least try to blend in with the locals.

Topless sunbathing, while not uncommon on some Tuscan beaches, is not *de rigueur* – women should look around before dropping their tops. Nude sunbathing is likely to be offensive anywhere other than on appropriately designated beaches (there are a couple on Elba).

The standard form of greeting is the handshake. Kissing on both cheeks is generally reserved for people who already know one another, sometimes after only a relatively brief acquaintance. There will always be exceptions to these rules, so the best thing on being introduced to locals is probably not to launch your lips in anyone's general direction unless you are pretty sure they are welcome. If this is the case, a light brushing of cheeks will do.

The police (*polizia* and *carabinieri*) have the right to arrest you for 'insulting a state official' if they believe you have been rude or offensive – so be diplomatic in your dealings with them!

On a minor note, cappuccino is a breakfast drink for Italians, and ordering one at any other time of day will immediately identify you as a tourist. Italians also take great pride in their cuisine, so if sitting down to a gourmet meal, try not to order a fizzy drink to go with it; the waiter or sommelier will be happy to advise on the appropriate beverage.

Renamed Florentia Viola in 2002, the club has begun to bounce back, and local support remains strong. They may no longer be able to afford the likes of Roberto Baggio and Gabriel Batistuta in the line-up, but if you want to catch a game, you can see them in action at Florence's Stadio Comunale Artemio Franchi. Find more information at www.florentiaviola.it (Italian only). As you might expect, tickets are a lot cheaper these days.

Rugby Union

'The Giro d'Italia is second only to the Tour de France in popularity'

While nothing quite competes with football, the popularity of rugby is at an all-time high, mainly thanks to Italy's entry into the Six Nations Championship in 2000. Italy's rugby team still has a long way to go before it can compete on equal terms with the world leaders in the sport, but it's constantly improving. You'll have to travel to Rome's Stadio Flaminio to catch a big game, but you may get a chance to see the Florence team play at the Centro Sportivo Universitario Val di Rose, in Sesto Fiorentino (www.firenzerugby.it), while other cities such as Perugia also have active teams. Perugia games can be seen at the Campo di Pian di Massiano. Further information is available at www.rugbyperugia.it (Italian only).

Cycling

The Giro d'Italia, held each summer since 1909, is second only to the Tour de France in popularity and media coverage on the international cycling circuit. The precise route changes, with foreign stages included, but it cuts through Umbria and the length of Tuscany. Italy's sports newspapers, the *Gazetta dello Sport* and the *Corriere dello Sport*, will have up-to-date details of the race if you want to follow the thrills and spills.

MEDIA

There has been considerable disquiet in Italy in recent years over press censorship and issues of conflict of interest. The country's current prime-minister, Silvio Berlusconi, is also the richest man in Italy and owner of AC Milan football club. He infamously owns several newspapers and TV stations; his Fininvest company runs Italia 1, Canale 5 and TG4. The three national channels, RAI 1, 2 and 3, are also, rather unsubtly, very much biased towards the media magnate/prime minister and are indirectly also under his control. He has avoided the normal restrictions on public office holders owning broadcasting licences by putting family members in charge of his various media interests. In 2002 two popular news presenters on RAI were dismissed after criticising Berlusconi and were accused of making 'criminal use' of state television. Satirical programmes about the prime minister have been pulled, as have news items unfavourable to his government.

In 2003 a row broke out over his attempts to directly nominate the head of McDonald's in Italy as president of RAI, the national channel, in contravention of Italian law, while another candidate, Paulo Mieli, withdrew because of 'political difficulties' after being attacked by right-wing politicians on the grounds of his being Jewish and socialist. Previously, the board of RAI had resigned after accusations of deliberate mismanagement and systematic censorship in the prime minister's favour. Berlusconi himself has been accused of deliberately trying to ruin RAI in order to win viewers over to his own populist channels. The quality of Italian TV's output is often staggeringly poor, with many tacky gameshows, soaps and imports.

The newspaper situation isn't much better. Italy's most prestigious national daily, the *Corriere della Sera*, and *La Stampa* are both controlled by the Agnelli family, who own Fiat automobiles. The country's leading daily financial paper, *Il Sole 24 Ore*, while meant to be independent, is actually owned by Confindustria, the national manufacturers' association, and another national daily, *Il Giornale*, is edited by Silvio Berlusconi's brother.

Most amazing is that most Italians seem unconcerned; only the political classes, especially on the left, are vocal about the situation, which former prime minister Massimo d'Alema has declared 'indecent'.

Tuscany's leading newspaper is *La Nazione*, which produces regional versions and is owned by media boss Andrea Monti Riffeser, while the *Corriere dell' Umbria* is the main read in that region. Italy's two national sports newspapers are very popular as well.

See www.regione.toscana.it (Italian only) – the official website of the regional government, with all the latest news and statistics.

See www.regione.umbria.it (Italian only) – the official website of Umbria's regional government.

Visit www.italianculture.net for a concise, multilingual guide to aspects of national culture including art, literature, wine and the press.

The Dark Heart of Italy by Tobias Jones is a searing investigation into the culture of corruption and political malpractice in Berlusconi's Italy.

RELIGION

As elsewhere in Italy, Catholicism is the dominant religion. It became the state religion at the time of Italian unification in 1870, and it wasn't until the 1929 Lateran Treaty between the Vatican and the Italian state was modified in 1985 that the Catholic Church lost that status. There are also Protestant and Jewish communities in the region.

Still as many as 85% of Italians profess to be Catholic and roughly the same figure can probably be applied to Tuscany and Umbria. However, that percentage doesn't translate into church attendance, which has declined steeply in recent decades. Ritual still plays an important part in the lives of Tuscans and Umbrians – first communions, church weddings and religious feast days are an integral part of society.

There is also a small Protestant population, made up of various denominations, including Anglicans and Baptists and consisting mostly of the expat community, especially in Florence. Interestingly, Florence is one of the country's biggest centres of Buddhism, which has about 5000 followers throughout Tuscany. The city also has a small Jewish population.

Environment

THE LAND

If you regard Tuscany's coast as the base, the region forms a rough triangle covering 22,992 sq km. Crammed within that triangle is a remarkable variety of land forms, from mountains in the north and east to flat plains in the south, from islands off the coast to hill country in the interior sliced up by river valleys.

Much of the coast facing the Tyrrhenian and Ligurian seas is flat, with the major exception of a stretch immediately south of Livorno and parts of the Monte Argentario peninsula.

The northern flank of the region, which runs roughly from east to west (with a gradual southwards drop), is closed off by the Apennines, which it shares with Emilia (part of the Emilia-Romagna region) and the Apuane Alps. These latter mountains in the northwestern corner of the region are renowned for their white marble deposits (see p163).

Lower hill ranges rise further south in the region, such as those of Monte Albano south of Pistoia and Monte Pratomagno in Arezzo province to the east. Separating them is a series of low river valleys, the most important of which is the Arno. In all, two-thirds of Tuscany is mountainous or hilly.

The most extensive lowlands are the Maremma Pisana, one-time swamps south of Pisa and in from the coast, and the Maremma, which covers a wide area down to the regional boundary with Lazio.

DID YOU KNOW?

The impressive Cascata delle Marmore, plunging from a height of 165m, is not a natural phenomenon – this waterfall was created by the Romans in the 3rd century BC.

The Arno River, at 240 windy kilometres long, is Tuscany's main river, although it is hardly one of the world's great natural wonders. It rises in Monte Falterona in the Apennines, flows south to Arezzo and then meanders northwest for a while. By the time it passes through Florence it is on a westwards course towards Pisa and finally the Ligurian Sea. Once an important trade artery, traffic on the river today is virtually nonexistent.

Of the seven islands scattered off Tuscany's coast, the central and eastern parts of Elba, along with Giannutri and parts of Giglio, are reminders of a great Apennine wall that collapsed into the sea millions of years ago. Capraia, Montecristo, western Elba and parts of Giglio are the creation of volcanic activity. The islands are surprisingly varied, from the unexciting flatness of Pianosa to the rugged and rocky coastline of much of Elba, broken up here and there by small but often enchanting little coves and beaches.

Neighbouring Umbria is a landlocked region with an area of over 8400 sq km. Around 53% of the region is mountainous with a further 41% covered in hills. The massive structure of the Umbrian-Marche Appenines is dominated by the Monti Sibillini, the highest peak of which is Monte Vettore reaching over 2000m. Other notable ranges include the Gubbio Appenines, the Monti Martani and the lower, yet still impressive, peaks of the Amerini and Spoleto clusters.

Less than 10% of the region is low lying. Elms, olive trees, vines, cypresses and fruit trees dominate these plain areas, giving the region its distinctive restful appearance.

The Tiber River, which has been navigable for many centuries, runs from the north to southwest, cutting the region into two sections. The second-longest river is the Nera, remarkable for the way it meets the Velino tributary and forms the magnificent Cascata delle Marmore (Marmore Waterfalls).

Umbria is also rich in both natural and artificial lakes. Lago di Trasimeno (p266), in the west, is the largest lake in central–southern Italy. Lake Corbara (p303) and Alviano are artificial.

WILDLIFE
Animals

Cinghiale, or wild boar, has been on Tuscan menus since the days of the Etruscans, and the rural areas of the region still teem with them. The only difference is that today most of them are the offspring of Eastern European boar imported to make up for the depletion of local species. They can also be found in many of the regional nature parks in Umbria. Although common enough, you will probably not spot them on walks in the countryside. They are busy avoiding their nastiest enemy – the hunter.

Among other animals fairly common in the Tuscan and Umbrian countryside are squirrels, rabbits, foxes, martens, weasels and hares. The badger and the black-and-white-quilled *istrice*, a porcupine supposedly imported from North Africa by the ancient Romans, are more rare. In parks such as the Parco Regionale della Maremma roe deer are frequently spotted, especially at dawn or dusk.

Wolves purportedly still roam the hills between Volterra and Massa Marittima, but some locals think they are actually only wild dogs. Either way, sightings are incredibly rare and you'd be very lucky to spot them. You've a better chance of seeing one in Parco Regionale del Monte Cucco, where there are more thanks to the mountainous environment. The wildcat is another predator that roams the scarcely populated areas of Tuscany and Umbria, but because there are very few they are hardly ever seen.

On a more slithery note, you can encounter several kinds of snake. Most are harmless and will glide out of your way if you give them warning (by treading heavily as you approach them). The only poisonous customer is the viper, which can be identified by its diamond markings. Rocky areas and the island of Elba are among its principal habitats.

Bird life is varied in Tuscany. The best time of year for fully appreciating it is from November to around March, when many migratory species hang about in nature reserves along the coast, including Lago di Burano, Laguna di Orbetello and Monti dell'Uccellina. As many as 140 species of our winged friends call Tuscany home or use it as a stopover. They include the blackbird, black-winged stilt, buzzard, crow, dove, falcon, hawk, hoopoe, jay, kestrel, kingfisher, osprey, thrush, tit, woodpecker and wren.

Umbria is also a great place to see a wide variety of bird life. The extensive marshlands are an important stopping-off place for migratory species such as the grey heron, purple heron, bittern, mallard and spoonbill. In other parts of the region birds of prey such as the golden eagle, goshawk, peregrine, eagle owl and osprey are also present.

The hunting season extends from early September to sometime in January. The opening and closure dates depend in part on what you want to hunt. Limits are imposed on how many of any given type of bird or animal you can bag in one day, and hunters are required to arm themselves with a licence and practise the activity in designated areas. Some game animals, such as wild boar, are considered pests in some areas and culled as such.

Plants

Tuscan and Umbrian farmland has long been appreciated as a visual treat, a pleasing mix of orderly human intervention and natural 'chaos'. In among the ubiquitous olive groves (olives were introduced in Etruscan times from the Middle East) and vineyards, a feast of trees and smaller plants thrives.

DID YOU KNOW?

The Dunarobba Fossil Forest, near Avigliano, is one of the oldest woods in the world, thought to date back almost two million years.

Check out www.lipu.it for the Italian Bird Protection League (LIPU); visit its UK branch at www.lipu-uk.org

The European Federation Against Hunting (LAC) can be found at www.anticaccia.it

Where to Watch Birds in Italy, published by the Italian Bird Protection League (LIPU), highlights over 100 recommendations for species spotting.

Tall, slender cypress and the odd flattened *pino marittimo* (or cluster pines, mainly on the coast) are among the most striking of the regions' call-sign trees. Driving down a cypress-lined country road on the way to a little village or vineyard is one of those pleasant daydreams that frequently become reality for the cross-country tourist. The cypress was introduced from Asia Minor in Roman times precisely for its decorative qualities.

Beech trees are common in the mountainous territory of the Apuane Alps, often competing for attention with chestnuts. Hunting for chestnuts and then cooking them is a favourite pastime on November weekends. In the Casentino and Vallombrosa areas of eastern Tuscany, deep, thick forests of pine, oak (one species of which is the cork, the bark of which is all-important to the wine industry) and beech still cover important tracts of otherwise little-touched land. Other species include maple, hazelnut, alder and imported eucalyptus.

In Umbria, other trees of note include willows, poplars and the black alder. Water lilies flourish in the rich marshlands while rare varieties of flora such as the yellow poppy can be found in Parco dei Monti Sibillini.

Springtime is obviously the brightest time of year in Tuscany and Umbria, when whole valley floors and upland plains are bathed in a technicolour sea of wild flowers. They can include jonquils, crocuses, anemones, gentians and orchids.

Tuscan coastal and island areas boast typical Mediterranean *macchia*, or scrub.

Flower spotters should equip themselves with specialist books such as Mediterranean Wild Flowers, by M Blamey & C Grey Wilson.

Try Paul Sterry's Complete Mediterranean Wildlife for a general guide to the flora and fauna of the region.

NATIONAL PARKS

Tuscany can claim two of Italy's 20 national parks. The Parco Nazionale dell'Arcipelago Toscano is Europe's largest marine park and includes the islands of Montecristo, Gorgona, Giannutri, Pianosa and part of Capraia, Elba and Giglio. It was set up in 1996 to protect a wild mountainous environment occupied by rare species of flora and fauna. Within Parco Nazionale delle Foreste Casentinesi Monte Falterona Campigna, on the border of Emilia-Romagna, you'll find one of the most extensive and best-preserved forests in central Italy.

The region also has three regional parks, one in the Apuane Alps, one in the Maremma and one on the heavily urbanised coast near Livorno.

Umbria has only one national park, Parco dei Monti Sibillini, which takes its name from the principal mountain range in the area. There are also the following regional parks: Parco Regionale di Colfiorito, Parco Regionale del Trasimeno, Parco Regionale del Monte Cucco, Parco Regionale del Monte Subasio, Parco Regionale del Fiume Nera and the Parco Regionale del Tevere. Other protected areas and places of naturalistic interest include La Valle Nature Oasis, La Cascata delle Marmore, Fonti del Clitunno (Clitunno Springs) and Foresta Fossile di Dunarobba (Fossil Forest).

The parks, reserves and wetlands all play a crucial part in the protection of the region's flora and fauna and there are regular conservation events and open days.

For further information on national parks and other protected areas in Tuscany and Umbria, visit www.parks.it

The World Wide Fund for Nature (WWF) has an Italian chapter at www.wwf.it

ENVIRONMENTAL ISSUES

One of the greatest ecological headaches in the region is the question of marble extraction in the mountains of the Apuane Alps. The great white scars (which from the seaside almost look like snowfalls) are the result of many centuries' work.

But today, the pace of removal has accelerated. About 1.5 million tonnes per year are scraped out and trundled away on heavy trucks. Before WWII, the level of incursion was much slighter and marble miners eased blocks down to nearby villages with complex pulley systems. The extraction is disfiguring part of a nature reserve, the waste produced is creating disposal problems and the heavy truck traffic is an ecological disaster. However, no-one dares seriously object to this prestigious industry. Carrara marble is sought after worldwide by everyone from architects to sculptors.

Heavy industry never really came to Tuscany or Umbria, so the associated problems of air and water pollution elsewhere in Italy are not as great here. That said, the medium- and light-industrial areas of Livorno, Piombino, suburban Florence, Perugia and along the Arno and Tiber rivers are far from hazard free. Heavy road traffic makes clean air a distant dream in Florence and in much of the heavily populated Prato-Pistoia area. Noise pollution can also be a problem in cities. Umbria is much less affected by pollution thanks to farming being the chief occupation. The introduction of several hydroelectric plants and the manufacturing of chemicals, iron, steel and processed food have all taken their toll on the countryside but on a much smaller scale and with a less detrimental impact on the environment.

www.blueflag.org lists the region's cleanest beaches.

The landscape of Tuscany and Umbria has long seemed something of a work of art, with farmers alternating a patchwork quilt of farmland with stretches of forest. The post-war crisis in agriculture saw many farmers leave the land and in more remote spots, where wringing results from the earth was always a challenge at best, forest or scrub is reclaiming its territory. Sometimes this uncontrolled regrowth has a downside, helping propagate bushfires as occurred in the summers of 1998 and 2001.

Regional government bodies in both Tuscany and Umbria are now taking a tougher line concerning the environment, partly in response to EU directives. Initiatives include reforestation measures with a view to the protection of natural areas and the promotion of environmentally friendly agricultural methods.

RESPONSIBLE TRAVEL

Thanks to the temperate climate and stunning landscape, both Tuscany and Umbria are becoming increasingly popular with walkers and hikers. Unfortunately, the increase in the number of visitors has placed a great pressure on the natural environment. Please consider the following tips when walking and help preserve the ecology and beauty of the region:

- Don't light fires unless you're absolutely sure it's safe.
- Don't pick alpine wild flowers – most of them are protected.
- Take all rubbish away with you, including cigarette butts, unless there are litter bins in the area. Don't bury your rubbish.
- Leave the wildlife alone.
- Don't make too much noise.
- Be careful about where you go to the toilet and be sure to bury waste.
- Ensure that you leave gates as you found them after you have passed through.
- Be attentive when passing through fields, particularly during periods of cultivation. Stick to the edges or obvious tracks and don't trample on crops.
- Keep to existing tracks to avoid causing erosion by disturbing the natural lay of the land.
- Don't pick grapes or olives on your way through vineyards or olive groves.
- Take note of and observe any rules and regulations particular to the national or state reserve that you are visiting.

Tuscany & Umbria Outdoors

The incomparably beautiful landscapes of Tuscany and Umbria beg to be explored and enjoyed. Those who tear through the regions on the highway miss out on a vast variety of outdoor activities that underscore the area's splendour.

Because Tuscany and Umbria are year-round destinations, there's something to do in every season. Everyone can find a suitable activity, from adrenaline-inspiring skiing to leisurely countryside walks. While travellers on holiday with the family will be delighted to discover how accessible these activities are, sojourners in search of more demanding pursuits won't be disappointed either.

So even if you had planned to lounge around the villa and sip chianti all day long, make an effort to get outdoors. Your holiday will be far better for it.

WALKING

Tuscany and Umbria are eminently suited to walking and a common sight throughout the region is large organised groups, most commonly from the UK. It must be something about those anoraks and floppy white sunhats that makes Brits so easy to spot.

This region is undeniably beautiful for walking. The patchwork country-side of the centre, the wilder valleys and mountains south and northwest, and the dramatic Apuane Alps and Apennine ranges offer a colourful variety of opportunities to the traveller with time and a desire to move on foot. A truly ambitious walker could undertake the 24-stage Grande Escursione Appenninica, an arc that takes you from the Due Santi pass above La Spezia southeast to Sansepolcro. Alternatively Umbria's Monti Sibillini is superb for walkers, using Castelluccio as a base, with a choice of demanding backpack hikes to the summit or casual day hikes (see p302).

'This region is undeniably beautiful for walking'

People have been traipsing across Tuscany since Adam was a boy, creating paths and trails as they went. One of the most important pilgrim routes in Europe during the Dark Ages was known as the Via Francigena (or Via Romea), which turned into something of a highway across Tuscany. Starting down the Magra River valley through the wild Lunigiana territory of the northwest, the trail hugged the coast for a while before cutting inland to Siena via San Gimignano and then turning south to the Christian capital, Rome. Parts of the route can still be walked today.

For information on walking and its effect on the natural environment, see the boxed text, p35.

Best Time of Year

Spring is undoubtedly the prettiest period to walk here, while the col-ours of autumn have their own mellow appeal. Given that summertime continues into late October, you have lots of light for longer walks. After Tuscany's mad summer tourist rush, things begin to ease off by late Sep-tember – all the more so out in the countryside.

If you're planning to go walking in the Apuane Alps or other mountain areas (such as Monte Vettore or the small Orecchiella reserve), the most pleasant (and safest) time is the summer, although August is to be avoided as this is when most Italians take their holiday and trails get busy. Inland, however, should be avoided during summer as the heat can be oppressive, making even a crawl to the nearest air-conditioned bar a bit of a strain.

What to Take

For your average walks in the Tuscany-Umbria area you will need only a minimum of items. Firstly, and pretty obviously, the right footwear is essential, either comfortable lace-up walking shoes or sturdy boots, depending on what kind of terrain you are planning to cover. A small daypack could contain an extra layer of clothing should temperatures drop and some kind of wet-weather gear. Depending on the season, sunblock, sunglasses and a hat are recommended. Obviously you need a map of the area you are walking in and a compass should be a standard item in any walker's pack.

For details of self-guided walking tours in Tuscany and Umbria, visit www.hiddenitaly.com.au /walks

Free camping is not permitted in the mountains. That may seem like bad news to some, because you need to plan your overnight stops around the availability of beds in *rifugi*. The upside is that you can leave tents, cooking gear and the like at your base accommodation. Bring your sleeping bag along as extra insurance against the cold.

On the subject of cold, you need to be prepared for all kinds of weather in the mountains. You may start the day in splendid sunshine and heat, but that can easily change to cold and wet – bear in mind that the Apuane Alps get the greatest concentration of rainfall in Tuscany. Take an extra pair of shoes to change into at the end of the day.

Prime Spots

The **Chianti** region continues to be one of the most popular for walkers of all levels. One of the classic walks would take you rambling over several days (perhaps as many as five or six) from Florence to Siena. The variations on this theme are numerous. Away from Chianti territory, another popular option is to walk from **San Gimignano** to **Volterra.** The start and end points are fascinating medieval towns with good transport links and plenty of accommodation. History buffs may want to walk in the tracks of the Etruscans, making a base in **Suvereto** or **Campiglia Marittima.** At the park of **San Silvestro** you can embark on a choice of archeological itineraries, guided or not. For more information, pick up the *Nature Walks* (Costa degli Etruschi) booklet at any tourist office in this area. For serious hikes, the **Apuane Alps** are stunning, and challenging, although there are possibilities for less arduous itineraries here. To get a feel for the area, hop on the *Treno nei Parchi*, which is specifically geared towards hikers.

The island of **Elba** is especially well geared for comparatively short walks and you will generally be able to plan your own routes quite easily. For more information contact **Il Genio del Bosco – Centro Trekking Isola d'Elba** (☎ 0565 93 08 37). In **Umbria**, hiking in the scenic **Sibillini** is wonderful, although there are relatively few marked trails. A good base for shorter day hikes is **Castelluccio** with a choice of trails leaving the village in several different directions; one of the most popular leads to the Lago di Pilato under Monte Vettore and, supposedly, where Pontius Pilate is buried.

Information

MAPS & BOOKS

Several publishers produce maps of varying quality that cover certain parts of Tuscany. The best regional map is probably Touring Club Italiano's (TCI's) 1:200,000 scale map. It is detailed and a more than sufficient tool for navigating around the region on wheels.

The next level down, but still not detailed enough for walking, is individual provincial maps. Edizioni Multigraphic Firenze publishes a series. Ask for the *Carta Stradale Provinciale* of the province(s) you want. They are scaled at 1:100,000.

Another publisher is Kompass, which produces 1:25,000 scale maps of various parts of Italy, including Tuscany and Umbria. In some cases it covers areas that Edizioni Multigraphic doesn't. Occasionally you will come across useful maps put out by the Club Alpino Italiano (CAI) as well.

You are unlikely to want to lug too many books along. An excellent one that includes over 50 walks and hikes of a not-too-strenuous nature is *Walking in Tuscany*, by Gillian Price (the text spills over into neighbouring Umbria and Lazio). This covers an ample selection taking you from Chianti country to the island of Elba, and to plenty of lesser explored parts of the Tuscan region as well.

Price does not cover the more arduous trekking possibilities in the Apuane Alps in Tuscany's northwest. For a couple of good suggestions, see Lonely Planet's specialist guide *Walking in Italy*, which includes several other walks in Tuscany and Umbria. *The Alps of Tuscany*, by Franceso Greco, describes in detail a good number of walks in the Apuane Alps. Tim Jepson's *Wild Italy* has some information on the Apuane Alps, but if your Italian is up to it you should go for one of several Italian guides on the mountains, such as *Alpi Apuane: Guida al Territorio del Parco* by Frederick Bradley and Enrico Medda. The series of *Guide dei Monti d'Italia*, grey hardbacks published by the TCI and CAI, are exhaustive walking guides containing maps. *Walking and Eating in Tuscany and Umbria* by James Lasdun and Pia Davis provides 40 varied itineraries across these two central regions of Italy.

Walking Holidays

There are plenty of options available. Reputable organisations with good websites include www.ramblersholidays.co.uk; www.sherpa-walking-holidays.co.uk; and www.inntravel.co.uk.

CYCLING

Italy is a cycle-friendly country. Most of the historic town and city centres are closed to traffic and there are plenty of places where you can rent a bike, buy your colour-coordinated lycra, and obtain advice on routes and itineraries. Whether you are looking for a gentle day's pedalling around town with kids in tow, a weekend winery tour in Il Chianti with a bunch of friends or to seriously work on that muscle tone over several weeks of pedal power, Tuscany and Umbria provide plenty of cycling-scope.

Cycling to Suit You

With such a varied landscape there is a wide choice of roads and routes. Paved roads are particularly suited to high-tech racing bikes or travelling long distances on touring bikes. Country roads, known as *strade bianche,* have dirt surfaces covered with gravel for stability and are a characteristic aspect of the landscape.

Backroads and trails are a further option, but only if you are fit and have a quality multi-gear bike, as this is mainly hilly terrain. Don't despair, as there are also itineraries with gentler slopes for amateur cyclists and even for families with children. Likewise, for the more ambitious cyclist, there are plenty of challenges: Monte Amiata is the perfect goal for aspiring hill climbers, while hilly itineraries with short but challenging climbs can be found from Umbria through to Il Chianti and Le Crete.

'With such a varied landscape there is a wide choice of roads and routes'

Best Time of Year

The best time of year for serious pedalling is in the spring, not only because of the obvious advantage of a cooler temperature, but also because the scenery is arguably at its most breathtaking at this time of year, with valleys drenched in poppies and wild flowers. However, Easter and holidays around 25 April and 1 May should obviously be avoided.

Autumn is also a good season, although it may be rainy, which can lead to slippery roads and poor visibility.

What Type of Bike?

The most versatile bicycle for most of the roads here is a comfortable all-terrain bike capable of travelling over both paved and country roads and, even more importantly, capable of climbing up hills. Ideally, it should afford a relaxed riding posture and be equipped with a gear system similar to a mountain bike. If you don't happen to have an all-terrain bike in your fleet of cycles, you can modify a mountain bike by substituting its wide grooved tyres with faster, narrower (1.4cm) tyres.

You may well find you are travelling along isolated roads that pass through fields or woodlands, so it's wise to be equipped with a kit for essential repairs. Always wear a helmet and have a detailed map of the area.

If you are bringing your own bike, check with your airline for costs and the degree of dismantling and packing required. Bikes can be transported by train in Italy, either with you or within a couple of days.

Prime Spots
IL CHIANTI

Hard to describe without serious superlative overdose – just check out a Tuscany calendar and you'll get the picture. More importantly, there are over 400km of traffic-free roads and, apparently, plans are underway to develop the sport further with more trails and special cycle signposts to indicate directions (how kind), as well as pertinent information regarding accommodation, mechanical assistance and even bicycle rental.

Il Chianti is also home to the annual **L'Eroica** (literally 'The Heroic') race, a day-long race organised by the **Parco Ciclistico del Chianti** (☎ 0577 74 94 11), which covers over 100km of primarily unpaved road. Not to be taken too seriously, the competitors ride on 'vintage' bikes with strictly no mountain bikes allowed.

Lago di Trasimeno abounds with water sports and outdoor activities. Ask for *Tourist Itineraries in the Trasimeno District*, a booklet of walking and horse-riding tracks, at the tourist office (p266).

AROUND SIENA

The hills around **San Gimignano** and **Colle Val d'Elsa** are very popular with cyclists. A challenging route here starts at Casole d'Elsa, following the road as it climbs to Monteguidi, then descending to cross the Cecina River before reaching the village of **Montecastelli** in the province of Pisa. An easier ride starts with a panoramic circuit around the town walls of **Monteriggioni**, carrying on to Colle Val d'Elsa and then towards San Gimignano and **Volterra**.

LE CRETE

The rolling landscape here is similar to Il Chianti, except that instead of woodlands there are vast swathes of wheat fields. Cycling here has been compared to sailing over a sea of land. Among the most stunning routes are the Monte Sante Marie road from Asciano to Torre a Castello and the Pieve a Salti road from Buonconvento to **San Giovanni d'Asso**. Both are unpaved and require all-terrain bikes or mountain bikes. An alternative for cyclists with racing bikes is the legendary Lauretana road from **Siena** to **Asciano** and onwards towards **Chiusure**, **Mont Oliveto Maggiore** and **Buonconvento**.

MONTE AMIATA

Only die-hard peddlers should attempt to climb this 1738m volcano. The good news is that, at a mere 1370m, there is accommodation and a restaurant (Prato Le Macinaie) some 4km from the peak. There are several routes available: the easiest are those leading up from Arcidossa and Abbadia San Salvatore; the latter is a 14km uphill ride with a steady but reasonably slight gradient. The most difficult approach is Castel del Piano, 15km uphill with a steady steep gradient over 7% to 8% for the first 10km.

UMBRIA

The broad valleys of the Umbria region around Orvieto, Spello and Lago di Trasimeno are not too physically demanding and are well suited for cyclists who want to experience the beauty of the unique and varied landscape at a more leisurely pace.

Information
MAPS & BOOKS

Edizioni Multigraphic publishes a couple of series of maps designed for walkers and mountain-bike riders (*mulattiere*, or mule trails, are especially good for mountain bikes), which are scaled at 1:50,000 and 1:25,000. Where possible you should go for the latter. Ask for the *Carta dei Sentieri e Rifugi* or *Carta Turistica e dei Sentieri*.

The *Guida Cicloturistica del Chianti* has 20 cycling itineraries and 32 detailed maps of the Chianti region. You can pick up a copy at the Siena tourist office. Another excellent reference for planning your cycling trip that you can pick up at most bookshops is *Toscana in Mountain Bike* (www.ediciclo.it - Italian only), covering 31 itineraries throughout Il Chianti, Montagnola, Crete Senesi, Val d'Orcia and Mont Amiata.

Lonely Planet's *Cycling in Italy* includes detailed itineraries for cycling in Tuscany and Umbria. *Garfagnana by Bicycle* by Lucia Giovannette and published by Tamari Montagna Edizioni has 32 colour photos, detailed descriptions of key route features, a contour map and 27 itineraries for mountain bikes, and five touring maps.

Check out www.parks.it for all the information you could ever want or need about Tuscany and Umbria's parks, nature reserves, mountains, rivers, lakes and coast.

CYCLING ASSOCIATIONS

The Siena-based **Gli Amica Della Bicicletta** (☎ 0577 4 51 59; www.comune.siena.it/adb; Via Campansi 32) is a very active, ecologically minded group that promotes cycling as a daily form of urban transport and organises day-long and sometimes longer bicycle trips. It also dedicates considerable effort to developing cycling paths and itineraries for visiting cyclists.

Cycling Holidays

There are numerous organisations that organise cycling trips to Tuscany and Umbria. The best idea is to check the web. The following sites are a good place to start: www.ciclismoclassico.com; www.xplus.com; www.ibikeitaly.com; www.bicycletuscany.com; www.sherpa-walking-holidays.co.uk; and www.alternative-travel.co.uk.

The approximate cost of a one-week cycling tour with meals and accommodation is €870.

SKIING

This region's skiing scene is centred on **Abetone**, on the border with the region of Emilia-Romagna. While it is true that the Apennines are smaller and less majestic than the Alps, they have a charm all their own.

There are some 51km of trails, 25 ski lifts (including the cabin lift that was closed for a couple of years in 2002 due to fire) and an average of 118cm annual snowfall, as well as artificial snowmakers (accounting for around 30% of the snow).

Prime Spots
If you need to rent equipment, there are a couple of shops on the main square in Abetone that hire out boots and skis – you'll have to supply your own woolly hat. From here it is just a couple of minutes' walk to the chair lift. This will carry you to the top of **Monte Selletta** (1711m) and a good choice of slopes rated blue (easy) and a couple rated red (difficult), although the latter should pose little problem to relatively novice skiers. On the contrary, they are exhilarating with alternating dips that allow you to pick up speed, followed by slower, flat sections where you can regain control.

Once you've warmed up with a couple of easy runs, ski across the face of the ridge to lift 17, then take lift 15 and whoosh down the trail to lift 18. This is the heart of the ski area with trails leading into all the valleys on the Tuscan side. It also serves as the access point for the **Val di Luce** (Valley of Light), a beautiful and appropriately named valley that contains most of the area's more interesting intermediate trails. If you head to the **Alpe Tre Potenze** (1940m), you will be rewarded with gorgeous panoramic views stretching all the way to the Tuscan coast.

Best Time of Year
The skiing season throughout Italy generally runs from December to late March, although at higher altitudes and in particularly good years it can be longer. Abetone gets pretty busy during weekends with people heading out here from Florence and other nearby cities, such as Lucca and Pisa.

If you are here in March you may catch the **Pinocchio Sugle Sci & Snowboard** national and international skiing and snowboarding competitions.

Information
For ski-lift tickets and more information, contact the **Ufficio Centrale Biglietti** (☎ 0573 6 05 56; Piazza Piramidi, Abetone; 1-day weekday/weekend €24/28, 3-day weekdays €58, 1 week €105; ☽ 8am-1pm & 3-7pm). You can also sign up for lessons with a couple of ski schools. **Scuola Sci Abetone** (☎ 0573 6 00 32) and the **Scuola Sci Montegomito** (☎ 0573 6 03 92) offer an hour's tuition for a minimum of €35.

WATER SPORTS
Enjoying the water doesn't necessarily involve any special effort or equipment but, if you want more than an idle paddle or swim, there are plenty of activities on offer. Diving facilities are generally of a high standard, and **scuba-diving courses** are not that expensive, with good rental gear widely available. **Snorkelling** is the low-tech alternative, and still allows you to get dramatically close to fascinating aquatic life. Although there are several areas that are excellent for diving, including **Monte Argentario** (Porto Ercole), the island of **Elba** is where most divers of all levels head. The main tourist office in Portoferraio can supply you with an extensive list of diving schools and courses available. Check that the school is a member of the **Circulo Subacqueri Association** (☎ 0565 9 30 46; Loc. Antiche Saline).

If you're into wrecks, you can dive at Pomonte where the *Elvisco* cargo boat is submerged at a depth of 12m. Alternatively, a Junker 52, an aeroplane from WWII, has also recently been discovered near Portoferraio at a more challenging depth of 38m.

'The island of Elba is where most divers of all levels head'

'You will
be rewarded
with
gorgeous
panoramic
views
stretching all
the way to
the Tuscan
coast'

The following prices are approximate: one dive €32; six dives €168; introductory snorkelling €68; and dive master course €468.

The coves of the Tuscan archipelagos and around Monte Argentario are superb for **sailing**, as well as **windsurfing** and **kitesurfing**. You can rent equipment and receive instruction at the major resorts. Typically, a six-day sailing or windsurfing/kitesurfing course costs from €130 (1½ hours per day).

Windsurfing is also very popular on the Costa Fiorita near Livorno. For information on sailing and windsurfing courses here, contact **Costa Fiorita Booking Centre** (☎ 0586 75 90 59; info@costafiorita.it), which also organises a large international-calibre **Regata Velica d'Altura (Trofeo Daniele Schena)** in early September (and can offer weekend 'regatta' training beforehand). Further up the coast, **Viareggio** holds several annual sailing regattas, including the **Coppa di Primavera** in March and the **Vela Mare Cup** in May. For more information, check out the website: www.circolovelamare.it. If you are planning to sail to Italy, you must report to the Port Authority of your first port to show passports and receive your Constito, which identifies you and allows you to purchase fuel tax-free. If you plan to moor your boat in Italy for an extended period, you are required to have a Navigation Licence.

All boats must pay a daily berthing fee in Italian ports. The national tourist office has a list of ports that charter yachts in Tuscan ports.

Fishing in the sea is unlikely to lead to a very plentiful catch, due to commercial over-fishing that (in turn) has led to regular fishing bans. You are better off heading for the trout farms and man-made lakes and streams, although you will need a permit, available from the Federazione Italiano della Pesca Sportiva ed Attività Subacuee (with offices in every province), before you cast your line.

Best Time of Year

In Monte Argentario and Elba it's possible to enjoy most water sports, including diving, throughout autumn and winter as the water tempera-ture remains relatively temperate year-round, thanks to the mild climate. For diving, however, it is still advisable to wear a semi-dry suit from November to October, whereas you should switch to a regular wet suit in the summer.

The Arts in Tuscany & Umbria

The undisputed beauty of the Tuscan and Umbrian countryside is matched only by the extraordinary artistic output of its people. While Tuscany gained worldwide fame as one of the foremost creators of all things artistic, from the Middle Ages through the Renaissance, Umbria was no slouch. A few millennia worth of some of the most impressive and well-known art on the planet blankets Tuscany and Umbria.

ARCHITECTURE
A Long, Long Time Ago...
While the most famous ancient architecture is found outside of the region, there is a decent smattering of pre-Etruscan, Etruscan and Roman urban centres and necropolises (burial grounds) left in Umbria and, to a lesser degree, Tuscany. In Umbria, Amelia boasts town walls that date to the 6th century BC. Outside of Perugia lies the Ipogeo dei Volumni burial site and outside of Orvieto is the Crocifisso del Tufo necropolis. Etruscans often buried their dead with their worldly possessions. Much of the recovered loot from these two sites is on display in museums, such as the Claudio Faina in Orvieto (p316) or the National Archaeological Museum in Perugia (p259). Perhaps the most imposing Etruscan monument is the Arco Etrusco (Etruscan Arch), built as a gateway into the city of Perugia.

The first technological advance that allowed the Etruscan civilisation to prosper was the advent of intricate drainage systems for the marshy valleys of Umbria and Tuscany, which allowed for a more complex agricultural system. The Etruscans wanted a strategic viewpoint to watch over their crops, which led to the building of towns on top of tufaceous plateaus, thus, the birth of the Italian hill town.

A few Roman ruins remain in Umbria, fewer in Tuscany. The most complete example is in Carsulae (p308), a Roman village outside of modern-day Terni, which was on the Via Flamini. Although you'd see much more intact Roman architecture in a place like Pompeii or, well, Rome, many towns have examples of Roman architecture. In Tuscany, there are Roman baths and a theatre in Volterra, an amphitheatre and smaller artefacts such as coins and vases in Arezzo and Roman bath ruins in Fiesole. In Umbria you'll find the grand amphitheatre in Spoleto, sections of a Roman bridge and aqueduct in Narni and the city gates and well-preserved walls in Spello. Bevagna (p290) in Umbria still has remnants of an amphitheatre and baths, and the town of Gubbio has a working Roman theatre (p273).

The Etruscans (Peoples of Europe) by Graham Barker and Tom Rasmussen is the foremost book on Etruscan culture, drawing upon centuries of archaeological and architectural research to contemplate this advanced civilisation.

Romanesque
Tuscany and Umbria weren't faring well for a few hundred years. After the collapse of the Roman Empire and through the early medieval centuries of barbarian hordes from the north, intertwined with a succession of foreign rulers, the region developed an architectural style classically influenced by Roman designs. The standard church ground plan, generally composed of a nave and two aisles, no transept, between one and five apses and topped by a simple dome, followed that used in Roman-era basilicas. Initially, at any rate, churches tended to be bereft of decoration except for the semicircular apses and arches above doorways and windows. The focus was on the architectural experience; how

one is manipulated by the space. Such churches were most commonly accompanied by a free-standing square-based bell tower, also adorned with layers of semicircular arched windows.

Check out
www.greatbuildings
.com/places/italy.html
for a comprehensive
list of prominent Italian
buildings.

One of the earliest Romanesque examples in Umbria is the Tempietto del Clitunno (p298), near Spoleto. It was built from the 5th to the 8th century AD but incorporated recycled materials from older structures. This is known in Latin (and among art historians) as *spolia*, literally re-using the 'spoils' from destroyed or looted monuments to build a new structure. In Spoleto, most of the cathedral has been reconstructed but features – including the impressive facade – remain.

In Tuscany, the early rediscovery of that favourite of Roman building materials, marble, led to a rather florid decorative style, the best examples of which you can see in Pisa and Lucca. The key characteristics of the Tuscan variant are the use of two-tone marble banding and complex rows of columns and loggias in the facade. The cathedral in Carrara (p164), begun in the 11th century, was one of the first medieval buildings to be constructed entirely of marble from the Apuane Alps.

The Battistero (p89) in Florence, embellished in its marble casing, is a fine example of the pure lines of the Romanesque style. Compare it with the Gothic mass of the Duomo (Cathedral; p87) next door. Also in Florence, the Chiesa di San Miniato al Monte is a splendid example of the Gothic style. The Pieve di Santa Maria (p243) in Arezzo is another fine version, although lacking the refinement of a marble facing.

Gothic

There was no one Saturday-23-January-1196-AD-at-6.35am kind of moment when Romanesque architecture ended and Gothic architecture began, but by the beginning of the 13th century, many of the buildings in Tuscany and Umbria were slowly inching their way towards Gothic.

Gothic architecture began in the Île de France area around Paris and quickly spread to Italy. Compared to their Romanesque predecessors, the newer Gothic churches and palaces are colossal. The description 'Gothic' came from 16th-century scholars who named the style after the Goths, the destroyers of the Roman Empire. The Gothic architectural style suppressed anything Roman in nature. The one element most Gothic structures have in common is their great height. Soaring structures, it was felt, would lift mortal eyes to the heavens and at the same time remind people of their smallness compared to the greatness of God. Rather than relying on the solidity of mass, priority was given to an almost diaphanous light pouring through tall pointed windows. These churches were bedecked to the hilt – pinnacles, statues, gargoyles and baubles, the busier, the better.

The central-Italian version of Gothic is somewhat different to the improbable lace stonework of the great Gothic cathedrals of northern Europe, such as Notre Dame in Paris. Although still of the same epic proportions, Gothic churches in Tuscany were relatively unadorned, but equally as impressive with rich marble decoration. Of particular note are the cathedrals of Florence, Siena and Orvieto, and the churches of Santa Croce (p102) and Santa Maria Novella (p97) in Florence.

Florence's Duomo was designed by Arnolfo di Cambio (1245–1302), the first great master builder in Florentine architectural history. Arnolfo was also responsible for applying the Gothic style to one of Florence's great civic structures, the Palazzo Vecchio (p92). Built of *pietra forte* (literally 'hard stone') with the rusticated surface typical of many grand buildings in Florence, it's one of the most imposing medieval Italian government buildings. Its rival could be only thought of as the Palazzo Pubblico (p192) in Siena, built at the turn of the 14th century, with its slender Torre del Mangia. Di Cambio also built the cathedral (p315) in Orvieto.

One of the most important and influential churches ever built was the Basilica di San Francesco in Assisi (p281). Touches from the Roman and Romanesque periods combined with Gothic designs, such as grand arches and vaulting, led to a change in architecture. The lower church was designed in a more classic Romanesque style – heavy walls, thick piers, etc – while the upper church is one of the best examples of Italian-Gothic architecture ever created.

Bad Boy Brunelleschi

Enter Filippo Brunelleschi (1377–1446), one of the hotter tempers in the history of Italian architecture. Brunelleschi launched the architectural branch of the Renaissance in Florence, but his greatest contribution to architecture, however, was the concept of the architect itself. Instead of acting as foreman, building on the fly, Brunelleschi designed formulae of perspective, mathematics and balance, and created buildings first on a drawing board.

His buildings are still found throughout Florence today: the Spedale degli Innocenti (Hospital of the Innocents, 1419; p101), considered the earliest work of the Florentine Renaissance, the Sagrestia Vecchia (Old Sacristy) in the Basilica di San Lorenzo (1428; p98), and the redesign of both the Basilica di San Lorenzo (1420) and the Basilica di Santo Spirito (designed in 1436; p106). The use of Corinthian columns, simple arches, a coffered ceiling over the wide nave (merely painted in Santo Spirito) and two-tone (greenish grey *pietra serena,* literally 'tranquil stone', and white plaster on the trim) colouring are common elements, but closer inspection soon reveals differences. But perhaps Brunelleschi's most important work was the revolutionary cupola on top of Florence's Duomo. He used his knowledge of architecture, science and art, along with a study of Roman construction – especially the dome of the Pantheon – to build this astonishing architectural feat.

Ross King's *Brunelleschi's Dome: How a Renaissance Genius Reinvented Architecture* chronicles how this hot-tempered Renaissance man constructed the largest bricks-and-mortar dome ever created.

Florence & the Renaissance

The Italian Renaissance thrived first and foremost in Florence, peaking in the mid-16th century. It is generally accepted that Michelozzo di Bartolomeo Michelozzi (1396–1472) was commissioned by Cosimo de' Medici to build a new residence that was in keeping with the family's importance (Palazzo Medici-Riccardi; p99). Three hefty storeys, with the air of a fortress, are topped by a solid roof with eaves jutting far out from the walls. The lowest storey features rustication (which can also be seen on the Palazzo Vecchio). This describes the rough-hewn, protruding blocks of stone used to build it, as opposed to the smoothed stone of the upper storeys. This building set the tone for civic building in Florence.

Other Renaissance palaces represent variations on the style and lend Florence its uniquely stern yet elegant feel. One example is the Palazzo Strozzi (p98), designed by Benedetto da Maiano (1442–97) with facade work by Giuliano da Sangallo (1445–1516). This particular aspect of Florentine Renaissance building was echoed in buildings in other parts of Tuscany, especially the nearby northern towns of Prato, Pistoia and Pisa – and often many years after the Renaissance had been left behind.

Francesco di Giorgio (1439–1502) was about the only architect of any note to come out of Siena during the Renaissance. An accomplished painter and sculptor as well, his only lasting building is the Chiesa di Santa Maria del Calcinaio, a few kilometres outside Cortona. His was an original vision – he dropped the use of pillars and columns to separate aisles from a central nave. Instead, the building is a solid, two-storey construction with tabernacle windows on the second level.

Two of the most important Renaissance buildings in Umbria are the Palazzo Ducale in Gubbio (c1470; p273) by Francesco Giorgio Martini and the Tempio di Santa Maria della Consolazione (1508; p304) in Todi, thought to have been designed by Donato Bramante (1444–1514).

Michelangelo
Born into a poor family, Michelangelo Buonarroti (1475–1564) got a lucky break early on, entering the Medici household as a privileged student of painting and sculpture. In later years he also turned his attention to building design, although his architectural activities in Florence weren't that extensive. Indeed, much of his greatest work was done in Rome, where the majesty of the High Renaissance left even Florence gasping in the dust.

Michelangelo did a few projects in Florence before he took off for Rome, including the Sagrestia Nuova (New Sacristy) and the grand staircase and entrance hall for the Biblioteca Medicea Laurenziana, both in the Basilica di San Lorenzo and neither completely finished as he wanted them. His work in Florence was seen as a precursor to Mannerism.

Mannerism
The High Renaissance ended around 1520. By 1527, with the sack of Rome by Charles V's imperial forces, it was all over, if only because war and suffering had depleted the funds and snuffed out the desire to continue creating in such quantity and grandiosity.

What followed was called Mannerism, which bridged the gap between Renaissance and Baroque. Antonio da Sangallo il Giovane (1485–1546), son of another Florentine architect and sculptor, worked mostly in Rome, although he returned briefly to Florence to build the Fortezza da Basso (p108) in 1534 for Alessandro de' Medici. Bartolomeo Ammannati (1511–92) expanded Florence's Palazzo Pitti (p104) into a suburban palace for the Medici dukes and designed the Ponte Santa Trinità (p98). He also had a hand in the design of the Giardino di Boboli (p105).

Arezzo-born Giorgio Vasari (1511–74) left his mark in Florence with the creation of the Uffizi (p94) and the Corridoio Vasariano (p96) which links Palazzo Vecchio with Palazzo Pitti across the Arno. Bernardo Buontalenti (1536–1608) succeeded Vasari as architect to the Grand Duke of Tuscany. He designed the Forte di Belvedere (p108) and the Palazzo Nonfinito (p89) on Via del Proconsolo, which differs from Renaissance predecessors principally in decorative flounces on the facade.

Baroque
The 17th century saw a construction slowdown throughout the region. This was the era of Baroque, which often had more impact on decor than on architectural design. At its most extreme, particularly in Rome, such decoration was sumptuous to the point of giddiness – all curvaceous statuary, twisting pillars and assorted baubles.

These are the exception rather than the norm in Tuscany, but some examples of the style can be found in the region, for example, the villas near Lucca, the cathedral in Pescia (p150) and the frenzied interior of the Basilica di Santa Maria del Carmine (p106) in Florence. The regional capital also boasts the Chiesa di San Gaetano (p98) and the facade for the Chiesa d'Ognissanti (p97). The former, finished by Gherardo Silvani (1579–1675), is considered the finest piece of Baroque in Florence and a demonstration of the restraint typical of the city.

Art and architecture were inextricably intertwined with mathematics and science in Renaissance Italy. Brunelleschi reinvented linear perspective by developing a system of drawing that allowed the accurate projection of three dimensions onto paper – science could now guide architecture.

Urban Renewal to the Present
Urban renewal took place in Tuscany and Umbria from the early 19th century. Napoleon's representative Elisa Baciocchi helped turn Lucca's walls into the velvet green garden area you see surrounding the old city today. Public works programmes got under way and many neoclassical buildings, bridges and *viali* (boulevards) were built. What had been the core of old Florence, where the Roman forum had once stood, was flattened to make way for the grandiloquent Piazza della Repubblica (p92) in the 1890s. Art Nouveau took off from the 1880s to the interwar period in the style known as Liberty (named after the eponymous London store). The town of Viareggio (p159) is crammed with Liberty buildings grand and simple.

'Tuscany and Umbria's art scene blossomed'

Sadly for a region so rich in the architecture of the past, the region has seen little flourishing of architectural talent or visionary town planning since WWII. In Tuscany, cities such as Livorno and the suburbs of Florence, and in Umbria, Terni and to a lesser extent Foligno, have seen block buildings replace the magnificent structures that came down during bombing campaigns in WWII. Nothing could be further from the ideals of Brunelleschi's finest structures than the soulless, fast-buck housing and light-industrial zones that now virtually fill the area between Florence and Prato.

PAINTING & SCULPTURE
Tuscany and Umbria were blessed – and cursed – with a collection of cities that were effectually owned by prominent families or the Church. These rulers commissioned hired hands – Raphael, Signorelli, Pinturicchio – to fresco their new palaces and churches. Tuscany and Umbria's art scene blossomed, spurred on not by an aesthetic need as much as a way of keeping alive in the minds of the faithful (and more often than not, illiterate) the stories and teachings of the Bible. Art was devotional and instructive, especially in the Byzantine, Romanesque and Gothic days, when art was commissioned (although not always paid for) by the

---

OFF THE BEATEN TRACK

Avoid the long lines to see David at the Accademia and the Uffizi Gallery (p94) by heading to these stunning examples of artistic genius.

- *Allegory of Good Government in the City and the Country* by Ambrogio Lorenzetti in the Palazzo Pubblico (p192) in Siena

- *The Legend of the True Cross* by Piero della Francesca at Chiesa di San Francesco (p241) in Arezzo

- The *Saint Francis Cycle* by Giotto and colleagues (p282) in Assisi

- The Cappella Brancacci by Masaccio, Masolino and Filippino Lippi at the Basilica di Santa Maria del Carmine (p107) in Florence

- *Fonte Gaia* by Jacopo della Quercia (p192) in Siena

- The Sagrestia Nuova (New Sacristy) by Michelangelo at the Basilica di San Lorenzo (p98) in Florence

- The architecture of the Basilica di Santo Spirito (p106) by Brunelleschi in Florence

- The Bardi and Peruzzi Chapels by Giotto in the Basilica di Santa Croce (p102) in Florence

- The Chapel of Santa Maria di San Brizio, Last Judgement, by Luca Signorelli in the Orvieto cathedral (p315)

- Cimabue's *Crucifixion* in the Basilica di San Francesco (p283) in Assisi

Church for religious institutions and purposes. The clergy instructed the artists – thought of as tradesmen – as to whom and how to paint. Whoever commissioned the work was thought of as the 'author', and it was often their signature found on the work.

Antiquities
Etruscan art is found mostly in the form of ceramics, painted in an Eastern geometrical style. The Greek influence was also strong, particularly along the southern coast of Tuscany and into Lazio, where the inhabitants interacted directly with Greek traders. Great examples of ancient ceramics, funerary decorations and sculpture can be seen in archaeological museums in Perugia (p257), Spoleto (p295) and Orvieto (p316) in Umbria.

Middle Ages
After the fall of Rome up until the 13th century, not much original art was created in Tuscany or Umbria. As the cities freed themselves from imperial or feudal control in the course of the 12th century, so art seems to have begun to free itself from the inherited rigidity of Romanesque and Byzantine norms. Gone were the solemn, otherworldly religious figures and the gold backgrounds representing heaven and in were paintings that displayed emotions and real people.

In Tuscany Pisa was in the ascendant. Master of Sardinia and a busy sea trade port, Pisa was more open to external influences and artistic interchange than inland cities such as Florence. The first artist of note to make an impact in Florence was Cimabue (c1240–1302). He began in Pisa but later travelled all over Tuscany. Cimabue painted the most realistic interpretation of St Francis in the lower basilica in the church of St Francis in Assisi (drawn from descriptions told to him by Francis' two nephews). Giorgio Vasari (see p52) identifies him as the catalyst for change in painting from the rigidity of Gothic and Byzantine models. In Florence, his *Maestà* (Majesty; in the Uffizi, p94) amply demonstrates the transition from Byzantine-style iconography to a fresh exploration of expression and life-like dimension.

The story goes that the master Cimabue 'discovered' the young shepherd boy Giotto while walking his sheep one day. He saw a sketch the young boy was drawing and the rest, as they say, is history.

Giotto di Bondone (known as Giotto, c1266–1337), born in the Mugello north of Florence, was the key figure in the artistic revolution that was gathering pace in the run-up to the Renaissance explosion. Most of his Florentine contemporaries were to some degree influenced by him, and his is one of the pivotal names in the Italian artistic pantheon. Fresco painting involves painting watercolours directly onto wet plaster, a tricky business.

Nicola Pisano (c1215–c1278), who left behind some of his best work in the baptistry (p155) in Pisa and the pulpit in Siena cathedral, was something of a master to all who followed in Tuscany and Umbria. He is the sculptor thought to have created the work on the Fontana Maggiore (the Great Fountain; p257) in the centre of Perugia. Despite his nickname (Pisano) he was actually born in southern Italy. He was succeeded by his son Giovanni Pisano (c1248–c1314), who worked on the cathedral in Siena.

Arnolfo di Cambio (c1245–1302), a student of Nicola Pisano, is best known as the architect of the Duomo and Palazzo Vecchio (p92) in Florence. He also had the task of decorating the facade of the Duomo. Some of this sculpture remains in the Museo dell'Opera del Duomo, but the bulk of his work was destroyed in the 16th century when the cathedral was remodelled.

Another outstanding sculptor was Andrea Pisano (c1290–c1348), who left behind him the bronze doors of the south facade of the Florence Battistero (p89). The realism of the characters combines with the fine linear detail of a Gothic imprint, revealing that this century was one of transition.

The Sienese School

Although the focus of artistic life in Tuscany was already shifting to Florence, its southern rival, Siena, enjoyed a brief period of glory.

The only artist in Siena to hold a candle to Giotto was Duccio di Buoninsegna (c1255–1318). Although still much attached to the Byzantine school, he mixed the style with Gothic ideas and introduced a degree of fluidity and expressiveness that has led some to compare him with Cimabue. Various examples of his work can be seen in Siena's cathedral and Florence's Uffizi (p94). Duccio's star pupil was Simone Martini (c1284–1344). Perhaps his most celebrated work is the *Annunciazione*, created for the cathedral in Siena but now hanging in the Uffizi.

Other artists of note in Siena included the brothers Pietro (c1290–c1348) and Ambrogio Lorenzetti (died c1348). Both worked in Siena and elsewhere – Pietro was particularly active in Assisi. Ambrogio's best-known work is the startling *Effetti del Buon e del Cattivo Governo* (Allegories of Good and Bad Government) in Siena's Palazzo Pubblico (p192).

As you trawl through the *palazzi* and galleries of Siena, it will sooner or later hit you that, for all the beauty of the masterpieces by Siena's greatest artists, they seem to stand still in time. While the Renaissance and subsequent movements gripped Florence, Siena remained supremely indifferent and plugged on with largely Byzantine and Gothic models. You can see this in the work of such painters as Taddeo di Bartolo (1362–1422) and even Giovanni di Paolo (1395–1482), who remained anchored in late Gothic, while in Florence people such as Uccello, Verrocchio and Filippo Lippi were turning painting on its head.

An extensive virtual museum, The Web Gallery of Art at www.kfki.hu/~arthp/, showcases over 6500 pieces of European Renaissance, Gothic and Baroque paintings and biographies on the artists.

The Basilica di San Francesco

All of the great masters of the day – Cimabue, Giotto, Pietro Lorenzetti, Simone Martini – were called in soon after St Francis' death to fresco the glorious new church being built in the new Italian Gothic style. The paintings revolutionised art. The former Byzantine style consisted of two-dimensional solemn religious figures painted on gold backgrounds representing heaven. In the fresco cycle in the upper church, as well as sky and nature, Giotto added something completely unheard of in art – emotions and expressions – into the frescoes.

Il Quattrocento & the Renaissance

As greater individuality and an aesthetic appreciation of painting, apart from its didactic or devotional purposes, emerged with the Renaissance, so its practitioners gained in social standing. In Florence especially, but also elsewhere in Tuscany and beyond, lay people began to commission art, either for public places or their own homes. This promoted a broadening of themes such as battle scenes, portraits (generally busts) and scenes from classical mythology, but even through the Renaissance and beyond, much of the output remained faithful to a series of stock religious icons. Innovation was not always easy under such conditions.

Many of the doors you'll see on Florence's Battistero were done by Lorenzo Ghiberti (1378–1455), dubbed Porta del Paradiso by an admiring Michelangelo. Donatello (c1386–1466) trained at Ghiberti's prestigious workshop, burst his banks and produced a stream of sculpture

MOSTLY MADONNAS

As so much of the art of medieval and Renaissance Europe falls into distinct thematic groups, the titles of many paintings are nearly always the same. You will rarely see such stock titles translated into English in Tuscany, so a handful of clues follows.

A *Crocifissione* (Crucifixion) represents the crucifixion of Christ, one of the most common subjects of religious art. Another is the *Deposizione* (Deposition), which depicts the taking down of the body of Christ from the cross, while the *Pietà*, a particularly popular subject for sculptors, shows the lifeless body of Christ in the arms of his followers – the characters can vary, but the theme remains the same. Before all the nastiness began, Christ managed to have an *Ultima Cena*, or Last Supper, with the Apostles.

Perhaps the most favoured subject is the *Madonna col Bambino/Bimbo* (Virgin Mary with Christ Child). The variations on this theme are legion. Sometimes they are depicted alone, sometimes with various *santi* (saints), *angeli* (angels) and other figures. The *Annunciazione* (Annunciation), when the Angel Gabriel announces to Mary the strange honour that has been bestowed on her, is yet another standard episode. When the big event occurred, lots of people, including the *Magi* (Wise Men), came to participate in the *Adorazione* (Adoration) of the newly born Christ.

hitherto unparalleled in its dynamism and force. The results swing from his rather camp bronze *David,* the first nude sculpture since classical times (Palazzo del Bargello; p90), to the racy *Cantoria,* a marble and mosaic tribune where small choirs could gather, created for the Duomo (now in the Museo dell'Opera del Duomo).

Meanwhile, Siena's Jacopo della Quercia (1374–1438) was cutting a temperamental swathe across Tuscany, working above all in Lucca and Siena where he designed the Fonte Gaia (p192) in Il Campo.

Although also active as a painter, Andrea del Verrocchio is best remembered for his sculpture (as well as being a teacher of Leonardo da Vinci). His virtuosity can be admired in the sarcophagus he carved in the old sacristy of the Basilica di San Lorenzo for the Medici family. His masterpiece, however, is the bronze equestrian statue of Colleoni in Venice.

Luca Signorelli (1450–1523) from Cortona painted the auspicious fresco cycle in the Orvieto cathedral detailing the Last Judgement, inspired by Dante's Divine Comedy.

The two most famous Umbrian painters were Pietro Vannucci (c1450–1523), known as Perugino, and Bernardo di Betto (c1454–1513), known as Pinturicchio. Perugino, born in Città della Pieve (which still houses much of his work), lived much of his life in Perugia, and is known for painting soft classical figures that signalled the changeover from mid-century linearity. He did many of the frescoes in the Collegio del Cambio (p258) in Perugia, but his most famous work adorns the Sistine Chapel in Rome – *Christ Delivering the Keys to St Peter.* The best example of his work is found in his hometown of Spello, in the Baglioni Chapel in Santa Maria Maggiore (p288), or in the Piccolomini Library (p195) in the cathedral in Siena. Another student of Perugino's, Pinturicchio also painted frescoes in the Sistine Chapel, as well as the Borgia apartments at the Vatican. One of Perugino's students was Raphael (1483–1520), who lived in Perugia from 1500 to 1504 as a student, and went on to study and paint in Florence, Siena and Rome.

'Leonardo da Vinci (1452–1519) stands apart from all his contemporaries'

Leonardo da Vinci

Born in a small town west of Florence, Leonardo da Vinci (1452–1519) stands apart from all his contemporaries. How do you categorise a man who hardly belonged in his own time? Painter, sculptor, architect, scientist and engineer, Leonardo brought to all fields of knowledge and art an original touch, often opening up whole new branches of thought. If one had to sum up what made him tick, it might be 'seeing is believing'. In the thousands of notes he left behind, he repeatedly extolled the virtue of sight and observation. Paying little heed to received wisdoms, either Christian or classical, Leonardo barrelled along with unquenchable curiosity.

All his studies took up much of Leonardo's time, but he found plenty more to devote to what he saw as the noblest art, painting. Leonardo did much of his work outside Florence (he stayed in Milan for 20 years). One of his outstanding early works, the *Annunciazione,* now in the Uffizi, already revealed his concern with light and shadow, and with its representation through chiaroscuro.

Michelangelo

While Leonardo was in Milan, Michelangelo Buonarroti (1475–1564) was asserting himself as a rival painter, albeit of a very different ilk. In contrast to Leonardo's smoky, veiled images, Michelangelo demonstrated a greater clarity of line. As a young lad he was taken in by Lorenzo de' Medici, who could spot talent when it presented itself. His greatest painting project was the ceiling of the Sistine Chapel in Rome. In Florence relatively little of his work can be seen, but the *Tondo Doni* (*tondo* means circular and Doni was the patron) in the Uffizi provides stunning insight into his craft.

Visit www.italian-art.org, site of the Italian Renaissance Art Project (IRAP) for details on the movement and its artists.

See www.michelangelo .com/buonarrotl.html – a site dedicated to the life and works of the artist.

However, Michelangelo was most prolific as a sculptor. And while he painted and built in Florence, his greatest gifts to the city were those he crafted from stone.

After a stint in Rome, where he carved the remarkable *Pietà*, Michelangelo returned to Florence in 1501 to carry out one of his most striking commissions, the colossal statue of *David*.

High Renaissance to Mannerism

Fra Bartolomeo (1472–1517) stands out for such paintings as the *Apparizione della Vergine a San Bernardo* (Vision of the Virgin of St Bernard), now in the Galleria dell'Accademia (p100), Florence. A follower of Savonarola (p24), Fra Bartolomeo's is a clearly devotional art, with virtually all incidental detail eliminated in favour of the central subject. Piero di Cosimo (c1461–1521), on the other hand, was interested in nature and mythology. Several of his works can be seen in Florence's Palazzo Pitti (p104).

Andrea del Sarto (1486–1531) painted *Madonna del Sacco*, which is in the large cloister at SS Annunziata (p101), as well as the remarkable set of frescoes in grey and white *grisaille* intended to suggest relief carving in the Chiostro dello Scalzo.

The experimentation associated with the likes of Jacopo Pontormo (1494–1556) makes his work emblematic of Mannerism – that troubled search for a freer expression. In one of his earlier works, the *Visitazione* (Visitation) in the SS Annunziata in Florence, the figures seem almost furtive or preoccupied. His most famous painting remains his *Deposizione* (Deposition) – a more mature work from the 1520s – one of his only in situ works, at Santa Felicità in Florence (p104).

Il Rosso Fiorentino (Florentine Redhead; 1494–1540) also worked on the SS Annunziata frescoes and several other projects elsewhere in Tuscany before heading to Rome. In his works, too, one detects a similar note of disquiet, although his style is different. The flashes of contrasting light and dark create an unreal effect in his characters.

The key events that affected Mannerist painting in Tuscany and Umbria were in 1527, when troops loyal to Holy Roman Emperor Charles V sacked Rome and the art movement there scattered. And then in 1530, Francis I from France brought Il Rosso to Fontainebleau to create a school of French painting, which began the dominance of court style for the next half-century in Italy and France and, to a lesser extent, England and Holland.

Down in Siena, Domenico Beccafumi (c1484–1551) was perhaps one of the leading exponents of Tuscan Mannerism. Among his better-known works, the *Caduta degli Angeli* (Fall of the Angels) is replete with disquiet and movement – to the point of blurring his images. It can be seen in the Pinacoteca Nazionale (p197) in Siena. Around the same time, Il Sodoma (1477–1549) was producing works of an altogether smokier style. (And yes, his nickname is exactly as it sounds, but it's debatable whether it was a horse racing nickname or because, as Vasari writes, he was always surrounded by 'beardless young men'.) Some critics see in him a follower, initially at least, of Leonardo da Vinci and later of Raffaello – his paintings have a matte quality suffused with Mediterranean light. You can compare several of his works with those of Beccafumi in Siena's Pinacoteca Nazionale.

The works of Giorgio Vasari (1511–74) and his students litter Florence – some are better than others. His particular boast seems to have been speed – with an army of helpers he was able to plough through commissions for frescoes and paintings with great alacrity, if not always with equal aplomb. Vasari and co were largely responsible for the decoration of the Palazzo Vecchio (p92). But Vasari's real claim to fame, and what he is most appreciated for today, is his somewhat factual *Lives of the Artists*. The book is a two-volume compendium of biographical 'facts' and juicy details about the lives of his fellow Italian artists (some even true), available in several English translations to this day.

Baroque, Neoclassicism & the Macchiaioli

Flocks of artists continued to work in Florence as the new century wore on, but few of enormous note. Giovanni da San Giovanni (1592–1636) was the leading light of the first half of the century and some of his frescoes remain in the Palazzo Pitti (p104). One much underestimated painter of the period was Cecco Bravo (1601–60), whose canvasses combine Florentine tastes of the period with a rediscovery of the soft, nebulous colours of Venice's Titian.

The arrival of artists from out of town, such as Pietro da Cortona and the Neapolitan Luca Giordano (1634–1705), brought the winds of Baroque tastes of hedonistic colour and movement to Florence. This was in contrast to the Mannerists, who had searched, often rather stiffly, for ways of breaking with Renaissance conventions.

The Florentine art scene remained sterile until the first signs of Impressionism wafted across from Paris around the middle of the 19th century. In Florence anti-academic artists declared that painting real-life scenes was the only way forward. The Macchiaioli movement lasted until the late 1860s and received its name (which could be translated as the 'stainers' or 'blotchers') in a disparaging newspaper article in 1862. Works by painters such as Livorno-born Giovanni Fattori (1825–1908), Neapolitan Giuseppe Abbati (1836–68) and the Emission painter Silvestro Alga (1826–95) can be seen in Florence's Galleria d'Arte Moderna.

By 1870 the movement had run out of steam. Splinter tendencies emerged separating realism from questions of style and Tuscany, to this day, hasn't witnessed the grandeur of earlier centuries.

In *Etruscan Places*, DH Lawrence traverses the Italian countryside, looking for ancient ruins and the meaning of life.

Don't go to central Italy without your copy of *Art and Architecture in Italy: 1250–1400* by John White, a preeminent art history professor.

The Penguin Book of the Renaissance by JH Plumb analyses the successes of this astounding movement.

Rudolf Wittkower's *Art & Architecture in Italy 1600–1750* is an excellent reference covering baroque art and architecture.

Modern

Several Umbrian artists have taken centre stage recently. Early in the century, futurist Gerardo Dottori (1884–1977), who was born and studied in Perugia, became known for *aeropittura*, or painting the sensation of flight. The most well-known Italian artist this century has been Alberto Burri (1915–95). Burri began painting on burlap while a prisoner of war in Texas, and continued to use textured media throughout his career. This abstract impressionist's work has been displayed in exhibitions all over the world, and he influenced a host of other artists such as Rauschenberg. Burri was born in Città di Castello (p276), where you can visit two art galleries housing much of his work (including an old tobacco warehouse for his larger pieces). Sculptor Leoncillo Leonardi (1915–68) worked mostly with ceramics and terracotta and dabbled in neo-cubism. Some of his work can be found in the Modern Art Gallery in Spoleto.

LITERATURE

Long after the fall of Rome, Latin remained the language of learned discourse and writing throughout Italy. The elevation of local tongues to literary status was a long and weary process, and the case of Italian was no exception.

The stirrings of Italian literature written in the vernacular began to thrive in Tuscany and Umbria in the beginning of the 13th century. One of the genres first created was spiritual poetry, which was concentrated in Assisi after the death of St Francis. Most notable was the genius of Dante Alighieri (1265–1321). Born in Florence to a wealthy family, Dante received an excellent education, became active in Florentine politics as a white Guelph and began to write in a number of different styles and genres, covering everything from philosophy and politics to love. He was exiled from Florence in 1301 when the opposing faction took the reigns of power, and spent the rest of his life, during which he wrote the *Divina Commedia* (Divine Comedy), wandering Europe.

Dante does not stand completely alone. Together with two fellow Tuscans, he formed the triumvirate that laid down the course for the development of a rich Italian literature.

Petrarch (Francesco Petrarca; 1304–74), born in Arezzo to Florentine parents who had been exiled from their city at about the same time as Dante, actually wrote more in Latin than in Italian. *Il Canzoniere* is the distilled result of his finest poetry. Although the core subject is the unrequited love for a girl called Laura, the whole breadth of human grief and joy is treated with a lyrical quality hitherto unmatched. So striking was his clear, passionate verse, filtered through his knowledge of the classics, that a phenomenon known as *petrarchismo* emerged across Europe – the desire of writers within and beyond Italy to emulate him. He remained influential up to 17th century England. John Donne, English poet and clergyman, wrote in the same kind of rhyme scheme and about the same subject matter.

Contemporary and friend of Petrarch was the Florentine Giovanni Boccaccio (1303–75), who ended his days in Certaldo, outside Florence. His masterpiece was the *Decameron*, written in the years immediately following the plague of 1348, which he survived in Florence. His 10 characters each recount a story in which a vast panorama of personalities, events and symbolism is explored.

The Medici Lorenzo the Magnificent dominated the second half of the 15th century in Florence and was also handy with a pen. His enlightened approach to learning and the arts created a healthy atmosphere for writers.

Check out www.artcyclopedia.com for a database describing the artistic movements and their major exponents.

Another outstanding writer of the Florentine Renaissance is Niccolò Machiavelli (1469–1527). He is known above all for his work on power and politics, *Il Principe*, but he was a prolific writer in many fields. His *Mandragola* is a lively piece of comic theatre and a virtuoso example of Italian literature. Tuscany and Umbria took a fairly long literary break during the 17th to 19th centuries, although Tuscany did give birth to Carlo Lorenzini (1826–90), better known to Italians of all ages under the pseudonym of Carlo Collodi, who was the creator of *Le Avventure di Pinocchio* – known to most audiences as the Disney-fied version, *Pinocchio*.

19th & 20th Centuries

Giosue Carducci (1835–1907) was one of the key figures of 19th-century Tuscan literature. Born in the Maremma, he actually spent the second half of his life in Bologna. Probably the best of his poetry was written in the 1870s; it ranged in tone from pensive evocation of death (such as in *Pianto Antico*) or memories of youthful passion (*Idillio Maremmano*) to a kind of historic nostalgia. In many of these latter poems he harked back to the glories of ancient Rome.

Reading *The Lives of the Artists* by Giorgio Vasari before you head out to churches and museums brings the paintings – and the artists – to life. This contemporary of the Renaissance artists includes all sorts of biographical (and often fictionalised) juicy tidbits about the regions' most famous artists.

Florence's Aldo Palazzeschi (1885–1974) was in the vanguard of the Futurist movement during the pre-WWI years. In 1911 he published arguably his best (although at the time little-appreciated) work, *Il Codice di Perelà* (Perelà's Code), an at times bitter allegory that in part becomes a farcical imitation of the life of Christ.

By the 1920s and '30s Florence was bubbling with activity as a series of literary magazines flourished, at least for a while, in spite of the Fascist regime. Magazines such as *Solaria*, which lasted from 1926 to 1934, its successor *Letteratura* (which began circulating in 1937) and *Il Frontespizio* (1929–40) gave writers from across Italy a platform from which to launch and discuss their work.

One of the founding authors of *Letteratura* was Alessandro Bonsanti (1904–84), much of whose writings are in essays and criticism. A contributor on *Letteratura* was Guglielmo Petroni (born 1911) from Lucca. Although a poet of some note in his day, his novel *Il Mondo è una Prigione* (The World is a Prison, 1948), a vivid account of political prison, was thought to be one of the best accounts of the Italian Resistance. Mario Tobino (born 1910), from Viareggio, used his experience as director of a lunatic asylum to great effect in *Le Donne Libere di Magliano* (Free Women of Magliano), which looks at life inside one such institution.

One of Italy's leading postwar poets was the Florentine Mario Luzi (born 1914). His poetry concentrates on the anguish arising from the contrast between the individual and the broader universe.

Few women writers have reached the limelight in Tuscany but an important exception was Anna Banti (1895–1985). Her prose approach is psychological, delving deep into the minds of her characters and analysing the position of women in society.

Dacia Maraini (born 1936) is with little doubt Tuscany's most prominent contemporary female author, with some 10 novels to her credit. An interesting one is *Voci* (Voices), in which the main character, a female journalist, embarks on the investigation of a murder. It is a mystery laced with disturbing social comment.

Pisa-born Antonio Tabucchi (born 1943) is emerging as a writer of some stature, with more than a dozen books to his name. Possibly one of his most endearing works is *Sostiene Pereira*, set in prewar Lisbon and made into a charming film starring Marcello Mastroianni.

CINEMA

Italian cinema has been enormously productive and has contributed an immense number of great works to the world of film. Tuscany's first claim to fame is as birthplace of the projector one year before the Lumiére brothers patented theirs in Paris. In 1895, poor Filoteo Alberini created his *kinetografo* (cinema projector) in Florence, but no-one paid much attention.

The biggest name to come out of Tuscany is Franco Zeffirelli (born in 1923). His career took him from radio and theatre to opera production and film. He created the television blockbuster *Jesus of Nazareth* (1977) and many film adaptations of operas, along with film hits *Romeo and Juliet* (1968), *Hamlet* (1990) and the semi-autobiographical *Tea with Mussolini* (1999), set in and around Florence.

More recently, the director and actor Roberto Benigni (born 1952) from Arezzo has made quite a name for himself, picking up three Oscars for successfully managing to create a genre all his own: Holocaust comedy. He directed and starred in *La Vita é Bella* (Life is Beautiful, 1998), about a father who protects his son in a concentration camp by pretending it's all a game. Charlie Chaplin's daughter, Geraldine, declared months after the Oscars that Benigni had inherited her father's cinematic poetry. Quite an accolade. Benigni shot parts of *La Vita é Bella* and his painful-to-watch rendition of Pinocchio (2001) at Papigno, an old factory near Terni converted into movie studios.

Umbria hasn't seen much in the way of the film industry. Their most recent claim to fame is actress Monica Bellucci, from Cittá di Castello, who starred in *Bram Stoker's Dracula* and across from Keanu Reeves in *The Matrix: Reloaded*. Zeffirelli's 1972 *Brother Sun, Sister Moon* (about the lives of St Francis and St Clare…if they were groovy 70s hippies) was shot in Assisi. Historical drama queen Dame Maggie Smith starred in yet another film with gratuitous Italian countryside shots, *My House in Umbria*, a made-for-TV movie in 2003.

> In 1991, Roberto Benigni achieved Italian box office success with Johnny Stecchino ('Johnny Toothpick'), a hilarious tale about mistaken identity.

MUSIC

Classical music didn't thrive in Tuscany or Umbria quite like it did in other parts of Italy. Giacomo Puccini (1858–1924), the man behind such well-loved opera classics as *Madame Butterfly*, *Tosca* and *La Bohème*, was born in Lucca. On a quite different note, one of Italy's former leading pop bands, Litfiba, was a Florentine product – its ex-singer, Pero Pelù, now continues solo – and both Jovanotti, the country's most popular rap singer, and the singer Irene Grandi are also Tuscan. Siena-born Gianna Nannini is an extremely popular, internationally acclaimed and politically active Italian artist whose work ranges from rock albums to film soundtracks.

Indeed, Tuscany has produced plenty of bands and musicians, ranging from Marasco – a gritty, folksy singer from Florence who was big in the 1950s, through to Dirotto Su Cuba, a trip hop band that has attracted a lot of attention around the country. In Umbria, jazz has gained an enormous following due to Umbria Jazz (p260) and the Spoleto festival (p297).

Food & Drink

For some, arrival in Tuscany and Umbria means having reached the pearly gates of food heaven. For others, the regional cuisines are rather overrated. The truth lies somewhere between the two. As with many (but not all) of the Mediterranean cuisines, it is essentially the result of poverty. Simple, wholesome ingredients have traditionally been thrown together to produce healthy but not always fascinating meals. The extraordinary excesses we read about of the tables of medieval barons, or later on those of the Medicis and their pals, were not passed down to us through the ages. One can only drool and dream about what concoctions must have been served up at such bacchanalian feasts.

Most common folk had to make do with limited ingredients. This is what has been passed down to us today, although the cuisine has been refined and enriched, particularly with other dishes and combinations from more widely flung parts of Italy. And all told it is very good – one of the keys remains the quality and freshness of the ingredients, upon which great store is placed.

STAPLES & SPECIALITIES
Tuscany

Tuscans love meat! Visit Florence's markets and you'll see more parts from more beasts than you previously thought existed. The pinnacle of all this carnivorous activity has to be the *bistecca alla fiorentina*, specially sourced from local white cattle, *la Chianina*. It's cut into T-bone steaks about 5cm thick and grilled over coals. *Bistecca* will come rare at a restaurant (forget well done as it will be burnt on the outside) and you pay by *l'etto* (100g). In even the humblest of restaurants, your *bistecca* will probably cost over €25 and is enough to feed two people. While Chianina beef is becoming scarcer, you can still find it at many restaurants, as well as at markets.

Stephanie Alexander & Maggie Beer's *Tuscan Cookbook* is a beautifully illustrated, authoritative tome.

Tuscans are jokingly called *mangiafagioli* or 'bean eaters', such is their passion for the humble legume. White *cannellini* beans and the dappled borlotti beans are favourites and often seen in soup, or served with sausages or braised meat.

Much of the food is also based on the *pane toscano*, the fine-textured salt-free bread. It's used to thicken soups, which the Tuscans are famous for, such as *ribollita*, a 'reboiled' bean-and-vegetable soup, flavoured with black cabbage and left to sit for a day before being served. The same *pane* is also used in *pappa*, a tomato-and-bread mush that has an extraordinary depth of flavour, and *panzanella*, a bread-and-tomato salad, which sometimes appears as runny as a thick soup.

One local pasta is *pinci*, similar to the Umbrian *umbricelli*, served with *ragù* or *sugo* (sauce). *Pappardelle*, fresh, flat egg noodles cut wider than *tagliatelle* and thinner than *lasagna* sheets, are also common. The noodles are mostly flat, but sometimes come with a crinkled edge, and may be served *alla lepre*, moistened with a little hare or rabbit *ragù*.

While meat can dominate, the seafood of Tuscany is also great, and you'll see it displayed in restaurant windows throughout the region. Livorno leads the region with seafood and it has created a seafood stew, *cacciucco*, which needs to have five types of fish, one for each 'c' in the name. The name comes from the Turkish *kukut*, meaning 'small fry'.

Cheese is central to the cuisine, particularly *caciotta*, the local name for cheese in general and *pecorino* in particular. In fact, cheese was considered so important that in days gone by women used cheese-making as a dowry skill. The cheese of Pienza, a town near the Umbrian border, is one of the greatest *pecorini* in Italy.

Local sweets are few but memorable. *Panforte*, the Sienese flat, hard cake with nuts and candied fruit is sensational. Instead of fancy sweets you'll see a range of dry-textured, often double-baked *biscotti* (biscuits) such as *cantucci*, which are usually studded with almonds. They're good, especially when dipped into *vin santo*, the local sweet wine. Another popular biscotti is *ricciarelli*, made with marzipan.

DID YOU KNOW?

Truffles produce a chemical that is similar to a sex hormone in pigs, which is why pigs are traditionally used to hunt them.

Umbria

The heart of Umbrian food is the hearth. Wood fires are used for everything from *porchetta* (spit-roasted pig) to tiny birds to *bruschetta* (grilled bread appetisers) and mushrooms. In Umbria it is the pig that reigns supreme, followed closely by lamb, sheep-milk cheeses, truffles and anything wild that hasn't been hunted out. Umbrians love to hunt and the *cinghiale* (wild boar) is fair game in autumn. Many species of wildlife, particularly small birds, deer and the *cinghiale*, have been hunted almost to extinction.

The local *porcini* mushrooms are some of the best in the land, and the elusive *tartufo nero* (black truffle) is found in winter, particularly around Norcia. *Tartufo bianco* (white truffle) is sometimes found near Orvieto, a town worth visiting for its wine alone.

Norcia, snuggled in the mountains to Umbria's east, is a food-lover's dream. Even if you're not there when the pungent truffles are in season, there are more than enough attractions. The local *pecorino* cheese is good, particularly the ricotta rolled in wheatgerm. *Pecorino di tartufo* is a semi-hard cheese studded with pieces of truffle.

The pork butchers of Norcia are famed around the country, giving the name *norcineria* (signifying quality) to good butchers elsewhere in Italy. Their *prosciutto* (cured ham) is saltier, coarser, but more fragrant and complex than those of Parma and San Daniele. *Cinghiale* makes a decent prosciutto, but the *salsicce* (cured sausages) from them are even better. About 30 minutes from Norcia is Castelluccio, set on a high plain, and home to the best *lenticchie* (lentils) in Italy.

Umbria has its own pasta, most notably *umbricelli* (sometimes called *ceriole* or *ombricelli*), and *stringozzi*. Both are made by hand with the same water-based dough. *Umbricelli* are round and string-like, but not as fine as spaghetti, while *stringozzi* are more squarish, but equally long. Both *stringozzi* and *umbricelli* are often served with a meat (perhaps including pork), truffle or tomato sauce.

Most of the bread in Umbria is the type made without salt, sometimes called *pane toscano*, here simply known as *pane*. Bread made with salt is called *pane con sale*.

Julia Della Croce's *Umbria* is one of the few books to focus specifically on this delightful regional cuisine.

TRAVEL YOUR TASTEBUDS

Cuisines born of poverty found a use for everything. As a result, offal became an integral part of the local diet. *Rognone*, a great plate of kidneys, is one favourite, although you might find it a little too much. Tripe is particularly prized by some and a common dish is *trippa alla fiorentina*, prepared with carrot, celery, tomato and onion mix. For true tripe fans, locals distinguish between various parts of the gut. One particular part of the tripe is known as *lampredotto*, just in case you are contemplating having some on a roll without knowing what it is.

Umbria isn't particularly famed for desserts, but the figs and plums are good in summer. Of more interest is the chocolate of Perugia. Chocoholics from around the world will know the brand name Perugina and associate it with Baci, or hazelnut 'kisses'.

DRINKS
Wine

Tuscany produces six of Italy's DOCG wines: Brunellodi Montalcino, Carmignano, Chianti, Chianti Classico, Vino Nobile di Montepulciano and Vernaccia di San Gimignano (the only white). It also boasts over 30 DOC wines.

Once, the bulk of wine coming out of Tuscany was rough and ready, if highly palatable, Chianti in flasks. The Chianti region remains the heartland of Tuscan wine production, but for a good generation winemakers have been concentrating more on quality rather than quantity.

The best of them, Chianti Classico, comes from seven zones in many different guises. The backbone of the Chianti reds is the Sangiovese grape, although other grape types are mixed in varyingly modest quantities to produce different styles of wine. Chianti Classico wines share the *Gallo Nero* (Black Cockerel) emblem that once symbolised the medieval Chianti League. Chianti in general is full and dry, although ageing requirements differ from area to area and even across vineyards.

DID YOU KNOW?

It's believed that the Sangiovese grape – the principal variety in Chianti – was used as far back as the Etruscan period.

The choice doesn't stop in the Chianti region. Among Italy's most esteemed and priciest drops is the Brunello di Montalcino (in Siena province). Until not so long ago only a handful of established estates produced this grand old red, but now over 140 vineyards are at it. The finished product varies a great deal and depends on soil, microclimate and so on. Like the Chianti reds, the Sangiovese grape is at the heart of the Brunello. It is aged in casks for four years and then another two years in bottles.

WINE CLASSIFICATION

Since the 1960s, wine in Italy has been graded according to four main classifications. *Vino da tavola* indicates no specific classification; *Indicazione Geografica Tipica* (IGT) means that the wine is typical of a certain area; *Denominazione di Origine Controllata* (DOC) wines are produced subject to certain specifications (regarding grape types, method and so on); and *Denominazione d'Origine Controllata e Garantita* (DOCG) shows that wine is subject to the same requirements as normal DOC but that it is also tested by government inspectors. These indications appear on labels.

A DOC label can refer to wine from a single vineyard or an area. DOC wines can be elevated to DOCG after five years' consistent excellence. Equally, wines can be demoted; the grades are by no means set in stone.

Further hints come with indications such as *superiore*, which can denote DOC wines above the general standard (perhaps with greater alcohol or longer ageing). *Riserva* is applied only to DOC or DOCG wines that have aged for a specified amount of time.

In general, however, the presence or absence of such labels is by no means a cast-iron guarantee of anything. Many notable wines fly no such flag. Many a *vino da tavola* or IGT wine is so denominated simply because its producers have chosen not to adhere to the regulations governing production. These sometimes include prestige wines.

Your average trattoria will generally only stock a limited range of bottled wines, but better restaurants present a carefully chosen selection from around the country. *Enoteche* (wine bars) usually present you with an enormous range of wines and a limited food menu.

Generally if you simply order the *vino della casa* (house wine) by the glass, half litre or litre you will get a perfectly acceptable table wine to accompany your food.

LE STRADE DEL VINO (THE WINE ROADS)

The kind wine-folk of Tuscany have made life that much easier for those with a healthy interest in wine by creating Le Strade del Vino, wine trails through rural Tuscany. These trails generally follow back roads, passing by a plethora of vineyards, where you can taste, buy and immerse yourself in wine (not literally though). It's a rewarding way to combine sampling a few wines and getting a glimpse of wine production and traditional farming life.

Each *strada* has its own distinct emblem which you'll see on signposts in towns and the countryside, but all are marked with a common logo of Le Strade del Vino di Toscana, a Pegasus atop six balls forming a downward-pointing triangle (much like a bunch of grapes).

To date 14 *strade* have been marked out, which crisscross famous wine-production areas, such as Rùfina and Montepulciano, to the not-so-famous, such as Massa Marittima and the Lunigiana. You can pick up maps and information at tourist offices or visit www.terreditoscana.regione.tos cana.it/stradedelvino.

Another Sangiovese-based winner is Vino Nobile di Montepulciano, another hill-top town in Siena province. The grape blend and conditions here make this a quite distinctive wine too, but it is not aged for as long as the Brunello.

Tuscany is largely, but not exclusively, about reds. Easily the best-known white is the Vernaccia of San Gimignano. Some of the best is aged in *barriques* (small barrels), while others are sometimes oaked.

The harsh terrain of much of Umbria isn't the best place to produce wine, but the region definitely has a few highlights. Wines from small producers around Lago di Trasimeno have interest, if not always loads of class, and much of the wine suits the pork-heavy food of the region. One of the country's best sparkling white wines comes from an Umbrian producer, Lungarotti. While you're in the region, Umbria's white Orvieto Classico is a must try.

'Tuscany is largely about reds'

An important development since the end of the 1980s has been the rise of Super Tuscans, a long-lived wine of high quality. Departing from the norms imposed by DOC and DOCG requirements, certain vineyards are finally doing the kind of thing that Australian and Californian vintners have been doing for ages – experimenting with different mixes. So now alongside the Sangiovese they are growing Sauvignon, Merlots, Syrahs and other grape varieties and mixing them with the Sangiovese. These wines are then aged in *barriques* – another break from tradition, but a process used all over the world for many modern premium wines.

Super Tuscan was a nickname given to the first red wines produced this way, and the name has stuck. This kind of experimentation has re-sulted in some first class wines that have been giving DOC and DOCG wines a run for their money – and often winning. Common names in the field of Super Tuscans include Sassicáia, Summus, Excelsus, Tignanello and Sammarco, some of which have been classed among the best wines in all Italy. Although Super Tuscans have sprung up all over Tuscany, they are generally found in and around Chianti Classico. Indeed, many Chianti producers have a Super Tuscan label in their portfolios.

A regional speciality that'll appeal to the sweet tooth is *vin santo* (holy wine), a dessert wine also used in Mass. Malvasia and Trebbiano grape varieties are generally used to produce a strong, aromatic and amber-coloured wine, ranging from dry to very sweet (even the dry retains a hint of sweetness). The wine takes four years to mature and a good one, which will set you back at least €13 for a 350ml bottle, will last years; it is traditionally served with almond-based *cantucci* biscuits.

Beer

The most common Italian beers are crisp and light Pilsener-style lagers, and younger Italians are happy to guzzle them down with a pizza. The main labels are Peroni, Dreher and Moretti, all very drinkable and cheaper than the imported varieties. If you want a local beer, ask for a *birra nazionale*, which will be either in a bottle or *alla spina* (on tap).

Coffee

Coffee in Italy isn't like anywhere else in the world: it's better.

An espresso is a small amount of strong black coffee. It is also referred to as *un caffè*. You can ask for a *caffè doppio* (a double shot), *caffè lungo* ('long coffee') or *caffè Americano*, though the last two will usually just be an espresso with extra water run through the grinds and can be bitter.

A *caffè corretto* is an espresso with a dash of grappa or some other spirit, and a *macchiato* ('stained' coffee) is espresso with a dash of milk. You can ask for a *macchiato caldo* (with a dot of hot, foamed milk) or *freddo* (with a spot of cold milk). On the other hand, *latte macchiato* is warmed milk 'stained' with a spot of coffee. *Caffè freddo* is a long glass of cold, black, sweetened coffee. If you want it without sugar, ask for *caffè freddo amaro*.

Then, of course, there is the cappuccino, coffee with hot, frothy milk. If you want it without the froth, ask for a *cappuccino senza schiuma*. Italians tend to drink cappuccino only with breakfast and during the morning, never after meals.

It will be difficult to convince bartenders to make your cappuccino hot rather than *tiepido* (lukewarm) – overheating the milk destroys its natural sweetness. If you must, ask for it *ben caldo* or *bollente* and wait for the same 'tut-tut' response that you'll attract if you order one after dinner.

Variations on the milky coffee menu include a *caffè latte*, a milkier version of the cappuccino with less froth. In summer the *cappuccino freddo*, a bit like an iced coffee, is popular. You will also find *caffè granita*, sweet and strong, which is traditionally served with a dollop of whipped cream.

Tea

Italians don't drink a lot of *tè* (tea) and generally do so only in the late afternoon, when they might take a cup with a few *pasticcini* (small cakes). You can order tea in bars, although it will usually arrive in the form of a cup of warm water with an accompanying tea bag. If this doesn't suit your taste, ask for the water *molto caldo* (very hot) or *bollente* (boiling).

Water

Rosemary & Bitter Oranges: Growing up in a Tuscan Kitchen by Patrizia Chen is a part cookbook, part memoir tale of post-WWII Livorno.

Despite the fact that tap water is reliable throughout the country, most Italians prefer to drink bottled *acqua minerale* (mineral water). This is available either *frizzante* (sparkling) or *naturale* (still) and you will be asked in restaurants and bars which you would prefer. If you just want a glass of tap water, you should ask for *acqua dal rubinetto*, although simply asking for *acqua naturale* will also suffice.

CELEBRATIONS

Italy celebrates an unprecedented number of festivals, many of them coming from the region's pagan past.

Italians have always celebrated a harvest, some god or other, a wedding, a birth or whatever. When Christianity arrived, they simply put their new God as the figurehead. Most of these festivals were wild affairs, such as the Saturnalia festival in Roman times, where a week of drunken revelry in honour of the god of disorder was marked by a pig sacrifice at the start and a human sacrifice at the end. Celebrations these days are more sedate affairs by comparison. But they can still be amazing. The biggest times for festivals these days centre around *Natale* (Christmas), *Pasqua* (Easter) and *Carnevale* (the period leading up to Ash Wednesday, the first day of Lent).

The classic way to celebrate any feast day is to precede it with a day of eating *magro* (lean) because the feast day is usually a day of overindulgence. While just about every festival has some kind of food involved, many of them are only about food. The general rule is that a *sagra* (feasting festival) will offer food (although you'll normally be expected to pay), and at a *festa* (festival or celebration) you may have to bring your own.

WHERE TO EAT & DRINK

Quality restaurants abound in Tuscany and Umbria, and making a choice can sometimes be a little daunting. Be sure not to judge an eatery by its tablecloth. You may well have your best meal at the dingiest little establishment imaginable.

Also worth noting are 'Slow Food' restaurants – establishments highly rated by the Slow Food Movement (see the boxed text below). Every two years the movement publishes *Osterie d'Italia*, which rates what it believes to be the top restaurants in the country. Look out for the 'Slow Food' sticker proudly displayed outside.

Some bars known as *vinai* are good places to either snack or put together a full meal from a range of enticing options on display. This is more of a lunchtime choice than for your evening meal.

'Quality restaurants abound in Tuscany and Umbria'

The standard name for a restaurant is *ristorante*. Often you will come across something known as a trattoria, which is traditionally, at least, a cheaper and simpler version of a *ristorante*. On pretty much the same level is the *osteria*. The *pizzeria* needs no explanation.

A *fiaschetteria* may serve up small snacks, sandwiches and the like, usually at the bar while you down a glass of wine or two. It is a particularly Tuscan phenomenon. A *tavola calda* (literally 'hot table') usually offers cheap, pre-prepared meat, pasta and vegetable dishes in a buffet.

Wine lovers should look out for their local *enoteca* (wine bar). These places offer snacks and sometimes full meals to accompany a selection of wines. Their primary business is the latter – food is viewed as an accompaniment (and often only cold dishes are available) to your chosen tipple(s). Generally the idea is to try the wines by the glass.

The problem with all this is that nowadays all the names seem to have become interchangeable. In all cases, it is best to check the menu, usually posted by the door, for prices. Occasionally you will find places with no written menu. This usually means they change the menu daily. Inside there may be a blackboard or the waiter will tell you what's on – fine if you speak Italian, a little disconcerting if you don't. Try to think of it as a surprise. If you encounter this situation in an overtly touristy area, you should have your rip-off antenna up.

A SNAIL'S PACE

Fast food as a concept doesn't sit easily with Italians and it was here in 1986 that the first organised, politically active group decided to tackle the issue head on. Symbolised by a snail, the Slow Food Movement now has chapters in 48 countries and over 77,000 members. It promotes good food and wine to be consumed (slowly, of course) in good company, and champions traditional cuisine and sustainable agricultural practices. The volunteer-run groups organise social programmes of feasting and frivolity. For more information check out www.slowfood.com.

FIESTAS FOR FOODIES

The following local fiestas all have something in common: they revolve around food. In most cases, one culinary delight (such as chocolate – see January!) will be singled out. Although the dates are as accurate as possible, call ahead and double check if you have a journey to make in case of changes.

January

Cioccolisti (☎ 0572 95 92 26; Monsummano Terme; last weekend of Jan) Artesan chocolate fair with top choco-makers and plenty of opportunities to taste.

February

Sagra della Polenta Dolce (☎ 0187 47 13 99; Pistoia; Sun of carnival) A giant sweet polenta is made with chestnut flour in the main piazza as part of annual carnival overdose.

Sagra del Chiodo di Maiale (☎ 0187 47 13 99; Aulla; last weekend in Feb) Typical Lunigianesi dishes made from pork are cooked on an open log fire.

March

Sagra della Polenta Dolce (☎ 0574 95 74 58; Prato; Easter Sun) Sweet polenta is eaten as part of a Renaissance festival, which is now in its 427th year!

Sagra del Gambellaio (☎ 0575 78 98 92; Arezzo; 18 Mar) Sausages all round, but only if you can take them with your mouth instead of using your hands. It's all part of the fun – apparently.

April

Rassegan dei Proddotori della Pastorizia della Montagna Pistoiese (☎ 05773 6 88 81; Pistoia; last weekend in Apr) Organised in collaboration with local cheese producers and the 'Slow Food' movement (see p61). There is plenty of tasting going on, as well as a large market.

Sagra della Fettunta (☎ 0572 6 71 94; Montecatini Alto; end Apr/early May) Celebration of the typical *bruschetta* with olives, accompanied by Tuscan wine.

May

Sagra delle Ciliegie (☎ 0587 68 55 15; Lari, Pisa; 24 May-2 Jun) Cherry festival with tastings of typical local dishes – sweet and savoury – made with cherries. Lots of food stands, music and entertainment.

June

Cena Medievale (☎ 0571 65 27 30; Certaldo, Florence; 14 Jun) Jolly medieval dinner with music and dancing. A long table is set for up to 500 people out in the village square.

Quick Eats

Global fast-food chains are becoming increasingly popular in Italy (you'll find all the usual ones), but seriously, why would you bother when Italian fast food – *pizza al taglio* (by the slice) for example – is so good?

The Tuscan Year: Life & Food in an Italian Valley by Elizabeth Romer describes the cuisine evocatively through the changing seasons.

VEGETARIANS & VEGANS

While menus around the region carry a bounty of vegetable-based dishes, vegetarians need to be aware of misleading names and the fact that many Italians don't think a little bit of prosciutto really counts as meat. But most eating establishments serve a good selection of *antipasti* (starters) and *contorni* (vegetables prepared in a variety of ways). Look for the word *magro* (thin or lean) on menus, which usually means that the dish is meatless. Vegans are in for a much tougher time. Cheese is used universally, so you have to say *'senza formaggio'* (without cheese) as a matter of course. Also remember that *pasta fresca*, which may also turn up in soups, is made with eggs. Vegetarian restaurants can be found in larger cities.

Palio dei Rioni (☎ 0575 65 82 78; Castignion Fiorentino, Arezzo; 3rd Sun) Gastronomic fair celebrating local produce.

Sagra del Pesce (☎ 0586 75 48 90; Caletta, Castiglioncello; 2nd Sun) A seafood celebration with plenty of fishy dishes available for tasting.

July

Festa del Calderone (☎ 0583 44 29 44; Altopascio, Lucca; 25 Jul) A stopping-off point for pilgrims in Medieval days, this festival commemorates the food hand-outs by cooking up enormous pots of pasta to feed the local folk.

Sagra del Pesce (☎ 0565 6 32 69; Piombino; last weekend in Jul) Typical local seafood dishes are prepared, culminating on the last Sunday with a giant feed-the-masses sized frying pan of fried fish for all the townsfolk to enjoy.

August

Sagra del Bombolone (☎ 0583 64 10 07; Sillicano-Camporgiano, Lucca; 1-3 Aug) Celebration of the famous *bombolone* (sweet doughnut).

Sagra delle Olive con Coniglio e Polenta (☎ 0583 80 58 13; Limano, Bagni di Lucca; 14-15 Aug) Local festival celebrating the traditional local dish: olives with rabbit and polenta.

Festa della Consuma (☎ 0575 54 20 13; Montemignaio, Arezzo; 18 Aug) Variety of pork dishes accompanied by local wine.

Sagra della Bistecca (☎ 0575 563 02 52; Cortona; 14-15 Aug) Thousands of Valdichiona steaks are cooked on a 14m-square grill in the local park.

September

Festa dell'uva e del vino (☎ 0575 44 03 23; Ciggiano, Arezzo; 3rd weekend in Sep) Open-air dinners with live entertainment and local wine.

October

Festa della Finocchiona (☎ 0555 00 24 26; Bivigliano, Vaglia, Florence; 1st Sun of Oct) Typical Florentine pork salami with wild fennel.

November

Mostra del Tartufo Bianco (☎ 0571 4 27 45; San Miniato, Pisa; last 3 weekends of Nov) White-truffle fair celebrated for over 30 years. The record is held here for the largest truffle ever!

December

Sagra del Vine Brulè (☎ 0573 6 02 31; Abetone, Pistoia; 30 Dec) At 9pm a giant cauldron of mulled wine is made and most people arrive on skis.

WHINING & DINING

You'll be hard-pressed to find a children's menu in most Italian restaurants. It's not that kids aren't welcome because, more than just about anywhere, they are. Local children are treated very much as adults and are taken out to dinner from a very tender age. You'll often see families order a *mezzo piatto* ('half-plate') off the menu for the smaller guests. Virtually all restaurants are perfectly comfortable tailoring a dish to meet your kid's tastes.

High chairs are available in many restaurants, but bring one along if you can, as some restaurants don't supply them. While children are often taken out, and the owner's kids may be seen scrambling about the room, it's expected that kids be well behaved and are disciplined if they are not.

For more information on travelling with your little ones, see p324.

Fred Plotkin's *Italy for the Gourmet Traveller* is an outstanding companion for your gastronomic tour.

HABITS & CUSTOMS

Italians rarely eat a sit-down *colazione* (breakfast). It's generally a quick affair taken at a bar counter on the way to work. They tend to drink a cappuccino, usually *tiepido* (warm), and eat a *cornetto* (croissant) or other type of pastry (generically known as a *brioche*).

Bars (in the Italian sense, ie, coffee-and-sandwich places) and cafés generally open from 7.30am to 8pm, although some stay open after 8pm and turn into pub-style drinking and meeting places. A few serve filling snacks with lunchtime and pre-dinner drinks. At others you can pick up reasonable *panini* (filled rolls or sandwiches).

You'll also find numerous outlets where you can buy *pizza al taglio* (by the slice) Another option is to go to an *alimentari* (delicatessen) and ask them to make a *panino* with the filling of your choice. At a *pasticceria* (cake shop) you can buy pastries, cakes and biscuits.

More suited to the coffee table than the kitchen, Jeni Wright's *Tuscan Food & Folklore* sets each recipe in its historical context.

For *pranzo* (lunch), restaurants usually operate from 12.30pm to 3pm, but many are not keen to take orders after 2pm. It's the main meal of the day and many shops and businesses close for two or three hours every afternoon to accommodate it. People generally start sitting down to dine around 7.30pm for *cena* (dinner). It will be difficult to find a place still serving after 11pm. Dinner's traditionally a simpler affair, but is becoming a fuller meal because of the inconvenience of travelling home for lunch every day.

Many restaurants and bars shut one or two days per week, but others don't. In some parts of Italy at least one day off is mandatory but ultimately the decision on whether or not to enforce that rule rests with the *comune* (local council). The Florence *comune*, for instance, does not care what restaurateurs do (unless they close for three days or more in a week) so some skip the weekly break altogether.

A full meal consists of an *antipasto* (starter), *primo piatto* (first course) and *secondo piatto* (second course), which is usually accompanied by a *contorno* (vegetable side dish). *Insalate* (salads) have a strange position in the order here. They are usually ordered as separate dishes and in some cases serve as a replacement for the *primo*.

Numerous restaurants offer a *menù turistico* or *menù a prezzo fisso*, a set-price lunch that can cost as little as €10 (usually not including drinks). Generally the food is breathtakingly unspectacular with limited choices. From your tastebuds' point of view (if you are not overly hungry) you'd be better off settling for a good *primo* or *secondo* at a decent restaurant. On the other hand, if you look at lunch as a mere refuelling stop, this could be the way to go.

COOKING COURSES

Many people come to Italy just for the food so it is hardly surprising that its cookery courses are among the most popular. The website www.italy cookingschools.com has hundreds of possibilities that you can consider. Here are a few of our choices:

Vallicorte (☎ 020 768 01 377; www.vallicorte.com) This is exactly what you need from a course: a good group of people (matched by the co-ordinators), a charismatic instructor and a pair of amusing hosts in an ancient villa in Tuscany.

Casa Ombuto (☎ 348 736 38 64; www.italiancookerycourse.com) High on the hills of the Casentino valley stands Casa Ombuto. Seven-day courses are run by an inspiring husband-and-wife team in their cave-like cantina.

Menfi (☎ 020 746 00 077; www.tastingplaces.com) Choose either a week in Tuscany, near Arezzo, or a week in Umbria, in Orvieto; wine tasting and tours of the area are all part of the package.

Lorenza de' Medici (☎ 0577 74 94 98; cuisineint@aol.com) Lorenza de' Medici teaches the art of Tuscan cuisine in an 11th-century former monastery in the Chianti. Students learn about agriculture, the seasonal influence on food and make excursions to local cheesemakers, wineries and food producers. This is a Rolls-Royce course with prices to match.

DOS & DON'TS

Just as an Italian at our table would make few faux pas, most visitors at an Italian table get it right. We simply aren't that different. That's the good news. The bad news is that what constitutes 'good manners' alters – as it does everywhere – depending not only on who you're with, but where you are eating and the part of the country you're in. But the *really* good news is that Italians are so hospitable that they will forgive virtually anything you do unwittingly.

- *Buongiorno* or *Buonasera* is the basic greeting in any bar or restaurant.
- Italians tend to dress with impeccable style at most meals, so do brush up when eating out.
- When eating pasta, any bits hanging down should be bitten through rather than slurped up. You'll probably never be offered a spoon to eat your pasta with, as this is considered quite rude, so you'll have to do your best to manage without one.
- If you're lucky enough to eat in an Italian home, remember that generosity at a meal is a sign of hospitality so refuse at your own peril! You can, and should, *fare la scarpetta* (make a shoe) with your bread and wipe plates clean of sauces – a sign you've really enjoyed the meal.

EAT YOUR WORDS

Get behind the cuisine scene by getting to know the language. For pronunciation guidelines see p350.

Useful Phrases

I'd like to reserve a table *Vorrei riservare un tavolo*
(vo-*ray* ree-ser-*va*-re oon *ta*-vo-lo)

I'd like the menu, please *Vorrei il menù, per favore*
(vo-*ray* eel me-*noo* per fa-*vo*-re)

Do you have a menu in English? *Avete un menù (scritto) in inglese?*
(a-*ve*-te oon me-*noo* (*skree*-to) een een-*gle*-ze)

What would you recommend? *Cosa mi consiglia?*
(*ko*-za mee kon-*see*-lya)

I'd like a local speciality *Vorrei una specialità di questa regione*
(vo-*ray* oo-na spe-cha-lee-*ta* dee *kwe*-sta re-*jo*-ne)

Please bring the bill *Mi porta il conto, per favore?*
(mee *por*-ta eel *kon*-to per fa-*vo*-re)

Is service included in the bill? *Il servizio è compreso nel conto?*
(eel ser-*vee*-tsyo e kom-*pre*-zo nel *kon*-to)

I'm a vegetarian *Sono vegetariano/a*
(*so*-no ve-je-ta-*rya*-no/a)

I'm a vegan *Sono vegetaliano/a*
(*so*-no ve-je-ta-*lya*-no/a)

For tasting notes and global events, see www.italianwinereview.com

You'll find information on Italian wines, olive oil and agritourism at www.agriline.it

Menu Decoder
SOUPS & ANTIPASTI
antipasti misto (an-tee-*pas*-tee *mis*-toh) – mixed appetisers
carpaccio (kahr-*pah*-cho) – very fine slices of raw meat

insalata caprese (in-sah-*lah*-tah kah-*pre*-ze) – sliced tomatoes with mozzarella and basil
insalata di mare (in-sah-*lah*-tah di *mah*-re) – seafood, generally crustaceans
minestrone (mi-nes-*tro*-ne) – vegetable soup
olive ascolane (o-*li*-ve ahs-ko-*lah*-ne) – stuffed, deep-fried olives
prosciutto e melone (pro-*shoo*-to e me-*lo*-ne) – cured ham with melon
stracciatella (strah-chah-*te*-lah) – egg in broth

PASTA SAUCES

There are literally hundreds of shapes of pasta and each region has its own variety. The straightforward long, thin strands of pasta, are omnipresent throughout the country and come with a variety of delicious sauces. Here are just a few – all equally delicious:

www.deliciousitaly.com is an excellent food and travel portal.

www.italianmade.com has recipes, extensive descriptions of regional specialities and downloadable booklets.

aglio e olio (*a*-lyo e *o*-lyo) – hot oil, garlic and sometimes chilli
amatriciana (ah-mah-tree-*chah*-nah) – salami, tomato, capsicum and cheese
arrabbiata (ah-rah-bee-*yah*-tah) – tomato and chilli
bolognese (bo-lo-*nye*-ze) – a meat sauce (minced veal or pork), vegetables, lemon peel and nutmeg
cacio e pepe (ka-cho e *pe*-pe) – black pepper and sheeps cheese
carbonara (kar-bo-*na*-ra) – bacon, butter, cheese, beaten eggs and sheeps cheese
partenopea (par-te-*no*-pe-a) – mozzarella, tomato, bread crust, capers, olives, anchovies, basil, oil, chilli and salt
pescatora (pes-ka-*to*-ra) – fish, tomato and sweet herbs
pommarola (po-ma-*ro*-la) – simple tomato sauce
puttanesca (poo-ta-*nes*-ka) – garlic, anchovy, black olives, capers, tomato sauce, oil, chilli and butter
tartufo di Norcia (tar-*too*-fo dee nor-cha) – black truffle, garlic, oil and anchovies
vongole (*von*-go-le) – tomatoes and clams

PIZZAS

All the pizzas listed below are made with a tomato (and sometimes also a mozzarella) base:

capricciosa (kah-pre-*sho*-sah) – olives, prosciutto, mushrooms and artichokes
frutti di mare (*froot*-i dee *mah*-re) – seafood
funghi (*fun*-gee) – mushrooms
margherita (mahr-ge-*ree*-ta) – oregano
napoletana (nap-ol-ee-*tan*-a) – anchovies
pugliese (pu-li-*eh*-se) – tomato, mozzarella and onions
quattro formaggi (*kwah*-tro for-*mah*-jee) – with four types of cheese
quattro stagioni (*kwah*-tro stah-*jo*-nee) – like a *capricciosa*, but sometimes with egg
verdura (ver-*doo*-rah) – mixed vegetables; usually courgette (zucchini) and aubergine, sometimes carrot and spinach

Glossary
BASICS

breakfast	*prima colazione*	*pree*-ma ko-la-*tsyo*-ne
lunch	*pranzo*	*pran*-zo
dinner	*cena*	*che*-na
knife	*coltello*	kol-*tel*-lo
fork	*forchetta*	for-*ke*-ta
spoon	*cucchiaio*	koo-*kya*-yo
(non) smoking	*(non) fumatori*	(non) foo-ma-*to*-ree
bill/cheque	*conto*	*kon*-to
waiter/waitress	*cameriere/a*	ka-mer-*ye*-re/a

METHODS OF PREPARATION

boiled	*bollito/a*	bo-*lee*-to/a
cooked	*cotto/a*	*ko*-to/a
fried	*fritto/a*	*free*-to/a
grilled	*alla griglia*	a-la *gree*-lya
raw	*crudo/a*	*kroo*-do/a
roasted	*arrosto/a*	a-*ro*-sto/a

STAPLES

bread	*pane*	*pa*-ne
butter	*burro*	*boo*-ro
cheese	*formaggio*	for-*ma*-jo
chilli	*peperoncino*	pe-pe-ron-*chee*-no
cream	*panna*	*pa*-na
egg/eggs	*uovo/uova*	*wo*-vo/*wo*-va
garlic	*aglio*	*a*-lyo
honey	*miele*	*mye*-le
jam	*marmellata*	mar-me-*la*-ta
lemon	*limone*	lee-*mo*-ne
milk	*latte*	*la*-te
oil	*olio*	*o*-lyo
olive	*oliva*	o-*lee*-va
pepper	*pepe*	*pe*-pe
rice	*riso*	*ree*-zo
salt	*sale*	*sa*-le
sugar	*zucchero*	*tsoo*-ke-ro
vinegar	*aceto*	a-*che*-to

MEAT, FISH & SEAFOOD

anchovies	*acciughe*	a-*choo*-ge
beef	*manzo*	*man*-zo
chicken	*pollo*	*po*-lo
clams	*vongole*	*von*-go-le
cod	*merluzzo*	mer-*loo*-tso
crab	*granchio*	*gran*-kyo
cuttlefish	*seppia*	*se*-pya
kid (goat)	*capretto*	ka-*pre*-to
lamb	*agnello*	a-*nye*-lo
liver	*fegato*	*fe*-ga-to
lobster	*aragosta*	a-ra-*go*-sta
mackerel	*sgombro*	*sgom*-bro
mussels	*cozze*	*ko*-tse
octopus	*polpi*	*pol*-pee
oysters	*ostriche*	*os*-tree-ke
prawns	*gamberoni*	gam-be-*ro*-nee
rabbit	*coniglio*	ko-*nee*-lyo
sardines	*sarde*	*sar*-de
sausage	*salsiccia*	sal-*see*-cha
seafood	*frutti di mare*	*froo*-te dee *ma*-re
snail	*lumache*	loo-*ma*-ke
squid	*calamari*	ka-la-*ma*-ree
steak	*bistecca*	bees-*te*-ka
swordfish	*pesce spada*	*pe*-she *spa*-da
tripe	*trippa*	*tree*-pa
tuna	*tonno*	*to*-no
veal	*vitello*	vee-*te*-lo

Burton Anderson's hardback pocket guide, *Wines of Italy*, is a handy little tool to have with you for hints on particular vineyards.

FRUIT & VEGETABLES

apple	*mela*	*me*-la
artichokes	*carciofi*	kar-*cho*-fee
asparagus	*asparagi*	as-*pa*-ra-jee
aubergines	*melanzane*	me-lan-*dza*-ne
cabbage	*cavolo*	*ka*-vo-lo
carrot	*carota*	ka-*ro*-ta
cherry	*ciliegia*	chee-lee-*e*-ja
fennel	*finocchio*	fee-*no*-kyo
grapes	*uva*	*oo*-va
green beans	*fagiolini*	fa-jo-*lee*-nee
cherry	*ciliegia*	chee-lee-*e*-ja
mushrooms	*funghi*	*foon*-ghee
orange	*arancia*	a-*ran*-cha
peach	*pesca*	*pe*-ska
pears	*pera*	*pe*-ra
peas	*piselli*	pee-*ze*-lee
peppers	*peperoni*	pe-pe-*ro*-nee
potatoes	*patate*	pa-*ta*-te
rocket	*rucola*	*roo*-ko-la
spinach	*spinaci*	spee-*na*-chee
strawberries	*fragole*	*fra*-go-le
tomatoes	*pomodori*	po-mo-*do*-ree

Lonely Planet's *World Food: Italy* takes an in-depth look at the whole country's food history and culture.

DRINKS

beer	*birra*	*bee*-ra
coffee	*(un) caffè*	ka-*fe*
tea	*(un) tè*	te
water	*acqua*	*a*-kwa
wine (red/white)	*vino (rosso/bianco)*	*vee*-no (*ro*-so/*byan*-ko)

Tuscany

DIANA MAYFIELD

Florence (Firenze)

Florence, cradle of the Renaissance, is a city like no other. With its staggering wealth of world-class art and architecture and its rich and dynamic history and culture, it's no wonder that this relatively small city on the banks of the Arno River is regularly besieged by tourists from around the globe. Dante, Michelangelo, Botticelli and Da Vinci are just some of the big names who once lived and worked here, and their influence remains to this day.

Despite the excessive traffic, stifling summer heat, pollution and industrial sprawl on the city's outskirts, Florence is immediately captivating. The French writer Stendhal was so dazzled by the magnificence of the Basilica di Santa Croce that he was barely able to walk for faintness. He is apparently not the only one to have felt thus overwhelmed by the beauty of Florence – they say Florentine doctors treat a dozen cases of 'stendhalismo' a year.

You will need at least four or five days to do Florence any justice at all, but remember, you can't see everything in just one visit.

HIGHLIGHTS

- Marvel at the art treasures of the Uffizi (p94) and Bargello (p90)
- Climb up to Piazzale Michelangelo (p108) for wonderful views of the city
- Visit Brunelleschi's greatest legacy, the Duomo (p87)
- Stand in awe before arguably the world's most famous artwork, Michelangelo's *David* (p100)
- Indulge in some of Italy's finest wines on a tasting tour through Il Chianti (p135)
- Take time out from Florence and explore the Etruscan and Roman remains in Fiesole (p133)
- Drop by Montecatini Terme (p129) for a spot of rest and relaxation

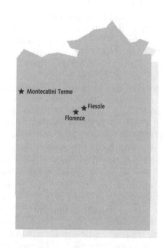

★ Montecatini Terme

★ ★ Fiesole
Florence

HISTORY

Florence's history stretches back to the time of the Etruscans, who based themselves in Fiesole and may have had a settlement of some kind on the spot where the city now stands. However, it was Julius Caesar who founded the colony of Florentia around 59 BC, making it a strategic garrison on the narrowest crossing of the Arno, controlling the Via Flaminia linking Rome to northern Italy and Gaul. Over succeeding centuries it grew to be an important centre of trade.

After the collapse of the Roman Empire, Florence fell under the sway of the invading Goths, followed by the Lombards and the Franks. The year 1000 AD marked a crucial turning point in the fortunes of Florence, when Margrave Ugo of Tuscany moved his capital from Lucca to the city, initialising a period of great expansion. In 1110, Florence became a free *comune* (city-state) and by 1138 was ruled by 12 consuls, assisted by the Consiglio di Cento (Council of One Hundred), whose members were drawn mainly from the prosperous merchant class. Agitation among differing factions in the city led to the appointment of a foreign head of state, known as the *podestà*, in 1207.

Medieval Florence was a wealthy and dynamic city-state, one of Europe's leading financial, banking and cultural centres and a major player in the international wool, silk and leather trades. The sizable population of moneyed merchants and artisans began forming guilds and patronising the growing number of artists who found lucrative commissions in this burgeoning city, but a political crisis was on the horizon.

The prolonged struggles between the pro-papal Guelphs (Guelfi) and the pro-imperial Ghibellines (Ghibellini) started towards the middle of the 13th century, with power passing from one faction to the other for almost a century. Into this fractious atmosphere was born the revolutionary artist Giotto and the poet Dante Alighieri, whose family belonged to the Guelph camp. In fact, young Dante even took part in the Battle of Campaldino (1289), which saw the defeat of Ghibelline Arezzo. Shortly afterwards the Guelphs themselves split into two factions, and the outspoken Dante ended up on the wrong side and was expelled from his native city in

1302, never to return. In exile, he wrote his best-known work, *The Divine Comedy*.

In 1348 the Black Death spirited away almost half the population. This terrifying period in the city's history, was used as a backdrop by Boccaccio for his *Decameron*.

The history of Medici Florence begins in 1434, when Cosimo de' Medici, a great patron of the arts, took the reins of power. His eye for talent and his tact in dealing with artists saw the likes of Alberti, Brunelleschi, Luca della Robbia, Fra Angelico and Filippo Lippi flourish under his patronage. Many of the city's finest buildings are testimony to his tastes. In 1439 the Church Council of Florence, aimed at reconciling the Catholic and Eastern churches, brought Byzantine scholars and craftsmen to the city, bringing with them the knowledge and culture of classical antiquity. The Council, attended by the pope and the Byzantine emperor, achieved nothing in the end, but it did influence what was later to be known as the Renaissance. Under the rule of Cosimo's popular and cultured grandson, Lorenzo the Magnificent (1469–92), Florence became the epicentre of this 'Rebirth', with artists of the calibre of Michelangelo, Botticelli and Ghirlandaio at work.

Unfortunately, Florence's golden age was not to last, effectively dying along with Lorenzo in 1492. Just before his death, the Medici bank had failed, and, two years later, the Medicis were driven out of Florence. In a reaction against the splendour and excess of the Medici court, the city fell under the control of Girolamo Savonarola, a humorless Dominican monk who led a stern, puritanical republic, surprisingly supported by many leading artists and intellectuals, as well as common folk. In 1497 the likes of Botticelli gladly consigned their 'immoral' works and finery to the flames of the infamous 'Bonfire of the Vanities' in Piazza della Signoria. The following year, Savonarola fell from public favour and was himself burned in the piazza as a heretic.

The republican government that followed was lead by Piero Soderini, who took on a role similar to the Venetian doge. However, its pro-French leanings brought it into conflict with the pope and his Spanish allies, and in 1512 Florence was defeated by the Spanish and the Medicis returned. Their tyrannical rule endeared them to very few and when Rome, ruled by the Medici

FLORENCE

pope, Clement VII, fell to the emperor Charles V in 1527, the Florentines took advantage of this low point in the Medici fortunes to kick the family out again. Two years later, though, imperial and papal forces combined to lay siege to Florence, forcing the city to accept Lorenzo's great-grandson Alessandro de' Medici, a ruthless transvestite whom Charles made Duke of Florence in 1530. Medici rule continued for another 200 years, during which time they gained control of all Tuscany, though after the reign of Cosimo I (1537–74), Florence drifted into steep decline, headed by a succession of increasingly ineffective, decadent or just plain unpleasant characters.

The last male Medici, Gian Gastone, died in 1737, after which his sister, Anna-Maria, signed the grand duchy of Tuscany over to the House of Lorraine (effectively under Austrian control). This situation remained unchanged, apart from a brief interruption under Napoleon from 1799 to 1814, until the duchy was incorporated into the kingdom of Italy in 1860. Florence became the national capital a year later, but Rome assumed the mantle permanently in 1871.

Florence was badly damaged during WWII by the retreating Germans, who blew up all its bridges except Ponte Vecchio. Devastating floods ravaged the city in 1966, causing inestimable damage to its buildings and artworks. However, the salvage operation led to the widespread use of modern restoration techniques that have saved artworks throughout the country.

FLORENCE IN...

Two Days

Start your day with a cappuccino in Caffè Gilli in Piazza della Repubblica. Take a look round the splendid Duomo and then the Battistero. If you have a head for heights, try the Campanile too. Visit Piazza della Signoria, stopping to admire the statuary in the Loggia della Signoria. This famous square is surrounded by restaurants where you can stop for lunch. Drop by the Uffizi Gallery to marvel at some of the world's greatest Renaissance art. After your visit take a leisurely stroll along the Arno, and cross Ponte Vecchio for a glimpse of the Oltrarno district. In the evening you can have dinner in one of the traditional Tuscan restaurants along Via Santo Spirito.

Start your second day with a visit to the Museo di San Marco, with its frescoes by Fra Angelico. There are a number of cafés in the square for a coffee or a light lunch afterwards. Next, call into the Galleria dell'Accademia to see Michelangelo's *David* before heading back to Via Cavour and Palazzo Medici-Riccardi. In the evening treat yourself to a meal in one of the swish restaurants on Piazza della Repubblica and round the day off with a *gelato* as you walk back to your hotel.

Four Days

Follow the itinerary for the first two days. On the third day, leave the city behind and take a day trip to Fiesole for great views over Florence. Spend the day exploring the Roman and Etruscan remains and relaxing in one of the restaurants on the main square.

On day four, visit Chiesa di Santa Croce, and stop by Enoteca Boccadama for a light lunch and a glass of wine. In the afternoon, cross again to Oltrarno and visit the fabulous collections of Palazzo Pitti, followed by a visit to the Boboli Gardens. In the evening you could take in a play or a concert at the Teatro Verdi.

One Week

Follow the previous itinerary and on the fifth day, visit Palazzo del Bargello. In the afternoon, take a tour of Palazzo Vecchio. Head down to the Arno and cross Ponte alle Grazie to the San Niccolò area. Climb up to Piazzale Michelangelo for superb views over the city before descending for dinner in one of the cafés on Via dei Renai.

On day six take in the Basilica di Santa Maria Novella and the Basilica di San Lorenzo, followed by a peek into the Cappelle Medicee. The Museo dell'Opera del Duomo is well worth a visit too.

On day seven explore more of the Oltrarno area, with a visit to the Basilica di Santa Spirito and the Basilica di Santa Maria del Carmine, with its frescoes by Masaccio.

ORIENTATION

However you arrive, the central train station, Stazione di Santa Maria Novella, is a good reference point. Budget hotels and *pensioni* are concentrated around Via Nazionale, to the east of the station, and Piazza Santa Maria Novella, to the south. The main route to the city centre is Via de' Panzani and then Via de' Cerretani, about a 10-minute walk. You'll know you've arrived when you first glimpse the Duomo.

Most of the major sights are within walking distance – you can stroll across the city centre in about 30 minutes. From Piazza di San Giovanni around the Battistero (Baptistry), Via Roma leads to Piazza della Repubblica and continues as Via Calimala then Via Por Santa Maria to Ponte Vecchio. Take Via de' Calzaiuoli from Piazza del Duomo for Piazza della Signoria, the historic seat of government. The Uffizi is on the piazza's southern edge, near the Arno. Cross Ponte Vecchio, or Ponte alle Grazie further east, and head southeast to Piazzale Michelangelo for a fantastic view over the city.

There is some reasonably priced public parking around the Fortezza da Basso, just north of the train station and a brisk 10-minute walk to the historic centre along Via Faenza.

Florence has two (somewhat haphazardly applied) street-numbering systems: red numbers usually indicate commercial premises while black denote a private residence. 'Black' addresses tend to be denoted by number only, though are sometimes followed by an 'n' *(nero)*, while 'red' addresses often carry an 'r' *(rosso)* after the number.

Maps

Lonely Planet also publishes a handy *City Map of Florence*, which includes greater Florence and its surroundings. One of the best commercial maps of the city is the red-covered *Florence* (€7), produced by the Touring Club Italiano and scaled at 1: 12,500. A cutaway of the centre is scaled at 1:6500. Its green-covered *Tuscany* is scaled at 1:200,000, and also costs €7.

INFORMATION
Bookshops

Edison (Map p84; ☎ 055 29 18 70; Piazza della Repubblica 27r; ▣ €2.50/hr) Sells a variety of maps and travel guides, as well as English novels and non-fiction.

Feltrinelli International Bookshop (Map p84; ☎ 055 21 95 24; Via Cavour 12r) Good selection in English, French and other languages.
La Librarie Francaise (Map pp82-83; ☎ 055 21 26 59; Piazza Ognissanti 1r; ☺ closed Tue) Good stock of French-language books.
Paperback Exchange (Map p81; ☎ 055 247 81 54; Via Fiesolana 31r) Vast selection of new and second-hand books in English.

Emergency

Police Station (Map pp78-79; ☎ 055 4 97 71; Via Zara 2) You can report thefts at the foreigners' office here.
Tourist Police (Polizia Assistenza Turistica; Map p80; ☎ 055 20 39 11; Via Pietrapiana 50r, Piazza dei Ciompi)

Internet Access

Internet Point (Map pp82-83; ☎ 055 24 07 80; Borgo degli Albizi 66r; €3/hr)
Internet Train (€4/hr) 12 branches including: Via dell'Oriuolo 40r (Map p80; ☎ 055 263 89 68); Via di Parione 11b (Map p84; ☎ 055 264 55 63); and Borgo San Jacopo 30r (Map p84; ☎ 055 265 79 35)

Internet Resources

www.comune.firenze.it A useful portal for information on the city.
www.firenze.net
www.firenze-oltrarno.net For a taste of things south of the river; it has lots of links to other sites.
www.florenceforfun.org Details of Florence's nightlife.
www.florenceitaly.net
www.studentsville.it Comprehensive information on life in the city from a student's perspective.

Laundry

Wash & Dry Laundrette (☎ 800 23 11 72; €3.10/ wash, €3.10/dry; ☺ 8am-10pm) 10 branches including: Via Nazionale 129 (Map pp78-79); Via della Scala 52-54r (Map pp78-79); Via dei Servi 105r (Map pp78-79), Via de' Serragli 87r (Map pp82-83); and Via del Sole 29r (Map p84)

Left Luggage

Stazione di Santa Maria Novella (☺ 6am-midnight; €3 per item for 12 hours, €2 for every 12 hours thereafter) The left-luggage office is on platform 16.

Media

La Nazione (http://lanazione.quotidiano.net – Italian only) Italian-language paper published in Florence; a useful source of local news.
La Repubblica (www.firenze.repubblica.it) Publishes a local version, which includes useful listings.
Toscana News (www.toscananews.com) A monthly tourist paper published in English and German, listing upcoming

regional events and places of interest. It usually comes with its sister publication, *Chianti News*. The cover price is €0.50, though tourist offices give them away free.

Medical Services

24-hour Pharmacies Farmacia Comunale (Map pp78-79; ☎ 055 21 67 61; inside Stazione di Santa Maria Novella); Molteni (Map p84; ☎ 055 28 94 90; Via de' Calzaiuoli 7r); All'Insegna del Moro (Map p84; ☎ 055 21 13 43; Piazza di San Giovanni 28).

Ambulance Station (Map p84; ☎ 055 21 22 22; Vicolo degli Adimari 1) The Misericordia di Firenze ambulance station is just off Piazza del Duomo. It also runs a medical-attention centre there for tourists, which operates 10am-7pm, Monday to Friday, and 9am-2pm on Saturdays.

Emergency Doctor (Guardia Medica; ☎ 055 47 78 91) For a doctor at night or on a public holiday.

Ospedale di Santa Maria Nuova (Map pp78-79; ☎ 055 2 75 81; Piazza Santa Maria Nuova 1) Just east of the cathedral.

Ospedali Riuniti di Careggi (Map p75; ☎ 055 427 71 11; Viale Morgagni 85) The main public hospital, north of the city centre.

Tourist Medical Service (Map pp78-79; ☎ 055 47 54 11; Via Lorenzo il Magnifico 59; ⏰ 11am-noon & 5-6pm Mon-Fri, 11am-noon Sat; no appointment required) Has English-, French- and German-speaking doctors, who will also make calls to hotels. The tourist office has lists of doctors and dentists who speak various languages.

Money

A number of banks are concentrated around Piazza della Repubblica. ATMs are commonplace throughout the city.

American Express (Map p84; ☎ 055 5 09 81; Via Dante Alighieri 22r; ⏰ 9am-5.30pm Mon-Fri, 9.30am-12.30pm Sat).

Thomas Cook (Map p84; ☎ 05528 97 81; Lungarno deglie Acciaiuoli 6r; ⏰ 8.30am-7.30pm Mon-Sat, 9.30am-5pm Sun) Bureau de change near Ponte Vecchio.

Post

Post Office (Map p84, B4; Via Pellicceria, off Piazza della Repubblica; ⏰ 8.15am-6pm Mon-Fri, 8.15am-noon Sat) Fax and telegram services are available.

Telephone

Public telephones can be found throughout the city. Both coins and phonecards are

(Continued on page 86)

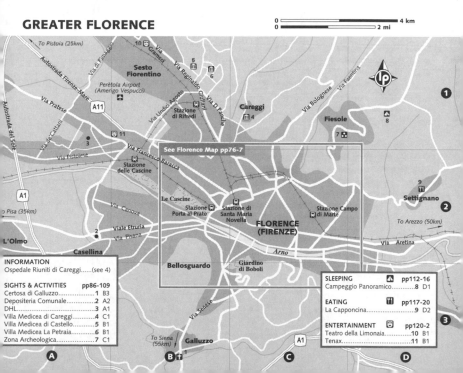

GREATER FLORENCE

0 — 4 km
0 — 2 mi

To Pistoia (25km)
Via di Pirmoggia
Via Gramsci
Via Reginaldo Giuliani
Sesto Fiorentino
Perètola Airport (Amerigo Vespucci)
Via Pratese
Autostrada Firenze-Mare
Via Undici Agosto
Via D Pantìe
Stazione di Rifredi
Careggi
Via Bolognese
Via Faentina
Fiesole
Autostrada del Sole
Via di Chitan
Via Pistolese
Via Francesco Baracca
See Florence Map pp76-7
Stazione delle Cascine
Le Cascine
Stazione Porta al Prato
Stazione di Santa Maria Novella
Stazione Campo di Marte
Settignano
A1
To Pisa (35km)
Via Canova
Viale Etruria
Via Pisana
FLORENCE (FIRENZE)
Arno
To Arezzo (50km)
Via Aretina
L'Olmo
Casellina
Bellosguardo
Giardino di Boboli
Via Senese
To Siena (55km)
Galluzzo
A1

A **B** **C** **D**

To Perétola
Airport (3km)

1

Viale Alessandro Guidoni

Via di Novoli

Via Francesco Baracca

**Ponte
di Mezzo**

Via Giovan Filippo Mariti

Rifredi

Via Circondaria

Via Crso

Via M Mercati

Via A Tavanti

Montughi

Via Vittorio Emanuele

2

Torente Mugnone

See Stazione & Around Map pp78-9

Viale Francesco Redi

Viale Corsica

Via Pietro Toselli

San Jacopino

Via dello Statuto

Canale Macinante

Piazzale
delle Cascine

**Ippodromo
delle
Cascine**

Via Benedetto Marcello

Via delle Porte Nuove

Via del Ponte alle Mosse

Via Belfiore

**Fortezza
da Basso**

Viale Spartac

Viale Filippo Strozzi

Piazza della
Indipendenza

3

To Anfiteatro
(1km)

Le
Cascine

Viale degli Olmi

Viale Abramo Lincoln

ARNO

Stazione
Porta al Prato

Viale Fratelli Rosselli

Porta
al Prato

Stazione
di Santa
Maria
Novella

Piazza
del Mercato
Centrale

Ponte della
Vittoria

Via de'Vanni

Lungarno del Pignone

Via Soleino

Corso Italia

Lungarno Amerigo Vespucci

Piazza della
Stazione

See Central Florence
Map p84

Via Bronzino

Pignone

Piazza di
Santa Maria
Novella

4

See Palazzo Pitti Map pp82-3

Via Pisana

Ponte Amerigo
Vespucci

Borgo San Frediano

Ponte alla
Carraia

Piazza della
Repubblica

Viale A Aleardi

**San
Frediano**

Ponte
Santa
Trinita

Ponte
Vecchio

Piazza
Tasso

Piazza
de' Pitti

5

INFORMATION
Swiss Consulate................................. 1 D6

SIGHTS & ACTIVITIES pp86-109
Azione Gay e Lesbica......................2 G4
Campo Sportivi ASSI........................3 F6
Museo Stibbert..................................4 D1
Piscina Bellariva...............................5 H5
Piscina Le Pavoniere.........................6 A3
Società Canottieri Comunali.............7 G5

SLEEPING pp112-16
Camp Site...8 H2
Ostello Villa Camerata...................(see 8)

ENTERTAINMENT pp120-2
Auditorium Flog.............................(see 9)
Cinema Poggetto...............................9 D1
Stadio Comunale Artemio Franchi.... 10 G3

BELLOSGUARDO

**Giardino
Torrigiani**

Viale Francesco Petrarca

Piazza
della
Repubblica

Piazza
de' Pitti

**Giardino
di
Boboli
(Boboli
Gardens)**

Forte
di
Belveder

Viale del Poggio Imperiale

Viale Senese

Via di San Leonardo

To Galluzzo
(3km)

6

0 — 1 km
0 — 0.5 mi

E **F** **G** **H**

1

2

3

4

5

6

arco di
illa
abbricotti

Via Bolognese

Via Faentina

Torrente Mugnone

8

Via San Domenico

See Le Cure & Around Map p81

Via Vittorio Emanuele II

Ponte
Rosso

Piazza
delle Cure

Viale Alessandro Volta

Viale Alessandro Volta

Viale Augusto Righi

ia XX Settembre

Lorenzo il Magnifico

avagnini

Viale Don G. Minzoni

Piazza
della
Libertà

Viale del Mille

Via Cairoli

Via A. Baldesi

Via G. Marconi

Viale Giacomo Matteotti

Piazza
Savonarola

Piazza
San Marco

Gardino
dei
Semplici

Gardino
della
Gherardesca

Via Giuseppe La Farina

Stazione Campo
di Marte

10

**Campo
di Marte**

Viale Pasquale Paoli

Via Lungo l'Affrico

Via Gabriele d'Annunzio

omo
d

Piazza M
d'Azeglio

Viale Antonio Gramsci

Via Mannelli

Viale Edmondo de Amicis

Via Andrea del Sarto

Via del Mezzetta

2

See Santa Croce Map p80

Via Vincenzo Gioberti

Piazza di
Santa Croce

Viale G. Amendola

Via Cimabue

Via Arnolfo

Via Piagentina

Via Campofiore

Via Aretina

Chianti

**Madonnone
Bellariva**

5

Ponte
alle
Grazie

ARNO

an Niccolò

Lungarno del Tempio

Ponte
San Niccolò

Lungarno Cristoforo Colombo

Lungarno Aldo Moro

Piazza
Giuseppe
Poggi

Lungarno Francesco Ferrucci

7

Ponte G
Da Verrazzano

5

Via di Villamagna

Piazzale
Michelangelo

Via Coluccio Salutati

Via dell'Erta Canina

Viale Michelangelo

Via Donato Giannotti

Cimitero
delle
Porte Sante

Viale Galileo
Galilei

Monte Alle Croci

3

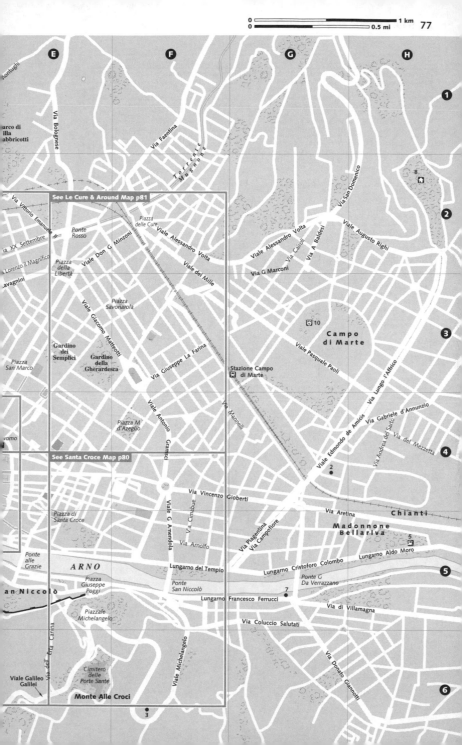

INFORMATION
24-hour pharmacy (Farmacia
  comunale)...........................1 E5
Belgian Consulate.....................2 H6
Box Office...............................3 D4
Comune di Firenze Tourist
  Office.................................4 E6
Consorzio ITA..........................5 E5
Danish Consulate......................6 H6
Deposito (left luggage)...............7 E5
Dutch Consulate.......................8 H4
German Consulate.....................9 D6
Ospedale di Santa Maria
  Nuova..............................10 H6
Swedish Consulate....................11 H3
Telecom phones.......................12 E5
Tourist Medical Service..............13 G3
Train Information......................14 E5
US Consulate..........................15 C6
Wash & Dry launderette.............16 H5
Wash & Dry launderette.............17 F5
Wash & Dry launderette.............18 D5
Wasteels...............................19 E5

SIGHTS & ACTIVITIES   pp86-109
Centro Lorenzo de'Medici......20 F5
Chiesa Russa Ortodossa........21 G3
Fortezza da Basso.................22 E3
Galleria dell'Accademia..........23 H5
Mercato delle Cascine...........24 A5
Museo di San Marco.............25 H5
Opificio delle Pietre Dure.......26 H5
Scuola Leonardo da Vinci......27 H6

SLEEPING   pp112-16
Florence & Abroad.................28 G4
Hotel Aprile...........................29 E6
Hotel Croce di Malta..............30 E6
Hotel Il Guelfo Bianco............31 G5
Hotel le Due Fontane............32 H5
Hotel Loggiato dei Serviti........33 H5
Ostello Archi Rossi................34 F5
Ostello Spirito Santo..............35 F5
Pensione Bellavista................36 F5

EATING   pp117-20
Il Vegetariano.......................37 H4
Mario..................................38 G5
Osteria dei Cento Poveri........39 E6
Restaurant ZàZà....................40 G5
Trattoria il Contadino.............41 H5

ENTERTAINMENT   pp120-2
Central Park..........................42 B5
Cinema Fulgor......................43 D6
Ex-Stazione Leopolda...........44 C5
Meccanò..............................45 B5
Teatro Comunale..................46 C6

SHOPPING   pp123-4
Mercato Centrale...................47 F5
Officina Profumo-Farmaceutica
  di Santa Maria Novella.....48 H6
Stockhouse Il Giglio...............49 D6

TRANSPORT   pp124-5
ATAF bus stop for nos 7, 13,
  62 & 70.............................50 E5
ATAF local bus stop..............51 E5
ATAF Ticket & information
  office.............................(see 50)
Avis Car Rental.....................52 D6
CAP & COPIT Bus station.....53 D6
CentralSita Viaggi..................54 E5
Florence By Bike...................55 G4
Happy Rent..........................56 D6
Hertz Car Rental...................57 D6
Lazzi Bus Station & ticket
  office...............................58 E5
Pre-booked train tickets
  pickup.............................59 E5
Sita Bus Station..................(see 54)
Ticket windows......................60 E5

Via G Lorengoni

Via del Ponte all'Asse
Via San Jacopino
Via Maragliano
Via A Catalani
Via G Luigi Spontini
Piazza San Jacopino
Via F Landini
Via Felice Fontana
Via D Cimarosa Via G Rossini Via B Cristofori
Via Cassia
Via Benedetto Marcello
Via delle Ghiacciaie
San Jacopino
Via della Carra Via A Scarlatti Via Luigi da Palestrina
Via delle Porte Nuove
Viale Belfiore
Via Guido V I Peri
Via Citadella
Via Guido Monaco

Le Cascine
Via del Ponte alle Mosse
Piazzale Porta al Prato
Viale Fratelli Rosselli
Via Jacoppo da Diacceto

Stazione Porta al Prato (Ex-Stazione Leopolda)
44
42
Viale Fratelli Rosselli
Porta al Prato
Via della Scala
18

Viale degli Olmi
Viale del Visarno
24
45
Piazza Vittorio Veneto
Via Abramo Lincoln
Via Solferino
Via il Prato
Via Montebello

Lungarno del Pignone
Via del Pignone
Ponte della Vittoria
Via de' Vanni
Via Magenta
46
Via G Garibaldi
Via Bernardo Rucellai
Via degli Orti Oricellari
Via S Lucia

Piazza Gaddi
Via G A Sogliani
Corso Italia
Via Palestro
52
56
Borgo Ognissanti
57
Via della Fonderia
Lungarno Amerigo Vespucci
Via Curtatone
15
9
49
43

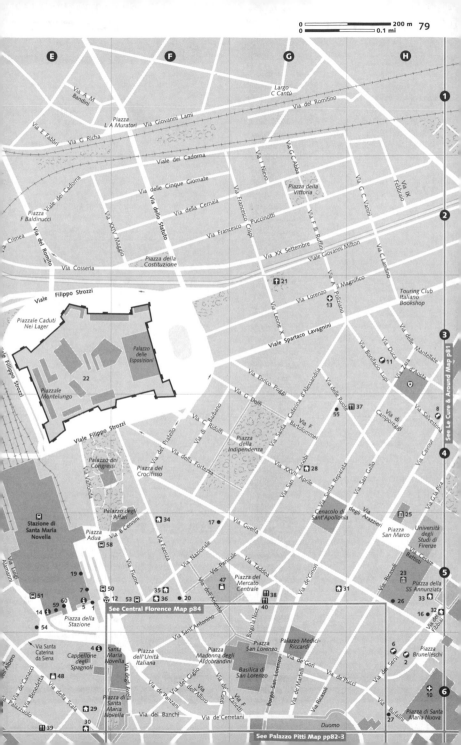

0 ──────── 200 m
0 ──────── 0.1 mi

E   F   G   H

1
2
3
4
5
6

Largo C Cantù
Via del Romitino
Via A M Bandini
Piazza L A Muratori
Via Giovanni Lami
Via E Fabbri
Via G Richa
Viale dei Cadorna
Via I Nievo
Via G C Abba
Piazza della Vittoria
Via G C Vanini
Via IX Febbraio
Via delle Cinque Giornate
Via Francesco Puccinotti
Via dello Statuto
Via della Cernaia
Via C Landino
Piazza F Baldinucci
Via del Romito
Via XXIV Maggio
Via Francesco Crispi
Via XX Settembre
Viale Giovanni Milton
Via Crimea
Via Cosseria
Piazza della Costituzione
Viale Spartaco Lavagnini
Via Il Magnifico
Touring Club Italiano Bookshop
Viale Filippo Strozzi
Piazzale Caduti Nei Lager
Palazzo delle Esposizioni
Via Leone X
Via Lorenzo
🛈 21
✚ 13
Poliziano
22
Piazzale Montelungo
Viale Filippo Strozzi
Via delle Mantellate
Via Bonifacio Lupi
⚕ 11
Via Duca d'Aosta
Via Zara
Via delle Ruote
✚ 55
📷 37
Via di Camporeggi
8 ⚕
Via Salvestrina
Via Enrico Poggi
Via G Dolfi
Via F Bartolommei
Via S Caterina d'Alessandria
Palazzo dei Congressi
Via Valfonda
Via del Pratello
Via C Ridolfi
Via della Fortezza
Piazza della Indipendenza
Via XXVII Aprile
🏠 28
Via Cavour
Palazzo degli Affari
Piazza del Crocifisso
Via B Cennini
Cenacolo di Sant'Apollonia
Via degli Arazzieri
Via C I A Pia
Stazione di Santa Maria Novella
Piazza Adua
🚌 58
17 ●
🏠 34
Via Guelfa
Via San Gallo
Via Santa Reparata
Piazza San Marco
📷 25
Università degli Studi di Firenze
Via Luigi Alamanni
19 ●
7 ●
🚌 50
12 ☎
53 📮
35 🏠
🏠 36
20 ●
Via Faenza
Via Fiume
Via Nazionale
Via del Ariento
Via Panicale
Via Taddea
Piazza del Mercato Centrale
📷 38
🏠 31
Via de' Ginori
Via Cesare Battisti
23 📷
Piazza della SS Annunziata
33 🏠
🚆 51
60 ●
59 ●
ℹ 5   1
🚌 14
54 ●
Piazza della Stazione
47 ●
40
26 ●
16 ●
32
Via de' Fibbiai
Via Santa Caterina da Siena
4 🛈
Cappellone degli Spagnoli
Santa Maria Novella
Piazza dell'Unità Italiana
Via Sant'Antonino
Borgo la Noce
Piazza Madonna degli Aldobrandini
Palazzo Medici-Riccardi
Piazza San Lorenzo
Via de' Gori
6 ⚕
Via dei Servi
2 ℹ
Piazza Brunelleschi
🏠 48
Via degli Avelli
Via della Scala
Via de' Panzani
Via del Giglio
Via dell'Alloro
Via F Zannetti
Via de' Conti
Basilica di San Lorenzo
Borgo San Lorenzo
Via de' Martelli
Via de' Pucci
Via de' Ricasoli
10 ✚
27 ●
Piazza di Santa Maria Nuova
🚆 39
29 🏠
30 ●
Piazza di Santa Maria Novella
Via dei Banchi
Via de' Cerretani
Duomo

See Le Cure & Around Map p81
See Central Florence Map p84
See Palazzo Pitti Map pp82-3

0 ——— 200 m
0 ——— 0.1 mi

See Le Cure & Around Map p81

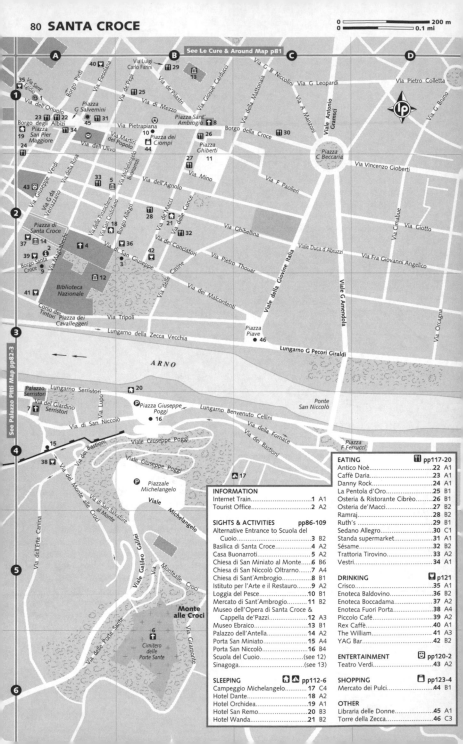

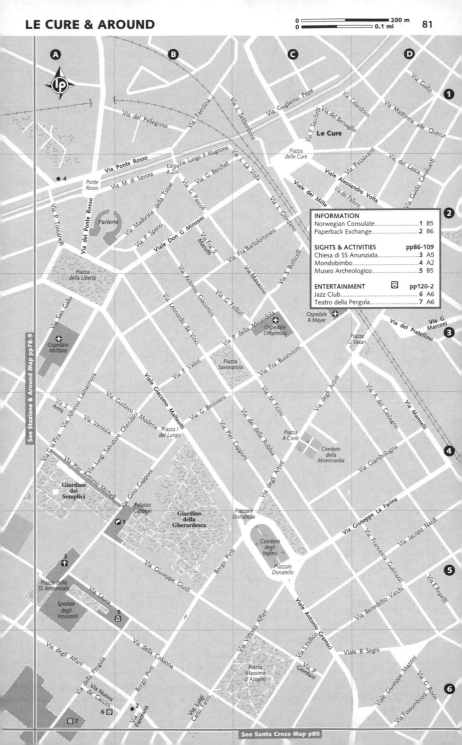

0 — 200 m
0 — 0.1 mi

A B C D

1

Via del Pellegrino
Via Faentina
Via L Settembrini
Via Guglielmo Pepe
Via F Sacchetti
Via del Bersaglio
Via Calandrino
Via Madonna alle Querce
Via Coito

Le Cure

Piazza delle Cure

Via del Lasca
Via Passavonti
Via Guido Cavalcanti

Via Ponte Rosso
Largo A Zoli
Via Lungo il Mugnone
Via G Berchet
Via L La Vista

Viale Alessandro Volta
Viale dei Mille
Via del Pallone

2

INFORMATION
Norwegian Consulate.....................1 B5
Paperback Exchange.....................2 B6

SIGHTS & ACTIVITIES   pp86–109
Chiesa di SS Anunziata................3 A5
Mondobimbo..............................4 A2
Museo Archeologico....................5 B5

ENTERTAINMENT   pp120-2
Jazz Club......................................6 A6
Teatro della Pergola....................7 A6

Ponte Rosso
●4
Via M di Savoia
Via del Ponte Rosso
Via P Toscanelli

Parterre

Via Madonna della Tosse
Via P Spano
Viale Don G Minzoni
Via Fra S Manetti
Via G Pascoli
Via Antonio Giacomini
Via Fra Bartolommeo
Via Masaccio
Via S Botticelli
Via L Giordano

Piazza della Libertà

Via San Gallo
Via Leonardo da Vinci
Via G Fattori
Via P della Mirandola

Ospedale Oftalmico

Ospedale A Mayer
Piazza G Vasari

Via del Pratellino
Via G Marconi

3

Ospedale Militare

Via F Valori
Piazza Savonarola
Via Fra Buonvicini
Via M Ficino
Via degli Artisti
Via A del Castagno
Via Mannelli

Viale Giacomo Matteotti
Via G Benivieni
Via dei della Robbia

Piazza A Conti

Cimitero della Misericordia
Via Giambologna

Via S Anna
Via Alfonso Lamarmora
Via Gustavo Modena
Via Venezia
Via Cherubini
Via Luigi Salvatore
Piazza I del Lungo
Via Pier Capponi
Via degli Artisti

4

Via G La Pira
Via Pier Antonio Micheli
Via Gino Capponi

Giardino dei Semplici

Palazzo Capponi
●1

Giardino della Gherardesca

Piazzale Donatello

Cimitero degli Inglesi
Piazzale Donatello

Via Giuseppe La Farina
Via Francesco Guerrazzi
Via Jacopo Nardi
Via E Repetti

5

●3
Piazza della SS Annunziata
Via Laura
Spedale degli Innocenti
5
Via della Colonna
Borgo Pinti

Viale Antonio Gramsci

Via Benedetto Varchi

6

Via degli Alfani
Via Nuova de' Caccini
Via della Pergola
6
●2
Via Fiesolana
Borgo Pinti

Piazza Massimo d'Azeglio

Via Vittorio Alfieri
Via S Pellico
Via P Giordani
Viale B Segni
Viale Giuseppe Mazzini
Via G Bovio
Via Fossombroni

●7
Via Luigi Carlo Farini

See Stazione & Around Map pp78-9

See Santa Croce Map p80

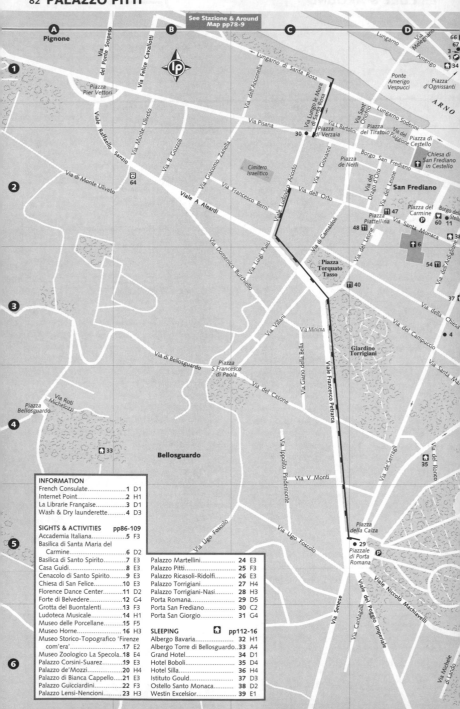

See Stazione & Around
Map pp78-9

INFORMATION

French Consulate.....................1	D1
Internet Point.........................2	H1
La Librarie Française..............3	D1
Wash & Dry launderette..........4	D3

SIGHTS & ACTIVITIES   pp86-109

Accademia Italiana..................5	F3
Basilica di Santa Maria del Carmine...............................6	D2
Basilica di Santo Spirito..........7	E3
Casa Guidi..............................8	E3
Cenacolo di Santo Spirito........9	E3
Chiesa di San Felice...............10	E3
Florence Dance Center...........11	D2
Forte di Belvedere.................12	G4
Grotta del Buontalenti...........13	F3
Ludoteca Musicale.................14	H1
Museo delle Porcellane..........15	F5
Museo Horne.........................16	H3
Museo Storico-Topografico 'Firenze com'era'.........................17	E2
Museo Zoologico La Specola..18	E4
Palazzo Corsini-Suarez..........19	E3
Palazzo de'Mozzi...................20	H4
Palazzo di Bianca Cappello....21	E3
Palazzo Guicciardini...............22	F3
Palazzo Lensi-Nencioni.........23	H3

Palazzo Martellini..................24	E3
Palazzo Pitti.........................25	F3
Palazzo Ricasoli-Ridolfi.........26	E3
Palazzo Torrigiani.................27	H4
Palazzo Torrigiani-Nasi.........28	H3
Porta Romana......................29	D5
Porta San Frediano...............30	C2
Porta San Giorgio.................31	G4

SLEEPING   pp112-16

Albergo Bavaria....................32	H1
Albergo Torre di Bellosguardo.33	A4
Grand Hotel.........................34	D1
Hotel Boboli.........................35	D4
Hotel Silla...........................36	H4
Istituto Gould.......................37	D3
Ostello Santo Monaca...........38	D2
Westin Excelsior...................39	E1

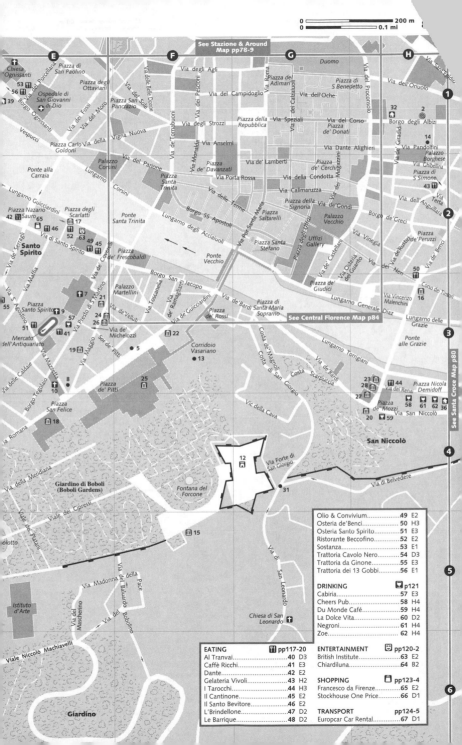

See Stazione & Around Map pp78-9

See Central Florence Map p84

See Santa Croce Map p80

EATING	pp117-20
Al Tranvai	40 D3
Caffè Ricchi	41 E3
Dante	42 E2
Gelateria Vivoli	43 H2
I Tarocchi	44 H3
Il Cantinone	45 E2
Il Santo Bevitore	46 E2
L'Brindellone	47 D2
Le Barrique	48 D2
Olio & Convivium	49 E2
Osteria de'Benci	50 H3
Osteria Santo Spirito	51 E3
Ristorante Beccofino	52 E2
Sostanza	53 E1
Trattoria Cavolo Nero	54 D3
Trattoria da Ginone	55 E3
Trattoria dei 13 Gobbi	56 E1

DRINKING	p121
Cabiria	57 E3
Cheers Pub	58 H4
Du Monde Café	59 H4
La Dolce Vita	60 D2
Negroni	61 H4
Zoe	62 H4

ENTERTAINMENT	pp120-2
British Institute	63 E2
Chiardiluna	64 B2

SHOPPING	pp123-4
Francesco da Firenze	65 E2
Stockhouse One Price	66 D1

TRANSPORT	pp124-5
Europcar Car Rental	67 D1

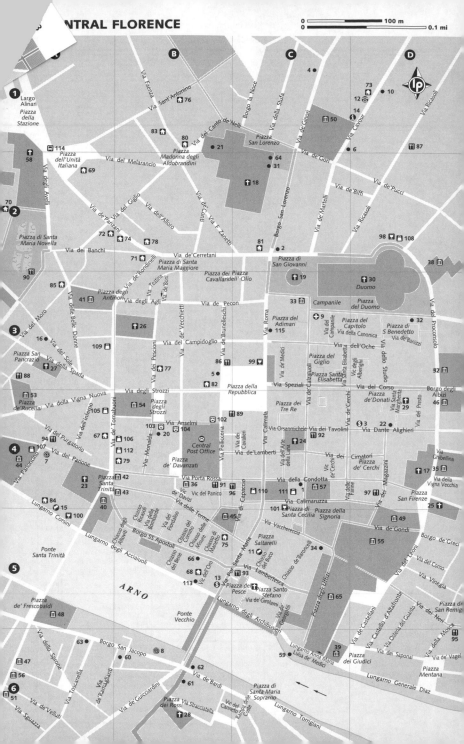

THE GRAND TOUR

The guest book of the now extinct Gabinetto Vieusseux, which from its foundation in 1819 in the Palazzo Buondelmont was something of a cultural institution in Florence, was a veritable who's who of VIPs who have passed through Florence. Some liked it, some hated it. In some respects one of the latter was Mark Twain, who in particular found the Arno a poor excuse for a river (after the Mississippi it must come as a bit of a letdown).

Stendhal, the French novelist, it is said, discovered 'stendhalismo' in the Basilica di Santa Croce, overwhelmed by the sheer concentration of art in Florence. Judging by his journal notes, he was equally overwhelmed by the need to pay little tips to an unending stream of attendants and small lads to get from one sight to another. His countryman, the Marquis de Sade, found the local women 'tall, impertinent, ugly, dishevelled and gluttonous'.

Percy Shelley composed his *Ode to the West Wind* in Le Cascine. Percy and pals, such as Lord Byron, the Brownings and Walter Savage Landor, all resided in Florence for a while, maintaining a haughty distance from the locals and indulging their whims.

Dickens, a little more down to earth, was fascinated by the city, and Anatole France opined that the 'god who created Florence was an artist'.

Fourteen-year-old Mozart popped by with his father in 1770. He stayed but a few days, just enough time to waltz from one engagement to the next, wowing all the nobs in town with his genius.

A century later, Queen Victoria visited three times. Not a great lover of museums or art, she preferred to spend her time in the city's parks and gardens and keep a low profile.

The list, as you can imagine, just goes on and on. So you are not in bad company at any rate!

FLORENCE

(Continued from page 75)
accepted at most. Phonecards (from €5) are available from *tabaccai* and newsstands.

Tourist Information

The police and tourist office combine to operate Tourist Help points for the disoriented at Ponte Vecchio and Piazza della Repubblica, open 8.30am to 7pm. From April to October, the tourist office also offers a special service known as Florence SOS Turista (☎ 055 276 03 82). Tourists needing guidance on matters such as disputes over hotel bills can phone from 10am to 1pm and 3pm to 6pm, Monday to Saturday.

Main Tourist Office (Map p84; ☎ 055 29 08 32; www.firenzeturismo.it; Via Cavour 1r; ☷ 8.15am-7.15pm Mon-Sat & 8.30am-1.30pm Sun Apr-Oct, until 1.30pm & closed Sun Nov-Mar) Just north of the Duomo; there is also a branch at Perètola Airport (☎ 055 31 58 74; ☷ 7.30am-11.30pm).

Comune di Firenze Tourist Office (Map pp78-79; ☎ 055 21 22 45; Piazza della Stazione 4; 8.45am-8pm Mon-Sat Apr-Sep, 9am-1.45pm Oct-Mar) Run by Florence's city council.

Tourist Office (Map p80; ☎ 055 234 04 44; Borgo Santa Croce 29r; ☷ 9am-7pm Mon-Sat, 9am-2pm Sun) Another useful office near the Basilica di Santa Croce.

Travel Agencies

CTS Viaggi (Map p84; ☎ 055 28 97 21; www.cts.it – Italian only; Via de' Ginori 25r) A branch of the national youth-travel organisation.

Sestante (Map p84; ☎ 055 239 87 66; Via Cavour 56r) You can book train and air tickets, organise guided tours and so on.

Wasteels (Map pp78-79; ☎ 055 28 06 83; www.wasteels.it – Italian only; Platform 16, Stazione di Santa Maria Novella) Head here for discounted international rail tickets (if you are under 26).

DANGERS & ANNOYANCES

The most annoying aspect of Florence is the crowds, which, along with the heavy traffic and the narrow roads, can make walking around the city a draining experience. While generally a safe city, single tourists should avoid the area around Stazione di Santa Maria Novella and the Parco delle Cascine after dark. Pickpockets are active in crowds and on buses.

SIGHTS

You'll never be lost for something to see or do in Florence. In fact, on one trip you'll only be scratching the surface of what this amazing city has to offer. With its numerous museums and galleries housing many of the most important and exquisite examples of Renaissance art, its unrivalled architecture and its warrens of narrow streets leading you off into the less explored but often fascinating side of modern Florentine life, your only problem will be deciding what you can squeeze into one day. Thankfully, Florence is a compact city and most of the sights are within walking distance.

Opening Times

Museums and monuments tend to be closed on Monday in Italy. Given the hordes of tourists that pour into Florence year-round, quite a few places *do* open here on Monday – you can get a list of them from the tourist office.

Opening times vary throughout the year, although many monuments stick to a vague summer/winter timetable. In the case of state museums, summer means 1 May to 31 October. For other sights it can be more like Easter to the end of September. It is impossible to be too precise, because timetables change from year to year and from summer to winter.

WARNING

At most sights the ticket office shuts up to 30 minutes before the advertised closing time. Also, in some places staff will usher you out at least 15 minutes before closing time. It would seem in such instances that closing time means not when you have to start heading out the door, but when the door has to be bolted shut. Take note that some churches enforce a strict dress code for visitors (no shorts, sleeveless shirts or plunging necklines), so remember to dress appropriately, or you may be refused admittance.

Free Entry

For one week of the year (usually in spring but the dates change), entry to *musei statali* (state museums) throughout Italy is made free. Since dates change it is impossible to plan a trip around this, but keep your eyes open.

In addition, admission to all state museums is supposed to be free for EU citizens under 18 and over 65. In some other museums EU citizens of differing ages get discounts. There are few discounts for non-EU

QUEUE JUMPING

If time is precious and money is not a prime concern, you can skip (or at least shorten) some of the museum queues in Florence by booking ahead. In summer especially, the long and winding queues can mean waits of two to four hours! For a €3 fee, you can book a ticket to the Uffizi by phoning **Firenze Musei** (☎ 055 29 48 83). You are given a booking number and agree on the time you want to visit. When you arrive at the gallery, follow the signs to a separate entrance for those with pre-booked tickets, which you pick up and pay for on the spot without queuing. You can book to visit any of the *musei statali* (state museums) this way. For the Uffizi, you can also buy the ticket in advance at the gallery itself (the booking fee still applies).

If you prefer the electronic age, **Weekend a Firenze** (www.weekendafirenze.com) is an online service for booking museums, galleries, shows and tours. For this you pay a small fee on top of the normal ticket price. You must book at least three days in advance. You will get an email confirmation that you will have to print out and present at the cashier's desk on the day you go. You can get tickets for the Uffizi, Galleria dell'Accademia, Galleria Palatina, Museo di San Marco, Museo del Bargello, Cappelle Medicee, Museo Archeologico and Galleria d'Arte Moderna. Many of the bigger hotels will also book these tickets for you.

citizens or nonresidents of Florence. Still, always ask to be sure.

Duomo & Around

The **Duomo** (Cathedral; Map p84; ☎ 055 230 28 85; 🕑 10am-5pm Mon-Wed & Fri, 10am-3.30pm Thu, 10am-4.45pm Sat, 1.30-4.45pm Sun) is one of those icons of Italy, ranking alongside Pisa's Leaning Tower and Rome's Colosseum. Brunelleschi's sloping, red-tiled dome dominates Florence's skyline, but it is only when you leave the crowded streets behind and approach the building from the piazza that you experience the breathtaking grandeur of the great church and the ordered vivacity of its pink, white and green marble facade.

The church's full name is Cattedrale di Santa Maria del Fiore and it is the world's fourth-largest cathedral. Begun in 1296 by Arnolfo di Cambio, it took almost 150 years to complete.

The present facade was only raised in the late 19th century. Its architect, Emilio de Fabris, was inspired by the design of the cathedral's flanks, which largely date from the 14th century. From the facade, you should do a circuit of the church to take in its splendour before heading inside.

The south flank is the oldest and most clearly Gothic part of the Duomo. The second doorway here is the **Porta dei Canonici** (Canons' Door); it's a mid-14th-century High Gothic creation (you enter here to climb up inside the dome). Wander around the trio of apses, designed to appear as the flowers on the stem that is the nave of the church (and so reflecting its name – Santa Maria del Fiore, St Mary of the Flower).

The first door you see on the north flank after the apses is the early-15th-century **Porta della Mandorla** (Almond Door), so named because of the relief of the Virgin Mary contained within an almond-shaped frame. Much of the decorative sculpture that graced the flanks of the cathedral has been removed for its own protection to the Museo dell'Opera del Duomo, in some cases to be replaced by copies.

INTERIOR

The Duomo's vast and spartan interior comes as a surprise after the visual assault outside. Down the left aisle you will see two immense frescoes of equestrian statues dedicated to two *condottieri* or mercenaries, who fought in the service of Florence. The one on the left is of Niccolò da Tolentino (by Andrea del Castagno) and the other is of Sir John Hawkwood (by Uccello).

The 'divine' poet Dante has always been revered in his native Florence, and Domenico di Michelino's *Dante e I Suoi Mondi* (Dante and His Worlds), the next painting along the left aisle, is one of the most reproduced images of the poet and his verse masterpiece.

The festival of colour and images that greets you as you arrive beneath Brunelleschi's dome is the work of Giorgio Vasari and Frederico Zuccari. The fresco series depicts the Giudizio Universale (Last Judgment). Below the frescoes is the octagonal

FLORENCE

coro (choirstalls). Its low marble enclosure surrounds the altar, above which hangs a crucifix by Benedetto da Maiano.

From the choirstalls, the two wings of the transept and the rear apse spread out, each containing five chapels. The pillars delimiting the entrance into each wing and the apse are fronted by statues of Apostles, as are the two hefty pillars just west of the choirstalls.

Between the left (north) arm of the transept and the apse is the **Sagrestia delle Messe** (Mass Sacristy), the panelling of which is a marvel of inlaid wood created by Benedetto and Giuliano da Maiano. The fine bronze doors were executed by Luca della Robbia – his only known work in the material. Above the doorway is one of his glazed terracotta compositions, of the Resurrection.

Some of the finest stained glass in Italy, by Donatello, Andrea del Castagno, Paolo Uccello and Lorenzo Ghiberti, adorns the windows.

A stairway near the main entrance of the Duomo leads down to the **crypt** (☎ 055 230 28 85; €3; ✆ 10am-5pm Mon-Sat, except during Mass), the actual site where excavations have unearthed parts of the 5th-century Chiesa di Santa Reparata. There's a small display of Roman pottery and architectural fragments, and sections of the original mosaic floor, typical of early Italian churches. Brunelleschi's tomb is also here, beside the gift shop.

DOME

You can climb up into the **dome** (☎ 055 230 28 85; enter by Porta dei Canonici; €6; ✆ 8.30am-7pm Mon-Fri, 8.30am-5.40pm Sat) to get a closer look at Brunelleschi's engineering feat; this was the biggest cupola then built. The view from the summit over Florence is breathtaking.

On 8 September every year, a walkway that stretches around atop the sides and facade of the dome is opened to the public. You access it by the same entrance as to the dome.

CAMPANILE

Giotto designed and began building the graceful and unusual **Campanile** (Map p84; ☎ 055 230 28 85; Bell Tower; €6; ✆ 8.30am-7.30pm) next to the Duomo in 1334, but died only three years later. The bell tower is 84.7m high and you can climb its 414 stairs.

Andrea Pisano and Francesco Talenti continued the work on the Campanile. The first tier of bas-reliefs around the base are copies of those carved by Pisano but possibly designed by Giotto, depicting the Creation of Man and the *attività umane* (arts and industries). The originals are in the Museo dell'Opera del Duomo. Those on the second tier depict the planets, cardinal virtues, the arts and the seven sacraments. The sculptures of the prophets and sibyls in the niches of the upper storeys are, again, copies of works by Donatello and others – the originals are in the Museo dell'Opera del Duomo.

Warning

People with heart conditions or who are otherwise unfit should not undertake the climb up the Campanile. There is no lift should you get into difficulties.

MUSEO DELL'OPERA DEL DUOMO

This **museum** (Map p84; ☎ 055 230 28 85; Piazza del Duomo 9; admission €6; ✆ 9am-7.30pm Mon-Sat, 9am-1.40pm Sun), behind the cathedral, features many of the sculptural treasures that at one time adorned the Duomo, Baptistry and Campanile.

The first main hall is devoted to statuary that graced Arnolfo di Cambio's original Gothic facade, which was never completed. The pieces include several by Arnolfo himself, among them *Pope Boniface VIII*, *The Virgin and Child* and *St Reparata*. The long flowing beard of Donatello's *St John* stands out among the four mighty statues of the evangelists.

Out in the courtyard are displayed five of the original 10 panels of Ghiberti's masterpiece, the *Porta del Paradiso* of the Battistero (what you see at the Battistero itself are copies). They were damaged in the 1966 floods and needed urgent restoration. It has taken a while but the end result is definitely worth it.

As you head up the stairs you approach what is the museum's best-known piece, Michelangelo's *Pietà*, a late work that he intended for his own tomb. Vasari recorded in his *Lives of the Artists* (see p52) that, unsatisfied with the quality of the marble or his own work, Michelangelo broke up the unfinished sculpture, destroying the arm and left leg of the figure of Christ. A student of Michelangelo later restored the arm and completed the figure of Mary Magdalene.

Continue upstairs to the next main hall, which is dominated by the two extraordinary *cantorie*, or 'singing galleries' (one by Donatello and the other by Luca della Robbia) that once adorned the Sagrestia in the Duomo. In the same hall is Donatello's carving of the prophet Habakkuk (taken from the Campanile and now under restoration) and, in an adjoining room, his extraordinary wooden impression of Mary Magdalene.

BATTISTERO

The Romanesque **Battistero** (Baptistry; Map p84; admission €3; ☺ noon-7pm Mon-Sat, 8.30am-2pm Sun) may have been built as early as the 5th century on the site of a Roman temple. It is one of the oldest buildings in Florence and dedicated to St John the Baptist (San Giovanni Battista).

The present structure, or at least its facade, dates to about the 11th century. The stripes of white and green marble that bedeck the octagonal structure are typical of Tuscan Romanesque style.

Even more striking are the three sets of bronze doors, conceived as a series of panels in which the story of humanity and the Redemption would be told.

The earliest set of doors, which is now on the south side, was completed by Andrea Pisano in 1336.

Lorenzo Ghiberti toiled away for 20 years to get his set of doors, on the north flank, just right. The top 20 panels recount episodes from the New Testament, while the eight lower ones show the four Evangelists and the four fathers of the Church.

Good as this late-Gothic effort was, Ghiberti returned almost immediately to his workshops to turn out the east doors. Made of gilded bronze, they took 28 years to complete (1424–52), largely because of Ghiberti's intransigent perfectionism. On 10 panels, the bas-reliefs depict scenes from the Old Testament. So extraordinary were his exertions that, many years later, Michelangelo stood before the doors in awe and declared them fit to be the Porta del Paradiso (Gates of Paradise), which is how they remain known to this day.

Most of the doors' panels are copies. The original panels are being restored and five from the Porta del Paradiso are on display in the Museo dell'Opera del Duomo.

The interior is reminiscent of a Byzantine church. The two-coloured marble facing on the outside continues within, made more arresting by the geometrical flourishes above the Romanesque windows.

The single most arresting aspect of the decoration is the mosaic-work. Those in the apse were started in 1225, and the glittering spectacle in the dome is a unique sight in Florence. It was designed by Tuscan artists, including Cimabue, and carried out by Venetian craftsmen over 32 years from 1270.

Donatello carved the tomb of Baldassare Cossa, better known as the antipope John XXIII, which takes up the wall to the right of the apse.

LOGGIA DEL BIGALLO

This elegant marble loggia was built in the second half of the 14th century for the Compagnia (or Confraternita) di Santa Maria della Misericordia, which had been formed in 1244 to aid the elderly, the sick and orphans. Lost and abandoned children were customarily placed here so that they could be reclaimed by their families or put into the care of foster mothers. Members of the fraternity transported the ill to hospital and buried the dead in times of plague. In 1425, the fraternity was fused with another that had been founded by the same person (San Pietro Martire), the Confraternita del Bigallo. The fusion lasted a century, after which the Misericordia moved to its present position on Piazza del Duomo, from where to this day they continue their charitable vocation.

The loggia houses a small **museum** (Map p84; admission €3; ☺ 8.30am-noon Mon, 4-6pm Thu) containing a collection of artworks commissioned by the two fraternities.

MUSEO STORICO-TOPOGRAFICO 'FIRENZE COM'ERA'

This **museum** (Map pp82-83; ☎ 055 261 65 45; Via dell'Oriuolo 24; admission €2.60; ☺ 9am-2pm Fri-Wed) may interest those who want to get an idea of how the city developed, particularly from the Renaissance to the modern day. Paintings, models, topographical drawings and prints help explain the history of the city.

From the Duomo to Piazza della Signoria (Map p84)
VIA DEL PROCONSOLO

Bernardo Buontalenti started work on **Palazzo Nonfinito** (literally 'Unfinished Palace'), a residence for members of the Strozzi family, in 1593. Buontalenti and others completed the 1st floor and courtyard, which is Palladian in style, but the upper floors were never completely finished, hence the building's name. The obscure **Museo dell'Antropologia e Etnologia** (☎ 055 239 64 49; Via del Proconsolo 12; admission €3.10; ☽ 10am-noon Wed-Mon) is housed here.

Across Borgo degli Albizi stands the equally proud **Palazzo dei Pazzi**, which went up a century earlier and is clearly influenced by Palazzo Medici-Riccardi. It now houses offices, but you can wander into the courtyard.

BADIA FIORENTINA
The 10th-century **Badia Fiorentina** (Florence Abbey; Via del Proconsolo; ☽ 3-6pm Mon) was founded by Willa, the mother of Margrave Ugo of Tuscany. Ugo continued her work after experiencing a hellish vision of the punishment awaiting him in the afterlife, should he not repent his sins. It is particularly worth a visit to see Filippino Lippi's *Appearance of the Virgin to St Bernard* (1485), to the left as you enter the church through the small (and scaffolding-cluttered) Renaissance cloister. At the left end of the transept is Mino da Fiesole's monument to Margrave Ugo. Stairs to the right of the altar lead up to an open gallery overlooking the cloister, decorated with 15th-century frescoes illustrating the life of St Benedict.

PALAZZO DEL BARGELLO
Just across Via del Proconsolo from the Badia is this grand mansion, also known as Palazzo del Podestà. Started in 1254, the palace was originally the residence of the chief magistrate and was then turned into a police station.

It now houses the **Museo del Bargello** (☎ 055 238 86 06; Via del Proconsolo 4; admission €4; ☽ 8.15am-1.50pm Tue-Sat & alternating Sun & Mon) and the most comprehensive collection of Tuscan Renaissance sculpture in Italy. The museum is one of Florence's true highlights.

You enter the courtyard from Via Ghibellina and turn right into the ticket office. From here you end up in the ground-floor Sala del Cinquecento (16th-Century Room), dominated by early works by Michelangelo. His drunken *Bacco* (Bacchus), executed when the artist was 22, a marble bust of Brutus

and a tondo of the *Madonna col Bambino* (Madonna and Child) are among his best here. Other works of particular interest are Benvenuto Cellini's playful marble *Ganimede* (Ganymede), Ammannati's sensuous *Leda*, and Giambologna's much-imitated *Mercurio Volante* (Winged Mercury).

Upstairs is the majestic Salone del Consiglio Generale (Hall of the General Council). At the far end, housed in a tabernacle, is Donatello's famed *San Giorgio* (St George), which once graced Chiesa di Orsanmichele. David (as in David and Goliath) was a favourite subject for sculptors, and in this hall you can see two versions by Donatello: a slender, youthful image in marble and the fabled bronze he did in later years. The latter is extraordinary – more so when you consider it was the first freestanding naked statue done since classical times. It is interesting to compare these slight, boyish Davids with Michelangelo's muscular warrior in the Accademia. Also in this room are a couple of masterpieces by Luca della Robbia, including his delightful *Madonna della Mela* (Madonna of the Apple, c1460), which once adorned Lorenzo the Magnificent's bedroom.

Up on the 2nd floor you will find a superb collection of terracotta pieces by the della Robbia family, including some of their best-known works such as Andrea's *Ritratto Idealizia di Fanciullo* (Bust of a Boy, c1475) and Giovanni's *Pietà* (1514). Also on this floor is a bronze collection, including another *Ganimede* by Cellini, and an arms gallery.

CHIESA DI SAN FIRENZE
The small medieval parish **church** (closed to public) of San Firenze is no longer recognisable in this Baroque complex that is today home to law courts. The original church of San Firenze, on the right, was reduced to an oratory when the church on the left, dedicated to San Filippo Neri was built. The late-Baroque facade that unites the buildings was completed in 1775.

Across the piazza (on the western side) is the main facade of **Palazzo Gondi**. It was once the site of the merchants' tribunal, a court set up to deal with their quarrels.

CASA DI DANTE & AROUND
Casa di Dante (Dante's House; ☎ 055 21 94 16; Via Santa Margherita 1; admission €3; ☽ 10am-5pm Wed-Mon,

FLORENCE

THE DELLA ROBBIA FAMILY

Some of the most beautiful and distinctive artworks of the Florentine Renaissance were produced by the prolific della Robbia family, headed by Luca (c1399–1482) who first developed the process of glazing terracotta in the 1440s. He started out as a sculptor in marble, and one of his first major commissions was designing the wonderfully detailed marble *cantoria* (singing gallery; 1438) for the Duomo, now in the Museo dell'Opera del Duomo. However, he soon turned his attention almost fully to the production of terracotta, and the system he employed long remained a closely guarded family secret. Essentially, it involved coating a terracotta statue in a thin layer of enamel, oxides and a lead glaze. Luca's workshop churned out a vast quantity of terracotta pieces, from simple blue and white Madonna reliefs for private homes to gigantic altarpieces for churches, as well as numerous *stemmi* (glazed heraldic emblems) for adorning the facades of guild houses across Florence. The durability of the new material made it ideal for decorating the outsides of public buildings.

Luca was aided by his nephew Andrea (1435–1525), whose most famous creations are the medallions of babies in swaddling clothes on the colonnade of the Spedale degli Innocenti (see p101). Many of his works are also on show in the Museo del Bargello (see p90). Like his uncle, Andrea produced many Madonna and Child reliefs in a fairly standard, conventional portraiture. One way of telling Andrea's work apart, though, is the fact that he usually placed the Child to the left of the Madonna, whereas Luca placed it on her right.

The family tradition was continued by Andrea's son Giovanni (1469–1521), many of whose finest pieces can be seen in the Museo del Bargello. Instantly recognisable, Giovanni's works are more elaborate than either Luca's or Andrea's, employing a larger palette of colours. His bright greens, yellows, blues and browns still seem fresh and vibrant, while the intricate garlands of fruit and flowers he used to frame some of his works exemplify his flamboyant touch.

Della Robbian works can be seen all around Florence and elsewhere in Tuscany and beyond, both inside and outside buildings, making them amongst the most accessible artworks of the Italian Renaissance.

10am-2pm Sun) was built in 1910, so you can be quite sure the claim that Dante lived here is utterly spurious. Those with an especial interest in the poet may find the limited display inside mildly diverting.

Just up the road is the small, 11th-century **Chiesa di Santa Margherita** (Via Santa Margherita), which houses some of the tombs of the Portinari family, relatives of Dante's muse, Beatrice, whom he first espied in the Badia.

CHIESA DI ORSANMICHELE
Originally a grain market, this **church** (Via Arte della Lana; closed for renovation at the time of writing) was formed when the arcades of the granary building were walled in during the 14th century and the granary moved elsewhere. The granary had been built on a spot known as Orsanmichele, a contraction of Orto di San Michele (St Michael's Garden). Under the Lombards, a small church dedicated to St Michael and an adjacent Benedictine convent had indeed been graced with a garden. The *signoria* (the city's government) cleared the lot to have the granary built. It was destroyed by fire 20 years later and a finer replacement constructed. Considered too good to be a mere granary, this was converted into a church.

The *signoria* ordered the guilds to finance the decoration of the church, and they proceeded to commission sculptors to erect statues of their patron saints in tabernacles placed around the building's facades.

The statues, commissioned over the 15th and 16th centuries, represent the work of some of the Renaissance's greatest artists. Some are now in the Museo del Bargello, though many splendid pieces remain, including Giambologna's *San Luca* (St Luke; third on the right on Via de' Calzaiuoli), and Ghiberti's bronze *San Matteo* (St Matthew; first on the left on Via Arte della Lana). Donatello's *San Giorgio* (St George; last on the right on Via Orsanmichele) is a modern copy.

The main feature of the interior is the splendid Gothic tabernacle, decorated with coloured marble, by Andrea Orcagna.

PIAZZA DELLA REPUBBLICA

This busy square was created in the 1880s after the demolition of the Mercato Vecchio and the surrounding slums and Jewish ghetto, as part of an ambitious plan of 'civic improvements'. A single column, once crowned with a statue by Donatello, is the sole reminder of the old market area still here. Vasari's **Loggia del Pesce** (Fish Market) was saved, though, and has been re-erected on Via Pietrapana (see p104). Today the square is flanked by a number of trendy and expensive restaurants and cafés.

MERCATO NUOVO

If you stroll south down Via Calimala you arrive at this loggia, built to cover the merchandise (including wool, silk and gold) traded here at the **Mercato Nuovo** (New Market; ☼ daily) in the mid-16th century. Nowadays, the goods on sale are aimed exclusively at tourists and range from tacky souvenirs to leather goods.

At its southern end is a bronze statue of a boar known as the Fontana del Porcellino (piglet's fountain), an early-17th-century copy of the Greek marble original that is now in the Uffizi. They say that if you toss a coin into the small basin and rub the boar's snout you will return to Florence.

PALAZZO DEI CAPITANI DI PARTE GUELFA

Just off to the southwest of the Mercato Nuovo, this palazzo (which is closed to the public) was built in the early 13th century and later added to by Brunelleschi and Vasari. The leaders of the Guelph faction raised this fortified building in 1265, taking up land and houses that had been confiscated from the Ghibellines.

PALAZZO DAVANZATI

About a block northwest is this remarkable 14th-century **mansion** (Via Porta Rossa 13). It has been closed for extensive renovation since 1995.

That the building has survived intact in its medieval state is largely due to the intervention of an antiquarian, Elia Volpi, who bought the building in 1904. By that time it had come down in the world, having been divided into small flats and shops and reduced to a pathetic state. Volpi had it restored to its former glory and it eventually became the seat of the **Museo dell'Antica**

Casa Fiorentina (closed to public), which aims to transmit an idea of what life was like in a medieval Florentine mansion.

Piazza della Signoria (Map p84)

The hub of the city's political life through the centuries and surrounded by some of its most celebrated buildings, the piazza has the appearance of an outdoor sculpture gallery.

Throughout the centuries, whenever Florence entered one of its innumerable political crises, the people would be called here as a *parlamento* (people's plebiscite) to rubber-stamp decisions that frequently meant ruin for some ruling families and victory for others. Scenes of great pomp and circumstance alternated with others of terrible suffering – it was here that the preacher-leader Savonarola was burned at the stake along with two supporters in 1498. A bronze plaque marks the spot.

Ammannati's huge *Fontana di Nettuno* (Neptune Fountain) sits beside Palazzo Vecchio. The pin-headed bronze satyrs and divinities frolicking about the edges of the fountain aren't the prettiest creations, and Il Biancone (Big White Thing), as locals derisively refer to it, was considered by Michelangelo to be a waste of good marble.

At the entrance to the palace are copies of Michelangelo's *David* (the original is in the Galleria dell'Accademia) and Donatello's *Marzocco*, the heraldic Florentine lion (the original is in the Museo del Bargello). To the right is a 1980 copy of Donatello's bronze *Giuditta e Oloferne* (Judith and Holofernes) – the original is inside the *palazzo*.

A bronze equestrian statue of Cosimo I de' Medici, created by Giambologna (1594), stands towards the centre of the piazza.

PALAZZO VECCHIO

Formerly known as Palazzo della Signoria and built by Arnolfo di Cambio between 1298 and 1314, this **palace** (☎ 055 276 82 24; Piazza della Signoria; admission €6; ☼ 9am-7pm, 9am-2pm Thu & holidays; disabled access on Via dei Gondi) is the traditional seat of Florentine government. Its **Torre d'Arnolfo** is 94m high and, with its striking crenellations, is as much a symbol of the city as the Duomo.

Built for the *priori* (city government) which ruled Florence, it came to be known as Palazzo della Signoria as the government took on this name.

In 1540, Cosimo I de' Medici moved from Palazzo Medici into this building, making it the ducal residence and centre of government. Cosimo commissioned Vasari to renovate and decorate the interior, but in the end, Cosimo's wife, Eleonora de Toledo, disliked it and bought Palazzo Pitti.

The latter took a while to expand and fit out as Eleonora wanted (she died before the work was finished), but the Medici family moved in anyway in 1549. Thus Palazzo Ducale became known as Palazzo Vecchio (Old Palace) as it still is today. It remains the seat of the city's power, and the mayor keeps his office here.

Coming in from Piazza della Signoria, you arrive first in the courtyard, reworked in early Renaissance style by Michelozzo in 1453. The decoration came more than a century later when Francesco de' Medici married Joanna of Austria. The cities depicted are jewels in the Austrian imperial crown.

From here you pass into the **Cortile della Dogana** (Customs Courtyard), off which you'll find the ticket office.

A stairway leads up to the magnificent **Salone dei Cinquecento** (16th-century Hall). It was created within the original building in the 1490s to accommodate the Consiglio dei Cinquecento (Council of 500) called into being in the republic under Savonarola. Cosimo I de' Medici later turned the hall into a splendid expression of his own power. In the 1560s the ceiling was raised 7m and Vasari added the huge battle scenes. Also here are a series of statues by Vincenzo de' Rossi, depicting the Labours of Hercules, including a painful-looking grapple between Hercules and Diomedes. The star-turn, though, is Michelangelo's *Victory*, left unfinished in the artist's studio at the time of his death.

From the Salone dei Cinquecento you enter **Quartiere di Leone X** (Leo X Area), named after the Medici pope. It's adorned with scenes from his life painted by Vasari. Upstairs is **Quartiere degli Elementi** (Elements Area), a series of richly decorated rooms and terraces dedicated to classical deities. Verrocchio's bronze *Putto col Delfino* (Cupid with Dolphin), mentioned in Vasari's *Lives of the Artists*, is in Sala di Giunone.

From here a walkway takes you across the top of the Salone dei Cinquecento into the

Quartiere di Eleonora, the apartments of Cosimo I's wife. The ceiling of the first room, the Camera Verde, was painted by Ridolfo del Ghirlandaio, and inspired by designs from Nero's *Domus Aurea* in Rome, while the small chapel, off to the side, contains vibrant frescoes by Bronzino.

Of the succeeding rooms, the most interesting is the Sala di Gualadra, decorated with views of 16th-century Florence by Giovanni Stradano, including a scene of a ball game in Piazza Santa Maria Novella and a jousting match in Piazza di Santa Croce.

You pass through the **Capella dei Priori** (Chapel of the Priors), which houses a lunette of the Annunciation by Ridolfo del Ghirlandaio, before reaching the **Sala dell'Udienza** (Audience Room), where the *priori* administered medieval Florentine justice.

The following room is the **Sala dei Gigli**, named after the lilies of the Florentine Republic that decorate three of the walls. Domenico Ghirlandaio's fresco on the far wall, depicting figures from Roman history, was meant to be one of a series by other artists including Botticelli. Donatello's restored original bronze of *Giuditta e Oloferne* stands in here. A small, bare study off this hall is the chancery, where Machiavelli worked for a while. The other room off the hall, the **Sala delle Carte Geografiche** (Map Room), houses Cosimo I's fascinating collection of 16th-century maps, of varying degrees of accuracy, charting everywhere in the known world, from the Polar regions to the Caribbean.

By paying a little extra you can join in small guided groups to explore the Percorsi Segreti (Secret Passageways; not open to disabled visitors) or head for the **Museo dei Ragazzi** (Children's Museum). The former consist of several options, including the possibility of visiting the **Studiolo di Francesco** and the nearby **treasury** of Cosimo I. Another choice takes you into the roof of the Salone dei Cinquecento, or you can also choose to be guided around the artworks by an actor portraying Giorgio Vasari.

In the **Museo dei Ragazzi**, you can interact with actors dressed up as Cosimo I and Eleonora de Toledo – children are invited to dress up as the ducal offspring (Bia and Garcia) and play with the kinds of toys they would have enjoyed. Other activities include building and taking apart models of Palazzo Vecchio, bridges and the like.

For any one of these options and the standard visit you pay €8. If you want to add on more of the extras, each one costs an additional €1. Family tickets (€16) for two adults and not more than three children are also available. Tickets and information on all these extra activities are available in a room just back from the main ticket area.

LOGGIA DELLA SIGNORIA

Built from 1376 as a platform for public ceremonies, this loggia eventually became a showcase for sculptures. It also became known as the Loggia dei Lanzi, as Cosimo I used to station his Swiss mercenaries, armed with lances, in it to remind people who was in charge around here.

To the left of the steps stands Benvenuto Cellini's magnificent bronze statue of *Perseus* (1545) holding the head of Medusa, one of the most recognizable masterpieces of Renaissance sculpture. The statue's troublesome creation is detailed by Cellini in his autobiography. To the right is Giambologna's Mannerist *Ratto delle Sabine* (Rape of the Sabine; 1583), his final work. Inside the loggia proper is another of Giambologna's works, *Ercole col Centauro Nesso* (Hercules with the Centaur Nessus), which originally stood near the southern end of Ponte Vecchio. Among the other statues are Roman representations of empresses.

RACCOLTA D'ARTE CONTEMPORANEA ALBERTO DELLA RAGIONE

The **collection** (Piazza della Signoria 5; closed at the time of writing) may interest the art buff with a passion for Italian 20th-century painting. Most of the works are by lesser-known artists, though there are a few by Giorgio Morandi and a modest De Chirico on show.

The collection was donated to Florence by the Genoese collector Alberto della Ragione on his death in 1970.

Uffizi Gallery & Around (Map p84)

Designed and built by Vasari in the second half of the 16th century at the request of Cosimo I de' Medici, Palazzo degli Uffizi, south of Palazzo Vecchio, originally housed the city's administrators, judiciary and guilds. It was, in effect, a government office building (*uffizi* means offices).

Vasari also designed the private corridor that links Palazzo Vecchio and Palazzo Pitti, through the Uffizi and across Ponte Vecchio. Known as the **Corridoio Vasariano**, it was long closed to the public but can now be visited by reservation (see p96).

Cosimo's successor, Francesco I, commissioned the architect Buontalenti to modify the upper floor of Palazzo degli Uffizi to house the Medicis' growing art collection. Thus, indirectly, the first steps were taken to turn it into an art gallery.

The Uffizi Gallery (Galleria degli Uffizi) now houses the family's private collection, bequeathed to the city in 1743 by the last of the Medici family, Anna Maria Ludovica, on condition that it never leave the city. Over the years sections of the collection have been moved to the Museo del Bargello and the city's Museo Archeologico. In compensation, other collections have joined the core group. Paintings from Florence's churches have also been moved to the gallery. It is by no means the biggest art gallery around, but the Uffizi still houses the world's single greatest collection of Italian and Florentine art.

Sadly, several artworks were destroyed and others badly damaged when a car bomb planted by the Mafia exploded outside the gallery's west wing in May 1993, killing five people. Documents cataloguing the collection were also destroyed. A massive clean-up enabled the gallery to reopen quickly.

Long queues are common – to avoid the worst of them, try to arrive in the morning when the gallery first opens, or during lunchtime. Alternatively, book ahead (see the boxed text, p87). In the high season especially, queuing can mean waits of three or more hours.

GALLERY

The **collection** (☎ 055 238 86 51; Piazza degli Uffizi 6; admission €8.50; ☼ 8.15am-7pm Tue-Sun) begins on the 1st floor, with the small **Galleria dei Disegni e delle Stampe** (Drawing and Print Gallery), in which sketches and initial drafts by the great masters are often shown. They tend to rotate the display frequently, as prolonged exposure can damage the drawings.

Upstairs in the gallery proper, you pass through two vestibules, the first with singularly unflattering portrait busts of several of the Medici clan, the second with some Roman statuary.

The long corridor has been arranged much as it appeared in the 16th century. Below the frescoed ceilings is a series of small portraits of great and good men, interspersed with larger portraits, often of Medici family members or intimates. Room 1, which holds some archaeological treasures, is closed.

The first accessible rooms feature works by Tuscan masters of the 13th and early 14th centuries. Room 2 is dominated by three paintings of the *Madonna in Maestà* (Madonna in Majesty) by Duccio di Buoninsegna, Cimabue and Giotto. All three were altarpieces in Florentine churches before being placed in the gallery. To look at them in this order is to appreciate the transition from Gothic to the precursor of the Renaissance. In the room also is Giotto's polyptych *Madonna col Bambino Gesù, Santi e Angeli* (Madonna with Baby Jesus, Saints and Angels).

Room 3 traces the Sienese school of the 14th century. Of particular note is Simone Martini's shimmering *Annunciazione*, considered a masterpiece of the school, and Ambrogio Lorenzetti's triptych *Madonna col Bambino e Santi* (Madonna with Child and Saints). Room 4 contains Florentine works of the 14th century.

Rooms 5 and 6 house examples of the International Gothic style, among them Lorenzo Monaco's polyptych *Santa Maria degli Angeli* (St Mary of the Angels).

Room 7 features works by painters of the early-15th-century Florentine school, which pioneered the Renaissance. There is one panel (the other two are in the Louvre and London's National Gallery) from Paolo Uccello's striking *La Battaglia di San Romano* (Battle of Saint Roman). In his efforts to create perspective he directs the lances, horses and soldiers to a central disappearing point. Other works include Piero della Francesca's famous profile portraits of the Duke and Duchess of Urbino, and *Madonna col Bambino* (Madonna with Child) painted jointly by Masaccio and Masolino. In the next room, devoted to a collection of works by Filippo and Filippino Lippi, is Filippo's delightful *Madonna col Bambino e due Angeli* (Madonna with Child and Two Angels).

Room 9 is devoted largely to Antonio de Pollaiuolo. His series of six virtues is followed by *Fortezza* (Strength) by Botticelli.

The clarity of line and light, and the humanity in the face, set it apart from Pollaiuolo's work. It's a taster for the Botticelli Rooms, Nos 10 to 14, which are considered the gallery's most spectacular. Highlights are the iconic *Nascita di Venere* (Birth of Venus) and the joyful *Allegoria della Primavera* (Allegory of Spring). The *Annunciazione* (Annunciation) is a beautiful and deeply spiritual work, while *Calunnia* (Calumny) is a disturbing reflection of Botticelli's late-life loss of faith in human potential.

Room 15 features Da Vinci's *Annunciazione*, painted when he was a student of Verrocchio. Perhaps more intriguing is his unfinished *Adorazione dei Magi*. Room 16 (blocked off, although you can peer in) contains antique maps. Room 17, the Sala dell'Ermafrodito, was closed at the time of writing, though again, you can peek inside at the collection of bronze statuettes.

Room 18, known as the Tribuna, houses the celebrated *Medici Venus*, a 1st-century BC copy of an earlier sculpture by Praxiteles. The room also contains portraits of various members of the Medici family by Bronzino.

The great Umbrian painter, Perugino, who studied under Piero della Francesca and later became Raphael's master, is represented in Room 19, as well as Luca Signorelli. Room 20 features works from the German Renaissance, including *Adorazione dei Magi by* Dürer (1471–1528) . His depictions of Adam and Eve are mirrored by those of Lucas Cranach. Room 21 has works by Giovanni Bellini and his pupil, Giorgione.

Room 22 is given over to various German and Flemish Renaissance artists, and houses, amongst others, a small self-portrait by Hans Holbein. The following room concentrates on the Veneto region in Italy's northeast, with paintings by Mantegna and Correggio. Peek through the railings of Room 24 to see the 15th- to 19th-century works in the Miniatures Room and then cross into the west wing, which houses works of Italian masters dating from the 16th century.

The star of Room 25 is Michelangelo's dazzling *Tondo Doni*, which depicts the Holy Family. It's his only known completed painting, and the composition is highly unusual, with Mary handing Jesus over her shoulder to Joseph. Thanks to restoration in the 1980s, the colours are as vibrant as when they were first applied. This masterpiece of the High Renaissance, still in its original frame, leaps out at you as you enter, demanding attention.

In the next room are works by Raphael (1483–1520), including his *Leo X* and *Madonna del Cardellino* (actually a copy as the original is being restored). The former is remarkable for the richness of colour and detail. Room 27 is dominated by the sometimes disquieting works of Florence's two main Mannerist masters, Pontormo and Rosso Fiorentino.

Room 28 boasts nine Titians, including *Madonna delle Rose* (Madonna of the Roses), a tender study in which the Christ child plays with flowers proffered by the infant John the Baptist, as Mary watches with a hint of amusement on her face. Also here is Titian's portrait of *Pope Sixtus IV*. Rooms 29 and 30 contain works by comparatively minor painters from northern Italy, but Room 31 is dominated above all by Venice's Paolo Veronese, including his *Sacra Famiglia con Santa Barbara* (Holy Family with St Barbara). Room 32 is mostly dedicated to Tintoretto, and houses his *Leda e il Cigno* (Leda and the Swan). He is accompanied by a few Jacopo Bassano canvasses. Room 33 is named the Corridor of the 16th Century and contains a mix of lesser-known artists. A couple of pieces by Vasari appear, along with some unexpected foreign contributions, including El Greco's *I Santi San Giovanni Evangelista e San Francesco* and a few French works by unknown artists. *Due Donne al Bagno* (Two Ladies Bathing), in which a pair of disrobed ladies are touching fingers, is typical of the saucy subject matter favoured by the French court at this time. The following room is filled mainly with 16th-century works by Lombard painters.

Next door comes as a bit of a shock as you are confronted with the enormous, sumptuous religious canvases of Lodovico Buti (c1560–1611) of Florence and Federico Barocci (1535–1612) of Urbino. Rooms 36 to 37 are part of the exit while the adjoining Room 38 was closed for renovation at the time of writing.

For some reason the counting starts at No 41 after this. This room is a showcase of Flemish art, dominated by two colossal tableaux sweeping with violence and power by Rubens, *Enrico IV alla Battaglia di Ivry* and *Ingresso Trionfale di Enrico IV a Parigi*, which represent the French King Henri IV at the Battle of Ivry and his triumphal march into Paris. This latter is virtually a scene of apotheosis as the Protestant monarch, dressed as a Roman emperor, is crowned by angels and borne along in a golden chariot. Van Dyck's *Self Portrait* looks very small next to these images. Room 42, with its exquisite coffered ceiling and splendid dome, is filled with Roman statues of the Niobe.

Caravaggio dominates Room 43. His most dramatic work here is undoubtedly the *Medusa*, painted on a shield. Rembrandt features in Room 44. Room 45 takes us back to Venice, with 18th-century views of the city by Canaletto and Guardi, and Crespi's arresting *Amore e Psiche* (Cupid and Psyche), with its interplay of light and shade.

Between rooms 25 and 34 is an entrance (not usually open to the public) leading down a staircase into the Corridoio Vasariano.

CORRIDOIO VASARIANO

When the the Medicis moved into Palazzo Pitti, they wanted to maintain their link – literally – with what from then on would be known as Palazzo Vecchio. And so Cosimo I commissioned Vasari to build this enclosed walkway between the two palaces that would allow the Medicis to wander between them with ease.

The corridor, lined with paintings by Vasari, Rubens, Raphael and others, was opened to the public in a limited fashion in 1999, and guided visits are by reservation only. A maximum of 30 people go through in any one visit, starting in the Corte Dogana in Palazzo Vecchio and emerging in the Boboli Gardens at Palazzo Pitti. It's very popular, and you are advised to book two months ahead by calling ☎ 055 238 86 51; tickets cost €26.50.

Visitors follow the corridor's twists and turns along the Arno, over Ponte Vecchio, around the Torre dei Mannelli (whose owners refused to allow Cosimo I to bulldoze through the medieval tower house), across the road and past Chiesa di Santa Felicità (where an enclosed balcony allowed the Medici to hear Mass without being seen) and on into Palazzo Pitti, emerging by the Grotta del Buontalenti in the Giardino di

Boboli. Along the way you can peer out for unusual views of Florence and various paintings are explained.

MUSEO DI STORIA DELLA SCIENZA
Telescopes that look more like works of art, the most extraordinarily complex-looking instruments for the measurement of distance, time and space, and a room full of wax and plastic cutaway models of the various stages of childbirth are among the highlights in this odd collection in the **Museum of the History of Science** (☎ 055 26 53 11; Piazza dei Giudici 1; admission €6.50; ☼ 9.30am-5pm Mon & Wed-Fri, 9.30am-1pm Tue & Sat, 10am-1pm 2nd Sun of every month).

Santa Maria Novella & Around
BASILICA DI SANTA MARIA NOVELLA (Map p84)
Just south of Stazione di Santa Maria Novella, this **church** (☎ 055 21 59 18; Piazza di Santa Maria Novella; admission €2.50; ☼ 9.30am-5pm Mon-Thu & Sat, 1-5pm Fri & Sun) was begun in the late 13th century as the Florentine base for the Dominican order. Although mostly completed by around 1360, work on its facade and the embellishment of its interior continued well into the 15th century. It was here that the Church Council of Florence was held in 1439. The tomb of the Patriarch of Constantinople, who died in the city, is near the **Cappella Rucellai**.

The lower section of the green-and-white marble facade is transitional from Romanesque to Gothic, while the upper section and the main doorway were designed by Alberti and completed in around 1470. The highlight of the Gothic interior is Masaccio's superb fresco *Trinità* (Trinity; 1428), one of the first artworks to use the then newly discovered techniques of perspective and proportion. It is about halfway along the north aisle.

The first chapel to the right of the choir, the **Cappella di Filippo Strozzi**, features lively frescoes by Filippino Lippi depicting the lives of St John the Evangelist and St Philip the Apostle (1489–1502). Another important work is Domenico Ghirlandaio's series of frescoes behind the main altar, painted with the help of artists who may have included the young student Michelangelo. Relating the lives of the Virgin Mary and St John the Baptist, the frescoes are notable for their depiction of Florentine life during

the Renaissance, and feature portraits of members of the Tornabuoni family who commissioned them. Brunelleschi's crucifix hangs above the altar in the **Cappella Gondi**, the first chapel on the left of the choir. Giotto's crucifix (c1288) hangs above the centre of the nave.

To reach the **Chiostro Verde** (Green Cloister), exit the church and follow the signs to the *museo*. Three of the four walls are decorated with fading frescoes recounting Genesis. The cloister actually takes its name from the green earth base used for the frescoes. The most interesting artistically, by Paolo Uccello, are those on the party wall with the church. *Il Diluvio Universale* (Great Flood) is outstanding.

Off the next side of the cloister is the **Cappellone degli Spagnoli** (Spanish Chapel), which was set aside for the Spanish retinue that accompanied Eleonora di Toledo, Cosimo I's wife, to Florence. It contains some well-preserved frescoes by Andrea di Firenze.

On the western side of the cloister is the **museum** (☎ 055 28 21 87; admission €2.60; ☼ 9am-5pm Mon-Thu & Sat, 9am-2pm Sun), which contains vestments and other ecclesiastical relics.

CHIESA D'OGNISSANTI (Map pp82-83)
This 13th-century **church** (☼ 7.30am-12.30pm & 3.30-7pm) was much altered in the 17th century and has a Baroque facade, but inside are works by Domenico Ghirlandaio and Botticelli. Note Ghirlandaio's fresco above the second altar on the right of the *Madonna della Misericordia*, protector of the Vespucci family. The young boy whose head appears between the Madonna and the old man is said to be Amerigo Vespucci, the explorer who allegedly gave his name to the American continent.

Ghirlandaio's masterpiece, *Ultima Cena* (Last Supper), covers most of a wall in the former monastery's *cenacolo* (refectory), while his detailed portrait *St Jerome* can be seen in the nave. Opposite, is Botticelli's pensive *St Augustine*. All three date from 1480.

LE CASCINE (Map pp76-77)
About 10 minutes' walk to the west along Borgo Ognissanti brings you to the **Porta al Prato**, part of the walls that were demolished in the late 19th century to make way for the ring of boulevards that still surrounds the city.

A short walk south from here towards the Arno brings you to the eastern tip of Florence's great green lung, Le Cascine (pastures). The Medici dukes made this a private hunting reserve, but Pietro Leopoldo opened it to the public in 1776, with boulevards, fountains and bird sanctuaries. Nowadays **Mercato delle Cascine**, a big market, is held in the park on Tuesday mornings.

CHIESA DI SAN PANCRAZIO & MUSEO MARINO MARINI (Map p84)

A church has stood here since the 9th century, though the present structure dates from the 14th and 15th centuries. The deconsecrated church now houses the **museum** (☎ 055 21 94 32; Piazza San Pancrazio; admission €7.50; ☽ 10am-5pm Mon & Wed-Sat, closed Aug) donated to the city of Florence by the sculptor Marino Marini (1901–80).

There are around 200 sculptures, portraits and drawings, mostly following the man-and-horse theme. It's unlikely to excite anyone not familiar with his work, especially given the hefty ticket price.

VIA DE' TORNABUONI & AROUND (Map p84)

Head east down Via della Vigna Nuova and turn down Via dei Palchetti; you'll pass the classically inspired **Palazzo Rucellai**, designed by Alberti for one of the city's wealthiest families. Continuing south, you reach Lungarno Corsini on the Arno.

For the best view of the Arno-side of **Palazzo Corsini**, head across Ponte alla Carraia. This grandiose late-Baroque edifice had belonged to the Medici family but they sold it in 1640, and work on the exterior wasn't completed until 1735. The most interesting feature inside the building is the spiral staircase known as the *lumaca* (literally the 'snail'). You can take a look at it by entering the building at Via del Parione 11b.

Head east for **Ponte Santa Trinità**, a harmonious and charming river crossing. Cosimo I de' Medici put Vasari in charge of the project and he in turn asked Michelangelo for advice. In the end the job was handed over to Ammannati, who finished it in 1567. The statues of the seasons are by Pietro Francavilla. It was painstakingly restored after being blown up by the Germans in 1944.

Turning inland, you next arrive at the 13th-century **Chiesa della Santa Trinità**. Although rebuilt in the Gothic style and later graced with a Mannerist facade of indifferent taste, you can still get some idea of what the Romanesque original looked like by looking at the facade wall from the inside. Among its more eye-catching art are frescoes depicting the life of St Francis of Assisi by Domenico Ghirlandaio in the Cappella Sassetti.

Across the road is the looming **Palazzo Spini-Feroni** (Via de' Tornabuoni), built in the 13th century for Geri Spini, the pope's banker, and now owned by the Ferragamo shoe empire. On the 2nd floor of the building is the **Museo Salvatore Ferragamo** (☎ 055 336 04 56; Via de' Tornabuoni 2; admission free; ☽ 9am-1pm & 2-6pm Mon-Fri; lift access). They advise booking by phone, but usually you can walk straight in. The rotating display shows off some of Ferragamo's classic shoes, many worn by Hollywood stars such as Marilyn Monroe, Greta Garbo and Katherine Hepburn, as well as the wooden model 'feet' upon which tailor-made shoes were crafted.

The city's most expensive shopping street, Via de' Tornabuoni itself, often referred to as the 'Salotto di Firenze' (Florence's Drawing Room), actually follows the original course of the Mugnone tributary into the Arno.

Piazza Santa Trinità is also faced by **Palazzo Buondelmonti**. The family of the same name was at the heart of the Guelph-Ghibelline feud in Florence. More imposing is **Palazzo Bartolini-Salimbeni**, an example of High Renaissance with a classical touch (columns flank the main door and the tympana are triangular).

By far the most impressive of the Renaissance mansions is **Palazzo Strozzi**, a great colossus of rusticated *pietra forte* raised by one of the most powerful of the Medici's rival families. It now hosts occasional art exhibitions.

Two blocks north stands the Baroque facade of **Chiesa di San Gaetano**. The church has been around since the 11th century, but the facade dates from 1683. Opposite and a few strides north, **Palazzo Antinori** was built in the 15th century by Giuliano da Maiano.

San Lorenzo Area

BASILICA DI SAN LORENZO (Map p84)

The Medici family commissioned Brunelleschi to rebuild this **church** (☎ 055 21 66 34; Piazza

San Lorenzo; admission €2.50; 🕑 10am-5pm Mon-Sat) in 1420, on the site of a 4th-century basilica. It is considered one of the most harmonious examples of Renaissance architecture. Michelangelo prepared a design for the facade that was never executed, which is why this, like so many other Florentine churches, appears unfinished from the outside.

It was the Medici parish church and many family members are buried here. The nave is separated from the two aisles by columns in *pietra serena* and crowned with Corinthian capitals.

Rosso Fiorentino's *Sposalizio della Vergine* (Marriage of the Virgin Mary; 1523) dominates the second chapel on the right aisle after you enter. As you approach the transept, you will see two bronze pulpits, adorned with panels of the Crucifixion (1466). These were Donatello's last works. You enter the **Sagrestia Vecchia** (Old Sacristy) to the left of the altar. It was designed by Brunelleschi and mostly decorated by Donatello.

From another entrance off Piazza San Lorenzo you can also enter the peaceful cloisters. Off the first cloister, a staircase leads up to the **Biblioteca Laurenziana Medicea** (admission €2.50; 🕑 8.30am-1.30pm Mon-Sat), commissioned by Guilio de' Medici (Pope Clement VII) to house the extensive Medici library. The real attraction is Michelangelo's magnificent vestibule and staircase. They are executed in grey *pietra serena* and the curvaceous steps are a sign of the master's move towards Mannerism from the stricter bounds of Renaissance architecture and design.

A separate entrance takes you to the **Cappelle Medicee** (Medicean Chapels; ☎ 055 238 86 02; Piazza Madonna degli Aldobrandini; admission €6; 🕑 8.15am-5pm Tue-Sun). After buying your ticket you first enter a crypt. The stairs from here take you up to the **Cappella dei Principi** (Princes' Chapel), a grand mausoleum of some of the Medici rulers.

It is sumptuously decorated top to bottom with various kinds of marble, granite and other stone. Breaking up the colossal splendour of the stone are the decorative tableaux made from *pietre dure*. It was for the purpose of decorating the chapel that Ferdinando I ordered the creation of the **Opificio delle Pietre Dure** (Map pp78-79), an artists' workshop, which still exists today.

Statues of the Medici were supposed to be placed in the still empty niches but, apart from the bronzes of Ferdinando I and Cosimo II, the project was never completed.

A corridor leads from the Cappella dei Principi to the **Sagrestia Nuova** (New Sacristy), so called to distinguish it from the Sagrestia Vecchia. It was the Medicis' funeral chapel.

It was here that Michelangelo came nearest to finishing an architectural commission. His haunting sculptures, *Notte e Giorno* (Night and Day), *Aurora e Crepusculo* (Dawn and Dusk) and the *Madonna col Bambino* adorn Medici tombs (1520–34), including that of Lorenzo il Magnifico.

PALAZZO MEDICI-RICCARDI (Map p84)

When Cosimo de' Medici felt fairly sure of his position in Florence, he decided it was time to move house. He entrusted Michelozzo with the design in 1444. The result is this **palace** (☎ 055 276 03 40; Via Cavour 3; admission €4; 🕑 9am-7pm Thu-Tue).

What Michelozzo came up with was ground-breaking and would continue to influence the construction of family residences in Florence for years to come. The fortress town houses with their towers that characterised Gothic Florence were no longer necessary, and Cosimo's power was more or less undisputed. Instead Michelozzo created a self-assured, stout, but not inelegant, pile on three storeys.

The rusticated facade of the ground floor gives a rather stern aspect to the building, though the upper two storeys are less aggressive, maintaining restrained classical lines – already a feature of the emerging Renaissance canon – and topped with a heavy timber roof, the eaves of which protrude well out over the street below.

The Medicis stayed here until 1540 and the building was finally acquired and remodelled by the Riccardi family in the 17th century.

You can wander inside to the courtyard and up to some of the rooms upstairs, although much of the building is now given over to public administration offices. The main hall you will want to inspect is the **Galleria** on the 1st floor. It's a rather overblown example of late-Baroque, dripping with gold-leaf and bursting with colour. The breathtaking, and none-too-modest, ceiling frescoes by Luca Giordano show the *Apotheosis of the Medici Dynasty* (1685),

FLORENCE

with members of the family reclining in saintly fashion around God, and surrounded by lavish and seemingly random scenes from classical mythology.

The highlight, however, is the tiny **Cappella dei Magi**, a chapel with outstanding frescoes (1459) by Benozzo Gozzoli. The bearded figure on horseback is said to be a portrait of the Byzantine Emperor, John VIII Paleologus, who attended the Church Council of Florence in 1439. Buy a ticket first from the office off the second internal courtyard. Only 15 people are allowed in at any one time, and visits are limited to 15 minutes.

MERCATO CENTRALE (Map pp78-79)
Built in 1874, the city's central produce market seems to disappear amid the confusion of makeshift stands of the clothes and leather market that fill the surrounding square and streets during the day. The iron and glass architecture was something of a novelty in Florence when the market was first built.

San Marco Area

GALLERIA DELL'ACCADEMIA (Map pp78-79)
No visit to Florence is complete without calling into this **gallery** (☎ 055 238 86 09; Via Ricasoli 60; admission €6.50; ☼ 8.15am-6.50pm Tue-Sun), if only because it contains one of the greatest masterpieces of the Renaissance, Michelangelo's giant *David*.

You first enter the grand **Sala del Colosso**, which is dominated by a plaster model of Giambologna's *Ratto delle Sabine* (Rape of the Sabine). Amongst the paintings here are a fresco of the *Pietà* by Andrea del Sarto, a couple of pieces by Fra Bartolommeo and a *Deposizione* by Filippino Lippi and Perugino.

Immediately to the left off this first room a doorway leads into a long hall, at the end of which is perhaps the most famous sculpture in the world, Michelangelo's *David* (1501–4). Carved from a single block of marble, the 5m tall statue originally stood in the Piazza della Signoria, and was installed here in 1882 in a purpose-built niche which hardly does this masterpiece justice. Nearby are Michelangelo's four *Prigioni* ('prisoners' or 'slaves'; 1530) and San Matteo (St Matthew; 1503), all unfinished. The four *Slaves*, who appear to be writhing and struggling to free themselves from the mar-

ble, were meant for the tomb of Pope Julius II, which itself was never completed.

Off to the left, the **Sala dell'Ottocento** (19th-Century Room) houses a collection of plaster models of some of Florence's public statuary, including Bartolini's *Machiavelli* (1846), now in the Uffizi arcade, and shelves full of nameless, ghostly busts commissioned by wealthy Victorian 'Grand Tourists' – members of the moneyed middle and upper classes who toured Europe, especially Italy, to soak up the culture and history, and round off their classical education (see the boxed text, p85).

In the surrounding rooms there is a mixed collection of paintings and sculptures, including works by Botticelli and Taddeo Gaddi.

MUSEO DI SAN MARCO (Map pp78-79)
Housed in the now deconsecrated Dominican convent and Chiesa di San Marco is the **museum** (☎ 055 238 86 08; Piazza San Marco 1; admission €6; ☼ 8.15am-1.50pm Tue-Fri, 8.15am-6.50pm Sat, 8.30am-1.50pm every 2nd Mon, 8.15am-7pm every 2nd Sun). Back in 1481 the Dominican friar Girolamo Savonarola came here as lector and later became the de facto head of a short-lived theocracy in Florence, before ending up on an Inquisitorial bonfire.

The church was founded in 1299, rebuilt by Michelozzo in 1437 and again remodelled by Giambologna some years later. It features several paintings, but they pale in comparison with the treasures contained in the adjoining convent.

Famous Florentines who called the convent home include the painters Fra (or Beato) Angelico (c1400–55) and Fra Bartolommeo (1472–1517). It now serves as a museum of Fra Angelico's works, many of which were moved there in the 1860s.

You first find yourself in the **Chiostro di Sant'Antonio**, designed by Michelozzo in 1440. Turn immediately to the right and enter the **Sala dell'Ospizio**. Paintings by Fra Angelico that once hung in the Galleria dell'Accademia and the Uffizi have been brought together here. Among the better-known works is the *Deposizione di Cristo* (1432), a commission taken on by Fra Angelico after the original artist, Lorenzo Monaco, died after finishing only a small section, in late Gothic style. Fra Angelico's attention to perspective and the realistic portrayal of nature marked a new development in art, and it has been suggested that this was one of the first true paintings of the Renaissance.

The eastern wing of the cloister, formerly the monks' refectory, is dominated at the far end by Giovanni Antonio Sogliani's fresco, *La Providenza dei Domenicani* (The Miraculous Supper of St Domenic; 1536), while just outside you can see Luca della Robbia's colourful *Madonna col Bambino* (c1460), one of his most expressive terracotta statues. Nearby, in the former kitchen, is a collection of fresco portraits by Fra Bartolommeo.

Next along is the former Chapterhouse, where Fra Angelico's huge *Crucifixion* fresco (1442) is on show, as well as the bronze church bell, known as 'La Pagnona', possibly made by Michelozzo

The main attractions, though, are upstairs. Fra Angelico was invited to decorate the monks' cells with devotional frescoes aimed as a guide to the friars' meditation. Most were executed by Fra Angelico, others by aides under his supervision, including Benozzo Gozzoli. You can peer into them today and wonder what sort of thoughts would swim through the minds of the monks as they prayed before these images.

The true masterpieces are on the walls in the corridors. At the top of the stairs is one of Fra Angelico's most famous works, the *Annunciazione* (c1440), faced on the opposite wall with a *Crocifisso* featuring St Dominic. His *Madonna delle Ombre* (Madonna of the Shadows) is to the right of cell No 25.

Savonarola's cell (actually a suite of three small rooms) is at the end of the opposite corridor, and is kept as a kind of shrine to the turbulent priest. It houses a portrait, a few personal items and a grand marble monument erected by admirers in 1873. In a nearby cell you can see the linen banner, painted with a scene of the Crucifixion, which Savonarola carried in processions.

PIAZZA DELLA SANTISSIMA (SS) ANNUNZIATA (Map p81)
Giambologna's equestrian statue of the Grand Duke Ferdinando I de' Medici commands the scene from the centre of this square. Some observers find it the city's loveliest square.

Chiesa di SS Annunziata
The **church** (Piazza SS Annunziata; ⏲ 7.30am-12.30pm & 4-6.30pm) that gives the square its name was established in 1250 by the founders of the Servite order and rebuilt by Michelozzo and others in the mid-15th century. It is dedicated to the Virgin Mary and in the ornate tabernacle, to your left as you enter the church from the atrium, is a so-called miraculous painting of the Virgin.

The painting, no longer on public view, is attributed to a 14th-century friar, and legend says an angel completed it. Also of note are frescoes by Andrea del Castagno in the first two chapels on the left of the church, a fresco by Perugino in the fifth chapel and the frescoes in Michelozzo's atrium, particularly the *Nascita della Vergine* (Birth of the Virgin), by Andrea del Sarto, and the *Visitazione*, by Jacopo Pontormo. Above the main entrance to the church is a mosaic lunette of the Annunciation by Davide Ghirlandaio, Domenico's little brother.

Spedale degli Innocenti
This 'hospital of the innocents' was founded on the southeastern side of the piazza in 1421 as Europe's first orphanage.

Brunelleschi designed the portico, which Andrea della Robbia then decorated with terracotta medallions of babies in swaddling clothes. Under the portico to the left of the entrance is the small revolving door where unwanted children were left. A good number of people in Florence with surnames such as degli Innocenti, Innocenti and Nocentini, can trace their family tree only as far back as the orphanage. Orphans were no novelty but the growing number of foundlings made a more systematic approach to the problem necessary. Undoubtedly life inside was hard, but the Spedale's avowed aim was to care for and educate its wards until they turned 18.

A small **gallery** (☎ 055 249 17 08; Piazza SS Annunziata 12; admission €2.60; ⏲ 8.30am-2pm Thu-Tue) on the 2nd floor features works by Florentine artists. The most striking piece is Domenico Ghirlandaio's *Adorazione dei Magi* (1488) at the right end of the hall.

MUSEO ARCHEOLOGICO (Map p81)
About 200m southeast of the Piazza SS Annunziata is the **Museo Archeologico** (☎ 055 23 57 50; Via Colonna 38; admission €4; ⏲ 2-7pm Mon, 8.30am-7pm Tue & Thu, 8.30am-2pm Wed & Fri-Sun), a

musty, old-fashioned place housing some of the Medici family's horde of antiquities. Further collections have been added in the centuries since.

On the 1st floor you can either head left into the ancient Egyptian display, or right into the section on Etruscan and Greco-Roman art.

The former is an extensive, though not well-labelled, collection of stelae inscribed with hieroglyphics, sculptures, painted wooden sarcophagi and an array of remarkably preserved everyday objects such as textiles and baskets.

The highlight of the Etruscan section is undoubtedly the wonderful 5th-century-BC bronze Chimera, found in Arezzo, and one of the best-known images of Etruscan art. There's also a large number of small Etruscan bronzes, as well as the life-size *Arringatore* (Orator). Dating from the 1st century BC, the figure, draped in a toga, illustrates the extent of Roman influence by this time.

From here you enter an enclosed corridor containing displays of ancient jewellery.

The museum's 2nd floor showcases Greek pottery and Roman bronze-statue fragments.

Santa Croce Area
PIAZZA DI SANTA CROCE (Map p80)
The Franciscan Basilica di Santa Croce stands haughty watch over the piazza of the same name. The square was initially cleared in the Middle Ages primarily to allow hordes of the faithful to gather when the church itself was full. In Savonarola's day, heretics were executed here.

Such an open space inevitably found other uses and from the 14th century on it was often the colourful scene of jousts, festivals and *calcio storico* matches. The latter was like a combination of football (soccer) and rugby with no rules. Below the gaily frescoed facade of **Palazzo dell'Antella**, on the south side of the piazza, is a marble stone embedded in the wall – it marks the halfway line on this, one of the oldest football pitches in the world. Today the square is lined with restaurants and souvenir shops.

Curiously enough, the Romans used to have fun in much the same area centuries before. The city's 2nd-century amphitheatre took up the area facing the western end of Piazza di Santa Croce. To this day, Piazza de' Peruzzi, Via Bentaccordi and Via Torta mark the oval outline of the north, west and south sides of the theatre.

BASILICA DI SANTA CROCE (Map p80)
Attributed to Arnolfo di Cambio, **Santa Croce** (☎ 055 244619; admission incl Museo dell'Opera €4; ☾ 9.30am-5.30pm Mon-Sat, 1-5.30pm Sun) was built between 1294 and 1385. The name stems from a splinter of the Holy Cross donated to the Franciscans by King Louis of France in 1258. Today the church is known as much for the celebrities buried here as for its captivating artistic treasures.

The magnificent facade is actually a 19th-century, neo-Gothic addition, as indeed is the bell tower. Like the contemporary job done on the Duomo, it's enlivened by a variety of coloured marble. A statue of Dante stands to the left of the main entrance.

The church's massive interior is divided into a nave and two aisles by solid octagonal pillars. The ceiling is a fine example of the timber, A-frame style used occasionally in Italy's Gothic churches.

Michelangelo's tomb, designed by Vasari (1570), is down the right aisle between the first and second altar. The three muses below it represent his three principal gifts – sculpture, painting and architecture. Next along is a cenotaph to the memory of Dante (1829), and a little further on is Machiavelli's tomb.

Beyond the next altar is an extraordinary piece of sculpture of the *Annunciazione* (1430–35) by Donatello. The striking tabernacle in grey *pietra serena* is brightened with gilded highlights. Between the sixth and seventh altars, a doorway leads into the cloister and Brunelleschi's Cappella de' Pazzi (see p103).

Continuing on, you pass the tomb of Giacchino Rossini, then turning right as you approach the transept, you find yourself before the delightful frescoes depicting the life of St Nicholas (later transformed into 'Santa Claus') by Agnolo Gaddi in the **Cappella Castellani** (1385). Taddeo Gaddi painted the frescoes illustrating the life of the Virgin in the adjacent **Cappella Baroncelli** (1332–38). Next, a doorway designed by Michelozzo leads into a corridor off which is the **Sagrestia**, an enchanting 14th-century room dominated on the left by Taddeo Gaddi's fresco of the Crocifissione. There are also a few relics of St Francis on show, including his cowl and belt.

Through the next room, which now serves as a bookshop, you can get to the **Scuola del Cuoio**, a leather school and mini shopping-mall, where you can see things being made and also buy finished goods. At the end of the corridor is a Medici chapel, which features a large altarpiece by Andrea della Robbia.

Back in the church, the transept is lined by five minor chapels on either side of the **Cappella Maggiore**. The two chapels nearest the right side of the Cappella Maggiore are decorated with fragmentary frescoes by Giotto; the best preserved, in the **Capella Bardi**, depict scenes from the life of St Francis (1315–20). A second Capella Bardi on the far left houses a wooden Crucifix (1412) by Donatello. According to Vasari, Brunelleschi complained that the figure of Christ, with movable arms, looked like a peasant, and created his own Crucifix, housed in Santa Maria Novella, to show the right way to do it.

Returning to the entrance, the first tomb in the left aisle is Galileo Galilei's (1737), featuring a bust of the great scientist holding a telescope and gazing skywards.

Cloisters & Cappella de' Pazzi

Brunelleschi designed the serene **cloisters** just before his death in 1446. His **Cappella de' Pazzi**, at the end of the first cloister, is a masterpiece of Renaissance architecture, built for, but never used by, the wealthy banking family destroyed in the Pazzi Conspiracy. Inside are terracotta medallions of the Apostles by Luca della Robbia. The **Museo dell'Opera di Santa Croce** off the first cloister, features a partially restored Crucifix by Cimabue, badly damaged during the disastrous 1966 flood, when the Santa Croce area was inundated. Other highlights include Donatello's gilded bronze statue *St Louis of Toulouse* (1424), originally placed in a tabernacle on the Orsanmichele facade, a wonderful terracotta bust of St Francis receiving the stigmata by the della Robbia workshop, and frescoes by Giotto, including an *Ultima Cena* (Last Supper; 1333).

MUSEO HORNE (Map pp82-83)

Herbert Percy Horne was one of those eccentric Brits abroad with cash. He bought this building in the early 1900s and installed his eclectic collection of 14th- and 15th-century Italian paintings, sculptures, ceramics, furniture and other oddments, creating this **museum** (☎ 055 24 46 61; Via de' Benci 6; admission €5; ☺ 9am-1pm Mon-Sat). Horne renovated the house in an effort to recreate a Renaissance ambience. There are a few works by masters such as Giotto, Filippo Lippi and Lorenzetti, though most are by minor artists. Perhaps more interesting than many of the paintings is the furniture, some of which is exquisite.

PONTE ALLE GRAZIE (Map pp82-83)

The first bridge here was built in 1237 by Messer Rubaconte da Mandella, a Milanese *podestà*. It was swept away in 1333 and on its replacement were raised chapels, one of them dubbed Madonna alle Grazie, from which the bridge then took its name. The Germans blew up the bridge in 1944, and the present version went up in 1957.

CASA BUONAROTTI (Map p80)

Two blocks north of Santa Croce is **Casa Buonarroti** (☎ 055 24 17 52; Via Ghibellina 70; admission €6.50; ☺ 9.30am-2pm Wed-Mon), which Michelangelo owned but never inhabited. Upon his death, the house went to his nephew and eventually became a museum in the 1850s.

Although not uninteresting, the collections are a bit disappointing given the entry cost. On the ground floor is a series of rooms on the left used for temporary exhibitions, usually held annually from May to September. To the right of the ticket window is a small archaeological display. The Buonarroti family collected about 150 pieces over the years, many of which were in the Museo Archeologico for a long time (see p101).

Upstairs you can admire a detailed model of Michelangelo's design for the facade of the Basilica di San Lorenzo – as close as the church came to getting one. By Michelangelo also are a couple of marble bas-reliefs and a crucifix. Of the reliefs, *Madonna della Scala* (Madonna of the Steps; c1490) is thought to be his earliest work.

Otherwise, a series of rooms designed by Michelangelo Il Giovane, the genius' grandnephew, are intriguing. The first is full of paintings and frescoes that together amount to a kind of apotheosis of the great man.

PIAZZA SANT'AMBROGIO & AROUND

From Casa Buonarroti, turn northwards up Via Michelangelo Buonarroti and proceed to **Piazza dei Ciompi**, these days the venue for a busy flea market.

The **Loggia del Pesce** (Fish Market; Map p80; Via Pietrapana) was designed by Vasari for the Mercato Vecchio (Old Market), which was at the heart of what is now Piazza della Repubblica. The loggia was moved to the Convento di San Marco when the Mercato Vecchio and the surrounding area were cleared in the 19th century and was set up here in 1955.

A block east, the plain **Chiesa di Sant'Ambrogio** (Map p80; Via Pietrapiana) presents an inconspicuous 18th-century facade on the square of the same name. The first church here was raised in the 10th century, but what you see inside is a mix of 13th-century-Gothic and 15th-century refurbishment. The name comes from Sant'Ambrogio (St Ambrose), the powerful 4th-century archbishop of Milan who stayed in an earlier convent on this site when he visited Florence. The church is the last resting place of several artists, including Mino da Fiesole and Verrocchio.

Nearby is the local produce market, the **Mercato di Sant'Ambrogio** (Map p80; Piazza Ghiberti).

Just north of Piazza Sant'Ambrogio is the **Sinagoga** (Synagogue; Map p80) ☎ 055 234 66 54; Via Farini 4; admission €4; ☼ 10am-5pm Sun-Thu, 10am-2pm Fri Apr-Oct, 10am-3pm Sun-Thu, 10am-2pm Fri Nov-Mar). It is an elaborate structure with Moorish and Byzantine elements. In the **Museo Ebraico** you can see Jewish ceremonial objects and richly embroidered vestments. A memorial in the garden lists the names of Florentine Jews who died in the Nazi concentration camps.

Oltrarno

PONTE VECCHIO (Map p84)

The first documentation of a stone bridge here, at the narrowest crossing point along the entire length of the Arno, dates from 972. The Arno looks placid enough, but when it gets mean, it gets very mean. Floods in 1177 and 1333 destroyed the bridge, and in 1966 it came close to being destroyed again. Many of the jewellers with shops on the bridge were convinced the floodwaters would sweep away their livelihoods but this time the bridge held.

The jewellers are still here. Their trade has been passed down from generation to generation since Grand Duke Ferdinando I de' Medici ordered them here in the 16th century to replace the rather malodorous presence of the town butchers.

The bridge as it stands was built in 1345 and was the only one saved from destruction by the retreating Germans in August 1944, supposedly on the orders of Hitler himself.

On the southern end of the bridge is the medieval **Torre dei Mannelli**, which looks rather odd, as the Corridoio Vasariano was built around it, not simply straight through it as the Medici would have preferred. Across Via de' Bardi as your eye follows the Corridoio, you can espy **Torre degli Ubriachi**, the Drunks' Tower.

CHIESA DI SANTA FELICITÀ (Map p84)

The most captivating thing about the facade of this 18th-century remake of what had been Florence's oldest (4th-century) **church** (Via de' Guicciardini; ☼ 9am-noon & 2.30-6.30pm Mon-Sat, 9am-1pm Sun) is the fact that the Corridoio Vasariano passes right across it; the Medicis could stop by and hear Mass without being seen.

Inside, the main interest is in Brunelleschi's small **Cappella Barbadori**, on the right as you enter. Here Jacopo Pontormo (1494–1557) left his mark with a fresco of the *Annunciation* and a *Deposizione*. The latter depicts the taking down of Christ from the Cross in disturbingly surreal colours. The people engaged in this operation look almost as if they've been given a fright by the prying eyes of the onlooker.

PALAZZO PITTI (Map pp82-83)

The wealthy banker Luca Pitti commissioned Brunelleschi to build this enormous, forbidding-looking palace in 1457, but by the time it was completed, the family fortunes were already on the wane, and they were later forced to sell the place to their great rivals, the Medici.

The original nucleus of the **palace** (☎ 055 238 86 14; Piazza de' Pitti) took up the space encompassing the seven sets of windows on the 2nd and 3rd storeys.

In 1549 Eleonora de Toledo, wife of Cosimo I de' Medici, acquired the palace from the by-then impoverished Pitti family. She launched the extension work, which continued for centuries, and through all that time the original design was respected – today you would be hard-pressed to distinguish the various phases of construction.

After the demise of the Medici dynasty, the palace remained the residence of the city's rulers, the dukes of Lorraine and their Austrian and (briefly) Napoleonic successors.

When Florence was made capital of the nascent kingdom of Italy in 1865, it became a residence of the Savoy royal family, who graciously presented it to the state in 1919.

Museums

The palace houses five museums; the most important is **Galleria Palatina** (Palatine Gallery; admission incl Appartamenti Reali €6.50; 8.15am-6.50pm Tue-Sun), containing paintings from the 16th to 18th centuries in lavishly decorated rooms. The works were collected mostly by the Medicis and their grand ducal successors.

After buying your ticket you head up a grand staircase to the gallery floor. The first rooms you pass through are a seemingly haphazard mix of paintings and period furniture.

The gallery proper starts after the **Sala della Musica** (Music Room). The paintings hung in the succeeding rooms – all decorated with stunning ceiling frescoes of mythological scenes – are not in any particular order. Among Tuscan masters you can see work by Filippo Lippi, Botticelli, Vasari and Andrea del Sarto. The collection also boasts some important works by other Italian and foreign painters. Foremost among them are those by Raphael, whose *Madonna della Seggiola* (Madonna of the Chair; 1515) is particularly intriguing. Caravaggio's *Amore Dormente* (Sleeping Cupid; 1608), Guido Reni's grinning *Bacco Fanciullo* (Young Bacchus; 1620), Guercino's dramatic *San Sebastian* and Tintoretto's *Deposizione* (Deposition) are just a few of the many highlights. Other important artists represented include Titian, Veronese, Velasquez, Rubens and Van Dyck. Among the lesser-known works, Dosso Dossi's *Ninfa e Satiro*, featuring a grotesque satyr snarling at a nervous-looking nymph, Lorenzo Lippi's gruesome portrait of *Santa Agata*, and Orazio Rimnaldi's *Amore Artifice* (False Cupid) are worth seeking out.

From the gallery you can pass into the **Appartamenti Reali** (Royal Apartments), a series of cloyingly opulent but rather dark and oppressively decorated rooms, where the Medicis and their successors slept and held court.

Of the other galleries, the most worthwhile is the **Museo degli Argenti** (Silver Museum; admission incl Boboli Gardens & Museo delle Porcellane €4; 8.15am-6.30pm Tue-Sat & alternating Sun & Mon Apr-May & Sep-Oct, 8.15am-7.30pm Jun-Aug, 8.15-4.30pm Nov-Mar). The collection of often bizarre and kitsch glassware, silver and jewellery is interesting enough, though it's the gorgeous, and humorous *trompe l'oeil* frescoes that fill the walls and ceilings that are the real attraction. Those in what was once the public audience chamber are particularly fine, with high terraces populated with a miscellany of people and animals, including a boy playing with a monkey and an elderly man adjusting his spectacles. **Galleria d'Arte Moderna** (Modern Art Gallery; admission incl Galleria del Costume €5; 8.15am-1.50pm Tue-Sat & alternating Sun & Mon) covers mostly Tuscan works from the 18th until the mid-20th century, and **Galleria del Costume** (Costume Gallery; admission €5, incl Modern Art Gallery; 8.15am-1.50pm Tue-Sat & alternating Sun & Mon) has high-class clothing from the 18th and 19th centuries, while the **Museo delle Carrozze** (closed at the time of writing) contains ducal coaches and suchlike.

Giardino di Boboli

Relax in the palace's Renaissance **Boboli Gardens** (Map pp82-83; admission incl Museo degli Argenti & Museo delle Porcellane €4; 8.15am-5.30pm Mar, 8.15am-6.30pm Apr-May & Sept-Oct, 8.15am-7.30pm Jun-Aug, 8.15am-4.30pm Nov-Feb), which were laid out in the mid-16th century and based on a design by the architect known as Il Tribolo. Buontalenti's noted artificial grotto (Grotta del Buontalenti), with a *Venere* (Venus) by Giambologna, is interesting. Note though that some of the paths are quite steep and rough, and can get slippery after a little rain.

Within the garden is the small **Museo delle Porcellane** (Porcelain Museum; admission incl Boboli Gardens & Museo degli Argenti €4; 8.15am-6.30pm Tue-Sat & alternating Sun & Mon Apr-May & Sep-Oct, 8.15am-7.30pm Jun-Aug, 8.15-4.30pm Nov-Mar), which houses some of the fine porcelain collected over the centuries by the tenants of Palazzo Pitti. The exhibits include some exquisite Sévres, Vincennes, Meissen and Wedgewood pieces, including

FLORENCE

a ceramic portrait of Napoleon, produced by the Sévres factory.

You can get into the **Forte di Belvedere** (see p108) from the southeastern end of the garden.

CHIESA DI SAN FELICE (Map pp82-83)

This unprepossessing church has been made over several times since the Romanesque original was constructed in 1066. The simple Renaissance facade was done by Michelozzo. Inside the church, you can admire an early-14th-century crucifix by Giotto's workshop.

At No 8 on this square is **Casa Guidi**, where Robert and Elizabeth Browning lived.

MUSEO ZOOLOGICO LA SPECOLA

A little further down Via Romana from Piazza San Felice, this rather fusty **zoological museum** (Map pp82-83; ☎ 055 228 82 51; Via Romana 17; admission €5; ⚲ 9am-1pm Thu-Tue) offers for your delectation, the stuffed-animal collection apart, a collection of wax models of various bits of human anatomy in varying states of bad health. An offbeat change from all that art and history anyway!

PORTA ROMANA (Map pp82-83)

Pilgrims to Rome headed down Via Romana as they left Florence behind them. The end of the road is marked by the Porta Romana, an imposing city gate that was part of the outer circle of city walls knocked down in the 19th century. A strip of this wall still stretches to the north from the gate. If you head along the inside of this wall (the area is now a car park) you will soon come across an entrance that allows you to get to the top of Porta Romana.

VIA MAGGIO

In the 16th century this was a rather posh address, as the line-up of fine Renaissance mansions duly attests. The following are all on Map pp82-83 unless otherwise noted. **Palazzo di Bianca Cappello**, at No 26, has the most eye-catching facade, covered as it is in graffiti designs. Bianca Cappello was Francesco I de' Medici's lover and eventual wife. Across the street, a series of imposing mansions more or less following the same Renaissance style include **Palazzo Ricasoli-Ridolfi** at No 7, **Palazzo Martellini** at No 9, **Palazzo Michelozzi** (Map p84) at No 11, **Palazzo Zanchini**

(Map p84) at No 13 and **Palazzo di Cosimo Ridolfi** (Map p84) at No 15. All were built and fiddled around with over the 14th, 15th and 16th centuries. Another impressive one is **Palazzo Corsini-Suarez** at No 42.

PIAZZA SANTO SPIRITO (Map pp82-83)

From Via Maggio you can turn into Via de' Michelozzi to reach the lively Piazza Santo Spirito. At its northern end, the square is fronted by the flaking facade of the **Basilica di Santo Spirito** (⚲ 8.30am-noon & 4-5.30pm, closed Sat & Sun morning & Wed afternoon), designed by Brunelleschi.

The entire length of the church inside is lined by a series of 38 semicircular chapels, and the colonnade of grey *pietra forte* Corinthian columns lends an air of severe monumental grandeur.

One of the most noteworthy works of art is Filippino Lippi's *Madonna con il Bambino e Santi* (Madonna with Child and Saints) in the Cappella Nerli in the right transept. Other highlights include Domenico di Zanobi's *Madonna del Soccorso* (Madonna of the Relief; 1485), in the Cappella Velutti, in which the Madonna wards off a little red devil with a club, and Govanni Baratta's marble and stucco *L'Arcangelo Raffaele e Tobiolo* (The Archangel Raphael and Tobias; 1698), illustrating an episode from the Apocrypha. The main altar, beneath the central dome, is a voluptuous Baroque flourish rather out of place in the spare setting of Brunelleschi's church.

Next door to the church is the refectory, **Cenacolo di Santo Spirito** (admission €2.20; ⚲ 9am-2pm Tue-Sun), home to the Fondazione Romano. Andrea Orcagna decorated the refectory with a grand fresco depicting the Last Supper and the Crucifixion (c1370). In 1946 the Neapolitan collector Salvatore Romano left his sculpture collection to Florence's council, the Comune di Firenze. Among the most intriguing pieces are rare pre-Romanesque sculptures and other works by Jacopo della Quercia and Donatello.

BASILICA DI SANTA MARIA DEL CARMINE (Map pp82-83)

West of Piazza Santo Spirito, Piazza del Carmine is an unkempt square used as a car park. On its southern flank stands the Basilica di Santa Maria del Carmine, high on many art lovers' list of must-sees because of the **Cappella Brancacci** (☎ 055 238 21 95; adult/child €3.10/2.30; ☽ 10am-5pm Wed-Mon, 1-5pm Sun).

This chapel is a treasure of paintings by Masolino da Panicale, Masaccio and Filippino Lippi. Above all, the fresco cycle illustrating the life of St Peter by Masaccio is considered among his greatest works, representing a definitive break with Gothic art and a plunge into new worlds of expression in the early stages of the Renaissance. His *Cacciata dei Progenitori* (Expulsion of Adam and Eve), on the left side of the chapel, is his best-known work. His depiction of Eve's anguish in particular lends the image a human touch hitherto little seen in European painting. Masaccio painted these frescoes in his early twenties, taking over from Masolino, and interrupted the task to go to Rome where he died aged only 28. The cycle was completed some 60 years later by Filippino Lippi. The scene of *St Peter Enthroned* is interesting for the self-portrait of Masaccio, standing beside the Apostle and staring out at the viewer. Figures standing around him have been identified as Brunelleschi, Masolino and Alberti. Filippino Lippi painted himself into the scene of *St Peter's Crucifixion*, along with his teacher, Botticelli.

That you can even see these frescoes today is little short of miraculous. The 13th-century church was nearly destroyed by a fire in the late 18th century. About the only thing the fire spared was the chapel.

Should you arrive too late for the chapel but find the church still open, you can wander in and get a distant look at the chapel from behind barriers – but the close-up inspection is what you need to appreciate the staggering detail.

BORGO SAN FREDIANO (Map pp82-83)
Heading northwards from Piazza del Carmine you reach Borgo San Frediano. The street and surrounding area retain something of the feel of what they have always been – a working-class quarter where artisans have been beavering away for centuries.

At the western end of the street stands the lonely **Porta San Frediano**, one of the old city gates left in place when the walls were demolished in the 19th century. Before you reach the gate, you'll notice the unpolished feel of the area neatly reflected in the unadorned brick walls of **Chiesa di San Frediano in**

Cestello (☽ 9-11.30am & 5-6pm Mon-Fri, 5-6pm Sun), its incomplete facade hiding a restrained Baroque interior.

BACK TO PONTE VECCHIO
From the front of Chiesa di San Frediano in Cestello you can wander along the river back towards Ponte Vecchio. Along the way you pass several grand family mansions, including **Palazzo Guicciardini** (Map pp82-83) at Via de' Guicciardini 7 and the 13th-century **Palazzo Frescobaldi** (Map p84) on the square of the same name. Round this *palazzo* you continue east along Borgo San Jacopo, on which still stand two 12th-century towers, the **Torre dei Marsili** and **Torre de' Belfredelli**.

PONTE VECCHIO TO PORTA SAN NICCOLÒ
Continuing east away from Ponte Vecchio, the first stretch of Via de' Bardi shows clear signs of its recent history. This entire area was flattened by German mines in 1944 and hastily rebuilt in questionable taste after the war.

The street spills into **Piazza di Santa Maria Soprarno** (Map p84), which takes its name from a church that has long ceased to exist. Follow the narrow Via de' Bardi (the right fork) away from the square and you enter a pleasantly quieter corner of Florence. The powerful Bardi family once owned all the houses along this street, but by the time Cosimo de' Medici married Contessina de' Bardi in 1415, the latter's family was well on the decline.

Via de' Bardi expires in **Piazza de' Mozzi** (Map pp82-83), which is also surrounded by the sturdy facades of grand residences belonging to the high and mighty. No 2, at the southern flank of the piazza, is occupied by the **Palazzo de' Mozzi**, where Pope Gregory X stayed when brokering peace between the Guelphs and Ghibellines. The western side is lined by the 15th-century **Palazzo Lensi-Nencioni**, **Palazzo Torrigiani-Nasi** (with the graffiti ornamentation) and **Palazzo Torrigiani**.

Across the square, the long facade of the **Museo Bardini** (closed for restoration at the time of writing) is the result of an eclectic 19th-century building project by its owner, the collector Stefano Bardini. The collection is a broad mix ranging from Persian carpets to paintings and Etruscan artefacts.

Next, turn east down Via dei Renai past the leafy **Piazza Nicola Demidoff** (Map pp82-83), dedicated to the 19th-century Russian philanthropist who lived nearby in Via San Niccolò. The 16th-century **Palazzo Serristori** (Map p80), at the end of Via dei Renai was home to Joseph Bonaparte in the last years of his life (he died in 1844). At the height of his career he had been made king of Spain under his brother Napoleon.

Turn right and you end up in Via di San Niccolò. The bland-looking **Chiesa di San Niccolò Oltrarno** (Map p80) is interesting if for nothing else than the little plaque indicating how high the 1966 flood waters reached – about 4m. If you head east along Via San Niccolò you emerge at the tower marking the **Porta San Niccolò** (Map p80), all that is left of the city walls here.

To get an idea of what the walls were like, walk south from Chiesa di San Niccolò Oltrarno through **Porta San Miniato** (Map p80). The wall extends a short way to the east and quite a deal further west up a steep hill that leads you to the Forte di Belvedere.

FORTE DI BELVEDERE
Bernardo Buontalenti helped design the rambling **fort** (Map pp82-83; admission free; ⊙ 9am-dusk) here for Grand Duke Ferdinando I towards the end of the 16th century. From this massive bulwark soldiers could keep watch on four fronts, and indeed it was designed with internal security in mind as much as foreign attack. The views are excellent.

The main entrance is near Porta San Giorgio, and you can approach, as we have, from the east along the walls or by taking Costa di San Giorgio from up near Ponte Vecchio. You can also visit the fort from the Boboli Gardens, which is what most people do (see p106).

PIAZZALE MICHELANGELO (Map p80)
From Porta San Miniato you could turn east instead of following the climb up to the Forte di Belvedere. A few twists and turns and you find yourself looking over Ponte San Niccolò. Several paths and stairways lead up from here to Piazzale Michelangelo, a popular spot that affords some of the best views over the city. Predictably, it's full of souvenir stalls.

Local bus No 13, which leaves from Stazione di Santa Maria Novella and crosses Ponte alle Grazie, stops at Piazzale Michelangelo.

CHIESA DI SAN MINIATO AL MONTE (Map p80)
The real point of your exertions is about five minutes further up, at this wonderful **Romanesque church** (⊙ 8am-7.30pm May-Oct, 8am-1pm & 2.30-7pm Nov-Apr), surely the best surviving example of the genre in Florence. The church is dedicated to St Minius (San Miniato), an early Christian martyr in Florence who is said to have flown to this spot after his death down in the town.

The church was started in the early 11th century; the typically Tuscan marble facade features a mosaic depicting Christ between the Virgin and St Minius, added 200 years later.

Inside you will see 13th- to 15th-century frescoes on the right wall, intricate inlaid marble designs down the length of the nave and a fine Romanesque crypt at the back, below the unusual raised *presbiterio* (presbytery). The latter boasts a fine marble pulpit replete with intriguing geometrical designs. The sacristy, to the right of the church (they suggest you donate €0.50 to get in), features marvellously bright frescoes. The four figures in the cross vault are the Evangelists. The **Cappella del Cardinale del Portogallo** to the left side of the church features a tomb by Antonio Rossellino and a tabernacle ceiling decorated in terracotta by Luca della Robbia.

Michelangelo made use of the church during the Medici siege of 1529 to 1530, and some of his battlements remain standing around here.

Bus No 13 stops nearby.

North of the Old City
FORTEZZA DA BASSO (Map pp78-79)
Alessandro de' Medici ordered this huge defensive fortress built in 1534 and the task went to a Florentine living in Rome, Antonio da Sangallo il Giovane. It was not designed to protect the city from invasion, but was rather a statement of Medici power aimed at overawing the potentially rebellious Florentines. Nowadays it is sometimes used for exhibitions and cultural events.

CHIESA RUSSA ORTODOSSA (Map pp78-79)
A couple of blocks east of Fortezza da Basso, the onion-shaped domes on this Russian Orthodox church are a bit of a giveaway. Built in 1902 for the Russian

populace resident here, it was designed in the northern-Russian style, with two interior levels decorated in part by Florentine artists but mostly by Russians who were expert in iconography.

MUSEO STIBBERT (Map pp76-77)

Frederick Stibbert was one of the grand wheeler-dealers on the European antiquities market in the 19th century and, unsurprisingly, had quite a collection himself. He bought the Villa di Montughi with the intention of creating a **museum** (☎ 055 47 55 20; Via Stibbert 26; adult/child €5/2; ☺ 10am-2pm Mon-Wed, 10am-6pm Fri-Sun) exuding the atmosphere of the various countries and periods covered by his collections. The result is certainly an intriguing mix.

An eye-opener is Stibbert's collection of armour and arms. In one room, the **Sala della Cavalcata** (Parade Room), are life-sized figures of horses and their soldierly riders in all manner of suits of armour from Europe and the Middle East. The exhibits also include clothes, furnishings, tapestries and paintings from the 16th to the 19th centuries.

You can join in on one of the tours (included in the admission price) led by actors portraying either Giovanni delle Bande Nere or the Ottoman sultan Suleyman the Magnificent, while one-hour tours for children take place on Saturday or Sunday; if you want English commentary, make reservations in advance.

The museum is north of the Fortezza da Basso. Bus No 4 from Stazione di Santa Maria Novella takes you as close as Via Vittorio Emanuele II, from where you have a fairly short walk.

South of the Old City

BELLOSGUARDO (Map pp82-83)

A favourite spot for 19th-century landscape painters was the hill of Bellosguardo (Beautiful View) southwest of the city centre. A narrow winding road leads up past a couple of villas from Piazza Torquato Tasso to Piazza Bellosguardo. You can't see anything from here, but if you wander along Via Roti Michelozzi into the grounds of the Albergo Torre di Bellosguardo, you'll see what the fuss was about. The hotel is the latest guise of what was once a 14th-century castle.

CERTOSA DI GALLUZZO (Map p75)

About 3km south of Porta Romana, along Via Senese, is Galluzzo, which is home to a remarkable 14th-century monastery, the **Certosa** (☎ 055 204 92 26; admission by donation; ☺ 9am-noon & 3-6pm Tue-Sun May-Oct, 9am-noon & 3-5pm Tue-Sun Nov-Apr). Its great cloister is decorated with busts from the della Robbia workshop and there are frescoes by Pontormo in the Gothic hall of Palazzo degli Studi.

The Certosa can only be visited with a guide. To get there catch bus No 37 from Stazione di Santa Maria Novella.

ACTIVITIES
Rowing

It may be possible to sign up for one of the two rowing clubs in Florence. Handier for the centre is **Società Canottieri Firenze** (Map p84; ☎ 055 28 21 30; Lungarno dei Medici 8). Further out is the **Società Canottieri Comunali** (Map pp76-77; ☎ 055 681 21 51; Lungarno Francesco Ferrucci 6). You are more likely to have luck getting in at the latter. Courses in rowing for beginners are available.

Swimming

The **Piscina Bellariva** (Map pp76-77; ☎ 055 67 72 51; Lungarno Aldo Moro 6; adult/child €6.50/4.50, carnet of 10 tickets €50; ☺ 10am-6pm Tue & Thu, 8.30am-11.30pm Jun-Sep) is 3.5km east of Ponte Vecchio along Lungarno Aldo Moro in Bellariva (bus No 14 from Piazza dell'Unità and the Duomo takes you closest to the pool). In summer, when they pull back the movable roof over the Olympic-size pool, it becomes a watery haven on those torrid Florentine days. Opening times tend to change from month to month; it's a good idea to ring up and check.

The **Piscina Le Pavoniere** (Map pp76-77; ☎ 055 36 22 33; Viale della Catena 2; adult/child €7/5, €7.50 Sun & holidays; ☺ 10am-6pm Jun–mid-Sep) opens late into the night on some evenings and has a pizzeria and bar.

From mid-September to June, access is restricted to certain times in Florentine pools. Ensure you'll be able to have a dip by calling ahead to check exact times.

Tennis

If you're interested in having a hit of tennis while on your trip, you can book courts (€12 per hour) at the **Campo Sportivo ASSI** (Map pp76-77; ☎ 055 68 78 58, Viale Michelangelo 64).

WALKING TOUR

Florence is best discovered on foot and this itinerary is designed to introduce you to the city's best. Begin in **Piazza Santa Maria Novella (1)**, dominated by the grand medieval basilica. Then take Via degli Avelli north, as far as the busy Piazza dell'Unità Italiana, and continue east on Via del Melarancio, past Piazza Madonna degli Aldobrandini and on to Piazza San Lorenzo, with its market stalls and the **Basilica di San Lorenzo (2)**, resting place of some of the Medici rulers. Walk south along Borgo San Lorenzo until you reach the junction with Via de' Cerretani. Cross the road and you will see Brunelleschi's breathtaking **Duomo (3)** and the **Battistero (4)**. Take a circuit around Piazza del Duomo before walking southwards along Via Roma, on into Piazza della Repubblica and then Via Calimala, before turning east into Via Orsanmichele, where you'll find the ornate **Chiesa di Orsanmichele (5)**.

At the end of this street you will come to a junction. Follow Via de' Calzaiuoli southwards and you will soon end up in Piazza della Signoria, with its **Loggia (6)** and the commanding presence of **Palazzo Vecchio**

(7), the home of the Florentine government since the Middle Ages. Just a few step south is the **Uffizi Gallery (8)**, housing one of the world's most precious collections of Renaissance art. Piazza degli Uffizi leads on to the Arno.

To the west you will see the instantly familiar **Ponte Vecchio (9)**, crammed with jewellery shops. Cross this bridge, which offers wonderful views up and down stream, and you will be in the Oltrarno district. Continue south along Via de' Guicciardini and you will shortly come upon the brooding hulk of **Palazzo Pitti (10)**, one-time seat of the Medici dynasty and today home to a vast collection of artworks. Behind lie the extensive **Boboli Gardens (11)**.

The walk is about 2.2km long and at a pace should take you a leisurely one hour.

COURSES

Florence has more than 30 schools offering courses in Italian language and culture. Numerous other schools offer courses in art, including painting, drawing, sculpture and art history, and several offer cookery courses.

While Florence is one of the most attractive cities in which to study Italian language or art, it is also one of the more expensive. Large numbers of British and American students do come here, so it may not be the best choice if you want to fully immerse yourself in the language and culture.

Brochures detailing courses and prices are available at Italian cultural institutes throughout the world, while the tourist office in Via Cavour has long lists of schools running language courses.

Non-EU citizens who want to study at a university or language school in Italy must have a study visa; the school will advise you.

Language Courses

The cost of language courses in Florence depends on the school, the length of the course (one month is usually the minimum duration) and its intensity. Among them are:

British Institute of Florence (Map p84; ☎ 055 267 78 200; Piazza Strozzi 2) This much-respected institution has been operating since 1917. Four-week beginners' courses cost €430, rising to €3520 for a full year's advanced study. There's also a numerous and diverse array of other specialist courses available, covering such subjects as opera, art and literature.

Istituto Europeo (Map p84; ☎ 055 238 10 71; www.istitutoeuropeo.it; Piazzale delle Pallottole 1) Courses here start at €202 for 20 hours (one week). A much better deal is to hang around for four weeks (€460).

Scuola Leonardo da Vinci (Map pp78-79; ☎ 055 26 11 81; www.scuolaleonardo.com; Via Bufalini 3) Courses offered range from two to 24 weeks, usually averaging four hours' class a day. Basic course costs start at €500 for four weeks.

Centro Lorenzo de' Medici (Map pp78-79; ☎ 055 28 73 60; Via Faenza 43) This school is popular with American students. Four hours a day for a month costs €500. They offer many levels and a variety of supplementary courses in acting, cooking, art history and suchlike, and will arrange home-stay accommodation from €25 per day.

Other Courses

Several of the schools already listed also offer courses on art history, cooking, art, music and so on.

Some schools specialise in particular courses. Art courses range from one-month workshops to longer-term professional diploma courses. Schools will organise accommodation for students on request and at cost, either in private apartments or with Italian families. As well as the following, many schools offer courses in applied arts, ceramics, cookery, theatre and fashion. The tourist office in Via Cavour has exhaustive lists.

Istituto per l'Arte e il Restauro (Map p80; ☎ 055 24 60 01; www.spinelli.it; Palazzo Spinelli, Borgo Santa Croce 10) Here, you can learn to restore anything from paintings to ceramics, interior and graphic design, fresco technique and gilding and marquetry. It also runs Italian-language courses.

Accademia Italiana (Map pp82-83; ☎ 055 28 46 16; www.accademiaitaliana.com; Piazza de' Pitti 15) This school offers a wide range of design programmes. They include one-month courses in drawing and painting, summer courses in fashion design, and more rigorous semester courses in painting, graphic arts and related fields.

Florence Dance Center (Map pp82-83; ☎ 055 28 92 76; www.florencedance.org; Borgo della Stella 23r) This centre offers a range of courses in classical, jazz and modern dance, including ballet, tango and flamenco.

Scuola del Cuoio (Map p80; ☎ 055 24 45 33; www.leatherschool.it; Piazza di Santa Croce 16) If you fancy trying your hand at a bit of leatherworking, this school, inside the Santa Croce church, is the place to go. It runs a wide variety of courses, lasting from half a day to a year, with prices starting at €125. Parchment-painting courses are also available.

FLORENCE FOR CHILDREN

As elsewhere in Italy, children are welcome pretty much anywhere in Florence. You will see families with young children out in the evenings, strolling with a *gelato* or sitting in a restaurant, while many designer clothes shops cater for kids, as well as their pampering parents. That said, however, Florence is not the best city to bring very young children; green spaces and playgrounds are scarce and while some of the pricier hotels can provide baby-sitters, there is no organised service of this nature available for tourists. Older children have rather more options, and there are several widely-available publications, in several languages, aimed at young teenagers, introducing the city, including *Florence for Kids* (Stefano Filipponi & Annalisa Fineschi; Lapis-snc 1998) and *Florence: Just Add Water* (Simone Frasca; Mandragora 2002).

Younger children will enjoy the various activities at the **Museo dei Ragazzi** at Palazzo Vecchio (see p93), while others might enjoy the weekend guided tours of the **Museo Stibbert** (see p109), aimed at children, or the **Museo di Storia della Scienza** (Map p84), where 'Galileo' will talk them through the exhibits. Some, no doubt, will relish the unsettling medical section. Advance reservation is needed for English commentary.

Mondobimbo (Map p81; ☎ 055 553 29 46; Via Ponte Rosso; admission €5; ☼ 10am-midnight May-Sep, 10am-7pm Oct-Apr) is a well-stocked playground with everything from bouncy-castles to a mini-railway, aimed at kids aged two to 10.

Ludoteca Musicale (Map pp82-83; ☎ 055 263 86 00; www.musicarte.it – Italian only; Via Pandolfino 18; admission free; ☼ 9.30am-12.30pm Tue, Wed & Fri) offers children – and their parents – demonstrations of various musical instruments and a chance to join in some hands-on activities and dancing.

The **Giardino di Boboli** (see p105) is a pleasant spot for a relaxing day out, while **Parco delle Cascine** (Via del Quercione; see p97), with its children's playground is popular with Florentine families. The **Piscina Bellariva** (see p109) swimming pool makes for a fun day out in the steamy Florentine summer.

TOURS

Walking Tours of Florence (Map p84; ☎ 055 264 50 33; www.artviva.com; Piazza Santo Stefano 2b) organises walks of the city for small groups, led by historians or art history graduates. It does several three-hour walks for €25 per person (reductions for children and students under 26), as well as half-day tours of the Tuscan countryside.

CentralSita Viaggi (Map pp78-79; ☎ 055 21 93 83; Via Santa Caterina da Siena 17) runs coach tours from the Sita bus station around Florence (€39). It also runs day trips to interesting destinations like Il Chianti, Siena, Pisa and others in Tuscany (€35 to €47).

CAF Incoming Tours (Map p84; ☎ 055 28 32 00; Via Roma 4) runs coach trips to the designer-clothes outlet malls (see p123) for €19, plus various tours around Florence and day excursions as far afield as Venice and Rome (€105 return).

FESTIVALS & EVENTS

Besides *carnevale* in February, major Florentine festivals include:

Scoppio del Carro (Explosion of the Cart) A cart of fireworks is exploded in front of the cathedral at noon on Easter Sunday.

Festa di San Giovanni (Feast of St John, Florence's patron saint) On 24 June, Florence celebrates with the lively *calcio storico* medieval football matches played on Piazza di Santa Croce, ending with a fireworks display over Piazzale Michelangelo.

Festa delle Rificolone (Festival of the Paper Lanterns) A procession of children carrying lanterns, accompanied by drummers, musicians and others in medieval dress, winds its way from Piazza di Santa Croce to Piazza SS Annunziata to celebrate the Virgin Mary's supposed birthday on 7 September.

Festa di Anna Maria Medici On 18th February, the death in 1743 of the last Medici, Anna Maria, is marked with a costumed parade from Palazzo Vecchio to her tomb in the Cappelle Medicee, honouring her gift to the city of the family's peerless art collection, meant as 'an ornament to the State... and to attract the curiosity of foreigners.' Some museums are free on this day.

Internazionale Antiquariato Every two years Florence hosts this antiques fair, held at Palazzo Strozzi (p98) and attracting exhibitors from across Europe. The next fair will be in September/October 2005.

SLEEPING

The city has hundreds of hotels in all categories and a good range of alternatives, including hostels and private rooms, though being Florence, rooms are constantly in demand and prices are higher than elsewhere in Tuscany.

You are advised to book ahead at any time of year, but especially in summer (from mid-April to October) and for the

GAY & LESBIAN FLORENCE

Florence, with its unrivalled artistic and creative history, has a long tradition of openness and tolerance. Its gay community is one of the most vibrant and well established in Italy, boasting a number of well-attended bars and clubs. That said, this is no Amsterdam, and there are no specifically 'gay areas' – what nightlife exists tends to be relatively low-key. **Azione Gay e Lesbica** (Map pp76-77; ☎ 055 67 12 98; www.azionegayelesbica.it – Italian only; Via Manara 12) is the city's main contact point for all information on the scene, while a free 'Gay City Map' is available from the tourist office, showing gay clubs, bars and gay-friendly shops and hotels. It also includes details of Pisa and Milan.

At the **Libreria delle Donne** (Map p80; ☎ 055 24 03 84; Via Fiesolana 2b) bookshop, you can get information to tune you into the lesbian scene in Florence.

Bars and clubs worth checking out include:

Piccolo Café (Map p80; ☎ 055 24 17 04; Borgo Santa Croce 23r; ☽ 5pm-1am) This is a relaxed little place to hang out and get acquainted with the gay and lesbian scene. It hosts occasional art exhibitions.

YAG Bar (Map p80; ☎ 055 246 90 22; Via de' Macci 8r; ☽ 5pm-2am) Barely a stone's throw from the Piccolo Café, this trendy gay bar is another relaxed and mixed location. It claims to be the largest gay bar in Florence and has regular live music. There are some computer terminals for going online and video games.

Crisco (Map p80; ☎ 055 248 05 80; Via Sant'Egidio 43r; ☽ 9pm-3am Sun & Tue-Thu, to 5am Fri & Sat) This is a strictly men-only club with dark rooms and a leather/jeans dress code.

Du Monde Café (Map pp82-83; ☎ 055 234 49 53; Via San Niccolò 103r; ☽ 7.30pm-4am Tue-Sun) Members-only cocktail bar, with drag acts on the weekend. It also has a restaurant, which closes at 1am.

Tabasco (Map p84; ☎ 055 21 30 00, Piazza di Santa Cecilia 3r; free entry, drinks €7; ☽ 10pm-4am, disco until 6am Tue, Fri & Sat) This is Florence's only serious gay club, Here, you can dance through the wee hours of the morning and then some. This place boasts a disco, cocktail bar and dark room. Wednesday is leather night. You are obliged to have at least one drink.

Easter and Christmas to New Year holiday periods.

In addition to the available hotels, about 175 houses have been registered as *affittacamere*. These are basically private houses offering beds for a fee. Both hotels and *pensioni* are concentrated in three principal areas: near Stazione di Santa Maria Novella, near Piazza Santa Maria Novella and in the old city between the cathedral and the Arno.

If you arrive at Stazione di Santa Maria Novella without a hotel booking head for the **Consorzio ITA office** (☎ 055 28 28 93; fax 055 24 78 22; ☺ 8.30am-7.30pm Mon-Sat), which can book rooms for a small fee.

You can also contact the tourist office for a list of *affittacamere* (private rooms), where you can sometimes find rooms for about €25 to €30. Most fill with students during the school year (from October to June), but are a good option if you are staying for a week or longer.

Prices listed here are for the high season. Many places, especially at the lower end, also offer triples and quads. If you are travelling in a group, these bigger rooms are generally the best value.

High season for those hotels that lift their prices starts on 15 April and fizzles out by mid-October (some dip a little in the hot months of July and August). Some hotels have an intermediate stage starting on 1 March. The Christmas and New Year period also signals price hikes. Others don't bother changing prices much at any time of the year.

If you have trouble finding a room in Florence, you might consider staying outside the city; places such as Arezzo, Pisa and Montecatini are just a short train trip away and often offer better value, while if you have your own transport, your options are clearly greater.

Hotel Associations

The following organisations can book you into member hotels. They usually offer a fair range of possibilities, but rarely drop below two stars.

Associazione Gestori Alloggi Privati (AGAP; ☎ 055 505 10 12; www.agap.it; Viale Volta 127). This organisation can get you a room in an *affittacamere* or *agriturismo*.

Florence Promhotels (☎ 055 55 39 41; www.promhotels.it; Viale Volta 72)

Gente di Toscana (☎ 0575 52 92 75; www.gentedotoscana.it; Via San Michele 9, Scandicci) This company offers inexpensive bed-and-breakfast accommodation in private homes or flats.

Top Quark (incorporating Family Hotels and Sun Rays Hotels; ☎ 055 33 34 03; www.familyhotels.com; Viale Fratelli Rossi 39r)

Inphonline (☎ 02 268 30 102 - Milan; www.initalia.it) This phone and online booking service operates Italy-wide and is free. You can book hotels, rent cars and organise conferences.

Budget

EAST OF STAZIONE DI SANTA MARIA NOVELLA

Many of the hotels in this area are well run, clean and safe, but there are also a fair number of seedy establishments. The area includes the streets around Piazza della Stazione and east to Via Cavour. If you have nothing booked and don't wish to tramp around town, the area has the advantage of being close to Stazione di Santa Maria Novella.

Ostello Archi Rossi (Map pp78-79; ☎ 055 29 08 04; fax 055 230 26 01; Via Faenza 94r; dm/s from €15/25.80) This private hostel, particularly popular with a young American set, is close to the train station and a reasonable option. It is generally full to the gunnels and you can't reserve in advance.

Ostello Spirito Santo (Map pp78-79; ☎ 055 239 82 02; fax 055 239 81 29; Via Nazionale 8; d €42; ☺ Jul-Oct) This is a religious institution near the train station, which offers beds to women and families only. Rooms come with two or three beds so you avoid the dorm situation. The place is predictably quiet.

Pensione Bellavista (Map pp78-79; ☎ 055 28 45 28; fax 055 28 48 74; Largo Alinari 15; s/d €60/80) Rooms in this hotel at the start of Via Nazionale are small, but a bargain if you can manage to book one of the two doubles with balconies that overlook the Duomo and Palazzo Vecchio.

Hotel Globus (Map p84; ☎ 055 21 10 62; www.hotelglobus.com; Via Sant'Antonino 24; s/d €70/90; ✺) This is a handy little place with 23 spotless, newly renovated rooms. Triples go for €140.

AROUND PIAZZA DI SANTA MARIA NOVELLA (Map p84)

This area is just south of the Stazione di Santa Maria Novella and includes Piazza di Santa Maria Novella, the streets running south to the Arno and east to Via de' Tornabuoni.

Hotel Abaco (☎ 055 238 19 19; www.abaco-hotel.it; Via dei Banchi 1; d from €72; 🔀) This is a smart and well-maintained establishment with plush, elegantly furnished rooms. Triples/quads are available for €95/135.

Albergo Scoti (☎ 055 29 21 28; www.hotelscoti.com; Via de' Tornabuoni 7; s/d €60/85) This friendly hotel, on the 2nd floor of an old *palazzo*, has a clutch of clean and simple rooms, all with bathroom. The communal lounge, with its 18th-century frescoes and chandelier, is stunning.

Pensione Ferretti (☎ 055 238 13 28; http://ferretti.hotelinfirenze.com; Via delle Belle Donne 17; s/d €60/98; 🖳) This simple hotel with 16 rooms is a quiet place, hidden away on a tiny intersection. Singles/doubles without bathroom go for €48/78.

BETWEEN THE DUOMO & THE ARNO

Pensione Bretagna (Map p84; ☎ 055 28 96 18; www.bretagna.it; Lungarno Corsini 6; s/d from €60/95; 🔀) One of the best options in this price range, it has 18 spotless, well-appointed rooms in the historic Palazzo Gianfigliazzi which overlooks the Arno. Only one room, though (34) has a view of the river, as does the frescoed breakfast room. Triples and quads go for €135/160.

Hotel San Giovanni (Map p84; ☎ 055 28 83 85; www.hotelsangiovanni.com; Via de' Cerretani 2; s/d €70/95; 🔀) Although the stairwell up to the 2nd floor isn't promising, the charming and often spacious rooms in this hotel, many with views of the Duomo, are well worth seeking out. Rooms without bathrooms are slightly cheaper while triples cost €120.

Albergo Bavaria (Map pp82-83; ☎ 055 234 03 13; Borgo degli Albizi 26; s/d €60/80) This hotel is housed in the fine Palazzo di Ramirez di Montalvo, built around a peaceful courtyard by Amannati. It is a good bet if you can get a room.

Hotel Orchidea (Map p80; ☎ /fax 055 248 03 46; Borgo degli Albizi 11; s/d €50/70) This is a fine, homey, old-fashioned *pensione* in a grand mansion. Rooms are clean and simple but those facing the street are plagued by noise well into the wee hours.

SANTA CROCE & EAST OF THE CENTRE

Hotel Wanda (Map p80; ☎ 055 234 44 84; www.hotelwanda.it; Via Ghibellina 51; dm/d from €25/50)

Quiet, friendly hotel with several large rooms near Piazza di Santa Croce, some with ceiling frescoes. Triples cost from €90. Rooms with bathroom cost slightly more, and long-term lets are available from €300 per week.

OLTRARNO

Campeggio Michelangelo (Map p80; ☎ 055 681 19 77; fax 055 68 93 48; Viale Michelangelo 80; person/tent/car €7/5/5; 🌓 Apr-end Oct) This is the closest camping ground to the city centre, just off Piazzale Michelangelo, south of the Arno. Take bus No 13 from Stazione di Santa Maria Novella. It's a big and comparatively leafy location and makes a lovely starting point for wanders down into the city (but a little arduous getting back!).

Ostello Santa Monaca (Map pp82-83; ☎ 055 26 83 38; www.ostello.it; Via Santa Monaca 6; dm €16) On a quiet street in the Oltrarno area, this old-fashioned hostel has single-sex dorms sleeping between four and 20 people. Be warned, you have to vacate your dorm by 9.30am and leave the hostel between 1pm and 2pm. There's also a 1am curfew.

Istituto Gould (Map pp82-83; ☎ 055 21 25 76; gould.reception@dada.it; Via de' Serragli 49; dm/s/d from €19/32/50) Housed in a 17th-century *palazzo*, this Protestant church-run hostel is popular with school groups. The rooms are simple but spotless, some overlooking a pleasant garden. Note that reception is only open 9am to 1pm and 3pm to 7pm Monday to Friday and 9am to noon Saturday.

Hotel Boboli (Map pp82-83; ☎ 055 229 86 45; www.hotelboboli.com; Via Romana 63; s/d €60/86; 🔀) Pleasant, homey and unpretentious little hotel right by the Boboli Gardens, with spotless and cosy rooms.

OUTSKIRTS OF FLORENCE

Campeggio Panoramico (Map p75; ☎ 055 55 90 69; www.florencecamping.com; Via Peramonda 1; person/car & tent €8/14) To get to this camping ground at Fiesole, take bus No 7 from the Stazione di Santa Maria Novella. It is a big rambling site and in the hot Tuscan summer has the advantage of being just a little cooler and more airy than down in Florence itself. There's a small supermarket on site.

Villa Camerata (Map pp76-77; ☎ 055 60 03 15; Viale Augusto Righi 2-4; person/tent €5/4.80) This camping ground is next to the HI hostel of the same name (see p115). It has space for 220 people and is well equipped in a congenial, verdant setting, but it is inconvenient for the city centre. One advantage is that it opens year-round, which the others do not.

Ostello Villa Camerata (Map pp76-77; ☎ 055 60 14 51; fax 055 61 03 00; Viale Augusto Righi 2-4; dm €14; ☺ 7am-9am, 2pm-midnight) This Hostelling International (HI) hostel, in a 16th-century house, is considered one of the most beautiful in Europe. Only members are accepted and the hostel is part of the International Booking Network (IBN), the online booking system for HI (see www.iyhf.org for more details). Breakfast is included. Take bus No 17B, which leaves from the right side of Stazione di Santa Maria Novella as you leave the platforms. The trip takes 30 minutes.

Mid-Range
EAST OF STAZIONE DI SANTA MARIA NOVELLA
Hotel Bonciani (Map p84; ☎ 055 2 60 90; fax 055 26 85 12; Via de' Panzani 17; s/d from €80/100; ❄) Elegant hotel near Piazza Santa Maria Novella, once patronised by Garibaldi. Rooms are comfortable and spacious and some come with frescoes.

Hotel Palazzo Benci (Map p84; ☎ 055 21 38 48; www.palazzobenci.com; Piazza Madonna degli Aldobrandini 3; s/d €100/155; ❄) This charming 16th-century *palazzo* near the Basilica di San Lorenzo was once home to one of Florence's leading political families. Rooms are comfortable and fully modernised and there's a quiet internal courtyard.

Hotel Decò (Map p84; ☎ 055 28 44 69; www.hoteldeco.it; Via de' Panzani 7; d from €90; ❄) Small, friendly hotel with cosy if rather uninspired rooms. Buffet breakfast included.

Hotel La Gioconda (Map p84; ☎ 055 21 10 23; gioconda@italyhotel.com; Via de' Panzani 2; s/d €105/170; ❄) This hotel shot to international fame in 1913 when the *Mona Lisa*, recently stolen from the Louvre, was recovered from under the bed in room 20. The small rooms are decent enough, though nothing special for the price. Singles without bathroom go for €70.

Hotel le Due Fontane (Map pp78-79; ☎ 055 21 01 85; www.leduefontane.it; Piazza SS Annunziata 14; s/d €110/160; ❄) This grand, fully renovated *palazzo* on one of Florence's most attractive piazzas offers neat, comfortable rooms, some with great views. Breakfast is included.

Hotel Accademia (Map p84; ☎ 055 29 34 51; www.accademiahotel.net; Via Faenza 7; s/d €85/150; ❄) This attractive hotel has pleasant rooms with TV, and incorporates an 18th-century mansion with magnificent, stained-glass doors and carved, wooden ceilings.

Hotel Casci (Map p84; ☎ 055 21 16 86; www.hotelcasci.com; Via Cavour 13; s/d €100/140; ❄) The charm of this hotel is the chance to stay in a 15th-century mansion on one of the city's main streets. The rooms are a little musty but large and comfortable. Prices come down considerably out of high season.

AROUND PIAZZA DI SANTA MARIA NOVELLA
Hotel Aprile (Map pp78-79; ☎ 055 21 62 37; fax 055 28 09 47; Via della Scala 6; d from €120; ❄) This pleasant 15th-century *palazzo* is just a stone's throw from the piazza, with small but comfortable rooms. There's also a walled garden.

BETWEEN THE DUOMO & THE ARNO (Map p84)
Hotel della Signoria (☎ 055 21 45 30; www.hoteldellasignoria.com; Via delle Terme 1; s/d from €90/155; ❄) A neat little hotel right in the heart of things, with smart, tastefully furnished rooms. Breakfast is included.

Pendini (☎ 055 21 11 70; fax 055 28 18 07; Via degli Strozzi 2; s/d €110/150; ❄) It has a rather musty, dated set of rooms on the 3rd and 4th floors of a 19th-century block overlooking Piazza della Repubblica. Rooms are furnished with antiques and reproductions. In low season they're willing to come down in price.

SANTA CROCE & EAST OF THE CENTRE
Hotel Dante (Map p80; ☎ 055 24 17 72; www.hoteldante.it; Via San Cristofano 2; s/d €84/123; ❄) Tucked away in a quiet street right by the Basilica di Santa Croce, the rooms are clean but unremarkable, with smallish bathrooms. Breakfast is a pricey extra at €12.

OLTRARNO
Hotel Silla (Map pp82-83; ☎ 055 234 28 88; www.hotelsilla.it; Via dei Renai 5; s/d €125/170; ❄) Set in a charming old *palazzo* in one of the most attractive and leafy parts of Florence, this hotel offers pleasant and impeccably maintained rooms that are a stone's throw from the centre.

Hotel San Remo (Map p80; ☎ 055 234 28 23; www.hotelsanremo-fi.it; Lungarno Serristori 13;

s/d €70/110; 🌡) Quiet 19th-century villa offering simply furnished rooms, some with great views across the Arno.

Top End
EAST OF STAZIONE DI SANTA MARIA NOVELLA (Map pp78-79)
Hotel Loggiato dei Serviti (☎ 055 28 95 92; fax 055 28 95 95; Piazza SS Annunziata 3; s/d €140/205; 🌡) This atmospheric hotel is housed in a historic 16th-century building mirroring Brunelleschi's Spedale, right opposite. Rooms are simply but comfortably furnished, while maintaining some of the original character of the place.

Hotel Il Guelfo Bianco (☎ 055 28 83 30; www.ilguelfobianco.it; Via Cavour 57r; s/d €135/180) This hotel's rooms are attractively laid out and comfortable. A handful of 'superior' and 'deluxe' doubles go for €210 and €235, and they have even better rooftop views than the others.

AROUND PIAZZA DI SANTA MARIA NOVELLA
Grand Hotel Baglioni (Map p84; ☎ 055 2 35 80; www.hotelbaglioni.it; Piazza dell'Unità Italiana 6; s/d €227/315; 🌡) This elegant, 19th-century hotel has 195 spacious and tastefully furnished rooms, while the rooftop terrace dining area affords some really fine views over the city. Suites start at €378.

Grand Hotel Minerva (Map p84; ☎ 055 2 72 30; www.grandhotelminerva.com; Piazza di Santa Maria Novella 16; s/d €212/276; 🌡 💻 🏊) Stylish four-star right beside the church, with elegantly furnished rooms and large suites starting at €340. There's a very good restaurant and wonderful views over the piazza from the rooftop swimming pool.

Hotel Croce di Malta (Map pp78-79; ☎ 055 21 83 51; www.crocedimalta.it; Via della Scala 7; s/d €205/270; 🌡 🏊) The spacious rooms are neat and plain, some with balconies. There are great views from the rooftop sitting area.

BETWEEN THE DUOMO & THE ARNO
Hotel Helvetia & Bristol (Map p84; ☎ 055 28 83 53; www.hotelhelvetiabristolfirenze.it; Via dei Pescioni 2; s/d from €205/310; 🌡) This inviting top-level hotel oozes charm and elegance from another era without being haughty. Prices lower considerably in the low season and all 56 well-appointed rooms are worthy choices. Suites start at €440.

Grand Hotel (Map pp82-83; ☎ 055 271 67 14; fax 055 21 74 00; Piazza d'Ognissanti 1; s/d from €339/519; 🌡) This luxury hotel overlooking the Arno certainly lives up to its name, with spacious and sumptuously decorated rooms; you can choose from Florentine Renaissance or French Empire style. Some come with frescoes and balconies.

Gallery Hotel Art (Map p84; ☎ 055 272 64 000; www.lungarnohotels.com; Vicolo dell'Oro 5; d/ste from €315/540; 🌡) Exclusive, chic hotel owned by the Ferragamo fashion house, with light, artfully designed rooms and a permanent display of contemporary artworks on the ground floor. The excellent on-site restaurant serves up a fusion of European and Asian cuisine.

Hotel La Residenza (Map p84; ☎ 055 21 86 84; www.laresidenzahotel.com; Via de' Tornabuoni 8; s/d €130/210; 🌡) In the heart of Florence's fanciest shopping street, this small hotel has big, individually styled rooms and a rooftop terrace. Breakfast is included.

Westin Excelsior (Map pp82-83; ☎ 055 2 71 51; www.westin.com; Piazza d'Ognissanti 3; s/d from €497/670; 🌡) One of Florence's plushest hotels, overlooking the Arno. The large rooms are stylishly furnished and luxurious suites start at €1209. Every Sunday an American brunch is served (€37) to the accompaniment of live jazz music. The hotel offers a complimentary baby-sitting service.

OLTRARNO
Albergo Torre di Bellosguardo (Map pp82-83; ☎ 055 229 81 45; info@torrebellosguardo.com; Via Roti Michelozzi 2; s/d €160/280; 🌡 💻 🏊) This is worth considering if only for its position. Long appreciated as a bucolic escape from the simmering heat of summertime Florence, the Bellosguardo hill to the southwest of the city centre offers not only enchanting views, but also enticing accommodation in what started life as a small castle in the 14th century.

Rental Accommodation
If you want an apartment in Florence, save your pennies and start looking well before you arrive, as apartments are difficult to come by and can be very expensive. **Florence & Abroad** (Map pp78-79; ☎ 055 48 70 04; www.florenceandabroad.com; Via San Zanobi 58) specialises in short- and medium-term rental accommodation in Florence and the Fiesole area for those with a fairly liberal budget.

FAST FOOD FLORENCE-STYLE

When Florentines feel like a fast snack instead of a sit-down lunch, they might well stop by a *trippaio* (often just a mobile stand) for a nice tripe burger (tripe on a bread roll). It may sound a little nauseating to the uninitiated, and this is probably one best left to the locals.

Savouring fine wines is one of the great pleasures of the palate in Florence, and for many there is nothing better than a couple of glasses accompanied by simple local snacks – sausage, cheeses, *ribollita* (vegetable stew) and suchlike. And the good news is that the tradition of the *vinaio* (wine merchant) has won new life in the past few years in Florence. You may never see the word 'vinaio' on the doorway, but the idea remains the same. The old traditional places still exist – often dark little bars where you can get a bite to eat too. Look out for the signs 'Mescita di Vini' (roughly 'wine outlet') and '*enoteca*' (wine bar).

Enoteca Fuori Porta (Map p80; ☎ 055 234 24 83; Via Monte alle Croci 10r; dishes around €5; ☻ Mon-Sat) In this fine old *enoteca* the wine list comprises more than 400 varieties (and an impressive roll-call of Scotch whiskies and other liquors). You can order from a limited list of *primi* (first course) for a pleasant evening meal. The desserts are also good.

Le Barrique (Map pp82-83; ☎ 055 22 41 92; Via del Leone 40r; meals with wine €30; ☻ Tue-Sun) Hidden deep in the San Frediano area, this charming little spot offers a limited *menù del giorno* (menu of the day) or, for those just stopping in for a quick drink or two, snacks at the bar. Again the emphasis is on wine, although the pasta dishes are good. It also offers a selection of Tuscan and French cheeses.

Olio & Convivium (Map pp82-83; ☎ 055 265 81 98; Via di Santo Spitito 4; meals around €12; ☻ Tue-Sat) As well as a small gastronomic restaurant and a well-stocked wine bar, this place also has a shop where you can purchase everything from fresh-baked bread to meats, pasta and cheeses.

Il Santo Bevitore (Map pp82-83; ☎ 055 21 12 64; Via di Santo Spirito 64/66r; dishes around €6-8; ☻ Mon-Sat) This modern, inviting little *enoteca* in Oltrarno is a great place to sample a wide variety of wines, with a selection of light pasta dishes.

Enoteca Boccadama (Map p80; ☎ 055 24 36 40; Piazza di Santa Croce 25-26r; dishes from €7.50; ☻ Tue-Sun) An excellent wine bar with outdoor seating on the piazza and a cosy lounge and restaurant indoors. The wine list is extensive and it serves light salads and pasta dishes. You'll also get complimentary olives, nuts and the like with your wine.

It seems barely conceivable that within about 10 seconds' walk off Piazza della Signoria, which is lined with tourist rip-off restaurants, the city centre's last surviving, more or less genuine, *osterie* (a restaurant offering simple dishes) should remain. **Vini e Vecchi Sapori** (Map p84; ☎ 055 29 30 45; Via dei Magazzini 3r; meals around €16) is a little den of 'wines and old tastes' where you can eat decently and taste some solid local wines at low prices. They also import *fragolino*, a strawberry-flavoured wine made in the northeast of Italy.

Osteria de' Macci (Map p80; ☎ 055 24 12 26; Via de' Macci 77r; ☻ 7am-1am Mon-Sat) A great little place to try a variety of wines, salads and *bruschetta*.

Enoteca Baldovino (Map p80; ☎ 055 234 72 00; Via di San Giuseppe 18r; ☻ Tue-Sun) This is a big place in a pleasant location, with footpath seating in the shadow of Santa Croce. You can taste fine wines accompanied by sophisticated snacks and salads.

EATING

There is no shortage of places to eat in Florence, and although Florentines have largely abandoned the city centre to the tourists, and prices here tend to be high while quality is often lacking. However, you can still dig up quite a few fine little eateries dotted about the place. Oltrarno has a number of good, economical options, while other places worth seeking out can be found in the Santa Croce area.

Budget

Eating at a good trattoria can be surprisingly economical – a virtue of the competition for customers' attention. Budget is a relative term in pricey Florence, so what follows is an arbitrary division. Anywhere you can fairly safely assume you will pay below about €25 for a full meal has been classed as 'budget' – ranging from sandwich joints (where you might pay around €3 for a filling roll) through trattorie serving respectable and good-value set meals (menù del giorno or menù turistico) and upwards into the modest categories of restaurant. Anything from around €25 up to €50 is classed here as mid-range and everything beyond that as top end, where obviously the sky's the limit.

EAST OF STAZIONE DI SANTA MARIA NOVELLA (Map pp78-79)

Mario (☎ 055 21 85 50; Via Rosina 2r; mains around €5; ⏲ Mon-Sat for lunch) This small bar and trattoria is usually heaving with people and attracts an interesting, eclectic mix of various foreign strays and local workers.

Ristorante ZàZà (☎ 055 21 54 11; Piazza del Mercato Centrale 26r; meals around €15; ⏲ Mon-Sat) This place is so popular that it has spread out into the open. It is the best place on the square for outdoor dining. The menu changes regularly and often sparkles with imaginative dishes.

Il Vegetariano (☎ 055 47 50 30; Via delle Ruote 30r; meals around €15; ⏲ Tue-Sat) One of the few veggie options in town, this is an unassuming *locale* with a limited (but changing) menu.

AROUND PIAZZA DI SANTA MARIA NOVELLA

Trattoria il Contadino (Map pp78-79; ☎ 055 238 26 73; Via Palazzuolo 71r; meals around €14; ⏲ Mon-Sat) This inexpensive and unpretentious place is popular with a young crowd. The food's not the best, but it's filling.

Il Grillo (Map p84; ☎ 055 28 24 38; Piazza di Santa Maria Novella 32; meals around €12) Another cheap and cheerful place serving up pasta and pizzas, with outdoor seating and a no-smoking interior.

BETWEEN THE DUOMO & THE ARNO

The streets between the Duomo and the Arno contain many pizzerias where you can buy takeaway pizza by weight – usually around €1.80 for a slice.

Queen Victoria (Map p84; ☎ 055 29 51 62; Via Por Santa Maria 32r) Busy place serving filling *panini* and focaccia from €4 and pizzas and salads from around €7. There's an outdoor seating area at the back.

La Grotta Guelfa (Map p84; ☎ 055 21 00 42; Via Pellicceria 5r; meals from €12.50) This popular place with outdoor seating serves up hearty Tuscan fare, with lots of beef and veal dishes, as well as pasta and salads.

Trattoria Pasquini (Map p84; ☎ 055 21 89 95; Via Val di Lamona 2r; meals around €20; ⏲ Thu-Tue) In this

tiny corner they offer a varied menu that includes Tuscan meals such as tripe or *bistecca alla fiorentina* (Florentine steak), and a mix of other national dishes. The *gnocchi al pomodoro* (gnocchio with tomato sauce) are good. Great wreaths of garlic and tomato grace the little bar, while the simple timber furnishing and dimly lit, vaulted ceiling all help to create a cosy atmosphere.

Trattoria da Benvenuto (Map p84; ☎ 055 21 48 33; Via della Mosca 16r; meals around €20; ⏲ Mon-Sat) Eating here, on the corner of Via dei Neri, is hardly an ambient dining experience, but the food is reliable and modestly priced. Mains include several Florentine favourites, including *lampredotto* (a type of tripe) and *bistecca*, while the pasta dishes are an interesting mix, including a decent *rigatoni alla siciliana*.

Caffè Daria (Map p80; ☎ 055 234 09 79; Borgo degli Albizi 36r; mains around €5) Popular place with the student crowd, serving sushi, snacks, buffet dinner and drinks.

AROUND OGNISSANTI

Da il Latini (Map p84; ☎ 055 21 09 16; Via dei Palchetti 6r; mains from €10; ⏲ Tue-Sun) This is an attractive trattoria just off Via del Moro and something of a classic for Florentines. The food is largely Tuscan and the speciality of the house is *bistecca alla fiorentina*.

Trattoria dei 13 Gobbi (Map pp82-83; ☎ 055 21 32 04; Via del Porcellana 9r; mains around €10; ⏲ Tue-Sat) There is a somewhat artificial, bucolic scene set inside this trattoria, but it's tastefully done. The courtyard out the back and the low ceilings all add atmosphere.

Sostanza (Map pp82-83; ☎ 055 21 26 91; Via del Porcellana 25; mains €7.50; ⏲ Mon-Fri) This traditional Tuscan eatery is a good spot for *bistecca alla fiorentina* if you're not fussy about your surrounds. A no-nonsense approach dominates.

SANTA CROCE & EAST OF THE CENTRE

Ramraj (Map p80; ☎ 055 24 09 99; Via Ghibellina 61r; meals from around €7; ⏲ Tue-Sun) Indian takeaway serving up tasty tandoori dishes, curries, rice and vegetarian options. There are a few seats inside too.

Osteria de' Benci (Map pp82-83; ☎ 055 234 49 23; Via de' Benci 13r; meals around €20; ⏲ Mon-Sat) This is a consistently good bet. It changes its menu quite often and serves up honest slabs of *bistecca alla fiorentina*. The food is well prepared, the atmosphere cosy and prices moderate.

Antico Noè (Map p80; ☎ 055 234 08 38; Arco di San Piero 6r; meals €15; ☻ Mon-Sat) This legendary sandwich bar, just off Piazza San Pier Maggiore, is another option for a light lunch. It has two sections: the sandwich bar is takeaway only, but next door is a cosy restaurant where you can enjoy fine cooking to slow jazz and blues tunes.

Danny Rock (Map p80; ☎ 055 235 03 07; Via Pandolfini 13r; meals around €10; ☻ noon-2.45pm & 7.30pm-1am) It might not sound promising, but inside it's an immensely popular place for pizza, pasta and baked potatoes.

Osteria Cibrèo (Map p80; ☎ 055 234 11 00; Via de' Macci 122r; meals around €20; ☻ Tue-Sat; closed Aug & Sep) This is a true delight to the palate, offering some enticing first courses, such as *ricotta al ragù* (ricotta cheese in a meat sauce). There follows a variety of seafood and meat options for the main course.

Ruth's (Map p80; ☎ 055 248 08 88; Via Luigi Carlo Farini 2a; meals around €10; ☻ Sun-Fri) For something a little different, try this place by the synagogue. It serves tasty kosher Jewish food, which bears a strong resemblance to other Middle Eastern cuisine and makes a good choice for vegetarians.

Sedano Allegro (Map p80; ☎ 055 234 55 05; Borgo della Croce 20r; dishes €7-10; ☻ Tue-Sun) Small place offering a wide range of vegetarian options and pasta, as well as traditional meat dishes. In the warmer months it opens up a garden at the rear.

OLTRARNO (Map pp82-83)

Al Tranvai (☎ 055 22 51 97; Piazza Tasso 14r; meals from €10; ☻ Mon-Fri) This is a small and wonderfully intimate rustic Tuscan eatery, mostly catering to locals. It serves up a limited range of pastas as *primi* and specialises in offal, including *trippa alla fiorentina* (tripe). You can also eat outside.

Caffè Ricchi (☎ 055 21 58 64; Piazza Santo Spirito 8; meals around €12; ☻ Mon-Sat) Welcoming little place with outdoor seating on the piazza, serving up pasta and veal dishes.

Trattoria da Ginone (☎ 055 21 87 58; Via de' Serragli 35r; meals around €11.50; ☻ 7-1am) This is a great place for inexpensive wholesome food, including pasta and vegetarian options. It's popular with a young student crowd.

L'Brindellone (☎ 055 21 78 79; Piazza Piattellina 10/11r; meals around €12.50; ☻ Thu-Tue) Surrounded

by dangling garlic strands and old Chianti bottles, this is a truly Tuscan spot with a slightly vegetarian bent too. Alongside such classics as *vitello tonnato* (veal in a tuna sauce) you can get vegetable cous cous.

I Tarocchi (☎ 055 234 39 12; Via dei Renai 12/14r; dishes from €6; ☻ Tue-Sat) This is a popular pizzeria/trattoria serving excellent pizzas. The first courses alone are substantial enough to satisfy most people's hunger.

Il Cantinone (☎ 055 21 88 98; Via di Santo Spirito 6r; meals around €13.50) This subtereannean trattoria, with a wine bar attached, serves up traditional Tuscan fare at reasonable prices.

Mid-Range
AROUND PIAZZA DI SANTA MARIA NOVELLA

Osteria dei Cento Poveri (Map pp78-79; ☎ 055 21 88 46; Via Palazzuolo 31r; meals around €25; ☻ Wed-Mon) A congenial little spot in a not-so-congenial part of town, the 'hostel of the hundred poor people' sits apart from most other places around here as a quality dining option. Tuck in to creative Tuscan food in a down-to-earth setting.

BETWEEN THE DUOMO & THE ARNO (Map p84)

Trattoria Coco Lezzone (☎ 055 28 71 78; Via Parioncino 26r; meals around €35; ☻ Mon-Sat) *Ribollita* is the house speciality here, but they will do you a genuine *bistecca alla fiorentina* if you book it ahead. It's a trendy place but service can be poor.

Fusion (☎ 055 2 72 63; Vicolo d'Oro 5; ☻ 11am-midnight Mon-Fri, noon-2pm Sat & Sun) The fashionable restaurant of the Gallery Hotel Art specialises in 'fusion' cuisine, in this case, French, Italian and Japanese, with such dishes as chicken teriyaki with rocket salad (€17). Brunch is served at weekends (€25).

SANTA CROCE & EAST OF THE CENTRE (Map p80)

La Pentola d'Oro (☎ 055 24 18 08; Via di Mezzo 24r; meals around €40; ☻ Mon-Sat) Long a jealously guarded secret among Florentine gourmands, this one-off has recently started to advertise itself. The menu involves all sorts of mixes, such as beef prepared with a black pepper and pear sauce.

Trattoria Tirovino (☎ 055 263 89 40; Via Ghibellina 70r; meals around €35; ☻ Mon-Sat) Intimate, traditional little trattoria, with friendly staff and a changing menu, featuring such items as chicken breast with truffles.

Sésame (☎ 055 200 13 81; Via delle Conce 20r; meals around €30; ☽ 8pm-1am) You'll think you've walked into the Casbah in this atmospheric place, which serves an interesting fusion of French and Moroccan cuisine.

OLTRARNO (Map pp82-83)
Osteria Santo Spirito (☎ 055 238 23 83; Piazza Santo Spirito 16r; meals around €28) If you prefer a slightly higher quality meal than in the bustling *locali* across the square, this cosy restaurant is the place. Try the *spagetthi con vongole* (spaghetti with clams; €14).

Trattoria Cavolo Nero (☎ 055 29 47 44; Via dell'Ardiglione 22; meals around €30; ☽ Tue-Sat) This place is hidden away in a back street. Try the entrecote of Angus steak prepared with herbs (€14).

Dante (☎ 055 21 92 19; Piazza Nazario Sauro 12r; meals around €16) This is an inexpensive place for great pizzas and pasta, in a vaguely rustic Tuscan atmosphere, with plastic hams dangling from the brick-vaulted ceiling.

Ristorante Beccofino (☎ 055 29 00 76; Piazza degli Scarlatti 1r; mains around €20) This stylish place has a very contemporary, trendy feel to it, and an innovative menu. Prices are quite high.

Top End
BETWEEN THE DUOMO & THE ARNO (Map p84)
Caffè Concerto Paszkowski (☎ 055 21 02 36; Piazza della Repubblica 6r; ☽ 7-2am Tue-Sun) More than 150 years old, this is one of the class café acts of the city. The interior alone is worth the trip, even if it's a little out of your way. It makes a stylish way to start the day. Pizzas are reasonably priced at around €12.

Giubbe Rosse (☎ 055 21 22 80; Piazza della Repubblica 13-14r; ☽ 8-2am) The early-20th-century Futurist artistic movement, although it didn't make as big an impact in Florence as elsewhere in Italy, nevertheless had its following – and this is where its die-hard members used to drink and debate. Inside, long vaulted halls lined with old photos, sketches and artwork make a great place for coffee over a newspaper – there are some hanging up for the customers' use.

SANTA CROCE & EAST OF THE CENTRE
Ristorante Cibrèo (Map p80; ☎ 055 234 11 00; Via de' Macci 118; meals around €60; ☽ Tue-Sat) Famous

---

GREAT GELATO
Once you've tasted real Italian *gelato*, you'll never touch the supermarket stuff again. *Gelato* can cost anything from €2 for a *coppetta* (small cup) to around €6 for a *cono* (massive cone). Florentines, like other Italians, like to round off the evening with a *gelato* while taking a leisurely stroll around town, and most *gelaterie* are open till late. Below are a few suggestions.

Gelateria Vivoli (Map pp82-83; ☎ 055 29 23 34; Via dell'Isola delle Stinche 7; ☽ 9-1am Tue-Sat) People queue outside this place, near Via Ghibellina, to delight in the *gelato* widely considered the city's best.

Vestri (Map p80; ☎ 055 234 03 74; Borgo degli Albizi 11r; ☽ Mon-Sat) This little place specialises in truly indulgent chocolate *gelato*, in a variety of combinations including cinnamon, orange and pistacchio.

Perchè No? (Map p84; ☎ 055 239 89 69; Via dei Tavolini 19r; ☽ Wed-Sun) This *gelateria*, off Via de' Calzaiuoli, has been operating since the 1930s, and is one of the city's best.

Carabè (Map pp78-79; ☎ 055 28 94 76; Via Ricasoli 60r; ☽ Thu-Tue) This family-run *gelateria* offers traditional Sicilian *gelato* and *granita* (sorbet).

Baroncini (☎ 055 48 91 85; Via Celso 3r; ☽ Thu-Tue) If you happen to be in the area, drop in to one of the best-known *gelaterie* in town. It also has a big range of sorbets.

---

in Florence and beyond, this is one of the city's most fashionable restaurants, with prices to match. Reservations are essential.

Self-Catering
You can save money by getting your own groceries from small shops, produce markets and small supermarkets, and throwing your own sandwiches and the like together.

Standa (Map p80; ☎ 055 234 78 56; Via Pietrapiana 4r) This is a handy central supermarket which is open from 8.30am to 9pm Monday to Saturday. There are also other branches around the city.

ENTERTAINMENT
Several publications list the theatrical and musical events and festivals held in the city and surrounding areas. The free, bimonthly *Florence Today*, the monthly *Firenze Information* and *Firenze Avvenimenti*, a monthly

brochure distributed by the council, are all available (sporadically) at the tourist offices. *Firenze Spettacolo*, the city's definitive entertainment publication, is available monthly at newsstands.

A handy centralised ticket outlet is **Box Office** (Map pp78-79; ☎ 055 21 08 04; Via Luigi Alamanni 39). Web ticket service **Ticket One** (www.ticketone.it – Italian only) allows you to book tickets for theatre, football and other events on the Internet.

Pubs & Bars

Astor Caffè (Map p84; ☎ 055 239 90 00; Piazza del Duomo 20r; ☽ 10-3am) You can take breakfast here if you will but the nocturnal folk gather around for loud music and cocktails both inside and out, right by the solemn walls of the Duomo. Live music features nightly.

Capocaccia (Map p84; ☎ 055 21 07 51; Lungarno Corsini 12/14r; ☽ noon-1am Tue-Sun) The beautiful people of Florence gather here, especially on balmy spring and summer evenings, for a riverside nibble and cocktail before heading on to dinner and clubs.

Caffè Gilli (Map p84; ☎ 055 21 38 96; Piazza della Repubblica 39r; ☽ 8-1am Wed-Mon) This is one of the city's finest cafés, elegantly decorated with Art Nouveau ceiling frescoes. Prices are very reasonable if you stand at the bar as the locals do.

The William (Map p80; ☎ 055 263 83 57; Via Magliabechi 7r; ☽ noon-1am) This is a loud English-style pub offering a selection of beers, which has found quite a following among young Florentines. Light meals are also served.

Rex Caffè (Map p80; ☎ 055 248 03 31; Via Fiesolana 25r; ☽ 5pm-1.30am, closed Jun-Aug) A hugely popular bar, this is a hip place to sip your favourite cocktail. The garishly decorated interior is certainly eye-catching. DJs perform at weekends.

Cabiria (Map pp82-83; ☎ 055 21 57 32; Piazza Santo Spirito 4r; ☽ 11-2am Wed-Mon) This popular café by day converts into a busy music bar by night. In summer the buzz extends on to Piazza Santo Spirito, which becomes a stage for an outdoor bar and regular free concerts.

La Dolce Vita (Map pp82-83; ☎ 055 28 45 95; Piazza del Carmine 6r; ☽ 11-2am) Just a piazza away from Santo Spirito, this small place attracts a young trendy crowd in the evenings, though at other times it's a quiet spot to enjoy an outdoor coffee or cocktail.

Zoe (Map pp82-83; ☎ 055 24 31 11; Via dei Renai 13r; ☽ 8.30-1am Mon-Sat) This narrow, and very red, bar heaves with young locals in the evenings. Thursday is 'fusion food & DJ night' (5pm to 11pm; €5), when it gets even more crowded than usual.

Negroni (Map pp82-83; ☎ 055 24 36 47; Via dei Renai 17r; ☽ 8-2am) A smart little place to hang out with a coffee or a cocktail. It also serves an inexpensive lunchtime buffet.

Cheers Pub (Map pp82-83; ☎ 055 24 58 29; Via dei Renai 27; ☽ 11-2am) In this small and seemingly always full British-style pub 'Happy Hour' is from 4pm to 9pm, when beer and cocktails cost €3.

Live Music

Some of the bigger venues are well outside the town centre. Depending on who is playing at these venues, admission costs from nothing to €20. Then the drinks will cost you on top of that – at least €5 for a beer. Note that many places close for the summer.

Jazz Club (Map p81; ☎ 055 247 97 00; Via Nuova de' Caccini 3; admission €6; ☽ 9.30pm-1.30am Tue-Fri, closed Jun-Sep) This is one of Florence's top jazz venues, in an atmospheric vaulted basement, with live music nightly.

Tenax (Map p75; ☎ 055 30 81 60; Via Pratese 46; ☽ 10.30pm-4am Tue-Sun, closed May-Sep) Florence's biggest venue for live bands, this place is well out to the northwest of town. Admission cost varies according to the act. Take bus No 29 or 30 from Stazione di Santa Maria Novella.

Auditorium Flog (Map pp76-77; ☎ 055 49 04 37; Via M Mercati 24b; ☽ 10pm-4am) Another venue for local bands, this place is in the Rifredi area, also north of the centre but a little closer than Tenax. It's not as big as Tenax but has a reasonable stage and dance area. Bus No 8 or 14 from the train station gets you here.

Discos/Clubs

Central Park (Map pp78-79; ☎ 055 35 35 05; Via Fosso Macinante 2; admission incl 1st drink €20; ☽ 11pm-4am Tue-Sat) This is one of the city's most popular clubs, with five dance floors and a different style of music each night, ranging from Latin and pop through to house.

Meccanò (Map pp78-79; ☎ 055 331 33 71; Viale degli Olmi; admission incl 1st drink €15; ☽ 11pm-4am Tue-Sat) Three dance spaces offer house, funk and mainstream commercial music to appeal to a fairly broad range of tastes. Occasionally it puts on special theme nights.

YAB (Map p84; ☎ 055 21 51 60; Via Sassetti 5r; admission €15; ☽ 9pm-4am Wed-Mon) One of the city's more established clubs, popular with local students and playing a variety of styles of music, with a particular fondness for hip-hop.

Classical Music & Opera

Teatro Comunale (Map pp78-79; ☎ 055 277 92 36; Corso Italia 16) Concerts, opera and dance are performed at various times of the year here. In May and June the theatre hosts Maggio Musicale Fiorentina, an international concert festival. Contact the theatre's box office for details.

Teatro Verdi (Map p80; ☎ 055 21 23 20; www.teatroverdifirenze.it; Via Ghibellina 99) There are seasons of drama, opera, concerts, musicals and dance here from January to April and October to December.

Teatro della Pergola (Map p81; ☎ 055 226 43 35; Via della Pergola 18) This theatre puts on a varied programme of opera and drama, with plays by writers as diverse as Pirandello, Pinter and Chekov.

In summer especially, concerts of chamber music are held in churches across the city. Keep an eye out for programmes of the Orchestra da Camera Fiorentina (Florentine Chamber Orchestra), whose performance season runs from March to October.

Cinemas

You have a few venue choices for seeing movies in the *versione originale* (original language). This generally means movies in English with Italian subtitles. At most cinemas there are three or four sessions a day; the latest starts between 10pm and 10.45pm. Wednesday is cheap day, when tickets cost around €4.60. Normally they go for around €7.50.

Odeon Cinehall (Map p84; ☎ 055 21 40 68; Piazza Strozzi) This is the main location for seeing subtitled movies, screened on Mondays and Tuesdays.

Cinema Fulgor (Map pp78-79; ☎ 055 238 18 81; Via Maso Finiguerra 22r) Here they screen movies in English on Thursday nights.

The British Institute of Florence shows movies in English at 6pm on Wednesdays at its **library** (☎ 055 267 78 270; Via de' Guicciardini 9). Admission costs €7.75 for nonmembers.

Yearly, from mid-June to September, several venues feature outdoor cinemas;

programmes available from tourist offices. Among them are **Chiardiluna** (Map pp82-83; ☎ 055 233 70 42; Via Monte Uliveto 1) and **Cinema Poggetto** (Map p76-77; ☎ 055 48 12 85; Via M Mercati 24b).

Theatre & Dance

The theatre season kicks off in October and continues into April/May. Which is not to say Florence then comes to a standstill, but many of the main stages stay quiet while more-festive cultural events take centre billing.

Ex-Stazione Leopolda (Map pp78-79; ☎ 055 247 83 32; Viale Fratelli Rosselli 5) One of the council's smarter ideas some years back was to convert this former train station (near Le Cascine) into a performance space – in fact several spaces. Theatre, most of it of an avant-garde nature, is frequently the star, although occasionally concerts are put on here too. For programmes and tickets it is easiest to go to Box Office (see p121) or any of the tourist offices in Florence.

The theatres mentioned above also frequently stage drama. You will find productions at these, and several other smaller theatres dotted about town, advertised in *Firenze Spettacolo*. As expected, most theatre is in Italian.

Teatro della Limonaia (Map p75; ☎ 055 44 08 52; Via Gramsci 426; Sesto Fiorentino) One of the leading avant-garde theatres in Italy is this place well beyond the centre of Florence (take bus No 28A or 28C).

Spectator Sports

FOOTBALL (SOCCER)

After premier league AC Fiorentina was relegated to the fourth division in 2002, it dissolved amid mounting debts and transformed into Florentia Viola (www.florentiaviola.it – Italian only). Florence's new football team has a strong following and has already lifted itself into the third division (Serie C1); the fans believe the only way is up.

If you want to see a match, tickets, which cost between €7 and €45, are available at **Stadio Comunale Artemio Franchi** (Map pp76-77; ☎ 055 262 55 37; Campo di Marte) or at **Chiosco degli Sportivi** ticket outlet (Map 84; ☎ 055 29 23 63; Via Anselmi, just off Piazza della Repubblica; ☽ 9am-1pm & 3-6pm Mon & Tue & Thu, 9am-7.30pm Wed, 9am-7pm Fri, 9am-1pm & 3-8pm Sat, 10am-12.30pm Sun).

You can also book tickets through Box Office or Ticket One (see p121 for details).

SHOPPING

It is said that Milan has the best clothes and Rome the best shoes, but Florence without doubt has the greatest variety of goods to choose from. The main shopping area is between the Duomo and the Arno, with boutiques concentrated along Via Roma, Via de' Calzaiuoli and Via Por Santa Maria, leading to the goldsmiths lining Ponte Vecchio. Via de' Tornabuoni is where the top designers, including Gucci, Armani and Trussardi, sell their wares.

There are two massive designer-clothes wholesale stores in the Tuscan countryside. The savings can be considerable, though don't expect huge bargains. Some tour companies organise coach trips to these outlets (see p112).

The Mall (☎ 055 865 77 75; Via Europa 8; ☺ 9am-6pm Mon-Sat, 1-6pm Sun) This enormous outlet for Gucci, Armani and others, is on the SS67 highway at the northern edge of Leccio, about 30 to 40 minutes southeast of Florence on the road to Arezzo.

Prada (☎ 055 919 05 80; ☺ 9.30am-12.30pm & 1.30-6pm Mon-Fri, 9.30am-7pm Sat, 4-7pm Sun) This outlet, which has the elegance of a high-street store with taxis waiting and a café, is just outside the village of Levanella, about another 30 minutes' drive down the same road from Leccio towards Arezzo. The quickest way from Florence by car is to take the A1 motorway, leave at the Valdarno exit and follow the signs for Montevarchi.

Should you prefer to shop for fashion without leaving Florence, a few classic starting points, all on Map p84, include:

Gucci (☎ 055 26 40 11; Via de' Tornabuoni 73r) This boutique is the oeuvre of one of the most successful families in Florentine-born fashion. Of course the soap-opera family saga has put a lot of spice into the name, but the fashion-conscious take little notice and keep on buying.

Ferragamo (☎ 055 29 21 23; Via de' Tornabuoni 16r) Another grand Florentine name, the one-time shoe specialists now turns out a range of clothes and accessories for the serious fashion aficionado. It also has a curious shoe museum – see p98.

House of Florence (☎ 055 650 53 34; Via de' Tornabuoni 6) This rather snooty boutique sells a range of conservative handmade accessories such as bags, scarves and ties.

Pucci (☎ 055 21 21 72; Via de' Tornabuoni 20/22r) The swirly, psychedelic patterns of Pucci's womenswear have been popular with the chic and wealthy since the 1950s.

Loretta Caponi (☎ 055 21 36 68; Piazza Antinori 4r) If nothing is too good for your infant or small child, particularly girls, this store sells exquisite small persons' clothing (and a

few things for big people too), some of it finely embroidered. Your three-year-old may not fully appreciate it, but will be dressed to impress.

If you are looking for labels without the snobbery, hunt around the so-called 'stockhouses' where designer wear is often on sale for affordable prices – if you cast around a little you will frequently find bargains. Try:

Stockhouse Il Giglio (Map pp78-79; ☎ 055 21 75 96; Borgo Ognissanti 86r) 'Cheap' is a relative term in Florence, but you can pick up some interesting men's and women's fashion items here and occasionally turn up some genuine bargains. Name labels can come in at a considerable discount. Florentines consider it one of the best 'stockhouses' for picking up labelled items at back-of-truck rates.

Stockhouse One Price (Map pp82-83; ☎ 055 28 46 74; Borgo Ognissanti 74r) Although more densely stocked (in a smaller space), this place is along similar lines to Stockhouse Il Giglio.

Leather and shoes are worth hunting out in Florence. You can try the markets (see p100) or some of the speciality stores, for instance:

Francesco da Firenze (Map pp82-83; ☎ 055 21 24 28; Via di Santo Spirito 62r) If only every shoemaker made shoes this way – hand-stitched leather is the cornerstone of this tiny family business. Expect to pay a fair amount for your footwear, but the investment will pay off. You can have shoes and sandals made to specification.

Scuola del Cuoio (Map p80; ☎ 055 24 45 33; Piazza di Santa Croce 16) If you get lucky you will see apprentices beavering away at some hide. Otherwise it is not a bad place to get some measure of quality–price ratios. When you arrive, access is either through the Basilica di Santa Croce or through an entrance behind the basilica at Via San Giuseppe 5r.

Il Bisonte (Map p84; ☎ 055 21 57 22; Via del Parione 31r) Here they concentrate on accessories, ranging from elegant bags in natural leather through to distinguished desktop items, leather-bound notebooks, briefcases and the like.

Florence is famous for its beautifully patterned paper, which is stocked in the many stationery and speciality shops throughout the city and at the markets.

Il Papiro (Map p84; ☎ 055 28 16 28; Piazza del Duomo 24r) One of six branches in Florence selling all manner of pretty paper and stationery.

Pineider (Map p84; ☎ 055 28 46 55; Piazza della Signoria 13r) This purveyor of paper and related products has been in business since 1774. It still sells a range of colourful stationery, but these days its other products, such as leather and glassware, dominate the store.

Officina Profumo-Farmaceutica di Santa Maria Novella (Map pp78-79; ☎ 055 21 62 76; Via della Scala 16) This venerable perfumery, established in 1612, is a Florentine institution, selling a range of high-quality, and high-priced, soaps, perfumes and lotions.

Mercato Centrale (central market; Map pp78-79; near Piazza del Mercato Centrale; ☽ Mon-Sat) This market offers leather goods, clothing and jewellery at low prices, but quality varies greatly. You could pick up the bargain of a lifetime, but check the item carefully before paying. It is possible to bargain, but not if you want to use a credit card.

Mercato dei Pulci (Map p84; flea market; off Borgo Allegri near Piazza dei Ciompi; ☽ Mon-Sat) Antiques and bric-a-brac are the speciality at this market.

GETTING THERE & AWAY
Air
Florence is served by two airports: Perè-tola, also known as **Amerigo Vespucci** (Map p75; ☎ 055 37 34 98), 5km northwest of the city centre at Via del Termine 11; and **Galileo Galilei** (☎ 050 50 07 07; www.pisa-airport.com), near Pisa and about an hour by train or car from Florence. Perètola caters for domestic and some European flights. Galileo Galilei is one of northern Italy's main international and domestic airports and has regular connections to London, Paris, Munich and major Italian cities.

Bus
The **SITA** (Map pp78-79; ☎ 055 4 78 21; www.sita-on-line.it – Italian only; Via Santa Caterina da Siena 15) bus station is just to the west of Piazza della Stazione. There is a direct, rapid service to/from Siena (€5.80, 1¼ hours) and buses leave here for Poggibonsi, where there are connecting buses for San Gimignano (€5.20, 1½ hours) and Colle di Val d'Elsa, where you change for Volterra (€6.20, 1¼ hours). Direct buses serve Arezzo, Castellina in Il Chianti, Faenza, Grosseto and other smaller cities throughout Tuscany.

Several bus companies, including **CAP** (Map pp78-79; ☎ 055 21 46 37) and **COPIT** (☎ 055 21 46 37), operate from Largo Alinari, at the southern end of Via Nazionale, with services to nearby towns including Prato (€2.20, 45 minutes) and Pistoia (€2.70, 50 minutes).

Lazzi (Map pp78-79; ☎ 055 21 55 55; www.lazzi.it; Piazza Stazione 3r), next to the Stazione di Santa Maria Novella, runs services to Rome, Pistoia and Lucca. Lazzi forms part of the Eurolines network of international bus services, running to destinations across Europe.

Car & Motorcycle
Florence is connected by the A1 to Bologna and Milan in the north and Rome and Naples in the south. The Autostrada del Mare (A11) connects Florence with Prato, Lucca, Pisa and the coast, and a *superstrada* (no tolls) joins the city to Siena. From the north on the A1, exit at Firenze Nord and then simply follow the bulls-eye 'centro' signs. If approaching from Rome, exit at Firenze Sud.

The more picturesque SS67 connects the city with Pisa to the west and Forlì and Ravenna to the east.

Train
Florence is on the Rome–Milan line, which means that most of the trains to/from Rome (€24.95, two hours), Bologna (€13.17, one hour) and Milan (€28.92, three hours 20 minutes) are Intercities or Eurostar Italia, for which you have to pay a supplement.

There are also regular trains to/from Venice (€26.60, three hours). For Verona you will generally need to change at Bologna. To get to Genoa and Turin, a change at Pisa is necessary.

The train information office (open 7am to 9pm) is in the main foyer at Stazione di Santa Maria Novella.

GETTING AROUND
To/From the Airports
There are no trains to Perètola airport. SITA and **Azienda Trasporti Area Fiorentina** (ATAF; ☎ 800 424500; www.ataf.net) run the 'Vola-in-Bus' shuttle bus service between the airport and Florence city centre. The bus runs every 30 minutes from outside Stazione di Santa Maria Novella to/from Perètola airport. The service from the airport runs from 6am to 11.30pm daily; from the train station the service runs from 5.30am to 11pm daily. The trip takes about 30 minutes. Tickets (€4) can be purchased on board or at the airport. From 8pm the service is hourly.

Regular trains leave from platform 5 at the *stazione* for Galileo Galilei Airport near Pisa. Check in your luggage 15 minutes before the train departs. Services are roughly hourly from 6.46am to 5pm, with a final service leaving at 11.07pm, from Florence and from 8.49am to 8.20pm from the airport. The trip takes 1½ hours and costs €4.85.

Bicycle

Cycling around Florence is one way to beat the traffic – though the cobbles may rattle your bones. **Florence By Bike** (Map p78-79; ☎ 055 48 89 92; www.florencebybike.it; Via San Zanobi 91r-120/122r) hires out a variety of bicycles. 'City bikes' cost €7 for five hours, €12 per day or €30.50 for three days. Mountain bikes go from €13 for five hours.

Bus

ATAF buses service the city centre, Fiesole and other areas in the city's periphery.

You'll find several main bus stops for most routes around Stazione di Santa Maria Novella. Some of the most useful lines operate from a stop just outside the southeastern exit of the train station below Piazza Adua. Buses leaving from here include: No 7 for Fiesole, No 13 for Piazzale Michelangelo and No 70 (night bus) for the Duomo and Uffizi.

A network of dinky little *bussini* (electric minibuses) operates around the centre of town. They can be handy for those getting tired of walking around or needing to backtrack right across town. Only Linea D operates 7am to 9pm daily. The others run 8am to 8pm Monday to Saturday. You can get a map of the routes published by ATAF from tourist offices.

Tickets cost €1 for one hour and €1.80 for three hours. A 24-hour ticket costs €4.50. A *biglietto multiplo* (four-ticket set, valid for one hour each) costs €3.90. You are supposed to stamp these in the machine when you get on your first bus. If you are hanging around Florence longer, you might want to invest in a *mensile* (monthly ticket) for €31 (€20.70 for students).

There is a special 30-day ticket (€14) for using the *bussini* (lines A to D) only.

Car & Motorcycle

Traffic is restricted in the city centre. A no-parking regime (except for residents) rules 7.30am to 6.30pm Monday to Friday. Nonresidents may only stop in the centre to drop off or pick up luggage from hotels or park in hotel or public garages (the latter will cost you a fortune).

There are several major car parks and numerous smaller parking areas around the fringes of the city centre; the most central is at Piazza della Stazione di Santa Maria Novella. If your car is towed away, call ☎ 055 783882 for the Depositeria Comunale (car pound; Map p75) at Ponte a Greve, which is some distance from the city centre. You will have to pay around €50 to recover it, plus whatever fine you are charged. Fines vary depending on the offence.

RENTAL

Several car-rental agencies cluster together in the Borgo Ognissanti area, all of which are on Map pp78-79, and include: **Avis** (☎ 055 21 36 29; Borgo Ognissanti 128r); **Europcar** (☎ 055 29 04 37; Borgo Ognissanti 53r); **Hertz** (Map pp82-83; ☎ 055 28 22 60; Via Maso Finiguerra 33r) and **Happy Rent** (☎ 055 239 96 96; Borgo Ognissanti 153r). Rates for small cars start at €52 per day.

Florence By Bike (Map pp78-79; ☎ 055 48 89 92; www.florencebybike.it; Via San Zanobi 91r-120/122r) hires out scooters and motorbikes, costing between €30 and €93 per day.

Taxi

Taxis can be found outside Stazione di Santa Maria Novella and several other ranks around town, or call ☎ 055 42 42, ☎ 055 47 98 or ☎ 055 43 90. The flagfall is €2.45, on top of which you pay €1 per kilometre within the city limits (€1.35 per kilometre beyond). There is a night-time (10pm to 6am) surcharge of €0.10. On public holidays you pay an extra €1.70. Each piece of luggage costs €0.55.

AROUND FLORENCE

One of the beauties of Florence, believe it or not, is leaving it behind. Whether it's just to check out less-visited towns to the north and west, to make a delicious lunchtime assault on the nearby towns of Fiesole and Settignano, or to explore the hilly wine region of Il Chianti to the south, there's no shortage of things to do. Public transport enables you to get to most places listed in this chapter without excessive difficulty, although you shouldn't be overly ambitious about how much you try to get done. With your own transport, you can, of course, see a lot more.

FLORENCE

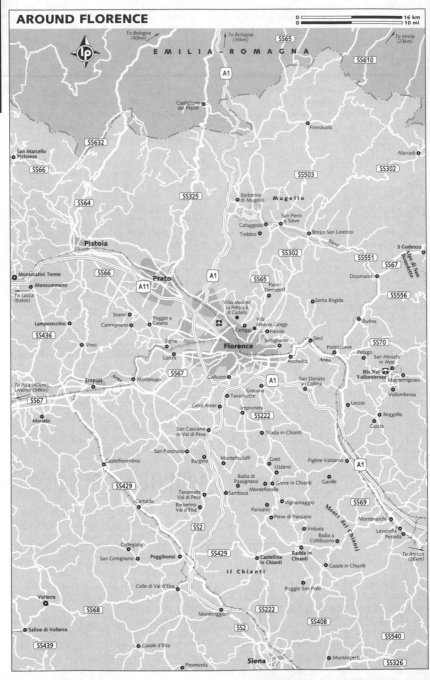

AROUND FLORENCE

PISTOIA

pop 83,500

A pleasant city at the foot of the Apennines and a half-hour northwest of Florence by train, Pistoia has grown beyond its well-preserved medieval ramparts and is today a world centre for the manufacture of trains. In the 16th century the city's metalworkers created the pistol, named after the city.

Orientation

Although spread out, the old city centre is easy to negotiate. From the train station in Piazza Dante Alighieri, head north along Via XX Settembre, through Piazza Treviso, and continue heading north to turn right into Via Cavour. Via Roma, branching off the northern side of Via Cavour, takes you to Piazza del Duomo and the tourist office.

Information

Hospital (Ospedale Riuniti; ☎ 0573 35 21; off Viale Giacomo Matteotti, behind the old Ospedale del Ceppo)

Police Station (☎ 0573 2 67 05; Via Macallè 23)

Post Office (Via Roma 5)

Tourist Office (☎ 0573 37 16 80; Piazza del Duomo; 🕑 9am-1pm & 3-6pm Mon-Sat)

Piazza del Duomo

Much of Pistoia's visual wealth is concentrated on this central square. The Pisan-Romanesque facade of the **Cattedrale di San Zeno** (☎ 0573 2 50 95; Piazza del Duomo; 🕑 8.30am-12.30pm & 3.30-7pm) boasts a lunette of the *Madonna col Bambino fra due Angeli* (Madonna and Child between two Angels) by Andrea della Robbia, who also made the terracotta tiles that line the barrel vault of the main porch. Inside, in the Cappella di San Jacopo, is the remarkable silver **Dossale di San Jacopo** (Altarpiece of St James; admission €2; 🕑 10am-noon & 4-7.30pm). Begun in the 13th century, artisans added to it over the ensuing two centuries until Brunelleschi contributed the final touch, the two half-figures on the left side. You can also climb the cathedral's Campanile (bell tower; adult/child €4/3; 🕑 10am-1pm & 2-6pm Sat-Mon) for splendid views of the town. It's by guided tour only and reservations must be made at the tourist office.

The venerable building between the cathedral and Via Roma is the **Antico Palazzo dei Vescovi** (Piazza del Duomo; admission €4; 🕑 10am-1pm & 3-5pm Tue & Thu & Fri, Oct-Jun). Guided tours four times a day take you through what little

remains of an original Roman-era structure on this site as well as displays of artefacts dating as far back as Etruscan times, which were discovered during restoration work. Reservations must be made through the tourist office.

Across Via Roma is the striking **battistero** (baptistry; admission free; 🕑 9.30am-12.30pm & 3.30-6pm). Elegantly banded in green-and-white marble, it was started in 1337 to a design by Andrea Pisano. The bare, red-brick interior is enlivened with an ornate square marble font.

Dominating the eastern flank of the piazza, the Gothic Palazzo del Comune houses the **Museo Civico** (☎ 0573 37 12 96; Piazza del Duomo 1; adult/child €3.10/1.55; 🕑 10am-7pm Tue-Sat, 9am-12.30pm Sun & holidays), with works by Tuscan artists from the 13th to 19th centuries.

The portico of the nearby **Ospedale del Ceppo** is worth seeking out for the incredibly detailed polychrome terracotta frieze by Santi Buglioni and Giovanni della Robbia. It depicts the *Virtù Teologali* (Theological Virtues) and the *Sette Opere di Misericordia* (Seven Works of Mercy) and is one of the best examples to come from the della Robbia family workshops. The medallions depict more conventional religious scenes, including a beautiful Annunciation.

Festivals & Events

For a weekend in mid-July Pistoia hosts **Pistoia Blues**, one of Italy's bigger music events. Check the website for ticket prices.

On 25 July Pistoia holds the so-called Joust of the Bear – Giostra dell'Orso – a grand medieval equestrian and jousting festival in the Piazza del Duomo in honour of the town's patron saint, San Giacomo.

Sleeping

Hotel Leon Bianco (☎ 0573 2 66 75; www.hotel leonbianco.it; Via Panciatichi 2; s/d €60/100; 🕸 🖵) This renovated 15th-century town house is right in the historical heart of town and offers spacious, comfortable rooms with all mod cons. If you show your Lonely Planet guide, you'll score a free breakfast!

Hotel Firenze (☎ 0573 2 31 41; www.hotel-firenze.it; Via Curtatone e Montanara 42; s/d €60/80; 🕸) Quiet, pleasant hotel in the centre of town, with small, cosy rooms. There's also one single and one double without private bathroom for €30 and €40.

FLORENCE

PISTOIA

0 _____ 1 km
0 _____ 0.5 mi

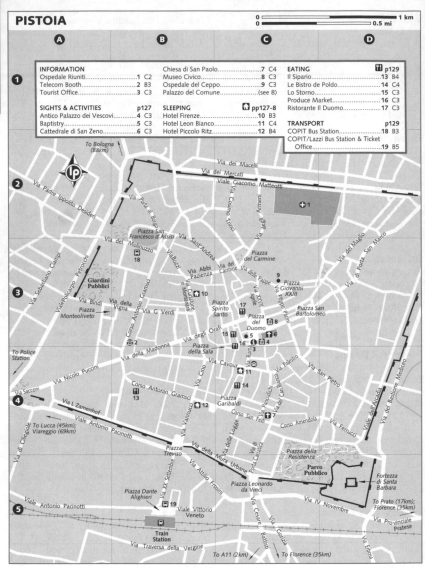

INFORMATION
Ospedale Riuniti.............................1 C2
Telecom Booth...............................2 B3
Tourist Office.................................3 C3

SIGHTS & ACTIVITIES p127
Antico Palazzo dei Vescovi............4 C3
Baptistry.......................................5 C3
Cattedrale di San Zeno.................6 C3

Chiesa di San Paolo.......................7 C4
Museo Civico.................................8 C3
Ospedale del Ceppo.......................9 C3
Palazzo del Comune.................(see 8)

SLEEPING pp127-8
Hotel Firenze...............................10 B3
Hotel Leon Bianco.........................11 C4
Hotel Piccolo Ritz.........................12 B4

EATING p129
Il Sipario.....................................13 B4
Le Bistro de Poldo........................14 C4
Lo Storno....................................15 C3
Produce Market...........................16 C3
Ristorante Il Duomo......................17 C3

TRANSPORT p129
COPIT Bus Station........................18 B3
COPIT/Lazzi Bus Station & Ticket
  Office......................................19 B5

Hotel Piccolo Ritz (☎ 0573 2 67 75; fax 0573 2 77 98; Via Vannucci 67; s/d €56/75; ⊠) Decent if unremarkable three-star, handy for the train station. All rooms have private bathroom.

Eating

Ristorante Il Duomo (☎ 0573 3 19 48; Via Bracciolini 5; meals from €12; ⊠ noon-3pm Mon-Sat) Try this

cheap, self-service buffet place for quick, filling meals.

Il Sipario (☎ 0573 3 33 30; Corso Antonio Gramsci 159; meals from €15; ⊠ closed Mon) Agreeable place specialising in traditional local fare, with live music and cabaret most nights.

Le Bistro de Poldo (☎ 0573 2 92 30; Via Panciatichi 4; meals from €13; ⊠ closed Wed & Thu lunchtime)

This place is situated on a quiet street in the centre, and serves up traditional Tuscan dishes.

Lo Storno (☎ 0573 2 61 93; Via del Lastrone 8; meals from €15; ✆ closed Sun & Mon evenings) If you are looking for something a little special but still affordable, try your luck here. An *osteria* of one sort or another has been documented on this site for the past 600 years! Today the chef prepares a continually changing array of dishes.

A **produce market** is open Monday to Saturday in Piazza della Sala, west of the cathedral.

Getting There & Around

Buses connect Pistoia with most towns in Tuscany. The main ticket office and bus station for COPIT and Lazzi buses is on the corner of Viale Vittorio Veneto and Via XX Settembre, near the train station. Buses for Florence (€3, 50 minutes) depart from Piazza Treviso, at the other end of Via XX Settembre. Other COPIT buses leave from Via del Molinuzzo, off Piazza San Francesco d'Assisi.

Trains connect Pistoia with Florence (€2.80, 40 minutes), Lucca (€3.20, 45 minutes) and Viareggio (€4.10, 1 hour). By car, the city is on the A11, as well as the SS64 and SS66, which head northeast for Bologna and northwest for Parma, respectively. Bus Nos 1, 3, 4 and 10 connect the train station with the town centre, although the city is easily explored on foot.

AROUND PISTOIA
Montecatini Terme & Around

The graceful little town of Montecatini Terme is one of Italy's foremost spa resorts, offering a wide range of health and beauty treatments. Verdi and Puccini found inspiration here, while Hollywood stars from Audrey Hepburn to Woody Allen have dropped by to unwind. These days it markets itself as the 'European Capital of Wellness', and is a pleasant place to spend a relaxing weekend, or longer if you want to partake of the spa programmes.

The **tourist office** (☎ 0572 77 22 44; Viale Verdi 66; ✆ 9am-12.30pm & 3-6pm Mon-Sat, 9am-noon Sun) has plenty of information on the town, including the guide *Liberty Seasons in Tuscany*, which includes a walking tour of Montecatini's rich Art Nouveau architecture. For more specifics on the *terme* (hot spring centres) and the various treatments available, try the **Terme di Montecatini information office** (☎ 0572 77 84 87; www.termemontecatini.it; Viale Verdi 41; ✆ 8am-noon & 3.30-6pm Mon-Fri, 8am-noon Sat).

Nine separate *terme* operate, many of them housed in grand Belle Époque buildings. They work from May to October, although services in some of the baths go on longer.

Excelsior's Centro di Benessere (Thermal Well-Being Centre; ☎ 0572 77 85 11; Viale Verdi; ✆ 8am-8pm Mon-Sat, 10am-8pm Sun) is the only one open year-round. The range of services, treatments and medical tests available is staggering – you could go for the two-day beauty programme and have a body and facial with mud and bath (€250), or indulge in a week of massages, manicures, face-packs and the like (€450). Alternatively, you could just get your eyebrows plucked (€5).

On the same road, the huge Art Nouveau complex of the **Terme Tettuccio** (€10.50) offers laxative waters, if you feel in need of purging. It has more than 400 toilets and beautiful gardens.

A pleasant distraction is the late-19th-century **funicolare** (funicular railway; ✆ 10am-1pm & 2pm-midnight daily, to 7.30pm March-Apr & Oct, every 30 mins; one way/return €3/5) uphill to Montecatini Alto, a pretty little village with great views of the surrounding countryside and several pleasant hotel and dining options. Although much fought-over, besieged and battered throughout the Middle Ages, the place retains an ancient, picturesque aspect, with several points of interest; look out for the 12th-century Chiesa di Santa Maria a Ripa with the bizarre, trophy-laden crucifix outside.

If you want to stay, try the well-appointed **Hotel Villa Gaia** (☎ 0572 7 86 37; www.villagaia.it; Via Mura P Grocco 11; d from €110) and ask for a room with a view.

Montecatini has more than 200 hotels, many of which offer half- and full-board as well as spa packages.

Hotel La Pia (☎ 0572 7 86 00; www.lapiahotel.it; Via Montebello 30; d from €56; ✆) is a friendly, family-run place with an excellent restaurant. Prices quoted are half-board, for stays of three days or more, and a range of spa packages are available.

Grand Hotel Plaza (☎ 0572 7 58 31; www.hotelplaza.it; Piazza del Popolo 7; s/d from €67/110; ✆ ✆) is a wonderfully atmospheric fin-de-siècle hotel, and past guests include Verdi, Rossini and Garibaldi. Half and full-board options are offered.

Apia (☎ 0572 7 56 61; www.apmmontecatini.it; Via delle Saline 88) is an agency that can find accommodation throughout the Pistoia province, and help organise wine tastings, cookery classes and suchlike. Those interested in *agriturismo* should contact **Turismo Verde** (☎ 0572 6 72 25 or 329 743 33 64; Molino delle Galere, Via Renaggio 12, Nievole; nievole@tin.it). The president, Giuseppe Mazzocchi, is an experienced chef who runs cookery classes (from €90) in an old mill in the nearby village of Nievole. Two- and three-day cooking courses and specialist courses, such as cooking with chocolate, are also offered. Large apartments at the mill cost €80 for two people.

One of the best places to eat is the stylish **La Cascina** (☎ 0572 7 84 74; Viale Guiseppe Verdi 43; mains around €15; ☽ Tue-Sun) set on the edge of the park. It also has a bar.

While in town, don't miss the opportunity to taste the local Cialde di Monticatini, large, round dessert wafers filled with crushed almonds. They are sold exclusively at **Bargilli** (☎ 0572 7 94 59; Viale Grocco 2; ☽ Tue-Sun); in summer the shop's open till midnight.

Montecatini Terme is on the train line between Lucca and Florence. Regular buses, running from the station next to the train station, service Florence (€3.50, 50 minutes), Pistoia, Lucca, Pescia, Monsummano (€1.35) and other nearby locations.

Monsummano

Diehard lovers of spa complexes could also wander over to Monsummano, a few kilometres away from Montecatini Terme by bus (€1.35). The main attraction is the **Grotta Giusti Terme** (☎ 0572 9 07 71; www.grottagiustispa.com; Via Grotta Giusti; ☽ 9am-1pm & 3-7pm Mon-Sat 21 Mar-8 Jan), just outside town. A vast range of treatments is on offer, from nasal irrigation (€20) to aromatherapy facials (€65) and full programmes of massages and baths. The bus goes right to the complex.

PRATO

pop 170,100

Virtually enclosed in the urban and industrial sprawl of Florence, Prato is one of Italy's main centres for textile production.

Founded by the Ligurians, the city fell to the Etruscans and later the Romans, and by the 11th century was an important centre for wool production. Today, it's a lively, down-to-earth provincial town, and while relatively few foreign tourists spend time here, it has a number of worthwhile sights and makes for a pleasant day trip from Florence.

Orientation

The old centre is small and is surrounded by the city wall. The main train station, on Piazza della Stazione, is to the east of the city centre.

Information

Hospital (Ospedale Misericordia e Dolce; ☎ 0574 43 41; Piazza dell'Ospedale) Southwest of Piazza del Comune.

Police Station (☎ 0574 55 55; Via Cino 10) Well out of the centre but there is a small station at Via B Cairoli 29.

Tourist Office (☎ 0574 2 41 12; Piazza Santa Maria delle Carceri 15; ☽ 9am-1.30pm & 2-7pm Mon-Sat) Two blocks east of Piazza del Comune.

Sights

MUSEO CIVICO

This **museum** (Piazza del Comune; closed for long-term restoration at the time of writing), with its small but impressive collection of largely Tuscan paintings, is housed in the imposing medieval Palazzo Pretorio. During the museum's restoration, part of its collection is on show at the Museo di Pittura Murale.

MUSEO DEL TESSUTO

The **textile museum** (☎ 0574 61 15 03; Via Santa Chiara 24; adult/child €4/2; ☽ 10am-6pm Wed-Mon) devotes itself to textiles through the ages. Unsurprisingly, the museum is slanted towards production and innovation aspects of local industry, but you'll also find examples of textiles (dating from as early as the 3rd century) from around Italy, Europe, and from as far afield as India, China and the Americas.

CATTEDRALE DI SANTO STEFANO

Head along Via Mazzoni from Piazza del Comune to the 12th-century **Cattedrale di Santo Stefano** (☎ 0574 2 62 34; Piazza del Duomo; ☽ 7am-noon & 3.30-7pm). The simple Pisan-Romanesque facade features a lunette by Andrea della Robbia and white-and-green marble banding. The most extraordinary element, however, is the oddly protruding **Pulpito della Sacra Cintola** jutting out over the

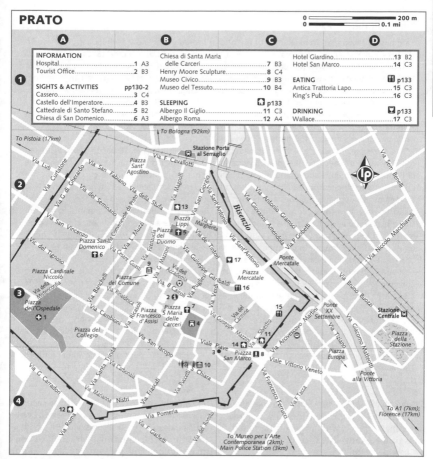

PRATO

0 ____ 200 m
0 ____ 0.1 mi

INFORMATION		
Hospital	1	A3
Tourist Office	2	B3

SIGHTS & ACTIVITIES	pp130–2	
Cassero	3	C4
Castello dell'Imperatore	4	B3
Cattedrale di Santo Stefano	5	B2
Chiesa di San Domenico	6	A3

Chiesa di Santa Maria		
delle Carceri	7	B3
Henry Moore Sculpture	8	C4
Museo Civico	9	B3
Museo del Tessuto	10	B4

SLEEPING	p133	
Albergo Il Giglio	11	C3
Albergo Roma	12	A4

Hotel Giardino	13	B2
Hotel San Marco	14	C3

EATING	p133	
Antica Trattoria Lapo	15	C3
King's Pub	16	C3

DRINKING	p133	
Wallace	17	C3

piazza on the right-hand side of the main entrance. The original panels of the pulpit, adorned with playful *putti* and designed by Donatello and Michelozzo in the 1430s, are housed next door in the **Museo dell'Opera del Duomo** (☎ 0574 2 93 39; Piazza del Duomo; combined ticket incl Castello dell'Imperatore & Museo di Pittura Murale €5; 9.30am-12.30pm & 3-6.30pm, closed Tue & Sun afternoon). The pulpit was expressly added on so that the *sacra cintola* (sacred girdle) could be displayed to the populace on certain days during the year. It is believed the girdle was given to St Thomas by the Virgin, and brought to the city from Jerusalem after the Second Crusade.

The museum is also home to a sizable collection of paintings, including a few masterpieces by Filippo Lippi, Caravaggio, Bellini and Santi di Tito.

Filippo Lippi's magnificent frescoes behind the cathedral's high altar, depicting the lives of John the Baptist and St Stephen, have been under restoration since 2001, a process set to take several more years. However, guided tours on the scaffolding are available (10am, 11am, 4pm and 5pm Saturday, 10am and 11am Sunday; €8) and must be booked at the tourist office. Agnolo Gaddi's fresco cycle of the *Legend of the Holy Girdle* is in the chapel to the left of the entrance.

CHIESA DI SANTA MARIA DELLE CARCERI

Built by Giuliano da Sangallo towards the end of the 15th century, the interior of this

THE MERCHANT OF PRATO

'Fate has so willed that, from the day of my birth, I should never know a whole happy day…' So wrote one of Prato's most celebrated sons, Francesco di Marco Datini, in the 1390s.

Datini, to whom a statue was erected in the shadow of Palazzo Pretorio after his death in August 1410, was neither a war hero nor a great statesman. Nor was he a man of learning or an inventor. Born in 1335 to a poor innkeeper, Datini grew up to become a highly successful international merchant.

Although he never reached the dizzy heights of the great Florentine trading families, Datini carved out a respectable business empire for himself that stretched from Prato and Florence to Avignon, Barcelona and the Balearic Islands. Not bad for a 15-year-old boy who arrived in the Papal city of Avignon with 150 florins in his pocket.

Prato was (and remains) a town of shopkeepers and small businesses. Datini rose above this and by the time he returned from Avignon 33 years later, he was the richest man in town. For the people of Prato, this made him something of a hero. Basing himself principally in Florence, he traded in just about anything that looked likely to turn a profit, from cloth and raw materials to slaves and armaments, through his branches and agents in France, Spain, England and Flanders.

Datini knew how to have fun, and the stories of his sybaritic lifestyle and womanising demonstrate he was no aesthete. On the other hand, he worked like a slave himself, often sleeping no more than four hours a night. Only at the end of his life did he seem to give thought to things other than the accumulation of money. In his will he left all his wealth (after bequests) to a new charitable foundation established in his name in his fine house on Via Rinaldesca.

It is not so much Datini's financial exploits that make him interesting today, but his extensive correspondence. He spent long hours every day writing not only to his branches but to his wife Margherita and friends too. He was meticulous about keeping all mail that came to him and ordered his branch managers to do the same. His charity, the Ceppo di Francesco di Marco, has kept the archive of this correspondence in one piece for more than 500 years. It provides a rare glimpse not only into the business life of a late medieval trader, but also into the daily life of middle-class Tuscans, especially in Prato and Florence.

Iris Origo distilled this wealth of material into a fascinating account of medieval life entitled *The Merchant of Prato* (1957).

church (☎ 0574 2 79 33; Piazza Santa Maria delle Carceri; ⊙ 7am-noon & 4-7pm) is considered a Renaissance masterpiece, with a frieze and medallions of the Evangelists by the workshop of Andrea della Robbia.

Nearby is the **Castello dell'Imperatore** (☎ 0574 3 82 07; Piazza Santa Maria delle Carceri; €2, combined ticket incl Museo dell'Opera del Duomo & Museo di Pittura Murale €5; ⊙ 9am-1pm & 4-7pm Apr-Sep). It was begun, though never completed, in the 1240s on the orders of Frederick of Antioch, son of the Holy Roman Emperor Frederick II. It's basically an empty shell, but there are good views of the town from the battlements. Just down the road is the **Cassero** (Viale Piave; free; ⊙ 10am-1pm & 4-7pm Wed-Mon), a much-restored medieval covered passageway that originally allowed access from the castle to the city walls.

CHIESA DI SAN DOMENICO

The main reason for dropping into this church is to have a look at the **Museo di Pit-**

tura Murale (☎ 0574 44 05 01; Piazza San Domenico; combined ticket incl Museo dell'Opera del Duomo & Castello dell'Imperatore €5; ⊙ 10am-6pm Mon & Wed-Sat, 10am-1pm Sun). A collection of 14th- to 17th-century frescoes and preparatory sketches for frescoes, it is reached through the church's cloister. Artists represented include Uccello, Bernardo Daddi, Lorenzo Monaco and Filippo and Filippino Lippi.

CONTEMPORARY ART

Prato's most striking piece of modern art is Henry Moore's **sculpture** *Forma Squadrata con Taglio*, an eye-catching white monolith smack bang in the middle of Piazza San Marco. South of the city walls is the **Museo per l'Arte Contemporanea** (Viale della Repubblica 277; closed at the time of writing). Part of a centre devoted to contemporary art, its permanent collection, comprised mainly of paintings and sculptures, is complemented by temporary exhibitions and performances throughout the year.

Festivals & Events
Outside town in Poggio a Caiano and in various locations around Prato they have been celebrating the **Festival delle Colline** (Hill Festival) since 1979. The concert series brings together class acts of world music from late June to late July.

Sleeping
Hotel San Marco (☎ 0574 2 13 21; www.hotel-sanmarco.com; Piazza San Marco 48; s/d €60/90; ✿ ☐) Reasonable three-star option on a very busy piazza. The small, neat rooms all have double-glazed windows and refrigerators.

Hotel Giardino (☎ 0574 60 65 88; fax 0574 60 65 91; Via Magnolfi 2; s/d €78/110; ✿ ☐) Very central hotel right beside the cathedral, though the rather dated rooms are disappointing for this price.

Albergo Roma (☎ 0574 3 17 77; fax 0574 60 43 51; Via Carradori 1; s/d €52/60) This is the cheapest hotel option in town. The rooms are neat and clean but could do with a bit of modernising.

Albergo Il Giglio (☎ 0574 3 70 49; fax 0574 60 43 51; Piazza San Marco 14; s/d €41/58, with bathroom €60/72) The same people run this place, of similar standard.

Eating & Drinking
Piazza Mercatale, with its popular restaurants and lively atmosphere, is a good place to eat out.

Antica Trattoria Lapo (☎ 0574 2 37 45; Piazza Mercatale 141; meals from €18) For a relaxed, informal atmosphere and service with a personal touch, head here. The menu has plenty of Tuscan dishes but if you turn up too late, you'll probably have to queue.

King's Pub (☎ 0574 2 86 41; Via Garibaldi 148; pizzas from €4.70; ✿ closed Wed) Ever-popular pizza and pasta joint, also serving up a variety of salads.

Wallace (☎ 0574 44 20 03; Piazza Mercatale 24; ✿ 6pm-2.30am) Lively Scottish pub offering live music nightly, as well as various theme and party nights. It also serves pasta and other light dishes.

Getting There & Around
CAP and Lazzi buses operate regular services to Florence and Pistoia from in front of the train station, on Piazza della Stazione. Prato is on the Florence–Bologna and Florence–Lucca lines. It's quicker and cheaper

to Florence (€1.80, 25 minutes) by train. By car, take the A1 from Florence and exit at Calenzano, or the A11 and exit at Prato Est or Ovest. The SS325 connects Prato with Bologna. Several buses connect the train station with the town centre, generally terminating at Piazza San Domenico.

FIESOLE
Perched in hills about 8km northeast of Florence, between the valleys of the Arno and Mugnone rivers, Fiesole with its cool air and lush olive groves continues to entice visitors away from muggy Florence – the views of the city from here are spectacular. Fiesole was founded in the 7th century BC by the Etruscans and long remained the most important city in northern Etruria. It makes a fabulous spot for a picnic and a short walk, and there's even a little sightseeing to be done.

The **tourist office** (☎ 055 59 87 20; www.comune .fiesole.fi.it; Via Portigiani 3; ✿ 8am-6pm Mon-Sat, 10am-1pm & 2-6pm Sun Mar-Oct, 8am-5pm Mon-Sat, 10am-4pm Sun Nov-Feb) can assist with information about the town, accommodation, walks and other activities. Most other services – including a bank, an ATM and a post office – are located on the main square, Piazza Mino da Fiesole.

Sights
Overlooking the main square is the **cathedral** (☎ 055 59 95 66; Piazza della Cattedrale 1; ✿ 7.30am-noon & 3-6pm May-Oct, 7.30am-noon & 3-5pm Nov-Apr). Begun in the 11th century, it was heavily renovated in the 19th century. Inside, one of the main points of interest is the tabernacle over the main door, housing a glazed terracotta statue of San Romolo (St Romulus; 1521) by Giovanni della Robbia, though it's not easy to see in the gloom. Behind the cathedral is the tiny **Museo Bandini** (☎ 055 5 94 77; Via Duprè; admission incl Zona Archeologica €6.50; ✿ 10am-7pm daily May-Oct, 9am-5pm Wed-Mon Nov-Apr), featuring an impressive collection of early Tuscan Renaissance works, including Taddeo Gaddi's *Annunciazione* (Annunciation).

Opposite the entrance to the museum, the **Zona Archeologica** (Map p75; ☎ 055 5 91 18; Via Portigiana 27; admission incl Museo Bandini €6.50; ✿ 9.30am-7pm May-Oct, 9.30am-5pm Wed-Mon Nov-Apr) features a 1st-century-BC Roman theatre that is used from June to August for the **Estate Fiesolana**, a series of concerts and performances. Also in the complex are a small Etruscan temple and Roman baths. The archaeological museum is worth a look for its rich collection of Etruscan, Roman and Lombard artefacts.

For some of the best views of Florence take Via di San Francesco west from Piazza Mino da Fiesole. After a few hundred metres you'll come across a small park and the panoramic views.

Sleeping & Eating

Hotel Villa Aurora (☎ 055 5 91 00; www.aurora fiesole.com; Piazza Mino da Fiesole 39; s/d €98/140; ☒) A very pleasant 19th-century hotel on the main square. Rooms are smart and spacious, and those at the back have superb views over Florence. A terrace restaurant is attached (meals are around €17).

Hotel Villa Bonelli (☎ 055 5 95 13; www.hotel villabonelli.com; Via Poeti 1; s/d from €67/111; ☒) This friendly, family-run place has large, airy rooms with a rustic feel, and a wide terrace, in a peaceful location.

Pizzeria Etrusca (☎ 055 59 94 84; Piazza Mino da Fiesole 2; pizzas around €5.50) Popular spot on the main square for pizza and pasta, with outdoor seating under the trees.

Getting There & Away

Fiesole is easily reached from Florence. ATAF bus No 7 from the Stazione di Santa Maria Novella in Florence connects with Piazza Mino da Fiesole (one way €5.50), the centre of this small town. If you are driving, find your way to Piazza della Libertà, north of the cathedral, and then follow the signs to Fiesole.

SETTIGNANO

Just 6km east of Fiesole, along a delightful back-country lane, Settignano offers even more splendid views of Florence than Fiesole (but be sure to come in the morning, as by early afternoon all you can see is glare). It is a pleasant little *borgo* (ancient town) worth visiting for the dining opportunity alone.

La Capponcina (Map p75; ☎ 055 69 70 37; Via San Romano 17r; meals about €35; ☾ Tue-Sun) This is one of the city's better-known restaurants, up in the hills overlooking Florence to the northeast. The kitchen is known in particular for its *tagliata di manzo*, succulent beef fillets sliced up and served on a bed of rocket. Sitting in the garden is a true pleasure in summer; you are sure of being several degrees cooler than down in Florence.

Also worth a look while you're here is **Chiesa di Santa Maria**, with a pulpit by Buontalenti and a della Robbia Madonna.

You can get bus No 10 from the Stazione di Santa Maria Novella or Piazza San Marco in Florence (this service is replaced from 9pm by bus No 67). The restaurant is a few steps off the central Piazza San Tommaseo, where the bus terminates.

THE MEDICI VILLAS

The Medicis built several opulent villas in the countryside around Florence as their wealth and prosperity grew during the 15th and 16th centuries. Most of the villas are now enclosed by the city's suburbs and industrial sprawl, and are easily reached by taking ATAF buses from the train station. Bus No 28 runs to La Petraia and Castello, and No 14 goes to Careggi.

One of the finest is the **Villa Medicea La Petraia** (Map p75; ☎ 055 45 12 08; Via della Petraia 40; admission incl Villa Medicea di Castello €2; ☾ 8.15am-8pm daily Jun-Aug, closes earlier Sep-May & 1st & 3rd Mon of the month year-round). Acquired by Cardinal Ferdinando de' Medici in 1575, this former castle, about 3.5km north of the city, was converted by Buontalenti and features a magnificent garden with a fountain by Giambologna.

Further north of the city is the **Villa Medicea di Castello** (Map p75; ☎ 055 45 47 91; Via di Castello 47; admission incl Villa Medicea La Petraia €2; ☾ 8.15am-8pm daily Jun-Aug, closes earlier Sep-May & 1st & 3rd Mon of the month year-round). It was the summer home of Lorenzo the Magnificent. You may only visit the park.

The **Villa Medicea di Careggi** (Map p75; ☎ 055 427 97 55; Viale Pieraccini 17; free; ☾ 9am-6pm Mon-Fri, 9am-noon Sat, admission by advance reservation only) is where Lorenzo the Magnificent breathed his last in 1492. Access is limited as it is used as administration offices for the local hospital, although you're free to visit the gardens.

Another Medici getaway was the **Villa di Poggio a Caiano** (Map p126; ☎ 055 87 70 12; Piazza Medici 14; €2, grounds free; ☾ 9am-6.30pm Jun-Aug, 9am-5.30pm Apr, May & Sep, 8.15am-4.30pm Mar & Oct, 8.15am-3.30pm Nov-Feb, closed 2nd & 3rd Mon of the month). About 15km from Florence on the old road to Pistoia, and set in magnificent sprawling gardens, the interior of the villa is sumptuously decorated with frescoes and furnished much as it was early in the 20th century as a royal residence of the Savoys. Visits inside are permitted every hour. The easiest way here without your own transport is with the COPIT bus service running between Florence and Pistoia – there is a bus stop right outside the villa.

IL MUGELLO

The area northeast of Florence leading up to Firenzuola, near the border with Emilia-Romagna, is known as Il Mugello and features some of the most traditional villages in Tuscany. The Sieve River winds through the area and its valley is one of Tuscany's premier wine areas. It's also a great area for walks.

For information on the area contact the **Comunità Montana del Mugello** (☎ 055 84 52 71; Via P Togliatti 45).

The Medicis originated from Il Mugello and some of their family castles, villas and palaces are open to the public, while others can be visited with a guide.

Just outside Pratolino, the **Parco della Villa Medici-Demidoff** (☎ 055 276 04 19; €3; 🕙 10am-8pm Thu-Sun Apr-Sep, 10am-7pm Thu-Sun Mar-Oct) was the focal point of one of the Medici family's villas, which was demolished in 1824. The Demidoff family acquired the land and transformed the property into a fine romantic garden. If you keep following the SS65 for another 13km you will reach a turn-off (east) for **Trebbio** and, a few kilometres further on, another for **Cafaggiolo**, both sites of Medici villas. Visits are by appointment only; contact the **Associazione Turismo Ambiente** (☎ 055 845 87 93; Piazza Dante 29, Borgo San Lorenzo).

IL CHIANTI

When most people think of classic Tuscan countryside, the lush, vine-and-poppy-speckled hills and valleys spreading out between Florence and Siena in the Chianti

---

DETOUR: VALLOMBROSA

An interesting little excursion, most easily accomplished with your own transport, has as its prime objective the cool forest of **Vallombrosa** and the *abbazia* (abbey) of the same name.

Exiting Florence eastwards along the SS67 (follow the blue signs for Arezzo), you first strike a **Commonwealth war cemetery** (8am-4.30pm daily) half a kilometre short of **Anchetta**. It is sobering to stop here and think of the soldiers who died in and around Florence in 1944.

You follow the road to **Sieci**, the Romanesque church of which is accompanied by a graceful, slender bell tower. A detour 6km north (signposted) would take you up to the one-time Pazzi family's **Castello del Trebbio** (☎ 055 830 49 00; Via Montetrini 10), a typical 12th-century fortified rural outpost that now operates as an *agriturismo*. You can go horse riding here and/or stock up on wine.

Back on the SS67, you next pass through **Pontassieve**, a busy little town that is picturesquely set on the Sieve River. Shortly after, take the SS70 for a short distance, turning off for **Pelago**, which is perched high on a ledge overlooking farming valleys. From here it's another 12km to **Vallombrosa**. As you wind higher, the forest thickens with the fir trees planted over the centuries by the Vallombrosan monks and the air freshens noticeably.

The **abbey** (☎ 055 86 20 74; free; 🕙 9am-noon & 3-6pm) is almost 1000m above sea level. Back in the 11th century, San Giovanni Gualberto formed this branch of the Benedictine order in the midst of what no doubt was an even more impressive forest. The monks set themselves the task of wiping out simony and corruption in the Church in Florence and eventually the abbey came to play an important role in the city's politics. The monks were booted out by Napoleon and only returned in the 1950s. You can wander into the grounds at any time or join a guided tour at 10.30am Tuesday or Friday in July and August. And like many monasteries in Tuscany, you can purchase ointments and elixirs produced within the monastery at their Antica Farmacia.

The surrounding area is great for picnics and walks, including one up to **Monte Secchieta** (1449m). At the abbey and in **Saltino**, 2km further down the road, you will find a few restaurants and places to stay.

From here we follow the road south to **Reggello** and **Cascia** (which has a small Romanesque church) and finally on to **Figline Valdarno**. The centre of this town, once known as Florence's granary, has a few interesting buildings, including the 14th-century Palazzo Pretorio, the seat of local power. Much of the city wall and its towers still stand.

From Figline Valdarno, you can follow the SS69 back up to Florence.

region usually spring to mind. The region suffered severe economic hardship and depopulation in the post-war period, but from the 1960s, waves of sun-hungry foreigners – mostly British and German – began arriving, snapping up holiday homes or moving in permanently. In some areas, British ex-pats now make up almost a third of the population – no wonder it's sometimes referred to as 'Chiantishire'.

The area is split between the provinces of Florence and Siena, and conveniently named Chianti Fiorentino and Chianti Senese. Apart from gentle countryside, Il Chianti is home to some of the country's best-marketed wines. Of the wines the oldest, and most famous, is Chianti Classico. It is a blend of red grapes, with a minimum 75% Sangiovese, and sold under the Gallo Nero (Black Cockerel) symbol. The rest of Il Chianti is split into a further six classified wine-growing regions; Colli Fiorentini, Colli Senesi, Colline Pisane, Colli Aretini, Montalbano and Rùfina, all with their distinct characteristics. As well as these wines, look out for *vin santo*, a sweet, aged dessert wine akin to sherry, produced by many wineries. It is often enjoyed with *cantucci* biscuits.

It's possible to catch buses around the Chianti countryside, but the best way to explore the area is by car. However, you might also like to do it by bicycle, or even on foot. You could take a few days to travel along the state road SS222, known as the Via Chiantigiana, which runs between Florence and Siena.

Budget accommodation is not the area's strong point, and you'll need to book well ahead since it is a popular area for tourists year-round. If you do have the time, though, Il Chianti is a truly rewarding area to explore.

Getting information about the area is easy. Virtually every tourist office in Tuscany has good information, but the best is at Radda in Chianti. For information online check out www.chiantionline.com. For more details about the region's wines, and Tuscan wines in general, see p58.

Chianti Fiorentino
GREVE IN CHIANTI
About 20km south of Florence on the Via Chiantigiana is Greve in the Chianti region, a good base for exploring the area.

You can get there easily from Florence on a SITA bus (€2.90). The unusual triangular 'square', Piazza Matteotti, is the old centre of the town. An interesting provincial version of a Florentine piazza, it is surrounded by porticoes. At the centre stands a statue of local boy Giovanni da Verrazzano, who discovered New York harbour and gave his name to a bridge in that city.

The **tourist office** (☎ 055 854 62 87; Via Giovanni da Verrazzano 33; ⊙ 10am-1pm & 2.30-7pm Mon-Fri, 10am-1pm & 2.30-5pm Sat) is 500m north of the piazza. It can provide maps and information in several languages, including English. Also useful is **Chianti Slow Travel** (☎ 055 854 62 99; Via Giovanni da Verrazzano 59; www.chiantiechianti.it – Italian only), which can book accommodation and arrange visits to wineries in the region. For a superb selection of local meat – including the traditional *cinta senese* pork – try the **Antica Macelleria Falorni** (☎ 055 85 30 29; Piazza Matteotti 69-71; ⊙ Mon-Sat).

If you're looking for accommodation in Greve, try **Giovanni da Verrazzano** (☎ 055 85 31 89; www.verrazzano.it; Piazza Matteotti 28; s/d €77/89; 🛏). Some rooms overlook the main square. Around 5km south is **Villa Vinamaggio** (☎ 055 85 46 61; Via Petriolo 5; d from €150; 🛏 💻 🏊), an exquisite 15th-century manor house said to be the birthplace of Mona Lisa, and used in Kenneth Branagh's film *Much Ado About Nothing*. Fully equipped villas and cottages with huge bathrooms and Jacuzzis are available (€200 to €250). There's a great Italian garden, outdoor pool and tennis courts.

Wine *aficionados* shouldn't miss the **Cantine di Greve** (☎ 055 854 64 04; Piazza della Cantine; ⊙ 10am-7pm), the biggest *enoteca* in Il Chianti, which operates a unique tasting system. You buy a refundable credit card (€10, €15 or €20) to insert into the various dispensing machines, offering over 140 different wines, from €0.80 a sip. The website www.comune.greve-in-chianti.fi.it (Italian only) is a source of local information.

MONTEFIORALLE
This ancient castle-village, only 2km west of Greve, is worth the walk, particularly to see its church of Santo Stefano, which contains precious medieval paintings. From Montefioralle, follow the dirt road for a few hundred metres, then turn off to the right to reach the simple **Pieve di San Cresci**. From here you can descend directly to Greve.

BADIA DI PASSIGNANO

About 7km west, in a magnificent setting of olive groves and vineyards, is the mighty Badia di Passignano, founded in 1049 by Benedictine monks of the Vallombrosan order. The abbey is a massive, towered castle encircled by cypresses.

The abbey church of **San Michele** was not open to visitors at the time of writing. If the two resident monks do decide to open up in the future, you could view early-17th-century frescoes by Passignano (so called because he was born here) and, in the refectory, *Ultima Cena* (Last Supper; 1476) by Domenico and Davide Ghirlandaio. The excellent **Osteria di Passignano** (☎ 055 807 12 78; Via Passignano 33; ☻ Mon-Sat) serves a creative menu, made from local ingredients, with three-course meals around €36. There's also an extensive wine list. Tours of the wine cellars cost €10 and the Osteria runs one-day cookery classes for €110.

PANZANO

Travelling south along the Chiantigiana you will pass the quiet medieval village of Panzano. It's a pleasant place to stop; don't miss the **Antica Macelleria Cecchini** (☎ 055 85 20 20; Via XX Luglio; ☻ Thu-Tue), an atmospheric butcher's shop run by local celebrity Dario Cecchini, who welcomes his customers with wine, platters of meat and Dante recitals. About 1km further on, turn off for Chiesa di San Leolino at **Pieve di Panzano**. Built in the 10th century, it was rebuilt in the Romanesque style in the 13th century. From here you can continue on to Chianti Senese.

Chianti Senese

With lots of hotels and restaurants, **Castellina in Chianti** is one of the best-organised Chianti towns for tourists. Its **tourist office** (☎ 0577 74 23 11) is at the central Piazza del Comune 1 and opens 10am to 1pm and 3.30pm to 7.30pm daily (morning only Sunday). The **Albergo Squarcialupi** (☎ 0577 74 11 86; Via Ferruccio 26; d from €85; ☒ ☙) has large, airy rooms in an atmospheric 14th-century *palazzo*. For traditional Chianti fare, try **Antica Trattoria La Torre** (☎ 0577 74 02 36; Piazza del Comune; mains from €9).

More charming is **Radda in Chianti**, which is east of Castellina in Chianti. It makes a handy springboard to many of Chianti's most beautiful spots. **Da Giovannino** (☎ 0577 73 80 56; Via Roma 6-8; s/d €50/60) is a charming family-run hotel in the centre of town, complete with wood-beamed ceilings and views of the countryside. There's an excellent little restaurant attached. For an extensive selection of local wines and olive oil, try **Enoteca Toscana** (☎ 0577 73 88 45; Via Roma 29); they will be happy to advise you and offer free tastings.

The **information office** (☎ 0577 73 84 94; proradda@chiantinet.it; Piazza Castello; ☻ 10am-1pm & 3-7pm Mon-Sat, 10am-1pm Sun Mar-Oct, 10am-1pm Nov-Feb) can help with suggestions for independent walking or tours to wineries. **ChiantiMania** (☎ 0577 73 89 79; www.chiantimania.com; Via Trento e Trieste 12), run by the helpful Alessandra and Lorenzo, offers a wide variety of excursions, from wine-tasting tours (from €45) and guided walks (€35) to ballooning (€235 for 3½-hour trip), and also arranges accommodation around the region. For a taste of rustic charm, you could try the four-star **Hotel Villa la Grotta** (☎ 0577 74 71 25; www.hotelvillalagrotta.it; d €230-325; ☒ ☙), a remote but luxurious place around 15km to the southeast of Radda.

For cooking courses in this area, you might consider trying the highly respected **Badia a Coltibuono** (☎ 0577 74 48 32; www.coltibuono.com), around 7km east of Radda, which offers four day/three night residential courses from €1200 and day courses for €148 (groups of six or more). Six-day/five-night courses go from €3300. If you just want to eat, it has an excellent restaurant on site, and the *menu di degustazione* (set menu) is €49.

Radda also makes a good base for exploring some of the best wineries in the area, including **Volpaia** (☎ 0577 73 80 66; www.volpaia.com; from €11 guided tour & tasting), around 6km to the north, a tiny village of 44 inhabitants, most of whom work in the winery. Tours of the cellars and olive-oil facility, and wine tasting are by appointment. It also has luxury apartments to let, with shared pool, for €903 per week.

GETTING THERE & AWAY

Buses connect Florence (€3.40, 1¾ hours) and Siena (€2.70), passing through Castellina and Radda, as well as other small towns. Chianti Senese is a much easier destination to get to from Siena than from Florence.

Florence to the Val d'Elsa

Another route south from Florence could start from the Certosa di Galluzzo (see p109). You could take the SS2 *superstrada* that

DETOUR: IL CHIANTI

Il Chianti is one of the most attractive and rewarding regions of Tuscany, but to appreciate it fully you need your own transport. From Greve in Chianti, take the SS222 – also known as the Via Chiantigina – southwards for roughly 1km, at which point you will see a local road on your right. Take this road, leading in a southeasterly direction through typical Chianti countryside of olive trees and vines, and after about 2km you will come upon Villa Vinamaggio. You can stop for a bite to eat and stock up on some wine. Continue eastwards, and after another 2km the road turns south and passes through the pretty village of Lamole, famous for its *vin santo*. Just over 2km further south, the road meets the SP118; turn eastwards (the road now becomes the SP112) and continue on this road as it turns south to the tiny village of Volpaia, with wonderful views of the surrounding countryside. The winery here is particularly good, and you can take a tour of the cellars and try some of the products.

From here, it's a 3km journey south along the SP112, passing vineyards and fields full of poppies along the way, to Lo Spiccio. Take the secondary road to the east, which after a little over 1km, joins the SS429. If you like, you can then double-back southwestwards for about 500m to visit Radda. Otherwise, continue travelling east on the SS429 for around 6km, at which point you will see a secondary road to the north, which soon leads to the remote and beautiful Badia a Coltibuono, which has an excellent restaurant and a shop selling the property's wine.

connects Florence with Siena, or the more tortuous and winding road that runs alongside it. Follow the latter to **Tavarnuzze**, where you could make a detour for **Impruneta**, about 8km southeast.

Impruneta is famed for its production of terracotta – from roof tiles to imaginative garden decorations. The centre of town is Piazza Buondelmonti. Not the most fascinating of Chianti towns, it has been around since the 8th century. Its importance historically was due above all to an image of the Madonna dell'Impruneta, supposedly miraculous, now housed in the Basilica di Santa Maria which looks onto the piazza.

Back at Tavarnuzze, you head south towards **San Casciano in Val di Pesa**. An important wine centre, the town came under Florentine control in the 13th century and was later equipped with a defensive wall, parts of which remain intact. The town centre itself is not overly interesting, however, so you could drink in the views and hit the road again. Before reaching San Casciano, you pass the **US war cemetery** (free; ☺ 8am-6pm mid-Apr–Sep, 8am-5pm Oct–mid-Apr), where the clean rows of white crosses are a powerful reminder of the carnage of WWII.

Just before Bargino, take the side road east for **Montefiridolfi**. It's one of those charming little detours that takes you winding up onto a high ridge through vineyards and olive groves. Along the way you pass the **Castello di Bibbione** (☎ 0545 824 92 31; www.castellodibibbione.com), a picturesque stone manor house, once owned by Niccolò Machiavelli. Two nights' accommodation for two here will cost from €550, and longer stays are possible. Another 1.5km brings you to a large Etruscan tomb. You can keep going until you hit a crossroads. From there turn west for **Tavarnelle Val di Pesa**, from where you can reach the charming little medieval borgo of **Barberino Val d'Elsa**, which is worth a stop for a brief stroll along the main street.

At Tavarnelle you have the option of staying at a modern youth hostel, the **Ostello del Chianti** (☎ 055 807 70 09; Via Roma 137; dm €12.50, incl breakfast €16; ☺ Mar-end Oct). It also has family rooms, and you can get main meals for €8.

Heading directly south from Barberino would take you to Poggibonsi, where you can make bus connections for San Gimignano (see p206). Some of the spots indicated above can be reached by bus (especially with the SITA company) from Florence, but progress can be painfully slow this way.

Certaldo

About 15km west of Barberino lies this pretty hilltop town, well worth the effort of a detour, although this move takes you out of Chianti territory. The upper town (Certaldo Alto) has Etruscan origins, while the lower town in the valley sprang up in the 13th century – by which time both had been absorbed into the Florentine republic.

The upper town was the seat of the Boccaccio family. Giovanni Boccaccio died and was buried here in 1375. Along the main street you can visit the largely reconstructed version of **Boccaccio's house** (☎ 0571 66 42 08; Via Boccaccio; €3.10; ☿ 10am-7pm May-Sept, 10.30am-4.30pm Oct-Apr, closed Tue). It was severely damaged in WWII. The library inside contains several precious copies of Boccaccio's Decameron, but there's little else directly linked with him. A couple of doors up, Chiesa di SS Jacopo e Filippo contains a cenotaph to the writer; his remains were disinterred and scattered in 1783 by townspeople who considered the poet's work scandalous.

The whole of the upper, walled *borgo* is commanded by the stout figure of **Palazzo Pretorio** (☎ 0571 66 12 19; €3; ☿ 9.30am-1pm & 2-7.30pm), the seat of power whose 14th-century facade is very richly decorated with family coats of arms. Frescoed halls lead off the Renaissance courtyard.

The steep climb to the upper town can easily be avoided using the *funicolare* (funicular railway; return €1), departing from Piazza Boccaccio in the new town.

An attractive place to stay in Certaldo Alto is **Albergo Il Castello** (☎ 0571 66 82 50; www.albergoilcastello.it; Via della Rena 6; s/d €60/100; ⊠), a charming old mansion with an attractive garden and cosy rooms; breakfast is included. Half-board is available for stays of three nights or more.

See Lonely Planet's *Walking in Italy* for details of a three-day walk from Certaldo to San Gimignano and on to Volterra.

WEST OF FLORENCE

West of Florence and south of Pistoia (see p127) lie several towns of secondary interest. If time is on your side you could include them in a trip between Pistoia and Florence. There is little reason to stay in any of these places, but all have hotels if you get stuck.

If you plan to visit a few museums in the area consider buying a joint €6 ticket that allows entry to Museo Leonardiano in Vinci, Museo della Collegiata di Empoli and Museo Archeologico e della Ceramica in Montelupo.

Vinci & Around

From Pistoia a small country road (the SP13) leads south towards Empoli. After a long series of winding curves through the forested high country of Monte Albano, you come across a sign pointing left to the **Casa di Leonardo** (Leonardo's House; Via di Anchiano 36; free; ☿ 9.30am-7pm Mar-Oct, 9.30am-6pm Nov-Feb) in **Anchiano**. It's about 1km up the hill. Here, it is believed, Leonardo da Vinci was born the bastard child of a Florentine solicitor, Piero, but there isn't a whole lot to see.

Back down on the SP13, you are about 1.5km short of arriving in Vinci itself. The **tourist office** (☎ 0571 56 80 12; Via della Torre 11; ☿ 10am-7pm) is near the commanding **Castello dei Conti Guidi**, named after the feudal family that ruled this town and the surrounding area until Florence took control in the 13th century. Inside the castle is the **Museo Leonardiano** (☎ 0571 5 60 55; adult/child €5/2; ☿ 9.30am-7pm Mar-Oct, 9.30am-6pm Nov-Feb), which contains an intriguing set of more than 50 models based on Leonardo's far-sighted designs, including a mirror-polishing machine, underwater breathing apparatus and a strikingly modern-looking bicycle. Down below the castle is the **Museo Ideale Leonardo da Vinci** (☎ 0571 5 62 96; Via Montalbano 2; adult/child €5/3.50; ☿ 10am-1pm & 3-7pm), a private competitor to the museum listed earlier, with a reasonably diverting collection of models, prints and documents.

Lazzi buses run regularly between Empoli and Vinci (€1.90, 30 minutes). To get to/from Pistoia you need to change at Crocifisso for the Pistoia–Lamporecchio bus. The drive from Pistoia is lovely, as indeed is the ride between Poggio a Caiano (see p134) and Vinci via the wine centre of **Carmignano**, famous for its DOCG wines. The Carmignano wine was first documented in 1396, so, unsurprisingly, the area reeks of history. The tourist office in Prato has information and maps pinpointing wineries in the area, if you wish to go on a tasting tour.

Empoli

From Vinci you can head south to Empoli, a pleasant, sleepy town, with a few points of interest. The Romanesque white-and-green-marble facade of the **Collegiata di Sant'Andrea** in Piazza Uberti is testimony that the medieval settlement that emerged from a place called Emporium must have been of some importance. Next door is the **Museo della Collegiata di Empoli** (☎ 0571 7 62 84; Piazza Uberti; adult/child €3/1; ☿ 9am-noon & 4-7pm Tue-Sun), which houses religious works, by Tuscan artists, dating from the 14th to the 16th centuries, including Lorenzo Monaco and Masolino.

On the western edge of town rises the somewhat worn profile of the 12th-century **Chiesa di Santa Maria a Ripa**. The original town, documented in the 8th century, lay here.

A regular Lazzi bus connects Vinci and Empoli. From Florence take the train (€4.50, 40 minutes), which is quicker and cheaper than the bus.

Montelupo

A short hop from Empoli by train (in the direction of Florence) is Montelupo, a market town on the confluence of the Arno and Pesa. The town has been a well-known centre of Tuscan ceramics production since medieval times and there is no shortage of shops here in which to browse or part with money.

Inspect the **Museo Archeologico e della Ceramica** (☎ 0571 5 13 52; Via Baccio da Montelupo 43; €3; ☼ 9am-noon & 2.30-7pm Tue-Sun), housed in the 14th-century Palazzo del Podestà opposite the tourist office. Examples of pottery from prehistoric times right up to the 18th century are displayed.

Across the Pesa stream, the Medici villa known as the **Ambrogiana**, and built for Ferdinando I, is now used as a psychiatric hospital which cannot be visited by travellers.

In the third week of every month, a pottery market is held in an exposition centre in Corso Garibaldi. In the last week of June Montelupo hosts an international pottery fair, which might be a good time for ceramics fans to turn up for a day.

To get to Florence the best bet is the train (€2.10, 25 minutes).

Northwestern Tuscany

CONTENTS

Aside from Pisa's seriously disorientated tower, tourists tend to ignore northwestern Tuscany en route to the equally grand-slam sights in Florence and Siena. It's a shame, as there is plenty to capture the imagination here. For example, after you have bought your fluorescent leaning tower, discover the backstreets of this mildly scuffed but seductive old lady. At nearby Lucca, it's love at first sight. This classy city has aged gloriously. Encased by 16th-century walls, butter-coloured buildings form a pedestrian maze of high, thin streets, Romanesque buildings and gracious piazzas; all within a high-heeled strut of stylish and sophisticated shops.

Further inland, the countryside is rugged and green, with tortuous roads that snake around the mountain peaks, dramatically descending into thickly-forested pine valleys. Picturesque riverside villages like Bagni di Lucca have a quasi-Alpine feel while, further north, lies Abetone, one of the country's foremost skiing resorts. Due west are the dramatic Apuane Alps, popular with both Italian and foreign walkers.

This is also marble territory, centred above all on the town of Carrara, known worldwide for its exquisite white stone. To this day, sculptors from all over the world seek their raw materials here, just as Michelangelo did five centuries ago.

On the coast, resorts like Viareggio fill up quickly with local families. There may not be much towel-space on the sand but, like much of the northwest, the atmosphere is intrinsically Italian, with not one 'I love Viareggio' T-shirt in sight.

HIGHLIGHTS

- Visit the tower of Pisa at dusk or dawn when there are no crowds or naff souvenir stands and you can marvel (and take pictures) in peace (p155)
- Rent a bike and explore the evocative walled city of Lucca (p143)
- Enjoy the Rio-style partying at Viareggio's *carnevale* in February and March (p160)
- Check out the most famous marble quarries in the world at Carrara (p163)
- Explore the wild beauty of the rural Garfagnana (p150) region and its northern neighbour, Lunigiana (p165)

NORTHWESTERN TUSCANY

LUCCA

pop 87,000

Lucca is a beautiful city with lashings of history, more than a hundred churches, and excellent shops and restaurants. Hidden behind imposing Renaissance walls, it also makes an ideal base for exploring the Apuane Alps and the Garfagnana.

Founded by the Etruscans, Lucca became a Roman colony in 180 BC and a free commune during the 12th century. In 1314 it fell to Pisa but, under the leadership of local adventurer Castruccio Castracani degli Anterminelli, the city regained its independence and began to amass territories in western Tuscany, including marble-rich Carrara. Castruccio died in 1325 but Lucca remained an independent republic for almost 500 years.

Napoleon ended all this in 1805 when he created the principality of Lucca. Unswerving in his democratic values, he handed control to one of the seemingly countless members of his family in need of an Italian fiefdom. In this case his sister Elisa who, in 1809, was entrusted with all of Tuscany. Twelve years later the city became a Bourbon duchy, before being incorporated first into the grand duchy of Tuscany in 1847 and subsequently into the Kingdom of Italy.

The long periods of peace Lucca enjoyed explain the almost perfect preservation of the city walls: they were rarely put to the test.

NORTHWESTERN TUSCANY

LUCCA

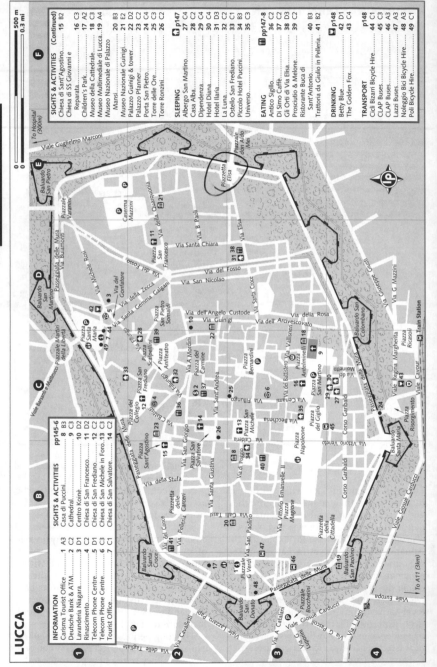

0		500 m
0		0.3 mi

Orientation

From the train station in Piazza Ricasoli walk northwest to Piazza Risorgimento and through Porta San Pietro. Head northwards along Via Vittorio Veneto to the immense Piazza Napoleone and on to Piazza San Michele, the centre of town.

Information

EMERGENCY
Police station (☎ 0583 44 27 27; Viale Cavour 38) Near the train station.

INTERNET ACCESS
Rinascimento (☎ 0583 46 98 73; Via C. Battisti 50; €1.50/2.50 30mins/hr) This place doubles as an art gallery. The Carisma tourist office (see below) also has an Internet kiosk which gobbles up coins at a rate of €6 for 15 minutes.

LAUNDRY
Lavanderia Niagara (Via Michele Rosi 26; washing & drying a load €4)

MEDICAL SERVICES
Main hospital (☎ 0583 97 01; Via dell'Ospedale) Beyond the city walls to the northeast.

MONEY
Deutsche Bank (Via Fillungo 76) One of several banks in town that have an ATM.

POST
Main post office (Via Vallisneri 2) Just north of the cathedral.

TELEPHONE
Telecom phone centres (Via Cenami 19 & Via del Gonfalone 5) Both phone centres are unstaffed.

TOURIST INFORMATION
Main tourist office (☎ 0583 91 99 31; www.luccatourist .it; Piazza Santa Maria 35; ❧ 9am-7pm) Just inside the main Porta Santa Maria gate. You can also pick up an audio-tour of the city that lasts around two hours, although you hire it for the day (thus giving you a little reprieve time for lunch) for €9 (€7 per person for two or more).
Carisma (☎ 0583 31 60 24; Piazzale Verde; ❧ 9am-7pm Jun-Sep, 9am-3pm Oct-May) Private tourist office that books accommodation and organises tours.

Sights & Activities

CATHEDRAL
Lucca's Romanesque **cathedral** (☎ 0583 49 05 30; Piazza San Martino; ❧ 7am-7pm Apr-Oct, 7am-5pm

Nov-Mar), dedicated to St Martin, dates from the 11th century. The exquisite facade, built in the Luccan-Pisan style, was designed to accommodate the pre-existing campanile (bell tower). Each of the columns in the upper part of the facade is different, and carved by a local artisan.

The interior was rebuilt in the 14th and 15th centuries with a Gothic flourish. Matteo Civitali designed the pulpit and, in the north aisle, the 15th-century *tempietto* (small temple) containing the **Volto Santo**, an image of Christ on a wooden crucifix said to have been carved by Nicodemus, who witnessed the crucifixion. It is a major object of pilgrimage and each year, on 13 September, is carried through the streets in a procession at dusk.

In the sacristy the **Tomba di Ilaria del Carretto** (admission €2; ❧ 7am-7pm Apr-Oct, 7am-5pm Nov-Mar) is a masterpiece of funerary sculpture for the wife of the 15th-century lord of Lucca, Paolo Guinigi, executed by Jacopo della Quercia. The church contains numerous other artworks, including a magnificent *Ultima Cena* (Last Supper) by Tintoretto, above the third altar of the south aisle.

Next to the cathedral is the **Museo della Cattedrale** (☎ 0583 49 05 30; Via Arcivescovato; admission €3.50; ❧ 10am-6pm daily Apr-Oct, 10am-2pm Mon-Fri, 10am-6pm Sat & Sun Nov-Mar), which houses religious art mainly of the 15th and 16th centuries, sculpture from the cathedral and illuminated manuscripts.

CHIESA DI SS GIOVANNI E REPARATA
The 17th-century facade of this one-time **Lucca cathedral** (☎ 0583 49 05 30; Piazza San Martino; €2.50; ❧ 10am-6pm daily Apr-Oct, 10am-2pm Mon-Fri, 10am-6pm Sat & Sun Nov-Mar) hides more than 1000 years of history. Parts of its archeological area have even been dated to the 2nd century BC. Remains of the original early-Christian church and baptistry, built in the 5th century, are visible in the present Gothic baptistry. Roman ruins have also been revealed below floor level and can be viewed. Today's church is largely the 12th-century remodelling of its 5th-century predecessor.

CHIESA DI SAN MICHELE IN FORO
As dazzling as the cathedral is this **Romanesque church** (Piazza San Michele; ❧ 7.40am-noon & 3-6pm), built on the site of its 8th-century

NORTHWESTERN TUSCANY

precursor over almost 300 years from the 11th century. The exquisite wedding-cake facade is topped by a figure of the Archangel Michael slaying a dragon. Keep a look out for Andrea della Robbia's *Madonna e Bambino* (Madonna and Child) to your right as you enter.

CASA DI PUCCINI
Near the church, off Via di Poggio, is the **Casa di Puccini** (☎ 0583 58 40 28; Corte San Lorenzo 9; adult/child €3/2; ☻ 10am-6pm daily Jun-Sep, 10am-1pm & 3-6pm Tue-Sun Mar-May, Oct-Dec). The composer's house is preserved in much the same way as he left it. His glasses and pen remain poised on the desk next to the piano where he wrote *Madame Butterfly* and much of his later work. The mildly morbid surprise is the tiny, elaborately marbled chapel, converted from a sitting room to house the composer's tomb.

VIA FILLUNGO
Lucca's busiest street, Via Fillungo, threads its way through the medieval heart of the old city and is lined with fascinating, centuries-old buildings. The **Torre delle Ore** (City Clock Tower; Via Fillungo; adult/child €3.50/2.50; ☻ 10am-6.30pm Mar, 10am-7pm Apr-Oct, 10.30am-5pm Nov-Feb) is about halfway along. It's a puff-you-out climb up 208 steps but the view from the top is stunning.

EAST OF VIA FILLUNGO
You would never guess it today but, just off to the east of Via Fillungo (accessed from Piazza Scalpellini), is the place where local thespians regularly gathered in Roman days for a spot of outdoor theatre. Centuries later the unique oval-shaped theatre became **Piazza Anfiteatro** as houses were built on the foundations of the imperial amphitheatre. In some respects it's a bit of a theatre even today. Idiosyncratic shops and cool cafés jostle to accommodate one another around the edges of the one-time stage.

Due southeast of Piazza Anfiteatro is **3o Guinigi** and its **torre** (tower; ☎ 0583 4 85 24; Via Sant'Andrea; adult/child €3.50/2.50; joint ticket for both towers adult/child €5/3; ☻ 9.30am-7pm Mar, 9am-8pm Apr, 9am-12pm May-Sep, 10am-4.30pm Oct-Feb). Intriguingly, an oak tree has managed to take root at the top of the tower, providing welcome shade after yet another steep climb.

After a short walk to the east you enter **Piazza San Francesco** and the attractive 13th-

century church of the same name. Further eastwards still is the Villa Guinigi, which houses the **Museo Nazionale Guinigi** (☎ 0583 49 60 33; Via della Quarquonia; adult/child €4/2; ☻ 8.30am-7pm Tue-Sat, 8.30am-1.30pm Sun & holidays) and the city's art collection, consisting of paintings, sculptures and archaeological finds.

WEST OF VIA FILLUNGO
Another example of Lucca's Romanesque influence is the facade of the **Chiesa di San Frediano** (Piazza San Frediano; ☻ 8.30am-noon & 3-5pm), which features a unique (and much-restored) 13th-century mosaic. The main feature of the beautiful basilica's interior is the **Fontana Lustrale**, a 12th-century baptismal font decorated with sculpted reliefs. Behind it is an *Annunciazione* by Andrea della Robbia.

Of some interest are the interior and artworks of the **Museo Nazionale di Palazzo Mansi** (☎ 0583 5 55 70; Via Galli Tassi 43; adult/child €4/2; combined ticket including Museo Nazionale Guinigi adult/child €6.50/3.25; ☻ 8.30am-7pm Tue-Sat, 8.30am-1pm Sun & holidays).

PALAZZO PFANNER
Erected in the late 17th century, the **palazzo** (Via degli Asili 33; garden & palace adult/child €4/2, garden or palace adult/child €2/1; ☻ 10am-6pm 1 Mar-15 Nov) is a fine example of how the other half lived in Lucca. A sweeping flight of stairs leads up to the Baroque residence, adorned with frescoes and furniture from the 18th and 19th centuries, or you can head straight for the ornate 18th-century garden.

CITY WALLS
If you have time, do the 4km walk, jog or cycle along the top of the city walls. These ramparts were raised in the 16th and 17th centuries. When you've finished torturing any kids you may have with churches and high culture, take them to the swings and things near the Baluardo San Donato.

Courses
Centro Koinè (☎ 0583 49 30 40; koinelu@tin.it; Via A. Mordini 60; 2-week summer course €355, month-long year-round course €500) offers Italian courses and can arrange accommodation.

Festivals & Events
Lucca has hosted the **Summer Festival** since 1998 and, each year, the series attracts top

international acts. Craig David, Simply Red, Elton John and Spanish crooner Julio Iglesias were among the performers in action in 2003. It is held in July and tickets cost around €30 for the whole festival. There is an information and ticket office in Piazza Napoleone from June onwards, otherwise check out the website at www.summer-festival.com, or ask at the main tourist office for further details.

On the third Sunday in July there is a torch-lit procession and crossbow competition at the **Festa di San Paolino**. On 14 September, Luminaria di Santa Croce sees another torch-lit procession.

Sleeping

Although hotels are limited within the old city, stay here if you can to appreciate this magical medieval ensemble after the coach tours have left. There are some *affitta-camere* (rooms to rent), although most are east of the centre around Via Romana.

BUDGET

Ostello San Frediano (☎ 0583 46 99 57; fax 0583 46 10 07; Via della Cavallerizza 12; dm/d €15/39; 🖳) This Hostelling International hostel has a lot going for it, including an ace location, near Chiesa di San Frediano. There's a leafy garden out back and the rooms are a good size and squeaky clean. You can have breakfast for a modest €1.55 and there are special needs and Internet facilities.

Hotel & Dipendenza Diana (☎ 0583 49 22 02; www.albergodiana.com; Via del Molinetto 11; hotel d €67; annexe s/d €75/93; 🕃) If you are here in the summer, the *dipendenza* (annexe) rooms have air-con, cool marble floors, satellite TV and hairdryers, whereas rooms in the original hotel are no-frills basic although everything works. The management speaks some English.

MID-RANGE

Piccolo Hotel Puccini (☎ 0583 5 54 21; www.hotelpuccini.com; Via di Poggio 9; s/d €55/80) This is a stylish three-star with a glossy marble lobby and modern rooms with all the trimmings. The location is unbeatable, right next to Piazza San Michele. Go for a room with a street view.

La Luna (☎ 0583 49 36 34; www.hotellaluna.com; Corte Compagni 12; s/d €75/90) This clean and tidy hotel has a handy pizzeria across the road.

Some rooms are old-style with beams and wardrobes, while others are modern and bland. There is limited parking available in a separate garage.

Casa Alba (☎ 0583 49 53 61; www.casa-alba.com; Via Fillungo 142; s/d €80/90) You will have to lug your cases up four flights of stairs but, once here, the rooms are small but sunny, washed in pastel colours with arty prints and fridges. If you are staying more than a couple of days, you may get a discount and prices decrease 10% in winter.

Albergo San Martino (☎ 0583 46 91 81; www.albergosanmartino.it; Via della Dogana 9; s/d/ste €73/98/145; 🕃) is an upbeat and welcoming hotel with just ten rooms decorated in warm peachy tones. Located in a quiet elbow off the grandiose Piazza Napoleone, available extras include fridges, car parks, bike rental and special needs facilities.

TOP END

Universo (☎ 0583 49 36 78; www.universolucca.com; Piazza del Giglio 1; s/d €120/170; 🕃) is a mildly moth-eaten, yet still grand, hotel with views of the tree-lined piazza and cathedral – this is about as close as you can get without attending confession. Former fans include Ruskin and his cronies; the place still gets booked up fast.

Hotel Ilaria (☎ 0583 46 92 00; www.hotelilaria.com; Via del Fosso 26; s/d €130/210; Ⓟ 🕃) Lucca's poshest hotel is housed in the former stables of the magnificent Villa Bottini next door (several concerts are staged here during the summer festival which, depending on your musical tastes, could be a real bonus or living hell). The hotel is executive-style slick with plenty of Internet terminals and meeting space for business bods. The bedrooms are modern and large, with bright marble bathrooms and terraces.

Eating

Lucca has an excellent variety of trattorie and restaurants and, while the majority tends to be red-tablecloth traditional, there is an increasing number of stylish eateries geared towards a more cosmopolitan clientele.

Prosciutto & Melone (☎ 0583 4 88 45; Via Anfiteatro 13/17; buffet €15; 🕃 closed Tue), just off the Piazza Anfiteatro, is a handy location for a spot of refuelling. The daily buffet is ideal for fussy families, with plenty of choice and pasta alternatives. Choose between scrubbed pine surrounds with interesting artwork on the walls, or the outside terrace.

Ristorante Buca Sant'Antonio (☎ 0583 5 58 81; Via della Cervia 3; mains €13.50; ☒ closed Sun eve & Mon) Founded in 1782, the setting is wonderful with whitewashed rooms, old beams, tiled floors and copper pots. The dishes sound deliciously innovative but are touted as traditional Luccan cuisine. Fatten your credit card on the ricotta-and-leek pie with chickpea sauce.

Trattoria da Giulio in Pelleria (☎ 0583 5 59 48; Via delle Conce 47; mains €7-9; ☒ closed Sun-Mon) An earthy inexpensive restaurant that packs them in at lunchtime. Don't be put off by the multilingual menu; the food here is solidly traditional with barely a french fry in sight. Photos of famous – and not so famous – customers line the walls.

L'Antico Sigillo (☎ 0583 39 10 42; Via degli Angeli 13; mains €8; ☒ closed Wed) Tucked into a quiet side street, this place is good for a light lunch with more salads than you can shake a carrot stick at, plus pizzas and pastas at wallet-friendly prices.

Di Simo Caffè (☎ 0583 49 62 34; Via Fillungo 58; snacks €2-4; ☒ closed Mon) This intimate little café hasn't changed since Puccini swapped gossip with his librettist Guiseppe Giacosa. Every room is gorgeous and stuffed with antiques. Try the local specialty *buccellato*, a kind of sweet bun typical of Lucca.

Also recommended is **Gli Orti di Via Elisa** (☎ 0583 49 12 41; Via Elisa 17) for its pizzas.

Drinking

Unless you arrive at festival time, Lucca goes to sleep early.

Betty Blue (☎ 0583 49 21 66; Via del Gonfalone 16/ 18) This lively, gay-friendly spot has a sixties feel, with op art on the walls and plenty of slouching space.

The Golden Fox (☎ 0583 49 16 19; Viale Regina Margherita 207; ☒ closed Mon) You can down a pint in pseudo-pub surroundings at this place near the train station.

Getting Around

Most cars are banned from the city centre. Tourists are allowed to drive into the walled city and park in the residents' spaces (yellow lines) if they have a permit from one of the hotels. There are parking areas (€1.20 per hour) in piazzas Bernardini, San Martino,

Santa Maria and Boccherini. There are few free parking places outside the walls.

CLAP bus No 3 connects the train station, Piazza Napoleone and Piazzale G Verdi, but it is just as easy, and more pleasurable, to walk.

You can hire bicycles from several outlets. **Noleggio Bici** rents out bikes next to the Carisma tourist office. Others, including **Poli** and **Cicli Bizarri** are virtually next door to each other on Piazza Santa Maria. Rates are similar wherever you go. A normal bicycle costs €2.10 per hour. You can hire tandems for around double (no surprises there).

For a taxi, call ☎ 0583 49 49 89.

Getting There & Away

CLAP buses (☎ 0583 58 78 97) serve the region, including the Garfagnana. **Lazzi** (☎ 0583 58 48 76) operates buses to Florence (€5, 1¼ hours), La Spezia, Carrara and Pisa (€2.20, 45 minutes). Both companies operate from near Piazzale G. Verdi.

Lucca is on the train line between Florence (€4.45, 1½ hours) and Viareggio, and there are also services into the Garfagnana. By car, the A11 passes to the south of the city, connecting it with Pisa and Viareggio. The SS12, which becomes the SS445 at Barga, connects the city with the Garfagnana.

EAST OF LUCCA
Villas

From the 16th to the 19th centuries, Luccan businessmen who had finally arrived built themselves country residences – some 300 of them all told. Today most have gone, have been abandoned or are inaccessible, but a dozen fine examples still dot the countryside to the northeast of Lucca. For more info on the following villas and others, check the website www.villelucchesi.net.

Villa Reale (☎ 0583 3 00 09; Via Fraga Alta; €6; ☒ closed Mon & Dec-Feb) at Marlia, about 7km from Lucca, is the most striking. Much of its present look, and that of the meticulously planned gardens, is owed to the tastes of Elisa Bonaparte, Napoleon's sister and short-lived ruler of Tuscany. You can only visit the villa on a guided tour (there are six from 10am to 7pm).

Just north of here is the neoclassical **Villa Grabau** (☎ 0583 40 60 98; Via di Matraia; €5.50; ☒ 10am-1pm & 3-7pm Tue-Sun) set in a vast nine-hectare parkland including traditional

THE REAL ADVENTURES OF PINOCCHIO

It is one of the best known children's classics and, no, the story of Pinocchio is not a Walt Disney invention. The story of a wooden puppet that turns into a boy is one of the most widely read and internationally popular pieces of literature ever to emerge from Italy. (At least Begnini's 2002 version of the film was more faithful to the original story, although the casting of the 50 year-old Roberto as the boy puppet was possibly just a tad far-fetched!)

This timeless tale has a long history, dating back to the early 1880s when Carlo Collodi, a Florentine journalist, wrote a series for one of united Italy's first children's periodicals entitled *Storia di un Burattino* (Story of a Puppet). Subsequently re-named *Le Avventure di Pinocchio* (The Adventures of Pinocchio), the tale would have made Collodi (real name Lorenzini) a multi-millionaire had he lived to exploit film and translation rights.

Collodi did not merely intend to pen an amusing child's tale. Literary critics have been trawling the text for the past century in search of ever more evidence to show that it was as much aimed at adult readers as children.

The character of Pinocchio is a frustrating mix of the likeable and the odious. At his worst he is a wilful, obnoxious and deceitful little monster who deserves just about everything he gets. Humble and blubbering when things go wrong, he has the oh-so-human tendency to return to his dismissive ways when he thinks he's in the clear. The wooden puppet is a prime example of flesh-and-blood failings. You thought Jiminy Cricket was cute? Pinocchio thought him such a pain, he splattered him against the wall (in the real, not the sanitised Disney, version).

Pinocchio spends a good deal of the tale playing truant and one of Collodi's central messages seems to be that only good, diligent school children have a hope of getting anywhere or, in this case, of turning into a fine human lad. But Collodi was not merely taking a middle-class swipe at naughty-boyish behaviour. He was convinced that the recently united Italy was in urgent need of a decent education system to help the country out of its poverty and lethargy. His text can be read in part as criticism of a society as yet incapable of meeting that need.

Indeed the story, weaving between fantasy and reality, is a mine of references, some more veiled than others, to the society of late-19th-century Italy – a troubled country with enormous socio-economic problems and the general apathy of those in power. Pinocchio waits the length of the story to become a real boy. But, while his persona may provoke laughter, his encounters with poverty, petty crime, skewed justice and just plain bad luck constitute a painful education in the machinations of the 'real' world.

English and Italian gardens, several fountains, more than 100 terracotta vases of centenary lemon trees and the 1700 Casa dei Limoni, still used to store lemons.

To get to the villas, take the SS435 towards Pescia, then turn northwards for Marlia (signposted 7km east of Lucca).

Collodi

If you stick to the SS435 you will, after another 8km, reach a turn-off north to this town. Alternatively, while heading south towards the SS435 from Villa Torrigiani, you could take a left-hand turn at the signpost for the village of **Petrognano**. This road winds its way uphill through olive groves and affords fantastic views of the valley below. In Petrognano, follow the signs to **San Gennaro** where the road starts its decent into Collodi. It is moderately interesting in its own right,

if only for the **Villa Garzoni** (☎ 0572 42 95 90; Piazza della Vittoria; adult/child €5.20/3.10; ☺ 9am-sunset), the majestic gardens of which rise away from the entrance on the town's main road. The Baroque building, richly frescoed inside, is closed until at least September 2004.

The **Parco di Pinocchio** (☎ 0572 429342; adult/child €8.50/6.50; ☺ 8.30am-sunset) is one for the kids. Pinocchio is quite a phenomenon in Italian literature (and considerably more meaningful than the Disney version – see the boxed text above). The Florentine Carlo Lorenzini, who spent some time when he was a child in Collodi, took the hamlet's name for a pseudonym, so the town felt it should repay the compliment with this children's theme park.

Be warned: buses between Lucca and Montecatini Terme don't stop often in Collodi; it's a lot easier by car.

Pescia

Pescia is the self-proclaimed Tuscan flower capital with national and international exports worth some €130 million annually. Every second September (even-numbered years) a flower fair is held in Pescia. The town, split by the north–south flow of the Pescia River, is enjoyable to stroll around.

The medieval heart of town is the unusually long and uneven Piazza Mazzini, which gets busy on Saturday with the weekly market. The northern end is capped by Palazzo Comunale and the 13th-century Palazzo del Vicario. A couple of other fine buildings around the church complete the picture on the western bank. The eastern bank is dominated by the Gothic Chiesa di San Francesco and the less interesting Baroque cathedral.

Boutique del Cibo (☎ 0572 47 61 76; Via Libria Andreotti 6; mains €8; ☽ closed Thu) is a fabulously friendly restaurant on a bustling corner in the centre. The atmosphere is kitchen-sink informal with a street-side terrace for alfresco dining.

CLAP buses (☎ 0583 58 78 97) connect Pescia with Lucca (€2.50, 45 minutes). Plenty of buses head east to Montecatini Terme too (€1.20, 20 minutes).

THE GARFAGNANA

The heart of the Garfagnana is in the valley formed by the Serchio river and its tributaries. Despite the raw beauty of this area, it is relatively undiscovered. Most visitors here are pursuing outdoor pursuits such as horse-trekking and hiking, while others use the area as a launch pad for treks into the Apuane Alps. For more information on the region, including lists of *rifugi* (mountain huts), check with the local tourist offices.

The SS12 sneaks away from the north walls of Lucca (follow the signs for Abetone) following the Serchio river valley. If you turn east at **Vinchiana** and follow the narrow and winding road for a few kilometres you will arrive at the **Pieve di Brancoli**, a fine 12th-century Romanesque church.

Further upstream you hit **Borgo a Mozzano**, with its wacky medieval Ponte della Maddalena (also known as Ponte del Diavolo, or Devil's Bridge). Each of its five arches is different – and extraordinary. Typical of the era (about all that *is* typical), the bridge rises to a midpoint and then descends to the other side of the Serchio – only the 'midpoint' here is well off centre!

Bagni di Lucca

A few kilometres further on as the SS12 curves east, just past the turn-off north for Barga, is the exquisite small town of Bagni di Lucca. In the early 19th-century, Bagni was famous for its thermal waters, both to the gentry of Lucca and to an international set. Byron, Shelley, Heinrich Heine and Giacomo Puccini were among the celebrity guests to take the waters. The dignified neoclassical buildings are an atmospheric reminder of the town's former splendour.

There are two distinct areas, known as the *ponte* (bridge) and the *villa* (town) which lie a confusing 2km apart. As the name suggests, the latter is the larger with more shops, restaurants, hotels and the small **tourist office** (☎ 0583 80 57 45; Via Angelina Wipple). The *ponte* is more of a hamlet centred around a bridge that crosses the Lima River.

SLEEPING & EATING

Hotel Roma (☎ /fax 0583 8 72 78; www.paginegialle.it/albergoroma-lu - Italian only; Viale Umberto I 110; s/d €35/50) This extraordinary hotel in *villa* dates back to 1690. Later it was converted to the summer residence of Elisa Bonaparte. Owner, Renato (who bears an uncanny resemblance to Jack Nicholson) is lovingly restoring the building without threatening its historical integrity. There are lovely shady gardens and one room has been turned into a small quirky museum.

Hotel Svizzero (☎ /fax 0583 80 53 15; Via Casalini 30; s/d €45/55) Svizzero is a lovely gracious building in *villa* with a quasi-colonial feel, right across from the park. The bedrooms have high ceilings and plain furniture, and the atmosphere is unbeatably welcoming. There are plans to build a pool, so be prepared for a price hike.

Albergo Bernabo (☎ 0583 80 52 15; Ponte a Serraglio; s/d €55/65) Located high above the bridge, this hotel has an air of gentility, as well as superb views of Bagni's golden buildings crowned by a church. Rooms are swing-a-cat size but have all the modern comforts, including hairdryers. There's a large sun terrace, and restaurants and bars are within short strolling distance.

Circolo dei Forestieri (☎ 0583 8 60 38; Piazza Jean Varraud 10; set menu €20; ☽ closed Mon) This 'foreigners club' in *villa* seems straight out of Victorian times, complete with high ceilings and chandeliers. You can dine exceedingly well here for a steal. Try the *crêpes ai funghi* (mushroom crepes).

Lazzi buses from Lucca run here on a regular basis (€2.50, 50 minutes).

The Lima Valley & Abetone

The SS12 proceeds northeast from the Garfagnana into Pistoia province. If you are heading for the ski slopes, this is the best and most picturesque, if windy, route. Possible minor detours en route are **San Cassiano**, with its 12th-century church, and **Lucchio**, spectacular for its position on the northeastern slope of a wooded ridge.

Abetone has some 30 hotels and is the centre of Tuscany's main ski resort, dating back to the 18th century, for more information see p40.

Ostello Renzo Bizzarri (☎ 0573 6 01 17; fax 0573 60 66 56; Via Brennero 157; dm €10.35 with breakfast, full board €25.80) This large Hostelling International hostel is well equipped for skiers with enthusiastic staff. It is also nicely secluded for those après-ski times. The prices are probably the most wallet-friendly in town.

Otherwise the town's hotels start at around €50/70 for a single/double. Also, at the height of the ski season the hotels tend to prefer bookings of at least three days and may also make half-board accommodation obligatory. Another dozen or so hotels are strung out in nearby towns. For those without their own transport, the easiest way up is to catch a bus from Pistoia (see p129).

Barga

The high point of the steep old town of Barga is quite literally the high point. Climb to the top of town for panoramic views and take a look inside the cathedral, built between the 10th and 14th centuries. The pulpit in particular is exquisitely carved by the idiosyncratic 13th-century sculptor Guido Bigarelli, and rests on four red marble pillars. The two front ones rest on lions that dominate a dragon and a heretic, while one of the back pillars rests on an unhappy-looking dwarf! Spread beneath the cathedral is the town, which is lovely: a patchwork of narrow streets, archways, ancient walls and small piazzas with very few foreigners around.

> ### DETOUR: LUCIGNANO
>
> From Bagni de Lucca to Barga (SS445), take the 9.5km turn, past Alpine meadows and just beyond Calavorno. It will be signposted to the picturesque stone village of Lucignano perched high above to your right. At 4.7km cross a bridge over the river and watch for the magnificent view of the medieval village of Montefegatesi (850m above sea level) to your right. At 10km you will enter the village. Conquer the narrrow ascent in first gear, squeeze your wing mirrors through the stone gateways and you'll find yourself in a world of leaning passages, cobbled squares and bent but welcoming old women. Park and ponder the magnificent view from the stone wall due north of here, before winding your way back to the main road.

SLEEPING & EATING

La Pergola (☎ 0583 71 12 39; fax 0583 71 04 33; Via San Antonio 1; s/d €65/75) is a good value hotel, which has recently had a makeover, in a pretty residential area. Rooms are prettily floral and several have good views of the village (try for No 43 if you can). There is also a 3rd-floor terrace for sunning or sketching. The management speaks English.

Albergo Alpino (☎ 0583 72 33 36; alpino@barga holiday.com; Via Pascoli 41; s/d €55/65) This 1920s lodge-style hotel has a great bar and restaurant to serve the glugging and gastronomic needs of the locals. The rooms are tidy, clean and comfortable, and the old town is around five minutes' walk away.

CLAP buses from Lucca run up to 10 times daily, but there are only three on Sunday (€3, 1¼ hours). The buses stop in Piazzale del Fosso by Porta Mancianella, the main gate into the old city. Other buses run to Bagni di Lucca twice daily.

Castelnuovo di Garfagnana

Apart from the formidable 14th-century **Rocca**, a castle built for the Este dukes of Ferrara, there is not a lot to see here. This is, however, one of the best centres to get information on walking in the Apuane Alps (see p36).

The **Pro Loco tourist office** (☎ 0583 64 10 07; www.garfagnanavacanze.it; Via Covalieri di Vittorio Veneto; ☯ 9.30am-12pm & 3.30-7pm Mon-Sat) and a

second **tourist office** (☎ 0583 6 51 69; Piazza delle
Erbe 1) operate similar opening hours. You
can stock up on maps and get information
on *rifugi*, walking trails, horse trekking
centres and other tips.

You can rent a bike from **Cicli Maggi**
(☎ 0583 63 91 66; Via Nicola Fabrizi 49; €10/day)
which also has reasonable week-long rates.

SLEEPING & EATING
Da Carlino (☎ 0583 64 42 70; www.dacarlino.it - Italian
only; Via Garibaldi 15; s/d €40/65) Across from the
park, this hotel is a good option. The rooms
are comfortable, chintzy and with balconies,
while the downstairs restaurant is one of the
best in town where trout is the speciality – as
well as home-made meringues.

Trattoria Marchetti (☎ 0583 63 91 57; Via Montalt-
issimo 2a; mains €6) An earthy and inexpensive
lunch spot with warm wooden innards and
a busy counter dishing up massive plates of
delicious local dishes. Try the *zuppe di farro*
(white-bean-and-potato soup) for starters.

There are up to 11 CLAP buses from
Lucca on weekdays (€3.50, 1½ hours).

Around Castelnuovo di Garfagnana
Several scenic roads fan out from Castelnuovo. If you have your own wheels and
steady nerves, a good route is to follow the
concertina of hairpin bends that constitute
the road leading, via Castiglione, to the
Foce di Radici pass across the Apennines
into Emilia-Romagna. The scenery in parts
is splendid. Occasional buses run this route.
The minor parallel road to the south leads
you to **San Pellegrino in Alpe**, site of a fine
monastery.

Walkers should head for the small **Riserva
Naturale dell'Orecchiella** park on the narrow
road via **Corfino**, itself a pleasant village with
several hotels. Seven kilometres further
north is the park's **tourist office** (☎ 0583 61
90 98; ☼ 10am-5pm Jun-Sep) where you can pick
up information and maps for walks within
the reserve. To reach here via one of the
most scenic routes, start on the main road
that takes you through Castiglione. Shortly
after, a tiny road leads off to the west (left)
to Villa Collemandine, after which you turn
right along the road for Corfino.

The SS445 road follows the Serchio
Valley to the east of the Apuane Alps and
into the Lunigiana region that occupies the
northern end of Tuscany (see p165). The

road is scenic and windy, and takes you
through lush, green countryside. About
8km north along this road from Castelnuovo at Poggio is a pretty turn-off to the
artificial Lago Vagli along the Torrente
Edron stream. You can undertake some
pleasant short walks in the area, or simply
some circular driving routes that can lead
you back to Castelnuovo.

PISA
pop 98,000
Once, if briefly, a maritime power to rival
Genoa (Genova) and Venice (Venezia), Pisa
now draws its fame from an architectural
project gone terribly wrong: its Leaning
Tower. But the city offers quite a deal more.
Indeed, the tower is only one element of the
trio of Romanesque beauties around the
green carpet of the Campo dei Miracoli –
along with Piazza San Marco in Venice, one
of Italy's most memorable sights.

Pisa has a centuries-old tradition as a
university town and there are plenty of
students around, still today. A perhaps
unexpectedly beautiful city, Pisa deserves
more than the usual off-the-coach/bus/
bicycle, take-the-photo, then-leave-again
experience that typifies most visitors here.

History
Possibly of Greek origin, Pisa became an
important naval base during the Roman
Empire and remained a significant port for
many centuries. The city's so-called Golden
Days began late in the 11th century when
it became an independent maritime republic and a rival of Genoa and Venice. The
good times rolled on into the 13th century,
by which time Pisa controlled Corsica,
Sardinia and all of the Tuscan coast. The
majority of the city's finest buildings date
from this period, as does the distinctive
Pisan-Romanesque architectural style.

Pisa's support for the Ghibellines during
the tussles between the Holy Roman Emperor and the Pope brought the city into
conflict with its mostly Guelph Tuscan
neighbours, in particular Florence, but also
Lucca. The real blow, however, came when
Genoa's fleet inflicted a devastating defeat
on Pisa in the Battle of Meloria in 1284. The
city fell to Florence in 1406 and, as if by way
of compensation, the Medici encouraged
artistic, literary and scientific endeavour

MARTIN HUGHES

Outside the **Uffizi Gallery** in Florence (p94)

DAMIEN SIMONIS

A view of a Florentine building across the Arno river from **Oltrarno** (p104)

The view over Florence from **Piazzale Michelangelo** (p108)

JULIET COOMBE

LEE FOSTER

Leaning Tower of Pisa
(Torre Pendente; p155)

NEIL SETCHFIELD

The Etruscan city of **Lucca** (p143)

View of the Garfagnana valley from the **Apuane Alps** (p167)

NICK

PISA

0 ———————— 400 m
0 ———————— 0.2 mi

INFORMATION
Hospital..................................1 B3
Internet Planet.........................2 C3
Onda Blu Laundrette.................3 D4
Pharmacy...............................4 D5
Ticket Office...........................5 C2
Tourist Office..........................6 C3
Tourist Office..........................7 B6

SIGHTS & ACTIVITIES   pp154-7
Battistero...............................8 B2
Cathedral...............................9 C3
Cemetery..............................10 B2
Chiesa di Santa Caterina..........11 D3
Chiesa di Santa Maria della Spina..12 B5
Chiesa di Santo Stefano dei
  Cavalieri.............................13 C4
Le Navi Antiche di Pisa.............14 A5

Leaning Tower (Torre Pedente)......15 C3
Museo dell Sinopie.................16 B3
Museo dell'Opera del Duomo....17 C3
Museo Nazionale di San Matteo....18 D5
Palazzo dei Cavalieri...............19 C4
Palazzo dell'Orologio..............20 C4
Torre Guelfa..........................21 A5

SLEEPING   pp157-8
Albergo Gronchi.....................22 C3
Albergo Helvetia....................23 C3
Albergo Milano......................24 B6
Hotel Francesco.....................25 B3
Hotel Il Giardino....................26 B2
Pensione Rinascente...............27 C4
Relais della Faggiola................28 C3
Royal Victoria Hotel................29 C4
Villa Kinzica..........................30 C3

EATING   p158
Antica Trottoria Il Campano.........31 C4
La Bottega del Gelato................32 C4
Numeroundica........................33 C5
Osteria dei Cavalieri.................34 C4
Produce Market......................35 C4
Ristorante La Clessidra..............36 D4
S Omobono.............................37 C4
Trattoria La Grotta....................38 D4

DRINKING   p158
Big Ben Pub............................39 D5
Caffè Federico Salza..................40 C4
Pick a Flower...........................41 C4
Pub Ambarabà.........................42 C4

ENTERTAINMENT   p158
Teatro Verdi...........................43 D5

TRANSPORT   pp158-9
CPT Buses...............................44 B6
Lazzi Buses.............................45 B6
Scooter & Bike Rental................46 C3

OTHER
Il Navicello.............................47 D5
University..............................48 C4

To Ostello della
Gioventù (500m);
Camping Torre
Pendente (800m)

Piazza
Manin

Via Contessa Matilde

Campo dei
Miracoli
(Piazza Duomo)

Via Card. Pietro Maffi

Via Galli-
Tassi

Piazza
Arcivescovado

Via Cardinale

Via Gaetano Boschi

Via Roma

Via Don

Via della Faggiola

Via Martiri

Piazza
Rivalto

Via San Zeno
Piazza
Santa
Caterina

Via Paolo Salvi

Via Derna

Via S Apollonia

Via S Caterina

Piazza Martiri
della Libertà

Botanical
Gardens

Piazza
Cavallotti

Piazza dei
Cavalieri

Via San
Frediano

Via C Oberdan

Via Santa Cecilia

Via San Lorenzo

Via San Francesco

Via Santa Maria

Via P Paoli

Via Poschi

Via Calafati

Via Risorgimento

Borgo Stretto

Via G
Verdi

Via Giovanni de Simone

Vicolo della
Croce Rosa

Via D
Cavalca

Piazza
Solferino

Via Enrico Fermi

Via Trieste

Via Volturno

Via Nicola Pisano

Lungarno R Simonelli

Ponte
di Mezzo

Via Palestro

Lungarno
delle
Belle Torri

Via San Martino

Lungarno Gambacorti

Saffi
Aurelio
Piazza

Lungarno Sonnino Sidney

Via S Paolo

Via Francesco Niosi

Via E Zerboglio

Via Lavagna

Via Nino Bixio

Piazza
S Antonio

Piazza
Vittorio
Emanuele II

Via Giuseppe Mazzini

Via P Trelli

Garibaldi
Piazza

Piazza
Cairoli

Lungarno Galileo Galilei

Piazza
XX September

Via San Martino

Lungarno Mediceo

Ponte
della
Fortezza

Via del Carmine

Corso Italia

Via Filippo Turati

Piazza
San Martino

Via A Ceci

Viale Gramsci

Viale Benedetto Croce

Via Giordano Bruno

Piazza
Fiorentina

Viale Bonaini

Piazza
Guerrazzi

To Airport (2km);
Livorno
(21km)

Vittoria
della
Ponte

Pisa Centrale
Train Station

To Casa della
Giovane (500m)

Arno

Piazza
Solferino

and re-established Pisa's university. The city's most famous son, Galileo Galilei, later taught at the university.

The medieval city underwent profound change under the grand dukes of Tuscany, who began a process of demolition to make way for wider boulevards to ease traffic. The single heaviest blow came in WWII, during the course of which about 50% of old Pisa was destroyed.

Orientation

By train you'll arrive at Pisa Centrale train station, which is at the southern edge of the old city centre. The main intercity bus terminus is Piazza Vittorio Emanuele, a short walk northwards along Viale Gramsci.

The medieval centre is a 15-minute walk northwards, across the Arno river, and Campo dei Miracoli (also known as Piazza del Duomo) is another 10-minute walk northwest. It is quicker to catch a city bus from outside the train station (p159).

Information

EMERGENCY
Police station (☎ 050 58 35 11; Via Mario Lalli)

INTERNET ACCESS
Internet Planet (☎ 050 83 07 02; Piazza Cavallotti; €3.10/hr) The most central place to get online.

MEDICAL SERVICES
Ospedali Riuniti di Santa Chiara (☎ 050 99 21 11; Via Roma 67) Hospital complex.
Farmacia Nuova Fantoni (pharmacy; Lungarno Mediceo 51; ☼ 24 hrs)

MONEY
Avoid the exchange booths near the cathedral. Change money at banks along Corso Italia, or at the train station.

POST
Main post office (Piazza Vittorio Emanuele II) Near the centre.

TOURIST INFORMATION
Main tourist office (☎ 050 56 04 64; www.comune .pisa.it; Piazza Duomo; ☼ 9am-7pm Mon-Sat, to 6pm in low season, to 4.30pm Sun) Facing the tower and next to the ticket office.
Tourist office (☎ 050 4 22 91; train station) Small office with little more than a map and list of hotels.
Consorzio Turistico (☎ 050 83 02 53; www.pisae.it

- Italian only) For accommodation advice and reservations contact the very efficient Consorzio Turistico, based in the main tourist office.

Sights
CAMPO DEI MIRACOLI

The Pisans can justly claim that the Campo dei Miracoli is one of the most beautiful sights in the world. Set among its sprawling lawns is surely one of the most extraordinary concentrations of Romanesque splendour – the cathedral, the baptistry (battistero) and the Leaning Tower. On any day the piazza is teeming with people – students studying or at play, tourists having their photos taken 'holding up the tower', and local workers enjoying a picnic lunch on the lawn. This is also the place to stock up on wonderfully kitsch 'tower' souvenirs, ranging from the inevitable cigarette lighters to the infinitely more exciting glowing (and flashing) lamps.

A staggered pricing system operates to visit the monuments in and around the square: €5 for admission to one monument, €6 to two, and €8.50 to four – the two museums, baptistry and cemetery (cimitero). The cathedral is not included in the joint tickets. Tickets are available from an **office** (☎ 050 56 05 47) next to the tourist office where, for security reasons, you will have to leave any personal belongings in a separate and guarded room.

CATHEDRAL

Pisa's **cathedral** (admission €2; ☼ 10am-7.40pm Mon-Sat, 1-7.40pm Sun Apr–mid-Oct, 10am-12.45pm & 3-4.45pm Mon-Sat, 3-4.45pm Sun mid-Oct–Mar) is majestic. So majestic, in fact, that it was made a model for Romanesque churches throughout Tuscany and even in Sardinia. Begun in 1064, it is covered inside and out with the alternating bands of (now somewhat faded) dark green and cream marble that were to become characteristic of the Pisan-Romanesque style.

The main facade, adorned with four tiers of columns, is striking. The bronze doors of the transept, facing the Leaning Tower, are by Bonanno Pisano. The 16th-century bronze doors of the main entrance were designed by the school of Giambologna to replace the wooden originals that were destroyed in a fire in 1596.

The huge interior is lined with 68 columns in classical style. This unusual feature is a remarkable reminder of the fact that among the artisans who worked on this church, many were Arabs. The forest of columns is reminiscent of many great Middle Eastern mosques.

After the 1596 fire, much of the inside was redecorated. Important works that survived the blaze include Giovanni Pisano's early 14th-century pulpit and an apse mosaic of *Il Redentore fra la Vergine e San Giovanni Evangelista* (Christ between the Virgin Mary and St John the Evangelist) completed by Cimabue in 1302.

LEANING TOWER

No matter how many postcards and holiday snaps of the **Leaning Tower** (Torre Pendente; €15, groups of around 30 people allowed at once,

advance bookings essential) you've seen, nothing prepares you for the real thing. It's, well, gravity defying. The cathedral's bell tower was in trouble from the start: its architect, Bonanno Pisano, managed to complete only three tiers before the tower started to lean on the south side (see the boxed text below).

BATTISTERO

The unusual, round **battistero** (baptistry; ⊙ 8am-7.40pm Apr-Oct, 9am-4.40pm Nov-Mar) was started in 1153 by Diotisalvi, remodelled and continued by Nicola and Giovanni Pisano more than a century later, and finally completed in the 14th century – which explains the mix of architectural styles. The lower level of arcades is in the Pisan-Romanesque style

---

BRACE, BRACE, BRACE

When architect Bonanno Pisano undertook construction work on the *campanile* (bell tower) for the Romanesque cathedral in 1173, he was on shaky ground. Barely 2m above sea level, what lies below the deep green lawns of the Campo dei Miracoli is hardly ideal for major building. A treacherous sand-and-clay mix sits atop a series of alternate strata of clay and sand to a depth of more than 40m.

Pisano had barely begun to build when the earth below the southern foundations started to give. By the time construction ground to a halt five years later, with only three storeys completed, Pisano's stump of a tower already had a noticeable lean.

A new band of artisans and masons set to work on it again in 1272. They attempted to bolster the foundations, but could not right the tower. Their solution was to keep going, compensating for the lean by gradually building straight up from the lower storeys, creating a slight but definite banana curve. The bell chamber at the top was built in 1370. At some point the process came to a halt and until the 18th century the lean remained stable.

Over the following centuries, the banana solution showed it was no solution, as the tower continued to lean a further 1mm each year. By 1993 it was 4.47m out of plumb, more than five degrees from the vertical.

In addition to the problems down on the ground floor, the structure is itself a little on the dodgy side. The tower is basically a pretty but hollow cylinder, cased on the inside and out with layers of marble. Between those layers is a loosely packed mix of rubble and mortar, very unevenly distributed. The stresses caused by the lean led some observers to fear they might be too much and simply cause the casing to crack and crumble.

In 1990 the tower was closed to the public. Two years later the government in Rome assembled a panel of experts to debate a solution. In 1993 engineers placed 1000 tonnes of lead ingots on the northern side in a bid to counteract the subsidence on the southern side. Steel bands were wrapped around the 2nd storey to try to keep it all together. For a while it seemed to have worked, until in 1995 it slipped a whole 2.5mm.

In 1999 a new solution was tried which consisted of slinging steel braces around the 3rd storey and attaching them to heavy hydraulic A-frame anchors some way from the northern side. These frames were later replaced by steel cables attached to neighbouring buildings. The tower thus held in place, engineers gingerly removed soil from below the northern foundations. After extracting some 70 tonnes of earth from the northern side, the tower had sunk to where it was in the 18th century, rectifying the lean by 43.8cm. This, say the experts, guarantees the tower's future (and the tourist dollar) for the next three centuries.

NORTHWESTERN TUSCANY

and the pinnacled upper section and dome are a Gothic add-on. Inside, the beautiful pulpit was carved by Nicola Pisano and signed in 1260, and the white marble font was carved by Guido da Como in 1246. The acoustics beneath the dome are quite remarkable too.

CEMETERY
Located behind the white wall to the north of the cathedral, this exquisite *cimitero*, also known as the **Camposanto** (🕑 same as baptistry), is said to contain soil shipped across from Calvary during the Crusades. Many precious frescoes in the cloisters were badly damaged or destroyed during Allied bombing raids in WWII. Among those saved were the *Trionfo della Morte* (Triumph of Death) and *Giudizio Universale* (Last Judgment) attributed to an anonymous 14th-century painter known as 'The Master of the Triumph of Death'.

MUSEO DELLE SINOPIE
Directly south of the baptistry, this **museum** (🕑 same as baptistry) houses some reddish-brown sketches drawn onto walls as the base for *sinopie* (frescoes), discovered in the cemetery after the WWII bombing raids. They have been restored and provide a fascinating insight into the process of creating a fresco.

MUSEO DELL'OPERA DEL DUOMO
In the line of fire if the tower should ever fall, this **museum** (Arcivescovado 8; 🕑 same as baptistry) features many artworks from the tower, cathedral and baptistry, including a magnificent ivory carving of the *Madonna e Crocifisso* (Madonna and Crucifix) by Giovanni Pisano. Another highlight is the bust known as the *Madonna del Colloquio* (Madonna of the Colloquium), by the same artist, taken from the exterior of the baptistry.

THE CITY
Once you've had your fill of the splendour and majesty of Campo dei Miracoli, a good thing to do is leave it behind. South of the Campo, the swarms of tourists are exchanged for quiet back alleys and vibrant shopping streets filled with locals going about their daily business.

Head southwards on Via Santa Maria and turn left at Piazza Cavallotti for the splendid **Piazza dei Cavalieri**, the centre of temporal power in the city remodelled by Vasari in the 16th century. The **Palazzo dell'Orologio**, on the northern side of the piazza, occupies the site of a tower where, in 1288, Count Ugolino della Gherardesca, his sons and grandsons, were starved to death on suspicion of having helped the Genoese enemy at the Battle of Meloria. The incident was recorded in Dante's *Inferno*.

The **Palazzo dei Cavalieri**, on the northeastern side of the piazza, was redesigned by Vasari and features remarkable graffiti decoration. The piazza and palace are named after the Knights of St Stephen, a religious and military order founded by Cosimo I de' Medici. Their church, **Chiesa di Santo Stefano dei Cavalieri**, was also designed by Vasari.

The **Chiesa di Santa Caterina** (Piazza Santa Caterina; 🕑 9am-noon & 3-7pm) is a fine example of Pisan Gothic architecture and contains works by Nino Pisano.

Wander southwards to the area around **Borgo Stretto**, the city's medieval heart. East along the waterfront boulevard, the Lungarno Mediceo, is the **Museo Nazionale di San Matteo** (☎ 050 54 18 65; Lungarno Mediceo; €4; 🕑 8.30am-7.30pm Tue-Sat, 8.30am-1pm Sun), an interesting enough art gallery housing mostly religious art, particularly from the 14th century. It features works by Giovanni and Nicola Pisano, Masaccio and Donatello.

Cross the Arno and head westwards to reach the **Chiesa di Santa Maria della Spina** (☎ 050 2 14 41; Lungarno Gambacorti; 🕑 10am-1.30pm & 2.30-7pm Tue-Fri, 10am-1.30 Sat & Sun Apr, May & Sep; 10am-1.30pm & 2.30-6pm Tue-Fri, 11am-8pm Sat & Sun Jun-Aug; 10am-2pm Tue-Fri, 11am-8pm Sat & Sun Oct-Mar), oddly perched on the road along the Arno and built in the early 14th-century to house a thorn purportedly from Christ's crown.

Cross to the northern bank of the Arno and continue westwards to **Le Navi Antiche di Pisa** (Ancient Navy of Pisa; ☎ 050 2 14 41; Lungarno R. Simonelli; €3; 🕑 10am-1pm & 2-7pm Tue-Fri, 11am-1pm & 2-9pm Sat & Sun May-Sep, 10am-1pm & 2-6pm Tue-Sun Oct-Apr). This small museum is devoted to the Roman Empire ships uncovered by builders at San Rossore in 1998. After the initial discovery, archeologists discovered 10 boats, ranging from a small warship through to cargo vessels, all of which had evidently been wrecked in storms at ancient Pisa's port. At the museum is a plethora of jugs, bowls and amphoras from the site, some of which have remained sealed and contain liquid residue thought to be wine or fruit. Near the pottery are animal bones, including the tooth from a lion thought to have been taken from Africa for gladiator matches. The boats are also well represented; small models and computer-generated 3D images give you a good idea of what condition the pieces were in when they were discovered.

A few paces west again is the **Torre Guelfa** (☎ 050 2 14 41; Lungarno R. Simonelli; adult/child €1.60/1; ☼ 10am-1.30pm & 2.30-7pm Tue-Fri, 10am-1.30pm Sat & Sun Apr, May & Sep; 10am-1.30pm & 2.30-6pm Tue-Fri, 11am-8pm Sat & Sun Jun-Aug; 10am-2pm Tue-Fri, 11am-8pm Sat & Sun Oct-Mar), where you can climb 200 steps for views over the city's rooftops.

Activities
BOAT TRIPS
Il Navicello (☎ 050 50 31 08; Marina de Pisa; from €8/hr) These boat trips cruise the Arno taking in the sights and have the normal on-board bar and audio commentary. The company also organises various other excursions, including fishing trips.

Festivals & Events
On 16 and 17 June, the Arno River comes to life with the Regata di San Ranieri, a rowing competition commemorating the city's patron saint. It is preceded by the Luminaria, a torchlit procession. On the third Sunday of the month is the Gioco del Ponte (Game of the Bridge), when two groups dressed in medieval costume battle over the Ponte di Mezzo, a bridge over the Arno.

Rotating between Pisa, Venice, Amalfi and Genoa is an annual race between the four – Palio delle Quattro Antiche Repubbliche Marinare (Historical Regatta of the Four Ancient Maritime Republics). It takes place in mid-June 2004, in Genoa.

Sleeping
Pisa has a reasonable number of hotels although they tend to get booked up fast.

BUDGET
Pensione Rinascente (☎ 050 58 04 60; Via dei Castelletto 28; d €51) This friendly place has a cluttered, homey feel, as well as being a lovely old building with frescoed vaulted ceilings and chandeliers. The rooms are huge and ideal for families or small groups. There are no singles.

Albergo Gronchi (☎ 050 56 18 23; Piazza Arcivescovado 1; s/d €35/38) This is a cheap sleep in a clean and tidy *albergo* (hotel) run by an elderly couple. The position, right on the square, more than compensates for the lack of sachets of shampoo – and style.

Albergo Helvetia (☎ 050 55 30 84; Via Don Gaetano Boschi 31; s/d €35/45, d with bath €62) Just south of the cathedral, this friendly place has large pleasant rooms, some of which look out onto the appealingly quirky courtyard with its hundreds of pots of cacti and private trampoline for the family's kids.

MID-RANGE
Hotel Il Giardino (☎ 050 56 21 01; www.pisaonline.it/Giardino; Piazza Manin 1; s/d €80/110; ☒) This place, just west of Campo dei Miracoli, has small but sparkling rooms with lots of shiny light wood and a classy cool colour scheme. Hotel Il Giardino has a large veranda and a reading room.

Villa Kinzica (☎ 050 56 04 19; fax 050 55 12 04; Piazza Arcivescovado 2; s/d €78/103; ☒) This place is a former private villa for a family with plenty of dosh. It has been tastefully revamped into a gracious hotel. A few rooms have tower views and there's a popular restaurant with terrace out front.

Royal Victoria Hotel (☎ 050 94 01 11; www.royalvictoria.it; Lungarno Pacinotti 12; s/d €95/115; ℗ ☒) This gorgeous old-fashioned hotel has a real *belle epoque* feel. It may cost more but room No 401 in the old tower is just fabulous. There are plans to renovate, let's hope that prices and atmosphere stay the same.

Hotel Francesco (☎ 050 55 41 09; www.hotelfrancesco.com; Via Santa Maria 29; s/d €105/115; ☒ ▢) In an ideal location (except for parking!) in the main bar/restaurant drag, this small hotel has recently had a total revamp and been given a slick modern look. There is a lounge and views over the botanical garden. Airport pick-up and bike rental are available.

Albergo Milano (☎ 050 2 31 62; www.pisaonline.it/hotelmilano; Via Mascagni 14; s/d €38/49, d with bath €70; ☒) A solid no-surprises hotel within stumbling distance of the train station, this is also recommended.

TOP END
Relais della Faggiola (☎ 050 83 03 61; www.hotelrelaisorologio.com; Via della Faggiola 12/14; s/d €225/326; ℗ ☒) If you are all set to splurge, you could

do a lot worse than this former 14th-century *palazzo*, which opened as a hotel in 2003. The rooms are elegantly furnished with floral frescoes, lashings of white linen, antique mirrors and complimentary champagne.

Eating

Pisa has a great range of restaurants, including those geared to students; those near the tower are more touristy and expensive.

Antica Trattoria il Campano (☎ 050 58 05 85; Via D. Cavalca 44; mains €8-10; ⏱ closed Wed) This trattoria, in an old tower, is full of atmosphere. The menu sports a myriad selection of vegetarian pizzas, while carnivores may prefer another speciality: a kilo of T-bone steak.

Trattoria la Grotta (☎ 050 57 81 05; Via San Francesco 103; mains €8-13; ⏱ closed Sun) As the name suggests La Grotta has a suitably cavernous interior and continues to keep customers happy with its top-quality food at bargain prices. The atmosphere is laid-back and friendly.

Ristorante la Clessidra (☎ 050 54 01 60; Via Santa Cecilia 34; mains €9-12; ⏱ closed Sun) This is a great place to come to for its choice of meat and fish dishes, while vegetarians may have to content themselves with the *rucola e parmigiano* salad, followed by a suitably girth-widening dessert.

Osteria dei Cavalieri (☎ 050 58 085 8; Via San Frediano 16; mains €9-11; ⏱ closed Sun) Although the size of portions may mean a siesta afterwards, the set meals (seafood or meat and veg) are worth the blow-out. Skip dessert and top it off with a shot of *limoncello* (lemon liqueur).

S. Omobono (☎ 050 54 08 47; Piazza S. Omobono 6/7; mains €8-9) Unpretentious traditional fare is on offer here. There are just a few tables (and one Roman column), and the menu is refreshingly short and sweet. If you're hungry, tuck into a bowl of *minestra di fagiola* for starters. The house wine is very drinkable.

Numeroundici (☎ 050 2 72 82; Via San Martino 47; mains €4-7; ⏱ closed Sat lunch & Sun) This place is well worth the hike from the centre but come prepared to share a table. Food is all self-service, with loads of choice including Indian fare (pretty rare in these parts), fat slices of *focaccine* (a kind of filled bread), grilled steak and superb salads.

La Bottega del Gelato (☎ 050 57 54 67; Piazza Garibaldi 11; ⏱ closed Wed) For seriously creamy *gelato*, head for this place just north of the river.

There is an open-air **produce market** in Piazza delle Vettovaglie, off Borgo Stretto.

Drinking

Many of the better restaurants have a bar attached, where you can enjoy an early evening aperitif, otherwise there is a fair number of bars and cafés around the centre.

Caffè Federico Salza (☎ 050 58 01 44; Borgo Stretto 46; ⏱ closed Mon) This is one of the city's finest bars and is popular with Pisa's shirt-and-tie sophisticates. The cakes, *gelati* and chocolates are worth stopping for too.

Big Ben Pub (☎ 050 58 11 85; Via Palestro 11) This place makes a decent attempt at impersonating a UK-style pub and has the advantage of Guinness on tap.

Pick a Flower (☎ 050 4 03 78; Via Serafini Angolo) This place has a great moody atmosphere inside with candlelight, high ceilings, good wines by the glass and tapas. The outside terrace attracts a lively chic crowd.

Pub Ambarabà (☎ 050 57 67 97; Vicolo della Croce Rossa 5; ⏱ closed Tue; 🖳) This popular bar specialises in sassy cocktails and international beer. There are also light veggie snacks and Internet access.

Entertainment

Teatro Verdi (☎ 050 94 11 11; www.teatrodi pisa.pi.it - Italian only; Via Palestro 40) Opera and ballet are staged here. Cultural and historic events include the Gioco del Ponte, a festival of traditional costume held on the last Sunday in June.

Getting There & Away

AIR

The city's **Galileo Galilei Airport** (☎ 050 50 07 07), about 2km south of the city centre, is Tuscany's main international airport and handles flights to major cities in Europe. **Alitalia** (☎ 8488 6 46 41) and other leading airlines are based at the airport.

BUS

Lazzi (☎ 050 4 62 88; Piazza S. Antonio) operates regular services to Lucca (€2.20, 45 minutes), Florence, change in Lucca (€6.10, three hours) and Viareggio. Less frequent services run to Prato, Pistoia, Massa and Carrara.

CPT (☎ 050 50 55 11; Piazza S. Antonio), also near the train station, serves Volterra, Livorno (Leghorn), Marina di Pisa and Tirrenia.

CAR & MOTORCYCLE
Pisa is close to the A12, which connects Genoa to Livorno and is being extended south to Rome. The city is also close to the A11 (tollway) and SS67 to Florence, while the north–south SS1, the Via Aurelia, connects the city with La Spezia and Rome.

There are several large car parks, including one just north of the cathedral.

TRAIN
The train station is on Piazza della Stazione south of town. The city is connected to Florence (via Empoli, €4.85, one hour) and is also on the Rome–La Spezia line, with frequent services.

Getting Around
To get to the airport, take a train (€1) from the main station for the four-minute journey to Stazione FS Pisa Aeroporto, or the more frequent CPT city bus No 3 (€0.80), which passes through the city centre and past the train station on its way to the airport.

To get from the train station to the cathedral, take CPT bus No 3 or 4, or walk 1.5km. Bus tickets cost €1 for an hour, €1.20 for two hours or €8 for a book of 10 one-hour tickets (you can change as often as you like within the validity of the ticket).

An excellent way to see Pisa is by bicycle or scooter. You can rent either at **Scooter & Bike Rental** (☎ 393 29 08 25 861; Via Santa Maria 129; €12.50/day) located in the centre.

For a taxi, call ☎ 050 54 16 00.

PONTEDERA
pop 25,000
Some 21km southeast of Pisa lies Pontedera. This good-size town is the place to come to, if you want to learn Italian (there are few tourists here) or buy a scooter – the town is home to the Piaggio company. If you want to ponder over your scooter purchase, there are a few hotels and plenty of restaurants serving up sturdy local dishes. The main pedestrian shopping street is Corsa Matteotti. The following hotel is in a good location in the centre, across from the 19th-century Santi Jacopo e Filippe church with its surprisingly Grecian-style facade.

Hotel Il Falchetto (☎ 0587 21 21 13; Piazza Caduiti di Cefalonia 3; s/d €45/64) If you like the stark anonymity of modern hotels, you won't go for this delightfully cluttered and ornate hotel. The owner is an art tutor in Florence and his paintings fill the walls.

DETOUR: CAPANNE

If you are travelling the well-trodden route from Pisa to Florence, take the 9.5km turn-off beyond Pontedera signposted to the charming Montópoli in Val d'Arno. You will pass through the nondescript hamlet of Capanne then become entangled in a confusing one-way system (and that's before you even get to Montópoli). Once in town, follow the signs to the centre and the tourist office. The restaurant **Quattro Gigli** is also well signposted. Grab a table on the delightful terrace in the back, overlooking the greener-than-green valley, and choose from an imaginative menu of traditional Tuscan dishes, including an Italian rarity – roast potatoes. After your blow-out meal, pick up the *Historical Footpaths* brochure from the tourist office and work off those calories exploring this lovely old town.

VIAREGGIO
pop 60,000
Viareggio is arguably the most popular sun-and-sand resort along the Versilia coastal strip. However the town's heyday was back in the 1920s, as witnessed by the celebrated art nouveau facades on the Passeggiata. It is equally famous for its flamboyant *carnevale*, second only to Venice in terms of party spirit.

Orientation
It's a short walk from the train station to the waterfront and main tourist office. The city is ranged roughly north to south on a grid pattern. South from the Canale Burlamacca, lined with pleasure boats, stretch the enticing woods of the Pineta di Levante. Another smaller wood, the Pineta di Ponente, occupies a large chunk of the northern end of town. Beyond it Viareggio merges seamlessly into the next beach resort of Lido di Camaiore.

Information
EMERGENCY
Police station (☎ 0584 4 27 41; Piazza S. Antonio)

VIAREGGIO

INFORMATION	
Floating Point	1 C1
Tourist Office	2 C1
Tourist Office	3 B2
Wash & Dry	4 C3

SIGHTS & ACTIVITIES	p160
Gran Caffè Margherita	5 B3

SLEEPING	p161
American Hotel	6 B2

EATING	p161
Brasserie Stuzzichino	7 B3
L'Oca Bianca	8 B3
Sergio	9 C2

DRINKING	p161
Flannery's	10 B3
Patchouly	11 B2

TRANSPORT	pp161-2
CLAP Buses	12 B3
Lazzi Buses	13 B3

INTERNET ACCESS
Floating Point (☎ 0584 43 30 25; Piazza Dante; €5/hr) Centrally located.

LAUNDRY
Wash & Dry (Corso Garibaldi 5; €2.20/load)

MEDICAL SERVICES
Main hospital (☎ 0584 60 51; Via Aurelia 335) The hospital has moved just east of the centre.

POST
Main post office (Corso Garibaldi)

TOURIST INFORMATION
Main tourist office (☎ 0584 96 22 33; www.versilia .turismo.toscana.it; Carducci 10; ⏲ 9am-1pm & 4-7pm Mon-Sat, 9am-1pm Sun Jun-Sep; 9am-1pm & 3-6pm Mon-Sat, Sun 10am-12pm Oct-May)
Tourist office (⏲ 9.30am-12.30pm) A smaller office located at the train station.

Activities
Apart from strolling along the tracks in the Pineta di Levante, around the Canale Burlamacca and along Via Regina Margherita,

there's not much to occupy your time but the beach.

A good deal of the waterfront area as it appears today was built in the 1920s and '30s, and some of the buildings, such as Puccini's favourite, the Gran Caffè Margherita, retain something of their ornate stylishness.

The beach costs. It has been divided up into *stabilimenti* – individual lots where you can hire cabins, umbrellas, recliners and the like. Two recliners with umbrellas will set you back about €19 a day. A keep-'em-quiet fun activity for families is dolphin watching with **CETUS** (☎ 356 56 44 69; www.cetus.supereva.it/ - Italian only; adult/child €40/30; ⏲ 9.30am-6pm) in the main harbour.

Festivals & Events
Viareggio's biggest moment of glory comes for about three weeks in mid-February to early March when the city goes wild at *carnevale* – a festival of floats (usually with giant and satirical effigies of political and other topical figures), fireworks and dusk-to-dawn fiesta spirit.

Sleeping
CAMPING
There's a choice of about half a dozen camping grounds spread out between Viareggio and Torre del Lago in the Pineta di Levante woods. Most open from April to September.

Campeggio dei Tigli (☎ /fax 0584 34 12 78; Viale dei Tigli; adult/tent €9/14) is one of the biggest camping grounds, and includes a restaurant and disco. Without a car from Viareggio, take CLAP bus No 1 or 2 from Piazza d'Azeglio.

HOTELS
Viareggio boasts more than 120 hotels of all classes, along with *affittacamere* and villas. They jostle for space on, or a couple of blocks in from, the waterfront and are mostly modern, clean – and bland. In high summer, especially July, many hotels charge at least *mezza pensione* (half board) and often *pensione completa* (full board).

Al Piccolo (☎ 0584 5 10 14; Via Duilio 16; alpiccolo hotel@cheapnet.it; s/d €45/60; 🖳) This place has large rooms in an older home on a quiet residential street. There's a TV lounge and Internet access but the best bonus of all is the bumper buffet breakfast, which makes a change from the packaged-croissant norm.

American Hotel (☎ 0584 4 70 41; fax 0584 4 70 43; Piazza Mazzini 6; s/d €110/180; 🅿 🛇) This slick modern hotel has lots of shiny marble and coral-coloured fabric. Rooms have king-size beds and views of the piazza, fountain and (with a little neck craning) the sea.

Gran Hotel Excelsior (☎ 0584 5 07 26; www.excelsior viareggio.it; Viale Carducci 88; s/d €70/180; 🅿 🛇) Here you'll find the last word in elegance; it has a glorious feel with plush furnished rooms accentuated by chandeliers and antiques.

Eating
If you dodge full board in the hotels, there are plenty of restaurant options around town, although the waterfront places tend to be expensive and uninspiring.

Brasserie Stuzzichino (☎ 0584 43 30 65; Viale Foscolo 3; salads €6.50-10.50; 🛇 closed Mon) Aside from a sound menu of familiar pasta dishes, this simply decorated restaurant, located on a bustling street, specialises in a jumbo selection of imaginative salads.

Sergio (☎ 0584 96 37 50; Piazza del Mercato 130; mains €7.75; 🛇 closed Mon) This fantastic place

is right in the centre of the market; just follow the tantalising aroma of spit-roasted chicken. It's more of a deli with excellent cheeses and cold meats, but there are a few tables inside.

L'Oca Bianca (☎ 0584 38 84 77; Via Coppono 409; menu €45-47; 🛇 closed Mon) This is a higher class of place with an air of gentility and a deliciously grand, if expensive, menu that includes a taste of three wines. Typical dishes include ravioli with white truffles.

Drinking
Viareggio has a healthy selection of bars and clubs for those who like to keep the tempo going after sundown. Pick up a copy of *Note* or the more comprehensive *Il Mangiarbere* from the tourist office for listings.

Patchouly (☎ 0368 353 99 00; Viale Foscolo 17) For cocktails and New Age music, float into this ambient café with its glassed-in terrace and photos of jolly-looking patrons papering the walls.

Flannery's (☎ 0584 4 58 46; Del Greco Lungomolo) Yet another suitably themed Irish pub, this is a lively place to enjoy a pint of Guinness, with a huge rooftop patio and live bands from midnight, Thursday to Sunday.

Agorà Café (☎ 0584 61 04 88; Viale Colombo 666, Lido di Camaiore) A cool and laid-back hang-out for those who like their tempo energetic rather than frenetic. Later in the evening it converts into a disco with plenty of space to get jiggy.

Getting There & Around
BOAT
From June to September **Navigazione Golfo dei Poeti** (☎ 0187 73 29 87; Via Minzoni 13), in La Spezia in the region of Liguria, puts on boats connecting Viareggio (along with Forte dei Marmi, Marina di Carrara and Marina di Massa) with coastal destinations in Liguria, such as the Cinque Terre and Portofino. It also operates day excursions from Viareggio to the islands of Capraia (see p174) and Elba (mid-July to August only). Boats leave for both at 9am and return at 6.15pm. Round trips cost around €35.

BUS
Lazzi (☎ 0584 4 62 34) and **CLAP** (☎ 0584 3 09 96) buses run from Piazza d'Azeglio to destinations around Tuscany, such as Florence (€6.70, 1½ hours).

CLAP has fairly regular buses up the coast to Pietrasanta and Forte dei Marmi, as well as up to 12 daily to Lucca and from three to six a day to Massa. CLAP also runs the town's local buses.

From June to September long-distance buses run to such destinations as Milan (€22.50).

TAXI
You can order a taxi 24-hours on ☎ 0584 4 70 00.

TRAIN
Local trains run to Livorno (€3, one hour), Pisa (€2.10, 20 minutes), and to La Spezia (€4, one hour) via Massa and Carrara. Regular Florence-bound trains run via Lucca. A couple of Eurostar Italia trains bound for Rome, Genoa and Turin stop here.

SOUTH OF VIAREGGIO
Torre del Lago
A few kilometres south of Viareggio on the other side of the Pineta di Levante, Torre del Lago is a quiet continuation of the seaside theme, but with one important difference. It is a further couple of kilometres inland to the **Lago di Massaciuccoli**, a shallow lagoon forming part of the **Parco Naturale Migliarino San Rossore Massaciuccoli** (see below). The lagoon hosts more than 100 species of permanent, migratory and nesting birds, including heron, egret, wild duck and moor buzzard. **Eco-Idea** (☎ 0584 35 02 52; www.laversilia.it/eco-idea/ - Italian only; adult/child €5/2) runs boat excursions across the lagoon for about an hour from Villa Puccini, with a minimum of 20 people.

The composer Puccini had a **villa** (adult/child €5/1.50; ☺ 10am-12.30pm & 3-6.30pm Tue-Sun, to 5.30pm in winter) built here by the lake, where he hammered out some of his operas, including *Madame Butterfly*. In July and August the open-air theatre by the lagoon is one of the stages for the Festival Pucciniano in July and August, in which his operas are performed (contact the Viareggio tourist office for details or check out the festival website at www.puccinifestival.it).

There are a couple of modest hotels here, which could make for a nice and calming base – although you'd need wheels to get around, otherwise the CLAP bus No 4 goes into central Viareggio.

Parco Naturale Migliarino San Rossore Massaciuccoli
Covering 24,000 hectares and stretching from Viareggio in the north to Livorno in the south, this park is one of the rare stretches of protected coastline in Tuscany.

Part swamp, part pine forest, the park plays host to particularly diverse birdlife, especially during the migratory periods, including species of falcon, duck, heron, cormorant and a series of other waterbirds. Deer, wild boar and goats constitute the bulk of the landed critter contingent.

The **centro visite** (visitors centre; ☎ 050 53 01 01; visitesr@tin.it; ☺ 8am-7.30pm, to 5.30pm in winter, weekends only) in Cascine Vecchie can provide more information.

A sliver of coast between the Arno River and Livorno is not part of the park, and for Pisans the small seaside towns of **Marina di Pisa** and the more attractive **Tirrenia** are the hub of the weekend beach-going experience. Beyond the park, the next stop south on the coast is the sprawling port town of Livorno (see p170).

LA VERSILIA
The coastal area from Viareggio north to the regional border with Liguria is known as La Versilia. Although popular with local holiday-makers and some foreigners (mainly Germans, French and Brits), it has been blighted by strip development along the beachfront.

It does however make a good gateway to the Apuane Alps (see p167), with roads from the coastal towns snaking their way deep into the heart of the mountains, and connecting with small villages and walking tracks.

Pietrasanta & Around
Pressing up the coast from Viareggio, you cross into **Lido di Camaiore**. The development becomes sparser as you head northwards and the beaches are usually less crowded.

When you reach **Marina di Pietrasanta,** turn inland 3.5km for the town of **Pietrasanta** itself. The centre of the old town is Piazza Duomo. If it's open, pop into the Chiesa di Sant'Agostino; its rather stark, Gothic facade won't necessarily appeal but the cloister inside is pleasant. Also here is a cathedral (13th century) and the Palazzo Moroni, which houses a modest archaeological museum.

With a car, or a circle-line CLAP bus from Piazza Matteotti, you could push further inland to **Seravezza**, since the 16th century an important centre for marble extraction (Michelangelo spent some time here looking for raw materials) and now a gateway to the Parco Regionale delle Alpi Apuane. The Parco delle Alpi Apuane **information centre** (☎ 0584 75 73 25; Via Corrado del Greco 11; ☯ 9am-1pm & 4-8pm daily summer, 9am-1pm & 2.30-4.30pm Mon-Sat winter) can supply you with maps and booklets on walks in the Alps.

Set on the confluence of the rivers Serra and Vezza into La Versilia, and with the Apuane Alps rising behind it, Seravezza is a pleasant small town. The cathedral has some superb works by Florentine goldsmiths, including a crucifix, while about 4.5km north, the Pieve della Cappella (parish church) in **Azzano** has a beautiful rose window nicknamed the 'eye of Michelangelo'. Also of interest is the Palazzo Mediceo, built by Cosimo I de' Medici as a summer getaway.

One recommended route is due southeast along the Vezza River (also accessible by CLAP bus from Piazza Matteotti) to the picturesque *frazione* (hamlet) of **Stazzema** high in the hills. The village entrance is marked by the Romanesque Chiesa di Santa Maria Assunta, and it makes a great base for walks in the Apuane Alps.

Procinto (☎ 0584 77 70 04; Via Novembre 21; d from €41) is a rural hotel in the heart of Stazzema and the obvious choice, although its management could use a course at charm school. The meals are huge and well priced. Rumbling tummies should fill up on the delicious *polenta con funghi*.

If you feel like a dip in the briny, return to Seravezza and take the direct road to **Forte dei Marmi**, where there are plenty of places to stay, eat and drink close to the waterfront. The **tourist office** (☎ 0584 8 00 91; Via Franceschi 8b) can provide you with a list.

Beyond Forte dei Marmi the seaside is fairly uninspiring, until you reach the border of Liguria and beyond.

Massa

Inland, the next town of note is Massa, the administrative centre of the province of the same name (the province is also known as Massa Carrara).

The main **tourist office** (☎ 0585 24 00 63; Viale Vespucci 24) is on the coast in Marina di Massa. Little remains of the old core of the town apart from the cathedral, itself of slight interest. Dominating the town is the **Castello Malaspina** (☎ 0585 4 47 74; adult/child €5/3; ☯ 9.30am-12.30pm & 5.30-8pm Tue-Sun mid-Jun–mid-Sep). The Malaspina family was in charge around here for hundreds of years from the mid-15th century onwards. From this high point they could keep a watch on the surrounding territory.

There are only two hotels in Massa, should you want to stay. Otherwise continue to Marina di Massa, a lively and fun place with a glut of restaurants and bars. North of the marina there are dozens of camping grounds.

Hotel Caprice (☎ 0585 86 80 28; www.hotel caprice.net; Via delle Pinete 237; s/d €55/60) is a hotel with lovely gardens and several terraces. The rooms are a little threadbare but comfortable enough and the English-Italian owners are cheery and helpful with info on the area.

GETTING AROUND

Buses for a good number of destinations around the northwest of Tuscany leave from the train station, which is in Massa itself. Buses to Lucca run five times a day (€3.50, 1½ hours).

Carrara

Carrara, about 7km northwest of Massa, is known as the world capital of both the extraction and working of white marble. Michelangelo made frequent trips to Carrara to select the best-quality material for his commissions. Watching the trucks rumble down from the quarries today makes you wonder just how back-breaking and treacherous a business the extraction and transport of marble must have been back then.

The marble quarries up in the hills behind Carrara were already being worked during the Roman Empire, so the tradition is a long one. In 1442 the town came under the control of the Malaspina family and shared the fate of Massa further south. Quarrying marble is no child's game and a monument to workers who have lost their lives in the quarries can be seen in Piazza XXVII Aprile. Although environmentalists oppose the continual massive quanity of marble that is extracted, quarry owners continue to fight back, protecting

NORTHWESTERN TUSCANY

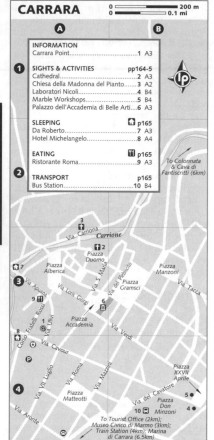

CARRARA

INFORMATION	
Carrara Point	1 A3

SIGHTS & ACTIVITIES	pp164-5
Cathedral	2 A3
Chiesa della Madonna del Pianto	3 A2
Laboratori Nicoli	4 B4
Marble Workshops	5 B4
Palazzo dell'Accademia di Belle Arti	6 A3

SLEEPING	p165
Da Roberto	7 A3
Hotel Michelangelo	8 A4

EATING	p165
Ristorante Roma	9 A3

TRANSPORT	p165
Bus Station	10 B4

their fourteen thousand or so employees. These tough men formed the backbone of a strong leftist and anarchist tradition in Carrara, something that won them no friends among the Fascists or, later, the occupying German forces.

The gracious little old centre of Carrara is tucked away in the northwestern corner of the town, almost 10km inland from its coastal counterpart, Marina di Carrara, and nuzzling up to the first hills of the Apuane Alps, many of them visibly scarred by centuries of marble extraction.

INFORMATION

The **tourist office** (☎ 0585 84 4 403; Via Settembre XX; ☻ 9.30am-7pm daily Jun-Sep, 10am-1pm & 4-7pm Mon-Sat Oct-May) is on the coast. If you are interested in visiting the *laboratori*, or marble workshops, they can provide you with a map.

The main post office is on the corner of Via Mazzini and Via Aronte. **Carrara Point** (☎ 0585 77 96 36; Ulivi 19) provides Internet access for €5 per hour, with discounts for students. The police station is on the corner of Via Cavour and Corso Fratelli Rossi.

SIGHTS

The **cathedral** (☎ 0585 7 19 42; Piazza Duomo; ☻ 7am-noon & 3.30-7pm), at the heart of the old town, is one of the earliest medieval buildings to have been constructed entirely of Apuane marble. Building began in the 11th century but it dragged on for two centuries. The facade, a mix of Romanesque (the lower half) and Gothic, was largely inspired by Pisan models.

The prettiest square in the town, with its festively painted houses, is the 15th-century **Piazza Alberica**.

The 'castle' on Piazza Gramsci started life as a fortified residence of the Malaspina clan and is now the **Palazzo dell'Accademia di Belle Arti** (☎ 0585 7 16 58; Via Roma 1; ☻ 9am-1pm Tue-Sat), housing a collection of Roman sculptural fragments and other odds and ends.

South of the centre towards Marina di Carrara is the **Museo Civico di Marmo** (☎ 0585 84 57 46; Via Settembre XX; adult/child €3.10/1.55; ☻ 10am-8pm Mon-Sat Jul-Aug, 10am-6pm Mon-Sat May, Jun & Sep, 8.30am-1.30pm Oct-Apr). Here you can find out everything you wanted to know about marble and were afraid to ask. On display are examples of no less than 310 types of marble, granite and other decorative stones found in Italy and a modest modern sculpture collection. Buses running between Marina di Carrara and Carrara will drop you off – it's near the *stadio* (stadium).

Colonnata and the **Cava di Fantiscritti** are home to quarries. Follow the *cava* (quarry) signs. Local buses make regular runs to Colonnata (€1.50, ½ hour), once home to the Roman slaves forced to extract marble. Nowadays mechanical saws are employed to carve out the enormous white blocks. At the Cava di Fantiscritti, there is a private **museum**, (☎ 0585 7 09 81; ☻ 9am-7pm Easter-Nov) where you can see the kinds of tools with which quarriers used to struggle. To get to this spot you cross the Ponti di Vara, a viaduct built in the 19th century for the railways. At the time it was considered one of the great feats of modern engineering.

You could also consider visiting some of the marble *laboratori*. The commissions can range from the banal to the bizarre. Artists frequently instruct the workshops on how they want a piece executed – or at least begun – thus cleverly avoiding the hard and dusty work themselves. A handy one is **Laboratori Nicoli** on Piazza XXVII Aprile. If nothing else, you could poke your nose into the dust-filled air of the workshops on either side of the square.

Over the summer, CAT buses provide a hop-on hop-off service that passes many of the *laboratori*, the museum and Colonnata. Tickets cost €8; pick up information at the tourist office.

SLEEPING & EATING
A couple of places are worth considering.

Da Roberto (☎ 0585 7 06 34; Via Apuana 3f; s/d €31/ 46.50) This is family run, pristine and good value although the location, at the junction of two busy roads, may mean sleeping with the window closed.

Hotel Michelangelo (☎ 0585 77 71 61; fax 0585 7 45 45; Corso Fratelli Rossi 3; s/d €60/90) This hotel is past its best but the rooms are still comfortable and filled with some lovely old furniture.

Ristorante Roma (☎ 0585 7 06 32; Piazza Cesare Battisti 1; mains €8) The decor here may be a little dated but the food makes up for it and the service is smiley and quick. Try the warming seafood risotto followed by a simple – yet memorable – vanilla *gelato*.

GETTING THERE & AWAY
The bus station is on Piazza Don Minzoni. **CAT buses** (☎ 0585 8 53 11) serve the surrounding area, including Massa (€0.90, ½ hour) to the south and, in the Lunigiana area, Fivizzano (€2.20, two hours), Aulla (€1.80, one hour) and Pontremoli (€2.80, two hours).

Trains along the coastal line (from Genoa, Rome, Viareggio and so on) stop nearer Marina di Carrara, from where local buses shuttle into Carrara itself (€0.75).

LUNIGIANA
North of here is one of the least-known pockets of Tuscany: the Lunigiana. This landlocked enclave of Tuscan territory is bordered to the north and east by Emilia-Romagna, to the west by Liguria and the south by the Apuane Alps. Pontremoli town makes a good central base for exploring the area.

The rugged territory abutting the mountains in Parma province to the north is great to explore. The medieval Via Francigena, a vital route connecting northern and central Italy in Roman days, and a key access to armies and Rome-bound pilgrims alike, roughly follows the modern A15 autostrada from the Cisa pass south to Sarzana (in Liguria) on the coast.

The following route is one of several options. From Carrara take the provincial SP446d road northwards and follow the signs to **Fosdinovo**.

The only reason for calling in here is to take a closer look at the formidable **castle** (☎ 0187 6 88 91; €3.10; ☼ tours only at 4pm, 5pm & 6pm Wed-Mon). Owned by the Malaspina clan since 1340 (it still belongs to a branch of the family), its defensive walls and towers were gradually modified from the 16th century when the family converted it into a residence. Legend has it that a young princess died of a broken heart within the castle walls and at full moon her shadow can be seen drifting from window to window.

From Fosdinovo, follow the SS446 until it reaches a T-junction with the SS63. Heading right (eastwards) will bring you to **Fivizzano** (buses serve this route). You could stop for a food break in this largely modern farming centre before proceeding up to the border with Emilia-Romagna and the Apennines.

CAT buses run regularly to Aulla and less so to Massa, Carrara, Fosdinovo and Passo Cerreto (the pass over the Apennines into Emilia). Indeed, beyond Fivizzano the mountain road offers wonderfully pretty country deep into Emilia-Romagna.

Heading in the opposite direction, southwest from Fivizzano, you hit **Aulla**, a drab town with a 16th-century *fortezza* as its only draw.

Proceeding northwards from Aulla, you arrive in **Villafranca**, a one-time waystation on the Via Francigena and, according to the stories, something of a medieval tourist trap, where the difference between local tax collectors and plain old thieves was vague, to say the least. The northern end is dominated by a mill, now housing a local ethnographic museum, and a bridge over the Magra River.

Albergo Manganelli (☎ /fax 0187 49 30 62; Piazza San Nicolò 5; s/d €32/37, with bath €37/42) is an inviting place at the southern end of the old village, below the train tracks. The rooms are big, airy and basic, and there's a decent restaurant attached.

Pontremoli

A primary halting place along the Via Francigena, the original old town is a long sliver of a place stretching north to south between the Magra and Verde Rivers. These watercourses served as natural defensive barriers in this, a key position for the control of traffic between northern and central Italy. In the 17th century the town enjoyed a boom and most of the fine residences date back to those times. The town has a definite charm, with small piazzas surrounded by colonnaded arches shading bars and cafés. The shops here are an eclectic mix of the old-fashioned and idiosyncratic next to the stylish and sophisticated.

The **tourist office** (☎ 0187 83 32 78; Piazza della Repubblica 6; ⊗ 9am-1pm & 3.30-6.30pm Mon-Fri, & 9.30am-12.30pm Sat) has plenty of information.

From the central Piazza della Repubblica and Piazza del Duomo (the latter is flanked by the 17th-century cathedral with its neoclassical facade), a steep and winding way takes you to the **Castello del Piagnaro** (☎ 0187 83 14 39; €3.10; ⊗ 9am-noon & 3-6pm Tue-Sun). Although originally raised in the 9th century, what you see today is largely the result of 14th- and 15th-century reconstruction. The views across the town are enchanting and inside you can visit the museum, which houses a number of striking prehistoric menhirs (carved standing stones) found nearby.

There are a couple of places to stay.

Golf Hotel (☎ 0187 83 15 73; golfhotel@tin.it; 1 Via della Pineta 32; s/d €62/99) Aside from the puzzling name (there's no golf course in sight) this is a sumptuous hotel with magnificent views of the pine-clad countryside. There is

---

BEGNINI'S WORLD

When people think about Italian cinema today, the image that undoubtedly comes to mind is Roberto Begnini's spirited and largely unintelligible Oscar acceptance speech in 1999. En route to the stage he conveyed his glee by jumping not just over, but on, the seats.

Until the momentous success of *Life is Beautiful*, Italian cinema had suffered an artistic and commercial slump. The Tuscan actor's approach to the delicate subject of the Holocaust quickly became the most successful foreign film ever in the US with a box office take of some $35.8 million. Benigni was also the first Italian and, indeed, non-English speaker to win the best actor award.

With the exception of films such as *Cinema Paradiso*, *Ciao Professore!* and *Il Postino*, very few Italian films had succeeded in the international market over the preceding decade; it had been a long time since films by such cinematic greats as Fellini, Rossellini, Visconti, Antonioni and De Sica had held foreign audiences in thrall.

Begnini's success was just the kickstart the Italian film world needed; in 2001 Nanni Moretti took top prize at Cannes for *La Stanza del Figlio* (The Son's Room) and Christian Comencini's *Il Piu bel Giorno della Mia Vita* (The Best Day of My Life) won the prize for best foreign film at the Montreal Film Festival the following year. In 2003 Begnini's *Pinnochio* was deemed one of the most beautiful of all Italian films with delightful costumes and storybook sets; the main criticism was that Begnini – at 50 – was just too old for the part.

Begnini was born in 1952 in Misericordia, a small village in the province of Arezzo, and moved shortly after to Vergaio, a village of 3,000 people 15 miles northwest of Florence. Here he joined the local virtuosos at the *casa del popolo* (town's social centre) perfecting that distinctly Tuscan dramatic technique of improvised rhyming stories. From this early training, he still maintains an admirable ability to improvise.

At age 20 Begnini moved to Rome where he worked in bars and theatres presenting his avant-garde monologue show to a bemused audience. Here he was discovered by Giuseppe Bertolucci, which eventually led to bringing Italian cinema, once again, to the screens of an international audience grown increasingly weary of the sanitised sentimentality of the Hollywood big screen.

a grand marble lobby leading to bright and spacious rooms.

Trattoria Da Bussè (☎ 0187 83 13 71; Piazza del Duomo 32; mains €8-12; ☺ lunch only Mon-Thu, lunch & dinner Sat & Sun) This restaurant, where you can dine on excellent local specialities, is in the shadow of the cathedral.

CAT buses run regularly south to Aulla and other destinations around the Lunigiana. You can also get to La Spezia (an important coastal town in Liguria). Pontremoli is also on the Parma–La Spezia train line.

Apuane Alps

This mountain range is bordered on one side by the Versilia coastline and on the other by the vast valley of the Garfagnana. Altitudes are relatively low – the highest peak, Monte Pisanino, is 1945m high – in comparison with the Alps further north, but the Apuane Alps are certainly not lacking in great walking possibilities with a good network of marked trails, as well as several *rifugi*. For further details of walking in this region, see p36.

Apart from a multitude of walking opportunities, the main attractions in the area are the underground caves. **Grotta del Vento** (☎ 0583 72 20 24; www.grottadelvento.com; tours €6.50-15) is a series of caves with stalagmites, stalactites and crystal-encrusted lakes. The caves are open all year-round and three possible guided itineraries are offered; they range in length from one to three hours and the first groups start at 10am. From November to March only the one-hour walk is available from Monday to Saturday. To get here by bus from Lucca, you travel via Gallicano with the last 1km only accessible by foot.

Antro del Corchia (☎ 0584 77 84 05; adult/child €11/10), to the north of Seravezza near Levigliani, is a relatively new cave and part of the deepest and longest cave in Italy. The first tours leave at 10am and last two hours. Bring something warm to wear as the caves maintain a chilly 7.6°C year-round. Buses do run from Pietrasanta via Seravezza (€1.45, 40 minutes), but there are no return services in the evening.

Central Coast & Elba

CENTRAL COAST & ELBA

CONTENTS

The Central Coast is a curious hotchpotch of ordinary working cities, intriguing medieval towns and well-preserved Etruscan sites. It is an interesting area for travellers, not only for its diversity, but also because eye-catching places like the ancient village of Suvereto have remained largely untainted by tourism. Livorno has never been on the tourist trail and yet there is a gritty individuality about the place that some may find oddly appealing. For those interested in Etruscan civilisation, Populonia and its medieval twin, Populonia Alta, make absorbing diversions. Livorno and Piombino are also departure points for ferries to the Tuscan islands and beyond.

Much of the coast south of Livorno, known as the Maremma Pisana, was once unpleasantly damp and mosquito infested. Although initial attempts to dry out these swamps were carried out in the 18th century, it was really only under Leopoldo II that serious land reclamation took place. As a result, agricultural and industrial activity prospered, along with roads and the infrastructure. The Maremma Pisana formally became a part of Livorno province in 1925.

Today another obvious plus of the Central Coast is the beach scene, with several worth exploring, especially on the southern Golfo di Baratti. Those seriously into sand and sea, however, should hop on a ferry to Elba which, although best enjoyed out of season, has all the classic appeal of a typical Mediterranean island without any high-rises fronting the beach.

CENTRAL COAST & ELBA

HIGHLIGHTS

- Chow down on a generous helping of *cacciucco*, a delicious and traditional seafood stew well worth shelling out for
- Combine a beach flop at Golfo di Baratti (p177) with an exploration of the Etruscan and medieval settlements of Populonia (p177)
- Catch a ferry to unspoilt Capraia (p174) – great for diving, walking or just a sunflop on the beach
- Exercise your calf muscles by climbing the torturous steep streets of Suvereto (p176), appreciating the village's heady Gothic feel
- Lace up those walking boots or saddle up a mountain bike to explore the western heights of the island of Elba around Monte Capanne (p184)

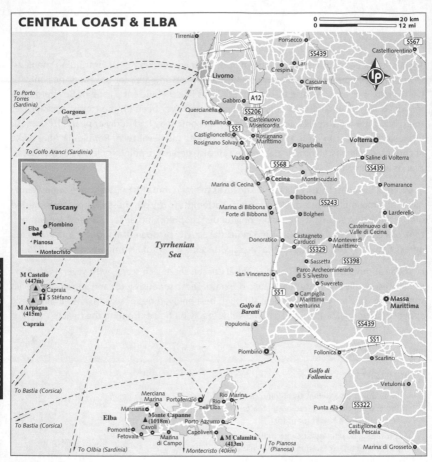

LIVORNO
pop 173,000

Tuscany's second-largest city, Livorno was heavily bombed during WWII (it was one of Fascist Italy's main naval bases) and there is something mildly melancholic about the centre of town. The post-war rebuilding program may be charitably described as unimaginative. On the plus side, this lack of wonderful old churches and buildings means that you can concentrate on other things – such as the seafood, reputedly the best on the Tyrrhenian coast. Be sure to tuck into a *cacciucco*, a remarkable mixed-seafood stew.

Earliest references to the town date to 1017. The port was in the hands of Pisa and then Genoa for centuries, until Florence took

control in 1421. It was still tiny – by the 1550s it boasted a grand total of 480 permanent residents. All that changed under Cosimo I de' Medici, who converted the scrawny settlement into a heavily fortified coastal bastion.

By the end of the 18th century, around 80,000 people lived in this busy port: it had become one of the main staging posts for British and Dutch merchants who were then operating between Western Europe and the Middle East. In the following century it was declared a free port, stimulating further growth and prosperity.

Information
EMERGENCY
Police Station (☎ 0586 23 51 11; Piazza Unità d'Italia)

INTERNET ACCESS
Internetcafé (☎ 0586 83 95 20; Vicolo delle Rimesse 13; €3/30mins)

LAUNDRY
Niagara (☎ Borgo dei Cappuccini 13; €3.60 for washing & drying a load)

MEDICAL SERVICES
Hospital (☎ 055 21 67 61, 0586 22 31 11; Viale Alfieri 36) Located between the town centre and the train station.

POST
Post Office (Via Cairoli 46)

TELEPHONE
Telecom (Largo Duomo 14) This office is unstaffed.

TOURIST INFORMATION
Main Tourist Office (☎ 0586 20 46 11; www.livorno.turismo.toscana.it; 2nd floor, Piazza Cavour 6; ☒ 9am-1pm & 3-5pm Mon-Fri) Just south of Piazza Grande; there is also a small tourist office on Piazza del Municipio; a third **tourist office** (☎ 0586 89 53 20; ☒ summer only) is near the main ferry terminal known as Calata Carrara.

Sights
The city has a few worthy sights. The **Fortezza Nuova** (New Fort), in the area known as Piccola Venezia because of its small canals, was built for the Medici in the late 16th century and based on the Venetian methods used to reclaim the land from the sea. Laced with canals, what this area lacks in gondolas and American tourists, it makes up for with a certain shabby charm: waterways flanked by faded, peeling apartments that are brightly decorated with strings of washing.

Close to the waterfront is the city's other fort, the **Fortezza Vecchia** (Old Fort), built 60 years earlier on the site of an 11th-century building. It is in pretty bad shape, with yawning chasms caused by obvious subsidence over the years.

A couple of modest museums can be found in Livorno. **Museo Civico Giovanni Fattori** (☎ 0586 80 80 01; Via San Jacopo 65; adult/child €4/2.50; ☒ 9am-1pm Tue-Sun) is in a pretty park south of the town centre and features works by the 19th-century Italian impressionist Macchiaioli school. Temporary exhibitions are also held occasionally.

If you still need a museum fix, try the **Museo di Storia Naturale del Mediterraneo** (☎ 0586 80 22 94; Via Roma 234; admission €2.60; ☒ 9am-1pm & 3-7pm

Tue-Sun), where you'll find a range of botanical and sea-faring creatures (specimens only) from the Mediterranean, including 'Annie', a common whale skeleton.

The city's unspectacular modern **cathedral** is on Piazza Grande.

South of Livorno is where the Etruscan Coast (Costa degli Etruschi) begins. The town's beaches stretch for some way south but they are pebbly and generally nothing special. The grand old seaside villas are worth seeing. The No 1 bus from the main train station heads down the coast road, passing via the town centre and Porto Mediceo.

Sleeping
Finding suitable accommodation in Livorno shouldn't be a problem.

Pensione Dante (☎ 0586 89 34 61; Scali d'Azeglio 28; s/d €35/40) Near the waterfront, this place has large, simply furnished rooms with basins. The place has a friendly rough-and-tumble family feel about it and is not a bad option if you are euro-economising.

Villa Morazzana (☎ 0586 50 00 76; fax 50 24 26; Via di Collinet 68; dm/d €16/45, with bathroom €75) This hostel-cum-hotel has a pleasant spot in the hills, only a couple of kilometres southeast of the town centre. It's a wonderful old building with spacious, bright rooms and plenty of easy-on-the-eye artwork hanging on the walls. Breakfast and a garden are thrown in to the budget-friendly price. To get here, take bus No 3 from Piazza Grande.

Hotel Gran Duca (☎ 0586 89 10 24; www.granduca.it; Piazza Micheli 16; s/d €86/124; P ☒) A modern plushly carpeted hotel with all the comforts and conveniences. The location is excellent, right across from the port, and there's an adjacent reasonably good restaurant.

Eating
For produce, the **market** is on Via Buontalenti, and the area around Piazza XX Settembre is encouraging for **bars** and **cafés**.

Il Travaso delle Idea (☎ 0586 21 94 15; Scali D'Azeglio 64; mains €6-8) Smart restaurant and bar with subdued lighting and alcoves for that locked-eyes-over-cocktail time. There is a tasty *antipasto* choice and the owner speaks English.

Cantina Senese (☎ 0586 89 02 39; Borgo dei Cappuccini 95; mains €6-8; ☒ closed Sun) Feels like a real local, and a great choice for food and

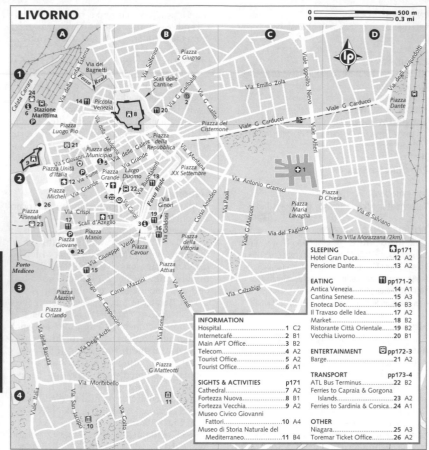

LIVORNO

SLEEPING 🛏 p171
Hotel Gran Duca...............12 A2
Pensione Dante..................13 A2

EATING 🍴 pp171-2
Antica Venezia..................14 A1
Cantina Senese.................15 A3
Enoteca Doc....................16 B3
Il Travaso delle Idea..........17 A2
Market...........................18 B2
Ristorante Città Orientale....19 B2
Vecchia Livorno................20 B1

ENTERTAINMENT 🎭 pp172-3
Barge............................21 A2

TRANSPORT pp173-4
ATL Bus Terminus..............22 B2
Ferries to Capraia & Gorgona
 Islands.........................23 A2
Ferries to Sardinia & Corsica..24 A1

OTHER
Niagara..........................25 A3
Toremar Ticket Office..........26 A2

INFORMATION
Hospital............................1 C2
Internetcafé.......................2 B1
Main APT Office..................3 B2
Telecom...........................4 A2
Tourist Office.....................5 A2
Tourist Office.....................6 A1

SIGHTS & ACTIVITIES p171
Cathedral...........................7 A2
Fortezza Nuova...................8 B1
Fortezza Vecchia.................9 A2
Museo Civico Giovanni
 Fattori...........................10 A4
Museo di Storia Naturale del
 Mediterraneo.................11 B4

low-key atmosphere. Trouble is everyone knows it. Try the *carbonara de mare* (pasta with a creamy seafood sauce).

Enoteca Doc (☎ 0586 88 75 83; Via Goldoni 40-44; mains €10-12; 🕑 closed Mon) The menu changes weekly at this *enoteca* (wine bar), and you can enjoy fresh pasta dishes and good *carpaccio*, as well as snacks. However, the main attraction is the gluggable choice of wines.

Vecchia Livorno (☎ 0586 88 40 48; Scali delle Cantine 34; mains €7.50; 🕑 closed Tue) Facing the Fortezza Nuova, this is a spit-and-sawdust place with long wooden tables and a buzzy neighbourhood feel. Expect hearty, filling food; the seafood dishes are particularly recommended.

Antica Venezia (☎ 0586 88 73 53; Piazza dei Domenicani; mains €14-15; 🕑 closed Sun) Attracts

a smart clientele with its imaginative menu of catch-of-the-day specials prepared with an innovative twist. The atmosphere is attractively upbeat. Book ahead.

Ristorante Città Orientale (☎ 0586 88 82 66; Via Ginori 23; mains €3.10-6.20) For a change from Italian, come to this Chinese restaurant offering a wide selection of dishes without the normal migraine-inducing decor. The set menus are great value.

Ristorante Aragosta (☎ 0586 89 53 95; Piazza Arsenale 6; mains €8-12) Also consider this place for its excellent seafood.

Entertainment
The Barge (☎ 0586 88 83 20; Scali Delle Ancore 6) Mickey Mouse's idea of an English pub that

attracts an effortlessly hip young crowd to its nightly live music mix.

Getting There & Away
BOAT
Livorno is a major west-coast port. Regular departures for Sardinia and Corsica leave from Calata Carrara, just north of Fortezza Vecchia. Ferries also depart from the smaller terminal, Porto Mediceo, near Piazza Arsenale. The port can be easily reached by bus from the main train station. There's a Toremar ticket office, for ferries to the islands of Capraia and Gorgona, on the opposite side of Piazza Arsenale to the ferry terminal.

Ferry services from Livorno:

Porto Mediceo
Toremar (☎ 0586 89 61 13; www.toremar.it) Services to Gorgona and Capraia leave from Porto Mediceo.

Porto Nuovo
Lloyd Sardegna Compagnia di Navigazione Marittima (☎ 0586 22 23 00; www.lloydsardegna.it) At Varco Galvani, Calata Carrara, with ferries to Olbia (Sardinia).
Grandi Navi Veloci (☎ 0586 40 98 04; www.grimaldi.it) At Varco Galvani, Calata Carrara, Darsena 1, with boats to Palermo in Sicily (one-way seats cost €56.25 to €87.25).

Stazione Marittima
Corsica Ferries (☎ 0586 88 13 80; www.corsicaferries.com) Regular services to Corsica (return daytime deck-class fares to Bastia cost €23 to €37).
Corsica Marittima (☎ 0586 21 05 07) Services to Corsica (to Bastia and Porto Vecchio) same price as above.
Sardinia Ferries (☎ 0586 88 13 80; www.corsicaferries.com) Regular services to Sardinia (return deck-class fares to Golfo Aranci, near Olbia, cost €23.48 to €58.48 – the higher fares on summer weekends only).
Moby Lines (☎ 0586 82 68 23/4/5; www.mobylines.it) Services to Corsica (one-way deck-class fares to Bastia cost €15.20 to €28.75 depending on the season) and Sardinia (one-way deck-class fares to Olbia cost €22 to €47.50).

BUS
ATL buses (☎ 0586 88 42 62) depart from Largo Duomo for Cecina (€2.80, one hour), Piombino (€5.85, 2¼ hours) and Pisa (€2.20, ¾ hour).

CAR & MOTORCYCLE
The A12 runs past the city and the SS1 connects Livorno with Rome. There are several car parks near the waterfront.

AMEDEO DOES PARIS
Modigliani's portraits of women with their long necks, African mask-like faces and tilted oblong heads are among the most readily recognisable in all of modern art.

Born in Livorno in 1884, Amedeo Modigliani showed talent as an artist at an early age and trained under the influence of the former Macchiaioli artists who had shaken up the Florentine, and indeed Italian, art scene in the years before and after Italian unity. Livorno's own Giovanni Fattori had been a leading light among the Macchiaioli.

Modigliani was soon drawn away from his home town. His early influences were the Renaissance masters, and he headed first to Florence and then to Venice. This was followed finally by a move in 1906 to Paris which, by then, was the epicentre of the art world, and where he was influenced by Cezanne, Picasso and Cocteau.

Modigliani returned to Italy briefly in 1909 but, from then until the end of his life in 1920, remained in Montparnasse in Paris. For the next five years he turned to sculpture, rapidly accelerating the process of simplification and emphasising the contours. This period was then reflected in his subsequent paintings – the long faces typical of his later work are a result of his venture into sculpture. In 1914 and 1915 he concentrated on portraiture and then, in the last years of his life, produced the series of nudes that figure among his best-known works and display a classical and serene eroticism.

Predictably, his work really only began to receive critical acclaim after his death, particularly in the wake of an exhibition of his paintings at the Venice Biennale in 1930. The bulk of his work has been scattered across art galleries in various parts of Italy and from Switzerland to France, Britain, the USA and beyond.

TRAIN
The main train station in Piazza Dante is on the Rome-La Spezia line. The city is also connected to Florence (€5.73, one hour 20 minutes) and Pisa (€1.29, 15 minutes). Trains are less frequent to Stazione Marittima, the second station near the main port. It's easier to catch a train to the main train station and then a bus to the ports.

Getting Around

During the summer there is a regular shuttle bus (€2) that run between Largo Duomo and the port. Otherwise take bus No 7. City buses cost €0.85, if bought in advance from *tabaccai* (tobacconists), or €1.10 if bought on the bus.

AROUND LIVORNO
Capraia & Gorgona

Toremar operates boats to the islands of Capraia and Gorgona from Livorno. Along with Elba, and four others further south still (Pianosa, Montecristo, Giglio and Giannutri), they form the Parco Nazionale dell'Arcipelago Toscano.

The elliptical, volcanic island of **Capraia** lies 65km from Livorno. Its highest point is Monte Castello at 447m and is covered mainly in *macchia*, various types of scrub. The third-largest island, it has changed hands several times over the course of its history, once belonging to Genoa, Sardinia, the Saracens from North Africa and Napoleon.

You can join boat trips around the 30km coastline (€12) or trek across the island. The most popular walk is to the Stagnone, a small lake in the south. There are also a couple of dive sites off the coast; contact **Capraia Diving** (☎ 0565 91 94 11; www.capraiadiving.it; from €37 a dive) for more information. The only beach worthy of the name is **Cala della Mortola**, a few kilometres north of **Capraia Isola** town.

The tiny island of **Gorgona** is the greenest and northernmost of the islands. At just 2.23 sq km, there's not much to it. Its two towers were built respectively by the Pisans and Medicis of Florence. Part of the island is off-limits as a low-security prison. You can effectively only visit the island on Tuesday, when the 8.30am Toremar ferry from Livorno stops there on the way to/from Capraia, giving you about five hours from the arrival time at 10am.

INFORMATION
Tourist office (☎ 0586 90 51 38; www.arcipelago. turismo.toscana.it/capraia; Via Assunzione 42; ☷ 9am-12.30pm & 3.30-6pm Apr-Sep, 9am-7.30pm Jul only)
Agenzia Turistica Parco/Agenzia Viaggi e Turismo (☎ 0586 90 50 71; www.isoladicapraia.it) Shares the same space as the tourist office and can advise on activities, such as trekking and boat trips.

SLEEPING & EATING
Accommodation on Capraia is tight, and there are no places to stay on Gorgona.

Da Beppone (☎ 0586 90 50 01; Via della Assunzione 78; s/d €40/70) A very friendly and reliable choice. The rooms are smallish but pleasant, and the bar and restaurant are a bonus. Pets accepted.

Il Saracino (☎ 0586 90 50 18; www.hotelilsaracino.it; Via Cibo 30; half-board s/d €110/220) Down near the beach, Il Saracino has bright modern rooms with plenty of wood and white paint. There is a snazzy roof-top bar with a small dance floor for late-night smooching under the stars.

Relais La Mandola (☎ 0586 90 51 19; www.laman dola.it; Via della Mandola 1; half-board s/d €135/270; P ✕) This money-no-object choice is a seriously swish new hotel with private beach (and beach bar). Rooms have balconies, sea views and all mod cons. Prices drop dramatically out of season.

GETTING THERE & AWAY
A daily boat to Capraia with Toremar sails from Livorno. On most days there is also a return trip but triple-check before you go. The one-way fare costs €10.40, whether you go to Capraia or Gorgona. In summer, excursions from Elba to Capraia are also organised.

THE ETRUSCAN COAST

The province of Livorno stretches down the coast to just beyond Piombino, and the ferry to the island of Elba.

Overall, Tuscany's beaches are the basic bucket-and-spade variety, although some have pebbles rather than sand. Watch out for the prices, as you can fork out plenty for the privilege of a sun bed and brolly.

Several attractive small towns are scattered about in the hilly hinterland of this slender province. A couple of archaeological parks and the possibility of discovering some of Tuscany's lesser-known, but often very good, wines complete the picture.

Livorno to Cecina

You can chug down the coast from Livorno by train or bus, but your own transport will give you greater freedom to explore.

There's a good beach a couple of kilometres short of **Quercianella**. Heading south from Livorno, keep a watch out for a tower and castle atop a promontory. The inlet directly north of this is where the beach is located. As you round a curve into the inlet there is a small sign indicating a path down to the beach. There is limited parking.

In leafy Quercianella you'll find a couple of little grey-stone beaches. At the northern end of the town, surfers gather even when an adverse wind is up. After another 5km or so, watch for the **Parco Comunale di Fortullino** sign. If you can find a place to park, walk down to the water's edge. The park is pleasant and a bar operates in summer. But again, the beach is disappointing and rocky.

Castiglioncello

This small seaside resort has a pleasing lack of pretension. In the late 19th century it was also the home of Digo Martelli, the famous Italian critic and patron of the arts who habitually invited the Florentine Impressionist artists of that period, giving birth to the legendary artistic period known as La Scuola di Castiglioncello.

The small sandy beaches on the north side of the town are the best, although sunbed rental is expensive (from €8). The town centres around the vast terrace of the Caffè Ginori (see below).

INFORMATION
There is a small **tourist office** (☎ 0586 75 48 90, Via Aurelia 967; 🕑 9.30am-12.30pm Mon-Fri, 9.30am-12.30pm Sat), located in the train station, which can help book accommodation.

SLEEPING & EATING
Pensione Bartoli (☎ 0586 75 20 51; Via Martelli 9; s/d €43/52, with bathroom €48/58; P) Old-fashioned 'let's stay with grandma' kind of place with well-dusted large rooms, lace curtains and heavy wood furniture. Go for room 19 if you fancy a sea view.

Villa Parisi (☎ 0586 75 16 98; www.emmeti.it/VillaParisi; Via Martelli 9; s/d €105/180; P 🌊) A special-occasion hotel in a former Roman villa. Rooms are stylish and good-sized, and most have a seamless sea view. There's a pool and large sun terrace, plus private access to the beach.

Caffè Ginori (☎ 0586 75 90 55; Piazza della Vittoria) This fin-de-siecle café is straight out of a Renoir painting, with its vast gracious terrace, where you can enjoy breakfast, drinks, snacks and, above all, the entertaining communal atmosphere. It was apparently a favourite hang-out of Italian heart-throb Marcello Mastroianni, who had a summer villa in town.

GETTING THERE & AWAY
The fastest and most convenient transport here is train; there is a frequent daily service from Livorno (€2, 25 minutes).

Inland from Castiglioncello
Perched high on a hill is **Rosignano Marittimo**. Already a small settlement in Lombard times, Rosignano was one of Lorenzo the Magnificent's preferred bases for hunting. Although there has been a castle here since the 8th century, the fortifications date from the days of Cosimo I de' Medici.

Back down on the coast, **Vada** is a typically characterless seaside spot. At least the beaches have sand. Another 8km south and you reach **Marina di Cecina**, where there is plenty of life, as well as hotels and restaurants that mainly front a beach. Children may enjoy the water park here (follow the signs; summer only).

About halfway between the sea and the modern centre of **Cecina** you can visit the **Parco Archeologico** (☎ 0568 26 08 37; Via Ginori; adult/child €3/2.50; 🕑 9am-noon & 5-9pm Tue-Fri, 3.30-6.30pm Sat & Sun Jul-Sep), which preserves Etruscan remains. At the time of research a new and grander **Museo Archeologico** was under construction and scheduled for completion in late 2004.

There are plenty of places to stay, including camp sites, in this area.

You can train or bus it to Cecina from Livorno. The train (€5, 30 minutes) is the better deal.

Cecina to Piombino
From Cecina you could follow the SS1 or minor coast roads south. Better still, head inland. Livorno's tourist office has come up with a Strada del Vino (wine route; p171), with a map and list of vineyards that moves from Cecina to **Montescudaio**. This is a pretty drive after the relatively drab coastal flats.

Head south from Montescudaio to **Bibbona**, a medieval hill town that dominates the plain running below to the coast. A little further south and on the coast is **Marina di Bibbona**, south of which stretches a narrow strip of sandy beach backed by *macchia* and pine woods.

There's plenty of accommodation to choose from.

Hotel Paradiso Verde (☎ /fax 0586 60 00 22; Via del Forte 9; s/d €90/120) is a small hotel located a frisbee throw from the beach, with spick-and-span rooms and a small bar/restaurant out the front. You pay more for a balcony and sea view.

A short way south of Marina di Bibbona is the small but important **Rifugio Palustre di Bolgheri** (☎ 0565 22 43 61; entrance just west off the SS1; adult/child €5/3; ☼ 9am & 2pm Fri & Sat Oct-May). This nature reserve is a key stop for migratory birds, and the best time for seeing them is from December to January. The two-hour visits are severely limited and must be arranged in advance. The entrance to the park is just south of the cypress-lined, arrow-straight road that leads eastwards to the village of **Bolgheri**. The castle that takes in the city gate and Romanesque Chiesa di SS Giacomo e Cristoro was restructured towards the end of the 19th century. Although very pretty, the village has been over-heritaged, with pricey restaurants and touristy shops. Have a quick look around, take a few photos and move on.

The next stretch of the Strada del Vino takes you through dense woodland along a minor road south of Bolgheri. The route becomes less interesting towards the end until you climb up into the hills to reach **Castagneto Carducci**.

Behind the town walls here lies a web of steep narrow lanes crowded in by brooding houses and dominated by the castle (turned into a mansion in the 18th century) of the Gherardesca clan that once controlled the surrounding area. The 19th-century poet Giosuè Carducci spent much of his childhood here.

Unfortunately there's nowhere to stay in town, but there are plenty of *agriturismo* (farmstay or country-inn accommodation) places in the surrounding countryside.

Traditional old recipes have been resurrected at the lovely **Ristorante Glorione** (☎ 0565 76 33 22; Via Carducci 6; mains €11-15; ☼ closed Thu), with its swish chandelier-lit dining room. There is a palm-shaded courtyard for atmospheric and soothing summertime dining.

Pick up some liqueurs, drinks and locally produced olive oil at the 100-year-old **L'Elixir** (☎ 0565 76 60 17; Via Garibaldi 7).

Next stop on the winding forested hill road is the tiny hamlet of **Sassetta**. Approaching from Castagneto, the houses here seem to be hanging on to their perches for dear life. There is a large map at the village entrance showing the main treks in the area.

Albergo La Selva (☎ /fax 0565 79 42 39; hotel.selva @tiscalinet.it; Via Fornaci 32; s/d €47/68) has squeaky-clean large plain rooms with a choice of bath or shower. There is a large terrace with positively swoony valley views, and the restaurant does an excellent six-course dinner for two.

Suvereto

The tortuous streets and steep stairways of nearby Suvereto have constituted a busy little centre since well before the year 1000. For a while it was the seat of a bishopric, only incorporated into the Tuscan grand duchy in 1815. The town has maintained an evocative Gothic feel.

INFORMATION
Tourist offices (☎ /fax 0565 82 93 04; Piazza Gramsci; ☼ 10am-12.30pm & 5-10pm daily, evening only Sun Jun-Sep) Also opens during the Sagra del Cinghiale (see below) The staff can provide information on walking in the surrounding hills.

SLEEPING & EATING
Apart from a handful of *affittacamere* (rooms for rent) and *agriturismo* places, the accommodation options are scarce.

Il Chiostro (☎ 0565 82 87 11; www.vacanzeilchiostro.it; Via del Crocifisso 14; apartments per week from €903, plus electricity used) This is a good choice if you plan to stay for a week. The apartments vary in size and quality, but even the smallest is lovely, complete with kitchen, wood-beamed ceilings and stone walls.

Enoteca dei Difficili (☎ 0565 82 80 18; Via San Leonardo; mains €5-8; ☼ closed Mon) This is an atmospheric brick-and-beam spot for a meal and, more critically, a drink. Alongside an array of delightful snacks, salads and main courses (including *carpaccio*), you can take a pick from the blockbuster selection of wines.

Mid-August sees the traditional **Corsa delle Botte**, when townsfolk race each other to push huge tumbling wine barrels along the cobbled lanes of the town. In December the people of Suvereto tuck into their **Sagra del Cinghiale** (Wild Boar Festival), which happily involves plenty of eating, drinking and a show of crossbow skills.

Campiglia Marittima to the Coast

From Suvereto you drop down onto the plains along the SS398 road to Piombino for about 5km before turning off right to head back into the hills, in which nestle the dun-coloured stone houses of **Campiglia Marittima**, another surprisingly intact and pretty medieval town, dating back to Etruscan times.

From the central Piazza della Repubblica, fronted by centuries-old mansions, head for the Palazzo Pretorio. Long the seat of government, its main facade, covered in an assortment of coats of arms, is akin to the bulky bemedalled chest of many a modern-day general. Accommodation options in the area consist of a camp site and several *affittacamere* and *agriturismo*.

A few kilometres northwest on the road to San Vincenzo is the **Parco Archeominerario di San Silvestro** (☎ 0565 83 86 80; Via di San Vincenzo 34b; adult/child €12/9 for both tours, adult/child €8/5 for one tour, family ticket €28; ☺ 9.30am-sunset Tue-Sun Jun-Sep, Sat & Sun only Oct-May). Just before the turn-off, look for the Etruscan smelting ovens that were used for copper production.

The park is dedicated to the 3000-year mining history of the area. The highlight for most is **Rocca di San Silvestro**, a medieval mining town abandoned in the 14th century. The surrounding Temperino mines produced copper and lead, some used for the mints of Lucca and later Pisa.

You can take two guided tours, one of Rocca di San Silvestro, the other to the Temperino mine and museum. The mine and museum (the latter is in the same building as the ticket office) are near the entrance, while Rocca di San Silvestro is about a half-hour walk away (or take the park shuttle). Tours of each location take place approximately every hour (timetables vary throughout the year).

The occasional bus runs to the park from San Vincenzo, about 6km down the road.

If you return on the road leading away from Campiglia, you would end up at this moderately attractive and popular (with Italians) seaside town of **San Vincenzo**. Yachties can park their vessels here, but there's not much to do after that. Sandy beaches stretch to the north and south of

---

DETOUR: SAN VINCENZO TO PIOMBINO

From the San Vincenzo tourist office on Via B Alliata, take the coast road towards Piombino. This is one of the most attractive stretches of asphalt in these parts, flanked by pine trees and dense woodland. Look for *tavoli* (picnic area) signs if you fancy stopping for a picnic with the luxury of tables and benches. After about 11km you'll see an old water tower to your left: park by the side and cross the road to a quiet and pleasant beach backed by wild brush and poppies (in season). Continue on to more good sandy stretches at Golfo di Baratti (see below) or follow the road to Piombino.

---

town; to the south backed by *macchia* and pine plantations. Although there are quite a few hotels, getting a room in summer is challenging and so are the prices. There is only one camp site.

Ristorante La Barcaccina (☎ 0565 70 19 11; Via Tridentina; mains €13-15; ☺ closed Wed) serves fine seafood that matches the restaurant's location on a great stretch of pale golden sand. This is not the kind of place where you stroll in wearing a thong, as it's glassed-in and on the smart side. From the coast road (not the SS1), follow the signs to the parking area near Parco Comunale.

Golfo di Baratti & Populonia

Twenty-three kilometres south of San Vincenzo, a minor road leads off to the southwest and the Golfo di Baratti. This must be one of the Tuscan coast's prettiest mainland beaches, although, as the weird and wonderful postures of the trees attest, it is often windy – so popular with windsurfers.

Inland from here is the **Parco Archeologico di Baratti e Populonia** (☎ 0565 2 90 02; Populonia; adult/child €12/9 for whole park, €8/5 for set areas, family ticket €28; ☺ 9am-8pm daily Jul & Aug, 9am-sunset Tue-Sun Apr-Jun, 9am-2pm Tue-Fri & 9am-sunset Sat & Sun Sep-Mar), where several Etruscan tombs have been unearthed, the most interesting of which are the circular tombs in the Necropoli di San Cerbone, between the coast road and the visitors centre.

Just beyond here is **Populonia Alta**, a three-street hamlet, walled in and protected by the castle. Built in the 15th century, the hamlet grew up on the site of a Pisan watchtower.

You can visit the small privately owned **Etruscan Museum** (adult/child €1.50/1) for an inspection of a few local finds; the opening times are sporadic. For superb views south along the coast, climb the **Torre di Populonia** (adult/child €2/1; 🕙 9am-12.30pm & 2-7pm) north of the museum. On the main street check out the **gallery** at No 19, with its permanent exhibition of glass sculptures and lamps by American artist Laura Pescae.

Next to the car park is the **Etruscan acropolis** (🕙 9am-7pm) of ancient Populonia, which was excavated from 1980 to 1990. If your Italian is up to it, join a guided visit (every half-hour). The digs have revealed the foundations of an Etruscan temple dating to the 2nd century BC, along with its adjacent buildings.

There's an expensive **restaurant** and an inordinate number of souvenir-shopping options, but no place to stay in Populonia. It appears the only way up here from the Golfo di Baratti (which can be reached by ATM buses from Piombino and San Vincenzo) is under your own steam (parking costs €1 for two hours).

Piombino

Poor old Piombino, it really gets a lot of lousy press. The smoke stacks to the south of the town are a rather disconcerting sight and only urge you to hop on the next ferry to Elba – which is probably why you are here in the first place. A Roman-era port, and from the late 19th century a centre of steel production, the city was heavily damaged during WWII and precious little remains of the walled historical centre.

If you have time, the town centre, whose focal point is the 15th-century **Torrione Rivellino**, and fishing port are not without a little charm.

Further north (along the coast in the direction of Populonia) are a couple of modest beaches (don't bother if you are going to Elba).

Should you need, for whatever emergency, to stay, **Hotel Roma** (🕿 0565 3 43 41; fax 3 43 48; Via San Francesco 43; s/d €37/55) is a reasonable, albeit monastically spartan, central choice two minutes' walk from the ATM bus stop.

GETTING THERE & AWAY
Piombino is on the Rome–Genoa train line. There are fairly regular connections

to Florence too. **ATM buses** (🕿 0565 26 01 80) leave from the town centre at Via Leonardo da Vinci 13.

For Elba ferry information, see p179.

GETTING AROUND
Piombino-based ATM buses running between Piombino and Cecina (€2.80, 1½ hours) usually stop at Castagneto Carducci (€2.60, one hour), Sassetta (€3, 1¼ hours), San Vincenzo (€2, 40 minutes) and Golfo di Baratti (€1, 15 minutes). Another bus line serves Suvereto (€2, 40 minutes) on a regular basis on its way to Monterotondo. Yet another connects Piombino with Campiglia Marittima. ATM buses also run to Massa Marittima (€3.60, 1½ hours).

For coastal stops, such as San Vincenzo, the train is a better bet, but the hill towns are generally a considerable hike from the nearest train station.

ELBA
pop 29,400
Napoleon should have considered himself lucky to be shunted off to such a pretty spot. He arrived in May 1814 and lasted a year – he just had to have another shot at imperial greatness. Nowadays people would willingly be exiled here, and the island attracts more than a million tourists per year. Just 28km long and 19km across at its widest point, Elba is well equipped with plenty of hotels and camp sites. The main towns are Portoferraio on the northern side and Marina di Campo on the southern. Don't come in August as it gets unpleasantly crowded and everything costs even more than usual.

HISTORY
Elba has been inhabited since the Iron Age and, coincidentally, the extraction of iron ore and metallurgy were the island's principal sources of economic wellbeing until the second half of the 20th century. You can still fossick around to your heart's content in museums dedicated to rocks.

Ligurian tribespeople were the island's first inhabitants, followed by Etruscans and Greeks from Magna Graecia. The iron business was well established by then, which made the island doubly attractive to the wealthier Romans who built holiday villas here.

Centuries of peace under the Pax Romana gave way to more uncertain times during the barbarian invasions, when Elba became a refuge for those fleeing mainland marauders. By the 11th century, Pisa (and later Piombino) was in control and built fortresses to help ward off attacks by Muslim raiders and pirates operating out of North Africa.

In the 16th century, Cosimo I de' Medici obtained territory in the north of the island, where he founded the port town of Cosmopolis (today Portoferraio). At the same time, the Spanish acquired control of the southeastern strip of the island.

Grand Duke Pietro Leopoldo II encouraged land reform, the drainage of swamps and greater agricultural production on the island in the 18th century. Nevertheless, iron remained the major industry. In 1917 some 840,000 tonnes were produced, but during WWII the industry was hit hard by the Allies and by the beginning of the 1980s production was down to 100,000 tonnes. The writing was on the wall: tourism had arrived to take the place of mining and smelting.

ORIENTATION
Although Elba is the largest and most heavily populated member of the Tuscan Archipelago, it measures just 28km long and 19km across at its widest point. The island is located 15km southwest of the ferry port of Piombino.

INFORMATION
Emergency
Police station (☎ 0565 91 95 11; Via Garibaldi, Portoferraio)

Laundry
Onda Blu (Viale Elba 51, Portoferraio; €6.20 washing & drying a load)

Medical Services
The following medical services all operate in summer.
Tourist medical service Portoferraio (☎ 0565 91 42 12; public hospital, Località San Rocco)
Marina di Campo (☎ 0565 97 63 21; Piazza Dante Alighieri 3)
Rio Marina (☎ 0565 96 24 07; Via Principe Amadeo)
Marciana Marina (☎ 0565 90 44 36; Viale Regina Margherita)
Capoliveri (☎ 0565 968995; Via Soprana)

Tourist Information
Tourist Office (☎ 0565 91 46 71; www.aptelba.it; Calata Italia 35, Portoferraio; ☼ 8am-8pm daily Apr-Oct, 8am-6pm Mon-Sat Nov-Mar) Close to the port. It has an extensive list of Internet cafés throughout Elba.
Associazione Albergatori Isola d'Elba (☎ 0565 91 55 55; agenziailva@elbalink.it; Calata Italia 20; ☼ 9am-5pm May-Sep) If you plan to visit in summer, this association can help with advance accommodation bookings. You can also look out for *camere* (rooms) or *affittacamere* signs.

ACTIVITIES
Popular activities on Elba include walking, mountain biking, windsurfing, diving and sailing. You can rent a motor boat from several operators, including **Enfola Rent Boats** (☎ 333 360 56 28; Loc. Enfola, Portoferraio; from €65 a day). Kids may enjoy the two-hour glass-bottom boat excursion with **Aquavision** (☎ 323 709 54 70; Portoferraio harbour; adult/child €15/8). For more information on outdoor activities in Tuscany and Umbria, see p36.

GETTING THERE & AWAY
During the summer, Lufthansa and several minor airlines operate regular flights from Vienna, Altenrhein, Zürich, Berne, Brescia, Parma and Milan to Elba's tiny **aerodrome** (☎ 0565 97 60 11) at La Pila. Prices start at around €350 return. There is only the occasional summer charter flight from mainland Italy; most folk opt for the ferry.

Ferries sail from Piombino to Elba. If you arrive in Piombino by train, get a connecting train to the port. Moby Lines and Toremar have offices in Piombino and Portoferraio. Except in August, you should be able to buy a ticket at the port. Fares (including port tax) start at around €6.20 per person or €26.75 for a small car plus driver. Both lines offer a special deal on certain runs (see timetables). The ferry trip takes an hour. Most ferries arrive at Portoferraio, Elba's capital and main transport hub, while a few call at Rio Marina, Marina di Campo and Porto Azzurro.

Toremar also operates a hovercraft service (€9.80, ½ hour) for passengers only throughout the year, and a fast vehicle and passenger service in the summer (two passengers/car from €54 return).

GETTING AROUND
Bus
Regular services are available with **ATL** (☎ 0565 91 43 92), which runs across the

CENTRAL COAST & ELBA

ELBA

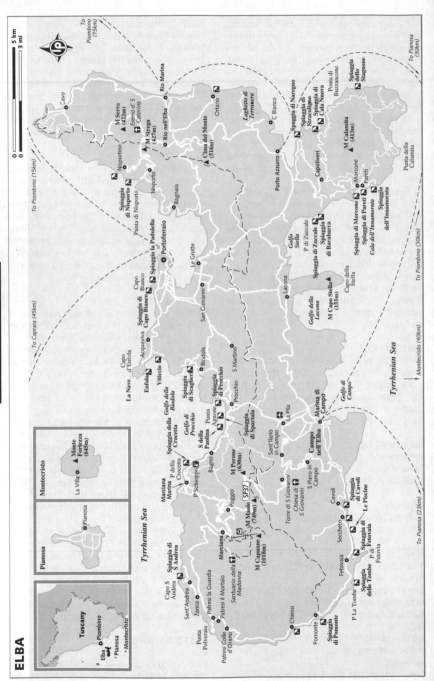

island. From Portoferraio you can reach all of the main towns and smaller resorts, including Marciana Marina, Marina di Campo, Capoliveri, Porto Azzurro, Bagnaia (all €1.80, ½ hour), Cavo (€2.60, 1¼ hours) and Fetovaia (€2.20, one hour). You can get a daily pass for €6.50. Timetables are available from the bus station (Viale Elba, Portoferraio) or tourist office.

Car, Motorcycle & Bicycle
The best way to see Elba is to rent a bike (from €11 per day, €52 per week), scooter (from €18/day) or motorbike (from €52 per day). **TWN** (Two Wheels Network; ☎ 0565 91 46 66; www.twn-rent.it; Viale Elba 32, Portoferraio), with branches at Marciana Marina, Marina di Campo, Porto Azzurro and other locations, and **Happy Rent** (☎ 0565 91 46 65; Viale Elba 7; www.renthappy.it), near the tourist office in Portoferraio, are two of many rental companies.

Portoferraio
Known to the Romans as Fabricia and later Ferraia (on account of its use as a port for iron exports), this small port was acquired by Cosimo I de' Medici in the mid-16th century, when the fortifications took shape. The walls link two forts (Stella and Falcone) on high points and a third tower at the port entrance (Linguella). In 1814 Napoleon took up residence here at the start of his exile on Elba; his enemies had generously turned the island into a Napoleonic statelet (see the boxed text, p183). Steelworks began operating in 1902 but were destroyed by the Allies in 1943.

SIGHTS
The old part of town picturesquely surrounds the fishing and pleasure port. You can wander around the forts, entering by Via Guerrazzi. Although the Falcone is closed indefinitely, you can visit **Forte Stella** (Via della Stella; admission €1.30; ☺ 9am-7pm). Down from the walls leading to Falcone is a narrow but inviting sliver of **beach**.

In the old town, up on the bastions between the two forts, is the worthwhile **Villa dei Mulini** (☎ 0565 91 58 46; Piazzale Napoleone; admission €5, includes Villa Napoleonica di San Martino; ☺ 9am-7pm Mon-Sat, 9am-1pm Sun), one of Napoleon's residences, which features a splendid terraced garden and his library.

The **Villa Napoleonica di San Martino** (☎ 0565 91 46 88; Loc. San Martino; adult/child €3/5, includes Villa dei

Mulini, parking €1.50; ☺ 9am-7pm Tue-Sat, 9am-1pm Sun), Napoleon's summer residence, is set in hills about 5km southwest of the town. The villa houses a modest collection of Napoleonic paraphernalia and also hosts an annual exhibition based on a Napoleonic theme.

The Linguella fortifications, near the port, house the modest **Museo Civico Archeologico** (☎ 0565 93 73 70; La Linguella; admission €2; ☺ 9.30am-2.30pm & 5pm-midnight mid-Jun–mid-Sep, 10.30am-1.30pm & 4-8pm Wed-Mon mid-Sep–mid-Jun), with a collection generally focussed on ancient seafarers.

SLEEPING
The closest camp sites are about 4km west of Portoferraio towards Viticcio.

Acquaviva (☎ /fax 0565 91 55 92; Località Acquaviva; adult/tent/car €11/9.50/3) A great choice for sunsets over the sea and about as close as you can get to the beach without getting your feet wet. The facilities are good, but the site fills up fast in summer.

Albergo Ape Elbana (☎ /fax 0565 91 42 45; apelbana@elba2000.it; Salita de' Medici 2; s/d €56/112) This is a fantastic old butter-coloured building with terraces overlooking buzzy Piazza della Repubblica. The position is its best point, as the rooms are large but a little soulless and tired looking.

Hotel Acquamarina (☎ 0565 91 40 57; www.hotel acquamarina.it; Loc Paduella; s/d €73/146) Knockout hotel within strolling distance of Portoferraio. Rooms are sunny and bright with large terraces overlooking the naturally wild gardens. A path leads down to a small cove.

Villa Ombrosa (☎ 0565 91 43 63; info@villa ombrosa.it; Via De Gasperi 3; s/d €91/182) This is one of Elba's classic hotels; a gracious 19th-century building near the park and across from the beach. Offers half-board only during the summer, which fortunately does not equal the standard bland buffet. The restaurant is good, serving tasty Tuscan dishes.

EATING
Trattoria da Zucchetta (☎ 0565 91 53 31; Piazza della Repubblica 40; mains €8-10; ☺ closed Wed lunch) A great people-watching position tucked in the corner of the Piazza, this Neapolitan eatery dates back to 1891. A huge menu offers the full range of pasta and more than 40 pizza toppings.

Trattoria La Barca (☎ 0565 91 80 36; Via Guerrazzi 60-62; mains €10-13; ☺ closed Wed) This is a good place to slurp a plate of *cacciucco* (fishy pasta). Popular with locals in the know, so there's not much elbow space between tables. Go for the terrace if you can.

ENTERTAINMENT
Sir William's Irish Bar (☎ 0565 91 92 88; Via Manganaro 28; ☻ 6pm-6am nightly) For a wee dram o' whiskey or a pint of bitter, head here. It generally doesn't start jumping till at least midnight and pulls in all sorts, from local punters to the casually hip.

West to Capo d'Enfola

Several modest beaches spread west from Portoferraio. Quite nice, although narrow and shelly, are **Spiaggia la Padulella** and its counterpart just west of Capo Bianco, **Spiaggia di Capo Bianco**. A couple of similar beaches dot the coast along the 7km stretch out to **Capo d'Enfola**. You can have a dip here or head south down the coast a few kilometres to **Viticcio**, which comprises a handful of restaurants and hotels, but is quieter than much of the island. You can walk from Viticcio to the beaches of the **Golfo della Biodola**.

SLEEPING & EATING
Hotel Scoglio Bianco (☎ 0565 93 90 36; www.scoglio bianco.it; Viticcio; half-board s/d €68/85) Rooms are spacious and bright, set around a central patio decorated with deckchairs and cats. The downstairs Pizzeria da Giacomino has a terrace over the sea; perfect for marriage proposals.

Hotel Paraiso (☎ 0565 93 90 34; www.elba turistica.it; Viticcio; d €90-120; ☒) Owned by a British-Italian couple, it has expansive seagull views and good-sized terraces with the more expensive rooms. Set high above the road, there is a vast outdoor bar, pool, tennis court and private beach access.

Emanuel (☎ 0565 93 90 03; Enfola; set menu €24.50; ☻ daily in summer, Thu-Tue rest of the year) New owner Alberto has maintained the excellent reputation of this restaurant with its beachfront terrace shaded by a magnificent fig tree. A lingering dinner is the best way to enjoy the seafood house delights.

West to Marciana Marina

From Portoferraio, a provincial road heads south and then forks westwards along the coast to Marciana Marina, via Procchio.

The pick of the beaches are the sandy strands lining the **Golfo della Biodola**. When

the Hermitage opened its doors in 1951, there were only five small *pensioni* scattered elsewhere on the island. Since then, a succession of other hotels has set up on this little gulf.

Hermitage (☎ 0565 93 69 11; www.hotelhermi tage.it; La Biodola; s/d €227/454; ☒) Pure Beverly Hills, this place is gorgeous – complete with infinity pool overlooking the sea. It's one of the island's first and only truly luxurious hotels.

PROCCHIO
A small bustling place with restaurants, shops and bars, and the added plus of sandy beaches.

Osteria del Piano (☎ 0565 90 72 92; Via Provinciale 24; mains €12; ☻ closed Wed) This unassuming restaurant is just beyond the Procchio junction heading towards Marciana Marina. The open-plan kitchen means you can watch the creative energy behind such innovative dishes as black-and-white spaghetti in crab sauce.

West from Procchio, the road hugs the cliffs, equalling fine views along the winding coast. If you can manage to park, **Spiaggia di Spartaia** and **Spiaggia della Paolina** are part of a series of beautiful little beaches, all requiring a steep clamber down.

Marciana Marina

Almost 20km west of Portoferraio, Marciana Marina is fronted by pleasant pebble beaches and makes a fine base for some of the island's best walking trails.

Hotel Marinella (☎ /fax 0565 9 90 18; Viale Margherita 36; s/d €75/150) Well-aged classic on the centre of 'main street' across from the sea. Rooms in the annexe overlook the garden but the best are at the front with balconies and sea views.

Casa Lupi (☎ /fax 0565 9 91 43; Località Ontanelli 35; s/d €41/82) Next to a vineyard a couple of kilometres from the beach, with a garden of peach trees and rose bushes, this small hotel is ideal for enjoying a little kick-back time in peaceful surroundings. The rooms are no-frills basic but comfortable and clean.

Poggio & the Interior

Following the inland road up into the mountains from Marciana Marina, the first town you reach is Poggio, an enchanting little place with a medieval core and

NAPOLEON IN EARLY RETIREMENT

At 6pm on 3 May 1814, the English frigate *Undaunted* dropped anchor in the Medici harbour of Portoferraio. The cargo was unusual to say the least. Under the Treaty of Fontainebleau, the emperor Napoleon who, since the beginning of the century, had held all Europe in his thrall, was exiled to the island of Elba.

It could have been a lot worse for the emperor; the Allies decided on a soft option, partly to short-circuit any possible adverse reaction in France. Napoleon was awarded the island as his private fiefdom, to hold until the end of his days.

His arrival was greeted with considerable pomp. The guns of Portoferraio shot off a 100-round salute, to which the English frigate replied. That at least is Alexandre Dumas' version. Others say the guns were actually firing *at* the frigate.

Whatever the case, Elba would never be quite the same again. Although undoubtedly watching the situation in Europe with a hawk's eye, Napoleon threw himself into frenetic activity in his new, somewhat humbler domain. After touring the island and making all the right noises to its inhabitants, he undertook a long series of public works. These included improving operations in the island's iron-ore mines (whose revenue now went to Napoleon), boosting agriculture, initiating a road-building program, draining marshes, overhauling the legal and education systems and so on. On some of the programs he often set members of his faithful 500 guardsmen to work.

A great deal of ink has been spilled over the Corsican's dictatorial style and seemingly impossible ambitions, but he can't have been all bad. To this day, they still say a Mass for his soul at the Chiesa della Misericordia in May.

Napoleon installed himself in the bastions of the city wall, in what became known as the Residenza dei Mulini. His so-called country or summer home, outside town in San Martino, was used as an occasional stopover on excursions – he never slept there. Some weeks after his arrival, Napoleon was joined by his mother Letizia and sister Paolina. But he remained separated from his wife Maria Luisa and was visited for just two days by his lover Maria Walewska.

On the Continent, things were hotting up. Rumours were rife that Napoleon's comfortable exile might be curtailed. At the Congress of Vienna, France called for Napoleon's removal to a more distant location. Austria, too, was nervous. Some suggested Malta, but Britain objected. London then suggested the South Atlantic islet of St Helena.

Napoleon could not be sure which rumours to believe. According to some, he would sooner or later be moved. Others suggested such reports were designed to induce him to some rash act in breach of the Treaty of Fontainebleau, which would provide the Allies with the excuse they needed to get rid of him. The Congress broke up with no official decision, although the Allies were well aware that Napoleon still had many supporters in and beyond France, and could easily raise a new army should he be of a mind to try.

He was. Under no circumstances was he going to allow himself to be meekly shipped off to some rocky speck in the middle of the Atlantic. A lifelong risk taker, he decided to have another roll of the dice. Perhaps, during his time on Elba, he always knew he would. For months he had sent out a couple of vessels flying his Elban flag on 'routine' trips around the Mediterranean. When one of them, the *Incostante*, set sail early in the morning of 26 February 1815 (a Sunday), no-one suspected he might be hidden on board. Sir Neil Campbell, his English jail warden, had only returned to Livorno the previous day under the impression that Napoleon was, as ever, fully immersed in the business of the island.

Elba lost its emperor and Napoleon his gilded cage. He had embarked on the Hundred Days that would culminate in defeat at Waterloo – he got the Atlantic exile after all, but at least he had tried.

winding cobblestone streets, and famous for its spring water.

Albergo Monte Capanne (☎ /fax 0565 9 90 83; Via dei Pini 13; s/d €52/84) Slum it in style at this lovely hotel with its ivy-clad main building and large terrace. The rooms have swoony views of Marciana Marina, plus a cosy and comfortable feel.

Publius (☎ 0565 9 92 08; meals €38; ⌣ closed Mon) If you want to spill money on a great meal, try this place, at the entrance to the village. The breathtaking views down to the coast should keep your mind off the high prices.

From Poggio choose from one of two options: either proceed west to Marciana then head around the coast (see the next section), or opt for the narrow SP37 road that winds through some of the highest, most densely wooded (and tourist-free) countryside on the island.

Park at the picnic site at the foot of **Monte Perone** (630m) – you can't miss it. Mountain bikers should proceed with caution. To the left (east) you can wander up to the mountain, with spectacular views across much of the island. To the right (west) you can scramble fairly quickly to a height that affords broad vistas down to Poggio, Marciana and Marciana Marina. From there you could press on to **Monte Maolo** (749m).

The road descends from this location into the southern flank of the island. On the way, you will notice the granite shell of the Romanesque **Chiesa di San Giovanni** and, shortly after, the ruined tower, **Torre di San Giovanni**

The two small hamlets here, **Sant'Ilario in Campo** and **San Piero in Campo**, are short on sights but still pleasant enough and little affected by tourism. The latter is a bit larger and boasts a few *osterie* (restaurants offering simple local dishes) and snack bars.

Albergo La Rosa (☎ 0565 98 31 91; Piazza Maggiore Gadani 17; s/d 48/63) is a quiet, old-fashioned hotel in a side street with large but rather dark rooms. The restaurant is popular, specialising in enormous plates of pasta at rock-bottom prices.

The hamlets lie on separate routes that lead south around to Marina di Campo, so are easily reached by drivers. Up to eight buses a day link the hamlets with Marina di Campo, where you can connect with most spots on the island.

Marciana & the West Coast

From Poggio, the other possibility is to continue west to Marciana (355m), the most engaging of the western interior towns. Once an important defensive position under Pisan rule, it subsequently passed to Piombino, the French and finally to the grand duchy of Tuscany.

The exterior of the **Fortezza Pisana** (closed) is a reminder of the town's medieval days, while about a 40-minute walk west out of town is the **Santuario della Madonna**, the most

important object of pilgrimage on the island. A much-altered 11th-century church houses a stone upon which a divine hand is said to have painted an image of the Virgin. The path to the church is known as the Via Crucis, because of 14 stations spaced along it. Each station represents a pause Jesus took while carrying the cross. The town also houses a modest **Museo Archeologico** (☎ 0565 90 12 15; Via del Pretorio; admission €2; ☿ closed Tue) behind the *fortezza*.

From near Marciana, a **cable car** (☎ 0565 90 10 20; one way/return €8/12) runs to the summit of **Monte Capanne** (1018m), the island's highest point. From here you can see across Elba and as far as Corsica to the west.

The road west out of Marciana pursues a course around the island, maintaining a prudent distance and altitude from the often precipitous coastline.

Sant'Andrea is a popular new resort with an astounding concentration of a dozen-or-so hotels winding back up the hill to the main road.

Hotel Barsalina (☎ 0565 90 80 13; Sant'Andrea; s/d €76/152) Just 20m from the beach, this hotel has been designed with a lot of TLC. The rooms are spacious, bright and comfortable, and the aquarium-flanked restaurant has an excellent and varied menu.

A series of small beaches appear as you follow the road round to the south side of the island. **Chiessi** and **Pomonte** have pebbly beaches, but the water is beautiful. The sandy **Spiaggia delle Tombe** is one of the few spots on the island with a nude-bathing scene.

At **Fetovaia**, **Seccheto** and **Cavoli** you will find further protected sandy beaches, accommodation and restaurants. West of Seccheto, **Le Piscine** is another mostly nudist stretch.

Marina di Campo

Elba's second-largest town, Marina di Campo is on Golfo di Campo to the south. The beaches are good and popular (venture west for fewer crowds). Many camp sites are located around here and the place gets ridiculously packed in the height of summer, but this is where some of the island's action can be found too; several discos help keep the brat-pack happy through the hot months.

Montecristo (☎ 0565 97 68 61; www.elbalink.it/ hotel/montecristo; Viale Nomelini; s/d €69/140) is a

Etruscan tombs at **Parco Archeologico di Baratti e Populonia** (p177)

DAMIEN SIMONIS

DAMIEN SIMONIS

Approaching **Marciana Marina** on the island of Elba (p182)

View over Portoferraio on Elba from **Forte Stella** (p181)

DAMIEN SIMONIS

Tuscan villa and vineyards near **Siena** (p190)

JEFF CANTARUTTI

JOHN HAY

San Gimignano in the Chianti region (p206)

Fonte Gaia (Happy Fountain) in Piazza del Campo in Siena (p192)

JOHN

pleasantly posh hotel on the beach, with flower-framed balconies and a bar/pool overlooking the sea. The large sunny rooms have Scandi-style light furnishings and king-size beds.

Capoliveri & the Southeast

High up on a majestic ridgeback in the southeastern pocket of the island, this is an enchanting village, all steep, narrow alleys with houses sardined together. At the height of summer it is jammed with tourists (at least one Italian newspaper writer has remarked tartly that one may as well hoist the German flag at Capoliveri). Come out of season and you can rediscover some of the peace of this hamlet, which used to live off iron-ore mining in the Punta della Calamita area.

There's nowhere to stay in the town, although there are several places just outside.

EATING

The tourists have brought an eating-and-drinking culture to Capoliveri, so there is plenty of choice whatever your culinary fancy.

Il Chiasso (☎ 0565 96 87 09; Via Cavour 32; set menu €32; ⚐ closed Tue) This is one of the best restaurants in town, with a limited classy set menu. The decor is a savvy combination of traditional and trendy, and there's an excellent wine list.

Freccia Azzurra (☎ 0565 96 89 68; Via Verdi 4; mains €8-10) There's not much squeeze-by space in the dining room but the Piazza terrace is vast. Dishes are predictable but good in this chaotic and popular restaurant. Try the *penne gamberetti e rucola* (shrimp-and-rocket penne) for a real tastebud treat.

DRINKING

Fandango (☎ 0565 93 54 24; Via Cardenti 1; drinks from €4; ⚐ closed Mon) Located downstairs just below the main square, this is an atmospheric place to taste fine Tuscan wines.

ENTERTAINMENT

Velvet Underground (Vicolo Lungo 14) This pub-style bar, a short stumble from the main square, feels like a real local.

Sugar Reef (☎ 0338 917 90 26; Località La Trappola) This is *the* place on the island for a little hip-swinging salsa, both live and DJ-mixed. It's about 1km south of Capoliveri on the road to Morcone.

Around Capoliveri

If you are driving, you can visit a series of pleasant little beaches. By bus it's possible, but not easy. Directly west of Capoliveri (take the Portoferraio road and watch for signs) are the beaches of **Zuccale** and **Barabarca**. You end up on a dirt track – leave your vehicle in the car park and walk the final stretch.

If you take the road heading south from Capoliveri, another three charming sandy little coves – Marcone, Pareti and Innamorata – come in quick succession. There are several hotel options here and some simple restaurants cater to rumbling tummies with typical local cuisine.

East of Capoliveri you have two choices. One road takes you to the comparatively long stretch of beach at **Naregno**, fronted by a series of discreet hotels.

The more adventurous should follow the signs for **Stracoligno**, which is one of the first in a series of beaches down the east coast from here. The road at this point becomes a dirt track and, if you don't mind dusting up your vehicle, you can push on to a couple of less-frequented beaches. **Cala Nuova** is a nice enough little beach with a good restaurant.

Ristorante Calanova (☎ 0565 96 89 58; mains €16-18; ⚐ summer only, closed Tue) is a table-for-two kind of place, because it is wonderfully secluded with only the gently lapping sea for company. Unsurprisingly, the menu is based on seafood.

Another 4km or 5km and you reach a path down to the **Spiaggia dello Stagnone**, which even in summer should not be too crowded, if only because of the effort required to rattle down this far.

Porto Azzurro

Dominated by its fort, built in 1603 by Philip III of Spain and now used as a prison, Porto Azzurro is a pleasant resort town, close to some good beaches.

Hotel Villa Italia (☎ /fax 0565 9 51 19; villaitalia @infoelba.it; Viale Italia 41; s/d €60/80) A fairly spartan family-run hotel on a quiet residential street. Its small but adequate rooms are about the cheapest in town, and there's a small terrace out the front.

Hotel Belmare (☎ 0565 9 50 12; fax 95 82 45; Banchina IV Novembre; s/d €55/90) With a good location on the main promenade, this traditional green-shuttered hotel is nothing fancy but the rooms are comfy enough, and there's a small bar and TV room for post-beach R&R.

Ristorante Cutty Sark (☎ 0565 95 78 21; Piazza del Mercato 25; mains €20; 🕙 closed Tue) Shift your credit card into overdraft and indulge in dinner here. *Ravioloni alla Cutty Sark* are large ravioli filled with zucchini and shrimp, and layered in a shrimp and tomato sauce. Simpler fare includes *gnocchetti dello scampi* (bite-size gnocchi with prawns).

La Lanterna Magica (☎ 0565 95 83 94; Lungomare Vitaliani 5; mains €15-18) Located on the waterfront, this place is also recommended.

The Northeast

If, on leaving Portoferraio, you swing around to the east and head for Rio nell'Elba and beyond, you will experience the least-visited part of the island, with lovely, albeit pebbly, beaches and glorious views.

This road hugs the coast on its way around to **Bagnaia**, the first worthwhile stop. En route you will scoot by **San Giovanni**, home to a rather expensive and dull mud spa, and **Le Grotte**, where a few stones still managing to stand on top of each other are all that remain of a Roman villa. At the Porto Azzurro and Bagnaia fork is **Elbaland** (☎ 0335 819 46 80; Località Fonte Murato; adult/child under 12 €6/3; 🕙 11am-7pm Tue-Sun), a low-key amusement park that is more like an outsize park with swings and minor attractions.

From Elbaland head north to Bagnaia, a lush and green part of the island with an attractive beach and some accommodation, including a camp site.

Pizzeria Sunset (☎ 0565 93 07 86; Bagnaia; pizzas from €5.15; 🕙 May-Oct) The views across the gulf to Portoferraio are wonderful and there's a pleasant beach-bum atmosphere, plus happy hour, sangria and surprisingly good pizza. At night, there's a head-thumping disco that spills out onto the beach.

From Bagnaia you can follow the 3km dirt road to **Nisporto** and on to **Nisportino**. The views along the way are quite spectacular in parts. In both places you will find a small beach and, in summer, snack stands and one or two restaurants. From Nisportino, head back down a few kilometres to the junction with the road that links Nisporto and Rio nell'Elba. About halfway along this road, stop for a short stroll to what little is left of the **Eremo di Santa Caterina**, a tiny stone hermitage, and more good views.

The road plunges down to the inland bastion of **Rio nell'Elba**, the heart of the island's iron-mining operations. It's a little gloomy, but the simple fact that it caters little to tourism has its appeal. The **Museo della Gente di Rio** (☎ 0565 93 91 82; Passo della Pietà; admission €2.60; 🕙 10am-1pm & 4-7.30pm Tue-Sun mid-Apr–Sep) has 200 rare mineral specimens from the east of the island and Monte Capanne. There is a handful of restaurants around the central Piazza del Popolo.

THE COUNT OF MONTECRISTO

This feel-good swashbuckling tale was born from author Alexandre Dumas' acquaintance with Jérome Bonaparte, Napoleon Bonaparte's brother, who accompanied Dumas on a trip to Elba. On their return, Dumas spotted another island, the deserted Montecristo, and determined to write a novel in remembrance of the trip. The story embodies the revenge of Napoleonic romanticism upon the restored royal house of Orleans. In the person of Dantés, a universal vigilante, Dumas is taking a dig at the corruption of the bourgeois world. The dashing officer is imprisoned for a crime he hasn't committed and vows to get even. He escapes and, after a tip-off, searches for treasure on the island of Montecristo where, after much adventure and jolly japes, our man wins all the prizes – getting rich, becoming the Count of Montecristo and exacting a full measure of revenge on those who framed him.

Of course, it's all a tall tale (and no-one has ever found any treasure on Montecristo) but this particular yarn has made a lot of loot for a lot of people. At least 25 film and TV versions of the story were made in the 20th century, with greater or lesser skill. Among the better ones are the oldies. Rowland Lee's 1935 film and the 1943 flick by Robert Vernay were equally good tales. In Italy, Andrea Giordana had women swooning at their TV sets in the 1966 series by Edmo Fenoglio. Richard Chamberlain had a go at the lead role in David Greene's 1975 *The Count of Montecristo*, as did Gérard Depardieu in *Montecristo* (1997).

Next, take the short run downhill to Rio nell'Elba's coastal outlet, **Rio Marina**. Oh goody, there's yet another mineral museum here! Apart from that, not a lot will hold you up.

Hotel Rio (☎ 0565 92 42 25; www.elbahotelrio.it; Via Palestro 31; s/d €70/140; ✆ Mar–mid-Oct) is a well-worn hotel with family-size rooms, some with a sea view, plus TV room, garden, lots of paintings of dubious quality and an overall homey, retro-1970s feel.

Lunch may be an idea at the attractive **Da Oreste La Strega** (☎ 0565 96 22 11; Via Vittorio Emanuele 6; mains €10; ✆ closed Tue) seafood restaurant, with large windows overlooking the harbour and an excellent wine list. Try the *frittura mista* (fried seafood).

The best beach is a little further down at **Ortano**. To get there, go back a couple of kilometres towards Rio nell'Elba and swing southwards. It's a nice location but, once again, the beach is that far-from-ideal part-sand part-pebble mix. If you want to stay here, choose between camping or a sprawling hotel complex.

Minor Islands

The island of Elba forms part of the Parco Nazionale dell'Arcipelago Toscano. Two out of the seven islands, Capraia and Gorgona, are covered earlier (p174) and the islands of Giglio and Giannutri are discussed in the Southern Tuscany chapter. The other three islands are Elba, Pianosa and Montecristo.

Pianosa, 14km west of Elba, is a remarkably flat, triangular affair measuring about 5.8km by 4.6km. From 1858 until the mid-1990s it was a penal colony; it's now part of the national park. **Trips** (adult/child €68/34; maximum of 110 people per day) to the island leave from Marina di Campo during summer at 9am and 11am, returning eight hours later. The island can also be reached on Tuesday only by Toremar ferry from Porto Azzurro. Unless you want to be stranded for a week, you have about two hours to explore before heading back! And if you go this way, you are not allowed into the grounds of the former prison (so two hours are probably more than sufficient).

There are no ferry services to **Montecristo**, 40km south of Elba. Montecristo was also a prison island, but that role was short-lived. Since 1979 it has been a marine biological reserve and can be seen only as part of an organised visit. You need special permission from the **Ufficio Forestale in Follónica** (☎ 0566 4 06 11) on the Italian mainland.

Central Tuscany

CONTENTS

This central region, with its impressionist-style landscape, its plunging valleys, forested slopes and the golden colour of its buildings, is the one that seems most to epitomise Tuscany. Lofty cypresses form a dramatic border to fields dotted with sheep and, if you visit here in spring, you have the additional treat of brilliant red poppy fields that sweep and fold into the sun-hazed green horizon. Some of Tuscany's best-known towns are here, from steep, straggling Montepulciano to the one-time defensive bulwark of Monteriggioni with its 14 defensive towers. Moving westwards, the pilgrim-route bastion of San Gimignano, with still more medieval towers, provides insight into the pomp and circumstance even relatively small towns enjoyed in the Middle Ages. Volterra, the ancient brooding successor to an Etruscan settlement, stands aloof watching over lunar expanses to the south while, at the heart of this region, lies Siena with its magnificent piazza, atmospheric stone-clad streets, and impressive black-and-white striped cathedral.

The hottest frontier in medieval Tuscany was the line separating Florence and its possessions from the county of Siena. This proud Gothic hilltop city, although long ago swallowed up by Florence to become the grand duchy of Tuscany, even today maintains a separate identity. In some respects the Sienese have neither forgiven nor forgotten.

HIGHLIGHTS

- Climb the 400 steps of the Torre del Mangia (p193) in Siena for glorious views, then treat yourself to a cold beer at one of the terrace bars in the Piazza del Campo (p192)

- Visit Italy's most astounding and elaborate Gothic church: Siena cathedral (p193)

- Explore the green pastureland of Le Crete (p202), visiting the imposing monastery of Abbazia di Monte Oliveto Maggiore and Il Sodoma's infamous frescoes

- Marvel at the medieval 'Manhattan' formed by the towers of the town of San Gimignano (p206)

- Stop by the *enoteca* in Montalcino's impressive Fortezza (p214) and sample a few vintages of the local Brunello wine

- Wander the streets of Montepulciano (p219), one of the prettiest of the area's medieval hill towns

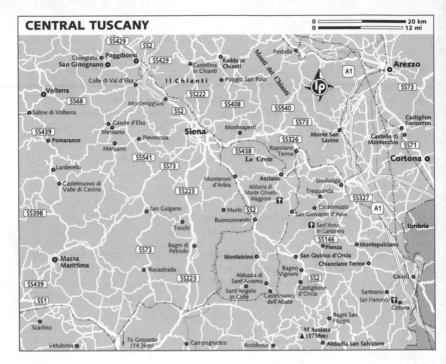

CENTRAL TUSCANY

SIENA
pop 59,200

Siena's pink and golden towers shimmer against the warm tones of ancient brick and stonework. This is one of Italy's most enchanting cities, its medieval centre bristling with majestic Gothic buildings. Like Florence, Siena offers an incredible concentration of things to see, which simply can't be appreciated in a day trip. Try to plan at least one night's stay or, better still, allow yourself a few days to take in properly the richness of the city's architecture and the art of the Sienese school.

History

According to legend Siena was founded by Senius, son of Remus, and the symbol of the wolf feeding the twins Romulus and Remus is as ubiquitous in Siena as it is in Rome. In reality, the city was probably of Etruscan origin and subsequently remained a minor outpost until the arrival of the Lombards in the 6th century AD. Under them, Siena became a key point along the main route from northern Italy to Rome, the Via Francigena. The

medieval town was an amalgamation of three areas (Città, Camollia and San Martino) that would come to be known as the *terzi* (thirds). The city was next under the control of local bishops and then to locally elected administrators, the *consoli* (consuls).

By the 13th century, Siena had become a wealthy trading city, producing textiles, saffron, wine, spices and wax. International traders and bankers (including the Piccolomini, Chigi, Malavolti and Buonsignori families) were increasingly active.

As the parallels with Florence grew, so did their rivalry. Both cities were bent on occupying more Tuscan territory, so war between the two was inevitable. Ghibelline Siena defeated Guelph Florence at the Battle of Monteaperti in 1260 but it was a short-lived victory. Nine years later the Tuscan Ghibellines were defeated by Charles of Anjou and, for almost a century, Siena was obliged to toe the Florentine line in international affairs, becoming a member of the Tuscan Guelph League (supporters of the Pope).

Siena reached its peak under the republican rule of the Consiglio dei Nove (Council of Nine), an elected executive dominated by the rising mercantile class. Many of the finest buildings in the Sienese Gothic style were constructed during this period, including the cathedral, the Palazzo Pubblico and the Piazza del Campo. The Sienese school of painting was born at this time, with Guido da Siena, and reached its peak in the early 14th century with the works of artists including Duccio di Buoninsegna and Simone Martini.

A plague outbreak in 1348 killed two-thirds of the city's 100,000 inhabitants and led to a period of decline for Siena.

At the end of the 14th century, Siena came under the control of Milan's Visconti family, followed the century after by the autocratic patrician Pandolfo Petrucci. Under his power, the city's fortunes improved but the Holy Roman Emperor Charles V conquered Siena in 1556 after a two-year siege that left thousands dead. Consequently, the city was handed over to Cosimo I de' Medici who, for a while, even barred the inhabitants from operating banks and thus definitively curtailed Siena's power.

Siena was home to St Catherine (Santa Caterina), one of Italy's most venerated saints. But saints don't make money. Siena today relies for its prosperity on tourism and the success of its Monte dei Paschi di Siena bank, founded in 1472 and now one of the city's largest employers.

That Siena has remained largely intact as a Gothic city is the silver lining in what was for the people of this city a particularly dark cloud. Its decline in the wake of the Medici takeover was so complete that no-one gave thought to demolition and/or new construction. As the population again finally grew in the years after WWII (it had dropped to 16,000 in the latter half of the 18th-century), the city became the first in Italy (in 1965) to ban motorised traffic in the old centre.

Orientation

Historic Siena, still largely surrounded by its medieval walls, is small and easily tackled on foot, although the way in which streets swirl in semicircles around the city's heart, Piazza del Campo (also known as 'Il Campo'), may confuse you, and be prepared for some steep climbs.

That the city once thrived on banking is evident by the name of two of its main central streets, Banchi di Sopra and Banchi di Sotto. Together they form part of the medieval Via Francigena pilgrims road from the north to Rome. Another artery is Via di Città, which joins the others just behind Piazza del Campo.

By bus you will arrive at Piazza Gramsci, north of the cathedral and Piazza del Campo. Walk south along Via dei Montanini, which turns into Banchi di Sopra which leads to Piazza del Campo.

From the train station you will need to catch a bus to Piazza Gramsci.

Those driving should note that streets within the walls are blocked to normal traffic – even if you are staying at a hotel in the centre of town, you will be required to leave your car in a car park after dropping off your bags.

You can enter Siena through any of eight city gates. Il Campo, south of the centre, is a good option; it's a relatively flat 10-minute walk to Piazza del Campo and there's a large underground carpark here. See Getting There & Away later in the chapter for details.

Information
BOOKSHOPS
Libreria Senese (☎ 0577 27 02 75; Via di Città 64) This bookshop has a good stock of English, Dutch and German books, and also sells international newspapers.

EMERGENCY
Police Station (☎ 0577 20 11 11; Via del Castoro)

INTERNET ACCESS
Engineering Systems (Via di Stalloreggi 8; €2/30 mins)
Internet Train (☎ 0577 24 74 60; www.siena web.com; Via di Pantaneto 54 & 121 Via di Città; €3/30 mins)

LAUNDRY
Onda Blu (Via del Casato di Sotto 17) Wash and dry 7kg for €6.

MEDICAL SERVICES
Hospital (☎ 0577 58 51 11; Viale Bracci) Just north of Siena at Le Scotte.

MONEY
Exact Change (☎ 0577 28 81 15; Via di Città 80-82 & ☎ 0577 22 61 33; Via Banchi di Sopra 33)

POST
Post Office (Piazza Matteotti 1)

TELEPHONE
Unstaffed Telecom phone offices are at Via dei Rossi 86, Via di Città 113 and Via di Pantaneto 44.

TOURIST INFORMATION
Tourist Office (☎ 0577 28 05 51; www.terresiena.it; Piazza del Campo 56; 🕑 8.30am-7.30pm Mon-Sat & 9am-3pm Sun) If you plan to see more than one sight, it can provide a list of ticket combinations that can save you a few euros.

Foreigners Office (Ufficio Stranieri; Jacopo della Quercia; 🕑 8.30-10.30am daily except Thu & Sun for everyone, & noon-1pm for EU citizens only)

Sights

PIAZZA DEL CAMPO
This shell-shaped, slanting square, on the site of a former Roman marketplace, has been the city's civic centre since it was laid out by the Council of Nine in the mid-14th century.

Today, tourists and locals alike gather in the square to take a break from the day's errands or sightseeing – backpackers and students lounge on the pavement in the square's centre, while the more well-heeled drink expensive coffee or beer at the outdoor cafés on the periphery.

The piazza's paving is divided into nine sectors, representing the number of members of the ruling council. In 1346 water first bubbled forth from the **Fonte Gaia** (Happy Fountain – for obvious reasons) in the upper part of the square. The fountain's panels are reproductions of those done by Jacopo della Quercia in the early 15th century. The much-worn originals are on display in the Complesso Museale di Santa Maria della Scala (see p196).

PALAZZO PUBBLICO
At the lowest point of the square, the impressive **Palazzo Pubblico** (☎ 0577 29 22 63; adult/student €6.50/4, combined ticket for Palazzo & tower €9.50; 🕑 10am-11pm Jul & Aug, 10am-7pm mid-Mar–Jun & Sept-Oct, 10am-4pm Nov–mid-Mar) includes a 102m bell tower, the **Torre del Mangia**, built in 1344.

Dating from 1297, the *palazzo* itself is one of the most graceful Gothic buildings in Italy. Its construction, as the nerve centre

of republican government, was planned to be an integral part of the piazza. The result is an amphitheatre effect with the Palazzo Pubblico as central stage.

The Council of Nine wanted to unite the offices of government and courts in one central building, thus further removing the instruments of power, symbolically and actually, from the hands of the feudal nobles.

Inside is the **Museo Civico**, a series of rooms on an upper floor of the *palazzo* with frescoes by artists of the Sienese school. As you will soon come to notice, the Sienese penchant for frescoes is unique. Here, as in other great buildings of Siena, and indeed elsewhere in the province (the Palazzo del Popolo and Collegiata in San Gimignano are sufficient confirmation), the decoration, often with a foundation of deep-blue hues on the ceiling, tends to be rich and full, leaving scarcely a millimetre uncovered.

Upstairs are five rather nondescript rooms filled with equally unarresting paintings, mostly by Sienese artists of the 16th to the 18th centuries. Check out the **Sala del Risorgimento** to your left with its more impressive series of frescoes from the late 19th-century serialising key events in the campaign to unite Italy.

From here, cross the central corridor into the **Sala di Balia** (or Sala dei Priori). The 15 scenes depicted in frescoes around the walls recount episodes in the life of Pope Alexander III (the Sienese Rolando Bandinelli), including his clashes with the Holy Roman Emperor Frederick Barbarossa.

You then pass into the **Anticamera del Concistoro**, remarkable above all for the fresco (moved here in the 19th century) of *Santi Caterina d'Alessandria, Giovanni e Agostino* (Saints Catherine of Alexandria, John and Augustine), executed by Ambrogio Lorenzetti.

The following hall, the **Sala del Concistoro**, is dominated by the allegorical ceiling frescoes by the Mannerist Domenico Beccafumi.

Back in the Anticamera del Concistoro, you pass to your right into the **Vestibolo** (Vestibule), whose star attraction is a bronze wolf, symbol of the city. Next door in the **Anticappella** are frescoes of scenes from Greco-Roman mythology and history, while the **Cappella** (Chapel), contains a fine *Sacra Famiglia e San Leonardo* (Holy

Family and St Leonardo) by Il Sodoma and intricately carved wooden choir stalls.

The best is saved till last. From the Cappella, you emerge into the **Sala del Mappamondo** where you can admire the masterpiece of the entire building – the powerful and striking *Maestà* (Majesty) fresco by Simone Martini, which is his earliest known work. It is one of the most important works of the Sienese school.

On the opposite wall, the equestrian fresco of Guidoriccio da Fogliano has also long been attributed to Martini, although there is some doubt about it now. Other large frescoes along the inside long wall depict famous Sienese victories.

The next room, the **Sala dei Nove** (or Sala della Pace) is dominated by Ambrogio Lorenzetti's fresco series depicting the *Effetti del Buon e del Cattivo Governo* (Allegories of Good and Bad Government). On the party wall with the Sala del Mappamondo are scenes of a charming serenity that lend a little insight into everyday life in medieval Siena and its countryside. This sunlit idyll is the result of good and wise government, symbolised by the figures on the narrow inner wall. Turning to the next long wall you see the symbolic figures of all the nasty vices that can come to rule the hearts of princes and lead to the misery depicted next to them. Unfortunately, this fresco has suffered considerable damage.

You can complete the visit by climbing the stairs to the **loggia** which looks out southeast over Piazza del Mercato and the countryside.

TORRE DEL MANGIA
Climb this graceful **bell tower** (admission €5.50, joint ticket for tower & Palazzo €9.50; ☺ same hours as Palazzo) for splendid views across the city. Note that the ticket office closes 45 minutes before the tower shuts and only 30 people are allowed up at any time.

CATHEDRAL
Despite the retention of some Romanesque elements, Siena's **cathedral** (Piazza del Duomo; ☺ 7.30am-7.30pm mid-Mar–Oct, 7.30am-1pm & 2.30-5pm Nov-Mar) is one of Italy's great Gothic churches. Begun in 1196, it was largely completed by 1215, although work continued on features such as the apse and dome well into the 13th century.

QUENCHING THE THIRST

In 1556 Emperor Charles V apparently claimed that 'Siena is as beautiful under the ground as it is above it'. As he had spent the two previous years plundering the city and slaughtering most of its inhabitants, this observation did not go down well at the time. Yet his seemingly wacky observation had an element of truth.

Beneath Siena lies an incredible 15-mile network of underground tunnels and interconnecting passages dating back to the 13th century. Back then, Siena was the main city on the much-travelled route through northern Italy to Rome. As the city prospered, the shortage of water became critical.

The resulting underground tunnels were an incredible feat of engineering. Two teams of workers started from opposite directions: one some 10 miles away at the source of the water in the hills, the other from underneath Siena. There was no communication and the only instruments the medieval builders had were plumb lines and pick axes. They also worked in the dark, apart from the flickering light of oil lamps. The tunnels were built with absolute precision, at a very low constant gradient which kept the water flowing at a constant rate. More than 700 years later, the network of tunnels is still working, flowing into many of Siena's fountains. Water from the main tunnel is also used to cool the fridge of Nannini (see p201), the famous ice-cream and pastry shop. It's a fitting example of how Siena's history lives on, complementing the medieval with the modern.

Underground tours in Siena can be arranged through the tourist office.

Exterior
After the cathedral's completion, work began on changing, enlarging and embellishing the structure. The magnificent facade of white, green and red polychrome marble was begun by Giovanni Pisano and finished towards the end of the 14th century. The mosaics in the gables were added in the 19th century. The statues of philosophers and prophets by Giovanni Pisano, above the lower section, are copies, the originals being preserved in the nearby Museo dell'Opera Metropolitana. The bell tower is Romanesque – exact date unknown.

SIENA

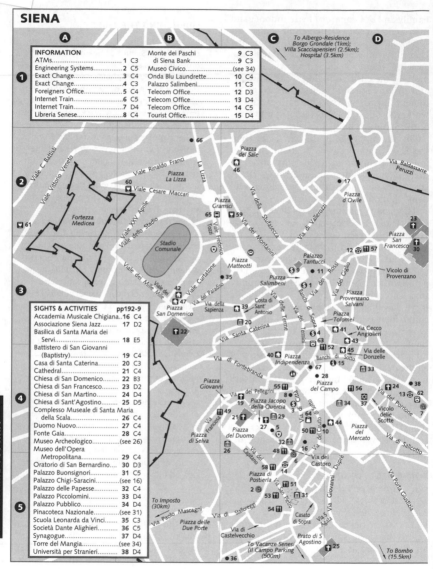

In 1339 the city's leaders launched a plan to create one of Italy's largest churches. Known as the Duomo Nuovo (New Cathedral), the remains of this unrealised project can be seen in Piazza Jacopo della Quercia, on the eastern side of the main cathedral. The plague of 1348 put a stop to this formidable scheme. You can climb to the top for great views from the Museo dell'Opera Metropolitana (see p196).

Interior

The cathedral's interior is truly stunning. Walls and pillars continue the black-and-white-stripe theme of the exterior, while the vaults are painted blue with gold stars. High

along the walls of the nave is a long series of papal busts.

After looking up, look down...and you'll see the cathedral's most precious feature – the inlaid-marble floor, which is decorated with 56 panels depicting historical and biblical subjects. The earliest panels are graffiti designs in simple black-and-white marble, dating from the mid-14th century. The latest panels were completed in the 16th century. Many of them are kept covered throughout the year, but a select few are uncovered and fenced off, allowing you a glimpse of these glorious panels. Between late August and September all the panels are generally revealed. Check with the tourist office for the latest dates. You can inspect the 19th-century drawings in the Museo dell'Opera Metropolitana (see p196), if you need another fix.

After the floor, the most exquisite item in the church is the beautiful octagonal pulpit carved in marble and porphyry by Nicola Pisano in the 13th century. Often compared with Pisano's hexagonal pulpit in the Baptistry in Pisa, this is, if anything, better still and is one of the outstanding masterpieces of Gothic sculpture. The more you behold the seven panels, laden with crowd scenes of remarkable reality, the more they seem to come to life. Unfortunately, you can't inch as close as you might like as barriers keep you at a respectful distance. To shed a little light on the subject, stick coins into the machine (€0.50 gets you a generous one minute of illumination).

Other significant artworks include a bronze statue of St John the Baptist by Donatello in the north transept.

Libreria Piccolomini
Through a door off the north aisle, the **Libreria Piccolomini** (admission €1.50; 9am-7.30pm mid-Mar–Oct, 10am-1pm & 2.30-5pm Nov–mid-Mar) is another of the cathedral's great treasures. Pope Pius III built this compact hall to house the books of his uncle, Enea Silvio Piccolomini, who was Pope Pius II; only a series of huge choral tomes remains on display.

The walls are truly impressive, covered by a series of richly coloured frescoes by Bernardino Pinturicchio, they depict events in the life of Piccolomini, starting from his early career days as a secretary to an Italian bishop on a mission to Basle, through to his ordination as pope and eventually his death in Ancona while trying to get a crusade against the Turks off the ground.

In the centre of the hall is a group of statues known as the *Tre Grazie* (Three Graces), a 3rd-century Roman copy of an earlier Hellenistic work.

CENTRAL TUSCANY

MUSEO DELL'OPERA METROPOLITANA

The **Museo dell'Opera Metropolitana** (☎ 0577 4 23 09; Piazza del Duomo 8; admission €5.50; ☺ 9am-7.30pm mid-Mar–Sept, 9am-6pm Oct, 9am-1.30pm Nov–mid-Mar) is next to the cathedral. Its great artworks formerly adorned the cathedral, including the 12 statues of prophets and philosophers by Giovanni Pisano that decorated the facade. Their creator designed them to be viewed from the ground level, which is why they look so distorted (they're all craning uncomfortably forward).

On the first floor is Duccio di Buoninsegna's striking early-14th-century *Maestà* (Majesty), painted on both sides as a screen for the cathedral's high altar. The front and back have now been separated and the panels depicting the *Passione* (Story of Christ's Passion) hang opposite the *Maestà*. It is interesting to compare Buoninsegna's work with Martini's slightly later *Maestà* in the Palazzo Pubblico. The closer you look at the Passion scenes, the more you are absorbed into the story. Remember, these were created for the largely illiterate masses who could not read. Duccio's narrative genius is impressive. Take the lower half of the bottom big middle panel. In one 'shot', three scenes take place: Christ preaches to the Apostles in the Garden of Gethsemane; he then asks them to wait up for him; and then is portrayed while in prayer. In the half-panel above, he is kissed by Judas while Peter lops off a soldier's ear and the remaining Apostles flee.

To the right of the *Maestà*, a door leads into a back room with statues by Jacopo della Quercia, while the door to the left leads to a room with 19th-century illustrations of the entire collection of marble floor panels in the cathedral.

On the upper floors other artists represented in the museum are Ambrogio Lorenzetti, Simone Martini and Taddeo di Bartolo. The collection also includes tapestries and manuscripts.

Follow the signs to the **Panorama del Facciatone** (which involves a claustrophobic climb up winding stairs) to come out on top of the facade of what would have been the huge extension of the cathedral. The views over Siena are marvellous.

BATTISTERO DI SAN GIOVANNI

Just behind the cathedral and down one flight of stairs is the **Battistero di San Giovanni** (Baptistry of St John; Piazza San Giovanni; admission €2.05; ☺ 9am-7.30pm mid-Mar–Sept, 9am-6pm Oct, 10am-1pm & 2.30-5pm Nov–mid-Mar). It has a Gothic facade which is unfinished at the upper levels, but is nonetheless a quite remarkable extravagance in marble.

Inside, the ceiling and vaults are bedecked with predictable lavishness in frescoes. The life of Jesus is portrayed in the apse of this oddly shaped rectangular baptistry. The one on the right showing Christ carrying the Cross is of particular interest. If you look at the city from which it appears he and the crowd have come, it is hard to escape the feeling that among the imaginary buildings have been illustrated Brunelleschi's dome and Giotto's Campanile in Florence. Is this a nasty little anti-Florentine dig suggesting Siena's rival as the source of Christ's tribulations?

The real attraction is a marble font by Jacopo della Quercia, decorated with bronze panels in relief depicting the life of St John the Baptist. The panels were carried out by several top-notch artists and include Ghiberti's *Cattura del Battistas* (St John in Prison) and Donatello's *Banchetto di Erode* (Herod's Feast).

COMPLESSO MUSEALE DI SANTA MARIA DELLA SCALA

Until a few years ago a working hospital with almost a millennium of history (it was originally a hospice for pilgrims), this immense space has been transformed into a major **arts centre** (☎ 0577 22 48 11, Piazza del Duomo 2; adult/child €5.20/3.10, groups of 15 with booking per person €4.20; ☺ 10am-7pm mid-Mar–Oct, 10.30am-4.30pm Nov–mid-Mar). Located on the southwestern side of Piazza del Duomo, the main attraction remains the vivid series of frescoes by Domenico di Bartolo in the former main ward.

Before entering the hospital proper, enter the **Chiesa della Santissima Annunziata** to the left. This is a 13th-century church remodelled two centuries later.

Turn right into the **Cappella del Manto**, decorated with frescoes, of which the most striking is that by Beccafumi (1514) portraying the *Incontro di San Gioacchino con Santa Anna* (Meeting of St Joaquim and St Anna), the supposed parents of the Virgin Mary.

You will pass into a long hall where, to the left, is the remarkable 14th-century

Sala del Pellegrinaio, the hospital's eventual main ward.

The bulk of the fresco series was done by Domenico di Bartolo in the 1440s. The first panel, by Il Vecchietta, depicts *gettatelli* (orphans) ascending to heaven. Taking in orphans was frequently one of the tasks of hospitals throughout Tuscany. Later panels show *balie* (wet-nurses) suckling orphans and other needy children. An entertaining panel depicts a doctor nodding off as his patient describes his symptoms.

Downstairs is the **Fienile**, once storage space for the hospital. The original panelling of the Fonte Gaia (and a few replicas) is now housed here. Through the Fienile is the **Oratorio di Santa Caterina della Notte** (Oratory of St Catherine of the Night), a gloomy little chapel for sending up a prayer or two for the unwell upstairs.

MUSEO ARCHEOLOGICO

After you've had enough of gloomy chapels, check out this museum housed in the Il Labirinti del Santa Maria (the Labyrinth of Santa Maria). Most of the collection consists of pieces found near Siena, ranging from elaborate Etruscan alabaster funerary urns to gold Roman coins. In between you'll see some statuary (much of it Etruscan and dating from several centuries BC), a variety of household items, votive statuettes in bronze and even a pair of playing dice. The collection is well presented, and the surroundings – twisting, arched tunnels – perfectly complement it and are a cool blessing on stifling-hot summer days.

Admission is included in the price for Santa Maria; opening hours are the same, except that it opens 10am to 1pm only on the second and fourth Sunday of the month.

PALAZZO DELLE PAPESSE

Head towards this contemporary **art gallery** (☎ 0577 2 20 71; Via di Città 126; adult/child €5/3.50; ☯ noon-7pm Mon-Sat) if you've had your fill of medieval religious art. The gallery houses a number of permanent pieces from the likes of Micha Ullman and Botto & Bruno, mixed in with ever-changing exhibitions. The rooftop terrace has stunning views.

PALAZZO CHIGO-SARACINI

The magnificent curving Gothic facade of this **palazzo** (Via di Città) is in part a travesty, the result of 'restoration' in the 18th and 19th centuries to re-create the medieval feel. From the tower, which is the genuine article, they say a young boy with particularly good eyesight watched the Battle of Monteaperti in 1260 and shouted down details of the home side's progress against the Florentines to eager crowds in the streets below (as you may remember, the home side won this round).

The *palazzo* is now home to the Accademia Musicale Chigiana (see p199). Call the **Monte dei Paschi di Siena bank** (☎ 0577 29 47 87) if you want to visit the sumptuously furnished rooms with their interesting collection of Sienese art.

PINACOTECA NAZIONALE

This **gallery** (☎ 0577 28 11 61; Via San Pietro 29; adult/child €4/2; ☯ 8.15am-7.15pm Tue-Sat, 8.15am-1.15pm Sun, 8.30am-1.30pm Mon), within the 14th-century Palazzo Buonsignori, constitutes the greatest concentration of Sienese art in the city and includes Gothic masterpieces. As you progress through the collection, you can only marvel at the gulf that lay between artistic life in Siena and Florence in the 15th century. While the Renaissance flourished 70km to the north, Siena's masters and their patrons remained firmly rooted in the Byzantine and Gothic precepts that had stood them in such good stead from the early 13th century. Stock religious images and episodes predominate, typically lavishly filled with gold and generally lacking any of the advances in painting (such as perspective, emotion or movement) that artists in Florence were indulging in.

Start your tour on the 2nd floor where, in the first two rooms, you can see some of the earliest surviving pre-Gothic works from the Sienese school, including pieces by Guido da Siena. Rooms 3 and 4 are given over to a few works by Duccio di Buoninsegna and his followers. The most striking exhibit in Room 6 is Simone Martini's *Madonna della Misericordia* (Madonna of Mercy), in which the Virgin Mary seems to take the whole of society protectively under her wing.

The brothers Pietro and Ambrogio Lorenzetti dominate Rooms 7 and 8, while the following three rooms contain works by several artists from the early 15th-century. Giovanni di Paolo dominates most of Rooms 12 and 13, and a couple of his

IL PALIO

This spectacular event, held twice yearly on 2 July and 16 August in honour of the Virgin Mary, dates back to the Middle Ages and features a series of colourful pageants, a wild horse race around Piazza del Campo and much eating, drinking and celebrating in the streets.

Il Palio is probably one of the only major medieval spectacles of its type in Italy, which has survived through the sheer tenacity of Sienese traditionalism. Most of the other charming displays of medieval tradition, although doubtless pleasing, have in fact been brought back to life in the 20th century out of a combination of nostalgia and the desire to earn a few more tourist bucks. The Sienese place incredible demands on the national TV network, RAI, for rights to televise the event.

Ten of Siena's 17 town districts, or *contrade*, compete for the coveted *palio*, a silk banner. Each has its own traditions, symbol and colours, and its own church and *palio* museum. As you wander the streets you will be hard-pressed to miss the various flags and plaques delineating these quarters, each with a name and symbol related to an animal. On the downside, competition is so fierce that fist fights sometimes break out between *contrade* and Il Palio jockeys often live in fear from rival *contrade*. Scheming rivals have been known to ambush jockeys and even drug their horses.

On festival days Piazza del Campo becomes a racetrack, with a ring of packed dirt around its perimeter. From about 5pm, representatives of each *contrada* parade in historical costume, each bearing their individual banners.

The race is run at 7.45pm in July and 7pm in August. For not much more than one exhilarating minute, the 10 horses and their bareback riders tear three times around Piazza del Campo with a speed and violence that makes your hair stand on end.

Even if a horse loses its rider it is still eligible to win and, since many riders fall each year, it is the horses in the end who are the focus of the event. There is only one rule: riders are not to interfere with the reins of other horses.

Book well in advance for a room and join the crowds in the centre of Piazza del Campo at least four hours before the start for a good view. Surrounding streets are closed off well before the race begins, except for Via Giovanni Dupré, which stays open right up until the flag drops. So if you arrive late you can try your luck reaching the Piazza via this street but don't count on it as everyone else has the same idea. If you'd prefer a more comfortable seat overlooking the race from one of the buildings lining the Piazza, ask around in the cafés and shops. They're as rare as hen's teeth but, if you do manage to find one, expect to pay around €220 for the privilege. If you can't find a good vantage point, don't despair – the race is televised live and then repeated throughout the evening on TV.

If you happen to be in town in the few days immediately preceding the race, you may get to see the jockeys and horses trying out in Piazza del Campo – almost as good as the real thing.

paintings show refreshing signs of a break from strict tradition. His two versions of the *Presentazione nel Tempio* (the Presentation of Jesus in the Temple) introduce new architectural themes, a hint of perspective, virtually no gold and a discernible trace of human emotion in the characters depicted.

The small **Collezione Spannochi** on the 3rd floor is a rather motley group of paintings with few highlights.

Down on the 1st floor, the Sienese roll-call continues and, although there are some exceptions, the interest starts to fade. The best rooms include Nos 27 to 32 and 37, which are dominated by works of the Mannerist Domenico Beccafumi and Il Sodoma. Of all these, Il Sodoma's *Cristo alla Colonna* (Christ Tied to the Pillar) in Room 31 is the

most disturbing. Christ's tears are a heart-rending human touch.

CHIESA DI SAN AGOSTINO

A few streets south of Pinacoteca Nazionale is this 13th-century **church** (☎ 0577 38 57 86; Prato di San Agostino; €2; ☽ 10.30am-1.30pm & 3-5.30pm mid-Mar–Oct). It was designed by the Dutch Vanvitelli, the chief architect for the King of Naples, and is richly representative of the rococo period. Its interior dates from the 18th century, after it was gutted by fire.

CHIESA DI SAN DOMENICO

This imposing 13th-century Gothic **church** (Piazza San Domenico; ☽ 7.30am-1pm & 3-6.30pm) has been altered time and time again over centuries past.

The bare, barnlike interior is in keeping with the Dominican order's spartan outlook. Near the entrance is the raised **Cappella delle Volte**, where St Catherine took her vows and supposedly performed some of her miracles. In the chapel is a portrait of the saint painted during her lifetime.

In the **Cappella di Santa Caterina**, on the south side are frescoes by Il Sodoma depicting events in the saint's life. St Catherine died in Rome and most of her body is preserved there. However, in line with the bizarre practice of collecting relics of dead saints, her head was given back to Siena and is contained in a tabernacle on the altar of the Cappella di Santa Caterina.

Another bit of her that managed to find its way here is a thumb on grisly display in a small window box to the right of the chapel. Also on show is a rather nasty-looking chain whip with which she used to apply a good flogging to herself every now and then for the well-being of the souls of the faithful.

FORTEZZA MEDICEA
Just west of the Chiesa di San Domenico, this **fortress** is typical of those built in the early years of the grand duchy. Also known as the Forte di Santa Barbara, the Sienese could have been given little more obvious a reminder of who was in charge than this huge Medici bastion, raised on the orders of Cosimo I de' Medici in 1560.

CASA DI SANTA CATERINA
This is the **house** (☎ 0577 4 41 77; Costa di Sant' Antonio 6; ⌚ 9am-12.30pm & 2.30-6pm) where St Catherine was born. The rooms were converted into small chapels in the 15th century and are decorated with frescoes of her life and paintings by Sienese artists, including Il Sodoma.

SYNAGOGUE
This 8th-century **synagogue** (Vicolo delle Scotte 14; admission €2.60; ⌚ 10am-1pm & 2-4pm Sun only) is the city's one and only. There's not a lot to see but it's worth a brief look around.

ORATORIO DI SAN BERNARDINO
Dating from the 1400s (☎ 0577 28 30 48; Piazza San Francesco 9; admission €2; ⌚ 10.30am-1.30pm & 3-5.30pm mid-Mar–end Oct), this chapel is notable for its frescoes by Il Sodoma and Beccafumi, plus a small museum of religious art.

Courses
Course prices are listed exclusive of accomodation.

LANGUAGE
Siena's **Università per Stranieri** (University for Foreigners; ☎ 0577 24 01 15; www.unistrasi.it; Via di Pantaneto 45; 10-week course €750) is open year-round and the only requirement for enrolment is a high-school graduation or pass certificate. (The four-week courses that run over summer have no prerequisites.)

The **Scuola Leonardo da Vinci** (☎ 0577 24 90 97; www.scuolaleonardo.com; Via del Paradiso 16; 12-week courses from €1330) runs courses varying from one-to-one tutorials to 12 students per class. It also offers culture, wine and cookery courses.

The **Società Dante Alighieri** (☎ 0577 4 95 33; www.dantealighieri.com; Via Tommaso Pendola 37; 4-week courses €610) Like da Vinci, this place runs language, culture and cookery courses. It's worth noting that it's the only government-recognised school of its kind in Siena.

MUSIC
The **Accademia Musicale Chigiana** (☎ 0577 4 61 52; www.chigiana.it; Via di Città 89; courses €160-454) offers eight- to 10-week classical-music classes in most instruments every summer, as well as seminars and concerts performed by visiting musicians, teachers and students.

The **Associazione Siena Jazz** (☎ 0577 27 14 01; www.sienajazz.it; Via di Vallerozzi 77; 2-week summer courses from €350) offers courses in jazz and is one of Europe's foremost institutions of its type.

Tours
The **Treno Natura** (☎ 0577 20 74 13; www.ferrovieturistiche.it - Italian only; €15) dates back to the early 1800s but nowadays runs exclusively for tourists. It is a great way to see the stunning scenery of Le Crete, south of Siena. The train line extends in a ring from Siena, through Asciano, across to the Val d'Orcia and the Monte Antico station, before heading back towards Siena. Pick up a timetable at the tourist office.

Ecco Siena (☎ 0577 4 34 97; www .guidedisiena.it; Piazza San Domenico 2; from €20; ☎ 9am-8pm Mon-Sat in summer & 9am-7pm in winter) runs city tours for groups and individuals. The group tours take around two hours and leave from outside the San Domenico Church at 4.30pm daily.

Festivals & Events

The **Accademia Musicale Chigiana** holds the Settimana Musicale Senese each July, as well as the **Estate Musicale Chigiana** (☎ 0577 2 20 91) in July and August. Tickets cost €5 to €35. Concerts are usually held at the Abbazia di San Galgano (a former abbey about 20km southwest of the city and regarded as one of Italy's finest Gothic buildings) and at Sant'Antimo, near Montalcino (see p204 and p216).

The city hosts **Siena Jazz** (☎ 0577 27 14 01; www.sienajazz.it - Italian only), an international festival each July and August, with concerts at the Fortezza Medicea as well as various sites throughout the city.

During the Festa di Santa Cecilia that takes place in November, concerts and exhibitions take place to honour the patron saint of musicians.

Sleeping

In Siena a decent range of accommodation is on offer – except during the Palio. To visit during Il Palio, make sure you make preparations well in advance. For assistance, contact the tourist office or **Siena Hotels Promotion** (☎ 0577 28 80 84; www.hotelsiena .com; Piazza San Domenico 2; ☎ 9am-8pm Mon-Sat in summer & 9am-7pm in winter) near the San Domenico Church. **Vacanze Senesi** (☎ 0577 4 59 00; info@vacanzesenesi.it; ☺ 10am-6pm Mon-Fri), located upstairs at the Il Campo underground carpark, can help with hotel and *agriturismo* reservations. There are also about 120 *affittacamere* (rooms for rent) in town.

BUDGET

Hotel Le Tre Donzelle (☎ 0577 28 03 58; fax 0577 22 39 33; Via delle Donzelle 5; s/d €33/46, d with bath €60) In a good central location, this small hotel is off Banchi di Sotto just north of Piazza del Campo. The rooms are monastically basic but spotlessly clean.

Locanda Garibaldi (☎ 0577 28 42 04; Via Giovanni Duprè 18; d €70) Brilliantly located just south of Piazza del Campo. The rooms are big, bright and modern, and the whole place has an individual, funky feel. The adjacent restaurant is pretty good, judging by the constant queue.

Piccolo Hotel Etruria (☎ 0577 28 80 88; hetruriqa@ tin.it; Via delle Donzelle 3; s/d €44/75) Always good value, this hotel has benefited from a recent facelift. There are large clean rooms and a central light, airy sitting area.

MID-RANGE

Albergo Bernini (☎/fax 0577 28 90 47; www.albergobernini.com; Via della Sapienza 15; d €62, s/d with bath €78/82) This old hotel is a bit frayed at the edges but has loads of character and atmosphere. Owner Mauro may even treat you to a tune on his piano accordion if you're lucky. The single rooms (and terrace) have stunning cathedral views.

Piccolo Hotel il Palio (☎ 0577 28 11 31; fax 0577 28 11 42; Piazza del Sale 19; s/d €60/85) Il Palio is housed in a 15th-century monastery; the rooms are still pretty small, but carpeted these days. It is a good 15-minute walk north of Piazza del Campo.

Albergo-Residence Borgo Grondaie (☎ 0577 33 25 39; www.borgogrondaie.com; Via delle Grondaie 15; s/d €70/120, 6-person apartments €209; P ⛄) Just a couple of kilometres north of the centre, this former farm still produces olive oil. Rooms are simple and tasteful, with lots of terracotta and earthy colours. The apartments are in the former stables and exquisite. There is a special-needs unit, saltwater pool and bicycles to rent.

Chiusarelli (☎ 0577 28 05 62; www.chiusarelli.com; Viale Curtatone 15; s/d €75/112; P ⛄) This place has solid, simply furnished rooms in a handsome old building. Fancy faux marble lobby leads to a vast popular restaurant where you'll be dodging elbows to find a seat among the locals.

Also recommended:

Albergo La Perla (☎ 0577 4 71 44; Via delle Terme 25; s/d €62/83) Simple clean rooms and ingenious matchbox-size toilet/shower en suites.

Albergo La Toscana (☎ 0577 4 60 97; fax 0577 27 06 34; Via Cecco Angiolieri 12; s/d €67/83) Clean basic doubles.

TOP END

Hotel Santa Caterina (☎ 0577 22 11 05; www.hscsiena.it; Via Enea Silvio Piccolomini 7; s/d €98/144; P ⛄) This is a very gracious hotel enhanced by friendly and welcoming staff. The rooms are tastefully luxurious and the garden is lovely, with plenty of shady magnolia (and similar) trees.

Villa Scacciapensieri (☎ 0577 4 14 41; www.villascacciapensieri.it; Via Scacciapensieri 10; s/d €128/235; P ⛄ ⛄) Around 2.5km north of Siena, overlooking the city walls. This 18th-century villa is gorgeous with carved wooden ceilings, oil paintings, antiques, formal gardens and an old family chapel. There are tennis courts and bicycles to rent.

Eating

The Sienese claim that most Tuscan cuisine has its origins in Siena, where the locals still use methods introduced to the area by the Etruscans.

Tuscans elsewhere may well dispute such boasting but the Sienese maintain that such dishes as *ribollita, panzanella* and *pappardelle al sugo di lepre* (hare sauce) are their own. *Pici*, a kind of bloated rough spaghetti, is also claimed by the Sienese, but also by Montalcino (see p214). *Panforte*, a rich cake of almonds, honey and candied melon or citrus fruit, has its origins in the city. Loosely translated, *panforte* is 'strong bread' and it was created as sustenance for the Crusaders to the Holy Land.

Spizzico-Ciao (☎ 0577 4 01 87; Piazza del Campo 77-81; mains €6-10; ☺ closed Tue) Despite the plastic fast-food feel, the self-service bars out back are good value and healthy (even), with bowls of fruit and salad for the same price as a couple of ice-cream scoops across the square.

Hostaria Il Carroccio (☎ 0577 4 11 65; Via Casato di Sotto 32; mains €7-10; ☺ closed Wed) The pasta at this place, which is off Piazza del Campo, is excellent. Try the *pici* followed by the *tegamate di maiale* (pork with fennel seeds). This restaurant is a member of the Slow Food movement (see p61) – always a good sign.

Osteria del Castelvecchio (☎ 0577 4 95 86; Via di Castelvecchio 65; mains €9-10; ☺ closed Tue) An unassuming small restaurant spread over a couple of rooms which packs in the locals and in-the-know tourists. Rumbling tummies should try the constantly changing *menu di degustazione* (€25).

Al Marsili (☎ 0577 4 71 54; Via del Castoro 3; mains from €11; ☺ closed Mon) This is one of the city's classiest restaurants where white-smocked waiters dish up traditional Sienese cuisine like *pici alla casareccia* (*pici* with a meat and mushroom sauce). The restaurant also offers more innovative dishes such as gnocchi in a duck sauce.

Ristorante da Mugolone (☎ 0577 28 32 35; Via dei Pellegrini 8; mains €10-12; ☺ closed Tue) This is another excellent restaurant, although the atmosphere is perhaps a little lacking in soul. You can easily get your fill on the *contorni* like *funghi fritti* (fried mushrooms) and *fagioli bianchi ali'olio* (white bean stew).

Kelly's English Tea Rooms (☎ 3485 54 20 25; Via San Pietro 19; snacks €2-3; ☺ closed Sat) For those who hanker after a filled baked potato or afternoon tea, this is the real McCoy with cucumber sandwiches (no crusts) or, for the more adventurous, rolls with blue cheese with pear and walnut filling.

Antica Osteria Da Divo (☎ 0577 28 43 81; Via Franciosa 29; mains €16-20) The atmosphere is memorable in this cavernous restaurant near the cathedral. This place has some serious Etruscan history happening – you can dine in a tomb dating back to 3000 BC. The inventive menu includes dishes like tarragon-scented lamb, beef fillet in basil crust followed by such girth-widening goodies as vanilla and pistachio pie with raspberry sauce.

Also recommended:

Osteria Da Cice (☎ 0577 28 80 26; Via San Pietro 32; mains €8-10) Go for the classic sage and butter ravioli.

SELF-CATERING

The most central supermarkets are at Via di Città 152–156 and Via Dei Rossi 88.

Nannini (☎ 0577 74 15 91; Banchi di Sopra 22 & 95; pastries from €0.75) This is the city's finest and most famous café and *pasticceria*.

Drinking

Enoteca Italiana (☎ 0577 28 84 97; Fortezza Medicea; ☺ closed Mon night) Within the fortress walls, the former munition cellars have been artfully transformed into a classy *enoteca* where you can also enjoy the Italian wine display, including some dusty *reservas*, the oldest dating back to 1944.

Dublin Post (☎ 0577 28 90 89; Piazza Gramsci 20-21) is always heaving, especially in summer when the overflow moves outdoors. This bar has a pseudo-Irish lilt and you can get cold dishes to accompany your Guinness on draught.

Robert the Bruce (Via Monte Santo 1; ☺ closed Wed) Italians love themed bars and here's another one; a bit of a hole in the wall but cosy enough, with British ale and cider on draught.

Entertainment

As elsewhere in Italy, the big dance venues are generally well outside town. Check ads for these places, for instance, at the uni noticeboard in the cloister of the Chiesa di San Francesco.

Caffé del Corso (Bianchi di Sopra 25; 🖳) During the day, this is the place for an espresso and croissant. At night the action moves upstairs to the moody plum-coloured music bar. There's Internet access for those who don't want to chat up-close.

Al Cambio (☎ 0577 22 05 81; Via di Pantaneto 48; ☺ closed Mon) This is one of the few dance spots in Siena where you can indulge in a little frenetic all-night air-punching.

Bombo (☎ 0577 37 50 21; Via Roma; admission including a drink €15.50; ☺ Jun-Aug only) This popular place is in Monteroni d'Arbia, about 15km southeast of Siena on the SS2.

Imposto (Località l'Imposto; admission €6; ☺ Jun-Aug only) This open-air club is about 30km south of Siena on the SS223, just north of Bagni di Petriolo. It also hosts the occasional concert.

Shopping

Via di Città is a chic shopping street (with a clear leaning to selling products to tourists) where you can buy ceramics, food items, antiques, jewellery and so on. If you're after clothes, there are more shops on Banchi di Sopra.

Siena Ricama (☎ 0577 28 83 38; Via di Città 61) This shop promotes the crafts that are practised in Siena, in particular embroidery, and is worth a visit.

Getting Around
BUS

Tra-in operates city bus services from a base in Piazza Gramsci. From the train station, you can catch bus No 3, 9 or 10 (€0.90) to Piazza Gramsci.

CAR & MOTORCYCLE

No cars, apart from those belonging to residents, are allowed in the city centre; however, there are several underground car parks outside the walls. Alternatively, look for free parking further away and be prepared for a bit of a walk. Technically, even to just drop off your luggage at your hotel it is necessary to get a special permit to enter the city by car. This can be obtained from the *vigili urbani* in Viale Federico Tozzi, but only if you have a hotel booking. Otherwise, phone your hotel for advice. Don't park illegally inside the city or around the city gates; you'll be towed quicker than you can yell 'where the *&@! is my car?' You can rent a

50cc scooter from **DF Moto Noleggi** (Via dei Gazzani 16/18) for €26 per day.

TAXI
For a taxi, call ☎ 0577 4 92 22.

Getting There & Away
BUS

From Siena, bus is generally the way to go. The hub for buses is Piazza Gramsci where up to seven SENA buses leave daily for Rome (€16, three hours).

Regular Tra-in buses race up to Florence (€6, 2¼ hours; *rapido* service €7, 1¼ hours), while LFI buses (as many as eight a day in summer) connect to Arezzo (€5).

Tra-in buses connect Siena with destinations around its province. Connections to San Gimignano (€5.20, one hour, half hourly, change at Poggibonsi) and Colle di Val d'Elsa (€2.50, 30 minutes, half hourly, change for Volterra) are frequent. Regular buses run to Montalcino (€3, 1¼ hours) and Montepulciano (€4.40, 1½ hours). Other destinations include Monterrigioni (€1.50), Chianciano, Radda in Il Chianti, Rapolano, San Quirico d'Orcia (€3), Pienza (€3.40), Grosseto (€5.60) and two daily to Bologna (€10).

At Piazza Gramsci, Tra-in and SENA operate an underground ticket sales and information service, along with left luggage (half-/full-day €2/3.50) and an ATM.

CAR & MOTORCYCLE

Take the SS2 which connects Florence and Siena, or take the SS222 ('la Chiantigiana'), which meanders its way through the Chianti hills. Follow the signs to Il Campo, south of the centre, where there's a large underground car park (€1.50 per hour) and a handy accommodation booking office.

TRAIN

Siena is not on a major train line so, from Rome, it is necessary to change at Chiusi and, from Florence, at Empoli, making buses a better alternative. Trains arrive at Piazza F Rosselli, north of the city centre.

AROUND SIENA
Le Crete

Just southeast of Siena, this area of rolling clay hills is a feast of classic Tuscan images – bare ridges topped by a solitary cypress tree flanking a medieval farmhouse, four hills silhouetted one against another as they fade off into the misty distance. The area of Le Crete changes colour according to the season – from the creamy violet of the ploughed clay to the green of the young wheat which then turns to gold. If possible, hire a car and spend a few days exploring Le Crete. Another option is the Treno Natura, a tourist train which runs from Siena through Asciano and along the Val d'Orcia.

RAPOLANO TERME
This is a relatively modern spa town that holds little interest for anyone not intent on taking an old-fashioned cure in the hot, bubbling waters here. One of the two bathing establishments operates year-round. There are more interesting places to take a sulphur bath elsewhere in central and southern Tuscany (such as Bagni di San Filippo, Bagno Vignoni and Saturnia – for the latter see p235).

ASCIANO
This pretty little hamlet is home to a trio of small museums dedicated to Sienese art and Etruscan finds in the area. It is most easily reached along the scenic SP438 road running southeast from Siena. The occasional slow local train passes through the town from Siena. While the town and its museums are interesting enough, the travelling is more rewarding than the arriving. Asciano is at the heart of Le Crete, so the trip there and beyond (such as south to the Abbazia di Monte Oliveto Maggiore) is a real treat. The small **tourist office** (☎ 0577 71 95 10; Corso Matteotti 18) has information on the town and surrounding area.

ABBAZIA DI MONTE OLIVETO MAGGIORE
This 14th-century **Olivetan monastery** (☎ 0577 70 70 61; ☒ 9.15am-noon & 3.15-6pm Apr-Oct, 9.15am-noon & 3.15-5pm Nov-Mar) is famous for the frescoes by Signorelli and Il Sodoma which decorate its **Choistro Grande** (Great Cloister). They illustrate events in the life of St Benedict. About 40 monks still live in the monastery.

The fresco cycle begins with Il Sodoma's work on the eastern wall, to the right of the entrance, and continues along the southern wall of the cloisters. The nine frescoes by Signorelli line the western side of the cloisters and Il Sodoma picks up again on the

northern wall. Il Sodoma's frescoes offer some ambiguous food for thought. At any rate, careful inspection of his frescoes reveals rather effeminate traits in many of the male figures represented. Part of the second fresco along the eastern wall, in which a potential new acolyte kneels before the severe St Benedict, who is holding up part of his habit, has a questionable air about it. Even if the sexual allusion is imaginary, it seems odd that the monastery's abbot should not have objected to the image. Further around on the southern wall, St Benedict is depicted giving a fellow friar a sound thrashing to exorcise a demon, again a rather kinky image, and what exactly is the demon on the right clutching through the monk's habit?

Note the decorations on the pillars between some of Il Sodoma's frescoes – they are among the earliest examples of 'grotesque' art, copied from decorations found in the then newly excavated Domus Aurea of Nero in Rome.

After viewing the frescoes you can wander into the **church** off the cloister. The Baroque interior is a pleasingly sober play of perspective and shape. You can also see further works by Il Sodoma here. Off the cloister is a staircase leading up to the Renaissance **library**, only visible through small windows in the door.

It is possible to stay at the monastery (☎ 0577 70 76 52; fax 0577 70 76 44; per night around €23; ☒ Dec-Oct only), although the literature makes clear that this is a silent order and you should approach your stay as a spiritual retreat.

From the monastery, head for **San Giovanni d'Asso**, where there's an interesting 11th-century church with a Lombardic-Tuscan facade, and a picturesque *borghetto* with the remains of a castle. Continue on to Montisi and Castelmuzio. Along a side road just outside Castelmuzio is the abandoned **Pieve di Santo Stefano in Cennano** 13th-century church which is usually open.

Around 2km past Castelmuzio on the road to Pienza is the 14th-century Olivetan monastery of **Sant'Anna in Camprena** (☎ 0578 74 80 37; ☒ 3.30-7.30pm Tue-Sun), the setting for the film, *The English Patient*. There are some lovely frescoes by Il Sodoma in the refectory.

The route from Monte Oliveto Maggiore to Pienza (p218) runs almost entirely along a high ridge, with great views of Le Crete.

CENTRAL TUSCANY

BUONCONVENTO

On first approaching Buonconvento down the SS2 highway, you could almost be forgiven for thinking it a large roadside rest stop. Lying perfectly flat in a rare stretch of plain, the low-slung fortified walls of this farming centre hide from view a quiet little town of medieval origins. One of its mega-historical moments came when the Holy Roman Emperor Henry VII, having shortly before captured the town, expired here in August 1313 and so put an end to any hopes the Empire might have had of reasserting direct control over Tuscany. About the only sight is the local **Museo d'Arte Sacra** (☎ 0577 80 71 81; Via Soccini 18; adult/child €3/2; ☼ 10.30am-1pm & 3-7pm Tue-Sat Mar-Oct, 10am-1pm & 3-5pm Sat & Sun Nov-Feb) in the main street. It contains religious art collected in the town and from neighbouring churches and hamlets.

If you're looking for a place to stay, move on to San Quirico d'Orcia (p217), just down the road, which is far more appealing.

Alternatively, head east via San Giovanni d'Asso to the pretty small village of **Castel-muzio** with its entrance lined with chestnut trees. Take a look at the 16th-century **Chiesa di Santa Maria** with its Romanesque Gothic facade.

Opened in 2001, **La Locanda della Moscadella** (☎ 0577 66 53 10; www.lamoscadella.it; Trequandafraz; s/d €95/160) is a former 16th-century monastery that has been artfully resurrected as an up-market hotel, restaurant and wine bar. There are minibus pick-ups from the airport, and the seclusion and views are sublime.

San Galgano & Around
ABBAZIA DI SAN GALGANO

About 20km southwest of Siena, just off the SS73, is the ruined 13th-century San Galgano abbey (☼ sunrise-sunset), one of the country's finest Gothic buildings in its day and now an atmospheric ruin.

A former Cistercian abbey, its monks were among Tuscany's most powerful, forming the judiciary and acting as accountants for the *comuni* (councils) of Volterra and Siena. They presided over disputes between the cities, played a significant role in the construction of the cathedral in Siena and built for themselves an opulent church.

As early as the 14th century, Sir John Hawkwood, the feared English mercenary, sacked the abbey on at least two occasions.

Things went from bad to worse and by the 16th century the monks' wealth and importance had declined and the church had deteriorated to the point of ruin. An attempt at restoration was made towards the end of the 16th century, but the rot had set in. In 1786 the bell tower simply collapsed, as did the ceiling vaults a few years later.

The great, roofless stone and brick monolith stands silent in the fields. Come on a rainy winter's day and you feel more like you are in France or England, surrounded by glistening green fields and confronted by this grey Gothic ruin. The French reference is no coincidence, since the style of building is reminiscent of French Gothic.

Next door to the church are what remain of the monastery buildings, as well as a brief stretch of cloister housing a small **tourist office** (☎ 0577 75 67 38).

The abbey is definitely worth a diversion if you are driving. Arriving by bus you will have to walk a few kilometres from the nearest stop.

The Accademia Musicale Chigiana in Siena sponsors concerts at the abbey during summer. See Special Events under Siena earlier in the chapter.

On a hill overlooking the abbey is the tiny, round Romanesque **Cappella di Monte Siepi**. This is the site of the original Cistercian settlement – from it came the impulse to build the great abbey below. Inside the chapel are badly preserved frescoes by Ambrogio Lorenzetti depicting the life of St Galgano, a local soldier who had a vision of St Michael on this site. A real life 'sword in the stone' is under glass in the floor of the chapel, placed by San Galgano, according to legend.

MURLO

You could continue across the valley towards this interesting medieval fortified village. This was once an important Etruscan settlement and apparently DNA tests show the locals are close relatives of these ancient people. There's not much to see but it's a quaint spot with a few walks branching out into the surrounding hills.

BAGNI DI PETRIOLI

About halfway along the SS223 highway between Siena and Grosseto, a side road leads down to the hot sulphur springs of Bagni di Petrioli. Scorching-hot spring water cascades into a few small natural basins. Anyone can come and sit in them, and there's usually a motley assortment of permanent campers making use of the natural shower.

About the only way to get here is with your own transport – unless you fancy the 9km walk from the highway.

Val d'Elsa
MONTERIGGIONI
This famous walled medieval stronghold is just off the SS2 about 12km north of Siena.

Established in 1203 as a forward defensive position against Florence, the walls and towers today constitute one of the most complete examples of such a fortified bastion in Tuscany. The walls were rebuilt in the 1260s and seven of the 14 towers were reconstructed in the 20th century. It appears from Dante's descriptions that they were considerably higher when the Florentines had reason to fear them and their Sienese defenders.

Monteriggioni is very pretty but in danger of being over-heritaged courtesy of the tidal wave of tourists which descends here each day. Aside from the coaches, regular buses run from Siena (€1.50).

There are plenty of places to stay and eat.

Hotel Monteriggioni (☎ 0577 30 50 09; www.hotelmonteriggioni.net; Via Primo Maggio 4; s/d €106/210; 🏊) The lovely gardens here are bordered by the original city walls. Originally two stone houses, the interior is lavishly decorated with antiques, and the rooms have picture postcard views. There's the added perk of a small pool.

Ristorante Il Pozzo (☎ 0577 30 41 27; Piazza Roma 20; mains €13-15; 🕙 closed Mon) Well worth a splurge, this restaurant in the main square has delicious food and is particularly known for its home-made desserts, including its legendary crêpes Suzette. There's a pleasant patio for dining alfresco.

COLLE DI VAL D'ELSA
All that the majority of visitors do here is change buses for Volterra. That's a shame because, unburdened by any notable church, museum or work of art, the town has kepts its character as a rural market town. The old town on its hill makes an ideal lunch spot, while the Friday market is a vast bustling affair selling everything from great wheels of cheese to frilly knickers. Colle has also long

been an important centre of Italian crystal production.

The most engaging part of town is historic **Colle Alta,** perched up on a ridge. From Piazza Arnolfo, if arriving by bus, it is a 10-minute climb up along Via San Sebastiano. By car, park near Porta Nova at the western end of town. It's still a 10-minute walk but there's no climb involved.

Eventually you will find yourself on Via del Castello 'high street'. At its eastern end is a medieval *casa torre* (tower house) where they say Arnolfo di Cambio was born. About halfway along the road is Piazza del Duomo, dominated by the neoclassical facade of the cathedral.

Three small museums are here. The **Museo Civico** and **Museo d'Arte Sacra** (☎ 0577 92 38 88; Via del Castello 31; €3 for both; 🕙 10am-noon & 4-7pm Tue-Sun Apr-Oct, 10am-noon & 3.30-6.30pm Sat, Sun & hols only Nov-Mar) are housed together, while the **Museo Archeologico** (☎ 0577 92 29 54; Piazza Duomo 42; admission €1.55; 🕙 10am-noon & 5-7pm Tue-Sun May-Sept, 3.30-5.30pm Tue-Fri, 10am-noon & 3.30-6.30pm Sat & Sun Oct-Apr) is right on Piazza del Duomo. The most interesting is the Museo d'Arte Sacra, with some good paintings by Sienese masters. In the newer part of town you'll find the **Museo del Cristallo** (☎ 0577 92 41 35; Via dei Fossi 8/A; admission €3; 🕙 10.30am-12.30pm & 3-7pm), which will provide everything you wanted to know about the history and production of crystal, plus some stunning pieces on display (leave your toddler at home).

You have a choice of four hotels, three in the lower part of town (Colle Bassa). The following are the better choices.

Hotel Arnolfo (☎ 0577 92 20 20; www.hotelarnolfo.it; Via Campana 8; s/d €53/75) is the only hotel in the historic part of town and has comfortable, sizable rooms. Downstairs, the corner bar, with its large leafy terrace, is an unbeatable place to sip a drink and watch local life.

La Vecchia Cartiera (☎ 0577 92 11 07; www.chiantiturismo.it; Via Oberdan 5-9; s/d €66/93) is a fairly modern hotel with all the extras, in a lively location, especially for the Friday market. The multilingual owner is a charmer and the breakfast buffet more lavish than most.

Regular buses run here from Siena (€2.50) and Florence (€4.70). Up to four connecting buses with the CPT company head west to Volterra.

CASOLE D'ELSA & AROUND
Southwest of Colle, this quiet fortified backwater was a key part of Siena's western defences against Volterra and Florence during the Middle Ages. Little remains to detain you but those with romantic tastes and a Swiss bank account could stick to the tiny road that winds south out of town to pretty hilltop **Mensano** and swing east to **Pievescola**.

Relais La Suvera (☎ 0577 96 03 00; www.lasuvera.it; Pievescola; s/d €350/780; 🕑 closed Nov–mid-Apr; P 🏊) This 12th-century former fortress and palace is still run by the Marchese Ricci family. The decor is heavily brocaded opulence with tapestries, dark and enormous oil paintings, roccoco mirrors and four-poster beds. There is a brand-new health centre with a Jacuzzi bubbling out of the palace's original well.

Il Colombaio (☎ 0577 94 90 02; Loc Il Colombaio; mains €18; 🕑 closed Mon & Tue lunch) Opposite vineyards with a distant view of Casole, this is an elegant place with stained glass and paintings. It also takes its wines seriously – 1400 at last count, including Japanese, Israeli and a Bodegas Vega Sicilia '90 for €500. The menu includes such goodies as quail salad and pecorino cheese soufflé with pear slices in chestnut honey sauce. There are apartments to rent.

POGGIBONSI
WWII managed to take care of what little was interesting about Poggibonsi, which takes line honours as one of the ugliest places in central Tuscany. If you are travelling by bus between Florence or Siena and San Gimignano, you can't avoid the town.

Ambassador Hotel (☎ 0577 98 29 22; www.toscana-ambassador.it; s/d €75/125; P 🏊) This glossy bland hotel is well placed for a quick getaway and has all the extras, including satellite TV and shoe polish.

SAN GIMIGNANO
pop 7100
As you crest the hill coming from the east, the 14 towers of this medieval walled town resemble a medieval Manhattan. And when you arrive you might feel half of Manhattan's population has moved in – San Gimignano is a tourist magnet. Come in the dead of winter, preferably when it's raining, to indulge your imagination a little. In summer, most of your attention will be focused on dodging fellow visitors.

There is a reason for all this, of course. The towers were symbols of the power and wealth of the city's medieval families and once numbered 72. San Gimignano delle Belle Torri ('of the Fine Towers') is surrounded by lush, productive land and the setting is altogether enchanting.

Originally an Etruscan village, the town later took its name from the bishop of Modena, St Gimignano, who is said to have saved the city from a barbarian assault. It became a *comune* in 1199 but fought frequently with neighbouring Volterra, and the internal battles between the Ardinghelli family (Guelph) and the Salvucci family (Ghibelline) over the next two centuries caused deep divisions. Most towers were built during this period – in the 13th century one *podestà* (town chief) forbade the building of towers higher than his (51m).

In 1348 plague decimated the town's population and weakened the power of its nobles, leading to the town's submission to Florence in 1353. Today, not even the plague would discourage the summer swarms.

Orientation
The manicured gardens of Piazzale dei Martiri di Montemaggio, at the southern end of the town, lie just outside the medieval wall and next to the main gate, the Porta San Giovanni. Via San Giovanni heads northwards to Piazza della Cisterna and the connecting Piazza del Duomo, in the city centre. The other major thoroughfare, Via San Matteo, leaves Piazza del Duomo for the main northern gate, Porta San Matteo.

Information
DISCOUNTS
There are two kinds of combination tickets. The €5.50 allows entry to the Collegiata and Museo d'Arte Sacra, and for €7.50 one gains access to the Museo Civico, Torre Grossa, Museo Archeologico & Speziera di Santa Fina and Collezione Ornitologico.

EMERGENCY
City Police (☎ 0577 94 03 46; Via Santo Stefano)
National Police (☎ 0577 94 03 13; Piazzale dei Martiri di Montemaggio)

INTERNET ACCESS
Tam Tam (☎ 0577 90 71 00; Via XX Settembre 4b; €6.20/hr; 🕑 10am-7pm)

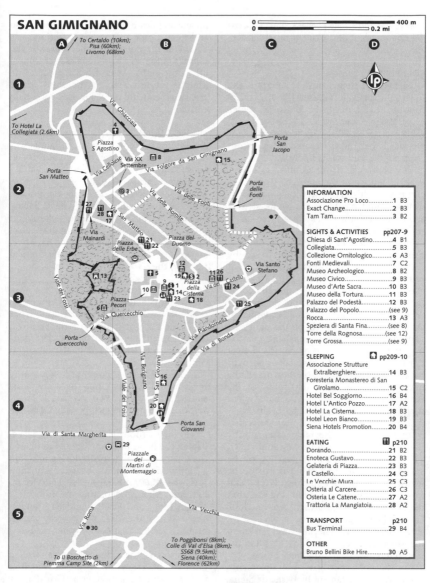

SAN GIMIGNANO

CENTRAL TUSCANY

POST
Post Office (Piazza delle Erbe 8)

TOURIST INFORMATION
Tourist Office (☎ 0577 94 00 08;
www.sangimignano.com; Piazza del Duomo 1;
🕙 9am-1pm & 3-7pm, to 6pm Nov-Mar) Very helpful,
with multilingual staff.

Sights
Start in the triangular Piazza della Cisterna,
named after the central 13th-century cistern.
The square is lined with houses and towers
dating from the 13th and 14th centuries.
In the adjoining Piazza del Duomo, the
Collegiata (cathedral) looks across to the
late-13th-century **Palazzo del Podestà** and its

tower, the **Torre della Rognosa**. The Palazzo del Popolo, right of the cathedral, still operates as the town hall.

COLLEGIATA

Up a flight of steps from the square is the town's Romanesque **cathedral** (☎ 0577 94 22 26; Piazza Luigi Pecozi 4; adult/child €3.50/1.50; ☼ 9.30am-7.30pm Mon-Fri, 9.30am-5pm Sat & 1-5pm Sun Apr-Oct, 9.30am-5pm Mon-Sat & 1-5pm Sun Nov-Mar), its simple facade belying the remarkable frescoes covering the walls of its interior.

Buy your ticket from an office in Piazza Pecori, south of the church. That first glimpse at this feast of (much restored) frescoes amid the black-and-white striped arches and columns separating three naves will take your breath away.

Head to the end of the church and the main entrance (and exit). The fresco by Taddeo di Bartolo covers the upper half of the rear wall and depicts the Last Judgment, while the lower half is dominated by Benozzo Gozzoli's rendering of the martyrdom of St Sebastian. Frescoes extend into the interior of the church, on the right side depicting *Paradiso* (Heaven) and on the left *Inferno* (Hell). Both are by Taddeo di Bartolo, who seems to have taken particular delight in presenting the horrors of the underworld. Remember that many of the faithful in these times would have taken such images pretty much at face value.

Along the left (southern) wall are scenes from Genesis and the Old Testament by Bartolo di Fredi, dating from around 1367. The top row runs from the creation of the world through to the forbidden fruit scene which, in turn, leads to the next level – and fresco – the expulsion of Adam and Eve from the Garden of Eden. Further scenes include Cain killing Abel, the story of Noah's ark and Joseph's coat. The last level picks up this story with the tale of Moses leading the Jews out of Egypt, and the story of Job.

On the right (northern) wall are scenes from the New Testament by Barna da Siena, completed in 1381. Again, the frescoes are spread over three levels, starting in the six lunettes at the top. Commencing with the Annunciation, the panels proceed through episodes such as the Epiphany, the presentation of Christ in the temple and the massacre of the innocents on Herod's orders. The subsequent panels on the lower levels summarise

the life and death of Christ, the Resurrection and so on. Some are in poor condition.

One of the delights of the church is the **Cappella di Santa Fina**, a Renaissance chapel off to the right. Apart from Benedetto da Maiano's tomb-altar to the saint, there are two beautiful frescoes by Domenico Ghirlandaio.

MUSEO D'ARTE SACRA

An interesting collection of religious art, including sculpture, can be seen at this **museum** (☎ 0577 94 03 16; Piazza Pecori 1; adult/child €3/1; ☼ 9.30am-7.30pm Mon-Fri, 9.30am-5pm Sat, 1-5pm Sun Apr-Oct, 9.30am-5pm Mon-Sat, 1-5pm Sun Nov-Jan). More curious than anything else is Sebastiano Mainardi's *Il Volto Santo Adorato* on the ground floor. Two hooded figures, looking suspiciously like KKK members, kneel at the feet of an incredibly well-dressed Jesus on the Cross.

PALAZZO DEL POPOLO

The other principal sight in San Gimignano is this seat of secular power. Dating from 1288, the present building is the result of expansion in the 14th century. The neo-Gothic facade was added in the late 19th century.

From the internal courtyard, containing frescoes and heralds, climb the stairs to the **Museo Civico** (☎ 0577 94 00 08; Piazza del Duomo; adult/child museum & tower €5/4; ☼ 10am-5.30pm Mar-Oct, 10am-5.30pm Nov-Feb).

The main room is known as the **Sala di Dante**. The great poet apparently addressed the town's council here, imploring it to join a Florentine-led Guelph League. You can't miss the *Maestà,* a masterful 1317 fresco by Lippo Memmi depicting the enthroned Virgin Mary and Christ child with angels and saints. Other frescoes portray jousts, hunting scenes, castles and other medieval goings-on.

Upstairs is the small **Pinacoteca**, with a limited collection of medieval religious works, including a *Crocifisso* (Crucifix) by Coppo di Marcovaldo and a pair of remarkable *tondi* (arches) by Filippino Lippi.

Opposite the Pinacoteca is a small frescoed room. Opinion is divided on what these frescoes, showing wedding scenes, are all about. It all looks like great fun, with the newlyweds taking a bath together and then hopping into the sack.

When you've had enough of high art, you can climb the **Torre Grossa** for a spectacular view.

MUSEO ARCHEOLOGICO & SPEZIERA DI SANTA FINA
There are actually two **museums** (☎ 0577 94 03 48; Via Fologore da San Gimignano 11; adult/child €3.50/2.50 for both; ☺ 11am-6pm) and a gallery here. The Speziera section includes ceramic and glass storage vessels from the original pharmacy of the 16th-century Speziera di Santa Fina (Hospital of Santa Fina). Many are beautifully painted and still contain curative concoctions. Follow your nose to the second room, called 'the kitchen', which is filled with herbs and spices used for elixirs.

Beyond here is a small archaeological museum divided into Etruscan/Roman and medieval sections with exhibits that have been found in the area.

The museum also houses a surprisingly good modern art gallery, including the distinctive swirly abstracts of Renato Guttuso and some excellent oils on canvas by Raffaele de Grada.

MUSEO DELLA TORTURA
This gruesome little **Museo della Tortura** (torture museum; ☎ 0577 94 22 43; Via del Castello 1-3; adult/child €8/5; ☺ 10am-6pm Mar-Apr, 10am-7pm rest of year) is (apparently!) a big hit with kids. It's all here, from gibbets to thumbscrews – over 100 ways to inflict unspeakable pain on your neighbour; obviously a popular pastime in the Middle Ages.

OTHER SIGHTS
Just to the west of the Piazza del Duomo, the **Rocca** is the atmospheric crumbling shell of the town's fortress with great views across the valley, a small playground – and not much else.

Due south is the **Collezione Ornitologica** (Via Quercecchio; adult/child €1.50/1; ☺ 11am-6pm Apr-Sep), whose collection of stuffed birds dates right back to 1886.

At the northern end of the town is the **Chiesa di Sant'Agostino** with a fresco cycle by Benozzo Gozzoli depicting the life of St Augustine.

If you head out of the town walls to the east you will be guided by signs to the **Fonti Medievali** – ruined arches around one-time springs.

Tours
If you're enthusiastic about one of Tuscany's best white wines, Vernaccia di San Gimignano, you can join a tour of vineyards in the surrounding area organised by the tourist office. Tours leave at 11am on Tuesday and 5pm on Thursday during summer, and cost €26. Advance reservations are essential.

Sleeping
Inside the walls of San Gimignano there are few hotels, mainly in the mid-range to top end price brackets. The tourist office also has a list of less expensive *affittacamere*.

The **Siena Hotels Promotion** (☎ 0577 94 08 09; www.sangimignano.com; Via San Giovanni 125) can place you in a hotel. It will make arrangements months in advance and charges a €2 fee. The **Associazione Strutture Extralberghiere** (☎ /fax 0577 94 31 90; Piazza della Cisterna 7) has information on alternative-style rural accommodation.

BUDGET
Foresteria Monastero di San Girolamo (☎ 0577 94 05 73; Via Folgore da San Gimignano; €25/person with bath) Accommodation doesn't come much cheaper than this inside the walls of a Tuscan hilltop town. The rooms are basic but spotless, roomy and comfortable. There are larger rooms for up to nine people. If you don't have a reservation, arrive between 9.30am and 12.30pm or between 3.30pm and 5.30pm and ring the Monastery bell (not the Foresteria which is never answered).

MID-RANGE
Hotel Bel Soggiorno (☎ 0577 94 03 76; www.hotel belsoggiorno.it; Via San Giovanni 91; d €90) Every room in this hotel is different, with lots of colour and an upbeat decor; go for one with a countryside view. The restaurant here has rave reviews from readers.

Hotel Leon Bianco (☎ 0577 94 12 94; www.leon bianco.com; Piazza della Cisterna 13; s/d €90/125; ☒) This is a smoothly run, good-looking hotel with an aesthetic use of space and plenty of glass, plants and columns. There is a pretty inner courtyard and some of the rooms have neck-craning tower views.

Hotel La Cisterna (☎ 0577 94 03 28; www .hotelcisterna.it; Piazza della Cisterna 24; s/d €95/103; ☒) Across the square, La Cisterna is in a wonderful 14th-century building with vaulted ceilings and chandeliers. Rooms are quiet, spacious and comfortable; you'll pay marginally more for a view.

Hotel L'Antico Pozzo (☎ 0577 94 20 14; www .anticopozzo.com; Via San Matteo 87; s/d €95/130; 🐾) The name derives from the old well *(pozzo)*, which is softly illuminated just off the lobby. Each room has its own personality, with thick stone walls, frescoes, antique prints and peach-coloured walls. No 20 has a magnificent domed ceiling.

TOP END

Hotel La Collegiata (☎ 0577 94 32 01; www .lacollegiata.it; Località Strada 27; s/d €200/340; P 🐾) This is a serious money-no-object place and you will need a car as it's outside town. A former Franciscan convent, the formal gardens are magnificent and surrounded by parkland, while the rooms are conservative yet elegant. At the time of research, there was a slight smell of drains – check the plumber has been before you hand over your Gold AmEx card.

Eating

Enoteca Gustavo (☎ 0577 94 00 57; Via San Matteo 29; snacks & wine from €2.10; 🕑 Sat-Thu) There's not much elbow space inside; go for one of the outside tables if you can. Snacks include fat focaccias and a plate of cheese with honey to go with your choice of tipple.

Il Castello (☎ 0577 94 08 78; Via del Castello 20; mains €11-15) This wine bar and restaurant has a delightful patio with views – perfect for sipping your glass of Vernaccia di San Gimignano. Dishes are macho-meaty, like *bistecca alla florentina* (grilled T-bone steak) and *cinghiale alla sangimignanese con polenta* (wild boar with polenta and tomato salad).

Osteria Le Catene (☎ 0577 94 19 66; Via Mainardi 18; mains €12-14; 🕑 closed Wed) Here you'll find a softly lit brick-barreled interior. Alongside many Tuscan stalwarts, it also experiments – for instance using saffron, a common spice in medieval times, in *zuppa medievale*. The carrot and leek soufflé is sublime.

Le Vecchie Mura (☎ 0577 94 02 70; Via Piandornella 15; mains €8-14; 🕑 evenings only, closed Tue) This popular restaurant has phenomenal views of the countryside, so book ahead for a terrace table. Choose from a delicious gastronomic choice of *primi piattis* like *gnocchi con tartufo e formaggio* (gnocchi with truffles and cheese).

Osteria al Carcere (☎ 0577 94 19 05; Via del Castello 5; soup €6.20; 🕑 closed Wed) This fine *osteria* offers great food at moderate prices. The reassuringly brief menu includes a half-dozen soups, including *zuppa di farro e fagioli* (pasta and white bean soup) which is a meal in itself.

Dorando (☎ 0577 94 18 62; Vicolo del Oro 2; mains €15-20) Recognised by the Slow Food movement, the classic menu has five courses with dishes based on authentic Etruscan recipes like carrot dumplings with zucchini, and *pecorino* blue cheese with puree of shallots. Atmosphere is swanky yet cool, with intimate corners and art work.

Gelateria di Piazza (☎ 0577 94 22 44; Piazza della Cisterna 4; gelato from €1.50) has heaven-sent ice cream lovingly made by master Sergio with only the choicest ingredients: pistachios from Sicily and cocoa from Venezuela. Try the saffron cream.

Also recommended is **Trattoria La Mangiatoia** (☎ 0577 94 15 28; Via Mainardi 5; mains €13; 🕑 closed Tue) for its succulent regional cuisine.

For your self-catering needs, a **produce market** is held on Thursday mornings in Piazza della Cisterna and Piazza del Duomo. The **alimentari** on Via Cellolese makes delicious *panini* (€1.50).

Getting There & Around
BUS

San Gimignano is accessible from Florence and Siena by bus – change at Poggibonsi. For Volterra, you need to change in Colle di Val d'Elsa, but there's a direct bus to Certaldo. Buses arrive in Piazzale dei Martiri di Montemaggio at Porta San Giovanni. Remember that connections are reduced on Sunday.

The closest train station is in Poggibonsi.

CAR & MOTORCYCLE

From Florence, it's easiest to take the SS2 to Poggibonsi and follow signs. Alternatively, take the SS68 from Colle di Val d'Elsa. From Volterra, take the SS68 east and follow the turn-off signs north to San Gimignano.

On arrival, there are various public carparks (€2 per hour) that you can go to. There is free parking in the new parts of town, just northwest of the old centre. You can hire scooters or motorbikes at **Bruno Bellini** (☎ 0577 94 02 01; www.bellinibruno.com; Via Roma 41; scooters/motorbikes per day from €51/62) It also rents out mountain bikes for €2 per hour.

VOLTERRA
pop 13,400

Straggling high on a rocky plateau, Volterra's well-preserved medieval ramparts give the windswept ridge town a proud, forbidding air.

The Etruscan settlement of Velathri was an important trading centre and senior partner of the Dodecapolis. It is believed that as many as 25,000 people lived here in its Etruscan heyday. Partly because of the surrounding inhospitable terrain, the city was among the last to succumb to Rome – it was absorbed into the Roman confederation in around 260 BC and it was renamed Volaterrae.

The bulk of the old city was raised in the 12th and 13th centuries under a fiercely independent free *comune*. The city first entered into Florence's orbit in 1361, but it was some time before it took full control. When this was first threatened in 1472, Lorenzo the Magnificent made one of his few big mistakes as well as lasting enemies of the people of Volterra when he marched in and ruthlessly snuffed out every vestige of potential opposition to direct Florentine rule.

Since Etruscan times, Volterra has been a centre of alabaster extraction and workmanship. The quarries lay fallow for several centuries until the Renaissance sculpture era. To this day, the traditions have been maintained and passed from generation to generation.

Orientation

Driving and parking inside the walled town are prohibited. Park in one of the designated parking areas (including a large multistorey) and enter the nearest city gate. All the main streets lead to the central Piazza dei Priori.

Information

DISCOUNTS

A €7 ticket, valid for a year, covers visits to the Museo Etrusco Guarnacci, the Pinacoteca Comunale and Museo Diocesano di Arte Sacra. Access to the Roman theatre and Parco Archeologico is free.

INTERNET ACCESS

Web & Wine (☎ 0588 8 15 31; Via Porta all'Arco; €3/30 mins) Surf your way through a creamy cappuccino while checking your inbox.

DETOUR:
SAN GIMIGNANO TO VOLTERRA

Instead of taking the normal road south of San Gimignano to Volterra, take the back road passing through some stunning countryside and potential picnic areas. Turn left out of the main San Gimignano car park (outside the main gate). At 2.3km, just past the Hotel San Michele, turn left again at the signpost to Páncole and Castelfalfe. Carry on along this road, passing Hotel La Collegiata, through green rolling valleys, wooded areas and vineyards. At 7.2km turn left to Volterra (15km). After around 10km turn right for the final 5km stretch into town.

MONEY

You can exchange money at several banks, including the Bancomat near the tourist office.

POST

Post Office (Piazza dei Priori)

TOURIST INFORMATION

Tourist Office (☎ 0588 8 72 57; www.volterratur.it; Piazza dei Priori 20; ⏰ 9am-1pm & 2-7pm Apr-Oct, 10am-1pm & 2-6pm Nov-Mar, closed last 3 weeks Nov) You can hire an audio guide for €5, which provides detailed information of the town and its history.
Viaggi Atuv Volterra (☎ 0588 8 63 33; fax 0588 8 63 03; Piazza Martiri della Libertà 4-6; ⏰ 10am-1pm & 3-6pm) Can help book accommodation.

Sights

PIAZZA DEI PRIORI & AROUND

Piazza dei Priori is surrounded by austere medieval mansions. The 13th-century **Palazzo dei Priori** (⏰ 10am-1pm & 2-6pm Sat & Sun; admission €1) is the oldest seat of local government in Tuscany and believed to have been a model for Florence's Palazzo Vecchio. The 13th-century **Palazzo Pretorio** is dominated by the Piglet's Tower, so named because of the wild boar sculpted on its upper section.

Behind the Palazzo dei Priori is the **cathedral** (☎ 0588 8 76 54; Via Turazza; ⏰ 8am-12.30pm & 3-6pm), built in the 12th and 13th centuries. Inside, highlights include a small fresco by Benozzo Gozzoli, the *Adorazione dei Magi* (Adoration of the Magi) in the oratory. The 15th-century tabernacle on the high altar is by Mino da Fiesole. The black-and-white

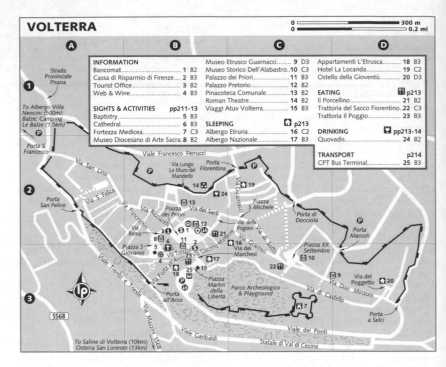

marble banding and Renaissance coffered ceiling add impact.

Facing the cathedral is the 13th-century **baptistry** with a font by Andrea Sansovino. On the western side of Piazza San Giovanni the porticoed **Ospedale di Santa Maria Maddalena** was once a foundlings hospital. Next to the cathedral is the **Museo Diocesano di Arte Sacra** (☎ 0588 8 62 90; Via Roma 13; combined ticket €7; ☼ 9am-1pm & 3-6pm mid-Mar–Oct, 9am-1pm Nov–mid-Mar), with its religious art and sculpture.

The **Pinacoteca Comunale** (☎ 0588 8 75 80; Via dei Sarti 1; €7 combined ticket; ☼ 9am-7pm mid-Mar–Oct, 9am-2pm Nov–mid-Mar) in the Palazzo Minucci Solaini, houses a modest collection of local, Sienese and Florentine art.

MUSEO ETRUSCO GUARNACCI
All the exhibits in this fascinating **Etruscan museum** (☎ 0588 8 63 47; Via Don Minzoni 15; combined ticket €7; ☼ 9am-7pm mid-Mar–Oct, 9am-2pm Nov–mid-Mar) were unearthed locally, including a vast collection of some 600 funerary urns.

The urns are displayed according to the subject and period. Be selective, as they all start to look the same after a while. The best

examples, from the later periods, are on the 2nd and 3rd floors.

Most significant are the *Ombra della Sera* sculpture, a strange, elongated nude figure that would fit in well in any museum of modern art, and the urn of the *Sposi*, featuring an elderly couple, their faces depicted in portrait fashion rather than the usual stylised method.

FORTEZZA MEDICEA & PARCO ARCHEOLOGICO
Further along, on the parallel Via di Castello, is the 14th-century **Fortezza Medicea**, later altered by Lorenzo the Magnificent and now used as a prison (you cannot enter unless you plan to stay for a while).

Near the fort is the pleasant **Parco Archeologico** (free; ☼ 8.30am-8pm May-Sep, 8.30am-5pm Oct-Apr), the archaeological remains of which have clearly suffered with the passage of time. This is where the heart of the ancient city, the Acropolis, was located. Little has survived, but the park has swings and things for kids and it's a good place for a picnic.

CENTRAL TUSCANY

MUSEO STORICO DELL'ALABASTRO

Set in a 12th-century convent, this museum (☎ 0588 8 68 68; www.museodellalabastro.it; Piazza XX Settembre 5; adult/child €2.50/1.50; ☺ 9.30am-12.30pm & 2.30-6.30pm) covers 12 richly decorated rooms as an appropriate backdrop for the permanent exhibition of alabaster. There are several exquisite sculptures of animals by 18th-century artist Raffaello, as well as plenty of Lladro-like sentimental pieces and some stunning furniture, like a mosaic table from the Palazzo Cenci in Rome. The Victorian dolls will appeal to some.

OTHER SIGHTS

On the city's northern edge is a **Roman theatre** (free; ☺ 11am-5pm), a well-preserved complex with a Roman bath.

Le Balze, a deep ravine created by erosion, a 3.5km drive northwest of the city centre, has claimed several churches since the Middle Ages, the buildings having fallen into its deep gullies. A 14th-century monastery is perched close to the precipice and is in danger of toppling into the ravine. To get there, head out of the northwestern end of the city along Via San Lino and follow its continuation, Borgo Santo Stefano and then Borgo San Giusto.

Sleeping
BUDGET

Ostello della Gioventú (☎ /fax 0588 8 55 77; Via del Poggetto 3; dm from €11, full board €32) This non-Hostelling International hostel looks more like a hospital, with clinically blue corridors and a real antiseptic feel. On a more positive note, the rooms are clean!

Albergo Etruria (☎ /fax 0588 8 73 77; Via Giacomo Matteotti 32; s/d €52/68) This is the cheapest hotel within the town walls. The rooms are a little dark, with ordinary furniture, but well dusted and quiet.

MID-RANGE

Albergo Nazionale (☎ 0588 8 62 84; www.albergona zionalevolterra.it; Via dei Marchesi 11; s/d €60/70) This late 19th-century hotel has benefited from a recent lick of paint. The rooms vary in size and style but most have terraces; No 403 is a real winner. The restaurant serves solid uncomplicated meals.

Albergo Villa Nencini (☎ 0588 8 63 86; www.villanencini.it; Borgo Santo Stefano 55; s/d €68/90; ⚙) This is a family-run hotel in a 16th-century villa. The new wing overlooks the Etruscan walls. There are shady grounds, a pool and valley views from the rooms and – what luxury – a choice of bath or shower.

Appartamenti L'Etrusca (☎ /fax 0588 8 40 73; letrusca@libero.it; Via Porta all'Arco 37-41; s/d €39/65) If you'd prefer an apartment, this is a good option – this place offers self-contained apartments suitable for up to three people for €77 per night. They are small but comfortable (with kitchenettes) and the rates come down marginally if you rent for a week or more.

TOP END

Hotel La Locanda (☎ 0588 8 15 47; www.hotel-lalocanda.com; Via Guarnacci 24-28; s/d €95/150; ⚙) This is the only four-star hotel in town and worth flexing your credit card for. A former nunnery, there is nothing austere about the classy rooms with a choice of massage shower or whirlpool. A room with sauna will cost you a cool €250.

Eating

Trattoria del Sacco Fiorentino (☎ 0588 8 85 37; Piazza XX Settembre 18; mains €10-12; ☺ closed Tue) This is a great place serving up imaginative dishes with a happy selection of local wines. Try the *coniglio in salsa di aglio e vin santo* (rabbit cooked in a garlic dessert-wine sauce) or the mouth-watering gnocchi with baby veg.

Trattoria Il Poggio (☎ 0588 8 52 57; Via Porta all'Arco 7; mains €12; ☺ closed Tue) is a low-key popular restaurant with a good set menu, outdoor terrace and dishes like risotto with clams, scampi and rocket, plus at least three different lasagnes.

Osteria San Lorenzo (☎ 0588 4 41 60; Via Massetana; mains €8-12; ☺ closed Tue) If you have wheels and would like to venture out of town a little, drive down to Saline di Volterra and then take the SS439 road south heading to Pomarance. About 3km out of Saline di Volterra you enter the tiny village of San Lorenzo, home to this place where you can get superb, home-style cooking.

Il Porcellino (☎ 0588 8 63 92; Vicollo delle Prigioni; mains €8-10; ☺ closed Tue) This is a local favourite with old-fashioned attentive, if gruff, service. The menu includes game dishes, seafood and some surprises – like roast pigeon and boar with olives.

Drinking

Quovadis (☎ 0588 8 00 33; Via Lungo Le Muro del Mandorlo 18) If you can't survive without your

CENTRAL TUSCANY

Guinness on draught, hightail it over here: it's the only place for miles around and, rumour is, there's even an Irish owner somewhere in the background.

Getting There & Away

BUS

Arriving from Florence (€6.50, two hours), Siena (€4.75, 1½ hours) or San Gimignano (€4.75, 1½ hours), change at Colle di Val d'Elsa. CPT has has four connections (€2.75, 50 minutes), Monday to Saturday.

Up to nine buses a day run to Pisa (€5, two hours) via Pontedera. Other buses head south in the direction of Massa Marittima but only go as far as Pomarance and Castelnuovo di Valle di Cecina.

CAR & MOTORCYCLE

By car, take the SS68, which runs between Cecina and Colle di Val d'Elsa. A couple of back routes to San Gimignano are signposted north off the SS68.

TRAIN

From the small train station in Saline di Volterra, 10km to the southwest of Volterra, you can catch a train to Cecina on the coast and change to the Rome–Pisa line. Up to five CPT buses a day run between Volterra and the train station.

SOUTH OF VOLTERRA

If you have a car and want to head for Massa Marittima (a worthwhile objective – see p229), the ride south from Volterra is very scenic.

The SS68 drops away to the southwest from Volterra towards Cecina. At Saline di Volterra (where you'll find the nearest train station for Volterra), the SS439 intersects the SS68 on its way from Lucca, south towards Massa Marittima. **Saline di Volterra** takes its name from the nearby salt mines; a source of wealth in the 19th century.

The lunar-landscape ride south passes through **Pomarance**, an industrial town. To the south, take the hilly road for **Larderello**, which is Italy's most important boric acid producer. The road out of here winds its way south to Massa.

SOUTH OF SIENA

You may already have had a taste of the strange undulating countryside of Le Crete

(see p202). For a while, similar countryside persists as you roam south and it's here you'll find the classic Tuscany of rolling hills of hay topped with a huddle of cypress trees. Gradually the landscape gives away to more unruly territory. This part of the province offers everything: the haughty hilltop medieval wine centres of Montalcino and Montepulciano; hot sulphurous baths in spots such as Bagno Vignoni; Romanesque splendours of the Abbazia di Sant'Antimo; and the Renaissance grace of Pienza – an early example of idealised town planning.

Montalcino

pop 5100

A pretty town perched high above the Orcia valley, Montalcino is best known for its wine, the Brunello. Produced only in the surrounding vineyards, it is famed as being one of Italy's best reds.

Plenty of *enoteche* (wine bars) around town allow you to taste and buy Brunello (minimum €20 a bottle). Top names in excellent years come with price tags up to the €105 mark, or break the bank with a bottle from the 1940s – a mere €5000. Price alone is not necessarily an indication of the wine's quality as all Brunello is made to strict regulations.

INFORMATION

Essepi Informatica (☎ 0577 84 61 05; Via Mazzini 30; Internet access €6/hr)

Pro Loco (☎ 0577 83 90 32; www.prolocomontalcino.it - Italian only; Costa Municipio 8) A better bet for booking accommodation.

Tourist Office (☎ 0577 84 93 31; www.prolocomontal cino.it - Italian only; Costa del Municipio 1; ☯ 10am-1pm & 2-5.40pm Apr-Oct & Tue-Sun Nov-Mar) Has plenty of information on the area. Confusingly, it shares the website with the Pro Loco tourist office.

SIGHTS & ACTIVITIES

The **Fortezza** (☎ 0577 84 92 11; Piazzale Fortezza; courtyard free, ramparts adult/child €3/1.50, combined ticket includes Museo Civico e Diocesano d'Arte Sacra €6; ☯ 9am-8pm Apr-Oct, 9am-6pm Tue-Sun Nov-Mar), an imposing 14th-century fortress that was later expanded under the Medici dukes, dominates the town from a high point at its southern end. You can sample and buy local wines in the *enoteca* inside, and also climb up to the fort's ramparts.

The **Museo Civico e Diocesano d'Arte Sacra** (☎ 0577 84 60 14; Via Ricasoli 31; adult/child €4.50/3, combined ticket including Fortezza €6; 10am-6pm Tue-Sun Apr-Oct, 10am-1pm & 2-6pm Nov-Dec, 10am-1pm & 2-5pm Jan-Mar), housed in the former convent of the neighbouring **Chiesa di Sant'Agostino**, contains an important collection of religious art from the town and surrounding region. Among the items on show are a triptych by Duccio di Buoninsegna and a *Madonna con Bambino* (Madonna with Child) by Simone Martini. Other artists represented include the Lorenzetti brothers, Giovanni di Paolo and Sano di Pietro.

None of the several churches in town is of especial interest. The **cathedral,** in particular, is an ugly 19th-century neoclassical travesty of what was once a fine Romanesque church.

If you want to visit **vineyards** in the Montalcino area, the tourist office can provide you with a list of some 141 producers (many smaller ones have little more than a hectare or two of land) and information on good and mediocre years. It can also advise on which vineyards are open to the public.

Montalcino hosts a week of **'Jazz and Wine'** in mid-July, which attracts both national and international acts. Ask at the tourist office for more details. There's a **Friday market** on Via della Libertà.

SLEEPING

Hotels are limited. If they are full, the tourist office can provide a list of *affittacamere* (around 10 in town) or *agriturismo* dotted around the countryside, and make a booking.

Il Giardino (/fax 0577 84 90 76; Piazza Cavour 4; s/d €42/53) This is your cheapest option – and it's spartan – to put it kindly. It is right next door to an excellent classy restaurant (see Osteria Il Giardino under Eating).

Hotel Il Giglio (/fax 0577 84 81 67; www .gigliohotel.com; Via Soccorso Saloni 5; s/d €53/80) This 16th-century building has been revamped artistically, with paintings and hand-painted frescoes in the rooms. Ask for room No 1 which has an enormous terrace at no extra cost.

Hotel dei Capitani (0577 84 72 27; deicapitani@tin.it; Via Lapini 6; s/d €83/103;) An option in town, this 15th-century hotel has rooms that vary greatly, ranging from super spacious to small with a view, so take a look first. There's a pretty terrace with a pool to splash around in.

Hotel Vecchia Oliviera (0577 84 60 28; www.vecchiaoliviera.com; Porta Cerbaia, Via Landi 1; s/d €83/150;) This former olive mill has been aesthetically restored with earthy colours and terracotta tiles, coupled with the modern efficiency of exec-style rooms with all mod cons. The back patio has stunning views.

EATING

There are several good options in town.

Osteria Il Giardino (0577 84 90 76; Piazza Cavour 1; mains €7-10; closed Wed) This restaurant is all light wood and arches and has a good selection of traditional dishes, including *risotto al radicchio rosso e pecorino* (risotto with red chicory and pecorino cheese) and wild boar.

Bar Mariuccia (0577 84 82 48; Via Matteotti 31; mains €6-8) The bread is made in-house and makes all the difference to the otherwise fairly basic menu of sandwiches and *bruschette*, salads and pizza. Get here early for a prime dining view from back terrace.

Osteria Porta al Cassero (0577 84 71 96; Via Ricasoli 32; mains €7; closed Wed) This is a simple place selling hearty peasant-style fare like bean and vegetable soup, and Tuscan pork sausage with white beans.

Les Barriques (0577 84 84 11; Piazza del Popolo 20-22; mains €5-12) This atmospheric place is lined with bottles where you can enjoy a nice wine accompanied by something light and tasty. Limited menu includes *bruschette*, *crostini* and at least five different salads.

DRINKING

Enoteca (0577 84 92 11; Piazza Fortezza; wine by the glass €4-6) This place, in the Fortezza, is perfect for trying out one of countless varieties of Brunello, buying a bottle and/or climbing up onto the ramparts. It also organises tasting evenings for €8 to €20 per person, accompanied by delectable nibbles.

Bar Circolo Arci (Via Ricasoli 2) This bar is worth seeking out for its fabulous interior, cobbled courtyard and atmosphere.

Fiaschetteria (0577 84 90 43; Piazza del Popolo 6; closed Thu) A fine tiled old café full of crusty locals, this is the perfect place for putting the world to rights over a bottle of wine.

GETTING THERE & AWAY

Montalcino is accessible from Siena by up to six buses (€3, 1¼ hours) a day. Buses leave from Piazza Cavour for the return journey. By car, follow the SS2 south from Siena and

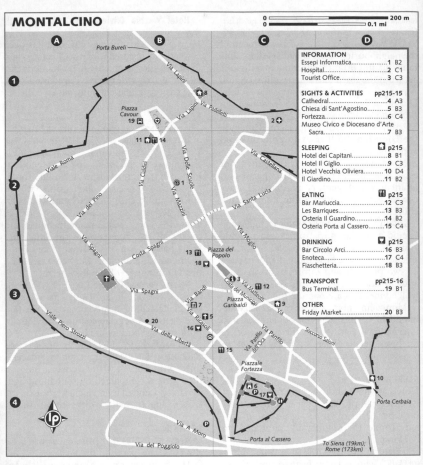

MONTALCINO

0   200 m
0   0.1 mi

INFORMATION
Essepi Informatica...................1 B2
Hospital................................2 C1
Tourist Office......................3 C3

SIGHTS & ACTIVITIES   pp215-15
Cathedral.............................4 A3
Chiesa di Sant'Agostino............5 B3
Fortezza...............................6 C4
Museo Civico e Diocesano d'Arte
  Sacra.................................7 B3

SLEEPING   p215
Hotel dei Capitani..................8 B1
Hotel Il Giglio......................9 C3
Hotel Vecchia Oliviera...........10 D4
Il Giardino..........................11 B2

EATING   p215
Bar Mariuccia.......................12 C3
Les Barriques.......................13 B3
Osteria Il Guardino...............14 B2
Osteria Porta al Cassero........15 C4

DRINKING   p215
Bar Circolo Arci...................16 B3
Enoteca..............................17 C4
Fiaschetteria......................18 B3

TRANSPORT   pp215-16
Bus Terminal.......................19 B1

OTHER
Friday Market.......................20 B3

Porta Bureli
Via Lapini
Piazza Cavour
Via Lapini Via Padelletti
Viale Roma
Via Caldini
Via Delle Scuole
Via Mazzini
Via Castellana
Via Santa Lucia
Via Moglio
Via del Pino
Via Spagni
Costa Spagni
Piazza del Popolo
Via Spagni
Via Bandi
Costa del Municipio
Via Matteotti
Viale Pietro Strozzi
Via Ricasoli
Piazza Garibaldi
Via della Libertà
Via Panfilo dell'Oca
Via Panfilo
Soccorso Saloni
Piazzale Fortezza
Via A. Moro
Porta al Cassero
Via del Poggiolo
To Siena (19km); Rome (173km)
Porta Cerbaia

take the turnoff for Montalcino, about 8km
after Buonconvento.

Abbazia di Sant'Antimo

Try and visit this superb and unusually
grand Romanesque church (☎ 0577 83 56
59; Castelnuovo dell'Abate; ⏰ 10.30am-12.30pm & 3-
6.30pm Mon-Sat, 9am-10.30pm & 3-6pm Sun & hols) in
the morning, when the sun shines through
the east windows to create an almost surreal
atmosphere. Even at night, it's impressive,
lit up like a beacon in the darkness. Set in
a broad valley, just below the village of
Castelnuovo dell'Abate, the architecture is
clearly influenced by northern European
versions of Romanesque, especially that of
the Cistercians.

It's thought Charlemagne founded the
original monastery here in 781. In subsequent centuries, the Benedictine monks
became among the most powerful feudal
landlords in southern Tuscany, until they
came into conflict with Siena in the 13th
century. Until the mid-1990s, the church
and abbey lay pretty much abandoned. Then
several monks moved in and supervised restoration work. There are daily prayers (7pm)
and Masses in the church open to the public.
This is a worthwhile exercise as the monks
sing Gregorian chants. If you can't make it,
they can sell you the CD.

Among the decorative features, note the
stone carvings of the bell tower and apse
windows, which include a *Madonna con*

Bambino and the various fantastic animals typical of the Romanesque style. Inside, take the time to study the capitals of the columns lining the nave, including one to the right representing Daniel in the lions' den.

If you're lucky, the attendant may let you into the **sacristy** where there are monochrome frescoes depicting the life of St Benedict. They probably date to the 15th century. The 11th-century crypt beneath the chapel is closed to the public but you can get a murky glimpse of it through the small round window at the base of the exterior of the chapel's apse.

Concerts are sometimes held here as part of Siena's Estate Musicale Chigiana (see p200).

Locanda Sant'Antimo (☎ 0577 83 55 46; Via Bassomondo 8; mains €6-9) If you're planning a visit to Sant'Antimo, stop for lunch at this restaurant which serves solid traditional cooking and is less than 1km away at Castelnuovo dell'Abate.

Agriturismo Aiole (☎ 0577 88 74 54; www .agriturismo-aiole.com; Strada Provinciale 22 della Grossola; d €65) This is a fabulous place in a 150-year-old farmhouse with knockout views. The rooms are large and there's a kitchen available for groups.

Three buses a day run from Montalcino (€1) to Castelnuovo dell'Abate, from where you can walk to the church.

If you have your own transport, you may want to consider an alternative lunch or dinner excursion west along a dirt road to **Sant'Angelo in Colle**. The views from the village are wonderful. Those without a car can get here by bus (three or four times a day Monday to Saturday; nothing on Sunday) from Montalcino.

You can eat excellent home-cooked food at **Trattoria Il Pozzo** (☎ 0577 84 40 15; full meals from €17; closed Tue), in the middle of Sant'Angelo, just off the square.

San Quirico d'Orcia

This fortified medieval town on the Via Cassia (SS2) is well worth a stopover. Its Romanesque **Collegiata**, dating from the 12th century, is notable for its unusual three doorways, decorated with extraordinary stone carvings. Inside is a triptych by Sano di Pietro. Wander around the **Horti Leononi**, a lovely Italian Renaissance garden at the other end of town. This is a gem of a place and

makes a good base for exploring the area, sitting just off the highway and at a crossroads between Montalcino and Pienza.

SLEEPING & EATING
There are several possibilities here. If you get stuck, contact **Consorzio Terra di Val d'Orcia** (☎ 0577 89 90 05; www.terradivaldorcia.it; Via Dante 33), which should be able to help you out.

Affittacamere L'Orcia (☎ 0577 89 76 77; Via Dante Alighieri 49; s/d €30/50) Right in the centre of town, this is another timeless classic with religious pictures and a no-frills old-fashioned feel.

Trattoria Al Vecchio Forno (☎ 0577 89 73 80; Via Piazzola 8; €9-13; closed Wed) You will eat well at this place, a few steps away from Via Dante Alighieri, with a lovely garden. Local dishes such as *Il pollo al Brunello* (chicken cooked in Brunello wine) are particularly good.

Café Central (Piazza della Libertà 6) Legendary kind of café where you can sit all day absorbing the atmosphere of the local menfolk playing cards and drinking grappa, while the outside terrace is more popular with the younger ice-cream-and-cola set.

GETTING THERE & AWAY
San Quirico is fairly easily accessible by bus from Siena (€3), Buonconvento, Pienza and Montepulciano.

Bagno Vignoni
About 5km from San Quirico along the SS2 towards Rome, this tiny spa town dates back to Roman times. The hot sulphurous water bubbles up into a picturesque pool, built by the Medici in the village's main square. Some 36 springs cook at up to 51°C and collect in the pool, although in winter the water is considerably cooler.

Unfortunately, you are not allowed to bathe in the pool but it is such a picturesque sight that it merits a quick stop regardless. If you do wish to take the waters you can go to the open-air Piscina del Sole at the **Hotel Posta Marcucci** (☎ 0577 88 71 12; www.hotelpostama rcucci.it; Via Ara Urcea 43a; day ticket adult/child €10/7, half day €7/5; closed Thu evening).

Alternatively, you can dangle your feet in the hot water streams in Il Parco dei Mulini di Bagno Vignoni just above the entrance to the hotel.

Albergo Le Terme (☎ 0577 88 71 50; www .albergoleterme.it; s/d €45/90) This 15th-century building was built by Rossellino for Pope Pius II who used it as a summerhouse. These days it's sumptuous, with lots of shiny wood and plush fabrics. Ask for rooms at the front, with views of the pool.

Osteria del Leone (☎ 0577 88 73 00; Piazza del Moretto 28; mains €10-15) Back a block from the pool, this is a fine choice for a lunch or dinner, whether you choose to stay or not. In a pleasantly lit rustic building with a heavy-beamed ceiling, you can eat solid Tuscan country fare, such as *faraona al vinsanto* (pheasant cooked in sweet white wine).

Buses serving the Siena–Grosseto route call in here.

Bagni San Filippo

Those who prefer free hot-water frolics could press on about 15km south along the SS2 to Bagni San Filippo. Most Siena–Grosseto buses call in here too. A park is signposted off the village's only road, uphill from the hotel. A short stroll down the lane brings you to a set of hot little tumbling cascades where you can plant yourself for a relaxing soak. It's best in winter, which is off-season for the hotel and when the water pressure is greatest.

Pienza

pop 2400

It was in this town that Renaissance town-planning concepts were first put into practice after Pope Pius II decided, in 1459, to transform the look of his birthplace (which he named after himself). He chose the architect Bernardo Rossellino, who applied the principles of his mentor, Leon Battista Alberti. This new vision of urban space was realised in the superb Piazza Pio II and the surrounding buildings. The only thing question today is: where do the locals go to buy a loaf of bread? Shops here are geared towards the gourmet tourist – cheese and preserves.

INFORMATION

Internet Point (☎ 0578 74 87 47; Via della Rosa 5; €4/30 mins)

Tourist Office (☎ /fax 0578 74 90 71; www.infinito.it/ utenti/ufficio.turistico; Piazza Pio II; 🕙 9.30am-1pm & 3-6.30pm) You can pick up an audio guide of the town here for €6, which lasts one hour.

SIGHTS

The most important buildings are grouped around the central Piazza Pio II. The square was designed by Rossellino, who left nothing to chance. The space available to him was limited so, to increase the sense of perspective and dignity of the great edifices that would grace the square, Rossellino set the Palazzo Borgia and Palazzo Piccolomini off at angles to the cathedral.

The **cathedral** (Piazza Pio II; 🕙 7am-1pm & 3-7pm) was built on the site of the Romanesque Chiesa di Santa Maria, of which little remains. The Renaissance facade, in travertine stone, is of clear Albertian inspiration.

The interior of the building is a strange mix of Gothic and Renaissance, and contains a collection of five altarpieces painted by Sienese artists of the period, as well as a superb marble tabernacle by Rossellino.

Perhaps the most bizarre aspect of the building is the state of collapse of the transept and apse. Built on dodgy ground, the top end of the church seems to be breaking off. The huge cracks in the wall and floor are matched by the crazy downwards slant of this part of the church floor. Various attempts to prop it all up have failed to solve the problem, as is quite clear from the major cracking in the walls and floor.

The **Palazzo Piccolomini** (☎ 0578 74 85 03; Piazza Pio II; adult/child 30-minute guided tour €3/2; 🕙 10am-12.30pm & 3-6pm Tue-Sun), to your right as you face the cathedral, was the Pope's residence and is considered Rossellino's masterpiece. Built on the site of former Piccolomini family houses, the building demonstrates some indebtedness on Rossellino's part to Alberti, whose Palazzo Rucellai in Florence it appears in part to emulate.

Inside is a fine courtyard, from where stairs lead you up into the papal apartments, now filled with an assortment of period furnishings, minor art and the like. To the rear, a three-level loggia faces out over the countryside.

To the left of the cathedral is the **Palazzo Borgia** (also known as Palazzo Vescovile), built by Cardinal Borgia, later Pope Alexander VI, and containing the **Museo Diocesano** (☎ 0578 74 99 05; Corso il Rossellino 30; adult/child €4.10/2.60; 🕙 10am-1pm & 3-6.30pm Wed-Mon mid-Mar–Oct, Sat & Sun only Nov–mid-Mar) which contains an intriguing miscellany of artworks, illuminated manuscripts, tapestries and miniatures.

Make time to visit the Romanesque **Pieve di Corsignano**, half a kilometre out of town along Via Fonti from Piazza Dante

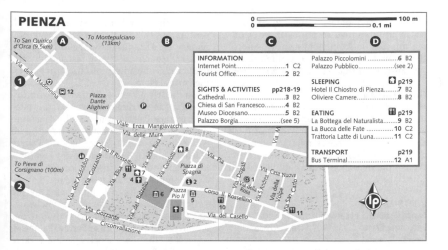

Alighieri. This church dates from the 10th century and boasts a strange circular bell tower. There are no fixed visiting times but it is usually open.

SLEEPING & EATING

There are a few good places to stay and to sample something delicious.

Oliviere Camere (☎ 0578 74 82 74; www.nautilus-mp.com/oliviera; Via Condotti 4; s/d/st €30/48/60) This former olive oil mill is squeezed into a side street. The rooms are modern and attractive, if a tad small.

Hotel Il Chiostro di Pienza (☎ 0578 74 84 00; fax 0578 74 84 40; Corso il Rossellino 26; s/d €120/180;) You can wallow in luxury – and history – at this hotel, in the former convent and cloister of the adjacent Chiesa di San Francesco. The decor is refreshingly unfussy and the manicured gardens have views and definite romantic appeal.

La Buca delle Fate (☎ 0578 74 84 48; Corso il Rossellino 38; mains €6.50-8; closed Mon) Despite its dress-for-dinner appearance, this restaurant is definitely for euro-economisers. There are no surprises on the menu but the standard is high. Save room for the dessert trolley.

Trattoria Latte di Luna (☎ 0578 74 86 06; Via San Carlo 6; mains €7-10; closed Tue) Popular with tourists, this restaurant, on a kind of squarette where the street splits off from Corso il Rossellino, has a lovely terrace with plenty of shady umbrellas. Try the *anatra arrosto alle olive* (roast duck with olives) topped off with home-made hazelnut ice cream.

La Bottega del Naturalista (☎ 0578 74 80 81; Corso il Rossellino 16) Pienza is renowned as a centre for that ever-so-Tuscan cheese, *pecorino*. If you want to get an idea of all the varieties available (from fresh to well-aged and smelly, from the classic *pecorino* to ones lightly infused with peppers or truffles), pop into this shop.

GETTING THERE & AWAY

Up to six buses run on weekdays from Siena to Pienza (€3.40, 1¼ hours). You can also make connections to San Quirico d'Orcia and Montepulciano. The buses stop just a short way off Piazza Dante Alighieri.

Montepulciano
pop 14,000

Set atop a narrow ridge of volcanic rock, Montepulciano combines Tuscany's superb countryside with some of the region's finest wines. This medieval town is the perfect place to spend a few quiet days and sample the local wines.

A late Etruscan *castrum* was the first in a series of settlements here. During the Middle Ages, it was a constant bone of contention between Florence and Siena, until in 1404, the city finally passed under the permanent jurisdiction of the former. And so the Marzocco, or lion of Florence, came to replace the she-wolf of Siena as the city's symbol on a column just off Piazza Savonarola. The new administration brought a new wind of construction taste as Michelozzo, Sangallo

CENTRAL TUSCANY

il Vecchio and others were invited in to do some innovative spring cleaning, lending this Gothic stronghold a fresh wind of Renaissance vigour. That mix alone makes this town an intriguing place for a stopover.

ORIENTATION

However you arrive, you will probably end up at the Porta al Prato (also known as the Porta al Bacco) on the town's northern edge. From here, buses take you through the town to Piazza Grande. Alternatively, the 15-minute walk is mostly uphill but well worth the effort.

INFORMATION

Banca Nazionale di Lavoro (Piazza Savonarola 14)
Fotociurnelli (☎ 0578 7 57 27; Via di Gracciano nel Corso 8; 🖳 €5/hr)
Police Station (☎ 0578 75 74 52; Palazzo Comunale)
Post Office (Via dell'Erbe)
Strada del Vino Nobile di Montepulciano Information Office (☎ 0578 71 74 84; Piazza Grande 7) Everything you need to know about the local tipple. It organises wine tours per €23 per person.
Tourist Office (☎ 0578 75 73 41; www.prolocomontepulciano.it; Via di Gracciano nel Corso 59a; 🕑 9am-12.30pm & 3-8pm Mon-Sat, to 6pm Oct-Mar, mornings only Sun & holidays; 🖳 €1/15 mins) Next door to the Chiesa di Sant'Agostino at the lower end of town.

SIGHTS & ACTIVITIES

Most of the main sights are clustered around Piazza Grande. If you arrive via Porta al Prato, you'll see the beelike banding of the facade of the **Chiesa di Sant'Agnese**. The

---

CENTRAL TUSCANY

DETOUR: MONTICHIELLO

From Pienza main junction (northern gate) take the minor road south out of town signposted to San Lorenzo Nuovo and Montichiello. Follow this road as it wiggles through green valleys and farmland. At 6.2km, just after you cross a small bridge, take the left turn signposted to Montichiello. At the 11km junction, turn right and continue for 500m until you reach the car park. Take an hour or so to wander around this pretty medieval village, stopping for an ice cream at Bar La Guardiola's outdoor terrace. When you leave, turn left and follow the signs to Montepulciano, passing a natural park with picnic tables on your left.

---

original church was built in the early 14th century but this version was the result of a remake by Antonio da Sangallo il Vecchio in 1511. He may also have restructured the medieval gate leading into the city proper, the **Porta al Prato**.

To the left near here is the 18th-century **Chiesa di San Bernardo**. Nearby is the late-Renaissance **Palazzo Avignonesi** by Giacomo da Vignola. Several **mansions** line Via di Gracciano nel Corso, including the **Palazzo di Bucelli** at No 73, whose facade features Etruscan and Latin inscriptions. Sangallo also designed **Palazzo Cocconi** at No 70.

Piazza Michelozzo is dominated by the striking Renaissance facade of Michelozzo's **Chiesa di Sant'Agostino**. Directly in front is a medieval tower-house, **Torre di Pulcinella**, topped by the town clock and the bizarre figure of Pulcinella (Punch of Punch & Judy fame), who strikes the hours.

Continue up the hill and take the first left past the **Loggia di Mercato** for Via del Poggiolo, which eventually becomes Via Ricci. In the Renaissance **Palazzo Ricci** is one of the town's wine *cantine*; a cavernous warren of ancient wine cellars which you can wander through, ending up (fortuitously) at the wine-tasting room and shop.

The town's **Museo Civico** (☎ 0578 71 73 00; Via Ricci 10; adult/child €4.15/2.60; 🕑 10am-7pm Tue-Sun summer, 10am-1pm & 3-6pm Tue-Sun winter) is opposite the Gothic Palazzo Neri-Orselli. The small collection features terracotta reliefs by the della Robbia family and some Gothic and Renaissance paintings.

Piazza Grande marks the highest point of the town and features the austere **Palazzo Comunale** (☎ 0578 75 74 52; Piazza Grande 1; 🕑 9am-1.30pm Mon-Sat), a 13th-century Gothic building remodelled in the 15th century by Michelozzo (the comparison with the Palazzo Vecchio in Florence, in form if not in colour, is hard to avoid). From the top of the 14th-century tower you can see the Monti Sibillini to the east and, they say, Siena to the northwest.

The other palaces in the piazza are the **Palazzo Contucci**, now a wine cellar, and the **Palazzo Tarugi**, attributed to Giacomo da Vignola, near the fountain. The **cathedral** (Piazza Grande; 🕑 temporarily closed) has a 16th-century facade that is noticeable by its absence. Inside there is a lovely triptych depicting the Assumption above the altar by

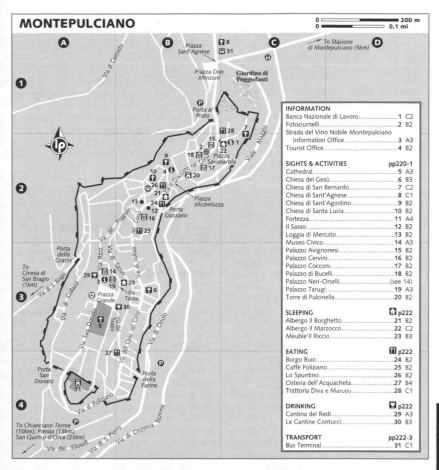

MONTEPULCIANO

INFORMATION	
Banca Nazionale di Lavoro	1 C2
Fotociurnelli	2 B2
Strada del Vino Nobile Montepulciano Information Office	3 A3
Tourist Office	4 B2

SIGHTS & ACTIVITIES	pp220-1
Cathedral	5 A3
Chiesa del Gesù	6 B3
Chiesa di San Bernardo	7 C2
Chiesa di Sant'Agnese	8 C1
Chiesa di Sant'Agostino	9 B2
Chiesa di Santa Lucia	10 B2
Fortezza	11 A4
Il Sasso	12 B2
Loggia di Mercato	13 B2
Museo Civico	14 A3
Palazzo Avignonesi	15 B2
Palazzo Cervini	16 B2
Palazzo Cocconi	17 B2
Palazzo di Bucelli	18 B2
Palazzo Neri-Orselli	(see 14)
Palazzo Tarugi	19 A3
Torre di Pulcinella	20 B2

SLEEPING	p222
Albergo Il Borghetto	21 B2
Albergo Il Marzocco	22 C2
Meublé'Il Riccio	23 B2

EATING	p222
Borgo Buio	24 B2
Caffè Poliziano	25 B2
Lo Spuntino	26 B2
Osteria dell'Acquacheta	27 B4
Trattoria Diva e Marceo	28 C1

DRINKING	p222
Cantina del Redi	29 A3
Le Cantine Contucci	30 B3

TRANSPORT	pp222-3
Bus Terminal	31 C1

Taddeo da Bartolo. At the time of research, the cathedral was undergoing restoration – check with the tourist office for updates.

If you take the low road from Piazza Michelozzi and follow Via di Voltaia nel Corso, you pass first, on your left, the Renaissance **Palazzo Cervini**, built for Cardinal Marcello Cervini, the future Pope Marcellus II. The unusual – most *palazzi* have austere, straight fronts – U-shape at the front, including a courtyard into the facade design, appears to have been another Sangallo creation. A few blocks further along on the left, is the **Chiesa del Gesù**, an elaborate Baroque job.

Outside the town wall, about 1km from the Porta della Grassa, stands the **Chiesa di San Biagio**, a fine Renaissance church built by (yet again) Antonio da Sangallo il Vecchio and consecrated in 1529 by the Medici Pope Clement VII.

Bravio delle Botti takes place on the last Sunday in August, when the streets are given over to barrel races.

COURSES

Il Sasso (☎ 0578 75 83 11; www.ilsasso.com; Via di Gracciano nel Corso 2; 1 hr from €28, 4 hrs/day for 2 weeks from €340) can organise language courses for you. The same place can also organise mosaic classes. By happy coincidence, the organisation doubles as an estate agency **Informazioni Turistiche** (☎ 0578 71 72 42; www.agriturismoonline .com) specialising in the rental of mainly rural accommodation to foreigners.

CENTRAL TUSCANY

SLEEPING

Montepulciano accommodation is limited. Several *affittacamere* are scattered about town. Get a list of them from the tourist office and expect to pay anything up to €77 for a double.

Meuble'll Riccio (☎ /fax 0578 75 77 13; www .ilriccio.net; Via Talosa 21; s/d €70/90) You enter this hotel via a 16th-century patio and it just gets better. There are large rooms, antiques, a solarium and a terrace bar for your glass of vino with a view.

Albergo Il Marzocco (☎ 0578 75 72 62; fax 0578 75 75 30; Piazza Savonarola 18; s/d €60/90) Run by a charming elderly couple, the rooms at this fabulous 16th-century building are large and comfortable; be sure to ask for one with a terrace and views (no extra cost).

Albergo Il Borghetto (☎ 0578 75 75 35; www .ilborghetto.it; Via Borgo Buio 7; s/d €93/105) It may look like every other 15th-century building on this street but once inside, this place is a gem, packed with antiques – including Napoleonic-era beds. There's even a tunnel, leading to the house across the street.

EATING

There are numerous places to sample Tuscan food and wine in Montepulciano.

Lo Spuntino (☎ 0578 75 77 68; Via Gracciano nel Corso 25; pizza slices €1.15-1.55; ☺ closed Tue) You can buy filling pizza slices here, and there is a small counter space if you don't fancy eating on the go.

Osteria dell'Acquacheta (☎ 0578 75 84 43; Via del Teatro 22; mains €5-6; ☺ closed Tue) This small eatery has the look and feel of a country trattoria. The food is excellent and ranges from *misto di salami Toscani* to huge steaks.

Trattoria Diva e Maceo (☎ 0578 71 65 91; Via di Gracciano nel Corso 92; mains €13; ☺ closed Tue) Here you can feast on Tuscan cuisine like *tagliatelle al tartufo* (tagliatella with truffles) in simple surroundings.

Borgo Buio (☎ 0578 71 74 97; Via Borgo Buio 10; mains €12-14; ☺ closed Thu) This is a rustic, low-lit place with a brick vaulted ceiling, where you can enjoy good Tuscan meals at reasonable prices. In addition, it functions as an *enoteca* (you can tipple from 10.30am to midnight) with a good selection of wines.

Caffè Poliziano (☎ 0578 75 86 15; Via di Voltaia nel Corso 27; mains €6-8) It's a justifiably popular restaurant, so get here early to grab a table on the balcony. There's a good choice of light lunches, including an omelette with artichokes, which makes a change from pasta.

DRINKING

There are plenty of places wet your palate on the local red, Vino Nobile, including the several long-established cantinas around town.

Cantina del Redi (Via Ricci 13; ☎ 10.30am-1pm & 3-7pm Apr-Sep) This place doubles as a wine cellar, which you can wander around at will. It's downhill from Piazza Grande along Via Ricci.

Le Cantine Contucci (☎ 0578 75 70 06; Palazzo Contucci, Piazza Grande) Vintners since Renaissance times, this is another active cellar where you can sample a drop of the local wine. The owner is a great character and will give you a personal tour, tasting and photo session – if he likes the look of you.

GETTING THERE & AROUND

Tra-in operates five bus services daily between Montepulciano and Siena (€4.40, 1½ hours), via Pienza. Regular LFI buses connect with Chiusi (€2.10, 50 minutes, half-hourly). One direct LFI bus goes to Siena (at 6.25am), while three go to Florence at 5.45am, 8.30am and 2.10pm. Two buses travel to Arezzo (change at Bettolle). It is possible to pick up the occasional bus to Rome here, too. Buses leave from Piazza Sant'Agnese, outside the Porta al Prato at the northern end of town.

The most convenient train station is at Chiusi-Chianciano Terme, 10km southeast, on the main Rome–Florence line. Buses for Montepulciano (€2.10) meet each train, so it's the best route from Florence or Rome. Stazione di Montepulciano, about 5km to the northeast, has less frequent local services.

By car, if you are not coming from Pienza, take the Chianciano Terme exit off the A1 and follow the SS166 for the 18km trip to Montepulciano.

Most cars are banned from the town centre and there are car parks near the Porta al Prato. Small town buses weave their way from here to Piazza Grande (€0.80).

Chianciano Terme

This place is a short trip south from Montepulciano by bus or car, but you could skip Chianciano Terme unless you think a local spa-water treatment for your liver is in order. The town is blessed with a small medieval core, which seems to recoil at all the surrounding development. Given its proximity to Montepulciano, however, it does make a great base as there are some 250 hotels here that cater to spa guests. Although most are fairly bland and modern, they are remarkably reasonable. However, be prepared for half or full board as, strangely, there are precious few bars and restaurants in town.

Chiusi

pop 9000

One of the most important of the 12 cities of the Etruscan League, Chiusi was once powerful enough to attack Rome, under the leadership of the Etruscan king Porsenna. These days it is a fairly sleepy country town but is highly recommended as a stopover. There is a **Pro Loco tourist information office** (☎ 0578 22 76 67; Piazza Carlo Baldini; ☼ 10am-12.30pm, 10am-12.30pm & 3.30-6.30pm Jun-Aug).

SIGHTS

Chiusi's main attractions are the **Etruscan tombs** which are dotted around the countryside. Unfortunately, almost all the tombs are in such a serious state of disrepair that they are closed to the public. Visits to the two accessible tombs, Tomba della Scimmia (the best) and Tomba del Leone, are with the custodian only, and leave from the **Museo Archeologico Nazionale** (☎ 0578 2 01 77; Via Porsenna 93; admission €4; ☼ 9am-8pm). The museum itself has a reasonably interesting collection of artefacts found in local tombs.

Also take a look at the Romanesque **cathedral** and adjacent **Museo della Cattedrale** (☎ 0578 22 64 90; Piazza Duomo; adult/child €2/0.52; ☼ 9.30am-12.45pm & 4.30-7pm Jun–mid-Oct; 9.30am-12.45pm Mon-Sat, 9.30am-12.45pm & 4.30-7pm Sun & hols mid-Oct–May), which has an important collection of 22 illustrated psalm books.

The **Labirinto di Porsenna** is a series of tunnels underneath the Piazza del Duomo which date back to Etruscan times and formed part of the town's water-supply system. Since ancient times, legend has associated the labyrinth with the Etruscan king Porsenna – it supposedly hid his grand tomb. A section of the labyrinth was excavated in the 1980s and can be visited with a guide (€3). Tickets can be bought at the Museo della Cattedrale.

It's also possible to visit a number of Christian **catacombs** (admission €5; ☼ guided tours 11am & 5pm Jun-mid-Oct; 11am Mon-Sat, 11am & 4pm Sun mid-Oct–May), 2km from Chiusi. Tours leave from the Museo della Cattedrale, where you buy your ticket.

SLEEPING & EATING

There are several *agriturismo* (farmstay or country inn accommodation) establishments in the countryside near Chiusi; contact the tourist office for details.

Albergo La Sfinge (☎ /fax 0578 2 01 57; www .albergolasfinge.com; Via Marconi 2; s/d €70/35) Just within the confines of Chiusi's historical centre, this hotel has adequate if smallish rooms with new bathrooms. Rooms with air-con cost a little more. Ask for a view.

La Solita Zuppa (☎ 0578 2 10 06; Via Porsenna 21; mains €12-14; ☼ closed Tue) This is arguably one of the better places to eat in Tuscany. The menu is heavily Tuscan and sports a wide range of soup options, which is the restaurant's forte. The food is wholesome and cooked to perfection, and the owners make you feel like a long-lost friend.

GETTING THERE & AWAY

Chiusi is easily accessible by public transport. Its train station, in the valley below the town, is on the main Rome-Florence line. The town is just off the A1.

Sarteano & Cetona

Heading into this part of the province, you definitely feel you have left the last of the tour buses well and truly behind you. This quiet rural territory is best explored with your own wheels. Both Sarteano and Cetona are curious little medieval towns, the former topped by a brooding castle. No specific outstanding sights present themselves but they are both fun to wander briefly around. At the camp site at Via Campo dei Fiori 30 in Sarteano, you can luxuriate in the warm waters of the Piscina Bagno Santo. Near Cetona is the modest mountain of the same name, which invites some vigorous meanderings in the clean country air.

Frateria di San Francesco (☎ 0578 23 82 61; www.mondox.it; Via di San Francesco; d/st €200/260; meals excluding wine €88; ☼ restaurant Wed-Mon; closed Jan-Feb) Those with wads of money and a desire for a special retreat should consider staying or eating at this place. A couple of kilometres along a side road (which leads

DETOUR: LAGO DI CHIUSI

Stock up on stale bread and exit Chiusi in the direction of Castiglione del Lago, passing the petrol station to your left. After 2km, just past the church on your right, turn left at the signpost marked 'Lago di Chiusi'. At the 2.6km fork, turn right to the lake, following the road to the right. Look for the 'Restaurant da Gino' sign and turn right along an avenue of pine trees. Park by the quay and have a stroll down to the lake to feed the ducks. Retrace your route until you reach the restaurant sign where, instead of turning left to Chiusi, carry on straight towards Montepulciano and Chanciano Terme. At 5.2km turn right to Chanciano. Just before you reach the town, take the left fork towards Sarteano (approximately 10km) and Cetona.

up to Monte Cetona) outside the northern entrance to Cetona, this former convent dating from 1212 has been lovingly restored and converted into a top-class restaurant with seven rooms added. You can expect a five-course dining experience of world-class standing. Look for the Mondo X signs when driving up.

Up to five buses a day (except Sunday) go to both towns from Montepulciano (some involve a change at Chianciano Terme).

Abbadia San Salvatore & Around

On your travels in this part of Tuscany you'd have to be shortsighted not to notice the village of **Radicófani** or, more precisely, its **Rocca** (☎ 0578 5 57 00; €3; 🕙 10am-7pm Tue-Sun Apr-Oct, 10am-6pm Nov-Mar). Built high on a blancmange-shaped hill, it's an impressive sight from any approach, and the views from its ramparts are stunning. It now houses a small museum devoted to medieval times. Radicófani itself is a pleasant village worth a stroll and is 17km southwest of Sarteano on the SS478.

La Torre (☎ 0578 5 59 43; Via G. Matteotti 7; s/d €30/52) is the only place to stay in town. Don't be put off by the bland red-brick exterior. The rooms, with balconies, are good value

and the restaurant is always full of locals here for the appetising home-made fare.

Eighteen kilometres further west is Abbadia San Salvatore, a largely ugly mining town that grew rapidly and tastelessly from the late 19th century. It does have a couple of saving graces, however. The old town, a sombre stone affair entered off the main Piazzale XX Settembre, is curious enough, although perhaps not really worth an excursion on its own. A small **tourist office** (☎ 0577 77 58 11; 🕙 9am-1pm & 4-7pm, closed Sun Sep-Jun) operates from Via Adua 25.

The **Abbazia di San Salvatore** (☎ 0577 77 80 83; Piazzale Michelangelo 8; 🕙 7am-6pm Mon-Sat, 10.30am-6pm Sun summer, 7am-5pm Mon-Sat, 10.30am-5pm Sun winter) was founded in 743 by the Lombard Erfo. It eventually passed into the hands of Cistercian monks, who still occupy it today. Little remains of the monastery, but the church is extremely interesting (for people into churches and architecture, at any rate). Built in the 11th century and Romanesque in style, it was reconstructed in a curious manner in the late 16th century, when the whole area from the transept to the apse was raised and adorned with broad, frescoed arches. Best of all, however, is the Lombard crypt, a remarkable stone forest of 36 columns. No-one is sure what purpose this hall served.

The town lies in the shadow of **Monte Amiata** (1738m) and serves as a base for local holidaymakers getting in a little skiing on one run on the peak (snow permitting) in winter or some walking in summer. You can, for instance, walk right around the mountain following a 30km-trail known as the Anello della Montagna. The path is signposted and maps are available from the tourist office (these also cover walks in the surrounding area). For this reason there are hotels aplenty in Abbadia San Salvatore and several others in towns dotted about the broad expanse of the mountain, so you should not have too much trouble finding a place to stay.

A handful of RAMA buses running between Grosseto and Bagni San Filippo call in at Abbadia San Salvatore (€4.50, 2½ hours). It is also possible to get down from Siena (€4.50, 1¼ hours, two daily).

Southern Tuscany

The landscape of this region can be quite beautiful: lush rumpled hills, distant smoky mountains and ancient hilltop villages. Several of Tuscany's most important Etruscan sites are here too, including Saturnia with its hot sulphur springs. For pure drama, the medieval town of Pitigliano is inimitable, looming above the mountainous cliff face pitted with the caves of former Etruscan tombs. On a lighter note, Grosseto's old town provides an atmospheric setting for the evening *passeggiata* while, along the coast, highlights include the Monte Argentario peninsula with its sophisticated harbours and good stretches of beach.

As in the Maremma Pisana south of Livorno, serious land reclamation and the drying out of the extensive swamps only began in the late-18th and early-19th centuries under the direction of the Lorraine grand dukes. Concurrently, there were reforms aimed at loosening the grip of the feudal-style landholders on this previously unproductive land. Roads were built and canals dug, agriculture was stimulated and dairy production encouraged – in a region as hilly and mountainous as Tuscany, the plains of the newly 'cleansed' Maremma were ideal for grazing. Today, agriculture still plays a big part here, although industry, and an increase in tourism revenue, has boosted the economy.

HIGHLIGHTS

- Explore the extraordinary town of Pitigliano (p235), rising dramatically from a rocky outcrop and with its perfectly preserved Jewish quarter
- Follow in the footsteps of the Etruscans in the necropolises around Sovana (p236) and their *vie cave* (sunken roads)
- Bathe in the natural hot springs at the waterfall of Saturnia (p235)
- Join a guided walk in the rugged, unspoiled surroundings of the Parco Regionale della Maremma (p231)
- Enjoy a special seafood moment at one of the waterfront restaurants in picturesque Porto Santo Stefano (p233)

SOUTHERN TUSCANY

GROSSETO

pop 71,600

Grosseto was the last of the Siena-dominated towns to fall into Medici hands in 1559. The walls, bastions and fortress were built on the orders of Florence to protect what was then an important grain and salt depot for the grand duchy.

The town has recently been spruced up. Ignore the modern sprawl and head straight for the old walls; they date back to 1559 and form a near-perfect hexagon. Within, the historic old town has plenty of unpretentious charm with few tourists around – probably because Grosseto has still not shaken off its former reputation as being a better place for scoring drugs than sightseeing.

Information

Tourist Office (☎ 0564 42 26 11; www.grosseto.turismo.toscana.it; Monte Rosa 206) Can book accommodation and provide information about the Parco Regionale della Maremma.

Sights

Within the city walls, Grosseto's **cathedral** (☎ 0564 42 01 43; Chiasso degli Zuavi 6; ☯ 8am-1pm & 3-7pm) was begun in the late 13th century and has a distinctive Sienese air. It has been added to, however, and much of the facade was renewed along neo-Romanesque lines in the 19th century; the bell tower dates from the early 1900s. The other interesting building on Piazza Dante is the Palazzo della Provincia. It appears to be Sienese Gothic, which is exactly what its early-20th-century architects hoped you might think. The **Museo d'Arte Della Diocesi di Grosseto** (☎ 0564 41 76 29; Piazza Baccarin 3; adult/child €5/1; ☯ 9am-1pm & 4.30-7pm 1 Mar-30 Apr, 10am-1pm & 5-8pm 2 May–31 Oct, 9am-1pm & 4.30-7pm 1 Nov–28 Feb) has an impressive collection, including Etruscan urns, bronze statuettes and Roman sculpture.

Sleeping & Eating

Hotel Ristorante l'Italiana (☎ 0564 2 84 19; Via Mazzini 78; s/d €40/80) Well-priced choice right in the heart of the old town, this older hotel with its traditional green shutters has small but adequate rooms. The adjacent restaurant is popular with locals – always a good sign.

Bastiani Grand Hotel (☎ 0564 2 00 47; fax 0564 2 93 21; Piazza Gioberti 64; s/d €82/142) A smart-looking

new hotel in a grand old building complete with *Gone with the Wind* staircase. The rooms are elegant and draped in warm coordinated colours and matching artwork. The location is excellent, within easy distance of some of the best bars and restaurants.

Dannbio Blu (☎ 0564 2 22 16; Via Cavour 6; mains €7-9) Hugely popular, noisy restaurant with cheery, frazzled staff and a dizzy choice of dishes, including the traditional – polenta and risotto – and occasional surprises like chicken curry.

Getting There & Away

Rama (☎ 0564 2 52 15; www.griforama.it – Italian only; Piazza Marconi) buses leave for points throughout the province. Most of the buses depart from the train station. Buses for Siena, where you can connect with either Tra-in or SITA buses to Florence, run roughly every 45 minutes from 5.40am. Alternatively there are three direct services. There is only one direct bus a day to Massa Marittima (€3, none on Sunday). Other destinations include: Piombino (€4.50), Magliano in Toscana (€2), Follonica (€3), Castiglione della Pescaia (€4), Porto San Stefano (€3) and Pitigliano (€5).

Grosseto is on the main coastal train line between Rome and Livorno. For places such as Pisa (€7.50, two hours), Florence (€10, three hours) or Siena (€5.80, 1½ hours), the train is probably a smarter bet.

AROUND GROSSETO
Roselle

Populated as early as the 7th century BC, Roselle was a middle-ranking Etruscan town which came under Roman control in the 3rd century BC.

Although no great monuments are left standing, the extensive **historic site** (☎ 0564 40 24 03; admission €4.50; ☯ 9am-sunset) retains Roman defensive walls, an oddly elliptical amphitheatre, traces of houses, the forum and streets; you'll also find remains of an abandoned medieval village. There are wonderful views down to the plains and out to sea.

If arriving by bus, ask the driver to let you off at the nearest spot and walk.

Vetulónia

This windswept mountain village seems to rise out of nothing from the surrounding

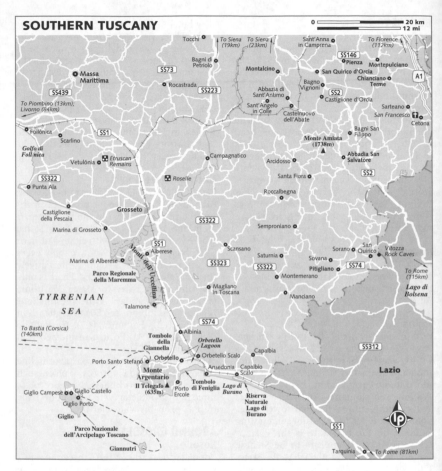

SOUTHERN TUSCANY

plains. You can see the sea from here, but Vetulónia seems to belong to another time dimension, making it obvious why the Etruscans set up shop here. The town sports what are purported to be some blocks from the ancient town wall and a small **Museo Archeologico** (☎ 0564 94 80 58; Via Garibaldi; adult/child €4.15/3; ☼ 10am-2pm & 4-8pm) dedicated to the Vetulónia remains. Near the town are two separate **sites** (☎ 0564 94 95 87; free; ☼ 9am-dusk) where excavations have revealed bits and bobs of the Etruscan settlement. The more extensive area, known as Scavi Città (Town Excavations), is just below the town as you leave by the only road.

More interesting are four unearthed **Etruscan tombs** (Via dei Sepolcri; ☼ 9am-dusk), a couple of kilometres further downhill and along a turn-off to the right. The most interesting of these is the last, about 1km down a rough dirt track.

Taverna Etrusca (☎ /fax 0564 94 98 02; Piazza Stefani 12; d €45) There's loads of atmosphere at this small hotel, with its excellent downstairs restaurant with panoramic views. The owner divides his time between here and Cuba, so you can expect a *Buena Vista* welcome. There are plans for a pool, so prices may increase.

There is just one other bar in the village, full of grizzled old men and oozing with small-town charm.

Buses run twice daily from Grosseto and once daily from Castiglione della Pescaia.

MASSA MARITTIMA
pop 9500

Massa is a compelling place with a pristine medieval centre. Briefly under Pisan domination, it thrived on the local metal mining industry but in 1225 became an independent commune, only to be swallowed up by Siena a century later. The plague in 1348, and the end of mining 50 years later, reduced the city almost to extinction. Not until the 18th century, with the draining of marshes and re-establishment of mining, did Massa Marittima finally come back to life.

Information
Banca Toscana (Piazza Garibaldi 17)
Post Office (Piazza Mazzini)
Tourist Office (☎ 0566 90 27 56; www.amatur.it – Italian only; Via Todini 315; ☼ 9.30am-1pm & 3.30-7pm Mon-Sat, 9.30am-1pm Sun Apr-Oct, & 10am-12.30pm Tue-Sun rest of year) Provides plenty of information on the area, including *Strada del Vino* maps.

Sights
The heart of medieval Massa is Piazza Garibaldi, dominated by the imposing bulk of the **cathedral** (Piazza Garibaldi; ☼ 8am-noon & 3.30-7pm), in Pisan Romanesque style. It is thought that Giovanni Pisano designed the church; the interior is graced with substantial remnants of frescoes and several paintings, including a *Madonna delle Grazie* by the workshop of Siena's Duccio di Buoninsegna.

Opposite is the **Palazzo Comunale**, the city's historic seat of government. The proud coat of arms of Florence's Medicis doesn't quite detract attention from the earlier symbol of rival Siena's one-time ascendancy here – the wolf with Romulus and Remus.

The 13th-century **Palazzo del Podestà** houses the **Museo Archeologico** (☎ 0566 90 22 89; Piazza Garibaldi 1; adult/child €3/1.50; ☼ 10am-12.30pm & 3.30-7pm Tue-Sun Apr-Oct, closes at 5pm Nov-Mar), visited above all for Ambrogio Lorenzetti's magnificent *Maestà* (Majesty). Paling into comparative insignificance is a modest collection of ancient Roman and Etruscan artefacts that have been dug up around town.

The Città Nuova (New Town) is dominated by the **Torre del Candeliere** (Piazza Matteotti; adult/child €2.50/1.50; ☼ 11am-1pm & 3-6pm). The tower is in turn joined to defensive bastions in the wall by the so-called **Arco Senese** (Sienese Arch). You can enter the tower and walk across the arch – the views over the Città Vecchia (Old Town) are stupendous.

At the **Museo della Miniera** (Via Corridoni; adult/child €5/3; ☼ 10am-5.45pm Tue-Sun) you can examine the city's mining history. The display includes a replica of a length of mine. Guided tours (1½ hours) are up to seven times daily from 10am. The **Museo di Arte e Storia delle Miniere** (Piazza Matteotti 4; adult/child €1.50/1; ☼ 10am-11.30am & 3-5.30pm Tue-Sun Apr-Oct) has more mining material, including a detailed history.

Festivals & Events
During the second week of July, the **Toscana Foto Festival** (www.toscanafotofestival.com – Italian only) is a biggie, with professional pics up all over town.

Sleeping
There are not many options here; check at the tourist office for a list.

Il Girifalco (☎ 0566 90 21 77; www.cometanet.it/girifalco; Via Massetana Nord 25; s/d €45/72) This low-key place just outside the walls is family friendly, with a playground and picnic area plus sweeping views. The rooms are clean and bright, and there is a new TV area.

Duca del Mare (☎ 0566 90 22 84; www.cometanet.it/duca; Piazza Dante; s/d €52/93) Around a 10-minute walk from the historic centre, this modern, sunny hotel has a definite Scandinavian look with lots of shiny light wood and Ikea-style furnishings. The adjacent ice-cream parlour adds appeal.

La Fenice Park Hotel (☎ 0566 90 39 41; www.lafeniceresidence.it; Via A. Diaz; s/d €76/140; P ☒) This seductive marble-clad hotel has some apartment-style rooms with mini-kitchen. Go for a room overlooking the croquet-quality lawn out back. This is the better of two hotels in the historic town centre.

Eating
As surprising as the lack of accommodation is the concentration of above-average restaurants.

Trattoria Vecchio Borgo (☎ 0566 90 39 50; Via N. Parenti 12; mains €9.50; ☼ closed Mon) In winter, you'll find a roaring fire in this brick-clad restaurant with a cavernous barrel-vaulted interior. There is an economically priced set menu and a good variety of dishes, although the basic *gnocchi al pomodoro* is hard to beat.

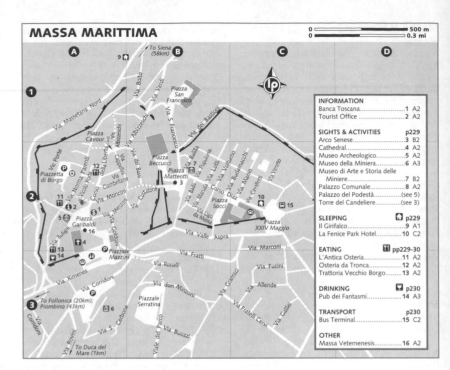

MASSA MARITTIMA

L'Antica Osteria (☎ 0566 90 26 44; Via N. Parenti 19; mains €8-9) Come here for the good-value dishes, including several lip-smacking vegetarian options like cheese-filled ravioli with mushrooms. Gets busy at weekends with discerning Germans.

Osteria da Tronca (☎ 0566 90 19 91; Vicolo Porte 5; mains €9; closed Mon) Squeezed into a side street, this intimate stone-walled restaurant is famously good. There is lots of antipasto (€2.50) to choose from. For mains try anything with *cinghiale* (wild boar).

Drinking & Entertainment

Pub dei Fantasmi (☎ 0566 94 02 75; Via N. Parenti 2/4; until 3am Thu-Tue) If you are feeling frisky after dinner, this is about the only place big enough to hold a crowd. There is occasional live jazz.

On the first Sunday after 19 May a crossbow competition – the Balestro del Girifalco – takes place here.

Getting There & Away

There are two daily buses to Siena at 7.05am and 4.40pm (€4.30 one way) and around four

to Volterra (changing at Monterotondo). The nearest train station is Massa-Follónica, served by a regular shuttle bus (€1.80). The bus terminal (Via Valle Aspra) is southeast of the new town. The most central place for purchasing train/bus tickets is **Massa Veternensis** (☎ 0566 902 20 16; Piazza Garibaldi 18).

THE COAST

There are no great swathes of sand when cruising the coast from Piombino south; occasional stretches of pine-backed beach are pleasant without being breathtaking. The best that this southern stretch of mainland Tuscan coast has to offer is down in the Parco Regionale della Maremma.

Golfo di Follónica

Take in the reassuring picture of chimney stacks and industry at work. All quite necessary, to be sure, but no reason to hang about. Hit the road and head south. The first town you will reach is **Follónica** with its cheap and scruffy high-rises. The outlook improves a few kilometres further around the gulf with a pleasant pinewood backdrop to the beaches; look for the turn-off signs inland for **Scarlino**.

There is a plentiful choice of camp sites, restaurants and hotels here.

A sadistic committee in **Punta Ala** succeeded in devising the most Kafkaesque road system when it set to designing this leafy but rather fake getaway for the seriously monied. On the plus side, the promontory is green and sparingly brutalised by building development and, along the northern flank, there is a pleasant pine-backed sandy beach.

Castiglione della Pescaia

At last, something seriously worth stopping for on the mad rush southwards. The modern sprawl around the foot of the hill on which this medieval stone village sits is surprisingly not too disturbing. The bustle where old meets new retains its life until mid-October.

The walled old town, brooding in its stony quiet, has no specific monuments of interest but has great stroll-around appeal, and the views out to sea are majestic.

The **tourist office** (☎ 0564 93 36 78; Piazza Garibaldi 6; www.castiglionepescaia.com; ☎ 9am-1pm & 4-8pm Mon-Sat & 10am-1pm Sun) is across from the harbour.

SLEEPING & EATING
Hotel Bologna (☎ /fax 0564 93 37 46, Piazza Garibaldi 8; d €47) This is a no-frills small hotel with no singles and shared bath only. The rooms are comfortable in a rough-edged kind of way but the location is five-star superb – across from the harbour with great views from the corner breakfast room and some rooms.

Hotel Lucerna (☎ 0564 93 36 20; Via IV Novembre 27; s/d €49/83) This attractive old-style hotel has been run by the same family for several generations. The rooms are cheerful, large and have balconies with sea or old-town views. The adjacent pizzeria is handy for staving off the midnight munchies.

Ristorante La Fortezza (☎ 0564 93 61 00; Via del Recinto 1/3; mains €9-12; ☎ closed Mon) If you want to sit outside (or anywhere after the steep climb here), this is a spacious place, serving up typical dishes of the Maremma, including pasta with lobster.

GETTING THERE & AWAY
Rama buses frequently run to/from Grosseto (€4) and connect with other places on the coast, such as Marina di Grosseto (€2). Up to five buses a day in the height of summer connect with Massa-Follónica train station, one of the main stops around here.

Marina di Grosseto

The beach is broad and sandy, but the resort is modern with slapped-together housing and an anonymous gridlike street system. At least it's predominately low rise and so well camouflaged by the umbrella pines typical of the Maremma coast. It's a favoured spot for locals to come and splash in the sea but there are more interesting places close by.

Parco Regionale della Maremma

Along the entire coastline from Piombino to Rome, this is arguably the main attraction. The park incorporates the Monti dell'Uccellina and a magnificent stretch of unspoiled coastline. Native animals include wild boar, wild cats, porcupines and hawks.

The park's main **tourist office** (☎ 0564 407098, fax 0564 40 72 78; ☎ 7am-6pm mid-Jun-end Sep, 8am-2pm Oct-mid-June) is at Alberese. There's a small office (same contact details and opening hours) located at the southern extremity of the park. A turn-off 1km before Talamone leads directly to it. **Talamone** itself is a fetching little fortress village with a camp site and several hotel and restaurant options.

Entry to the park is limited and cars must be left in designated areas. Walking is the best way to explore the park and nine trails have been marked out within its borders.

A number of companies run canoeing and horse-riding tours in certain areas, costing around €20 and €25 respectively. It's also possible to ride with the legendary *butteri*, cowboys who still work the area in and around the park. (see the boxed text p232) The tourist office in Alberese has a list.

There are no shelters within the park, so make sure you wear sunblock and carry water. The Marina di Alberese gets crowded in summer, especially at the weekend.

You can't stay in the park, but there are *agriturismo* options nearby.

Trattoria Romoli (☎ 0564 40 50 33; Via Provinciale; Alberese; main €10-15; ☎ closed Tue) is a fantastic place just outside Santa Maria di Rispescia on the road to Alberese. Specialities include home-made tiramisu, *cinghiale* (wild boar) in a red-wine sauce and anything fresh from the sea.

COWBOY CULTURE

The fascination Europe held for the cowboy culture of the American West was never more apparent than in the late 1800s when Colonel William Cody (alias Buffalo Bill) took his fabulously successful Wild West show on two grand European tours. The crowds were unprecedented; everyone was eager to see the fabled buffalo hunter, the sharp-shooting Annie Oakley and bands of real Sioux warriors, many the very same braves who had fought Custer at the battle of Little Big Horn. In Britain, Queen Victoria liked the show so much she went to see it twice.

When Buffalo Bill brought the show to Italy, the troupe was invited to the Vatican to attend the celebration of the 10th anniversary of the coronation of Pope Leo XIII. Then, in Verona, Cody fulfilled his ambition of exhibiting his Wild West in the ancient Roman amphitheatre where the high point was a bronco-busting challenge match between Buffalo Bill's cowboys and the *butteri*. These were Tuscany's legendary cowboys who survived under the harsh nature of the Maremma: the swampland breeding ground of malarial mosquitoes. The Maremma was divided between landowners of vast estates where the *butteri* tended herds of Cajetan horses, one of the most unmanageable and wild breeds in Europe. In front of a crowd of some 20,000 spectators, the *butteri* challenged the American cowboys to break the Cajetans. The Rome correspondent of the *New York Herald* wrote: 'The brutes made springs into the air, darted hither and thither in all directions, and bent themselves into all sorts of shapes, but all in vain. In five minutes the cowboys *[butteri]* had caught the wild horses with the lasso, saddled, subdued and bestrode them. Then the cowboys rode them around the arena while the dense crowds applauded with delight.'

Today, longhorn cattle and horses still graze free in the Maremma and, on the first Sunday in August, the *butteri* gather and brand the cattle. The **Equinos Association** (☎ 0564 24988; www.cavallomaremmano.it) organises *butteri* shows and equestrian tourism, and even information on buying – presumably tamed – Maremma horses. There is also an official organisation, **Butteri di Alta Maremma** (www.butteri-altamaremma.com), which protects and promotes the remaining *butteri* and also arranges rodeo-style events.

MONTE ARGENTARIO

Once an island, this promontory came to be linked to the mainland by an accumulation of sand that is now the isthmus of Orbetello. Further sandy bulwarks form the Tombolo della Giannella and the Tombolo di Feniglia to the north and south. They enclose a lagoon that is now a protected nature reserve. Intense building has spoiled the northern side of the promontory, but the south and centre have been left in peace (forest fires aside). It is something of a weekend getaway fave with Romans in summer so inevitably is packed to the gunwales.

Orbetello

In 1559 Orbetello was called Presidio and was a Spanish military base. The occupation lasted until 1707 and had a strong impact on the town. Orbetello's main attraction is its **cathedral**, which has retained its 14th-century Gothic facade, despite being remodelled in the Spanish style in the 16th century. Further reminders of the Spanish garrison include the fort and city wall; parts of the latter belong to the original Etruscan wall.

The best place for observing the birdlife (as many as 140 species have been identified) on Orbetello's lagoon is out along the **Tombolo della Feniglia**, the southern strip of land linking Monte Argentario to the mainland. It is blocked to traffic – you can park your car near the camp site (see p233) and proceed on foot or bicycle. The beach on the seaward side is one of the best on the peninsula.

Around the Peninsula

Porto Santo Stefano and **Porto Ercole** are the main resort towns and you can expect to see a few Ferraris and G-strings. Porto Ercole, in a picturesque position between two Spanish forts, retains some of its fishing village character.

Information

Internet Provider (Via Martiri d'Ungheria 35; ☐ €5/hr)

Tourist Office (☎ 0564 81 42 08; Monte dei Paschi di Siena Bldg; Corso Umberto I 55, Porto Santo Stefano; ☺ 9am-1pm & 4-6pm Mon-Sat Sep-Jun, 9am-1pm & 5-7pm Mon-Sat Jul & Aug)

Sights & Activities

The **Acquario Mediterraneo** (☎ 0564 81 59 33; Lungomare dei Navigatori 44/48; €4.50; ⏰ 5pm-midnight), on the waterfront in Porto Santo Stefano, has a small but interesting collection of marine life. **Fortezza Spagnola** (☎ 0564 81 06 81; Piazza del Governatore; €4.50; ⏰ 6pm-midnight Jun-Sep, Sat & Sun only Oct-May) is a little overpriced for the underwater archaeological finds it houses but the breathtaking views of Porto Santo Stefano are worth the dosh.

For a pleasant drive, follow the signs to Il Telegrafo, one of the highest mountains in the region, and turn off at the **Convento dei Frati Passionisti**, a church and convent with sensational views across to the mainland. Another good drive is the Via Panoramica, a circuit running out from Porto Santo Stefano.

There are several good beaches, mainly of the pebbly variety. Near Porto Ercole the beach is serviced, so it's clean but cluttered with deck chairs and umbrellas. Further away, the beach becomes less crowded but, as with most public beaches in Italy, it also gets dirtier.

Sleeping

Accommodation on the peninsula is generally expensive and popular over the summer months.

ORBETELLO

Albergo Piccolo Parigi (☎ 0564 867 23 33; fax 0564 86 72 11; Corso Italia 169; d €62) If you don't mind the extra exercise on the stairs, this is a friendly well-run hotel with plain rooms that won't bust the budget. It's at the quiet end of town but near enough to the action.

Hotel Sole (☎ 0564 86 04 10; Via Colombo; d €80) This slightly scuffed older hotel has rusty orange (sorry, ochre) exterior and good-sized rooms. Its location is superb, near cafés, bars and the charmingly historic Piazza Groe dei due Mondi.

PORTO SANTO STEFANO

Pensione Weekend (☎ /fax 0564 81 25 80; www.pensioneweekend.it – Italian only; Via Martiri d'Ungheria 3; d from €55) This fine hotel, poised on a hill going out of town, is one of your best bets. The rooms don't exactly sparkle but they are airy, comfortable and have a lot of character. The owner is warm, welcoming and speaks enough languages to satisfy most people. Ask for the discount deals at local restaurants.

Hotel La Caletta (☎ 0564 81 29 39; caletta@nevib.it; Via del Fortino 51; s/d €84/96; P ❄) The private sandy beach is a welcome perk at this three-star hotel. Floral and white decor may be a bit girly for some but, overall, this is a fair-priced place in a choice location.

Torre di Cala Piccola (☎ 0564 82 51 11; www.torredicalapiccola.com; Località Cala Piccola; s/d €201/268; P ❄) For splendid isolation and good views over the sea, fatten your credit card and head for this place, out on the Via Panoramica. The dining setting in the gardens is particularly glorious on a sunny day.

Another good mid-range choice is **Albergo Belvedere** (☎ 0564 8126 34; Via Fortino 51) on the approach to town.

PORTO ERCOLE

Feniglia (☎ 0564 83 10 90; fax 0564 86 71 75; on the northern fringe at Feniglia beach; adult/tent €8/10.75) If you want to camp, this is the best choice; it has all the amenities you need.

Eating

The peninsula is full of its fair share of restaurants and, unsurprisingly, seafood is the staple.

ORBETELLO

Osteria del Lupacante (☎ 0564 86 76 18; Corso Italia 103; mains €9-13; ⏰ closed Tue) This restaurant is Sicilian-run, with imaginative and spicy dishes. The *spaghetti alla messinese* (Messina style) comes with swordfish meat, tomato, peppers, sunflower seeds and spices. The chef is admirably versatile and you can also find reasonably authentic paella on the menu.

Osteria il Nocchino (☎ 0564 86 03 29; Via dei Mille 64; mains €10-12; ⏰ closed Wed) This is another excellent choice, albeit with about as much seating capacity as a glorified matchbox (in summer there's outdoor seating). Prices are moderate and the food is like mamma used to make.

PORTO SANTO STEFANO

Il Veliero (☎ 0564 81 22 26; Via Panoramica 149; menu degustativo €40; ⏰ closed Mon) Expect to find fresh fish on the menu every day here – the owner's father runs a local fish shop. If that doesn't tempt you to tackle the steep climb to Via Panoramica, then the restaurant's outdoor seating with views should. The *scampi flambati al cognac* (prawns flambé) comes highly recommended.

Trattoria La Locandina (☎ 0564 81 44 57; Via del Molo 25; mains €12-15; ✆ closed Mon) This semi-smart place serves predictably fishy fare on the waterfront. Goodies on the menu include seafood kebabs with crayfish, penne with crab sauce and squid risotto.

Lo Sfizio (☎ 0564 81 99 52; Corso Umberto I 26; mains €12) Another good bet on the waterfront is this restaurant. You can have pasta, pizza, or seafood such as *sauté di cozze e vongole veraci* (sautéed mussels and clams).

PORTO ERCOLE
Gatto e la Volpe (☎ 0564 83 52 05; Via dei Cannoni 3; mains €20; ✆ closed Wed) Sweeping down the road to the harbour, this restaurant is a brake-squealing stop on the right. The harbour views are wonderful. Try the speciality *linguine all'astice* (lobster in aspic), leaving room for the home-made desserts.

Getting There & Around
Rama buses connect most towns on the Monte Argentario with Orbetello (coinciding with train arrivals) and Grosseto. By car, follow the signs to Monte Argentario from the SS1, which connects Grosseto to Rome.

THE ISLANDS
More than a few locals skip Monte Argentario altogether and choose to head off on excursions to one of two islands off the coast. The islands of Giglio and Giannutri are both part of the **Parco Nazionale dell'Arcipelago Toscano**.

Giannutri
This tiny island, just 5km long, has a grand old ruin of a Roman Villa (1st century AD) but not much else, aside from a pleasant shady bay, Cala Spalmatoio, on the eastern side.

Giglio
The hilly island of Giglio lies 14km off Monte Argentario. Regular boat services from Porto Santo Stefano make getting to this pretty little spot easy. You arrive at colourful Giglio Porto, once a Roman port and now the best spot to find accommodation. A local bus service will take you 6km to the inland fastness of Giglio Castello, dominated by a Pisan castle.

Aside from a couple of patches of sand the size of a beach towel, the only beaches are on the western side of the island, in and around

the modern resort of Giglio Campese built around the old watch tower.

Toremar (☎ 0564 81 08 03) and **Maregiglio** (☎ 0564 81 29 20) run around three to four daily ferries to the island during the summer and less frequently in winter. The one-way trip costs €5.20 Monday to Friday and €6.20 Saturday and Sunday.

LAGO DI BURANO
Little more than 10km further east along the coast, and about 5km short of the regional frontier with Lazio, this saltwater flat has since 1980 been a nature reserve run by the World Wide Fund for Nature (WWF) – the **Riserva Naturale Lago di Burano** (☎ 0564 89 88 29; Capalbio Scalo; €5.15; guided visits 10am & 2.30pm Sun Sep-Apr). Covering 410 hectares, it is typical of the Maremma in its flora, but interesting above all for its migratory birdlife. Tens of thousands of birds of many species winter here, including several kinds of duck and even falcons. Among the animals, the most precious is the beaver. A path dotted with seven observation points winds its way through the park.

To get here you take the Capalbio Scalo exit from the SS1 (some trains stop at the station here, too).

INLAND & ETRUSCAN SITES
The deep south of Tuscany is home to thermal springs, medieval hill towns and Etruscan archaeological finds.

Magliano & Scansano
From **Albinia**, at the northern tip of the Orbetello lagoon, take the SS74 in the direction of Manciano and make a detour up the SS323.

The first stop is **Magliano in Toscana**, impressive above all for its largely intact city walls. Some date from the 14th century, while most were raised by Siena in the 16th century. The town is a little scrappy on the inside.

Lunch at **Antica Trattoria Aurora** (☎ 0564 59 20 30; Via Chiasso Lavagnini 12/14; mains €12; ✆ Thu-Tue) is a good idea, but its pretty sheltered garden is only open for dinner. Cutting-edge menu concepts include *cinghiale al finocchio sevatico* (wild boar tortellini with wild fennel).

A few buses connect with Grosseto, Scansano and Orbetello. Next, proceed up to **Scansano**. Although there are no monuments of great importance, the old centre is a pleasure to wander around, all narrow lanes and archways with some great views over the surrounding countryside.

Montemerano, Saturnia & Manciano

Heading towards Manciano, you first hit the small walled medieval town of **Montemerano**. Pick up a bottle of local wine at **La Vecchia Dispensa** (Via Italia 31) then visit the town's Chiesa di San Giorgio, decorated with 15th-century frescoes of the Sienese school. Finally, stroll up to the Piazza del Castello for one of the best camera shots of your travels. There are some exceptional *agriturismo* places in the surrounding valleys.

Le Fontanelle (☎ 0564 60 27 62; Poderi di Montemerano; d €73) is a wonderful place with cabinlike accommodation, a large pond, plenty of shady trees and even some deer. Daughter Daniella is a sparkling hostess for the evening meals which cost an extra €19 but are worth the splurge for the chance to practise your Italian with the other guests.

From here it's 6km to **Saturnia** and its sulphur spring and thermal baths at **Terme di Saturnia**, just outside the village. Bring along a bathing costume and towel for a restorative dip. You can either fork out for the high-tech private spa with all the services typical of such establishments (from €14 for the privilege) or go for a free hot (but crowded) shower under the sulphurous waterfall and a dip in its hot pools where the temperature remains a constant 37.5°C.

Saturnia's Etruscan remains, including part of the town wall, are worth a diversion if you are into that sort of thing. A tomb at **Sede di Carlo**, just northeast of the town, is one of the area's best preserved.

Getting here by bus is a real hassle and virtually impossible on our route, as about the only service is by the occasional bus running between Grosseto and Pitigliano. Many hitchhike from Montemerano.

Manciano is another former Sienese fortress and could end up being a compulsory transport stop on your travels around here. Apart from the much-interfered with Rocca (the Fortress), there is not much to keep you.

Pitigliano

From Manciano head east along the SS74 for Pitigliano. The visual impact of this town of just 4,300 inhabitants is hard to forget. It seems to grow organically out of a high

---

DETOUR: MONTE ARGENTARIO TO MANCIANO

Travelling from Monte Argentario to Manciano, turn right after 18.8km at the Vallerana sign. Turn left at 1.4km, in the direction of Pitardi. You'll pass vineyards on your left as the road continues through seamless rolling countryside with the town of Manciano straddled on a hilltop in the distance. At 3.2km, turn into the farm on your left (look for the *vendita vino-olio* sign) and ask for Renalto, the farmer, who has excellent olive oil, and red and white wine for sale. After you have made your purchases, turn left out of the gate and continue past a pastoral scene of fields of cows and sheep. Turn left at 3.9km then, at 8.3km, rejoin the main road to Manciano happily weighed down with vino.

---

volcanic rocky outcrop that towers over the surrounding country. The gorges that surround the town on three sides constitute a natural bastion, completed to the east by the man-made fort.

Originally built by the Etruscans, the town remained beyond the orbit of the great Tuscan city states, such as Florence and Siena, until it was finally absorbed into the grand duchy under Cosimo I de' Medici.

In the course of the 15th century, a Jewish community settled here, increasing notably when Pope Pius IV banned Jews from Rome in 1569. They moved into a tiny ghetto, where they remained until 1772. From then until well into the following century, the local community of 400 flourished and Pitigliano was dubbed Little Jerusalem. By the time the Fascists introduced their race laws in 1938, most Jews had moved away (only 80 or so were left; precious few survived the war).

INFORMATION
The main **tourist office** (☎ 0564 6 71 11; Piazza Giribaldi 51; ☼ 9.30am-1pm & 3-7pm May-Sep, to 6pm rest of year) has lots of information.

SIGHTS
Apart from the spectacle of viewing the town from the Manciano approach road (arrive at night and you see it lit up – quite breathtaking), it is a joy to wander around

the narrow lanes. Perched on a sharp out-crop surrounded by gorges, the place feels like it could have inspired Escher. Twist-ing stairways disappear around corners, cobbled alleys bend out of sight beneath arches and the stone houses seem to have been piled up one on top of the other by a drunk giant playing with building blocks.

As you enter the town, the first intriguing sight is the aqueduct, built in the 16th cen-tury. Keeping watch over the interlocking Piazza Garibaldi and Piazza Petruccioli is the 13th-century **Palazzo Orsini** (☎ 0564 61 44 19; €3; ☒ 10am-1pm & 5-7pm (8pm Aug) Tue-Sun Apr-Sep, 10am-1pm & 3-5pm Tue-Sun Oct-Mar). Eight-een of its rooms are open to the public, decked out with sacred art, including two works by Francesco Zuccarelli, who was born here. Much of what you see was built over the following centuries. Now seat of the local bishopric, it is a true citadel, a city within a city – fortress, residence and supply dump.

In a separate area of the palace you'll find the **Museo Archeologico** (☎ 0564 61 40 67; Piazza della Fortezza; adult/child €2.60/1.55; ☒ 10am-1pm & 4-7pm Tue-Sun Apr-Sep, 10am-1pm & 3-6pm Tue-Sun Oct-Mar), with an instructive display rather than just the usual glass containers full of all sorts of unexplained ancient odds and sods. In the cellars of the palace is the **Museo della Civilta Giubonnai** (☎ 3477 2 89 65; ☒ only groups of 8 or more with advance reservation) dedicated to agricultural equipment specific to the Maremma.

If you wander down Via Zuccarelli deep into the town, you will see a sign pointing left to the **La Piccola Jerusalemme** (☎ 0564 61 60 06; Vicolo Manin 30; adult/child €2.50/1.50; ☒ 10am-12.30pm & 4-7pm Tue-Sun Jun-Sep, 10am-12.30pm & 3-7pm Tue-Sun Oct-May), at the heart of the town's once-busy little ghetto. It had largely gone to seed until 1995, when it was restored using old photos and other material to reconstruct it. Of particular interest is the museum of Jewish culture dating from 1598 with its ko-sher butcher and original matzo bakery, last used in 1939. You can also visit the Jewish cemetery by appointment.

The town's **cathedral** dates back to the Middle Ages but its facade is Baroque and its interior has been modernised. Older is the oddly shaped **Chiesa di Santa Maria**.

The local drop, Bianco di Pitigliano, is a lively dry white wine of DOC calibre (see p58 for details on wine classification). The

shops lining Via San Chiara, off Piazza Petruccioli, are good places to get some.

SLEEPING & EATING
Several *affittacamere* (rooms for rent) oper-ate in and around town; information is avail-able from the tourist office or look for signs.

Hotel Valle Orientina (☎ 0564 61 66 11; www .valleorientina.it; Località Valle Orientina; s/d €55/90) In lovely pastoral surroundings, this is a real kick-back place with its very own 7th-century thermal baths, plus pool, tennis courts and archery for the movers and shakers.

Osteria Il Tufo Allegro (☎ 0564 61 61 92; Vico della Costituzione 2, just off Via Zuccarelli; mains from €12; ☒ closed Tue) This is definitely the place to eat. The service and food are superb but the seating limited, so book ahead.

ENTERTAINMENT
Jerry Lee Bar (☎ 0564 61 60 66; Via Roma 28; ☒ closed Mon; ☒ €3/30 mins) This is the best place to catch any nightlife in town. There's a young vibe and occasional live music.

Il Ghetto (Via Zuccarelli 47) This smart new flagstone and brick wine bar has cheese and salami tapas to accompany that favourite tipple.

GETTING THERE & AWAY
Rama buses stop just outside Piazza Petru-ccioli, on Via San Chiara. Up to five buses a day run to Grosseto (€5) via Manciano Monday to Saturday, but no buses run on Sunday. Quite a few buses run to Sorano, while only two go to Sovana (none on Sun-day). To get to Saturnia you need to change at Manciano. Enquire at the terminal in ad-vance to make sure of the connections.

Sovana
This pretty little village has more than its fair share of important Etruscan sites and historical monuments. There is an **informa-tion office** (☎ 0564 61 40 74; Palazzo Pretorio, Piazza del Pretorio; ☒ 9am-1pm & 3-8pm daily Jul & Aug, to 7pm rest of year, Fri-Sun only Nov-Feb) here.

If you plan to visit all the archaeological sites in and around Sovana and Sorano, it's worth purchasing a €6.50 combined ticket. This allows entry to Tomba della Sirena and Tomba di Ildebranda, the Fortezza Orsini in Sorano, the Necropoli di San Rocco, and the Vitozza rock caves outside San Quirico. Tickets can be purchased at any of the sites.

VIE CAVE

There are at least 15 rock-sculpted passages spreading out in every direction from the valleys below Pitigliano. These sunken roads *(vie cave)* are enormous, up to 20m deep and 3m wide, and believed to be sacred routes linking the *necropoli* and other sites associated with the Etruscan religious cult. A less popular, more mundane explanation is that these strange megalithic corridors were used to move livestock or as some kind of defence, allowing people to move from village to village unseen. Whatever the reason, every spring on the night of the equinox (19 March) there is a torchlit procession down the Via Cava di Giuseppe which culminates in a huge bonfire in the Piazza Garibaldi (Pitigliano), as a symbol of purification and renewal marking the end of winter.

The countryside around Pitigliano, Sovana and Sorano is riddled with *vie cave* and they make great excursions from any of the towns. Two particularly good examples, half a kilometre west of Pitigliano on the road to Sovana, are Via Cava di Fratenuti, with high vertical walls and Etruscan graffiti, and Via Cava di San Giuseppe, which passes the Fontana dell'Olmo. This fountain is carved out of solid rock with the sculpted head of Bacchus, the mythological god of fruitfulness, from whose mouth water flows. Via Cava San Rocco is another fine example, near Sorano. It winds its way through the hills for 2km between the town and the Necropoli di San Rocco.

Pope Gregory VII was born here. Medieval mansions and the remains of a fortress belonging to his family are at the eastern end of the town, where you enter. Proceed west along the main street (this is essentially a one-street town) and you emerge into the broad Piazza del Pretorio. Here the **Chiesa di Santa Maria** (Piazza del Pretorio; 🕑 10am-1pm & 2.30pm-7pm May-Sep, to 6pm Oct-Apr, Sat & Sun only Jan) is a starkly simple Romanesque church (although interfered with in parts in later centuries) featuring a magnificent 9th-century ciborium in white marble, one of the last remaining pre-Romanesque works left in Tuscany. It is a highly curious piece of work placed over the altar. The church also contains some frescoes from the early 16th-century.

Walk along the Via del Duomo to reach the imposing Gothic-Romanesque **cathedral** (☎ 0564 61 65 32; same opening times as Chiesa di Santa Maria), at the far-western end of the town. The original construction dates back to the 9th century.

A couple of kilometres out of town proceeding west along the road to Saturnia you come to a series of **archaeological sites** (€5.50 for both sites; 🕑 9am-7pm Mar-Oct, 9am-6pm Fri-Sun Nov-Feb). Look for the yellow sign on the left for the **Tomba della Sirena**. At the first site you can follow a trail running alongside a series of monumental tomb facades cut from the rock face, as well as walk along a *via cava*.

The second site, 300m further west along the same road, is dominated by the **Tomba di Ildebranda**, by far the grandest of Etruscan tombs, and still preserving traces of the columns and stairs that made up this resting place. Due east just outside the tiny hamlet of San Quirico and signposted from the main square, are the **Vitozza rock caves** (€2; 🕑 9am-7pm Mar-Oct, 9am-6pm Fri-Sun Nov-Feb) situated along a high rock ridge. There are more than 200 caves. This is one of the largest rock dwellings in Italy, first inhabited in prehistoric times when wooden posts were embedded in holes cut in the rock for foundations.

SLEEPING & EATING

Taverna Etrusca (☎ 0564 61 61 83; fax 0564 614193; Piazza Pretorio 16; s/d €49/80) If you'd like to stay in Sovana, try this place. Its fine **restaurant** (mains around €13; 🕑 closed Mon) serves typical Maremma cuisine.

Scilla (☎ 0564 61 65 31; www.scilla-sovana.it; Via Siviero 1/3; s/d €63/92; 🅿 ✸) There is an uncluttered elegance about this choice hotel. The eight terracotta-and-white rooms have marshmallow soft pillows. Scilla also boasts a classy glassed-in **restaurant** (closed Tuesday) with well-priced set menus (€26), including vegetarian and fish options.

Sorano

From Sovana, go back and pass the turnoff for Pitigliano to proceed northeast to Sorano. Two kilometres before you arrive at the village are the **Necropoli di San Rocco** (€2; 🕑 9am-7pm Mar-Oct, Fri-Sun only Nov-Feb), another Etruscan burial site. From here you can proceed on foot to Sorano through a *via cava*.

High on a rocky spur, the small medieval town of Sorano has largely retained its original form. Its houses seem to huddle together in an effort not to shove one another off their precarious perch. Many of the backstreets in the town's medieval heart are rather forlorn and only inhabited by our feline friends. There's a small **tourist office** (☎ 0546 63 30 99) on Piazza Busati.

The town's main attraction is the partly renovated **Fortezza Orsini** (☎ 0564 63 37 67; admission €2, guided tours €3 only at 11am & 5pm, in English by prior arrangement; ☽ 9am-1pm & 3-7pm Mar-Oct, Fri-Sun only Nov-Feb), with its museum devoted to the medieval era.

You could also climb up **Masso Leopoldino** (€2; ☽ 10am-1pm & 3-7pm Apr-Nov), a large platform at the top of the village, for absolutely spectacular views of the surrounding countryside.

SLEEPING & EATING

Hotel della Fortezza (☎ 0564 63 20 10; www.fortezza hotel.it; Piazza Cairoli; s/d €72/123; ☒) If you like the fortress so much that you want to stay there, you can. It has a heady historical feel with wood-beamed ceilings and tapestries, as well as fantastic views.

Talismano (☎ 0564 63 32 81; Via San Marco 29; mains €5-7; ☽ closed Tue) This cavernous place comes highly recommended by locals. The menu has an excellent selection of pizzas and Tuscan dishes, so you'll be hard-pressed not to find something to your liking.

Eastern Tuscany

An easy train ride from Florence puts the capital of this region, Arezzo, within tempting reach even of many fleeting tourists in Tuscany, but relatively few get beyond this former Etruscan city. The old centre, dominated by one of the most inspiring examples of Tuscan Romanesque construction, has more than enough to warrant a day trip or weekend stopover, while the city also makes an excellent base for exploring the surrounding countryside. Another popular destination is Cortona, the spectacularly located hilltop eyrie that looks out over the surrounding Tuscan and Umbrian plains.

Art lovers will no doubt be attracted by the Piero della Francesca trail. Starting with his fresco cycles in Arezzo itself, you can head out into the country in search of his other masterpieces in towns such as Monterchi and Sansepolcro.

Beyond the towns, one of the least-visited corners of Tuscany is the hill country of the Casentino on the frontier with the region of Emilia-Romagna, a lush forested landscape dotted with castles and monasteries.

HIGHLIGHTS

- Join in the medieval fun of the Giostra del Saracino in Arezzo's Piazza Grande (pp243-4)
- Gaze in awe at Piero della Francesca's magnificent fresco cycle in the Chiesa di San Francesco, Arezzo (p241)
- Explore the back roads of the little-visited Casentino region (pp246-8)
- Follow the Piero della Francesca trail from Arezzo to Sansepolcro (p245)
- Discover the Etruscan heritage of Cortona and enjoy the splendid views across the Tuscan and Umbrian countryside (pp248-50)

EASTERN TUSCANY

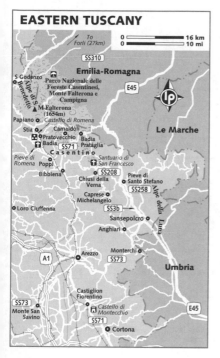

AREZZO
pop 91,400

Arezzo was heavily bombed during WWII, and while the modern part of town may not provide the most inspiring urban landscape in Tuscany, the small medieval centre retains some real character and a number of rewarding highlights. The best known is the fresco cycle by Piero della Francesca in the Chiesa di San Francesco, while the charming Piazza Grande and the Romanesque jewel that is the Pieve di Santa Maria are also worth seeking out. The pedestrianised, shop-lined Corso Italia is Arezzo's main promenade where locals gather each evening to stroll, chat, eat *gelato* and generally pass the time.

An important Etruscan town, Arezzo was later absorbed into the Roman Empire, remaining an important and flourishing centre of trade. It became a free republic from the 10th century and supported the Ghibelline cause in the prolonged and bloody conflict between pope and emperor. Arezzo eventually lost its independence in 1384, when it was effectively bought by Guelph Florence.

Sons of whom Arezzo can be justly proud include the poet Petrarch, the artist Vasari, most famous for his book *Lives of the Artists*, and comic actor and producer Roberto Benigni, who created and starred in the Oscar-winning *Life is Beautiful* – locations used in the film are marked by signboards featuring stills and dialogue in Italian and English.

Orientation
From the train station on the southern edge of the walled town, walk northeastwards along Via Guido Monaco to the piazza of the same name. The old city is to the northeast and the modern part to the southeast along Via Roma.

Information
Hospital (☎ 0575 3051; Via Paolo Toscanelli) Nuovo Ospedale San Donato
Police Station (☎ 0575 3181; Via Fra Guittone 3)
Post Office (Via Guido Monaco 34)
Tourist Office (☎ 0575 37 76 78; Piazza della Repubblica 28; ☺ 9am-1pm & 3-7pm Mon-Sat, 9am-1pm Sun Apr-Oct, 9am-1pm & 3-6.30pm Mon-Sat Nov-Mar)

Chiesa di San Francesco
The apse of this 14th-century **Gothic church** (☎ 0575 35 27 27; Piazza San Francesco; ☺ 8.30am-noon & 2-7pm) houses one of the greatest works of Italian art, Piero della Francesca's fresco cycle of the *Leggenda della Vera Croce* (Legend of the True Cross, 1452–56). This masterpiece relates in 10 episodes the story of the cross upon which Christ was crucified. Its 15-year restoration was finally completed in 2000.

The illustration of the medieval legend begins in the top right-hand corner and follows the story of the tree that Seth plants on the grave of his father, Adam, and from which, eventually, the True Cross is made. A scene on the opposite wall shows the cross being discovered by Helena, mother of the emperor Constantine; behind her, the city of Jerusalem is represented by a medieval view of Arezzo.

The chapel of the cross is cordoned off, so if you want a closer view you need to purchase a ticket (€5.10). Viewing times are 9am to 6pm Monday to Friday, 9am to 5.30pm on Saturday and 1pm to 5.30pm on Sunday. A half-hour audio-guide tour is included in the price. The ticket office is to the right of the main entrance to the church,

AREZZO

0 —————— 200 m
0 —————— 0.1 mi

A | **B** | **C** | **D**

INFORMATION
Tourist Office.................................1 A5

SIGHTS & ACTIVITIES   pp241-4
Casa di Petrarca............................2 C4
Casa Museo di Ivan Bruschi..........3 C4
Cathedral......................................4 C3
Chiesa di San Bernardo.................5 B6
Chiesa di San Domenico...............6 C3
Chiesa di San Francesco...............7 B4
Fortezza Medicea..........................8 D4
Museo Archeologico.....................9 B5
Museo di Casa Vasari..................10 B3

Museo Statale d'Arte Medioevale
   e Moderna...............................11 B3
Palazzo dei Priori........................12 B3
Palazzo della Fraternità dei Laici.....13 C4
Palazzo delle Logge Vasariane......14 C4
Pieve di Santa Maria...................15 C4
Roman Amphitheatre...................16 B6

SLEEPING   p244
Hotel Continentale......................17 A5
Hotel Europa...............................18 A5
Hotel I Portici.............................19 B5
Il Patio.......................................20 B4

EATING   pp244-5
I Tre Bicchieri.............................21 B5
La Torre di Gnicche.....................22 C4
La Tua Piadina............................23 B5
Lancia dell'Oro...........................24 C4
Trattoria Il Saraceno...................25 C4

DRINKING   p245
Al Canto de'Bacci.......................26 C4
Crispi's.......................................27 B5
Vita Bella...................................28 B4

TRANSPORT   p245
Bus Station................................29 A5
Bus Ticket Office........................30 A5

and at busy times such as the summer season it is suggested to make reservations in advance (☎ 0575 90 04 04) though you can usually walk straight in. Combined tickets (€10), which include the frescoes, plus the Museo Archeologico, Museo Statale d'Arte Medioevale e Moderna and Museo di Casa Vasari, are also on sale.

Pieve di Santa Maria & Around

This 12th-century **church** (☎ 0575 295254; Corso Italia; ♥ 8am-1pm & 3-7pm) has a magnificent Romanesque arcaded facade reminiscent of the cathedral at Pisa. Each column is of a different design. The 14th-century bell tower, with its 40 windows, is something of an emblem for the city, though the interior is rather stark – the only colour comes from the polyptych (1324) by Pietro Lorenzetti on the raised sanctuary at the rear of the church.

Below the altar is a 14th-century silver bust reliquary of the city's patron saint, San Donato, while other treasures on display include a 13th-century Crucifix by Margherito di Arezzo and a carved marble bas-relief of the *Adoration of the Magi* from the same period.

Opposite the church is the **Casa Museo di Ivan Bruschi** (☎ 0575 90 04 04; Corso Italia 14; admission €4; ♥ 10am-1pm & 2-6pm Tue-Sun) where you can cast an eye over the varied collection of art and antiques amassed by the man who founded the Arezzo antiques fair.

Piazza Grande & Around

This cobbled sloping piazza, the venue for the Giostra del Saracino (see the boxed text p244), is lined at its upper end by the porticoes of the **Palazzo delle Logge Vasariane**, completed in 1573. The **Palazzo della Fraternità dei Laici** on the western flank dates from 1375. It was started in the Gothic style and finished after the onset of the Renaissance. The southeastern flank of the square is lined by a huddle of medieval houses.

Via dei Pileati leads to **Casa di Petrarca**, the former home of the poet, which contains a small museum and the Accademia Petrarca. Visits are by appointment and really only for serious Petrarch fans. Enquire at the tourist office for further details.

Cathedral & Around

At the top of the hill is the **cathedral** (☎ 0575 2 39 91; Via Ricasoli; ♥ 7am-12.30pm & 3-6.30pm), built

between the 13th and 15th centuries. The Gothic interior houses several artworks of note, the most important being the fresco of the *Maddalena* (Mary Magdalene) by Piero della Francesca. Off to the left, the Capella della Madonna del Conforto is adorned with a number of fine glazed terracotta images from the della Robbia workshop. Also in the cathedral is the tomb of Pope Gregory X, who died in Arezzo in 1276.

To the southeast of the cathedral, across the peaceful English-style gardens of the **Passeggio del Prato**, stands the **Fortezza Medicea** (free; ♥ 7am-8pm Apr-Oct, 7.30am-6pm Nov-Mar), completed in 1560. The grand views of the town and surrounding countryside are best at sunset.

Chiesa di San Domenico & Around

It's worth walking to **Chiesa di San Domenico** (☎ 0575 2 29 06; Piazza di San Domenico; ♥ 8.30am-1pm & 3.30-7pm), with its unusual, asymmetrical facade, to see the Crucifix painted by Cimabue between 1265 and 1270, which hangs above the main altar. It was replaced in January 2002 after restoration. Cimabue's other Crucifix, in Florence's Santa Croce, was badly damaged in the 1966 floods and is in a much poorer state of preservation. Other points of interest include frescoes by Spinello Aretino (1350–1410) and a della Robbia statue of San Antonio.

West of San Domenico, the **Museo di Casa Vasari** (☎ 0575 40 90 40; Via XX Settembre 55; admission €2; ♥ 9am-7pm Wed-Mon, 9am-1pm Sat & Sun) was built and sumptuously decorated by the man himself.

Further west again, the **Museo Statale d'Arte Medioevale e Moderna** (☎ 0575 409050; Via di San Lorentino 8; admission €4; ♥ 9am-7pm Tue-Sun, 9am-1pm Sat & Sun) houses works by local artists, including Luca Signorelli and Vasari. The small gallery on the ground floor mostly contains sculptures from local churches, while on the first floor is a display of medieval paintings, including works by Neri di Bicci and Domenico Peccori, a collection of glazed terracotta pieces by the della Robbia family, and colourful majolica plates. Upstairs, the art continues into the 19th century.

Museo Archeologico & Roman Amphitheatre

The **archaeological museum** (☎ 0575 2 08 82; Via Margaritone 10; admission €4; ♥ 8.30am-7.30pm) is in

THE GIOSTRA DEL SARACINO

With origins going back to the time of the Crusades, the 'Joust of the Saracen' is one of those grand, noisy affairs involving extravagant fancy dress and neighbourhood rivalry that Italians delight in. The tournament was revived in its present form only in 1931 after long neglect. The day begins with a proclamation being read by a herald, followed by a procession of 311 people in 14th-century dress and 31 horses. Those taking part in the joust are then blessed on the steps of the cathedral by the Bishop of Arezzo. It's the highlight of the year for the four Quartieri (Quarters) of the city, which each put forward a team of knights armed with lances. The 'knights' try their hand jousting at a wooden effigy in the Piazza Grande, known as the 'Buratto', representing a Saracen warrior. In one hand the Buratto holds a shield, etched with various point-scores, which the knights aim for while trying to avoid being belted with the *mazzafrustro* – basically three heavy leather balls on ropes – which dangles from the Buratto's other hand. The winning team takes home the coveted Golden Lance, bringing glory to their Quartiere. In 2003, the honour went to the Quartiere Sant'Andrea; its website (www.portasantandrea.com) gives some interesting information on the joust and the life of the Quartiere in English.

Arezzo's division into Quartieri dates back to the 11th century or even earlier, and there's still a strong sense of neighbourhood pride and loyalty in the city, with heraldic flags fluttering from shops and homes and communal events taking place throughout the year. The Quartieri are named after the four gates of the city and have their own distinctive colours: yellow and blue for Porta San Spirito; white and green for Porta Sant'Andrea; yellow and cerise for Porta del Foro; and green and red for Porta Crucifera. They are the centre of social and cultural life for their inhabitants, and are in many ways like extended families, throwing dinners, running sports events and excursions, and generally fostering community spirit.

a former convent overlooking the remains of the 2nd-century AD Roman amphitheatre, which once seated up to 10,000 spectators. Inside, there's a sizable collection of Etruscan and Roman artefacts, including locally produced ceramics and bronzes. Among the highlights are the Cratere di Euphronios, a large Etruscan vase dating from the 6th century BC and decorated with vivid scenes showing Hercules in battle, and a tiny, and very rare, portrait of a bearded man executed on glass in the 3rd century AD.

Festivals & Events

Over five or six days in late June/early July the town hosts **Arezzo Wave** (www.arezzowave.com - Italian only; free), a music festival featuring artists and bands from Italy and abroad, occasionally including some top international acts.

The **Giostra del Saracino** (Joust of the Saracen; see the boxed text above) takes place on the second-last Sunday of June and again on the first Sunday of September; it's a colourful and exciting time to be in town.

The first Sunday of every month sees the centre of Arezzo converted into one of Tuscany's biggest **antique fairs**, which is well worth checking out.

Sleeping

Il Patio (☎ 0575 40 19 62; fax 0575 2 74 18; Via Cavour 23; s/d/ste from €130/176/224; ✗) This is Arezzo's most characterful hotel with seven 'themed' rooms, each dedicated to one of Bruce Chatwin's travel books. Each has original furnishings from the various countries represented, including Australia, Morocco and China. There's also a good restaurant and a re-creation of a 1930s Chicago bar.

Hotel I Portici (☎ 0575 30 09 34; Via Roma 18; d/ste from €155/260; ✗) This elegant four-star place consists of just eight rooms on the 4th floor of a city-centre apartment block. It offers luxurious, individually designed suites with large bathrooms; some have Jacuzzis.

Hotel Continentale (☎ 0575 2 02 51; www.hotel continentale.com; Piazza Guido Monaco 7; s/d €67/98; ✗ 💻) This modern, central three-star is a decent option, with comfy, spotless rooms, though service is somewhat impersonal.

Hotel Europa (☎ 0575 35 77 01; Via Spinello 43; s/d €52/90) This drab high-rise is in need of modernisation, but it's serviceable and handy for the train and bus stations.

Eating

La Torre di Gnicche (☎ 0575 35 20 35; Piaggia San Martino 8; mains around €6; ✌ closed Wed) Not far off the

Piazza Grande is this fine old *osteria* (restaurant offering local dishes), with fine outdoor seating and a superb wine selection.

Trattoria Il Saraceno (☎ 0575 2 76 44; Via G Mazzini 3a; mains €6.80-35; ☒ closed Wed) This place is recommended by locals for no-nonsense Tuscan food at moderate prices. Pizzas (from €5) are served evenings only.

I Tre Bicchieri (☎ 0575 2 65 57; Piazzetta Sopra I Ponti 3-5; mains €15; ☒ closed Wed) Upscale restaurant in a little square off Corso Italia, serving such dishes as roast quail in chianti, as well as pasta options. It's a nice place for a quiet drink, too.

Lancia d'Oro (☎ 0575 2 10 33; Piazza Grande 18-19; mains around €10.50; ☒ closed Mon & Sun evening) Typical Tuscan cuisine is on the menu at this pleasantly appointed trattoria, under the loggia with commanding views of the piazza.

La Tua Piadina (☎ 0575 2 32 40; Via de' Cenci 18) Very popular takeaway place hidden away down a side-street, where you can get a range of hot, tasty filled sandwiches, from around €3.

Drinking

Crispi's (☎ 0575 2 28 73; Via Francesco Crispi 10/12) For an evening tipple with a young crowd, try this place. There's also a good restaurant (pizzas from around €5.50).

Al Canto de' Bacci (☎ 0575 40 14 40; Logge Vasari 16) A pleasant little wine shop, where you can taste some of the local produce and sit outside, under the loggia.

Vita Bella (☎ 0575 35 37 96; Piazza San Francesco 22) An agreeable place opposite the church, where you can sip a Negroni and watch the world go by.

Getting There & Away

Buses depart from and arrive at Piazza della Repubblica, serving several towns around Tuscany, including Cortona (€2.30, 1 hour), Siena (€4.50, 1½ hours) and Florence (€5.40, 2½ hours). The city is on the Florence (€4.80, 1¼ hours) to Rome train line. The town of Arezzo is a few kilometres east of the A1, and the SS73 heads east to Sansepolcro.

NORTHEAST OF AREZZO

The art lovers' trail in search of masterpieces by Piero della Francesca leads away northeast of Arezzo to the towns of Monterchi and Sansepolcro, both easy day trips from Arezzo.

Monterchi & Anghiari

Visit **Monterchi** to see Piero della Francesca's fresco **Madonna del Parto** (Pregnant Madonna; ☎ 0575 7 07 13; Via della Reglia 1; adult/child under 14/ pregnant women €3.10/free/free; ☒ 9am-1pm & 2-7pm Tue-Sun Apr-Sep, to 6pm Oct-Mar). The Pregnant Madonna is considered one of the key works of 15th-century Italian art and the only such representation known from the period.

A few kilometres north of Monterchi along the way to Sansepolcro lies the pretty medieval village of **Anghiari**, which is worth a brief stop-off just to meander along its narrow twisting lanes. There are a few hotels if you want to stay longer, including **La Meridiana** (☎ 0575 78 81 02; www.hotellameridiana.it; Piazza IV Novembre 8; s/d €34/52).

An infrequent local bus runs the 17km north to **Caprese Michelangelo**, birthplace

---

DETOUR: THE PIERO DELLA FRANCESCA TRAIL

The so-called Piero della Francesca trail is a pleasant if rather circuitous journey into the Valtiberina (High Tiber Valley), one of the least-explored corners of Tuscany. From Arezzo take the SS71 north for about 4km, as far as Ponte alla Chiassa. Turn eastwards, through the hilly countryside of the Alpe di Catenaia, passing through the village of Chiaveretto. Continue onwards to the well-preserved medieval village of Anghiari, which makes a rewarding stopover. From here it's a straight, though not particularly scenic, 6km drive northeastwards to Sansepolcro, where a number of the great artist's works are on show.

Head southwestwards from Sansepolcro along the SS73 and after roughly 12km you will see a sign for the Madonna del Parto (Pregnant Madonna); take the minor road leading east for 3km and then turn south for about 500m and you'll be in Monterchi, home of della Francesca's Madonna del Parto. Retrace your route back to the SS73 and continue westwards back to Arezzo.

John Pope-Hennessy's book *The Piero della Francesca Trail* (1993) is an interesting source of information on the painter and the region.

of the great artist. The town's castle plays host to the **Museo Michelangelo** (☎ 0575 79 37 76; Via Capoluogo 1; adult/child €2.58/1.55; ☯ 9.30am-6.30pm Tue-Sun mid-Jun–Oct, 10am-5pm Nov–mid-Jun), a rather lacklustre affair devoted to the man and his works.

Sansepolcro

Sansepolcro is best known as the birthplace of Piero della Francesca (c.1420–92), though the artist left town when he was quite young and returned only when he was in his seventies to work on his treatises, which included *On Perspective in Painting*. Today, while the surrounding light-industrial sprawl doesn't make for the most picturesque of settings, the town's medieval heart is a pleasant place to wander.

The **tourist office** (☎ 0575 74 05 36; Piazza Garibaldi 2; ☯ 9.30am-1pm & 3.30-7pm) is a useful source of local information.

In the former town hall, just outside the main city gate, the **Museo Civico** (☎ 0575 73 22 18; Via Aggiunti 65; adult/child €6.20/3; ☯ 9am-1.30pm & 2.30-7.30pm Jun-Sep, 9.30am-1pm & 2.30-6pm Oct-May) features a couple of Piero della Francesca's masterpieces. The most famous is the *Resurrezione* (Resurrection), in which the newly risen Christ stares out impassively at the viewer, banner in hand like a triumphant warrior. Other important works by the master include the splendid *Madonna della Misericordia* polyptych, painted between 1455 and 1458 for the charitable Sansepolcro Misericordia brotherhood.

Other local artists represented in the collection include Luca Signorelli and Santi di Tito, whose *Riposa durante la fuga in Egitto* (Rest during the flight into Egypt) shows the Holy Family in a tender and humanistic light.

Upstairs there's a display of 14th- and 15th-century frescoes, including a haunting portrait of St Sebastian, while the basement holds a small gathering of archaeological finds and ecclesiastical knick-knackery.

A little further along is the **Aboca museum** (☎ 0575 73 35 89; Via Aggiunti 75; adult/child €8/4; ☯ 10am-1pm & 3-7pm Tue-Sun Jun-Sep, 10am-1pm & 2.30-6pm Oct-May), housing displays dedicated to the history of pharmacy and herbal medicine and a re-creation of a 17th-century laboratory. Given the high ticket price, it's likely to appeal only to those with a specialist interest in the subject.

Nearby is the **cathedral**, founded in the 11th century. Its most celebrated treasure is the *Volto Santo* (Holy Visage), a striking wooden crucifix with a wide-eyed Christ, dating back to at least the 12th century.

On the second Sunday in September there is a rematch of the **Palio della Balestra**, a crossbow contest between the men of Gubbio and Sansepolcro. The men dress in medieval costume and use antique weapons.

If you wish to stay we recommend these options:

Orfeo (☎ 0575 74 20 61; Viale Armando Diaz 12; s/d €30/50) This decent budget option is just outside the old town's western gate.

Albergo Fiorentino (☎ 0575 74 03 50; fax 0575 74 03 70; Via Luca Pacioli 60; s/d €50/70) This venerable and characterful establishment has neat rooms. Its atmospheric restaurant (mains about €8.50; open Saturday to Thursday) serves traditional Tuscan food such as baked pork with fennel flowers.

SITA buses connect Arezzo with Sansepolcro (€3.10, one hour, hourly), and the town is on the Terni–Perugia train line.

THE CASENTINO REGION

A tour through the remote forest and farming region of Casentino will take you through a little-visited area boasting two of Tuscany's most important monasteries and some wonderful walking in the Parco Nazionale delle Foreste Casentinesi, Monte Falterona e Campigna.

Buses and a private train line from Arezzo make it possible to get around the Casentino region slowly, but having your own transport makes it a whole lot easier.

Pratovecchio & Around

From Arezzo, you can follow the SS71 north as far as Bibbiena. From here you can take the SS310, which goes through Poppi and on to Pratovecchio. The town itself is of minimal interest; the spacious porticoed Piazza Garibaldi is about all there is to it. La Ferroviaria Italiana (LFI) private train line runs through here with regular trains that connect Arezzo (via Bibbiena and Poppi) with Stia.

There's an **information office** (☎ 0575 5 03 01; Via Brochi 7; ☯ 9am-1pm & 3-5pm Mon-Thu, 9am-1pm Fri) for the Parco Nazionale delle Foreste Casentinesi in the centre of town.

Just west of town, follow the brown signs for the **Castello di Romena** and the Romanesque

Pieve di Romena; both are well worth the visit. The only way to get there is by car or your own two feet – a Club Alpino Italiano (CAI) walking trail meanders through the area.

The privately owned **castle** (☎ 0575 58 13 53) houses a small archaeological museum. Erected around AD 1000 on the site of an Etruscan settlement, the castle in its heyday was an enormous complex surrounded by three sets of defensive walls. Supposedly Dante got his inspiration for the Circles of Hell from observing the castle's prison tower. Call ahead for opening times, which are subject to change.

Stia, a couple of kilometres up the road, marks the end of the train line. Like Pratovecchio, there is nothing of extraordinary interest here, although the porticoed central square is pretty.

Parco Nazionale delle Foreste Casentinesi

This national park spreads over both sides of the Tuscany–Emilia-Romagna border, taking in some of the most scenic stretches of the Apennines. The Tuscan half is gentler territory than on the Emilian side.

One of the highest peaks, **Monte Falterona** (1654m) marks the source of the Arno River. The park authorities have laid out nine short nature walks. Apart from the human population, which includes the inhabitants of two monasteries, the park is also home to a rich assortment of wildlife, including foxes, wolves, deer and wild boar, plus around 80 bird species. The dense forests are a cool summer refuge, ideal for walking and also escaping the madding crowds. The Grande Escursione Appenninica (GEA) passes through here, and several other walking paths (such as those marked by the CAI) criss-cross the park area. Approach the park office in Pratovecchio (see p246) for more details.

Camaldoli

A winding hill road sneaks westwards out of Pratovecchio (crossing the train line on the northern side of the station) towards Camaldoli. The drive itself is a pleasure; the lush forest and superb views easily make up for the energy exerted coping with the corners. Where it emerges at a crossroads you are directed left to the **Eremo di Camaldoli** and right to the **Monastero di Camaldoli** (☎ 0575 55 60 12; www.camaldoli.it; 🕙 8.30am-12.30pm & 2.30-6.30pm). Free guided tours are available on request.

According to the story, Conte Maldolo handed the land for this isolated retreat to St Romualdo in 1012. From the name of the count came that of the location, and around 1023 Romualdo set about building the monastery, which became home to the Camaldolesi, an ascetic branch of the Benedictines and a powerful force in medieval Tuscany. Through a fence you can see 20 small tiled houses – they are the cells of the monks who still live here to this day.

Follow the road 3km downhill and you come to the monastery. The monks cultivated the forests that still stand around the monastery and developed all sorts of medicinal and herbal products. You're free to wander about the place, and be sure to take a look inside the **Antica Farmacia** (🕙 9am-12.30pm & 2.30-6pm Thu-Tue). The monks still make all manner of products, including liqueurs, honey, perfumes and chocolate. If it is closed, the bar in the Albergo Camaldoli has some of their products for sale, and they're also available in other towns in the region, including Arezzo.

If you want to stay, the basic **La Foresta** (☎ 0575 55 60 15; Via Camaldoli 5; s/d from €19/31) is just across the road.

Poppi & Bibbiena

Easily the most striking town of the Casentino region is Poppi, perched up on a hill in the Arno plain and topped by the commanding presence of the **Castello dei Conti Guidi** (☎ 0575 52 05 16; Piazza Repubblica 1; adult/child including audio-guide €4/3; 🕙 10am-6pm Jun-Oct), built by the same counts who raised the Castello di Romena. The main attraction is the chapel on the second floor, with frescoes by Taddeo Gaddi. The scene of *Herod's Feast* shows Salome apparently clicking her fingers as she dances, accompanied by a lute player, while John the Baptist's headless corpse lies slumped in the corner. Also of interest is the Sala della Feste, with its restored medieval frescoes. Speculation surrounds the origins of this fortified medieval residence. Vasari attributes it to the father of Arnolfo di Cambio, who subsequently used it as a model for the Palazzo Vecchio in Florence. Others claim Arnolfo built a section of this one here and modelled it on his own work in Florence, but no-one knows for sure.

Should you wish to stay, the **Albergo Casentino** (☎ 0575 52 90 90; www.albergocasentino.it; Piazza della Repubblica 6; s/d €47/62) has pleasant rooms within sight of the castle. There's also a restaurant with a shaded garden.

Poppi is on the LFI train line between Arezzo and Stia. LFI buses also connect with several destinations throughout the province.

The attraction of **Bibbiena** is its transport links to the national park. There are six buses daily to both Camaldoli (€1.60) and Verna (€2.10), both taking around 45 minutes. They generally leave a few minutes after trains pull into the town's station.

Santuario di San Francesco (Verna)

Of more interest than the Camaldoli monastery to many modern pilgrims is this Franciscan monastic complex 23km east of Bibbiena. It marks the southern edge of the national park, 5km uphill from Chiusi della Verna, at a spot called Verna. This is where St Francis of Assisi is said to have received the stigmata and in a sense, this place is closer to the essence of the saint than Assisi itself.

When you enter the complex follow the signs around to the **sanctuary** (☎ 0575 5341; ☼ 6.30am-9pm). You will find yourself first at the Chiesa Maggiore (also known as the Basilica), decorated with some remarkable glazed ceramics by Andrea della Robbia. Also on display are reliquaries containing items associated with the saint, including his walking stick and clothing stained with blood from stigmatic wounds.

By the entrance to the Basilica is the Cappella della Pietà, off which the Corridoio delle Stimmate (with frescoes recounting the saint's life) leads you to the core of the sanctuary – a series of chapels associated with St Francis's life. The masterpiece is the Cappella delle Stimmate, beautifully decorated with terracotta works by Luca and Andrea della Robbia.

Pilgrims can stay in the Foresteria of the monastery. For more information, call the sanctuary.

SOUTH OF AREZZO
Castiglion Fiorentino

If you have time, this commanding hillside village makes an interesting stop-off on the bus route between Arezzo and Cortona.

Fought over throughout the Middle Ages for its strategic position, it finally fell to Florentine rule in 1384.

The main point of interest is the **Pinacoteca** (☎ 0575 65 74 66; Via del Cassero; admission €3; ☼ 10am-12.30pm & 4-6.30pm Tue-Sun), containing medieval paintings, including works by Taddeo Gaddi. Nearby you'll find the **Museo Archeologico** (☎ 0575 65 94 57; Via del Tribunale 8; admission €3, including Pinacoteca €5; ☼ 10am-12.30pm & 4-6.30pm Tue-Sun), housing a small collection of local finds.

A few kilometres further south along the road to Cortona, you can't miss the **Castello di Montecchio**, a formidable redoubt that Florence gave to the English mercenary Sir John Hawkwood (c.1320–94) in return for his military services. You can see the knight's portrait in the Duomo in Florence (see p87). The privately owned castle is presently closed to visitors.

Cortona
pop 22,000

Set into the side of a hill covered with olive groves, Cortona offers stunning views across the Tuscan countryside and has changed little since the Middle Ages. It was a small settlement when the Etruscans moved in during the 8th century BC and it later became a Roman town. In the late 14th century, it attracted the likes of Fra Angelico, who lived and worked in the city for about 10 years. The city is small, easily seen in a few hours, and well worth visiting for the sensational view alone; on clear days you can see as far as Lago di Trasimeno in Umbria.

ORIENTATION & INFORMATION

Buses arrive at Piazza Garibaldi, on the southeastern edge of the walled town, after a long winding climb out of the valley. The square has a car park, and offers some splendid views over the surrounding Tuscan and Umbrian countryside. From the piazza, walk up Via Nazionale to Piazza della Repubblica, the centre of town.

The **tourist office** (☎ 0575 63 03 52; Via Nazionale 42; ☼ 9am-1pm & 3-6pm, to 7pm Jul-Sep) has a few local brochures.

SIGHTS & ACTIVITIES

Start in Piazza della Repubblica with the crenellated **Palazzo Comunale**, which was renovated in the 19th century.

MARTIN MOOS

The thermal waters of **Terme di Saturnia** (p235)

DIANA MAYFIELD

Via Cava (sunken Etruscan pathway) at **San Rocco** (p237)

The town of **Pitigliano** (p235)

DAMIEN SIMONIS

The **Piazza Grande** in Arezzo (p243)

Looking towards the Gothic **Chiesa di San Domenico** in Arezzo (p243)

Chiesa di Santa Margherita in Cortona (p250)

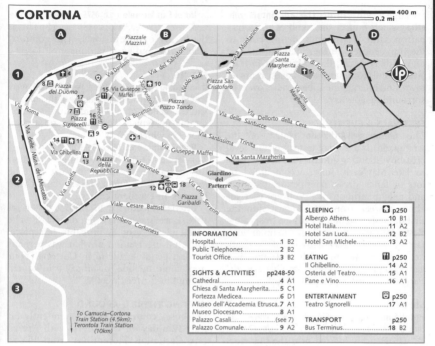

CORTONA

INFORMATION	
Hospital.................................1 B2	
Public Telephones...................2 B2	
Tourist Office.........................3 B2	

SIGHTS & ACTIVITIES	pp248-50
Cathedral...............................4 A1	
Chiesa di Santa Margherita.....5 C1	
Fortezza Medicea....................6 D1	
Museo dell'Accademia Etrusca..7 A1	
Museo Diocesano....................8 A1	
Palazzo Casali.....................(see 7)	
Palazzo Comunale..................9 A2	

SLEEPING	⌂ p250
Albergo Athens.....................10 B1	
Hotel Italia...........................11 A2	
Hotel San Luca.....................12 B2	
Hotel San Michele.................13 A2	

EATING	⊞ p250
Il Ghibellino.........................14 A2	
Osteria del Teatro.................15 A1	
Pane e Vino..........................16 A1	

ENTERTAINMENT	⊡ p250
Teatro Signorelli...................17 A1	

TRANSPORT	p250
Bus Terminus.........................18 B2	

To the north is Piazza Signorelli, named after the artist and dominated by the 13th-century **Palazzo Casali**. Inside is the **Museo dell'Accademia Etrusca** (☎ 0575 63 04 15; Piazza Signorelli 9; admission €4.20; ☼ 10am-7pm Apr-Oct, 10am-5pm Nov-Mar), which displays an eclectic array of art and antiquities, including Etruscan bronzes, medieval paintings and 18th-century furniture. One of the most intriguing pieces is an elaborate 5th-century-BC bronze Etruscan oil lamp decorated with mythological figures, while the Egyptian collection includes remarkably preserved papyri and mummies. There are also paintings by Ghirlandaio and Neri di Bicci, as well as works by the local Futurist painter, Gino Severini. The ornately decorated Medici Room houses a pair of early-18th-century globes, the terrestrial globe showing the *Isola di California* separated from the western coast of America. Upstairs, you can see some of the material excavated from local Etruscan tombs. Guided tours (€7) of the museum, for groups of six or more, leave from the ticket booth at 10.30am, while you can also take a guided tour (€10.50, reserve

a day in advance) of three Etruscan tombs in the surrounding countryside.

The **cathedral** in Piazza del Duomo, northwest of Piazza Signorelli, is largely 18th century and houses an array of workmanlike paintings. Opposite, in the former church of Gesù, is the **Museo Diocesano** (☎ 0575 6 28 30; Piazza Duomo 1; adult/child €5/3; ☼ 10am-7pm Apr-Oct; 10am-5pm Nov-Mar) housing a small but important collection of artworks. Room 1 houses a remarkable Roman sarcophagus decorated with a frenzied battle scene between Dionysus and the Amazons. Also here are a number of paintings by Luca Signorelli, continuing into the adjoining Room 4. His *Compianto sul Cristo Morto* (Grief over the Dead Christ, 1502) is the most arresting. The star work of the collection is found in Room 3. Fra Angelico's *Annunciazione* (1436) is one of the most recognizable images of Renaissance art, and by its sheer luminosity leaves all the surrounding works in the shade. Downstairs, the Oratorio is decorated with Biblical frescoes by Vasari's workshop.

The eastern part of town is a sleepy warren of steep cobbled lanes, where you'll find the largely 19th-century **Chiesa di Santa Margherita**, which houses the tomb of Cortona's patron saint, Margherita, dating back to the 14th century. Further uphill, at the end of Via di Fortezza, the forbidding **Fortezza Medicea** still dominates the highest point in town, and offers some superb views over the surrounding country.

FESTIVALS & EVENTS
The **Giostra dell'Archidado** (Joust of the Archidado) is a 10-day festival of medieval crossbow shooting and theatre, taking place in late May/early June, accompanied by lots of fancy dress, trumpeting, parading and neighbourhood rivalry. Every year for about a week from late August into the first days of September, Cortona hosts a big **Mostra Antiquaria**, one of Italy's main antique fairs. The **Sagra della Bistecca** (Steak Festival), held on the 14th and 15th of August, is a gastronomic celebration, with Giardino del Parterre becoming an open-air grill.

SLEEPING
Hotel San Luca (☎ 0575 63 04 60; www.sanluca cortona.com/english; Piazza Garibaldi 1; s/d €70/100; ✗ 🖳) Handily located near the bus stop, this pleasant, modern hotel has spacious rooms, some with great panoramic views. There's a restaurant attached.

Albergo Athens (☎ 0575 63 05 08; fax 0575 60 44 57; Via Sant'Antonio 12; s/d €29/42) A decent cheap option, if you don't mind the hike up the very steep hill. Rooms are simple, some with commanding views. Those without a private bathroom are slightly cheaper.

Hotel Italia (☎ 0575 63 02 54; fax 0575 60 57 83; Via Ghibellina 5; s/d €70/97; ✗) Rooms at this old mansion, just off Piazza della Repubblica, are neat and comfortable and there's a restaurant onsite.

Hotel San Michele (☎ 0575 60 43 48; www.hotel sanmichele.net; Via Guelfa 15; s/d €83/150; ✗) This is the luxury option in town, with comfortable rooms and guest parking.

EATING
Il Ghibellino (☎ 0575 63 02 54; Via Ghibellina 9; mains from €6.20) Atmospheric place in the barrel-vaulted cellar of a 17th-century *palazzo*, serving up typical Tuscan fare and a good choice of wines.

Pane e Vino (☎ 0575 63 10 10; Piazza Signorelli 27; mains around €20) This is a hugely popular dining hall in the heart of Cortona. The *lambatine di cinghiale brasato* (cured wild boar) is an excellent choice.

Osteria del Teatro (☎ 0575 63 05 56; Via Giuseppe Maffei 2; meals around €25; ✓ closed Wed) The nicest of the crop is probably this place, the latest incarnation of what was perhaps the last genuine *osteria* in Cortona. Your meal could include *ravioli ai fiori di zucca* (pumpkin-flower ravioli).

GETTING THERE & AROUND
LFI buses connect Cortona frequently (at least 12 a day on work days) with Arezzo (via Castiglion Fiorentino) from Piazza Garibaldi.

Two train stations serve the town. Trains coming from Arezzo (€2) stop at the Camucia-Cortona station, which is around about 5km away in the valley below Cortona, and trains going to Rome stop at Terontola, which is located about 10km to the south of town. Shuttle buses connect Camucia (€1, 10 minutes) and Terontola (€1.60, 25 minutes) with Piazza Garibaldi. By car, the city is on the north–south SS71, which runs to Arezzo, and it is also close to the superstrada that connects Perugia to the A1.

Umbria

JEFFREY N. BECOM

Northern Umbria

CONTENTS

Italy has a green heart: Umbria.

Umbria's tourist slogan rings true – it's the only province in Italy that borders neither the ocean nor another country. Italy's most rural region, Umbria is a collection of medieval hilltowns, sloping farmlands and the occasional ancient ruin. It's certainly been discovered, but Umbria doesn't see anywhere near the number of tourists as its more famous neighbour Tuscany...yet.

Except for a few blighted exceptions along the major highways and in sprawling suburbs, most of Umbria is incredibly picturesque and Umbrians celebrate everything from Renaissance painters to Roman coins to olive oil. Umbria hosts more *manifestazioni* – festivals, events, outdoor movies, concerts, parades, fairs, medieval tournaments, trade shows, etc – than any other place on the planet. The most well-known Umbrian town is Assisi, but Perugia's wide range of activities and sights makes it a cosmopolitan destination. Umbria's real heart can be found in the smaller towns – Todi, Spoleto and Spello – not to mention the countless tiny villages and hamlets in which one could get lost for days exploring. Umbria is small enough to drive its perimeter in less than a day. You can wander off on side roads, and then take side roads off those side roads.

If you have a car, you can stay just about anywhere. Those without their own wheels would be best to stay in a major transport hub, such as Perugia; Foligno, Spello and Assisi are also on the main train line. Lago di Trasimeno is equidistant between Rome and Florence, and the views of the lake from most of the surrounding towns are remarkable.

HIGHLIGHTS

- Eat *cinghiale* (wild boar) and *tartufo* (truffles) and drink Umbrian *sagrantino* (type of wine) in a 'tipica' restaurant in Montefalco (p289)
- Take in some jazz during the Umbria Jazz festival in Perugia (p260)
- Watch an outdoor movie at the Pinacoteca in Città di Castello (p278)
- Marvel at the legacy of St Francis at his eponymous Basilica in Assisi (p281)
- Attend festivals celebrating everything including history, dance, chocolate, gnocchi and snails

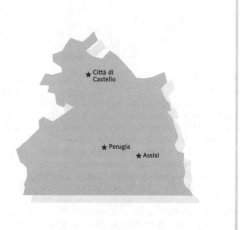

NORTHERN UMBRIA

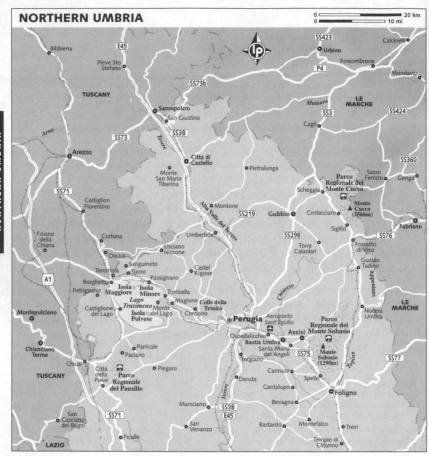

PERUGIA
pop 149,350

One of Italy's best-preserved medieval hill towns, Perugia is also a hip student town with a never-ending stream of cultural events, restaurants to try and concerts to attend.

Perugia has a lively and bloody past. The Umbrii tribe inhabited the surrounding area and controlled land stretching from present-day Tuscany into Le Marche, but it was the Etruscans who founded the city, which reached its zenith in the 6th century BC. It fell to the Romans in 310 BC and was given the name Perusia. During the Middle Ages the city was racked by the internal feuding of the Baglioni and Oddi families and violent wars against its neighbours. In the mid-13th century Perugia was home to the Flagellants, a curious sect, whose members whipped themselves as a religious penance. In 1538 the city was incorporated into the Papal States under Pope Paul III, remaining under papal control for almost three centuries. It was during this time as a Guelph city that it warred against many of its neighbouring towns.

Perugia has a strong artistic and cultural tradition. In the 15th century it was home to fresco painters Bernardino Pinturicchio and his master Pietro Vannucci (known as Perugino), who was to teach Raphael. This city also attracted the great Tuscan masters Fra Angelico and Piero della Francesca. Today, the Università per Stranieri, established in 1925, offers courses in Italian and attracts thousands of students from all over the world.

Orientation

Old Perugia's main strip, Corso Vannucci (named after Pietro Vannucci, aka Perugino), runs south to north from Piazza Italia through Piazza della Repubblica and finally ends in the heart of the old city at Piazza IV Novembre, bounded by the cathedral and the Palazzo dei Priori. Almost everywhere listed in this section is within a few small blocks of this square. Intercity buses will drop you off at Piazza dei Partigiani, from where you can take a *scala mobile* (escalator) up to Piazza Italia. Several city buses go straight from the train station, Stazione Fontivegge, west of the city centre, to Piazza Italia.

Information

BOOKSHOPS

La Libreria (☎ 075 573 50 57; Via Oberdan 52) Stocks a selection of English-language books.

EMERGENCY

Police Station (☎ 075 5 06 21; Piazza dei Partigiani)

GAY & LESBIAN TRAVELLERS

Solidarietà Totale (☎ 075 572 31 75; Via A Fratti 18) Information on gay and lesbian events.

INTERNET ACCESS

InformaGiovani (see Tourist Information)
InfoUmbria (see Tourist Information)
Tempo Reale (see Telephone)

INTERNET RESOURCES

www.perugia.it Information on the area surrounding Perugia, including Lago di Trasimeno.
www.umbria2000.it
www.bellaumbria.net This is the most comprehensive website on Umbria – the Events and Traditions page allows you to search for festivals by either town or date. Information is translated into English, French, German and Spanish.
www.umbria.org
www.argoweb.it
www.umbriaonline.it
www.umbriatrasporti.it Useful for train and bus information – you can also dial ☎ 800 51 21 41 while in Italy to get instant information.
www.perugia.it Handy information on the area surrounding Perugia, including Lago di Trasimeno.
www.tourinumbria.com A complete listing to assist travellers with physical disabilities to navigate Umbria.

www.abitarelastoria.it A loose association of grand historic hotels, country houses and castles, with over a dozen in Umbria and Tuscany.

LAUNDRY

67 Laundry (Via Pinturicchio; ☼ 8am-10pm daily) It sells single serves of detergent.
Onda Blu (Corso dei Bersaglieri 4; ☼ 8am-10pm daily)

LEFT LUGGAGE

InfoUmbria (see Tourist Offices) It charges €1.30 for the first hour, €0.80 for each additional hour and €3 a day to leave luggage at its offices next to the Intercity bus station at Piazza dei Partigiani.

MEDICAL SERVICES

Emergency Doctor (☎ 075 3 40 24)
Farmacia San Martino (pharmacy; Piazza Matteotti 26; ☼ 24 hrs)
Monteluce Hospital (☎ 075 578 34 22; Piazza Monteluce)

MONEY

The currency exchange machines don't work now that the euro has been introduced in Italy. Corso Vannucci is lined with banks, all of which have ATMs.

POST

Mail Boxes Etc (☎ 075 50 17 98; Via D'Andreotto 71; ☼ 8.30am-12.30pm & 3-6pm) Try this place to send packages via FedEx or Airborne Express.
Post Office (Piazza Matteotti; ☼ 8.10am-6pm Mon-Sat)

TELEPHONE

Centro Omnitel (☎ 075 572 37 78; Piazza Danti 17) One of the cheapest places to buy a mobile phone in Perugia. Phones go for as much as €500, but you can find one here for €79.
Tempo Reale (☎ 075 573 55 33; Via del Forno 17; ☼ 8am-10pm daily; 🖳) Phone calls from the booths here cost €0.11 to Australia, Canada, the USA, the UK and most places in Europe, and €0.21 to South Africa. Internet access will cost you €1.50 for an hour, prorated to whatever you have used.

TOURIST INFORMATION

InformaGiovani (☎ 075 572 06 46; Via Idalia 1, off Via Pinturicchio; ☼ 10am-1.30pm Mon-Fri, 3.30-5pm Mon-Wed; 🖳 €1/30min) Assists young travellers and students living in Perugia with information on Italian culture, work opportunities, education and travelling abroad. It's got a host of flyers and signs all over the walls displaying every concert, apartment for rent and other youth-related event available.

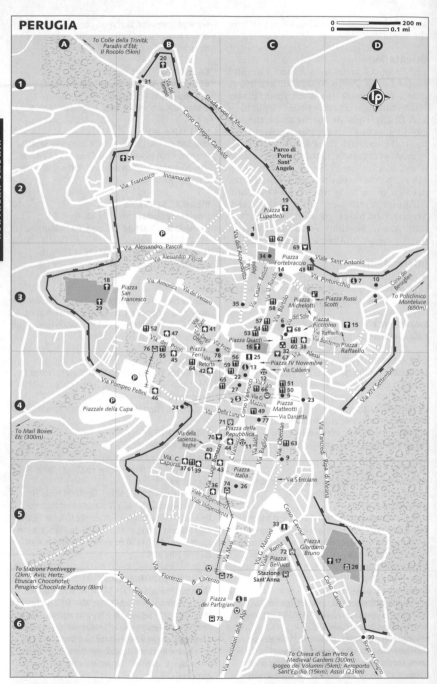

NORTHERN UMBRIA

InfoUmbria (☎ 075 5757; www.infoumbria.com; Largo Cacciatori delle Alpi 3, at the Piazza dei Partigiani Intercity bus station; ☉ 9am-1.30pm & 2.30-6.30pm Mon-Fri, 9am-1pm Sat, closed Sun; 🖳 €1/30min) Private InfoUmbria, also known as Infotourist, offers information on all of Umbria, and is a fantastic resource for *agriturismi* (farm stay or country inn accommodations), festivals, sights, hotels and general information. Keep in mind that the service is free because it's sponsored by hotels and other businesses. InfoUmbria checks for quality at all of its sponsors, but you're only hearing about a segment of what's available.

Tourist Information Office (☎ 075 573 64 58; info@iat.perugia.it; Palazzo dei Priori, Piazza IV Novembre 3, opposite the cathedral; ☉ 8.30am-1.30pm & 3.30-6.30pm Mon-Sat & 9am-1pm Sun) Surprisingly, many employees at Umbrian tourist offices don't speak English. The monthly publication Viva Perugia (€0.80) lists all events and useful information. You must go next door to the public relations office (the door that reads: 'This is not the tourist office') to buy a copy.

Train Information (☎ 800 51 21 41) For train information throughout the whole of Umbria, try this extremely helpful information line. You will rarely be connected to someone who speaks English, but if you're well practised in your numbers, and can tell them the city, they'll usually patiently tell you the prices and times of day that trains leave.

TRAVEL AGENCIES

CTS (☎ 075 572 70 50; Via del Roscetto 21) Specialises in budget and student travel and sells International Student Identity Cards (ISIC) to students studying at the university.

Il Periscopio (☎ 075 5730808; Via Sole 6) A travel agency and tourist 'Welcome Point' that arranges excursions, escorted tours and trips within Italy or abroad. The owner speaks fluent English and French.

Sights

HISTORIC CENTRE

The centre of Perugia – and therefore of the centre of Umbria – is Piazza IV Novembre. For thousands of years, it was the meeting point for the ancient Etruscan and Roman civilisations. In the medieval period, it was the political centre of Perugia. Now students and tourists come here to congregate and eat *gelato*. In the very centre of the piazza stands the **Fontana Maggiore** (Great Fountain). It was designed by Fra Bevignate, and father-son team Nicola and Giovanni Pisano built the fountain between 1275 and 1278. Along the edge are bas-relief statues representing scenes from the Old Testament, the founding of Rome, the 'liberal arts', and a griffin and a lion. Look for the griffin all over Perugia – it's the city's symbol. The lion is the symbol for the Guelphs, the Middle Ages faction that favoured rule by the Papacy over rule by the Holy Roman Empire.

The **Palazzo dei Priori** houses some of the best museums in Perugia. The foremost art gallery in Umbria is the **Museo Archeologico**

Nazionale dell'Umbria (National Gallery of Umbria; ☎ /fax 075 572 10 09; www.gallerianazionaledellumbr ia.it; Corso Vannucci 19, Palazzo dei Priori; adult/reduced €6.50/3.25, free for EU citizens under 18 or over 65; ⌚ 8.30am-7.30pm Mon-Sun & public holidays, closed 1st Mon of each month) is the building across from the cathedral, which runs the length of Corso Vannucci. Designs for the building began as early as 1270 and finished seven centuries later, in 1902. You'll see an enormous doorway. The National Gallery has 30 rooms of artwork dating back to the 13th century, including rooms dedicated to works from Pinturicchio and Perugino.

The **Collegio del Cambio** (Exchange Guild; ☎ 075 572 85 99; Corso Vannucci 25, Palazzo dei Priori; adult/students €2.60/1.60; ⌚ 9am-12.30pm & 2.30-5.30pm Mon-Sat, 9am-12.30pm Sun & public holidays) consists of three rooms: the Sala dei Legisti (Legist Chamber), with wooden stalls carved by Zuccari in the 17th century; the Sala dell'Udienza (Audience Chamber), with frescoes by Perugino; and the Chapel of San Giovanni Battista, painted by a student of Perugino's Giannicola di Paolo. Next door is the **Collegio della Mercanzia** (Merchant's Guild; ☎ 075 573 03 66; Corso Vannucci 15, Palazzo dei Priori; adults/reduced €1.03/0.52; ⌚ 9am-1pm & 2.30-5.30pm Mon-Sat, 9am-1pm Sun & public holidays Mar-Oct & Nov 20-Dec 6; 8am-2pm Tue-Thu & Fri, 8am-4.30pm Wed & Sat, 9am-1pm Sun & public holidays Nov 1-Dec 19 & Jan 7-Feb 28), which highlights an older audience chamber, from the 13th century, covered in wood panelling by northern craftsmen. A combined ticket for both *collegi* is €3.10/ 2.10 adult/reduced.

The fourth museum in the Palazzo dei Priori is the **Sala dei Notari** (Notaries' Hall; admission free; ⌚ 9am-1pm & 3-7pm Tue-Sun & public holidays, closed Mon except Jul-Sep), which was built from 1293 to 1297 as a citizens' assembly chamber. The arches supporting the vaults are Romanesque, covered with frescoes depicting Biblical scenes and Aesop's fables. On the north end of the piazza is the **Cathedral of San Lorenzo** (☎ 075 572 38 32; Piazza IV Novembre). Although a church has been on this land since the 900s, the version you see was begun in 1345 from designs created by Fra Bevignate in 1300. Building of the cathedral continued until 1587, and the doorway was built in the late 1700s; however, the main facade was never completed. Inside you'll find dramatic Gothic architecture.

At the southern end of Corso Vannucci is the tiny **Giardini Carducci**, with lovely views of the countryside. This is where the antiques market takes place on the third weekend of each month. The gardens stand atop a once-massive 16th-century fortress, now known as the **Rocca Paolina**, built by Pope Paul III in the 1540s and standing over a medieval quarter formerly inhabited by some of the city's most powerful families. Destroyed by the Perugini after Italian unification, the ruins remain a symbol of defiance against oppression. A series of *scala mobile* run through the Rocca and you can wander around inside the ruins, which are often used for art exhibitions.

You can buy a combined ticket called the **Perugia City Museum Circuit** (valid 1 week; adult/seniors/children €2.50/2/1) at any of the three following museums. First, you can venture down into the 3rd-century-BC **Pozzo Etrusco** (Etruscan Well; ☎ 075 573 36 69; Piazza Danti 18; ⌚ 10.30am-1.30pm & 2.30-6.30pm daily Apr-Oct; 10.30am-1.30pm daily & 2.30-4.30pm daily Nov-Mar). The 36m-deep well was the main water reservoir of the Etruscan town. The second stop is the **Cappella di San Severo** (☎ 075 573 38 64; Piazza Raffaello; ⌚ same hours as Pozzo Etrusco), decorated with Raphael's *Trinity with Saints* (thought by many to be his first fresco) and frescoes by Perugino. The third museum included is the **Cassero di Porta Sant'Angelo** (Panoramic Tower; ☎ 075 573 36 69; Porta Sant'Angelo; ⌚ 11am-1.30pm & 3-6.30pm daily Apr-Oct, 11am-1.30pm & 3-5pm daily Nov-Mar). The panoramic view facing back on to Perugia is the main reason to come out here, plus it offers a historical briefing of the three city walls.

Walking down towards the Università per Stranieri takes you on either one of the two **Arco d'Augusto**, one of the ancient city gates. Its lower section is Etruscan, dating from the 3rd century BC; the upper part is Roman and bears the inscription 'Augusta Perusia'. The loggia on top dates from the Renaissance.

North along Corso Giuseppe Garibaldi is the **Chiesa di Sant'Agostino** (Piazza Lupattelli; admission free; ⌚ 8am-noon & 4pm-sunset daily), with a beautiful 16th-century choir by sculptor and architect Baccio d'Agnolo. Small signs forlornly mark the places where artworks once hung before they were carried off to France by Napoleon and his men. Further north along the same thoroughfare, Via del Tempio branches off to the Romanesque

Chiesa di Sant'Angelo (☎ 075 57 22 64; Via Sant'Angelo; admission free; ☻ 10am-noon & 4-6pm), said to stand on the site of an ancient temple. The columns inside the round church were taken from earlier buildings. Corso Giuseppe Garibaldi continues through the 14th-century wall by way of the **Porta Sant'Angelo**. Built in the 13th century, Chiesa di San Francesco delle Donne is now the headquarters for the **Giuditta Brozzetti fabric company** (☎ 075 4 02 36; fax 500 24 92; www.brozzetti.com; Via T Berardi 5/6; ☻ 9am-1pm & 3-6pm Mon-Fri), operating since 1921. You can buy hand-woven linens produced using traditional techniques dating back a thousand years. It's also possible to take classes from one day to three weeks in hand weaving, embroidery and lace making.

Along Corso Cavour, the early-14th century **Chiesa di San Domenico** (☎ 075 573 15 68; Piazza Giordano Bruno; admission free; ☻ 8am-noon & 4pm-sunset) is the city's largest church. Its Romanesque interior, lightened by the immense stained-glass windows, was replaced by austere Gothic fittings in the 16th century. Pope Benedict XI, who died after eating poisoned figs in 1325, lies buried here. The adjoining convent is the home of the **Museo Archeologico Nazionale dell'Umbria** (☎ 075 572 71 41; Piazza Giordano Bruno 10, in the former San Domenico monastery; adult/reduced €2/1, free to EU citizens under 18 or over 65; ☻ 8.30am-7.30pm Tue-Sun, 2.30-7.30pm Mon), which has an excellent collection of Etruscan pieces and a section on prehistory. The most important item in the collection is the *Cippo Perugino*, the Perugian Memorial Stone, a travertine stone with one of the longest Etruscan language engravings.

OUT OF TOWN

A fabulous way to wile away the afternoon is to stroll or picnic at the **Medieval Gardens** (☎ 075 585 64 20 for information from the University of Perugia's Department of Plant Biology or for guided tours; Borgo XX Giugno 74; admission free; ☻ 8am-6.30pm), behind the Chiesa di San Pietro, 300m southeast of the city. During the medieval period, monasteries often created gardens reminiscent of the Garden of Eden and Biblical stories, complete with plants that symbolised myths and sacred stories. Numbered locations through this garden include 3) the Cosmic Tree, symbolising the forefather of all trees; 6) the Tree of Light and Knowledge and 7) the Tree of Good and Evil; 11) and 12) medicinal and edible plants used for

centuries; 16) remnants from an ancient fish pond; 20) the Cosmogonic Ovulation Spring (a lily-pad pond); ending in 24) the exit of the Medieval Gardens, symbolising the elevation of man from the natural plane. Be sure to check out the groovy alchemist's studio tucked into the corner near 20) the Yggdrasil Incline.

In front of the medieval gardens is the medieval 10th-century **Chiesa di San Pietro** (☎ 075 3 47 70; Borgo XX Giugno; admission free; ☻ 8am-noon & 4pm-sunset), entered through a frescoed doorway in the first courtyard. The interior is an incredible mix of gilt and marble and contains a *Pietà* by Perugino. Many of the paintings in this church feature depictions of Biblical women.

About 5km southeast of the city, at Ponte San Giovanni, is the **Ipogeo dei Volumni** (☎ 199 10 13 30 for information; Via Assisana; admission €2.05, free to EU citizens under 18; ☻ 9am-1pm & 3.30-6.30pm daily Sep-Jun, 9am-12.30pm & 4.30-7pm daily Jul-Aug), a 2nd-century-BC Etruscan burial site. An underground chamber contains a series of recesses holding the funerary urns of the Volumnio family. It's part of the larger Palazzone Etruscan necropolis. Visits are limited to seven people every five minutes, so there can be delays. Take the APM bus from Piazza Italia to Ponte San Giovanni and walk west from there.

If chocolate is your thing, don't miss the **Perugino chocolate factory** (☎ 075 527 67 96; Van San Sisto; admission free; ☻ 8.30am-1pm & 2-5pm Mon-Fri). Granted, you'll learn more than you'd ever want to know about the business practices of a chocolate company, but you get free samples, and there's a shop filled with all sorts of chocolate goodies.

Courses

The list of courses available to locals and foreigners in and around Perugia could constitute a book in itself. You can learn Italian, take up ceramics, study music or spend a month cooking. The tourist office has details of all available courses.

On Wednesday and Saturday you can take a one-day cooking class with **Angela Pitteri** (☎ 0742 4 88 77 for information or to book). This school arranges transport to/from Perugia.

Università per Stranieri (☎ 075 5 74 61; www.unistrapg.it; Palazzo Gallenga, Piazza Fortebraccio 4, Perugia 06122) is Italy's foremost academic institution for foreigners, offering courses in language, literature, history, art, music and opera, and architecture, to name a few. It also offers a one-month refresher course for teachers of Italian abroad for €233. A series of degree courses are available, as well as one-, two- and three-month intensive language courses. The basic language course costs €233 per month.

Istituto Europea di Arti Operative (☎ 075 573 50 22; www.iaeo.it; Via dei Priori 14; ✆ 10am-12.30pm for questions) runs courses in fashion, graphic design, industrial and interior design, architecture, restoration, drawing and painting. All classes are taught in Italian.

Organised Tours
From April until September, **Guide in Umbria** (at InfoUmbria office; ☎ 075 573 29 33; www .guideinumbria.com; Largo Cacciatori delle Alpi 3) offers small eight-person coach tours to surrounding towns in Umbria. If you don't want to rent a car or your schedule doesn't fit in with the train or bus times, this is a perfect solution. Prices are reasonable, from €20 to €39 for a full-day trip. The tours visit Assisi, Orvieto and Gubbio, but they're especially beneficial for places like the Valnerina or the areas around Lago di Trasimeno because you'll be able to see things that wouldn't be accessible without a car.

Festivals & Events
Perugia – and Umbria in general – has no less than 80 gazillion events, festivals, concerts, summer outdoor movies, *sagre* (traditional festivals) etc. Not surprisingly, most festivals are between May and October, but tourist offices will have a list of all the festivals throughout the year.

Sagra Musicale Umbra (Holy Music Festival; ☎ 075 572 13 74; fax 075 572 76 14; www.sagramusicaleum bra.com - Italian only) is one of the oldest music festivals in Europe. Begun in 1937, it's held in Perugia in mid-September and features world-renown conductors and musicians.

Umbria Jazz (☎ 075 572 86 85, 075 572 86 77; www.umbriajazz.com) festival attracts top-notch international performers for 10 days each July, usually around the middle of the month. In the past, the festival has featured performances by hundreds of jazz greats, including Sonny Rollins, the Buena Vista Social Club, Chick Corea and Al Jarreau. Check with the tourist office for details on where to buy tickets. Single tickets cost €10 to €100,

but you can also buy passes: full-week passes cost from €100 to €310 and weekend passes cost from €50 to €150. Not all performances sell out, but hotels do, so arrange your accommodation well in advance.

Serious chocoholics might want to plan a trip to Italy around **Eurochocolate**, which occurs from mid- to late October each year. Hundreds of booths associated with chocolate set up for the week. Taste, learn, eat, drink and indulge. There's always a fun component, like the first ever chocolate wedding in 2003 or, in 2001, a chocolate trial.

Sleeping
Perugia has a fine array of hotels and *pensioni*, and is a good place to stay if you're using public transport for the entire time or just part of your trip. You can get a 10-pass bus ticket (€7.20) to travel to the train station and take one- or two-day trips to virtually anywhere in Umbria, and many places in Tuscany. There's no reason to stay outside the historic centre: it's noisier, less charming and not much cheaper.

High-season rates are listed here, but almost every hotel offers a discount during the low season, which varies from place to place, but is usually January to March, November to early December and possibly August.

BUDGET
The city has two camp sites, both in Colle della Trinità, 5km northwest of the city and reached by taking bus No 9 from Piazza Italia (ask the driver to drop you off at the Superal supermarket, from where it's a 300m walk to the camp sites).

Paradis d'Été (☎ 075 517 31 21; www.camping paradisdete.com; Via del Mercato 29/A, Str Fontana, Colle della Trinità; per person/tent/car €6.20/4.65/2.84; ✆ year-round) This camp site has 50 well-shaded sites in a park-like setting with good facilities and a swimming pool. If you're tentless, you can rent a bungalow for up to six people.

Il Rocolo (☎ /fax 075 517 85 50; ilrocolo@ilrocolo.it; Str Fontana 1/n, Loc. Colle della Trinità; per person/tent/car €6/5/2.50; ✆ mid-Apr–end of Sep) Il Rocolo has over 100 sites with a bit of shade and all the standard facilities, including an onsite restaurant, minimarket, bocce and playground. It's 6km from the city centre, near highway E-45. A minibus makes the journey back and forth several times a day.

Centro Internazionale per la Gioventù (☎ /fax 075 572 28 80; www.ostello.perugia.it; Via Bontempi 13; dm €13.50, sheets €1.50; 💻) If the 9.30am to 4pm lockout and the midnight curfew (*no exceptions*) don't scare you off, then you'll appreciate the sweeping countryside view and wafting sounds of church bells from the hostel's terrace, where guests often gather after making dinner in the well-stocked kitchen. Enjoy the 16th-century frescoed ceilings and the best view from a hostel bathroom anywhere on the planet.

Casa Spagnoli Bed & Breakfast (☎ 075 573 51 27, 340 350 38 93; fabkation@yahoo.it; Via Caporali 17; s/d/t €31/48/60; shared bathroom; 🗙 💻) Feel like you're staying with your long-lost Italian third cousins at this comfortable and spacious private home. Do some yoga in the yoga salon, play with the baby or discuss Italy with international Spagnolis, who speak fluent Italian, Spanish, French and English. Internet access, laundry facilities, photocopier and use of the kitchen are available. It offers a small weekly discount and it's perfectly located near Piazza Italia, so it makes an ideal base for exploring Umbria by public transport from Perugia. Only one of each room is available, so email or call ahead.

Primavera Mini-Hotel (☎ 075 572 16 57; www .primaveraminihotel.com; Via Vincioli 8; s/d/t €48/70/90) This central and quiet hotel run by a dedicated English- and French-speaking mother-daughter team is the most upscale of the budget listings. The magnificent views complement the bright and airy rooms and common areas. All rooms come with private bath, telephone and TV.

Pensione Paola (☎ 075 572 38 16; Via della Canapina 5, s/d €31/48; 🅿) It's a great bet if you want use of your own kitchen without the lockout of the hostel. And you get to play this fun game: Can I find anyone in all of Perugia nicer than Paola? Eight simply furnished rooms. Take bus No 6 or 7 heading towards Piazza Italia and get off at the Pellini car park. Signs will point you up the steps to the right. From the city centre, walk down Via dei Priori.

Also available:

Pensione Anna (☎ /fax 075 573 63 04; annahotel@ hotmail.com; Via dei Priori 48; s/d without bathroom from €26/42; 🅿) A decent four-floor walk up.

Hotel Eden (☎ 075 572 81 02; fax 075 572 03 42; Via C. Caporali 9; s/d/t €36/57/77) Convenient and basic with incredibly stiff and starchy sheets.

Hotel Morlacchi (☎ 075 572 03 19; morlacchi@ tiscalinet.it; Via Tiberi 2; s/d/t/q with bathroom €38/60/ 78/96, s without bathroom €28) This friendly, family-run two-star hotel is a popular choice, so phone ahead for reservations.

MID-RANGE

Hotel Fortuna (☎ 075 572 28 45; fortuna@umbriahotels .com; Via Luigi Bonazzi 19; s/d €79/114; 🗙 💻) In an excellent location, the charming Fortuna offers well-appointed rooms, all with air-con; a few frescoed suites have private balconies. Free Internet access for guests from 8pm to midnight.

Hotel la Rosetta (☎ /fax 075 572 08 41; larosetta@ umbriaonline.com; Piazza Italia 19; s/d €77.50/117; 🅿 🗙) One of Perugia's top hotels in the city centre, the restaurant alone is worth a stay (see p262). Both a tourist and business hotel, Rosetta has frescoed ceilings, a meeting room, elevator, satellite TV and parking.

Etruscan Chocohotel (☎ 075 583 73 14; etruscan@ chocohotel.it; Via Campo di Marte 134; s/d €70/110; 🅿 🗙) The only one of its kind in the world: a hotel based entirely on chocolate. Try items from the restaurant's 'chocomenu', shop at the 'chocostore' or swim in the rooftop pool (sadly, filled with water). Just east of the train station, take bus No 2 or 13d.

Also available:

Hotel Priori (☎ 075 572 33 78; www.hotelpriori.it; Via Vermiglioli 3; s/d €66/91; 🅿) Not the most exciting rooms, but the garage parking (€14) and full buffet breakfast might make it worth it to some.

TOP END

Brufani Palace (☎ 075 573 25 41; www.sinahotels.com; Piazza Italia 12; s/d €205/307, ste €423-800; 🅿 🗙 🏊) Not only is the Brufani one of the only five-star hotels in Umbria, it's a five-star-plus. Special touches include frescoed main rooms, impeccably decorated rooms and suites, a garden terrace to dine in during summer, and a helpful trilingual staff. The only place in the city centre with its own parking facilities, this hotel has all amenities, but the real gem is the fitness centre, with a sauna, Turkish bath and a subterranean pool situated over Etruscan ruins. Twenty-four hour concierge. Wheelchair accessible.

Locanda della Posta (☎ 075 572 89 25; novelber@ tin.it; Corso Vannucci 97; s/d €108/170; 🗙) The service is less than friendly and the amenities are scarce, but this centrally located, well-advertised hotel is very popular. You coul save money by staying at the almost-as-centrally located Hotel la Rosetta or Hotel Fortuna, or upgrade for an experience of a lifetime at Brufani Palace.

RENTAL

If you are planning to staying in Perugia at least one month, **Atena Service** (☎ 075 573 29 92; www.atenaservice.com; Via del Bulagaio 38) can arrange accommodation, from €200 per month for a shared room in an apart-ment, and from €550 per month for a one-bedroom apartment to yourself. The rooms are completely furnished, equipped with bed linen and kitchen implements, and are within a 15-minute walk from the university and city centre. It can also help with other student or traveller needs, such as finding a dentist, arranging a cooking course or a night out on the town.

Once in town, you can check posted flyers at the Università per Stranieri or at Informa-Giovani for rental accommodation.

Eating

Because of the great number of students and tourists, the amount of places to eat in Perugia is staggering. A pizzeria is around every corner, and there are dozens of res-taurants. There's not a lot of choice, though: most serve an extremely similar array of Umbrian pasta, such as *strangozzi* (a square-shaped spaghetti-like pasta) and meat dishes like *cinghiale* (wild boar), but a few excellent restaurants stand out for their food, value or location, or all three.

RESTAURANTS

Il Falchetto (☎ 075 573 17 75; Via Bartolo 20; meals around €25; ☟ closed Mon) In a great location just behind the cathedral, this restaurant (named 'the eagle') offers some of Peru-gia's better dishes. Try its house speciality, *falchetto verde,* a spinach and gnocchi dish served in a bubbling hot casserole dish.

La Rosetta (☎ 075 572 08 41; Via del Sette 2, just off Corso Vannucci; meals around €25; ☟ closed Wed) Hotel restaurants usually garner an 'also has a res-taurant', but this restaurant could get an 'also has a hotel' mention. During summer, meals are served on a private outdoor patio, romantically decorated with wrought-iron roses and candles. It serves a slight varia-tion on the typical Umbrian repertoire and

includes some international flavours. Try anything with the saffron sauce.

Ristorante Il Bacio (☎ 075 572 09 09; Via Boncampi 6; meals around €11; ☟ closed Wed) This rather smoky cavernous pizzeria and restaurant serves decent pizza at decent prices, but its selling point is that it's one of the only late-night restaurants in the historic centre, open until 12.30am.

Ristorante del Sole (☎ 075 573 50 31; Via della Rupe at Via Oberdan; meals around €27; ☟ closed Mon) Ristorante del Sole is a popular spot. It's actually down a side alley and, if you aren't dazzled by the views, you'll probably want to just roll around in the *antipasto* and des-sert displays. The food tastes as good as it looks, but expect to pay for it.

La Cambusa (☎ 075 572 13 83; Via dei Priori 82; meals around €15; ☟ closed Tue) This inexpensive and reliable restaurant is mostly populated by locals. It specialises in seafood dishes, including a swordfish *carpaccio* (thinly sliced meat, dressed and eaten raw).

Ristorante Giancarlo (☎ 075 572 43 14; Via dei Priori 36; meals around €20; ☟ closed Fri) Giancarlo himself might seat you at this cosy restau-rant. He serves mostly typical Umbrian food, with delicious lentil soup and several sausage dishes.

Ristorante Altromondo (☎ 075 572 61 57; Via Caporali 11; meals around €25; ☟ closed Sun) A popular restaurant with locals, Altromondo cooks typical Umbrian dishes in gracious surroundings.

Ristorante dal Mi'Cocco (☎ 075 573 25 11; Corso Giuseppe Garibaldi 12; set meals €13; ☟ closed Mon) This place, popular with students, serves local specialities on rustic tables with bright-red checked covers. The menu changes daily, so basically you eat what you're given.

CAFÉS

Many of the restaurants that line Corso Vannucci open up sidewalk cafés in the warmer months. Don't expect the food to be top-notch, as you're paying for atmos-phere. You'll find the best (and priciest) food at Caffè di Perugia.

Sandri (Corso Vannucci 32) Just try to walk by this café, a Perugian staple, without having your mouth water at the sight of chocolate cakes and candied fruit.

Caffè di Perugia (☎ 075 573 18 63; Via Mazzini 10) This is the fanciest café in town and makes delectable desserts. It also serves a fine array of basic pasta and meat dishes.

SELF-CATERING
Coop (Piazza Matteoti; ☺ 9am-8pm daily) is the largest grocery store in the historic centre. You can buy all sorts of pasta, vegetables and staples here, as well as prepared food from the deli.

Below Coop is a **covered market** (☺ 7am-1.30pm Mon-Sat), down the stairs from Piazza Matteotti, where you can buy fresh produce, bread, cheese and meat.

PIZZERIE
Pizzeria Etrusca (☎ 075 572 07 62; Via Ulisse Rocchi 31; pizza from €3.10) Etrusca is a popular student haunt.

Pizzeria Mediterranea (☎ 075 572 1322; Piazza Piccinino 11/12; pizza from €4.15; ☺ Wed-Mon) Very trendy and in a good location, Mediterranea can get fairly busy at times so be prepared to queue.

SWEETS
Augusta Perusia Cioccolato (☎ 075 573 45 77; Via Pinturicchio 2) Handmade chocolate bars come in a box with old paintings of Perugia, so it's a perfect gift to bring home. Wonderful homemade *gelato*, including flavours such as mascarpone, baci, pinoli, cinnamon and, of course, chocolate.

Gelateria degli Sciri (Via dei Priori) Some of the best *gelato* in town; it serves the rare dairy-free *gelato* (made with soy milk). Try a frappé, which is like a thin milkshake.

Entertainment
Much of Perugia's nightlife parades outside the cathedral and around Fontana Maggiore. Practically every night, hundreds of local and foreign students congregate here, playing guitars and drums and chatting with friends. Tourists mix in easily, slurping *gelati* and enjoying this version of outdoor theatre. When the student population grows, the Università per Stranieri offers a bus that leaves from Palazzo Gallenga to some of the clubs, on the outskirts of town, which are difficult to get to on foot (especially since the *scala mobile* stop running just after midnight). Check with the university for details.

Bottega di Vino (☎ /fax 075 571 61 81; Via del Sole 1; ☺ wine bar 6pm-1am, wine shop 9am-1pm & 4-8pm, closed Sun) This is a fantastic place to take in the atmosphere. Flaming torches light the way and a fire burns on the terrace. Inside, live jazz and hundreds of bottles of wine lining the walls add to the romance of the setting. You can taste dozens of Umbrian wines, and can then purchase them from the wine bar with the help of sommelier-like experts.

Joyce's Pub (☎ 075 573 46 95; Via Luigi Bonazzi 15; ☺ noon-3pm Mon-Fri & 7.30pm-2.30am daily) A more convivial, airy pub with a decent restaurant.

Shamrock Pub (☎ 075 573 66 25; Piazza Danti 18; ☺ 6pm-2am) For late-night drinks, sample a Guinness at the Shamrock, down an appropriately dank but atmospheric alley off Piazza Danti.

Velvet (☎ 075 572 13 21; www.velvetfashioncafe .com; Viale Roma 20) Come to where the beautiful people play and party. It doesn't open until after midnight, but you can party here until the wee hours.

Teatro del Pavone (Corso Vannucci 67) This movie theatre screens Italian and foreign films. On Monday night, it often shows original-language films, usually in English.

Shopping
If you're lucky enough to be in Perugia on the last Sunday of the month, spend a few hours in the **antiques market** around the Piazza Italia and in the Giardini Carducci. It's a great place to pick up old prints, frames, furniture, jewellery, postcards, stamps etc. The second week of January sees steep discounts, as prices can be reduced by as much as 75%.

Getting There & Away
AIR
Aeroporto Sant'Egidio (☎ 075 59 21 41), 15km east of the city, has flights to/from Milan and Palermo, but no international service. A train is cheaper and much more convenient.

BUS
Intercity buses leave from Piazza dei Partigiani (take the *scala mobile* from Piazza Italia). The Perugia–Rome service is operated by **Sulga** (☎ 800 09 96 61); there are roughly five buses daily (€14.50, three hours) in each direction and three continue on to Fiumicino airport (€18.75, 3¾ hours). Buses usually leave from Fiumicino at 12.30pm, 2.30pm and 5pm. Sulga also

operates the Perugia–Florence service (€10.35, two hours), which runs daily in each direction, leaving Perugia at 7.30am and Florence at 6pm (from Piazza Adua at Santa Maria Novella). Buses also depart from Piazza dei Partigiani for Siena (€7.25, 1½ hours, twice daily, once on Sunday) and cities throughout Umbria, including Assisi (€2.60, 50 minutes, 10 daily with a gap between 3pm and 7.45pm) and Gubbio (€4, one hour 10 minutes, 15 daily). To get to Narni or Amelia, take an ATC Terni bus from Piazza dei Partigiani and switch in Terni (€6.40, one hour 15 minutes, 2pm and 6.10pm). Check the TV monitors above the terminals. It's best to take the train to Spello, Foligno, Spoleto, Orvieto or Assisi.

Current train and bus routes, company details and timetables are listed in the monthly booklet *Viva Perugia* (€0.80), available next door to the public-relations office.

CAR & MOTORCYCLE

From Rome, leave the A1 at the Orte exit and follow the signs for Terni. Once there, take the S3B-E45 for Perugia. From the north, exit the A1 at Valdichiana and take dual carriageway S75b for Perugia. The S75 to the east connects the city with Assisi.

You'll find three car-rental companies at the main train station.

Avis (☎ /fax 075 500 03 95; alvalrent@hotmail.com; Piazza Vittorio Veneto 7, Stazione Ferroviaria; ⊗ 8.30am-1pm & 3.30-7pm Mon-Fri, 8.30am-1pm Sat, closed Sun) has the cheapest rates and its staff speak fluent English. Rates cost about €233 for a manual transmission (about €400 for an automatic). Smart Cars are available for about €40 a day. Ask for Pino.

Also available:

Maggiore (☎ 075 500 74 99; www.maggiore.it; Via Fontivegge, Stazione Ferroviaria; ⊗ 8.30am-1pm & 3.30-7pm Mon-Fri, 8.30am-1pm Sat, closed Sun)

Hertz (☎ 075 50 024 39; hertzperugia@tiscali.it; Piazza Vittorio Veneto 4, Stazione Ferroviaria; ⊗ 8.30am-1pm & 3.30-7pm Mon-Fri, 8.30am-1pm Sat, closed Sun)

Give **Scootyrent** (☎ 075 572 07 10, 333 102 65 05; scootyrent@scootyrent.com; Via della Volpe 5) a call for scooter hire. For about €20 a day, you can feel like a real Italian, transporting yourself and taking your life in your hands, all at the same time.

TRAIN

The main train station, **Stazione Fontivegge** (for train information, call Tren Italia ☎ 848 88 88 08), is on Piazza Vittorio Veneto, a few kilometres west of the city centre and easily accessible by frequent buses from Piazza Italia. The ticket office is open from 6.30am to 8.10pm, but you can buy tickets at the automated machines any time of day with a credit card or cash. There are seven direct services to Rome daily (€10.12 to €18.45, two hours and change on Eurostar, over three hours on regional trains). Even if your ticket doesn't indicate a change, ask, as you mostly have to change in Terontola or Foligno. Trains to Florence run about every two hours, more so in the morning (€7.90 to €12.50, two hours). Other destinations and fares include Assisi (€1.55, 20 minutes, hourly), Gubbio (€4.30, 1½, seven daily, change in Foligno), Spello (€1.95, 30 minutes, hourly) and Arezzo (€4.50, one hour 10 minutes, every two hours).

Some trains leave from the private **Ferrovia Centrale Umbra railway** (☎ 075 57 54 01). These adorable 'Thomas the Tank Engine' trains run from Stazione Sant'Anna on Piazzale Bellucci and serve Deruta (€1.30, 20 minutes, seven daily), Sansepolcro (€3.80, one hour 20 minutes, 12 daily), Terni (€4.25, 1½ hours, hourly), Todi (€2.90, one hour, hourly) and Città di Castello (€2.90, one hour 10 minutes, 15 daily).

Getting Around

Getting around Umbria is a little more difficult on public transport and requires a little more forethought. Conversely, having a car is a hindrance in several congested hill towns. The best way to see Umbria is to take the train or buses to Assisi, Spoleto, Perugia, Orvieto or Gubbio and rent a car for a week and wander throughout the countryside.

Perugia's main train station is Stazione Fontivegge, but if you arrive by train, look for the stop that reads simply: Perugia. It's a steep climb uphill, so a bus is highly recommended, especially for those with luggage. The city bus costs €0.80 (€0.65 seniors) and takes you as far as Piazza Italia in the historic centre. Be sure to validate your ticket upon boarding or you will be fined on the spot. If you haven't bought a ticket, you can buy one on the bus for €1.50. Bus Nos 6 and 7 are the most immediate, but bus Nos 11, 13 and 15d will also get you to Piazza Italia. Buy your bus ticket from the small green bus kiosk in front of the train station (or in Piazza Italia, or at many *tabacchi* (tobacconists) throughout the city). If you're going to stick around for a while, buy a 10-ticket pass for €7.20.

An airbus connects Piazza Italia with Aeroporto Sant'Egidio (€3, 30 minutes, three daily) to coincide with flights.

CAR & MOTORCYCLE
If you arrive in Perugia by car, following the Centro signs along the winding roads up the hill will bring you to Piazza Italia. Driving and parking in Perugia is expensive, time-consuming and a headache. The best bet is to reach Perugia (and Assisi) by public transport and then rent a car to explore smaller villages and the countryside. Most of the city centre is largely closed to normal, nonresidential traffic, although tourists may drive to their hotels to drop off luggage. Rumour has it that parking police are more lenient on tourist cars, but if you park illegally for too long you run the risk of getting towed. Perugia has six paid car parks: Piazza Partigiani, Viale Pellini, Mercato Coperto, Briglie di Braccio, Viale Sant'Antonio and Piazzale Europa. *Scala mobile* or *ascensori* (lifts) lead from each car park towards the city centre, but take note: they don't operate 24 hours, and usually stop between about midnight or 1am and 6am or 7am. Parking fees cost €0.80 to €1.05 per hour, 24 hours daily. If you intend to use the car park a lot, buy an *abbonamento* (unlimited parking ticket pass) from the ticket office at the car park for about €7.75 for the first day and €5.20 for each successive day. For general parking information, contact **SIPA** (☎ 075 572 19 38).

Call the **Deposito Veicoli Rimossi** (☎ 075 577 53 75) if your car has been towed; be prepared to pay around €105 to retrieve your car.

TAXI
For a taxi, dial ☎ 075 500 48 88. A ride from the city centre to the main train station, Stazione Fontivegge, will cost about €10.

AROUND PERUGIA
Deruta
pop 8082
Just south of Perugia along the S3B/E45, Deruta is a mildly interesting hill town that

would hardly be visited if it wasn't considered the centre of ceramics in Umbria and, according to some, Italy. Derutans have been creating majolica ceramics here for more than 600 years. Some shops are still in the walled medieval historical centre, but for serious shopping, try the main road leading from the highway, Via Tiberina.

Museo Regionale Della Ceramica (☎ 075 971 10 00; adult/reduced/children €2.58/1.81/1.03; ☺ 10.30am-1pm & 2.30-5pm Oct-Mar, 10.30am-1pm & 3-6pm Apr-Jun, 10am-1pm & 3.30-7pm Jul-Sep, closed Tue Oct-Mar), in the majestic town-hall building, this museum lists all information in Italian and English. Although the museum has over 6,000 ceramic pieces, its showcases include archaeological restoration, ceramic works in each stage of production and Etruscan pottery.

At **Maioliche Nulli** (☎ /fax 075 97 23 84; Via Tiberina 142), Rolando Nulli creates each ceramic item by hand while his brother Goffredo finishes them with intricate paintings, specialising in reproductions of classic medieval designs. They ship all over the world.

Maioliche CAMA Deruta (☎ 075 971 11 82; www.camaderuta.com; Via Tiberina 112) is a bigger operation, but one of the most respected in Deruta. You can order most of its products online.

For a great and cheap meal, try **Hotel Ristorante Asso di Coppe** (☎ 075 971 02 05; SS E-45, Km 73,400), a place, populated by locals, that serves basic but delicious Umbrian cuisine.

Torgiano
Torgiano doesn't offer much in the way of sights or activities except for its great wine museum and wine-making history. Then again, isn't that enough? The most famous export from Torgiano is its Rosso Riserva, awarded with the DOCG (Controlled and Guaranteed Designation of Origin) label.

Torgiano is worth a quick visit to stop in at the different *enoteche* (wine bars), and also for the **Museo del Vino** (☎ 075 988 02 00; www.lungarotti.it; Corso Vittorio Emanuele 23; adult/student €4/2.50; ☺ 9am-1pm & 3-7pm Mon-Sat in summer, 9am-1pm & 3-6pm in winter). This wine museum, sponsored by the Lungarotti Foundation (prolific vintners in Umbria), has several well-documented collections in 20 rooms, including information on everything to do with wine drinking, wine making and wine tasting. It displays wine-related archaeological finds, ceramics, books, artwork and ethnography.

In the same vein, the **Museo dell'Olivo e dell'Olio** (The Olive Oil Museum; ☎ 075 988 03 00; Via Garibaldi 10; adult/student €4/2.50; ☺ 10am-1pm & 3-7pm Mon-Sat in summer, 10am-1pm & 3-6pm in winter) displays everything you had no idea you needed to know about olive oil. Combined tickets to both museums cost €7 for adults and €4 for students.

Umbria's most exclusive restaurant is in Torgiano, **Le Melagrane** (☎ 075 988 04 47; www .3vaselle.it; Via Garibaldi 48; meals around €39) at the five-star hotel Le Tre Vaselle (the only other five-star hotel is the Brufani Palace in Perugia). Owned by the famous wine-producing Lungarotti family (who own many vineyards and the wine museum), it serves deluxe Umbrian cuisine amid luxurious furnishings and beautiful brick floors. Dishes include veal *carpaccio* topped with black truffles and risotto cooked with Rubesco red wine produced by, of course, the Lungarottis.

LAGO DI TRASIMENO

Lago di Trasimeno's main draw is its plethora of outdoor activities and natural beauty, but it offers an equal amount of cultural and architectural history as well. Hiking and trekking are popular pastimes in the area, the fourth-biggest lake in Italy. During spring, flowers blanket the area. Sunflowers are grown for their oil, which is used for frying because it's less expensive than olive oil. Historically, the area bounced back and forth between various factions, but is now perfectly situated, literally at the crossroads of Tuscany and Umbria. Two major highways (well, major for Umbria) run to the west and north sides of the lake – the S71 goes from Chiusi in the south to Arezzo in the north – and the A1/75 bis connects in Tuscany with the A1 (which connects Florence and Rome) and meets up with Perugia in the east.

The communities that surround Lago di Trasimeno have banded together with various governmental organisations to bring to life a sustainable plan for maintaining the ecological purity of the area. Many of the lake's activities involve environmentally friendly water sports, such as kayaking or windsurfing. There's an environmental educational lab on Isola Polvese.

Orientation

The *comune* (municipality) of Trasimeno is closer to Cortona in Tuscany than it is to

Perugia, so it makes a perfect base to explore both regions. If you're using public transport, your best bet is to stay in Passignano or Castiglione del Lago. If you've got a car, try any of the towns or go further afield. The region known as Lago di Trasimeno is made up of eight different *comuni*: Castiglione del Lago, Città della Pieve, Magione, Paciano, Panicale, Passignano, Piegaro and Tuoro. Castiglione del Lago and Passignano are the nicest towns to spend a few days in, especially if you're using public transport, but all of the towns – with the exception of Magione – are lovely. Tourist offices can provide you with *Le Mappe di Airone per il Trekking* or *Le Mappe di Airone per il Cicloturismo* – foldout maps. The trekking guide has 13 maps and the *cicloturismo* ('cycle tourism') guide has six maps. They're free at the tourist offices, or you can buy them ahead of time for €5.16 (postage included).

Information

INTERNET ACCESS
Alisé Café (☎ 075 95 31 41; Piazza della Stazione 5) Across from the Castiglione del Lago train station.

INTERNET RESOURCES
www.trasinet.com A good website with listings of hotel accommodation and things to do.

MEDICAL SERVICES
Emergency First-aid Castiglione del Lago (☎ 075 9 52 61); Passignano & Tuoro (☎ 075 829 87 51)

POST
Post Offices (☺ 8.10am-1.20pm Mon-Fri, 8.10am-12.30pm Sat); Castiglione del Lago (Via F lli Rosselli); Città della Pieve (Via Veneto 6); Passignano (Via Rinascita 2); Tuoro (Via Baroncino 1)

TOURIST INFORMATION
You can buy a **percorso museale** (museum ticket; adult/child €6.20/4.15) from any tourist office if you're planning on visiting the entire lake area, including Città della Pieve.

Trasimeno Area Tourist Office (☎ 075 965 24 84; info@iat.castiglione-del-lago.pg.it; Piazza Mazzini 10, Castiglione del Lago; ☺ 8.30am-1pm & 3.30-7pm Mon-Fri, 9am-1pm & 3.30-7pm Sat, 9am-1pm & 4-7pm Sun) Has most of the maps on hiking and biking in the area, along with information on accommodation throughout the region.

Città della Pieve tourist office (☎ 075 829 93 75; ⏱ 10am-2.30pm & 3.30-6pm in winter, 10.30am-12.30pm & 3.30-6pm in summer)

Pro Loco (☎ 075 82 76 35; Piazza Trento e Trieste 6, Passignano; ⏱ 10.30am-12.30pm & 4-7pm Mon-Sat, 10.30am-12.30pm Sun)

Tourist Office (☎ 075 825 42 22; Via Guglielmi, Isola Maggiore; ⏱ 9am-12.30pm & 1-6pm Mon-Sat)

Tourist Office (☎ 075 847 60 27; Via Sergio Cocchini 43, San Feliciano; ⏱ 10am-1pm & 4.30-7.30pm Mon-Sat, 10am-1pm Sun)

Sights

CASTIGLIONE DEL LAGO

Castiglione del Lago is one of the oldest towns around Lago di Trasimeno, and is the most popular with travellers today. In Etruscan times, the area produced wheat. In the 7th century, the town became an important defensive promontory for the Byzantine Perugia. It was fought over and traded between the papacy, the emperor and various territories for about 1000 years.

Castiglione del Lago's attractions include the **Palazzo della Corgna** (☎ 075 965 82 10; Piazza Gramsci; admission €2.60, includes entrance to Rocca del Leone; ⏱ 10am-1pm & 4-7.30pm in summer, 9.30am-4.30pm weekends only in winter), an ancient ducal palace housing an important series of 16th-century frescoes by Giovanni Antonio Pandolfi and Salvio Salvini. It was built in the 16th century by Jacopo Barozzi, who incorporated parts of ancient houses once owned by the feudal Baglioni family from Perugia. A covered passageway connects the palace with the 13th-century **Rocca del Leone**, ('the fortress of the lion'), a pentagon-shaped fortress built in 1247 and an excellent example of medieval military architecture. Seen from the lake, rearing up on a rocky promontory, it cuts a striking pose.

CITTÀ DELLA PIEVE

Città della Pieve is culturally and geographically considered part of Lago di Trasimeno, but it's about 20km to the south.

Although he became known as 'Il Perugino' ('the Perugian'), the famous Renaissance painter Pietro Vannucci was born here in 1445 and his paintings adorn all over the town. The **Cattedrale di San Gervasio e Protasio** houses more Perugino works and was developed from the ancient baptismal church (known as a *pieve*). Perhaps Perugino's most famous work in his hometown is

Adoration of the Magi, on view at the **Oratory of Santa Maria dei Bianchi**.

The head of the della Corgna family was appointed as governor of the town by his uncle, Pope Julius III, and subsequently commissioned artists to paint works for the town, known then as Castel della Pieve (it was elevated to a city in 1600). The frescoes in the statuesque **Palazzo della Corgna** include ones by Il Pomarancio and Salvio Savini.

ISOLA MAGGIORE

The lake's main inhabited island, Isola Maggiore, near Passignano, was reputedly a favourite with St Francis. The hill-top **Chiesa di San Michele Arcangelo** contains a Crucifixion by master painter Bartolomeo Caporalimaster. The island is famed for its lace and embroidery production and you can see examples in the **Museo del Merlotto** (Lace Museum; ☎ 075 825 42 33; Via Guglielmi, near the port, Isola Maggiore; admission €2.60; ⏱ 10am-1pm & 2.30-6pm daily). Be sure to stop by **Castello Guglielmi**.

ISOLA POLVESE

There's not much to do in Isola Polvese, which, to some, is its charm. The main draw is that the entire island is a scientific and educational park. Many school groups come here to use the environmental labs devoted to teaching preservation of biodiversity and sustainable technologies. Be sure to visit the **Garden of Aquatic Plants** and see biodiversity at work. Also of interest are the **Monastery of San Secondo** and the **Church of St Julian**. There are also remains of a 14th-century castle. For information or booking a guided tour of the island, you need to call ahead on ☎ 075 965 95 46.

MAGIONE

You might end up here – the least attractive town on the lake – if you suddenly realise you need a heap of groceries, a lawnmower or a mosaic table. However, the train stops here and it does have an interesting past. Originally constructed between 1160 and 1170, the Templars used Magione's fortified abbey as a hospital for crusaders going back and forth to fight in the crusades in Jerusalem. The Knights of Malta took the abbey from the Templars and, to this day, still own it. You can drive up to the **Castle of the Knights of Malta** (☎ 075 84 38 59; admission free), which is only open from 22 June to 24 August.

PASSIGNANO

Passignano feels like the most holiday-ish of the Trasimeno towns, with many restaurants, hotels and souvenir shops. The medieval castle on the top of the hill is closed to visitors, but the view from in front of it is as good as it gets. Check out the 16th-century **Chiesa della Madonna dell'Uliveto** (☎ 075 82 71 24; ✆ 5-7pm Wed & Thu, 4-8pm Fri & Sat, 10am-noon & 5-7pm Sun). A must-see for anyone stopping here on the last Sunday of July is the **Palio delle Barche** (Boat Race), when groups of neighbourhood men carry a boat to the castle on the top of the hill, probably thinking that they need to move to a different town.

SAN FELICIANO

This working town still sees fishermen leave to trawl for fish in the morning. Mostly a strip of hotels catering to Northern Europeans on a sun holiday, San Feliciano does have a few worthwhile stops. For those that are into this sort of thing, the **Fishing Museum** (☎ 075 847 92 61; www.museodellapesca.it; Via Lungolago della Pace e del Lavoro 20; adult/reduced/children €3/2/1; ✆ 10am-1pm & 2.30-5pm Sat & Sun Nov-Jan, 10.30am-12.30pm & 2.30-5.30pm Thu-Sun Feb-Mar & Oct, 10am-12.30pm & 3-6pm Tue-Sun Apr-Jun & Sep, 10am-1pm & 3-7pm daily Jul-Aug) showcases fishing techniques from ancient times until modern days. Although the thought of spending two hours strolling through the history of ancient fishing techniques doesn't seem enthralling, this museum is actually extremely popular as it shows an unusual peek into history.

TUORO

The only reason to go to Tuoro is to visit the site of one of the deadliest battles in ancient history. In 217 BC this area witnessed one of the bloodiest battles in Roman history. The first Punic war had ended in 241 BC, when the Romans defeated the Carthaginians at Aegadean Islands, winning back Corsica, Sardinia and Sicily. Hannibal's father, Hasdrubal Barca, began planning for revenge. The second Punic war began in 219 BC. The following year, Hannibal chose to march by land, also in order to stir up hatred for the Romans and partially to gather more troops along the way, from Spain across the Pyrenees and the Alps (oh yes, along with 50,000 troops, 9000 horses and 37 elephants). They marched in a southerly manner so it would look like they were planning to attack Rome itself. When they arrived at the lake, Hannibal had his men run back to Tuoro to light fires so it would look like they were further away from the lake than they were. In fact, behind thick fog, they were slowly surrounding the local Roman troops, led by Consul Caius Flaminius. They ambushed the ill-prepared Romans, killing 16,000 men, including Flaminius himself. There were so many killed that the local stream was renamed Sanguineto (The Bloody) after it flowed blood for three days.

You can visit the **Permanent Documentation Centre** (☎ 075 82 52 20) and take an historic archaeological tour.

Also visit **Field of the Sun** (Campo del Sole; near Loc. Navaccia Lido, close to the lake's edge), a group of 28 sand sculptures made by 28 celebrated artists which looks like a modern-day Stonehenge.

Activities

Lago di Trasimeno abounds with water sports and outdoor activities. From April to September, the water is tested for purity each month. Ask at one of the tourist offices for *Tourist Itineraries in the Trasimeno District*, a booklet of walking and horse-riding tracks.

Horse-riding centres include the **Maneggio Oasi** (☎ 0337 65 37 95; Loc. Orto, in Castiglione del Lago); and the **Poggio del Belveduto** (☎ 075 82 90 76; www.poggiodelbelveduto; Via Donato, Loc. Campori di Sopra, Passignano), which also has archery, if you're feeling particularly medieval. Ask about other riding centres, and sporting activities such as kayaking, at either the tourist offices or your hotel or camp site.

Canoe, windsurfing and sailboat rentals can be found in Castiglione del Lago at **La Merangola** (☎ 075 965 24 45; Loc. Lido Arezzo) or in Tuoro at **Belneazione Tuoro** (☎ 328 454 97 66; Loc. Punta Navaccia). La Merangola also has a small beach and restaurant, and turns into a **discoteca** at night.

To rent **scooters**, try **Marinelli Ferrettini Fabio** (☎ 075 95 31 26; Via Buozzi 26, Castiglione del Lago; ✆ 7am-8pm Mon-Sat). **Bicycles** can be rented in Castiglione del Lago at **Valentini** (☎ 075 95 1663; Via Firenze 68/B), which also rents children's bikes, and in Passignano at **Eta Beta Modellismo** (☎ 075 82 94 01; Via della Vittoria 58). Many local camp sites and *agriturismi* rent bicycles and water-sports equipment.

For a fun cultural and gastronomic experience, don't miss the **weekly markets**, which have all sorts of fresh local produce and basic goods. They take place from 8.30am to 1pm at the following locations: Castiglione del Lago (Wednesday), Magione (Thursday), Tuoro (Friday) and Passignano (Saturday). Ask at each town's tourist office for more information.

Festivals & Events

No different from the rest of festival-happy Umbria, Lago di Trasimeno hosts countless events throughout the year. The region has its share of unique festivals, though. See p268 for more about the **Palio delle Barche**.

In Città della Pieve, the first weekend in June is the **Art and Culture festival**. In mid-August, the **Palio dei Terzieri** showcases the town's Renaissance past with some serious revelry, including acrobatics, fire-eating and archery.

Sleeping

The Lago di Trasimeno area is filled with every type of lodging imaginable, from an environmental hostel on Isola Polvese to your own private rental villa in Lisciano Noccione, where you can take classes in fresco painting or Italian cooking.

BUDGET

Camping Badiaccia (☎ 075 965 90 97, in winter 075 823 01 03; camping@badiaccia.com; www.badiaccia.com; Via Trasimeno I 91, Bivia Borghetto; sites per person/tent/car €6.50/6/2, caravans & bungalows €35-93; ☐ ⚒) You don't need camping equipment to stay here; you can rent a bungalow or caravan, some with kitchens. The tennis courts, two pools, basketball courts, ping pong, bocce, 200m of beach, convenience store and Internet access means you hardly have to leave. This is a fabulous place for kids. The restaurant is surprisingly good.

Listro (☎ /fax 075 95 11 93; listro@listro.it; www.listro .it; Via Lungolago, Castiglione del Lago; sites per person/tent €4.15/4.15; ✆ Apr-Sep) This camp site is 500m from Castiglione del Lago, with 100 tent sites.

Il Poggio (☎ 075 965 95 50; ostelloilpoggio@libero .it; www.isolapolvese.it; Isola Polvese; €16 per person, meal supplement €8; ✆ end Mar-end Oct) This old farmhouse uses the latest techniques in sustainable development, such as phytopurification and natural troughs to purify waste water.

A pool carved out of rock holds regional aquatic plants. Lots of activities are available, including kayaking, ping pong, beach volleyball and various games, as well as hammocks to soak up the sunsets. The easiest way to reach the island is from San Feliciano. Call ahead, especially if you have heavy luggage, and staff will pick you up in their car.

Albergo Il Torrione (☎ 075 95 32 36; iltorrione@ trasinet.com; www.trasinet.com/iltorrione; Via delle Mure 4/8, Castiglione del Lago; d €55-65) This tranquil setting near the heart of Castiglione del Lago is a sweet little oasis. Each room and the public areas are decorated with beautiful artwork painted by the owner. The rooms are tastefully furnished and have their own bathroom and shower. A beautiful private garden overlooks the lake, where you can sit on chaise lounges and enjoy the scent of flowers while watching the sunset.

Pensione del Pescatore (☎ 075 829 60 63; fax 075 829201; Via San Bernardino 5, Passignano; s/d €28.40/ 43.90) This family-run *pensione* has 11 simple but appealing rooms above a charming local trattoria (a simple restaurant). It was closed for renovation in 2003, so expect prices to go up in 2004.

Hotel Da Sauro (☎ 075 82 61 68; fax 075 825130; Via Guglielmi 1, Isola Maggiore; d €65). This family-run establishment has just 10 rooms in a rustic stone building at the northern end of the main village on the island. The restaurant downstairs is very popular so expect a lot of noise at mealtimes.

Paola's B&B (☎ 075 573 08 08, mobile 335 6247240; Città del Pieve; per person €30-50) For an authentic Italian experience, stay in Paola's home. She rents out two rooms in her 17th-century flat (be sure to take a peek at the frescoes in her daughter's bedroom). Paola also offers cooking and Italian lessons (usually at the same time) in addition to B&B. During winter, she cooks in her open-hearth fireplace. Paolo speaks French and a bit of English.

MID-RANGE

Hotel Miralago (☎ 075 95 11 57; www.hotelmiralago.it; Piazza Mazzini 6, Castiglione del Lago; s/d €65/77) The Miralago is very central and top-floor rooms have magnificent lake views. It's rather austere, but it's got amenities such as satellite TV and room service. There's also a good restaurant downstairs, La Fontana, a perennial favourite.

CASA SAN MARTINO

There's no other word than 'perfection' for this farmhouse in the hills north of Lago di Trasimeno (☎ 075 84 42 88; casam@tuscanyvacation.com; San Martino 19, Lisciano Noccione). The owner has completely restored this 250-year-old stone building (she lives in the old pigsty) to accommodate up to eight friends or family members at a time. It's incredibly private and quiet, but less than an hour from most destinations in Tuscany and Umbria. The main building is impeccably decorated with terracotta tile floors, wood-beam ceilings and open-hearth fireplace, and comes with a completely stocked kitchen, washer and dryer, and four bedrooms with en suite. Outside is a pool facing an expansive countryside view (with a few castles thrown in) and a stone barbeque grill. Your hostess – an American resident of Italy for almost 15 years – can provide itineraries of the area, put you in touch with a retired English-army captain for a guided tour of Hannibal's battlefield, and tell you which are the best restaurants and shops in the area. During the off season, you don't even have to gather a group of eight, as the rooms are sometimes rented separately as B&B accommodation.

The best time to come would be during special events, such as cooking classes taught by former New York chef Faye Hess, who teaches guests to cook meals they can easily prepare for themselves at home, such as polenta with roasted tomatoes and thyme, homemade gnocchi, and Italian basics like *bruschetta* (garlic bread with tomatoes and herbs served as an appetiser) or red sauce. There are also classes in fresco painting and writing, and guided hiking trips.

To book for summer, call months in advance. The cost is reasonable: €2000 during winter, €2500 during autumn and spring, and €3000 a week during summer. Winter can be a great time to visit, as it has central heating and an open-hearth fireplace.

Hotel La Torre (☎ 075 95 16 66; latorre@trasinet .com; www.trasinet.com/latorre; Via Emanuele 50, Castiglione del Lago; s/d €55/75) Located in the heart of Castiglione del Lago, this building is a restored palace, but the rooms are rather basic. The breakfast is fabulous, as the hotel owners also run a bakery downstairs. They'll pick you up at the train station for a small fee.

TOP END

Relais La Fattoria (☎ 075 84 53 22; www.relaislafattoria .com; Castel Rigone; d from €78, junior ste in high season €186) This impeccably furnished castle up on the hills above the lake offers a spectacular setting for a holiday. The 17th-century building has been outfitted with satellite TV, and has a fantastic restaurant.

AGRITURISMO

Locanda del Galluzzo Agriturismo (☎ 075 84 53 52; locandagalluzzo@hotmail.com; Loc. Castel Rigone) This *agriturismo* on the hills above the lake is in a beautiful setting and, unlike an increasing number of places that call themselves *agriturismi*, food is actually grown onsite, and cooked and served in the restaurant. Each mini-apartment holds two to four people and costs from €310 to €480 a week, or from €60 a double. The restaurant specialises in wild game. There's a pool, view of the lake, and you can rent mountain bikes.

Eating

Ristorante La Corte (☎ 075 84 53 22; Via Rigone 1, Castel Rigone; dishes about €30) This is one of the more upscale restaurants in the area. Its appetisers are the best part of the meal; try the *bruschetta*, the swordfish *carpaccio* or the sweet lentil soup. It also serves a delectable tagliatelle with black Norcia truffles and freshly made *strangozzi* (the Umbrian square-shaped version of spaghetti) with *porcini*.

Da Settimio (☎ 075 847 60 00; Via Lungolago Alicata, San Feliciano; dishes about €21; ☒ closed Thu & throughout Nov) This little restaurant, which also has a small hotel on the 2nd floor, serves many local fish dishes, including *risotto alla pescatora* (fisherman's risotto) or grilled local tench. Try its appetiser fish platter with 'little fried fishes'. Directly across from Da Settimio towards the lake is the simply named **Bar Gelateria**, which has some of the best *propio produzione gelato* in the area.

La Locanda del Castello (☎ 075 829 64 25; Piazza Garibaldi 13; dishes about €25) Excellent restaurant with very well-priced meals. Specialities are its many fish and meat dishes, as well as a grilled *pecorino* salad.

Lido (☎ 075 82 8472; Via Roma 3, Passignano; dishes about €20; ☒ Mar-Oct) One of the oldest restaurants in Passignano, it's located right on the water, above the lake, facing Isola Maggiore. It serves local cuisine, including specialities such as *crostini* with carp eggs and *taglierini al profumo di lago* (which translates, very roughly, as 'pasta with lake perfume').

Ristorante L'Acquario (☎ 075 965 24 32; Via Emanuele 69, Castiglione del Lago; meals around €25; Jun-Oct only, closed Wed) This is the oldest restaurant in Castiglione del Lago and cooks up traditional dishes, including (surprise!) local fish specialities based on ancient recipes.

Ristorante La Cantina (☎ 075 965 24 63; Via Emanuele 93, Castiglione del Lago; meals around €21; closed Mon during winter) Relax in the secluded garden, enjoy the beautiful view and eat cheap pizza (€5). Try the gnocchi with saffron, and its crayfish sauce is delicious. Many types of wine, several from the Lago di Trasimeno area, are served here.

Getting There & Around

There are two main train lines that go past the lake. The slow train goes from Terontola to Perugia, Assisi and Foligno and makes stops in Tuoro, Passignano, Torricella and Magione. You can travel from Perugia to Passignano (€2, 30 minutes, nine daily), to Magione (€1.60, 20 minutes, eight daily), or to Tuoro (€2.20, 30 minutes, eight daily).

Buses connect Perugia with Passignano (€2.60, one hour, five daily) and Castiglione del Lago (€4.15, one hour 20 minutes, eight daily). Passignano is also served by regular trains from Perugia (€1.95, 25 minutes, hourly) via Terontola (€1.30, 10 minutes, hourly), making it the most accessible part of the lake.

The ferry is operated by **APM** (☎ 075 50 67 81). Check the listings at each town's ferry terminal, as times vary with the season, holiday schedule or day of the week. From Passignano, you can get to Isola Maggiore (one way/return €3.30/5.40, 14 daily). There are far fewer direct ferries from Passignano to Castiglione del Lago (one way/return €3.80/6.90, two daily), but you can go through Isola Maggiore. The best way to get to Isola Polvese is to go from San Feliciano (€2.70/4.30, nine daily), but you can also get there from Isola Maggiore (€3.30/5.90, six daily). You can also go from Tuoro to Isola Maggiore (€2.70/4.30, 17 daily).

The latest bus, train and ferry schedules are listed in the booklet *Intorno al Trasi-meno*, available at any tourist office within 20km of the lake.

GUBBIO

pop 31,651

Hitched onto the steep slopes of Monte Ingino and overlooking a picturesque valley, the centuries-old *palazzi* of Gubbio exude a warm ochre glow in the late afternoon sunlight. You don't need much imagination to feel that you have stepped back into the Middle Ages, while meandering along the town's quiet, treeless lanes and peering into some of the city's many fine ceramic shops.

Gubbio is famous for its Eugubian Tables, which date from 300–100 BC and constitute the best existing example of ancient Umbrian script. In 295 BC Gubbio was the site of an important battle, where the Romans fought the Umbri, Etruscans and Gauls. Because Gubbio didn't participate, Rome elevated its status and the town became Romanised. It was fought over many times, given to the church, and entered into the Battle of Montaperti between the Guelphs and the Ghibellines. In the 14th century it fell into the hands of the Montefeltro family of Urbino and was later reincorporated into the Papal States in the late 1500s. It didn't gain its independence until 1831, and quickly saw Italian unification in the 1860s.

Gubbio now has a thriving tourist industry. One of the most famous festivals in all of Italy is here on 15 May (Corsa dei Ceri; see p273). Gubbio can be overcrowded at times, especially on summer weekends. But it's possible, even on a Sunday, in August to venture further afield and find your own serene cobblestone street flanked by grey limestone buildings.

Orientation

The city is small and easy to explore. The immense traffic circle known as Piazza Quaranta Martiri, at the base of the hill, is where buses to the city terminate, and it also has a large car park. The square was named in honour of 40 local people who were killed by the Nazis in 1944 in reprisal for partisan activities. From here it is a short, if somewhat steep, walk up Via della Repubblica to the main square, Piazza Grande, also known as the Piazza della

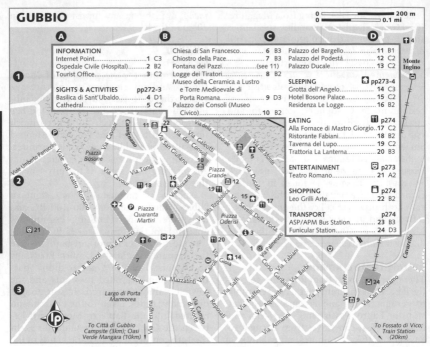

GUBBIO

INFORMATION		
Internet Point	1	C3
Ospedale Civile (Hospital)	2	B2
Tourist Office	3	C2

SIGHTS & ACTIVITIES	pp272-3	
Basilica di Sant'Ubaldo	4	D1
Cathedral	5	C2

Chiesa di San Francesco	6	B3
Chiostro della Pace	7	B3
Fontana dei Pazzi	(see 11)	
Logge dei Tiratori	8	B2
Museo della Ceramica a Lustro		
e Torre Medioevale di		
Porta Romana	9	D3
Palazzo dei Consoli (Museo		
Civico)	10	B2

Palazzo del Bargello	11	B1
Palazzo del Podestà	12	C2
Palazzo Ducale	13	C2

SLEEPING	pp273-4	
Grotta dell'Angelo	14	C2
Hotel Bosone Palace	15	C2
Residenza Le Logge	16	B2

EATING	p274	
Alla Fornace di Mastro Giorgio	17	C2
Ristorante Fabiani	18	B2
Taverna del Lupo	19	B2
Trattoria La Lanterna	20	B3

ENTERTAINMENT	p273	
Teatro Romano	21	A2

SHOPPING	p274	
Leo Grilli Arte	22	B2

TRANSPORT	p274	
ASP/APM Bus Station	23	B3
Funicular Station	24	D3

Signoria. Corso Garibaldi and Piazza Oderisi are to your right as you head up the hill.

Information

EMERGENCY
Police Station (Via XX Settembre 97)

INTERNET RESOURCES
www.gubbio.com The best website to find tourist information on Gubbio.

MEDICAL SERVICES
Ospedale Civile (hospital; ☎ 075 9 23 91; Piazza Quaranta Martiri)
Emergency Doctor (☎ 075 923 94 68)

POST
Post Office (Via Cairoli 11; ⏰ 8.10am-5pm Mon-Sat)

TOURIST INFORMATION
Tourist Office (☎ 075 922 06 93; Piazza Oderisi; ⏰ 8.30am-1.45pm & 3.30-6.30pm Mon-Fri, 9am-1pm Sat, 9.30am-12.30pm Sun & public holidays) Can help with accommodation and information on festivals and surrounding towns.

Sights

Gubbio's most impressive buildings look out over Piazza Grande, where the heart of the Corsa dei Ceri takes place (see p273). The piazza is dominated above all by the 14th-century **Palazzo dei Consoli**, attributed to Gattapone. The crenellated facade and tower can be seen from all over the town. The building houses the **Museo Civico** (☎ 075 927 42 98; Piazza Grande; adults/reduced €4/2.50 including gallery; ⏰ 10am-1pm & 3-6pm Apr-Oct, 10am-1pm & 2-5pm Nov-Mar), which displays the Eugubian Tables, discovered in 1444 near the Teatro Romano (Roman Theatre) southwest of Piazza Quaranta Martiri. The seven bronze tablets are the main source for research into the ancient Umbrian language. Upstairs is a picture gallery featuring works from the Gubbian school. Across the square is the **Palazzo del Podestà**, also known as the Palazzo Pretorio, built along similar lines to its grander counterpart. Now the city's active town hall, you can take a peek in to see the impressive vaulted ceilings.

From Via San Gerolamo you can ride the **funicular** (adults/children €5/4 return trip; ⏰ 10am-

1.15pm & 2.30-6.30pm daily, 9.30am-1.15pm & 2.30-7pm public holidays) to the **Basilica di Sant'Ubaldo**. The church is fairly uninspiring, but you'll never forget the ride there. One of several sweaty men throws you into a moving metal contraption that looks somewhat like a ski lift for giant birdcages. Believe the man when he tells you to stand on the dots. You're whisked instantly away, dangling dozens of metres precariously above a rocky hill. The ride up is as frightening as it is utterly beautiful. There's a restaurant on top of the hill and the aforementioned church, but the nicest way to spend the day is to bring a picnic and have a wander.

Just below the birdcage funicular is the **Museo della Ceramica a Lustro e Torre Medioevale di Porta Romana** (☎ 075 922 11 99; Via Dante 24; admission €2; � 9am-1pm & 3.30-7pm). *Il lustro* ceramics came from the Arab influence in Spain in the 11th century. On the 2nd floor, ceramics from prehistoric times share space with medieval and Renaissance pieces. There's also a collection of crossbows from the 18th century, some that have a target range as far as 50m. Check out the really un-fun-looking chastity belt on the 4th floor and appreciate that you're alive today instead of 300 years ago.

Perugia's Fra Bevignate is said to have designed the **Chiesa di San Francesco** (Piazza Quaranta Martiri; admission free; � 7.15am-noon & 3.30-7.30pm). It features impressive frescoes by a local artist, Ottaviano Nelli. Built in a simple Gothic style in the 13th century, it has an impressive rose window. Wander into the **Chiostro della Pace** (Cloister of Peace) in the adjoining convent to view some ancient mosaics and wander around the peaceful garden.

Via Ducale leads up to the 13th-century pink **cathedral** (Via Federico da Montefeltro; donations welcome; � 9am-7pm Mon-Sat, 9am-1pm Sun), a plain beast with a fine 12th-century stained-glass window and a fresco attributed to Bernardino Pinturicchio. Opposite the pink cathedral, the 15th-century **Palazzo Ducale** (☎ 075 927 58 72; Via Federico da Montefeltro; adult/child €3/free; � 8.30am-7.30pm Tue-Sun) was built by the Duke of Montefeltro and his family as a scaled-down version of their grand palazzo in Urbino, and its walls hide an impressive Renaissance courtyard.

From Piazza Grande, Via dei Consoli leads west to the 13th-century **Palazzo del Bargello**, the city's medieval police station

and prison. In front of it is the **Fontana dei Pazzi** (Fountain of Lunatics), so named because of a belief that if you walk around it three times, you will go mad – on summer weekends the number of tourists carrying out this ritual is indeed cause for concern about their collective sanity.

Southwest of Piazza Quaranta Martiri, off Viale del Teatro Romano, are the overgrown remains of 1st-century-AD **Teatro Romano** (☎ 075 922 09 22; admission free; � 8.30am-7.30pm Apr-Sep, 8am-1.30pm Oct-Mar). Most of what you see is reconstructed.

Festivals & Events

The centuries-old **Corsa dei Ceri** (Candles Race) is held each year on 15 May to commemorate the city's patron saint, Sant'Ubaldo. The event starts at 5.30am and involves three teams, each carrying a *cero* (these 'candles' are massive wooden pillars weighing about 400kg, each bearing a statue of a 'rival' saint) and racing through the city's streets. This is one of Italy's liveliest festivals and warrants inclusion in your itinerary, but be wary if you have small children as the crowd gets excited and scuffles between the supporters of the three teams are common.

On the last Sunday in May, there's the annual **Palio della Balestra**, an archery competition involving medieval crossbows, in which Gubbio competes with its neighbour Borgo San Sepolchro. Every tourist store in Gubbio sells some sort of miniature crossbow (if you're travelling home on an airplane, it might be difficult to explain your purchase to an airline security employee).

Sleeping

BUDGET

Città di Gubbio (☎ /fax 075 927 20 37; Loc. Ortoguidone; sites per person/tent €7.75/8.25; � Apr-Sep) For camping, try this site in a southern suburb of Gubbio, about 3km south of Piazza Quaranta Martiri along the S298 (Via Perugina).

Residenza Le Logge (☎ 075 927 75 74; Via Piccardi 7-9; s/d €47/57, mini-apartments €62-80) This is one of those rare little perfect locations, where you'll either appreciate the great value or feel luxurious on a tight budget. Decorated with homey antiques and comfortable beds, it's quiet, tranquil and central. Three rooms feature garden views – try to get one of these, but the view of Gubbio is also beautiful. During summer, you can take your breakfast (included in the price) in the garden. The two mini-apartments are even more perfect than the rooms, and have kitchenettes and room for four people. One has a gracious blue-and-white porcelain-and-ceramic bathtub big enough to park a Fiat in.

Grotta dell'Angelo (☎ 075 927 17 47; grottadellangelo@jumpy.it; Via Gioia 47; s/d €35/50; ☒ closed 7 Jan–7 Feb) Clean, simple and welcoming, this two-star hotel has modern rooms and a charming garden restaurant.

MID-RANGE

Hotel Bosone Palace (☎ 075 922 06 88; hotelbosonepalace@mencarelligroup.com; Via XX Settembre 22; s/d/ste €73/99/181; ☒) This chic three-star hotel has 17th-century frescoes in the breakfast room and benefits from its central position. Parking is 300m away, but it's best to stop here first and drop off your things, and staff will explain where to park. Suites are a big jump up, but worth it if you've always wondered what it truly means to sleep like a queen or king.

AGRITURISMO

Oasi Verde Mengara (☎ 075 922 70 04; direzione@oasiverdemengara.it; www.oasiverdemengara.it; Loc. Mengara Vallingegno 1) This *agriturismo* is just 10km south of the city. Its fine restaurant is open to the public, and you can eat a memorable and very filling meal for around €17. It also organises horse riding (€13 per hour). It's easily accessible from Gubbio using the regular APM bus to Perugia, which stops right outside (ask the driver to tell you when to get off).

Eating

Taverna del Lupo (☎ 075 927 43 68; Via Ansidei 21; meals about €32; ☒ closed Mon) Il Lupo was the wolf that St Francis domesticated, who supposedly came back to this restaurant to dine. The wolf made an excellent choice. Don't be put off by the waiters in penguin suits, but you will be more comfortable (and better served) if you're smartly dressed. Most of what is served is locally produced in the surrounding Apennines, including its cheese, truffles and olive oil.

Ristorante Fabiani (☎ 075 927 46 39; Piazza Quaranta Martiri 26; meals around €15.50; ☒ closed Tue) This place is a large traditional *trattoria* with garden seating.

Trattoria La Lanterna (☎ 075 927 66 94; Via Gioia 23; meals about €20; ☒ closed Thu) Here, where local specialities are on hand, many meals feature delicious *tartufi*.

Alla Fornace di Mastro Giorgio (☎ 075 922 1836; Via Mastro Giorgio 2; meals about €24; ☒ closed Tue) One of the better restaurants in town, this is also one of the more expensive, with dining in elegant surroundings.

Shopping

Leo Grilli Arte (☎ 075 922 22 72; Via dei Consoli 78; ☒ 9.30am-1pm & 3-7pm Tue-Sun) In the Middle Ages, ceramics were one of Gubbio's main sources of income and there are some fabulous contemporary samples on display in this crumbly 15th-century mansion. Artist/owner Leo Grilli works here almost every day, as he has for decades. You can watch him work at a ministudio in the shop.

Getting There & Around

APM buses (☎ 075 927 46 39) run to Perugia (€3.80, one hour 10 minutes, 10 daily), Gualdo Tadino (€2.25, 50 minutes, 10 daily) and Umbertide (€2.60, 50 minutes, three daily) and a service to Rome (€14.45, four hours) leaving daily at 5.50am. Buses depart from Piazza Quaranta Martiri. You can buy tickets at **Easy Gubbio** (Via della Repubblica 13).

The closest train station is at Fossato di Vico, about 20km southeast of the city. Trains run from Fossato to Rome (€10.10, 2½ hours, eight daily), Ancona (€4.20, one hour 20 minutes, nine daily) and Foligno (€2.40, 40 minutes, roughly hourly), where you can pick up connections to Arezzo, Perugia and Florence. Hourly APM buses connect the station with Gubbio (€1.95, 30 minutes), although there are delays between train and bus connections of anything between five minutes and an hour.

By car or motorcycle, take the S298 from Perugia or the S76 from Ancona, and follow the signs. Parking in the large car park in Piazza Quaranta Martiri costs €0.50 per hour.

Walking is the best way to get around, but ASP buses connect Piazza Quaranta Martiri with the funicular station and most main sights.

For a taxi, dial ☎ 075 927 38 00.

AROUND GUBBIO

South on the S3, on the way from Parco Regionale del Monte Cucco, **Gualdo Tadino** is a fairly industrial town. Although it doesn't offer much in the way of tourist attractions, it does have the best-named site, the 13th-century **Rocca Flea**. One of its major industrial outputs is ceramics; in August the town celebrates a month-long exhibition of ceramics. Slightly more enticing than its neighbour Gualdo Tadino, **Nocera Umbra** is mostly known for its spring water, and still has a few vestiges from the past. Its most notable monument is the **Torre dei Trinci**, a medieval tower built by the seigniory Trinci family (p290).

PARCO REGIONALE DEL MONTE CUCCO

East of Gubbio, this park is a haven for outdoor activities and is dotted with caves, many of which can be explored. It is well set up for walkers, rock climbers and horse riders, and has many hotels and *rifugi* (mountain huts). **Costacciaro**, accessible by bus from Gubbio (€1.95, 30 minutes) via Scheggia or Fossato di Vico, is a good base for exploring the area and is the starting point for a walk to the summit of Monte Cucco (1566m).

Monte Cucco is a fantastic place to go caving or spelunking. The Monte Cucco karst system is the largest in Italy and the fifth deepest in the world (922m). Sinkholes, wells and dolines create unique geological formations and lush habitats for various species of birds and plants.

Club Alpino Italiano (CAI) produces a walking map, *Carta dei Sentieri Massiccio del Monte Cucco* (€12), for sale in local bookshops and newsagents. The free booklet *Monte Cucco Park: Country Walks Through History* is available in English at *rifugi* and tourist offices throughout Umbria. Use this as a guide to the best of Umbria's nature and history. The booklet describes in detail 11 walks in the area that take you through some of Umbria's most picturesque terrain, more Alpine-like than the typical rolling hillside. The guides detail the estimated time needed while walking at a good pace (most take at least four hours and are far from civilization, so take lots of water and emergency supplies), presence of water sources on the trail and a thorough map of each route. If you don't have your hiking gear, Tour #6 is a 62km driving route through ancient abbeys and monasteries in the region.

The **Centro Escursionistico Naturalistico Speleologico** (☎ 075 917 04 00; mail@cens.it; www.cens.it; Via Calcinaro 7A, Costacciaro) can help with infor-

THE UBIQUITOUS UMBRIAN OLIVE TREE

If you know what you're looking for, it's easy to spot the difference between a young and an old olive tree. After about 60 years, olive trees start to split. If you see an olive tree with what looks like two, three or even four smaller trees growing out of separate places in the ground, it's still just one tree (some trees have been known to live for 1000 years or more). The five major sub-zones of Umbrian olive-growing areas are Assisi-Spoleto, Colli Martini, Colli Amerini, Colli del Trasimeno and Colli Orvietani.

mation about exploring local caves, walking and mountain-bike routes. You can get information at the **park office** (☎ 075 917 73 26; parco.montecucco@libero.it; Via Matteotti 52, 'Villa Anita', Sigillo). Online, look for information at www.parks.it/parco.monte.cucco.

The **Campeggio Rio Verde** (☎ 075 917 01 38; www.campingrioverde.it; 3km west of Costacciaro; adult/child/tent/car €5/3/4.50/2.50) camp site offers horse riding (€13 per hour, during the summer), rock climbing and speleology. Many *agriturismo* establishments in the area can also arrange horse riding. Don't even consider coming here on a weekend in August – the rates more than quintuple. A good mountain inn is the **Rifugio Escursionistico Dal Lepre** (☎ /fax 075 917 77 33; Pian del Monte, Sigillo, Montecucco; €15 with breakfast), also featuring a decent restaurant.

It is possible to hire **mountain bikes** at the **Coop Arte e Natura** (☎ 075 917 07 40; Via Stazione 2) in the village of Fossato di Vico, about 8km southeast of Costacciaro.

ALTA VALLE DEL TEVERE

The northernmost reaches of Umbria, clamped in between Tuscany and Le Marche and known as the Alta Valle del Tevere (Upper Tiber Valley), is regarded as Museum Valley for its extraordinary collection of art and history, especially in the town of Città di Castello.

The area's more interesting spots are **Città di Castello**, which was a powerful centre during the Renaissance; **Umbertide**, with a couple of castles and dominated by a 14th-century fortress; tiny **Monte San Maria Tiberina**, where there's a great camp site and an imposing castle; and **Montone**, a vertical medieval town where Braccio Fortebracci was born. The area is connected with Perugia by the private Ferrovia Centrale Umbra railway and several buses. SITA buses also connect the valley with nearby Arezzo in Tuscany and travels on to Florence.

Città di Castello
pop 36,921

Città di Castello is surrounded by some pretty awful suburbs, but if you can look past this, it's got a beautiful historic centre, many grand buildings and the second most important art museum in Umbria after the National Gallery in Perugia. Known as Tifernum Tiberium in the Roman era, Castrum Felicitatis (Town of Happiness) in the Medieval period and Città di Castello today, it doesn't have a castle, nor is it much of a city. The town was economically depressed until the 1960s, but is now known for its thriving paper, book, ironworks and furniture industries. The town's favourite son is Alberto Burri, and two galleries proudly display much of his lifetime's work. (The town's current favourite daughter is actress Monica Bellucci.)

Note: Don't bother visiting Città di Castello on a Monday. Practically every museum is closed, as are many restaurants.

ORIENTATION
A rarity in Umbria, the entire town, including its historic centre, is within a valley, so it's almost all on flat ground and easily walkable. People using wheelchairs will have less of a problem getting around here.

From the train station, walk straight ahead for 200m. Turn right under Porta Santa Maria Maggiore and take Corso Vittorio Emanuele to Piazza Matteotti, the centre of town. Driving is mostly forbidden in the walled city, but there's piles of free parking just outside the walls, much of it around Porta San Giacomo and Piazza Garibaldi.

INFORMATION
EMERGENCY
Police (☎ 0758 52 92 22; Piazza Garibaldi)

INTERNET RESOURCES
www.cdcnet.net
www.cittadicastello.com

Medical Services
Hospital (☎ 075 8 50 91; Largo Giovanni Muzi Betti)

Money
There is a Cassi di Risparmio ATM machine to the left of the tourist office at 3a.

Post
Post Office (☎ 075 855 44 89; Via Gramsci; ☑ 8.10am-6pm)

Tourist Information
Tourist Office (☎ 075 855 49 22; info@iat.citta-di-castello.pg.it; Logge Bufalini, Piazza Matteotti)

SIGHTS
The collection at the **Pinacoteca Comunale** (☎ 075 855 42 02; Via della Cannoniera; adults/reduced/children €5/3/1.50; ☑ 10am-1pm & 2.30-6.30pm Tue-Sun Apr-Oct, 10am-12.30pm & 3.30-5.30pm Tue-Sun Nov-Mar), in the imposing 15th-century Palazzo Vitelli alla Cannoniera, is well regarded as the second most important art collection in Umbria. Ask for the detailed information booklet in English, which will guide you through the paintings, giving explanations and context to the more prominent works. The art gallery began in the 1860s after the liberation of Città di Castello from Papal rule. There are important works by masters such as Raphael, Vasari and Signorelli. The furniture collection is small but includes some beautiful inlaid Gothic work from monasteries in the 1500s. Admire the immensely cool astrological fresco cycle in the staircase, filled with depictions of Apollo and the Muses, Erudites and Emperors, seahorses and winged cherubs. The halls include wall frescoes from Cristoforo Gherardi depicting historical subjects such as Hannibal, Caesar and Alexander the Great.

Collezione Burri (☎ 075 855 46 49; Palazzo Albizzini, Via Albizzini 1; secondary exhibit: Ex Seccatoi del Tabacco, Via Pierucci; ☑ 9am-12.30pm & 2.30-6pm Tue-Sat, 9am-12.30pm & 2.30-5pm Tue-Sat Oct-May, 10.30am-12.30pm & 3-6pm public holidays; adult/reduced/chldren €5/3/2) Collezione Burri houses Alberto Burri's main collection. The artist began his art career in 1946 after a stint as a prisoner of war in Texas. His contemporary work with paint and physical materials has been immensely popular throughout the world. His early work influenced the New Dada and Pop Art movements, and artists such as Rauschenberg, Christo and Jasper Johns

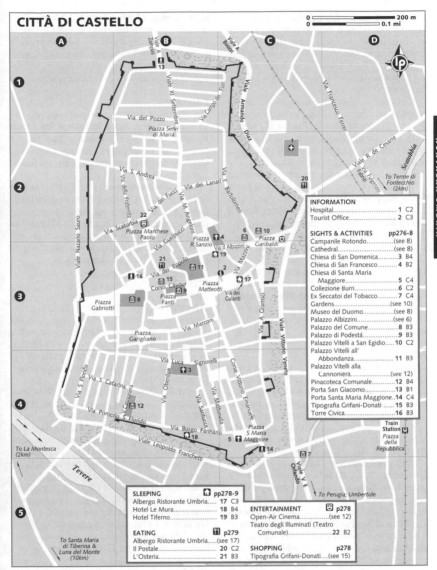

CITTÀ DI CASTELLO

credit him as inspiration. A secondary exhibit of mostly larger pieces is housed in the old tobacco-drying warehouses – a site in itself to see – and is closed from November to March, except by special requests made three days in advance.

Not much remains of the original Romanesque cathedral, but the building still houses some treasures. **Museo del Duomo** (Museo Capitolare; ☎ 075 855 47 05; Piazza Gabriotti 3; ☻ 9.30am-1pm & 2.30-7pm Tue-Sun summer, 10am-1pm & 2.30-6.30pm Tue-Sun winter; adult/reduced/child €4/3/2) houses the most impressive collection of sacred artefacts in all of Umbria. In the same building complex is the **Palazzo del Comune**. In the council chamber you can still see the official bricks dating back to medieval times when citizens could compare the size of their bricks to make sure they weren't being ripped off. Across the way is the **Torre Civica** (Piazza Gabriotti; ☉ 10.30am-12.30pm & 3-6.30pm Tue-Sat summer, 10am-12.30pm & 2-5.30pm Tue-Sat winter).

Città di Castello also has many other impressive buildings. Facing the main square, Piazza Matteotti, is the **Palazzo di Podestá**, with a facade by Nicola Barbioni. The **Chiesa di San Francesco** dates back to 1291; the main attraction to this church is Raphael's *The Marriage of the Virgin*, which was painted when he was quite young. **Chiesa di Santa Maria Maggiore** dates to the 1400s and also has some fine frescoes. The **Palazzo Vitelli a San Egidio** is a stately home, dating from the 1500s, built by the Vitelli family. The ceilings feature frescoes in the grotesque style. **Chiesa di San Domenico** was built in 1271 by Domenican friars and features an impressive display of frescoes by painters in the Umbria school. The **Teatro degli Illuminata** (☎ 075 855 50 91; Via dei Fucci) is a civic theatre which features musical and all kinds of live-arts performances.

ACTIVITIES
During the summer, the Pinacoteca's large lawn is the perfect place to take in an open-air film at **Cine Città di Castello Estate** (☎ 075 852 92 49; adult/child €5/4). All genres of movies are shown – from Harry Potter to art-house films to Italian classics. Movies are usually screened on Friday and Saturday at 9.15pm from July to the end of August.

A day of relaxation can be had at **Terme di Fontecchio** (☎ 075 852 06 14; www.termedifontecchio.it; Loc. Fontecchio), one of the five areas of Umbria known for its curative waters (the others being San Gemini, Acquasparta, Nocera Umbra and San Faustino di Massa Martana). The area was known for its spas back in the Roman times. Good prices and a beautiful setting make this excellent value. A Turkish bath costs €17 and a 30-minute massage is €27. It also offers two-, three- and seven-day wellness retreats. Check the Sleeping section for information about its hotel and unfortunately named retreat, Beauty Farm.

FESTIVALS & EVENTS
From the first Sunday in November until the following Friday, the town plays host to the

Mostra Mercato Tartufo e Prodotti del Bosco, a festival dedicated to the area's ubiquitous white truffle. Farmers and growers bring every type of truffle product imaginable to this epicurean trade show, as well as honey, mushrooms and many other local delicacies.

SHOPPING
On the third weekend of every month the town hosts the **Retro Antiques & Old Things Market**. Not as big as the one in Perugia, it's still a great place to get a hands-on history lesson (and purchase unique gifts not found anywhere else).

Tipografia Grifani-Donati (☎ 075 855 43 49; Corso Cavour 4; ☉ 8.30am-12.30pm & 3-7pm, closed Sun) sells paper and artwork using the same printing techniques as when it opened in 1799. It has a small museum on the 2nd floor. At the time of writing, the store was planning to relocate elsewhere on the street.

SLEEPING
Budget
La Montesca (☎ 075 855 85 66; fax 075 852 07 86; Loc. Montesca; per person/tent/car €8/6.50/3; ☉ May-Sep; P ☒) La Montesca is fully stocked with a restaurant and swimming pool, surrounded in the verdant hills of the Alta Valle di Tevere. Accessible to people with disabilities. Dogs are allowed.

Luna del Monte (☎ /fax 075 857 00 54; camping@tline.net; Voc S Pietro 10, Santa Maria del Tiberina; adult/children/tent/car €5.50/3.50/5/2; ☒ P) A bit further afield but worth it for the fantastic setting. The camp site has a swimming pool, children's playground and bocce. Bungalows with veranda, kitchen and private parking for up to four people cost €36 a night.

Hotel Umbria (☎ 075 855 49 25; umbria@hotelumbria.net; Via S Antonio 6; s/d €35/55) The least expensive hotel within the city walls, the Hotel Umbria is a fairly charming place to spend the night and is well located. All rooms have bathrooms, TV and IDD telephone.

Mid-Range
Hotel Tiferno (☎ 075 855 03 31; info@hoteltiferno.it; Piazza R Sanzio 13; s/d €96/148; ☒ P) Opened in 1985, this is one of Città di Castello's top hotels. The building was a monastery for the nearby Chiesa di San Francesco, then became a palace in the 17th century and has been upgraded to a four-star hotel, but rooms still include period details of its

past lives, great views, as well as artwork by Burri himself. Each room has a hairdryer, minibar and satellite TV.

Hotel Le Mura (☎ 075 852 10 70; direzione@hotel lemura.it; Via Borgo Farinario 24; s/d €48/80; 🔀) In a beautiful location, the Hotel Le Mura is a modern affair, with modernist architecture and efficiently designed rooms. It's quiet, perfectly located and has a very good restaurant.

Top End

Terme di Fontecchio (☎ 075 852 06 14; www.terme difontecchio.it; Loc. Fontecchio; at hotel spa s/d €51/80; at Cappucchin hermitage s/d €150/175; 🔀 P 🔀) The spa complex has a fancy hotel, but it's more charming to stay in the city centre and come here for the day. However, the spa has a few rooms at its 'Beauty Farm', located at an ancient Cappuccin hermitage 1km up the hill from the spa, with a breathtaking view of the valley below. The seven-room hermitage still has a Romanesque crypt and monastically decorated rooms.

Pratto di Sotto (☎ 075 941 73 83; www.umbria holidays.com; Santa Guiliana, 10km south of Città di Castello; from €600 for 2 people in low season to €2500 for 8 people in high season weekly; P 🔀) Stay at this serene weekly rental with two, eight or up to 16 people. Set far back among forested hills with an 11th-century ruin as one of its nearest neighbors, Prato di Sotto is less than an hour from most towns in Umbria. A classically furnished stone farmhouse with terracotta-tiled floors, international antiques, Prato di Sotto practically forces you to relax. Outside, each building has either a terrace, ivy-covered trellis or barbeque, and the four apartments share a pool. The owners can arrange sailing on their sailboat at Lago di Trasimeno or itineraries in Umbria and Tuscany. Kitchens come fully stocked. Check its website for last-minute cancellations.

EATING

Il Postale (☎ 075 852 13 56; Via Raffaele 8; 3-course meal €30-40; 🕑 closed lunch Sat & all day Mon) If there's such a thing as nouvelle Umbrian cuisine, this is the place to try it. It serves dishes such as duck with fennel compote, or carp with hazelnuts. Specialities are its lentil dishes and, of course, truffles.

L'Osteria (☎ 075 855 69 95; Via Borgo di Sotto; meals around €13) Nothing fancy, but good typical

Umbrian food. Friday features fish specialities. Try the asparagus gnocchi.

GETTING THERE & AWAY

Città di Castello is just east of the E45. The Ferrovia Centrale Umbra railway connects the Perugia Santa Anna station with Città di Castello (€2.90, 50 minutes, 10 daily) and Umbertide (€2.30, 40 minutes, 10 daily).

For a taxi, dial ☎ 337 65 31 67/65 24 76.

ASSISI

pop 25,346

Assisi is the quintessentially perfect Italian hill town. It's so perfect, in fact, that millions upon millions of the visitors who come here agree, turning it into the most crowded spot in Umbria. But it's still well worth a visit of several days, as the history, architecture and art are some of Umbria's best.

Since Roman times, its inhabitants have been aware of the visual impact of their city, perched halfway up Monte Subasio (1290m). From the valley, its pink and white marble buildings shimmer in the sunlight.

There is perhaps no other place on Earth that is as tied to its famous son as Assisi is with St Francis, who was born here in 1182. He renounced his father's wealth in his late teens to pursue a life of chastity and poverty. After his renunciation of worldly goods he began founding the order of mendicant friars known as the Frati Minori (Order of Minors; they became known as the Franciscans after St Francis' death), which attracted a huge following in Europe. With one of his disciples, St Clare (Santa Chiara), he co-founded the Franciscans' female Ordine delle Clarisse (Order of the Poor Clares). St Francis became the patron saint of Italy in 1939.

The Basilica di San Francesco is Assisi's, and possibly Umbria's, main draw. Don't be put off by the prospect of huge crowds, but do check before coming here that your trip doesn't coincide with a religious celebration, when hotels are likely to be booked out.

Orientation

Piazza del Comune is the centre of Assisi. At the northwestern edge of this square, Via San Paolo and Via Portica both eventually lead to the Basilica di San Francesco. Via Portica also leads to the Porta San Pietro and the Piazzale dell'Unità d'Italia, where most intercity buses stop, although APM buses

NORTHERN UMBRIA

ASSISI

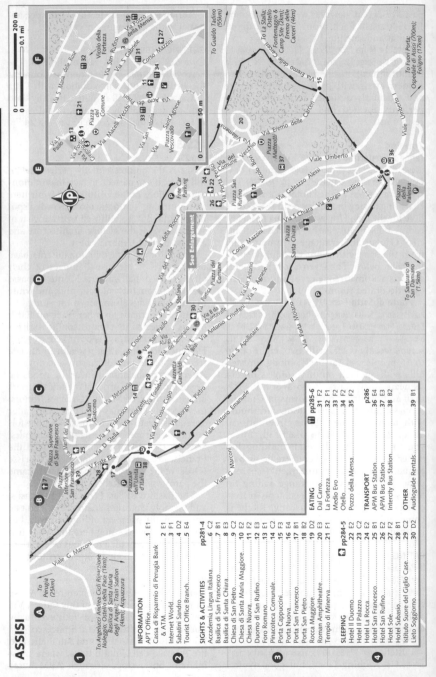

To Perugia
(25km)

To Angelucci Andrea Cicli Riparazione
Noleggio; Ostello della Pace (1km);
Basilica di Santa Maria
degli Angeli; Train Station
(4km); Acquazzura

Via G. Marconi

Piazza
Inferiore di
San Francesco

Piazza Superiore
di San Francesco

V Frate Elia

Via S. Francesco

Via San
Giacomo

Via Metastasio

Via S Francesco

Via D. Stella

Via Giorgetti

Via del Fosso CUPO

Via Borgo S. Pietro

Piazzale
dell'Unità
d'Italia

Viale C. Marconi

Viale Vittorio Emanuele

Piazzetta
Garibaldi

Via San Croce

Via S Agata

Via San Paolo

Via del Seminario

Via B. da
Quintavalle

Via A.
Aluigi

Ponte Piazza del
Comune

Via San Antonio

Via S. Agnese

Corso Mazzini

Via Porta Moiano

Via Stefano

Via del Colle

Via della Rocca

Free Car
Parking

Rocca

Via Porta Perlici

Via Porta
Comune Vecchio

Via Eremo delle Carceri

Via del
Comune

Via San Rufino

Piazza
San Rufino

Via Galeazzo Alessi

Via S. Chiara

Via Borgo Aretino

Piazza
Santa Chiara

Via S Apollinare

Via Antonio Crisofani

Via Villamena

Piazza
Matteotti

Viale Umberto I

Viale Umberto I

Piazza
della
Palestra

To La Stalla; Ostello
Fontemaggio &
Campsite (1km);
Eremo delle
Carceri (4km)

To Gualdo Tadino
(55km)

To Fuori Porta;
Ospedale di Assisi (200m);
Foligno (17km)

To Santuario di
San Damiano
(1.5km)

See Enlargement

Enlargement:

Via S Maria delle Rose

Vicolo della
Fortezza

Via San Rufino

Via S. Gabriele

Corso Mazzini

Via S
Paolo

Via S.
Gregorio

Via S. Paolo

Piazza
del
Comune

Via Arco dei Priori

Via Macelli Vecchi

Via San Antonia

Piazza Sant'Agnese
Piazza Vescovado

Via Pozzo
della Mensa

0   200 m
0   0.1 mil

0   50 m

Locally produced ceramics in **Gubbio** (p271)

DAMIEN SIMONIS

GLENN BEANLAND

A main thoroughfare in **Gubbio** (p271)

The **Basilica di San Francesco** in Assisi (p281)

CHRISTOPHER WOOD

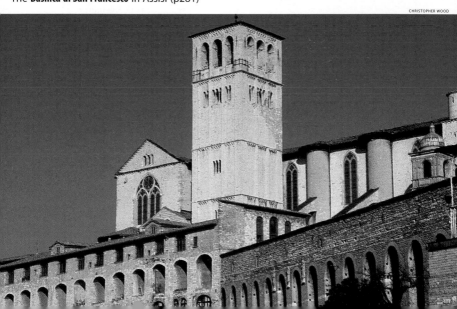

The **Piano Grande** near Castelluccio (p302)

DIANA MAY

The facade of the **cathedral** in Orvieto (p315)

DAMIEN SIMONIS

Rock caves in **San Quirico** (p237)

JUDI WILLOU

from smaller towns in the area terminate at Piazza Matteotti. The train station is 4km southwest of the city in Santa Maria degli Angeli, and a city bus runs between the two towns at least every 30 minutes (€0.80).

Information

EMERGENCY
Police Station (Piazza Matteotti)

INTERNET ACCESS
Internet World (☎ 075 81 23 27; Via San Gabriele dell'Addolorata 25; €0.20/min, minimum 10 min; 🕑 11am-1pm & 3-10pm Mon-Sat, 4-10pm Sun, shorter hours in winter) You can upload and print photographs from your digital camera here.
Sabatini Sandro (29b Via Portica; €2.50/3.50 15/30 min) A bar in the centre of town with Internet connection.

INTERNET RESOURCES
www.assisi.com A good website for tourist information.
www.assisiaccessibile.com Access information for people with disabilities.

LAUNDRY
Acquazzura (☎ 075 804 09 27; Via San Bernardino da Siena 6, Santa Maria degli Angeli; 🕑 8am-10pm) A self-service laundromat near Basilica di Santa Maria degli Angeli.

MEDICAL SERVICES
Ospedale di Assisi (hospital; ☎ 075 804 36 16) About 1km southeast of Porta Nuova, in Fuori Porta.

MONEY
Assisi has half a dozen banks, all with ATMs. You can also change money at the Porta San Pietro post office.
Banca dell' Umbria (Piazza del Comune; 🕑 usually around 8.20am-1.20pm & 2.20-3.30pm) Currency-exchange machines don't work anymore so you'll need to go inside during business hours to change cash or travellers cheques.

POST
Post Office (☎ 075 81 51 78; Piazza San Pietro 4, just inside Porta San Pietro; 🕑 8.10am-6.30pm Mon-Fri & 8.10am-12.30pm Sat)
Post Office Branch (Porta Nuova)

TOURIST INFORMATION
Tourist Office (☎ 075 81 25 34; fax 075 81 37 27; info@iat.assisi.pg.it; Piazza del Comune 22; 🕑 8am-6.30pm Mon-Sat, 10am-1pm & 2-5pm Sun & public holidays in summer; 8am-2pm & 3.30-6.30pm Mon-Fri, 9am-1pm & 3-6pm Sat, 9am-1pm Sun in winter) It has all the information you'll need on hotels, sights and events.

MODERN RESTORATION

The 1997 earthquake caused some of the frescoes in the upper church of the Basilica di San Francesco to crumble, seemingly lost forever. Technology has resolved this. Led by art restoration expert Paola Passalacqua, a team of art historians are busy at work next to the basilica, piecing these frescoes back together. That's 300,000 pieces, some weighing not much more than a grain of sand.

Tourist Office Branch (☎ 075 81 67 66; just outside Porta Nuova, 🕑 Easter to November) Has information on accommodation.

Basilica di San Francesco
The **Basilica di San Francesco** (☎ 075 81 90 01; Piazza di San Francesco; admission free; 🕑 9am-12pm & 2-5pm) is the main draw in Umbria, and one of the most visited religious sites in the world. People come here on pilgrimages from all corners of the planet. It has its own **information office** (☎ 075 819 00 84; assisisanfrancesco@libero.it; www.sanfrancescoassisi.org; across from entrance to lower church; same opening hours as above). An audio tour guide (€5) is available from an office across from the **Basilica** (☎ 075 81 28 50; acousticguide@yahoo.com) in the Piazza Inferiore. Or you can call the office a day or two in advance (or drop in) and see if there's an English-language tour you can pay to hitch on to. They're usually led by resident African, English or North American Franciscan friars.

The basilica saw heavy damage during a series of earthquakes on 26 September 1997. Two friars and two Italian governmental inspectors died during a second major earthquake when the vaulted ceiling of the upper church they were inspecting collapsed.

At the end of 1999, after two years of restoration work, the reopening of the basilica was celebrated with a mass of rededication. New technology was used to make the basilica as earthquake-proof as possible. Since the frescoes are being restored, you can buy one of the guidebooks to the basilica (in the bookshop or at the information centre) for photographs of the intact paintings.

St Francis gained a lot of fame and quite a following during his lifetime. When he died in 1226 at age 44, his followers knew they

NORTHERN UMBRIA

ST FRANCIS OF ASSISI TIMELINE

1182	Born in Assisi to Pietro Bernardone and Madonna Pica
1205	Converted
1206	Disinherited by his father
1210	Approval of the Franciscan Order
1219	Preached peace and goodness in Egypt among crusaders and Muslims
1223	Recreates the nativity scene and the crib of Jesus for Christmas Eve at Greccio
1224	Receives the stigmata on Monte La Verna in Arezzo
1225	Writes the *Canticle of the Creatures*
1226	Dies at Santa Maria degli Angeli
1228	Canonised in Assisi; the building of the lower church of the Basilica di San Francesco begins
1230	His body is buried in a hidden crypt in the basilica
1253	The upper church completed
1939	St Francis is named patron saint of Italy

had to hide his body as soon as possible, since the long-held Roman belief in the area was that God was on the side of whomever possessed the corpse of a holy person. Ghibelline (pro-emperor) Assisi was warring with Guelph (pro-papal) Perugia at the time, so they had to build quickly. Construction of the lower church began almost immediately, and Pope Gregory IX himself laid the first stone in 1228. St Francis' body was hidden so well under this church that it wasn't found again until 1818.

The basilica was built on a hill known as Colle d' Inferno ('Hell Hill'). People were executed at the gallows here until the 13th century. St Francis asked his followers to bury him here in keeping with Jesus, who had died on the cross among criminals and outcasts. The area is now known as Paradise Hill.

The **lower church** (🕑 6.30am-6.50pm Easter-Nov, 6.30am-6pm Nov-Easter, 6.30am-7.15pm public holidays) was built between 1228 and 1230. The stained-glass windows are the work of master craftsmen brought in from Germany, England and Flanders during the 13th century, and were quite an architectural feat at that time.

In the centre of the lower church, above the main altar, are four frescoes attributed

to Maestro delle Vele, a pupil of Ghiotto, that represent what St Francis called 'the four greatest allegories'. The first was the victory of Francis over evil, and the other three were the precepts his order was based on: obedience, poverty and chastity.

Lorenzetti's triptych in the left transept ends with his most famous and controversial, *Madonna Who Celebrates Francis*. Mary is seen holding the baby Jesus and indicating with her thumb towards St Francis. On the other side of Mary is the apostle John, whom we're assuming is being unfavourably compared with Francis. In 1234 Pope Gregory IX decided that the image was not heretical because John had written the gospel, but Francis had lived it.

Cimabue was the most historically important painter because he had personally known St Francis. In the *Madonna in Majesty*, in the right transept, much has been tampered with, but Cimabue's intact depiction of St Francis is considered the most accurate, as he painted it from eyewitness accounts from St Francis' two nephews. Francis appears peaceful and calm in this painting. The first biographer of St Francis, Thomas of Celano, wrote in the middle of the 13th century that Francis was an eloquent man, of cheerful countenance and of a kindly aspect.

The basilica's **Sala delle Reliquie** (Relics Hall; 🕑 9am-6pm daily, 1-4.30pm public holidays) contains items from St Francis' life, including his simple tunic and sandals and fragments of his celebrated *Canticle of the Creatures*. The most important relic here is the Franciscan Rule parchment, the *Book of Life* composed by Francis.

The **upper church** (🕑 8.30am-6.50pm daily Easter-Nov, 8.30am-6pm daily Nov-Easter, 8.30am-7.15pm public holidays) was built between 1230 and 1253. It contains a 28-part fresco cycle detailing St Francis' life, as well as corresponding images from the Bible. The frescoes in the basilica literally revolutionised art in the Western world, on several levels. They were painted by all of the most famous painters at the time – Cimabue and Giotto from the Florentine school were the most prolific, but also Cavalini, Rusuti, and artists from the Tuscan and Sienese schools. The frescoes represented a shift in art style: from the majestic *Divine Judge* Jesus of the Byzantine and Romanesque art to a Minore

NORTHERN UMBRIA •• Assisi **283**

Christ, suffering and humbled. Instead of gold backgrounds symbolising heaven, the basilica artists painted natural backgrounds, with the stars, sky and clouds. This was in keeping with Francis' idea that the human body was 'brother' and the earth around him mother and sister. Some of these frescoes were the first paintings to ever depict third-class citizens, such as shepherds. At the time, the only people who could afford to commission paintings of themselves were noblemen and the very wealthy class, so no one had ever bothered to paint anyone but religious icons or powerful figures before the basilica.

These fresco painters were the storytellers of their day, turning Biblical passages into *Bibliae Pauperum* – open public Bibles for the poor, who were mostly illiterate. Cimabue painted a good number of what is displayed in the upper church, including the Marian scenes in the upper and lower section of the apse, the *Apocalypse* and the *Acts of the Apostles* in the left and right transepts, and the *Crucifixion* in the left transept – an example of both the Minore Christ and what can happen when a lead-white fresco oxidises (it has become a negative of its former image).

Giotto, trained under Cimabue, was responsible for most of the 28-part fresco cycle. Francis appears in concordance with images from both the Old and New Testaments. His life is depicted on the lower portion of the church while the biblical themes are on top: on the right, stories from Genesis, and on the left, stories from the life of Jesus. The upper paintings were done by a host of great artists, including Giotto and Cimabue. In the centre nave vault appears Francis, glorified as the convergence of both Testaments. This symbolism was another way the paintings were used to translate stories of the Bible. The scenes in St Francis' life were tied to the scenes as a way to translate the Bible through images. For instance, the fifth fresco shows St Francis renouncing his father, while the corresponding Biblical fresco shows the disobedient Adam and Eve in the Garden of Eden.

Dress rules are applied rigidly – absolutely no shorts, miniskirts, sleeveless tops or low-cut dresses. Please adhere to the no-flash photography rule – over the years, some of the paintings have been damaged by chemical interactions due to human interference.

Other Sights

The **Chiesa Nuova** (☎ 075 81 23 39; fax 815 50 50; ✆ 6.30am-12pm & 2.30-6pm in summer, 6.30am-12pm & 2-6pm in winter) was built by King Philip III of Spain in the 1600s on the spot reputed to be the house of St Francis' family. Mass is said daily at 7am, with an extra service on holidays at 10am.

The **Tempio di Minerva**, facing Piazza del Comune, is now a church but retains its impressive pillared facade. Wander into some of the shops on the piazza, which open their basements to reveal Roman ruins. The city's **Pinacoteca Comunale** (☎ 075 81 20 33; Palazzo Vallemani Via San Francesco 10; adult/child €3/2; ✆ 10am-1pm & 3-6pm 16 Mar–15 Oct, 10am-1pm & 3-5pm 16 Oct–15 Mar) displays Umbrian Renaissance art and frescoes from Giotto's school.

Off Via San Antonio is Piazza Vescovado and the Romanesque **Chiesa di Santa Maria Maggiore** (☎/fax 075 81 30 85; ✆ 8.30am-7pm Easter-Nov, 8.30am-5pm Nov-Easter), which was formerly the city's cathedral. South of Piazza del Comune, along Corso Mazzini and Via Santa Chiara, is the pink and white 13th-century Romanesque **Basilica di Santa Chiara** (☎ 075 81 22 82; Piazza Santa Chiara; admission free; ✆ 6.30am-12pm & 2-7pm in summer, 6.30am-12pm & 2-6pm in winter), with steep ramparts and a striking facade. The white and pink stone that makes up the exterior here (the same stone that makes many buildings in Assisi look like they glow in the sunlight) came from nearby Subasio. The daughter of an Assisian nobleman, Saint Clare was a spiritual contemporary of St Francis and founded the Order of the Poor Ladies, now known as the Poor Clares. She's buried in the church's crypt. The Byzantine cross that is said to have spoken to St Francis is also housed here.

Assisi does have a few remaining Roman ruins, most notably the **Foro Romano** (Roman Forum; ☎ 075 81 30 53; entrance on Via Portica; admission adult/reduced €2.50/2; ✆ 10am-1pm & 2-7pm daily, 10am-1pm & 2-6pm in winter). There's really not much to see here unless you're really, really into reading Latin script. It's an underground forum, now rather dank.

Northeast of the Basilica di Santa Chiara, the 13th-century Romanesque **Duomo di San Rufino** (☎ 075 81 60 16; Piazza San Rufino; ✆ 7am-noon & 2-7pm), remodelled by Galeazzo Alessi in the 16th century, contains the fountain where St Francis and St Clare were baptized.

The facade is festooned with grotesque figures and fantastic animals.

Dominating the city is the massive 14th-century **Rocca Maggiore** (☎ 075 81 30 53; Via della Rocca; admission adult/reduced €1.70/1; ☼ 10am-sunset), a hill fortress offering fabulous views over the valley and across to Perugia. Most of the fortress is closed for a long restoration that will eventually see it converted into an immense art gallery.

A 30-minute walk south from Porta Nuova, the **Santuario di San Damiano** (☎ 075 81 22 73; admission free; ☼ 10am-noon & 2-6pm in summer, 10am-noon & 2-4.30pm in winter, vespers at 7pm in summer & 5pm in winter) was built on the spot where St Francis first heard the voice of Jesus and where he wrote his *Canticle of the Creatures*. The convent founded by St Clare is still located here.

In the valley southwest of the city, near the train station, the imposing **Basilica di Santa Maria degli Angeli** (☎ 075 8 05 11; Santa Maria degli Angeli; ☼ 6.15am-7.45pm in summer, 9-11pm Jul, Aug & Sep, 6.15am-12.30pm & 2-7.45pm in winter) was built around the first Franciscan monastery. St Francis died in its **Cappella del Transito** on 3 October 1226.

About 4km east of the city, reached via the Porta Cappuccini, is **Eremo delle Carceri** (☎ 075 812301; admission free; ☼ 6.30am-7.15pm daily Easter-Nov, 6.30am-sunset daily Nov-Easter), the hermitage that St Francis retreated to after hearing the word of God. The *carceri* (prisons) are the caves that functioned as hermits' retreats for St Francis and his followers. St Francis was known to spend time here and preach sermons to the local animals (the ilex tree where the bird audience sat is still alive). Apart from a few fences and tourist paths, everything remains as it was in St Francis' time, and a few Franciscans live here. Eremo delle Carceri is a great jumping-off point for walks through Monte Subasio.

Activities

Local bookshops sell maps (€7.75) of walks on nearby Monte Subasio, produced by Club Alpino Italiano (CAI). None of them are too demanding and the smattering of religious shrines and camp sites could make for an enjoyable two-day excursion.

Bicycle rentals are available at **Angelucci Andrea Cicli Riparazione Noleggio** (☎ 075 804 25 50; VG Becchetti 31) in Santa Maria degli Angeli.

Courses

Accademia della Lingua Italiana Corsi di Lingua e Cultura Italiana (☎ /fax 075 81 52 81; www.aliassisi.it; Via San Paolo 36) runs a variety of courses, including Italian language and culture and creative writing. It arranges group courses and Certificazione di Italiano come Lingua Straniera (CILS; Italian-proficiency benchmark exam taken by Italian teachers abroad) twice a year.

Festivals & Events

The **Festa di San Francesco** falls on 3 and 4 October and is the main religious event in the city. **Easter week** is celebrated with processions and performances. **Ars Nova Musica** festival, held from late August to mid-September, features local and national performers. The colourful **Festa di Calendimaggio** celebrates spring in medieval fashion and is normally held over several days at the end of the first week of May. The multi-denominational **Marcia per la Pace** (March for Peace; www.tavoladellapace.it) has been bringing together thousands of marchers from around the world each June to walk from Assisi to Perugia in a show of solidarity for peace.

Sleeping

Assisi is well appointed for tourists, but in peak periods, such as Easter, August and September, and the Festa di San Francesco, you will need to book accommodation well in advance. Even outside these times, many of the hotels will often be full. There are a phenomenal amount of hotels in Assisi, so prices are extremely reasonable. The tourist office on Piazza Comune has a complete list of private rooms, religious institutions (there are 17), flats and *agriturismo* options in and around Assisi. Otherwise, keep an eye out for *camere* (rooms for rent) signs as you wander the streets. If you fail to find anything in Assisi itself, consider staying in Santa Maria degli Angeli, 4km southwest of Assisi – you'll be near the train station and a half-hourly shuttle bus runs to the city centre.

BUDGET

Ostello Fontemaggio (☎ 075 81 36 36; fax 81 37 49; Via San Rufino Campagna; dm €18.50, per person/tent/car €7/6/3; [P]) To reach this hostel and camp site, just east of town at Fontemaggio, walk about 2km uphill along Via Eremo delle

Carceri. There's a playground for children and parking.

Ostello della Pace (☎ /fax 075 81 67 67; Via Valecchie 177; dm from €14, private rooms available; ☺ Mar–10 Jan; P ⬜) Assisi's HI hostel is located in a 17th-century farmhouse and has tonnes of extras: bicycle hire, laundry room, football, ping pong, a restaurant and a piano. It offers discounts for guests to all of Assisi's museums. It's on the shuttle-bus route between Santa Maria degli Angeli and Assisi.

Istituto Suore del Giglio Case Religiose di Ospitalità (☎ 075 81 22 67; fax 81 62 58; Via San Francesco 13; s/d €24/42, several family rooms with up to 5 beds) There's well over a dozen religious institutions that offer rooms, but this one is centrally located, has an incredibly friendly staff (including several English-speaking Zambian nuns) and a terrace with a view calming enough to inspire a religious experience. Two rooms even have their own balconies. Look for the sign that reads: Casa di Ospitalità 'Maria Immacolata'. Curfew is 10.30pm.

Hotel Il Duomo (☎ 075 81 27 42; prenotazioni@hotelsanrufino.it; Via San Lorenzo 2; s/d €32/42, d without bathroom €36) At these prices, there aren't too many extras (rooms are without TV or phone, and two of the rooms share a bath), but it's clean and comfortable. On a stairway to the Rocca Maggiore, it's a bit of a climb but pin-drop quiet. It's extremely popular, and has only two singles and seven doubles, so call ahead.

Hotel San Rufino (☎ 075 81 28 03; prenotazioni@hotelsanrufino.it; Via Porta Perlici 7; s/d €41/50) Owned by the same people as Il Duomo, the San Rufino is a slightly higher-end hotel, with phones and TVs in the slightly larger rooms.

Hotel La Rocca (☎ 075 81 22 84; info@hotellarocca.it; Via Porta Perlici 27; s/d/t/q €35/43/61/69; P) In a beautiful location far away from the crowds, the Hotel La Rocca is a low-priced little gem that seems to rise directly out of the landscape. Simple but amply outfitted rooms come with a hairdryer, elevator access, TV and IDD phone. Some rooms have disability access. Breakfast is included.

Hotel Sole (☎ 075 81 23 73; Corso Mazzini 35; s/d €42/62) Recently renovated with 35 comfortable, modern rooms, the real draw is this hotel's popular restaurant downstairs. The hotel is good value and has a great location, but rooms near the restaurant won't be quiet until about 10.30pm.

Lieto Soggiorno (☎ 075 81 61 91; Via Portica 26; s/d without bathroom from €26/38, d with bathroom €50) If you don't mind a rather fascinating lack of charm, this is one of the cheapest, most centrally located places in town.

MID-RANGE

Hotel Il Palazzo (☎ 075 81 68 41; www.hotelilpalazzo.it; Via San Francesco 8; s/d €75/120) A stately historic building, it began its life in the 1500s and many remnants from that time are still evident. Room decor features wrought-iron and canopied beds, half-a-millennium-old oak beams and views of the countryside. It's smack dab between the basilica and the Piazza del Comune.

Hotel Ristorante La Fortezza (☎ 075 81 24 18; Via Piazza del Comune) This place has seven decent mid-priced rooms that aren't as charming as the associated wonderful restaurant around the corner.

TOP END

Hotel San Francesco (☎ 075 81 22 81; info@hotelsanfrancescoassisi.it; Via San Francesco 48; s/d/t/q €110/155/207/232, discounts in low season & for children; ☒) For travellers who are looking for a serious view of the basilica, you've got a postcard shot just outside most of the hotel's rooms. Amenities include satellite TV (with BBC, CNN, France 2), minibar, elevator, hairdryer, double windows and a hotel shuttle service that will come and collect you at any of the car parks (you can also drive in and drop off your luggage first). Its enormous breakfast buffet is included in the price, and is the perfect way to start a day of travelling.

Hotel Subasio (☎ 075 81 22 06; fax 81 66 91; www.umbria.org/hotel/subasio; Via Frate Elia 2; s/d €114/181; ☒ P) The Subasio is one of the top hotels in Umbria. All the impeccably decorated rooms are furnished in Florentine Renaissance style, and distinguished former guests include Herman Hesse, Greta Garbo and Charlie Chaplin.

Eating

Assisi offers a good selection of traditional Italian and Umbrian delicacies.

Hotel Ristorante La Fortezza (☎ 075 81 24 18; Via Piazza del Comune; mains €7-16) Run by a chef-owner and his wife and two sons, this wonderful little restaurant just up the Vicolo della Fortezza stairway serves dishes featuring black truffles and game meats.

Otello (☎ 075 81 32 25; Vicolo San Antonio 1; pizza €7) This restaurant is a local favourite. It serves simple but good pizza, and a wide selection of pasta dishes.

Medio Evo (☎ 075 81 30 68; Via Arco dei Priori 4; mains €12-21; ☯ closed Wed) This is one of Assisi's better restaurants, serving traditional Umbrian dishes in fabulous vaulted 13th-century surroundings.

La Stalla (☎ 075 81 36 36; Via Eremo Caceri 8; meals €15.50; ☯ Tue-Sun) This eatery is in the same complex as the camp site at Fontemaggio. You can have filling meals under an arbour.

Dal Carro (☎ 075 81 52 49; Vicolo dei Nepis 2; pizza from €5) Off Corso Mazzini, Dal Carro is a good bet – the *strangozzi alla norcina* (pasta with a black truffle sauce) is a marvel and so is the homemade *tiramisu* (dessert made with sponge-finger biscuits, marscapone cheese, chocolate, liqueur and cream). Watch as your meal is cooked over an open fire.

Pozzo della Mensa (☎ 075 815 52 36; Via Pozzo della Mensa 11; meals around €20.65; ☯ closed Wed) This place specialises in Umbrian dishes. It's charming, fairly laid-back and has a good vegetarian option.

Shopping

Assisi is one of the best towns to shop in, as it's geared towards tourists. A few shops and attractions shut in the middle of the day, but it's barely a blink compared to the veritable daytime hibernation of most Umbrian towns. While most of the ceramics here are made in Assisian factories rather than handmade and handpainted like they are in Deruta, let's face it: you could save you money and relatives wouldn't notice the difference anyway. Open-air **markets** take place in Piazza Matteotti on Saturday and Santa Maria degli Angeli on Monday.

Getting There & Away

APM buses connect Assisi with Perugia (€2.60, 50 minutes, 10 daily) and other local towns, leaving from the bus station on Piazza Matteotti. Most APM buses also stop on Largo Properzio, just outside Porta Nuova. Piazzale dell'Unità d'Italia is the terminus for **SULGA buses** (☎ 075 500 96 41) for Rome (€16.55, three hours, three daily), Florence (€11.65, 2¾ hours, one daily at 6.45am, returning at 5pm) and other major cities.

Although Assisi's train station is 4km away at Santa Maria degli Angeli, the train is still the best way to get to many places as the services are more frequent than the buses. It is on the Foligno–Terontola train line, with regular services to Perugia (€1.55, 30 minutes, hourly). Change at Terontola for Florence (€9, two hours, 10 daily) and at Foligno for Rome (€11.20, two hours, 11 daily).

To reach Assisi from Perugia by road, take the S75, exit at Ospedalicchio and follow the signs.

Getting Around

A shuttle bus (€0.80) operates every half-hour between Piazza Matteotti and the train station. Normal traffic is subject to restrictions in the city centre and daytime parking is all but banned. There are six major pay car parks just outside the city centre: Porta San Pietro; Porta Moiano; Porta Nuova; Piazza Matteotti; Porta San Giacomo; and Ponte San Vittorino. If you object to paying for one of the several car parks (and connected to the city centre by orange shuttle buses), head for the car park on Via della Rocca, the road that leads up to Rocca Maggiore. There are no restrictions beyond the 'P' (parking) sign. This leaves you a fairly short, if steep, walk to the Basilica di San Francesco and Piazza del Comune. Santa Maria degli Angeli has one free car park at Piazza del Mercato.

For a taxi, dial ☎ 075 500 48 88.

SPELLO
pop 8303

Sometimes it seems like there's no way any town you visit could be more beautiful than the last. But Spello, an often passed-by little town between Assisi and Foligno, is a lovely place to spend a day or two. The town is surrounded by so many blooming flowers, the entire town actually smells good, especially during spring and autumn. The town rightly uses these flowers for one of its most important festivals – the Infiorate di Corpus Domini (see p288). The town is located at the foothills of Monte Subasio, so there are many good walking trails in the area. Emperor Augustus developed much of the land in the valley, and there is still a smattering of Roman ruins in the area, as well as some spectacular paintings by Pinturicchio, among others. But Spello's main draw is wandering its narrow cobblestone streets.

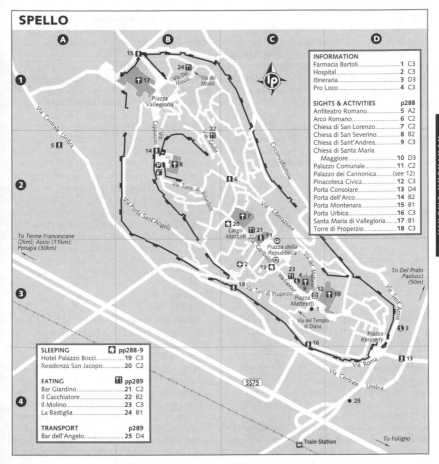

SPELLO

NORTHERN UMBRIA

INFORMATION
Farmacia Bartoli.....................1 C3
Hospital..................................2 D3
Itineraria................................3 D3
Pro Loco................................4 C3

SIGHTS & ACTIVITIES p288
Anfiteatro Romano.................5 A2
Arco Romano.........................6 C2
Chiesa di San Lorenzo............7 C2
Chiesa di San Severino............8 B2
Chiesa di Sant'Andrea.............9 C3
Chiesa di Santa Maria
  Maggiore..........................10 D3
Palazzo Comunale.................11 C2
Palazzo dei Cannonica........(see 12)
Pinacoteca Civica.................12 C3
Porta Consolare....................13 D4
Porta dell'Arco......................14 B2
Porta Montenara...................15 B1
Porta Urbica.........................16 C3
Santa Maria di Vallegloria.....17 B1
Torre di Properzio................18 C3

SLEEPING pp288-9
Hotel Palazzo Bocci...............19 C3
Residenza San Jacopo............20 C2

EATING pp289
Bar Giardino.........................21 C2
Il Cacchiatore.......................22 B2
Il Molino..............................23 C3
La Bastiglia..........................24 B1

TRANSPORT p289
Bar dell'Angelo....................25 D4

Information

EMERGENCY
Police Station (☎ 0742 65 11 15; Piazza della Repubblica)

INTERNET RESOURCES
www.spellonet.com A well-organised site that has online information about accommodation, restaurants, history and special events.

MEDICAL SERVICES
Doctor (☎ 0742 30 20 16) Dial this number to locate a local doctor.
Farmacia Bartoli (☎ 0742 30 14 88; Via Cavour 63; ⏰ closed Sat morning)
Hospital (☎ 0742 33 91; Via dell' Ospedale, Piazza dell'Ospedale)

POST
Post Office (☎ 0742 65 29 18; Piazza della Repubblica; ⏰ 8am-6.30pm Mon-Fri, 8am-12.30pm Sat)

TOURIST INFORMATION
Itineraria (☎ 0742 30 23 01, 328 220 93 81; www.itineraria.biz; Via Sant'Anna 2) This private, top-end tourist office provides information about classes, health tourism, wine and guided tours. Catering mostly to groups and travel agencies, it can also arrange tours and itineraries for independent travellers, and translation services.
Pro Loco (☎ 0742 30 10 09, if closed ☎ 0742 65 14 08; Piazza Matteotti 3; ⏰ 9.30am-12.30pm & 3.30-5.30pm) It can provide you with a list of accommodation and has maps of walks in the surrounding area, including an 8km walk to Assisi. It sells a good tourist map of the area for €0.52.

Sights

Perhaps the best sight in all of Spello is to head up to the **Arco Romano**. From here you can get the best view of the **anfiteatro Romano** (closed to the public) and the surrounding countryside. Nearby is the **Chiesa di San Severino**, a Cappuccin monastery with a Romanesque facade.

As you enter Spello, you'll come across **Piazza Kennedy**, the main entrance to the town, with a partially Roman gate, **Porta Consolare**. The first main piazza features two enormous churches: the austere **Chiesa di Sant'Andrea** (Piazza Matteotti; 8am-7pm), where you can admire a fresco by Bernardino Pinturicchio. A few doors down, you'll reach the 12th-century **Chiesa di Santa Maria Maggiore** (Piazza Matteotti; 8.30am-12.30pm & 3-7pm summer, 8.30am-12.30pm & 3-6pm winter) and the town's real treat, Pinturicchio's beautiful frescoes in the Cappella Baglioni. The fresco is in the righthand corner as you enter, behind glass, but be aware that you need to pay to illuminate the fresco. This is done not just to make money; constant light damages the paint. Also of note is the Cappella's exquisite floor (dating from 1566) made of tiles from Deruta. The **Pinacoteca Civica** (0742 30 14 97; Palazzo dei Cannonica, Piazza Matteotti; 10.30am-1pm & 3-6.30pm Apr-Sep, 10.30am-12.30pm & 3-5pm Oct-Mar, closed Mon all year) was closed at the time of writing for renovation but should reopen by the time you read this.

Continuing in to town, you'll reach Piazza della Repubblica. Further along, in the same piazza as the **Palazzo Comunale**, is the **Chiesa di San Lorenzo** (8.30am-12.30pm & 3-7pm in summer, 8.30am-12.30pm & 3-6pm in winter), with a collection of sacred works. At the far north of town is yet another imposing church, **Santa Maria di Valleglòria**, built in the 1320s in Gothic style with frescoes by Spacca. The **Torre di Properzio**, or the Porta Venere, stands guard over the western Roman walls. Named for the Roman poet Propertius, the gate and its towers are a hodgepodge of Roman, medieval and 20th-century re-constructionist architecture.

Activities

The Pro Loco (and the tourist office in Assisi) has a badly drawn map of a walking trail between Spello and Assisi called the *Passeggiata Tra Gli Ulivi* down the Via degli Ulivi (Road of Olives). Give yourself several hours. It's not a long walk (8km) and is fairly flat, considering the rest of the region's terrain. If you like flowers, ancient gnarled olive trees and breathtakingly beautiful scenery, you won't be disappointed.

Festivals & Events

Spello, like nearby towns, has no shortage of festivals. The most beautiful – and best smelling – is **L'Infiorata del Corpus Domini**, which happens on Corpus Domini, the Sunday 60 days after Easter. Those familiar with Semana Santa in Guatemala and other Latin American countries will recognise the similarity to the *alfombras* (flower carpets) that decorate the streets in colourful artistic displays. If you want to enjoy it, come on the Saturday evening before to see the floral fantasies being laid out (from about 8.30pm) and participate in the festive atmosphere. On the festival day, the Corpus procession begins at 11am, and can be extremely crowded. Make sure you have a hotel reservation, or just come for the day from Assisi or Perugia.

Sleeping

BUDGET

Residenza San Jacopo (0742 30 12 60; Via Borgo di via Giulia 1; d €63) This vacation house saw its first incarnation in 1296 as the hospice of San Jacopo, a way station for pilgrims heading to Compostella in Galicia. Much has been rebuilt over the last eight centuries and San Jacopo is as comfortable as it is charming. Seven mini-apartments feature a kitchenette, bathroom and TV, and are furnished with rustic antiques. Vanya, the owner, also runs a nearby *enoteca* (wine shop), and knows everything about local wine and delicacies.

Del Prato Paolucci (0742 30 10 18; Via Brodolini; s/d €45/62; P) Paolucci is just outside the main town centre. Rooms aren't anything special, but it's the best-priced accommodation in Spello. The incredibly friendly owners are a hoot. Call ahead and they'll pick you up at the train station. As of writing, plans were underway to add a pool. It's Italy, so expect that pool to be installed in, oh, say 2012.

MID-RANGE

Terme Francescane (0742 30 11 86; Via Delle Acque; s/d €70/90; P) After a few weary weeks on the road, a spa might be just what you need. A few kilometres from town, it's set in beautiful grounds.

TOP END
Hotel Palazzo Bocci (☎ 0742 30 10 21; fax 30 14 64; bocci@abitarelastoria.it; www.palazzobocci.com; Via Cavour 17; s/d €90/150 ste €200-250; ﹩) This 18th-century hotel is in the Abitare La Storia association of grand hotels and is truly exquisite. Benvenuto Crispoldi frescoes appear in many bedrooms and public spaces. An outdoor terrace begs to host a romantic breakfast.

Eating & Drinking
La Bastiglia (☎ 0742 65 12 77; Via dei Molini 17; about €47 for a tasting menu; ⊗ closed Wed, lunch Fri) This stuffy hotel (pricy but not worth it) has one of the more unique restaurants in all of Italy. The food is beyond outstanding and a rare example of Umbrian nouvelle cuisine. If you've been too scared to try pigeon before, try its burned pigeon breast in cherry sauce in a potato puff pastry.

Il Cacciatore (☎ 0742 65 11 41; fax 30 16 03; Via Giulia 42; ⊗ closed Mon) Also a hotel, this place has a great restaurant with a large terrace, perfect for a summer lunch. The rooms are large and traditional.

Il Molino (☎ 0742 65 13 05; Piazza Matteotti 6/7; ⊗ closed Tue) Owned by the Hotel Palazzo Bocci, the Molino is set in a 700-year-old building. It specialises in truffles, legumes, winter game meats, wild asparagus and cooking with local mountain-grown herbs.

Bar Giardino (Via Garibaldi 10) This simple bar has decent snacks and *gelato*, but the best thing is the back veranda, where you could wile away hours admiring the view.

Getting There & Away
APM buses connect Spello with Perugia (€2.90, one hour, five daily) and Foligno (€0.60, 15 minutes, nine daily), and there are connections to Assisi (€1.30, 15 minutes, six daily, Monday to Saturday). In June, the ride passes by fields of majestic sunflowers.

Trains are a better option, as Spello is on the Perugia–Assisi–Foligno train line. Starting at 7.32am, trains run at least every hour and connect Spello with Perugia (€2, 30 minutes), Assisi (€1.10, 10 minutes) and Foligno (€0.80, 15 minutes). If the train station isn't staffed, there's a self-service ticket machine in the waiting lounge. If that doesn't work, you can buy tickets at the Bar dell'Angelo around the corner on Viale Gugliemi Marconi.

For a taxi, dial ☎ 0742 65 15 82/336 24 44 99.

AROUND SPELLO
The area around Spello is picture perfect: hillsides covered in wildflowers; fields of sunflowers in June; and stone villas quietly placed among the natural terrain. Wine is the major drawcard of this region, the most well-known is the *sangrantino* from Montefalco. The area is quite upscale, as most travellers are here to taste wine and enjoy the good life, but there are many good camp sites, rooms to let and some inexpensive hotels.

Montefalco
pop 5640
The main reason to come to Montefalco is the wine. Umbria doesn't have the tasting setup at the vineyards like you would find in Tuscany, or in California's Napa Valley or Australia's Hunter Valley. Most of the tasting travellers are likely to do is at places with names such as *enoteca* or *degustazione* at any one of a number of *enoteche*. An excellent recent innovation in the area is olive-oil tasting, which is becoming quite popular. This is one of the main olive-growing regions in Umbria, and tasting is a fun way for nondrinkers and children to join in the fun. You can play along with the big kids by saying things like 'this extra virgin has a bitter aftertaste' or 'lots of artichoke with overtones of oak'.

The **Museo Civico** (☎ 0742 37 95 98; ⊗ 10.30am-1pm & 2.30-5pm Nov-Feb, 2-6pm Mar-May & Sep-Oct, 3-7pm Jun-Jul, 3-7.30pm Aug) is housed in the deconsecrated St Francis Church, with a moving fresco cycle about the life and works of St Francis.

Villa Pambuffetti (☎ 0742 37 94 17; villabianca@interbusiness.it; Viale della Vittoria 20; s/d €105/163; ﹩) This stone and woodbeam-ceiling hotel is 'an oasis within an oasis'. It's got all the four-star amenities, plus extras such as soundproof rooms and an excellent restaurant.

Hotel Ristorante Ringhiera Umbra (☎ 0742 37 91 66; Via Mameli 20; s/d €47/60) This basic hotel has a fantastic inexpensive restaurant located in a cosy stone-and-brick cave, and serves excellent *strangozzi* with truffles and a *sagrantino* red-wine sauce.

GETTING THERE & AWAY
Buses from Montefalco travel to Perugia (6.20am, 7.25am and 1.15pm daily), Foligno (nine daily), Spoleto (five daily), Terni

(9.30am and 3.16pm daily) and Bevagna (6.20am, 8.10am and 6.10pm daily).

Bevagna
pop 4797

Bevagna began first as an Umbrian settlement, then became Etruscan and eventually became a Roman municipium on the Via Flaminia. The heart of Bevagna is in the Piazza Filippo Silvestre, where you'll find a Roman column of San Rocco.

The **Pro Loco tourist office** (☎ 0742 36 16 67; pbevagna@bcsnet.it) can help with accommodation and wine tasting. Parking just outside the city centre is free.

The **Pinacoteca Comunale** (☎ 0742 36 00 31; Corso Matteotti 70; adult/reduced/child €3/2/1; ☾ 10.30am-1pm & 2.30-5pm summer, Fri-Sun only in winter) features a very rudimentary exhibit on local archaeology and ceramics. The nearby asymmetrical **Piazza Silvestri** is a marvel of medieval urban planning.

The ticket price for the *pinacoteca* also includes entrance into the **Roman Mosaic Museum of Antiquities** (☎ 075 572 71 41; Via di Porta Guelfa), a well-preserved tile floor from ancient Roman baths. There's also the remains of an old Roman theatre, and a Roman and medieval wall.

At the end of June, Bevagna goes medieval with the **Festival of the Gaite**. For two days, the town goes back in time a few hundred years, selling all sorts of medieval-inspired handicrafts and food. If you happen upon the area during the last third of August and feel that slime is lacking in your diet, the little town of Cantalupo di Bevagna celebrates its **Sagra della Lumaca** (Festival of the Snail) with snail dishes cooked in every way imaginable (and unimaginable), as well as exhibits, dancing and general slug-related merriment.

Agriturismo/Camping Pian di Boccio (☎ 0742 36 01 64; piandiboccio@tiscalinet.it; www.piandiboccio.com; per person/tent/car €6.50/6/2.50; apts €75-120, sleeps 4-6 people; ℗ ☂) An *agriturismo* that produces its own olive oil, canned fruit, jam and honey. The camp site has archery, a swimming pool and a pizzeria, and nine rustic but comfortable apartments that come with firewood, fully equipped kitchen and TV.

Ristorante L'Orto Degli Angeli (☎ 0742 36 09 67; www.ortoangeli.it; Via Dante Aligheri; rooms €130-230; ☾ restaurant closed Wed; ℗ ☂) This historic hotel also has one of the most popular

resturants in town. The menu changes weekly, but you're guaranteed it will be Umbrian dishes made with local produce. The homemade *strangozzi* is excellent.

Foligno
pop 51149

Foligno was one of the major centres of power in medieval Umbria, but has lost most of its history and charm to industry. Still, if you decide to stay (or get stuck here due to public-transport mishaps), or you're sick of postcard-perfect Italian hill towns, there are some worthwhile activities. The youth hostel alone is worth a stay.

At the horrendously unhelpful **tourist office** (☎ 0742 35 44 59; info@iat.foligno.pg.it; Corso Cavour 126; ☾ 9am-1pm & 4-7pm Mon-Sat, 9am-1pm Sun), no one speaks English, but it has information behind the desk for Foligno, as well as the surrounding towns of Bevagna, Gualdo Cattaneo, Montefalco, Spello and Trevi. It's located near the Porta Romana. Pass up the smaller, equally unhelpful **tourist office** (☾ 10am-1pm & 3-7pm Wed-Sun) at the train station.

The **cathedral** is in **Piazza della Repubblica**, in which Saint Feliciano is buried. The building dates from the 12th century and is a hodgepodge of many architectural styles, from Roman-Gothic to Renaissance additions added in the 16th century. There are some stunning 16th-century Vespasiano Strada frescoes. **Palazzo Trinci** (☎ 0742 35 07 34; admission free; ☾ 10am-7pm Tue-Sun) still has some paintings and frescoes from the 15th century. The Trinci family was part of the feudal lordship, also known as the *seigniories*, which ruled over much of Papal-controlled Umbria in the later medieval period. (You'll notice buildings all over Umbria named after these families: the Baglionis in Perugia or the Vitellis in Città di Castello.) The Trincis paid Ottaviano Nelli to decorate their palace (although they didn't score like the Vitellis in Città di Castello, with Raphael and Giorgio Vasari). There's a small museum in the palazzo, all in Italian, which features some of the historic costumes you might find at the Quintana festival.

If you're in the area during the beginning of June or in September, the main festival is **La Giostra della Quintana** (☎ 0742 35 40 00; www.quintana.it), a medieval equestrian tournament reinvented from the 1400s. Ten neighborhoods vie against each other in a friendly jousting competition complete with elaborate velvet-and-lace traditional costumes, and dishes from the 15th century.

Ostello per la Gioventú (☎ 0742 34 35 59; folhostel@ tiscali.it; Via Pierantoni 23; dm & breakfast €14, bed in private f €16; reception ☺ 7am-noon & 2pm-midnight) Five hundred metres from the station, this full-service hostel has 199 beds, washer/dryer, Internet facilities, outdoor garden, bike rental, access for people with disabilities and a restaurant. It feels like a palace with frescoed, echo-high ceilings, but it was actually a monastery for some extremely comfortable monks.

Il Barbablu (☎ 0742 35 46 97; Via Umberto I 46; pizza slice €1) On the way to the hostel is this fantastic cheap pizza place. Try the corn or zucchini.

Trevi
pop 7797
Trevi has miraculously avoided any sort of bowing to the burgeoning tourist industry in Umbria, and would feel downright foreign to anyone just coming from San Gimignano or Siena. Trevi allied itself with Perugia against Spoleto during the papal rule – it was a papal state until the Unification of Italy. It witnessed several exciting firsts: the first press association and the first pawn shop. Nowadays, you can actually hear the z-z-z-zip as it rolls itself up for siesta, and nary a local soul ventures out between 1pm and 4pm. The town calls itself a 'Slow City', and residents pride themselves on its utter mellowness. Greenish-grey olive trees swathe every inch of hillside around Trevi, and the olive oil here is reputedly some of the best in Italy. In the spring, the entire town smells of blooming flowers.

The **Pro Loco office** (☎ /fax 0742 78 11 50; Piazza Mazzini 5; ☺ 9am-1pm & 4-8pm) has an interactive Internet computer display out the front, so if it's closed, you can still get information from its website www.protrevi.com.

Trevi was a theatre town, all the way back to Roman times. The **Teatro Clitunno** (☎ 0742

DETOUR: OLIVO DI SAN EMILIANO

In the town of Bovara you can see the oldest olive tree in the region. Take the road through Bovara back to the highway. Across from the La Foccaccia ristorante on the left is a side road. Turn right and just 50m down the road you'll find the Olivo di San Emiliano, a grandfatherly tree 9m in diameter, 5m tall and estimated to be over 1700 years old.

38 17 68; Piazza del Teatro) remains the town's most important gathering point. The **Flash Art Museum** (☎ 0742 38 19 78; Palazzo Luncarini; adult/ reduced €4/2.50; ☺ 3-7pm Wed-Fri, 10am-1pm & 3-7pm Sat-Sun, closed Mon-Tue) is a funky collection of modern art. Remnants of concentric rings of a **Mura Romana** (Roman Wall) and a **Mura Medievali** (Medieval Wall) still encircle the historic centre of the town. The **Museo della Civiltá dell' Ulivo** (Olive Museum; ☎ 0742 33 22 22; ☺ 10.30am-1pm & 3.30-7pm Tue-Sun Jun-Jul, 10.30am-1pm & 3-7pm Tue-Sun Aug, 10.30-1pm & 2.30-5pm Fri-Sun Oct-Mar, 10.30am-1pm & 2.30-6pm Tue-Sun Apr-May & Sep) is a must-see while in the area, as it details the history of olive-oil production in Umbria for millennia.

Albergo Ristorante Il Terziere (☎ 0742 7 83 59; info@ilterziere.it; Via Coste 1; s/d €52/70; P) This beautiful hotel and restaurant is outside the city centre, just behind the parking area in Piazza Garibaldi. The views are better than the rather austere rooms, but with a stunning garden and terrace, you won't want to spend much time inside here anyway.

Antica Dimora alla Rocca (☎ 0742 38 54 01; Piazza della Rocca; s/d €110/160; ☒ P) This is a breathtakingly decorated *relais* (hotel) with palatial furnishings and frescoed hallways. It feels palatial for a reason: the hotel was actually built in the 1500s as a prince's palace. It offers three rooms that are completely accessible for wheelchairs.

Maggiolini (☎ 0742 38 15 34; Via San Francesco 20) Try this beautiful restaurant in summer when you can dine al fresco on several different reasonably priced truffle dishes.

Southern Umbria

SOUTHERN UMBRIA

Southern Umbria isn't as well travelled as its northern counterpart, but it's equally as beautiful and historically significant. The biggest tourist draw is Orvieto, known for its magnificent cathedral. But the area has some quintessentially perfect hill towns: Spoleto, famous for its Festival di Due Mondi; Norcia, a meat-lover's paradise; Narni, charming but undiscovered; Amelia, unassumingly friendly; and Todi, about to become very popular now that it's been called 'the most livable city in the world'.

Most of Southern Umbria is sleepy, slow and laid-back. Everything closes from 12.30pm or 1pm to 3.30pm or 4pm. Locals pride themselves on this relaxed atmosphere and – as there is virtually nothing to do for three hours every day but eat a tenth of your body weight in pasta and then stroll it off – tourists begin to adapt to this lifestyle as well.

History, art and culture dominate the sights and attractions in the area. Near Orvieto lies an Etruscan necropolis dating from the 6th century BC. Carsulae, outside of the south's industrial capital of Terni, is a well-preserved Roman town, once a major stopping-off point on the Roman Via Flaminia. You won't find the artistic masterpieces of Perugia or Città di Castello, but each town has several galleries and historically important artwork in its churches and cathedrals.

If you need to get your adrenaline junkie fix, Southern Umbria offers activities and sports of all kinds. Outdoor enthusiasts can indulge in just about any sport they desire. Fancy hanggliding? Try Castelluccio, near the Piano Grande. Rafting? Several companies along the Nera and Corno rivers offer white-water rafting, kayaking or canoeing. You can rent bikes outside of Orvieto, rock climb in Ferentillo or go spelunking (caving) in the Valnerina.

SOUTHERN UMBRIA

HIGHLIGHTS

- Take in a concert or performance at the Spoleto Festival (p297)
- Wander through the ancient village of Amelia (p311)
- Picnic in fields of flowers flanked by snow-capped peaks in the Piano Grande (p302) near Castelluccio in May or June
- Experience the majesty of the black-and-white marble facade of the Orvieto cathedral (p315)
- Savour the view from the top of La Rocca Albornoz in Narni (p309)

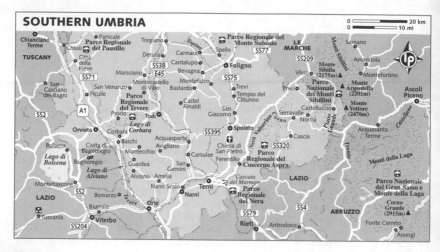

SOUTHERN UMBRIA

SPOLETO
pop 37,918

Spoleto was one of those sleepy Umbrian hill towns until, in 1958, Italian-American composer Giancarlo Menotti changed everything. For a while, Spoleto saw its tourist season peak for only 10 days from the end of June to the beginning of July during its immensely popular Spoleto Festival (see p297), when this otherwise quiet town takes centre stage for an international parade of drama, music, opera and dance.

So many people have discovered the town via the festival that it's become a popular destination for most of the year (although as in the rest of Umbria, you'll have the town mostly to yourself in winter). Even outside the festival season, Spoleto has enough museums, Roman ruins, wanderable streets and vistas to keep you busy for a day or two.

The surrounding Umbra Valley is a masterpiece of well over two thousand years of agricultural practice. From the Umbrian tribes to the Romans and farmers in the medieval period, the Vale di Spoleto, as it was known then, has been drained using an intricate system of hydraulics and agricultural techniques.

Umbria was first divided in half between the Etruscans and Umbrians. After Rome fell, it was divided again: Byzantines on the east of the Tiber river, Lombards to the west. Spoleto, which was just to the west of the Tiber, became the capital of the Lombardy Duchy. Although much of its pre-Lombard artwork has been lost, you'll see many of the signature religious buildings and hermitages in the area.

If you plan to visit during the Spoleto Festival (see p297), book accommodation and possibly even tickets months in advance.

Orientation

The old part of the city is about 1km south of the main train station – take the orange shuttle bus marked A, B or C for Piazza della Libertà in the city centre, where you'll find the tourist office and the Teatro Romano. Piazza del Mercato, a short walk northeast of Piazza della Libertà, marks the engaging heart of old Spoleto. Between here and Piazza del Duomo you'll find the bulk of the city's monuments and some fine shops.

Information
BOOKSHOPS

Il Libro (Corso Mazzini 63) A wide selection of maps, cookbooks, guidebooks and novels in English.

EMERGENCY

Police Station (☎ 0743 2 32 41; Viale Trento e Trieste) It's a block south of the main train station.

INTERNET ACCESS

A Tuta Birra (Via di Fontesecca 7) There's an Internet terminal at this pub, which opens at 7.30pm.
Pizzeria (Corso Mazzini 31; €2/hr) There's one computer with Internet access here.

MEDICAL SERVICES
Ospedale di Madonna di Loreto (hospital; ☎ 0743 2101; Via Madonna di Loreto) It's west of Porta San Matteo.

POST
Post Office (faces Piazza della Libertà, but the entrance is off Viale Giacomo Matteotti; ☻ 8am-6.30pm Mon-Fri, 8am-12.30pm Sat)

TOURIST INFORMATION
Tourist Office (☎ 0743 23 89 20; Piazza della Libertà 7; info@iat.spoleto.pg.it; ☻ 9am-1pm & 4-7pm Mon-Fri in summer, 9am-1pm & 3.30-6.30pm Mon-Fri in winter, 10am-1pm & 4-7pm Sat & Sun year-round) This friendly office has many brochures of local tourist sites and places to stay.
Con Spoleto (☎ 0743 22 07 73; info@conspoleto.com; Piazza della Libertà 7) A privately owned service that can book accommodation.

Sights
Make your first stop the **Museo Archeologico e Teatro Romano** (☎ 0743 22 32 77; http://www.archeop g.arti.beniculturali.it/musei/spoleto.htm - Italian only; Via S Agata 18; adult/reduced/EU student €2/1/free, includes museum; ☻ 8.30am-7.30pm) on the western edge of Piazza della Libertà. Since 1985, this former Benedictine monastery and prison has been used as a museum. Exhibited are many artefacts from ancient and Roman Spoleto, including two marble sculptures of Augustus and possibly Caesar. The Spoleto Festival ingeniously uses the dramatic stage setting here to put on ballet performances.

East of Piazza della Libertà, around Piazza Fontana, are more Roman remains, including the **Arco di Druso e Germanico** (Arch of Drusus and Germanicus; sons of the Emperor Tiberius). The grandiose archway marks the entrance to where the old Roman forum used to be. The excavated **Casa Romana** (Roman House; ☎ 0743 4 37 07; Via di Visiale; adult/child €2/1; ☻ 10am-1pm & 3-6.30pm Oct-Mar, 10am-8pm Apr-Oct, closed Tue) dates from the 1st century. It's a good example of a fairly typical Roman house from this time, and still has vestiges of tile and painting decoration.

The city boasts an **Anfiteatro Romano** (Roman Amphitheatre), one of the country's largest. Unfortunately it is within military barracks and closed to the public. Wander along Via dell'Anfiteatro, off Piazza Garibaldi, in search of a glimpse.

The **Rocca Albornoziana** (☎ 0743 4 37 07; Piazza Campello; adult/reduced €5/3; ☻ 10am-1pm & 3-6pm Mon-Fri, 10am-6pm Sat-Sun 15-31 Mar, 10am-1pm &

3-7pm Mon-Fri Apr-10 Jun, 10am-8pm daily 10 Jun-15 Sep, 2.30-5pm Mon-Fri, 10am-5pm Sat-Sun Nov-Dec) is an example of a Albornoz-built fortress from the mid-1300s. Cardinal Albornoz led Pope Innocent VI's forces in the fight to take back control of Umbria. He fostered the building of many of the *rocche* (fortresses) in the area, including the one still standing in Narni, the ruins of one in Orvieto, and one in Perugia that was destroyed in an uprising against the Pope just three years after it was built. For hundreds of years, until as recently as 1982, this *rocca* was used as a high-security prison housing such notables as Pope John Paul II's attempted assassin, Ali Agca. It's now used as a museum and to host open-air theatre performances.

Inside the town hall on Piazza del Municipio is the **Pinacoteca Comunale** (☎ 0743 21 82 70; Via A Saffi; adult/child €2.05/1; ☻ 10.30am-1pm & 2.30-5pm in winter, 10.30am-1pm & 3-6.30pm in summer, guided tour only). It is a sumptuous building, with some impressive works by Umbrian artists. To check out more modern artwork head towards the **Galleria D'Arte Moderna** (☎ 0743 4 64 34; in the Palazzo Collicola on Piazza Collicola; ☻ 10.30am-1pm & 3-6.30pm 16 Oct-26 Mar, 10am-8pm 27 Mar-15 Oct).

Churches
The **cathedral** (☎ 0743 4 43 07; Piazza del Duomo; admission free; ☻ 7.30am-12.30pm & 3-6pm in summer, 7.30am-12.30pm & 3-5pm in winter) in Spoleto was consecrated in 1198 and remodelled in the 17th century. The Romanesque facade is fronted by a striking Renaissance porch. In the 11th century, huge blocks of stone salvaged from Roman buildings were put to good use in the construction of the rather sombre bell tower. The mosaic floors are from a 12th-century reconstruction effort. Inside, the first chapel to the right of the nave (Chapel of Bishop Constantino Eroli) was decorated by Bernardino Pinturicchio, and Annibale Carracci completed an impressive fresco in the right transept. The frescoes in the domed apse were executed by Filippo Lippi and his assistants, and decorated the apse with his *Life of the Virgin*. This was Lippi's last piece of artwork, as he died before completing the work. Lorenzo de Medici travelled to Spoleto from Florence and ordered Lippi's son, Filippino, to build a mausoleum for the artist. This now stands in the right transept of the

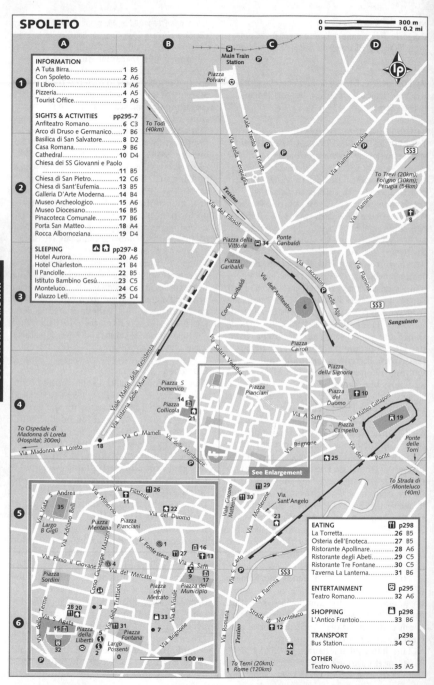

SPOLETO

0 300 m
0 0.2 mi

INFORMATION
A Tuta Birra.....................1 B5
Con Spoleto.....................2 A6
Il Libro.........................3 A6
Pizzeria........................4 A5
Tourist Office..................5 A6

SIGHTS & ACTIVITIES pp295-7
Anfiteatro Romano...............6 C3
Arco di Druso e Germanico.......7 B6
Basilica di San Salvatore.......8 D2
Casa Romana.....................9 B6
Cathedral......................10 D4
Chiesa dei SS Giovanni e Paolo
...............................11 B5
Chiesa di San Pietro...........12 C6
Chiesa di Sant'Eufemia.........13 B5
Galleria D'Arte Moderna........14 B4
Museo Archeologico.............15 A6
Museo Diocesano................16 B5
Pinacoteca Comunale............17 B6
Porta San Matteo...............18 A4
Rocca Albornoziana.............19 D4

SLEEPING 🏠 🏠 pp297-8
Hotel Aurora...................20 A6
Hotel Charleston...............21 B4
Il Panciolle...................22 B6
Istituto Bambino Gesú..........23 C5
Monteluco......................24 C6
Palazzo Leti...................25 D4

Main Train Station

Piazza Polvani

To Todi (40km)

Piazza della Vittoria 34
Ponte Garibaldi

Piazza Garibaldi

Piazza Cairoli

To Trevi (20km); Foligno (30km); Perugia (54km)

Sanguineto

SS3

Piazza S Domenico

Piazza Collicola

14
21

Via G Mameli

Via delle Montanze

Piazza Pianciani

Piazza della Signoria

Piazza del Duomo
10

Via A Saffi

Brignone

Piazza Campello

25

19

Ponte delle Torri

Via del Ponte

To Strada di Monteluco (40km)

To Ospedale di Madonna di Loreta (Hospital; 300m)

Via Madonna di Loreto

18

See Enlargement

29
30

Via Sant'Angelo

23

Via S Carlo

SS3

Via Flaminia

Strada di Monteluco

To Terni (20km); Rome (120km)

Via S Andrea
35

Via Filitteria 26

11

22
Via del Duomo

Piazza Mentana
Piazza Pianciani

V Fonte sseca

1

27
16
13

Via A Saffi

9
17

Piazza del Mercato

Piazza del Municipio

Largo B Gigli

Piazza Sordini

Via Plinio il Giovane

4
Via del Mercato

28 20
15
32

Piazza della Libertà

31
Piazza Fontana

33

7

Largo Possenti

100 m

EATING 🍴 p298
La Torretta...................26 B5
Osteria dell'Enoteca..........27 B5
Ristorante Apollinare.........28 A6
Ristorante degli Abeti........29 C5
Ristorante Tre Fontane........30 C5
Taverna La Lanterna...........31 B6

ENTERTAINMENT 🎭 p295
Teatro Romano.................32 A6

SHOPPING 🛍 p298
L'Antico Frantoio.............33 B6

TRANSPORT p298
Bus Station...................34 C2

OTHER
Teatro Nuovo..................35 A5

cathedral. No 8 on Piazza del Duomo is the house where composer Giancarlo Menotti stays when in town. The spectacular closing concert of the Spoleto Festival is held on the piazza.

On Via Filitteria, you'll come across the tiny and ancient **Chiesa di SS Giovanni e Paolo** (10am-1pm & 4-8pm sporadically), an example of an early Romanesque church. If you can get in, you'll see an early painting of St Francis.

Along Via del Ponte is the **Ponte delle Torri**, erected in the 14th century on the foundations of a Roman aqueduct. The bridge is 80m high and 230m across, built in an imposing set of 10 arches. It's a beautiful walk across the bridge to the eponymous tower on the other side, although the structure is not much more than ruins.

If you feel like a walk, cross the bridge and follow the lower path, Strada di Monteluco, to reach the **Chiesa di San Pietro** (0743 4 48 82; Loc. San Pietro; admission free; 9.30-11am & 3.30-6.30pm). The 13th-century facade, the church's main attraction, is liberally bedecked with sculpted animals.

Festivals & Events

The Italian-American composer Giancarlo Menotti conceived the Festival dei Due Mondi (Festival of the Two Worlds) in 1958. Now known simply as the **Spoleto Festival**, it has given the city a worldwide reputation and brought great wealth to the small population, which basks in its reflected glory. During the three weeks from late June to mid-July, all sorts of performances take place, from opera and theatre to ballet and art exhibitions. A special **Spoleto Cinema** component showcases old and new films. A fairly new but inventive performance tradition has been to re-enact either famous or historical court proceedings. Tickets cost €5 to over €100, depending on the performance and whether you want luxury seats or standing room. Try to buy your tickets as early as possible, as some performances sell out months in advance, but if you arrive empty-handed, ask at the **Box Office** (0743 4 47 00; fax 4 05 46; www.spoletofestival.it; Piazza della Libertà 12, 06049 Spoleto, Italy), as there are often still tickets available for many smaller performances. There are also usually several free concerts in various churches.

For information, call or write to the festival office. You can find further details and book tickets online at its website.

Sleeping

The city is well served by cheap hotels, *affitta-camere* (rooms for rent), hostels and camp sites, although if you're coming for the festival, book a room well in advance.

BUDGET

Monteluco (/fax 0743 22 03 58; www.geocities.com/monteluco2002; Via Giro del Ponte; Loc. San Pietro; site per person/tent/car €5/5/3) This leafy, quiet camp site is just behind the Chiesa di San Pietro, in easy walking distance of the town centre. The area is filled with pedestrian paths and lots of oak groves, so it's a wonderful place for strolling and hiking.

Istituto Bambino Gesù (0743 4 02 32; Via Sant'Angelo 4; s/d €36/70) The nuns at this religious institution keep up a beautiful central garden and the convent itself is very attractive, but it's a bit of a schlep up the hill to the town centre.

Il Panciolle (/fax 0743 4 56 77; Via del Duomo 3-5; s/d €40/55; P) A perfectly reliable and comfortable bet, rooms come with hairdryer and minibar, and are well located near the cathedral. A parking permit allows you to park your car in the city centre. No credit cards.

Hotel Aurora (0743 22 03 15; info@hotelaurora spoleto.it; www.hotelauroraspoleto.it; Via Apollinare 3; s/d €57/80; P) Just off Piazza della Libertà, the Aurora is very central. Some rooms have pleasant balconies, and breakfast is excellent.

MID-RANGE

Hotel Charleston (0743 22 00 52; info@hotelcharleston .it; www.hotelcharleston.it; Piazza Collicola 10; s/d €64/105; P) The Charleston has a relaxed chalet feel with an open fireplace in the hall and wood-panelled rooms. It has many special touches, such as a hotel sauna, and staff are wonderful at arranging activities and excursions throughout the area, whether you want to hunt for truffles, take a one-day cooking class or go wine- or olive-oil tasting. There's a great little terrace outside for breakfast. Air-conditioning in only half the rooms.

TOP END

Palazzo Leti (0743 22 49 30; info@palazzoleti.com; Via degli Eremiti 10; s/d/ste €119/170/258, higher during Spoleto Festival; P) This gorgeous location opened in April 2003. In the southeast part of town facing the hills, this former noble palace exudes romance and charm down to the last detail, from the delicate breakfast china to the historical oak and wrought-iron furnishings. With the view and perfect silence, you'll feel like you're staying in the country, but you're a three-minute walk from the centre of Spoleto.

Eating

Spoleto is one of Umbria's main centres for the *tartufo nero* (black truffle), used in a variety of dishes. Trying them can be a costly exercise, so check the price before digging in. On Via dell'Arco Druso is a gathering of five shops selling meat, bread, sauces and wine, perfect to pick up supplies for a picnic.

Ristorante Apollinare (☎ 0743 22 32 56; Via Sant' Agata 14; meals about €40; ☺ closed Tue) A delight for the senses, Apollinare is an extraordinary culinary experience set amid ancient 12th-century walls and low oak beam ceilings. You can choose to go with one of its tasting menus – vegetarian, truffle or traditional – or choose from its *nouvelle* menu. Appetiser specialities are millet puffed pastry topped with yellow pumpkin (€13) and a rolled cheese and truffle dish. Yum.

Osteria dell'Enoteca (☎ 0743 22 04 84; Via A Saffi 7; tourist menu €14.99; ☺ closed Tue) A small but good-value spot, Osteria dell'Enoteca's set menus incorporate local ingredients. It serves many good wines by the glass. You can also buy some typical Umbrian wine and food products here.

Ristorante degli Abeti (☎ 0743 22 00 25; Via B Egio 3/5) Its prices are some of the most reasonable in town. A delicious *cinghiale* (wild boar) with *porcini* (a type of mushroom) is served for €8.50.

Taverna la Lanterna (☎ 0743 4 98 15; Via della Trattoria 6; meals around €15; ☺ closed Wed) A great place with extremely reasonable prices in the town centre, La Lanterna serves a variety of Umbrian pasta dishes. Tasting menus include vegetarian for €11, regular for €13, and *porcini* and *tartufo* (truffle) for €15.

Ristorante Tre Fontane (☎ 0743 22 15 44; Via Egio 15; pizza from €4; ☺ closed Wed) This is a great spot for pizza in an informal but pleasant garden dining area.

La Torretta (☎ 0743 4 49 54; Via Filetteria 43) This casual restaurant serves Spoletan cuisine and cooks with many locally grown herbs. Try the steak or truffle fondue.

Shopping

Gathered Via dell'Arco Druso are several shops that sell locally produced meats, wines or delicacies. **L'Antico Frantoio** (Via dell'Arco Druso 8) sells plenty of pasta, wine, oil and cheese for a great gift or picnic. The owner of the store, Sandra, makes many of the sauces she sells herself. She makes a delectable pesto, as well as several sauces made with local black and green olives, or truffles. She will carefully package and Fed Ex any purchases you make to anywhere in the world.

Getting There & Away

Most **Società Spoletina di Imprese Trasporti (SSIT)** (☎ 0743 21 22 11) buses depart from Piazza della Vittoria (some leave first from the train station). They travel to Perugia (€5.60, one hour) at 6.23am, 7.14am and 10.44am (the latter just from the train station), and Foligno (€3.70, 40 minutes, hourly) and Terni (€3.10, 30 minutes, five daily).

Trains from the **main station** (☎ 0743 21 22 08; Piazza Polvani) connect with Rome (€8.10 to €14.20, one to 2½ hours, hourly), Ancona (€8.60, two hours, 10 daily), Perugia (€4.50, one hour, hourly) and Assisi (€3.20, 30 minutes, hourly).

The city is easily explored on foot, though local buses weave through the streets. Orange shuttle buses A, B and C run between the train station, Piazza Garibaldi and Piazza della Libertà (€0.80). It's a vertical hike up to the city centre, so you'll want to take one of these if you've got luggage.

CAMPELLO SUL CLITUNNO

Heading towards Foligno from Spoleto on the Via Flaminia you'll come across the area known as the Campello sul Clitunno, where you'll find the **Fonti del Clitunno** (☎ 0743 52 11 41; Loc. Pissignano), the source for the Clitunno river. This Zen-like garden setting proffers crystal clear springs, a tranquil lake and exquisitely lush foliage. In ancient times, it was a popular site for religious pilgrimages. Caligula was known to come here to consult the god of the Clitunno river. It was also used for theatre performances, feasts and gladiator matches. It's open daily but on an incredibly complex schedule; call for opening hours.

In the same area is the **Tempietto del Clitunno** (☎ 0743 27 50 85; Via Flaminia, Km 139; ☺ 9am-8pm April-Oct, 8am-6pm Nov-Mar). This Paleo-Christian

OUTDOOR ADVENTURES

Umbria has plenty of outdoor activities to keep you busy for months.

The **Club Alpino Italiano** (Italian Alpine Club; ☎ 075 914 22 13; www.cai.it) is an authority on all things mountainous in the region, but its website is Italian only.

Every tourist office carries a brochure entitled *The Environment and Sports*. All sports and activities are listed, along with companies, outfitters and contact information at the back of the brochure.

Here's just a sample of the outdoor activities you can try in Umbria (and the best locations to experience them):

Hang-gliding & Paragliding With vertical cliffs and soft rolling hills, Umbria is a great place to learn how to do either, or get in a little practice if you're already certified. The hang-gliding capital of Italy – Castelluccio and the Monti Sibillini – has two popular hang-gliding schools. Courses can be long (up to 15 days) and expensive, so a good alternative is paragliding. You can take a five-day course with several companies in the Monti Sibillini area.

Rafting/Canoeing The Nera, Tiber and Corno rivers offer wild rides in beautiful settings for those who want a leisurely canoe ride or a white-water thrill.

Horse Riding Many places around Lago di Trasimeno in the north of Umbria lead walks or rent horses by the hour.

Spelunking/Caving Monte Cucco in the north of Umbria has an extensive karst system of caverns to explore.

Rock Climbing Ferentillo and the Valnerina are the climbing hotspots.

Hiking & Walking One of the most popular Umbrian pastimes for locals and tourists alike is trekking, hiking or simply strolling in the outdoors. Italy's national park system is a well-maintained group, with marked trails, outdoor activities and a system of *rifugi* (mountain huts). Check www.parks.it for more information or at any tourist office in Umbria.

building was first thought to be an ancient Roman ruin, but artefacts have shown that it was built sometime between the 5th and 8th centuries AD. It has many of the classic Roman features, such as Corinthian columns and neo-Augustan inscriptions (in big block lettering).

THE VALNERINA

Incorporating most of the lower eastern parts of Umbria, along the Nera river, the Valnerina is one of the most geographically striking areas in Umbria. Instead of rolling hillsides and vineyards, it has jagged cliffs and forests full of beech trees that hide the Apennine wolves, wild boar and golden eagles that thrive here. Stretching northeast to the barren summit of Monte Sibilla (2175m) in neighbouring region Le Marche, it makes for great walking territory.

The area is criss crossed by walking trails and you might try to pick up a copy of the aptly titled *20 Sentieri Ragionati in Valnerina* (20 Well-Thought-Out Routes in Valnerina; in Italian), available for free from local tourist offices in the region.

The S395 from Spoleto and the S209 from Terni join with the S320 and then the S396, which passes through Norcia. The area is also accessible from Ascoli Piceno in Le Marche.

NORCIA

pop 4872

This inherently walkable town is the commercial and tourist hub of the surrounding Valnerina. It's certainly a pleasant enough town, but rather inexplicably, Norcia receives an enormous number of tourists. They are mainly day-tripping Italians or Germans, so avoid visiting on a Sunday (and Saturday, if you can help it) and you'll be able to explore the town – which has several fine elements – at a more leisurely pace.

Orientation

The main gate for Norcia is the Porta Ascolana, also known as the Porta Massari, which is where buses arrive. Most of Norcia is pedestrian-only, but there are many pay car parks around the city walls, including one near Porta Ascolana.

Information

INTERNET RESOURCES

www.norcia.com An Italian-only website.

POST

Post Office (next to Porta Romana)

TOURIST INFORMATION

Casa del Parco (☎ 0743 81 70 90; cpnorcia@yahoo.it; Via Solferino 22; 🕙 9.30am-12.30pm & 3-6pm Mon-Fri,

NORCIA

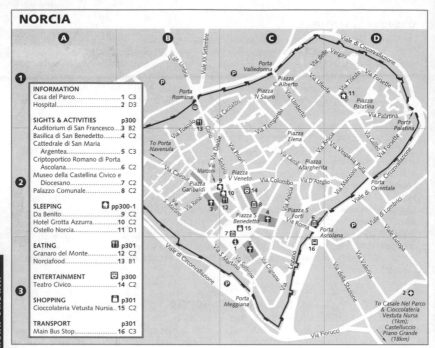

INFORMATION	
Casa del Parco	1 C3
Hospital	2 D3

SIGHTS & ACTIVITIES	p300
Auditorium di San Francesco	3 B2
Basilica di San Benedetto	4 C2
Cattedrale di San Maria Argentea	5 C3
Criptoportico Romano di Porta Ascolana	6 C2
Museo della Castellina Civico e Diocesano	7 C2
Palazzo Comunale	8 C2

SLEEPING	pp300-1
Da Benito	9 C2
Hotel Grotta Azzurra	10 C2
Ostello Norcia	11 D1

EATING	p301
Granaro del Monte	12 C2
Norciafood	13 B1

ENTERTAINMENT	p300
Teatro Civico	14 C2

SHOPPING	p301
Cioccolateria Vetusta Nursia	15 C2

TRANSPORT	p301
Main Bus Stop	16 C3

9.30am-12.30pm & 3.30-6.30pm Sat & Sun, 9.30am-12.30pm & 3-7pm Jul-Aug) Offers tourist information and plenty of Monti Sibillini information, including guided trips, public transportation to the area, various maps and local products.

Sights

Norcia's lack of worthwhile sights isn't a problem, as it's much more fun to wander around, checking out all the boar heads lining the shops on the streets.

The **Basilica di San Benedetto** (Piazza San Benedetto) is an impressive show of architectural know-how. Named after St Benedict, who was born in Norcia, it was built in the shape of a Latin cross with a polygonal apse. The bell tower dates back to 1389 and its portico is Gothic. Frescoes inside the church date to the 16th century, including *Resurrezione di Lazzaro* (Resurrection of Lazarus) by Michelangelo Carducci (not *the* Michelangelo, but one from Norcia) and *San Benedetto e Totila* (St Benedict and Totila) by Filippo Napoletano, completed in 1621.

The **Museo della Castellina Civico e Diocesano** (La Castellina Diocesan Civic Museum; ☎ 0743 81 70 30;

Piazza San Benedetto; adult/reduced €4/2.50; 🕑 10am-1pm & 4-7pm Apr-Sep, 10am-1pm & 4-7.30pm & 9-11pm Aug) is an Umbrian anomaly: it's a terrible museum. There's almost no information given (and what is available is in Italian), nor are the small archaeological exhibits very good. However, the admission price also gains you entrance to the **Criptoportico Romano di Porta Ascolana** (Roman Crypt of Porta Ascolana), which is an interesting look into a Roman tomb.

Also on Piazza San Benedetto is the **Palazzo Comunale**, parts of which date back to the 14th century. Its bell tower dates to 1713. The **Cattedrale di Santa Maria Argentea** was built in 1560 but heavily modified after an earthquake in 1703.

You can see a performance at either the **Teatro Civico** or the **Auditorium di San Francesco** (☎ 0743 816 44 88).

Sleeping
BUDGET

Ostello Norcia (☎ 0743 81 74 87; Via Ufente 1/b; ostellonorcia@montepatino.com; www.montepatino.com; dm €13 with breakfast) This new and modern hostel is in an old and beautiful building. It has only recently opened, so it's incredibly clean. Open year-round, it sleeps 52 in four-, six- or eight-person rooms. It can also arrange many local outdoor and sporting outings. Try calling ahead to book as it closes intermittently during the day. Sheets are included.

Hotel Da Benito (☎ 0743 81 66 70; ristorante.benito@libero.it; Via Marconi 5; s/d with bathroom €40/55) Located perfectly in the centre of town, it's a friendly one-star hotel with eight modest rooms. The attached restaurant is excellent.

MID-RANGE
Hotel Grotta Azzurra (☎ 0743 81 65 13; info@bianconi.com; www.bianconi.com; Via Alfieri 12; d €100-150; 🏊) The Bianconi Ospitalità group also owns three McHotels outside the city centre (including a rare Umbrian chain hotel, a Best Western). This one has the most personality by far, and you can take advantage of all the activities the group offers: baby-sitting, evening events, gym classes and outdoor activities, such as truffle hunts. The building dates back to the 16th century and has been an inn since 1850.

AGRITURISMO
Casale Nel Parco (☎ /fax 0743 81 64 81; agriumbria@casalenelparco.com; Loc. Fontevena 8; d €70 or €110 with dinner for 2; 🅿) Only 1km from Norcia towards Castelluccio, this working organic *agriturismo* (farm holiday) grows its own lentils, spelt and vegetables (which you can sample at dinner). Swim in the terracotta-tiled pool under the eye of snow-capped Monte Patino, ride the horses through the foothills of Monti Sibillini or ask your hosts to arrange one of many outdoor activities. Eight rustic double rooms all come with private bathroom.

Eating
The town is full of Norcineras – butchers serving Norcia-produced dried meats. In fact, the word *norcinera* is now used to mean a butcher throughout all of Italy. Famous food items from the area also include *cinghiale*, lentils and *pecorino* cheese.

Granaro del Monte (☎ 0743 81 65 13; Via Alfieri 12; tourist menu €18.08, dishes €7-24) One of the most famous restaurants in Umbria. It's filled with tourists, but the food is impeccably good. With an enormous banquet-sized interior

and pleasant outdoor dining area during summer, this is the place to try some of the trumpeted Norcinera specialities, including pork, sausage and *cinghiale*. Its speciality is Filetto Tartufato del Cavatore, a filleted veal dish sautéed in butter, black truffles and red wine – as rich as it is delicious.

Da Benito (☎ 0743 81 66 70; ristorante.benito@libero.it; Via Marconi 5; 🕑 closed Mon; meals around €16) This simple but delicious restaurant offers many dishes served with local meats and truffles.

Cioccolateria Vestusta Nursa (☎ 0743 81 73 70; Viale della Stazione 41/43; 🕑 daily, including public holidays & Sun) A kilometre outside Norcia on the road to Castelluccio you'll pass what looks like a boring warehouse. Step inside and you'll find the best prices on a huge selection of chocolate, wine, lentils and local (non-meat) products. Best of all, there is always something available to taste. There's a smaller and more expensive shop in town (☎ 0743 82 80 70; Via Mazzini 6).

Norciafood (☎ 0743 82 83 62; Via dei Priori 38; www.norciafood.com) This is one of the largest and most complete Norcinera and local produce shop. They ship to anywhere in the world and you can order many of their products on their website.

Getting There & Away
The closest train station is in Spoleto, so the best way to get to Norcia is by bus. **SSIT** (Spoletina; ☎ 0743 21 22 11) is Norcia's intercity bus company. You can go to Cascia (€2, 20 minutes, 10 daily), Spoleto (€4.40, 45 minutes, seven daily), Perugia (€6.80, one hour and 20 minutes, one daily at 6.15am), Foligno (€5.20; one hour, two daily at 6.15am and 2.05pm), Preci (€2, 20 minutes, two daily at 7.20am and 2.20pm).

You can travel to Castelluccio only once a week, and Norcia is the town to do it from. The bus leaves Norcia at 6.25am and 1.30pm on Thursday only (€2.80, 40 minutes). It originates in Castelluccio, returning at 7.20am or 2.20pm, so if you just wanted to take a drive through the region, you could technically buy a return ticket and take it straight through.

MONTI SIBILLINI
Monti Sibillini is one of those places it would be great to discover by accident, but there's no way you're going to haul yourself up from Norcia (if you make it to Norcia

at all) unless you hear how beautiful this area is.

This area is really, really, *really* beautiful. Really. Go. Even during summer, its jagged peaks keep a healthy dusting of snow. Mt Vettore – the highest peak in Monti Sibillini – stands at 2476m. In May and June, infinite expanses of wildflowers blanket the **Piano Grande**, the great plain surrounding Castelluccio. Wolves run free, icy streams flow and fairies dance. Well, so the story goes. During the Middle Ages, the Sibillini mountains were known throughout Europe as a place that held demons, necromancers and fairies. A woman named Sybil was said to live in a cave and tell fortunes. These days, the area is home to peregrine falcons, royal eagles and porcupines (brought over in the last few decades). Eighteen hundred botanical species have been counted just in this one area.

Before going off into the Monti Sibillini, you can pick up or buy a host of maps at the Casa del Parco in Norcia (see p299), depending on how strenuous or leisurely you want to be. Any level of activity is possible here, spanning from day paths for families to week-long survival treks circling the mountain chain.

For information online, try the official Parco Nazionale dei Monti Sibillini website, www.sibillini.net, or email informazioni@sibillini.net.

CASTELLUCCIO

Visiting this little hamlet in the middle of the Piano Grande is like going back in time a few decades. There's only one hotel in town (and a bad *agriturismo*). Stone buildings that were once houses and stores have fallen into artistically charming ruin.

Albergo Sibilla (☎ 0743 82 11 13; Via Piano Grande 2; s/d €34/55) This hotel has very basic rooms with fairly primitive bathrooms. But they're clean and it's whisper quiet at night. The view is the reason you're staying here (that, and it's also the only hotel in town). There's a good restaurant downstairs, so it's best to go with the half-board option.

Pro Delta (☎ 0746 82 11 56, mobile 339 5635456; www.prodelta.it; summer location Via della Fate 3) Pro Delta is one of the most well-respected hang-gliding institutions in Europe and has a solid reputation for safety. A basic five-day hang-gliding or paragliding course costs €400. If you want to try paragliding but don't have a lot of time, consider taking a two-person flight with an instructor. The flight costs more the higher you take off. A paragliding ride costs €25 to €50, and hang-gliding is €50 to €70. Check the requirements page of its website before arriving for a course.

Another school is **Fly Castelluccio** (☎ 0736 3 44 20; info@flycastelluccio; www.flycastelluccio.com; Via Iannella 32, Ascoli Piceno), in the neighbouring region of Le Marche. It teaches paragliding and hang-gliding, as well as paramotoring.

CASCIA

The entire historical centre of Cascia is devoted to Santa Rita, and thousands of religious pilgrims (and historically curious) make the trek every year. There's a gloomy pall over Cascia, as most of its visitors seem to wear a rather depressed countenance. This might be because St Rita is the patron saint of – among other things – the impossible, spousal abuse, parenthood, infertility, illness, and lost or desperate causes.

St Rita's own life was an uphill battle of impossible suffering. The story goes that Rita Lotti was born in 1381 in nearby

---

THE PASSEGGIATA

One of the very best things to take advantage of while a tourist in Umbria is the *passeggiata* (evening stroll). No matter how big or small a town, locals and visitors of all ages take to the streets with friends or family, by themselves or, these days, attached to a mobile phone. Most towns in Umbria are built concentrically around a main square or gathering place that might have started out as a Roman forum or medieval gathering place. Best of all, '*un passeggio*' is free, doesn't require any pre-planning and practically forces you to eat a double *gelato*. Think of it as improvised urban street theatre. In Perugia, watch as the students preen and flirt, jostling their way towards adulthood. In Orvieto, sit with older locals around the cathedral, who come to deliver Italian lessons to unsuspecting visitors. In Castelluccio, your *passeggiata* will most likely be shared with the town's herd of goats.

Roccaporena, the only child of an older devout Christian couple. She wanted to enter the convent, but obedience to her parents' will dictated that she marry. Her husband, who was cruel and abusive towards Rita, was eventually ambushed and killed. She appealed to heaven for her sons not to seek revenge for their father's murder. Both sons died that year. She then turned to her first desire, to enter a convent, but no-one wanted to accept her, as they were worried one of their own family members might have murdered her husband. Rita approached both her husband's family and their rivals and persuaded them to make peace. Impressed by her level of commitment and forgiveness, the sisters at the Convent of St Mary Magdalene invited her to live with them. For 40 years, she lived as an Augustinian nun, caring for the poor and sick of her community. After 15 years of service, St Rita received a stigmatisation, a wound that appeared to be from Jesus' holy crown of thorns, which stayed on her forehead for the rest of her life.

Information

Tourist Office (☎ 0743 7 14 01; info@iat.cascia.pg.it; Via G. Da Chiavano) Offers information about Cascia or the surrounding Valnerina.

Sights & Activities

The body of St Rita was buried in the church now known as the **Basilica di Santa Rita di Cascia** (☎ 0763 7 62 02). Rita became canonised as a saint in 1900 and the main basilica was built shortly thereafter in the mid-20th century.

The opening schedule varies from month to month. Call for details. Priests are always available for confession. Masses are said on the hour from 7am to 5pm or 5.30pm (with a break between noon and 4pm) year-round.

To see **Monasterio di Santa Rita** (☎ 0763 7 62 02), you will need to go on a guided tour led by a resident monk. From April to October, guided tours are conducted every half-hour from 8.30am until noon, and at 2.30pm, 3.30pm and 4.30pm (plus 5.30pm May to September) during holidays. For the rest of the year, guided tours are conducted at 9am, 10am, 11.15am, 2.30pm, 3.30pm and 4.30pm. Tours are conducted only in Italian.

On 21 and 22 May, Cascia holds **St Rita's Feast**, a grand festival honouring St Rita.

Sleeping

Ostello San Antonio (☎ /fax 0743 75 10 53; Via Porta Leonina; dm €17) This hostel has 161 beds and mostly caters to those on pilgrimage. It offers meals.

Hotel Delle Rose (☎ 0743 7 62 41; hdr@netgen.it; Via del Sanctuario 2; s/d €32/52; P) This is a completely standard hotel set up to get guests in and out. It has several rooms for guests with disabilities, offers baby-sitting and accommodates animals.

FERENTILLO

This is a fairly good-sized town in the Valnerina known mainly for two things: mummies and rocks. The nearly perfectly preserved bodies can seen be seen at **Le Mummie de Ferentillo** (☎ 0743 5 43 95; ex-Chiesa di San Stefano, Via delle Torre; adult/reduced €2.60/1.55; 9am-12.30pm & 2.30-7.30pm Apr-Sep, 10am-12.30pm & 2.30-6pm Oct & Mar, 10am-12.30pm & 2.30-5pm Nov-Feb), one of the more ghastly museums in the area.

The second thing Ferentillo is known for is its fantastic rock climbing. You can contact certified rock climbing guide Kathleen Scheda at **Duka Duka Outdoors** (☎ 0765 6 32 02; dukadukaoutdoors@libero.it) to arrange climbing expeditions. Kathleen's family owns a B&B just across the border in Lazio called **La Torretta** (☎ /fax 0765 6 32 02; www.latorrettabandb.com; Casperia, Lazio; s/d with a 2-night minimum €60/80, f €140). It's in a medieval town about an hour from Rome and close to the best climbing spots in Lazio and Umbria. The B&B offers one-week rock-climbing trips, as well as cooking courses and hiking excursions.

Ostello Il Tiglio (☎ 0744 38 87 10; fax 40 23 76; Via Abruzzo; dm €12, f €14.50; P) This hostel is perfectly situated to reach many different parts of the Valnerina, Norcia and La Cascata delle Marmore for river rafting and rock climbing.

LAGO DI CORBARA

This man-made lake was created to control the overflow of the Tiber river. It doesn't offer too much in the way of scenery or activities, but it can be a nice half-day stop, as it's off a major road on the way between Todi and Orvieto. **Cycling** is popular here. Try www.ciclietrekking.it for information.

Scacco Matto (☎ 0744 95 01 63; fax 95 03 73, Lago di Corbara; sites per person/tent €4.15/4.65) The closest camp sites are about 10km east of Orvieto, on Lago di Corbara near Baschi. Scacco Matto is tiny (just 12 pitches) and fairly basic, but stays open year-round.

La Penisola – Villa Bellago (☎ 0744 95 05 21; www.villabellago.it; SS448 Baschi; d per person €50; P ☒ ☒) This lakefront resort is situated between Orvieto and Todi next to Lago di Corbara. It offers tennis, volleyball, mountain bike rental and baby-sitting services. Its restaurant – La Dolce Vita – specialises in home-made pasta and gnocchi and fish caught in the lake.

TODI
pop 16,694

Many monikers have been used recently for Todi: 'the ideal city' or 'the most livable city in the world'. If some disagree now, they might not in five years. For more information about Todi's commitment to the Città Lenta (Slow City) movement, see p306.

As a traveller in Todi, you'll quickly adapt to its pace of life. Restaurants take longer, the entire town shuts down for a three-hour (or more) midday break and people seem to walk a little slower. Todi was seemingly built to wander around aimlessly in, breathing in the fresh air and taking in the beauty of one of the most historically preserved towns in Umbria. There are a good amount of museums, churches and monuments to keep a visitor occupied for a day, but if you take it as leisurely as the locals, you just might want to spend a week or two.

The Umbrian tribe settled in Todi as far back as four millennia ago. Etruscans and Romans have also once called Todi home. Todi was sacked during the fall of the Roman Empire, but blossomed during the late Middle Ages, which is visible through many buildings still standing today.

Information
DISCOUNTS
Biglietto Cumulativo (adult/15-25 years & over 60s/child €6/5/4) If you'll be spending a day or two in Todi, it's a good idea to buy a cumulative ticket, which will allow you to gain entry into the Museo Pinacoteca, Cisterno Romano and the Tempio di San Fortunato.

INTERNET ACCESS
Paolo M Fedrighini Centro Grafica Digitale (☎ 075 894 22 27; Piazza Umberto I 17-18; €1.55/15 min) Across the street from the Tempio di San Fortunato.

INTERNET RESOURCES
www.iat.todi.pg.it The official governmental tourist site.
www.todi.net

MEDICAL SERVICES
Hospital (☎ 075 8 85 81)

EMERGENCY
Police (☎ 075 895 62 43; Piazza Jacopone)

POST
Post Office (Piazza Garibaldi; ☒ 8.10am-1.25pm)

TOURIST INFORMATION
Tourist Office (☎ 075 894 33 95; info@iat.todi.pg.it; Piazza Umberto I 6; ☒ 9am-1pm & 4-6.30pm Mon-Sat) It also serves Monte Castello di Vibio, which is located just behind the cathedral. Here you'll also find telephone booths and bus timetables.

Sights & Activities
One of the most renowned medieval squares in all of Italy is the **Piazza del Popolo**. On this square, you'll find Todi's **Museo Pinacoteca** (☎ 075 894 41 48; ☒ 10.30am-1pm & 2.30-6pm), located within the **Palazzo del Popolo** and the **Palazzo del Capitano**. Within the *pinacoteca* (art gallery), there's a Museo della Città that includes history about the city of Todi and its surroundings. There are also exhibits on archaeology, numismatics (coins), weaving and ceramics. The *pinacoteca* part of the museum displays some impressive frescoed rooms and paintings by Giovanni di Pietro (Lo Spagna). A copy of an Etruscan statue of Mars can be found here (while the original bronze is now at the Vatican).

At the northwestern end of the square, and across from the gloomy **Palazzo dei Priori**, is the **cathedral** (☎ 075 894 30 41; Piazza del Popolo; admission free; ☒ 8.30am-12.30pm & 2.30-6.30pm), which has a magnificent rose window and intricately decorated doorway. The 8th-century crypt is worth visiting for the inlaid wooden stalls in the chancel.

Wander through Todi's medieval labyrinthine streets and pop into some of the other churches, including the lofty **Tempio di San Fortunato** (Piazza Umberto 1; admission free; ☒ 9.30am-12.30pm & 3-6pm), with frescoes by Masolino da Panicale and the tomb of San Jacopone, Todi's beloved patron saint. Just outside the city walls is the late-Renaissance **Tempio di Santa Maria della Consolazione**, considered one of the top architectural masterpieces of the

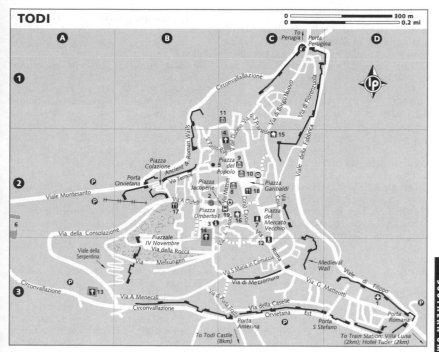

TODI

SOUTHERN UMBRIA

16th century. Possibly designed by Donato Bramante in 1508 but not completed until 99 years later, the construction was a veritable modern feat in early Renaissance Italy and its Greek cross design was considered geometrically perfect.

The **Parco della Rocca** is at the highest point in Todi. It's got magnificent views of the surrounding countryside and ruins of the old *rocca*. From here you can see part of the old Roman wall, called the **Nicchioni**. Todi features a staggering amount of old city walls, some of them medieval, some Roman and some pre-Roman. The gates are a magnificent example of ancient architecture, especially the Porta Romana (Roman Gate), Porta Perugina (Perugia Gate) and Porta Marzia (Gate of Mars).

Just outside the main town walls you can see the **Convento di Montesanto,** now a working convent but built as a fortress in 1325 to guard against Orvieto.

Festivals & Events

The **Todi Arte Festival** (☎ 199 10 99 10; www.todi artefestival.it), held for 10 days usually around

INFORMATION	
Hospital...1	D3
Internet Access..2	B2
Tourist Office...3	B2

SIGHTS & ACTIVITIES	pp304-5
Cathedral..4	C2
Cisterno Romano.....................................5	B2
Convento di Montesanto........................6	A2
Nicchioni Romani....................................7	C2
Palazzo dei Priori....................................8	C2
Palazzo del Capitano...............................9	C2
Palazzo del Popolo.................................10	C2
Palazzo Landi Corradi............................11	C1
Porta Marzia...12	C3
Tempio della Maria Consolazione..........13	A3
Tempio di San Fortunato.......................14	B2

SLEEPING	p306
Casa per Ferie L Crispoliti......................15	C2
Hotel Fonte Cesia...................................16	C2

EATING	p306
Il Giardinetti...17	B2
Ristorante Cavour..................................18	C2

TRANSPORT	p307
Main Bus Stop.......................................19	C2

the end of July and beginning of August, is a mixture of classical and jazz concerts, theatre, ballet and cinema.

At the end of March to the beginning of April, Todi hosts an **antiques fair** in the Palazzo Landi Corradi.

Sleeping

Todi has a freakishly small amount of hotels, and almost all of those are four-stars. It's a good place to take a day trip from Perugia, although arrive early, as Todi shuts down for the midday siesta.

BUDGET

Hotel Tuder (☎ 075 894 21 84; tuder@perugiaonline.it; www.perugiaonline.it; Via Maesta dei Lombardi 13; s/d from €47/77; ☒) A functional three-star hotel that has clearly made an effort, but the result is a bit soulless. It's about 2km east of the historic centre.

Casa per Ferie L. Crispoliti (☎/fax 075 894 53 37; info@crispolitiferie.it; Via Cesia 96; children under 12 €15, s/d €36/57) This former monastery-cum-orphanage is the least expensive place to stay in Todi. It's institutional and depressing, but if you don't mind feeling a little bit like Little Orphan Annie, the views are superb and it's centrally located.

MID-RANGE

Hotel Fonte Cesia (☎ 075 894 37 37; www.fontecesia.it; Via Lorenzo Leoni 3; s/d €109/152; breakfast included; ☐ ☒) The top hotel in Todi, the exquisitely decorated rooms have all the amenities: satellite TV, hairdryer, minibar etc. You can upgrade to a junior suite, some of which have private balconies and claw-footed bathtubs.

Villa Luisa (☎ 075 894 85 71; fax 894 84 72; Via A Cortesi 147; s/d €51.65/77.45; ℗ ☒ ☒) This place is well out of the city walls, but it's set in its own park-like grounds with a swimming pool.

WEEKLY

Todi Castle (☎ 0744 95 21 28; www.todicastle.com; Vocabolo Capecchio, Morre; €1900-7000/week for 4- to 8-room villa; ℗ ☒ ☒) Here's your chance to live in an honest-to-goodness castle for a week. If you can swing it, this place is almost perfect. The eight-room castle has an 11th-century turret (make sure you get dibs on that bedroom). Two other villas on the property are still lovely and a little more financially accessible. Services are available at a price, including a full-time Italian cook who will prepare and serve a meal in a medieval banquet hall.

Eating

Ristorante Umbria (☎ 075 89 43 90; Via Santa Bonaventura 13; meals about €25; ☯ closed Tue) Relax on the terrace while enjoying the beautiful view. This restaurant serves typical Umbrian cuisine, including the difficult-to-find pigeon, once a staple of medieval cuisine.

Ristorante Cavour (☎ 075 894 37 30; Corso Cavour 21; meals around €15; ☯ until 2am, closed Wed) A much more casual setting than Ristorante Umbria, Cavour serves excellent pizza and pasta at decent prices. Try the delicious *tagliatelle al tartufo*, local pasta with truffles.

Il Giardinetti (☎ 0758 94 54 76; Via A Ciuffelli) Just across from the park, this *gelateria* makes scrumptious fresh yogurt, frappés and *gelato* with fresh fruit.

SLOW FOOD, SLOW CITY

In 1986 McDonald's was about to open a restaurant at the famed Spanish Steps in Rome. Carlo Petrini, a wine writer, was so appalled that he started a movement that has grown to include around 70,000 members on five continents. Called 'Slow Food' (see p61), about half of the members are based in Italy, but conviviums are opening around the world at a rapid pace, as people are adopting the Italian and, more so than any other province, Umbrian way of cooking and eating.

From the Slow Food movement grew the Slow City movement, whose current president is the mayor of Orvieto. Its members are concerned that globalisation is wiping out differences in traditions and culture and replacing it with a watered-down homogeneity.

To become a Slow City (or Città Lenta as they're known in Italy, where most of the Slow Cities are located), towns have to pass a rigid set of standards, including having a visible and distinct culture. The towns must follow principles such as relying heavily on autochthonous (from within) resources instead of mass-produced food and culture, cutting down on air and noise pollution, and relying more and more on sustainable development, like organic farming and public transport. Umbria boasts six Slow Cities: Trevi, Todi, San Gemini, Orvieto, Città di Castello and Castiglione del Lago.

As you travel through these towns, you will never hear a car alarm, you can be assured you'll find plenty of public space and there will never, ever be a McDonald's.

Getting There & Away

By road, Todi is easily reached on the S3B-E45, which runs between Perugia and Terni.APM buses from Perugia (€4.75, 1½ hours, seven daily) terminate in Piazza Jacopone, just south of Piazza del Popolo. Other buses may terminate in Piazza Consolazione (from here take city bus A or B or walk uphill 2km to the town centre). There is one daily service to Orvieto (€4.15, 1½ hours) at 5.50am, which returns at 1.55pm.

Todi is on the Ferrovia Centrale Umbra train line, but the train station is inconveniently located 3km east of the town centre in the valley below. City bus C runs there (€0.80, 20 minutes).

For a taxi, dial ☎ 075 894 23 75.

MONTE CASTELLO DI VIBIO

pop 1700

The real draw in this tiny speck of a town about 20km from Todi is its even tinier speck of a theatre. Throw in sleeping (or dining) in a castle, gorgeous views and a working *agriturismo* and you're set for one or two days.

Monte Castello di Vibio feels like it's in the middle of nowhere, but it's just a few kilometres from the S3B-E45 that links Perugia and Terni (just north of Todi). Tourist information can be found at the **Associazione Culturale** (Via Roma 1) behind the theatre.

In keeping with the proportions of the tiny town, **Teatro della Concordia**, (Teatro Piccolo; ☎ 075 878 07 37; admission free but contributions appreciated; ☯ 10am-12.30pm & 3.30-6.30pm Nov-Mar, 10am-12.30pm & 4-7.30pm Apr-Oct; audio in English available) is billed as the smallest theatre in the world. It seats 99 people, 67 on the main floor and 32 in stalls. The theatre was built in 1808, when nine Monte Castello di Vibio families decided that their town needed a theatre. In 1850 the theatre was frescoed, resulting in an incredible combination along with its red velvet seats. Gina Lollabrigida acted in her very first play here. In 1951 the theatre was almost shut down for lack of revenue, but the community voted to pay extra taxes to keep the theatre going. In 1993 this small theatre teamed up with the theatre in Parma – one of the world's largest – to put on a series of events.

A brilliant marketing campaign (and honestly, a really fun way to spend a day and a half) is to take advantage of the **Weekend in Umbria** (Fulginium Viaggi; ☎ 0742 35 70 91; fulginium@fulginiumviaggi.it) package. Available only on Saturday night, you arrive in Monte Castello di Vibio and you will be provided with accommodation at either Hotel il Castello or one of the local *agriturismi*, dinner, a show at the theatre and breakfast on Sunday morning (all for about €89/146 for one/two people). If you don't have your own transport, you can even arrange to be picked up.

Hotel Il Castello (☎ 075 878 06 60; info@hotelilcastello.it; www.hotelilcastello.it; Piazza Guglielmo Marconi 5, Monte Castello di Vibio; d €98/119 low/high season; ℗ ☙) A fascinating place to spend the night or, especially, to eat. The hotel isn't anything great – rooms feel historical, but not necessarily in a good way – but the restaurant (Ristorante Lo Scudo) feels almost theme-park-like in its castle-ness.

Take the S3B-E45 from Todi to Perugia. Exit at the Monte Vibio sign and continue for about 4km (at the roundabout that doesn't tell you where to turn, veer left). It's on the S397 between Todi and Marsciano.

TERNI

pop 104,938

Terni is a major industrial city, virtually obliterated in WWII bombing raids and subsequently rebuilt. Known as 'the steel city' or 'the Manchester of Italy', it used to have steel and iron factories that attracted tourists in the early part of last century. Now, there's not much to see and the factories make the outskirts feel dreary and depressing rather than modern and industrial. If you're using public transport, you might need to pass through here on the way to the Valnerina, Norcia and the Monti Sibillini.

Terni's **tourist office** (☎ 0744 42 30 47; info@iat.terni.it; Viale Cesare Battisti 7; ☯ 9am-1pm Mon-Fri, 3-6pm Tue-Thu) is south of the main train station and just west of Piazza C Tacito, near Largo Don Minzoni.

One of Terni's charms is its devotion to that famous Umbrian pastime, the festival. Its most famous hometown hero is St Valentine, who was the bishop of Terni until Placidius Furius, on orders of Emperor Aurelius, got really angry and had St Valentine executed in AD 269. Well after Valentine's martyrdom, a legend was created. It was said that he would often give gifts of flowers from his own garden to his young visitors. Two of these visitors fell in love and married, forever linking St Valentine with love. Now, a huge feast engulfs the city on 14 February, but the entire month is dedicated to love and romance.

At Easter, Terni's theatres, churches and streets are given over to the **Gospel & Soul Festival**, a spin-off of the Umbria Jazz festival (see p260), which attracts international performers. Ask at the tourist office or the main Umbria Jazz office in Perugia.

From Terni, you can catch an ATC Terni bus to Perugia (€6.40, 1¼ hours, three daily) and Narni (€1.60, 30 minutes, two daily). If you arrive in Terni by train and need to get to the bus station on Piazza Europa, or vice versa, catch local bus No 1 or 2.

LA CASCATA DELLE MARMORE

About 6km east of Terni, this waterfall was created by the Romans in 290 BC when they diverted the Velino river into the Nera river. These days the waterfall provides hydroelectric power and its flow is confined to certain times of the day. If you're without a car, it's worth catching a bus to see it, particularly to witness the arrival of the water after it has been switched on. Local bus No 7 runs from Terni to the falls.

Whenever the waterfalls are operational, the S209 (connecting Terni and Perugia to Norcia and Ferentillo) and the S79 (connecting Terni and Perugia to Piediluco and Rieti) come to a virtual standstill. Car parks exist on both roads, so you can stop and walk through the area. There's quite a lot of interesting vegetation and geological formations in the area, so it's a good idea to give yourself a few hours here, especially as you never quite know when the falls will be operational.

The falls operate on a bizarrely complex scheduling system, and in the past few years they haven't operated when there was a danger of low water levels. Just about any tourist office in Umbria will have the schedule for the waterfall, but the local tourist offices – Terni, Narni, Spoleto, Norcia and Perugia – are most likely to know the correct data, or you can call ☎ 0744 6 29 82. Generally, the falls only run on weekends or holidays in winter for just a few hours a day, but from March to September, they often run every day for much of the day (but not during the morning in June). Your best bet is to catch them around noon or 4pm, or late in the evening when they're illuminated by a spectacular light show.

The skittish and the completely insane are both welcome at **Centro Canoe e Rafting 'Le Marmore'** (☎ 330 75 34 20; www.rafting marmore.com; Via Carlo Neri, Terni). One can try 'hydrospeeding'– the white-water equivalent of bobsledding – or take what is called an 'Easy Rafting' excursion.

CARSULAE

The most complete example of a Roman city in Umbria, **Carsulae** (☎ 0744 33 41 33; ☼ 10am-1pm & 4-7pm Tue-Fri, 10am-7pm Sat-Sun & public holidays) isn't anywhere near the size or scope of Pompeii or Rome, but it does offer some spectacular Roman history in a beautiful setting. During the reign of Augustus in the 3rd century BC, Romans took to the task of building the strategically important road, the Via Flaminia. Carsulae was one of the many outposts systematically built along this Roman version of a highway. It was on the part of the road that joined Narnia to Vicus Martis Tudertium (Narni to the Todi region), so when reconstruction started on a more easterly route, Carsulae fell into decline. Then, barbarians from the north began using this part of the road to head towards Rome, and Carsulae had no chance.

To arrive here, take the road to Perugia from Terni. Look for the sign indicating S75/San Gemini and you'll then see signs for Carsulae. The closest place to spend the night around Carsulae is in San Gemini.

THE ROMANS INVADE UMBRIA

One of the most important battles in the beginning of the Roman conquest of Italy was in Sentinum in 295 BC, near the modern day town of Sassoferrato, in Le Marche. The Roman troops divided and conquered an alliance between the local Etruscans and Umbrians and their southern counterparts the Gauls and Samnites. The most important Roman settlements in Umbria over the next few hundred years were Perugia, Orvieto, Todi, Bevagna, Spello, Assisi, Gubbio, Terni, Narni, Carsulae and Ocriculum (where the small town Otricoli, 12km south of Narni and almost on the Lazio border, now sits).

NARNI

pop 20,054

While Umbria is called the 'Green Heart of Italy', the town of Narni could be called the true heart of Italy. Actually, it's the closest town to the geographic centre of the Italian peninsula, a symbolic position not lost on its inhabitants. Umbria is one of the more rural provinces in Italy, and Narni exudes the friendly, laid-back charm that's so pervasive throughout the region. You're not just imagining it: people here *are* friendlier.

However, as one Narni local puts it, 'We have the bread, but we don't have the teeth'. He's referring to the amazing array of tourist sites – a 13th-century hill top *rocca* guarding mightily over the town, Narni Sotterranea, a subterranean world of caves that used to house Inquisition prisoners (with remnants of their graffiti), churches and palaces galore – but practically no tourist structure. That *rocca* is difficult to get to, Narni Sotterranea is only open on public holidays and weekends (one entrance is through a preschool playground), and the tourist office has practically no literature or maps, and nothing in English. Despite the effort it takes to explore Narni, this is a wonderfully friendly town. Within 10 years, it could find its calling as a hill town tourist mecca, so go as soon as possible. Just make sure you plan your trip carefully (ie go on a weekend) so as to not miss their bread for lack of teeth.

Orientation

Narni is centred around the **Fontana di Piazza dei Priori** in the Piazza Cavour, where the tourist office, cathedral, Palazzo del Podestà and Palazzo dei Priori are located. Everything is a short walk away, except for the *rocca*, which is either a drive or a pretty decent hike up the hill.

Information

EMERGENCY
Police Station (☎ 0744 71 52 34; Via Portecchia)

INTERNET RESOURCES
www.comune.narni.tr.it The government website for Narni.

MEDICAL SERVICES
Hospital (☎ 0744 7401; Via Cappuccini Nuova)

TOURIST INFORMATION
Tourist Office (☎ 0744 74 72 47; www.comune.narni.tr.it, Piazza dei Priori 3; ☼ 9.30am-12.30pm & 3.30-6.30pm)

Sights

The fortress **La Rocca Albornoz** (admission free; ☼ 10am-7pm by appointment; P) was built by Cardinal Albornoz, who was the heavy charged with imposing Papal control on Narni. The Pope needed an imposing bastion to guard against the pro-Emperor Ghibellines and scare the people into submission. Albornoz went about building this *rocca,* and several others throughout the region, in the mid-1300s. Some original frescoes still exist, but its use as a prison for hundreds of years took its toll on the building. The climb up the stairs is treacherous but worth it for the 360° quintessentially perfect Umbrian view at the top. La Rocca now opens its doors to choirs and orchestras and has a collection of photos from its medieval festival. Also housed is the **motorcycle collection** of a local resident who had nowhere else to store his priceless antiques, one of the biggest collections in Europe. If you like motorcycles (actually, even if you don't like motorcycles), this is a fascinating look back into history. On display is a 1906 foldable motorcycle, a rare surviving joint venture from Aermacchi (a popular Italian manufacturer) and Harley Davidson. Imagine yourself sitting in the 1938 BMW sidecar.

It's a complete shame, but the best tourist site in Narni is hardly ever open. **Narni Sotterranea** (☎ 0744 72 22 92; www.narnisotterranea.it; Via S Bernardo 12; ☼ 3-6pm Sat, 10am-1pm & 3-6pm some Sun & public holidays Apr-Oct, 11am-1pm & 3-5pm some Sun & public holidays Nov-Mar) is the subterranean galleries from the convent San Domenico. If you arrive and it's open, you'll see drawings on the walls made by prisoners held here during the Inquisition. If you arrive with a group of three or four people, you might be able to talk the tourist office into arranging an opening. Call at least a day or two in advance.

The Romans built the **Ponte d' Augusto** in 27 BC, part of the ancient route of the Via Flaminia. The bridge now has only one remaining arch, but imagine it in its heyday, with three or even four arches.

Around what was the Roman forum is now the municipal and social centre of

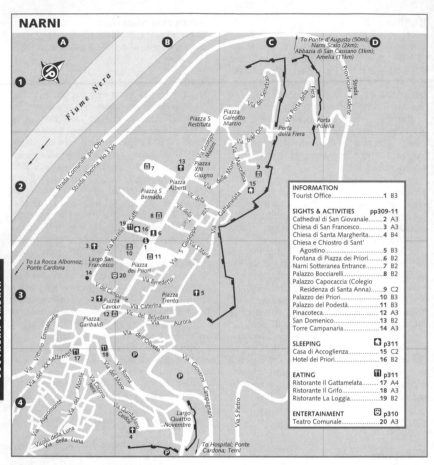

NARNI

INFORMATION
Tourist Office.............................1 B3

SIGHTS & ACTIVITIES   pp309–11
Cathedral di San Giovanale........2 A3
Chiesa di San Francesco............3 A3
Chiesa di Santa Margherita........4 B4
Chiesa e Chiostro di Sant'
   Agostino................................5 B3
Fontana di Piazza dei Priori.......6 B2
Narni Sotteranea Entrance........7 B2
Palazzo Bocciarelli.....................8 B2
Palazzo Capocaccia (Colegio
   Residenza di Santa Anna)......9 C2
Palazzo dei Priori.....................10 B3
Palazzo del Podestà.................11 B3
Pinacoteca..............................12 A3
San Domenico..........................13 B2
Torre Campanaria....................14 A3

SLEEPING   p311
Casa di Accoglienza................15 C2
Hotel dei Priori.......................16 B2

EATING   p311
Ristorante Il Gattamelata........17 A4
Ristorante Il Grifo...................18 A3
Ristorante La Loggia...............19 B2

ENTERTAINMENT   p310
Teatro Comunale....................20 A3

Narni. The **Palazzo dei Priori** (🕐 10am-1pm & 3-7pm) construction is attributed to Gattapone in 1275. Look up at the balcony called the *loggia colpire*, from where a town crier used to yell the equivalent of the evening news. Attached to the Palazzo dei Priori is the **Palazzo Comunale** (Municipal Palace; ☎ 0744 74 72 58; Piazza Cavour 8; admission free; 🕐 10am-1pm & 3-7pm Tue, 11am-1pm & 3-7pm Wed-Thu, 10am-1.30pm & 2.30-7pm Fri-Sun), a 13th-century building formed by the union of three towers. If no-one is inside, you can take a peek in the council chamber to see the *Pala di Ghirlandaio*, the artist's representation of the coronation of the Virgin Mary. Next door is the **Palazzo Bocciarelli**. The 12th-century **Cathedral di San Giovanele** (Piazza Cavour, Palazzo Garibaldi; 🕐 9am-

7pm) is dedicated to Narni's patron saint, San Giovenale, who became the first bishop of Narni in AD 386.

The **Teatro Comunale** (☎ 0744 72 52 62; Via Garibaldi; admission free; 🕐 4-7pm Sat, 9am-1pm & 4-7pm Sun) is a glorious 19th-century theatre that can accommodate up to 500 patrons. You can visit it for free on the weekends, and it's also a lovely place to see a performance.

The simple **Chiesa di San Francesco** was built several years after the death of St Francis on the same site of a place where the Assisian himself had briefly lived.

The geographic centre of Italy is just outside Narni at the **Ponte Cardona** (☎ 0744 72 22 92 for information or to book a guided tour), a Roman bridge that is the only remnant of an old

Roman aqueduct dating to the 1st century AD. It's off the road heading towards Terni.

Abbazia di San Cassiano is an imposing abbey dating back to the 11th century, built in the plan of a Greek cross. It's thought to have been the first Benedictine abbey constructed in the area.

Festivals & Events

The town's major festival of the year is the **Corso all'Anello** (☎ 0744 72 62 33) held from the end of April to the beginning of May. The town goes all out for this festival. As a rare foreign tourist, you will be welcomed with open arms. There's all sorts of feasts, competitions and performances by the Anerio Choir, an ancient choir formed by Palestrina, who was one of the founders of baroque music.

The **International Folklore Festival** is held from mid-July to mid-August and sees folklorist groups from all over the world perform nightly on a stage in the Piazza dei Priori.

Sleeping

Narni has very few hotels within the historic centre, but the Hotel dei Priori is practically perfect, and the 700-year-old Casa di Accoglienza, attached to a convent, is inexpensive and comfortable.

BUDGET

Casa di Accoglienza (Suore di Santa Anna; ☎ 0744 71 52 17; Via Gattemelata 74; s/d €19/34) This quiet and tranquil religious house is near the town centre along the ancient walls. It's got an internal garden used for reflection and meditation, as well as a view of the Nera river. It's in an austere 14th-century building.

Camping Monti del Sole (☎ 0744 79 63 36; Str di Borgaria 22; SS Flaminia, Km 80.800; site per person/tent/ car €5.50/4.50/1.50; ⓟ ⓡ) This camp site 5km south of Narni has a pool, restaurant and tennis courts. It's open from the beginning of April until the end of September.

MID-RANGE

Hotel dei Priori (☎ 0744 72 68 43; www.loggia deipriori.it; Vicolo del Comune 4; s/d €50/70; ⓧ) This charming three-star hotel is in a 15th-century building in the centre of town. It's got 17 beautiful rooms with incredible views, and some have balconies from which to enjoy those views. Try to snag the *camere di torre* (tower room).

Eating

Ristorante La Loggia (☎ 0744 72 68 43; Vicolo del Comune 4) Owned by the Hotel dei Priori, this restaurant serves excellent dishes at even better prices. Try its house speciality, *tortellini al loggia* (pasta stuffed with *porcini* and truffles) for €8, or one of its *farro* (type of grain) dishes, or the flavourful lamb with artichokes.

Ristorante Il Gattamelata (☎ 0744 71 72 45; Via Pozzo della Comunità 4; meals €28; ⓨ closed Mon) This simply decorated restaurant serves wonderful meals, a little more inventive than the typical Umbrian cuisine. You can order from two tasting menus that feature foods served during medieval times.

Ristorante Il Grifo (☎ 0744 72 66 25; Via Roma 3) It specialises in Umbrian and international cuisine, all set in a busy restaurant with an expansive view through enormous windows.

Getting There & Away

To get to Narni from the A1 *autostrada*, take the Magliano Sabina exit if you're coming from the south. Take the Orte exit if you're coming from the north.

ATC Terni (☎ 0744 71 52 07) buses leave from Piazza Garibaldi, just outside the main gate. From Narni, you travel by bus to Amelia (€1.60, 30 minutes, nine daily from Piazza Garibaldi, plus another 10 from Narni Scalo), Terni (€1.60, 30 minutes, almost hourly with a gap between 10.30am and 1pm) and Orvieto (€4.80, one hour and 20 minutes, five daily). To get to Perugia, switch in Terni (€6.40, 1½ hours).

AMELIA

pop 11,090

Few other words describe this town as aptly as 'sweet'. Perhaps 'quaint', 'delightful' or 'adorable' come close. It's a tiny little village, unassuming and unspoiled, with one of the oldest histories in Umbria. The legend goes that Amelia was founded by a mythological king named Ameroe in the 12th century BC. Latin texts mention the existence of Amelia as a settlement as early as the 11th century BC (four centuries before Rome was founded). A good chunk of the original walls (believed to have been constructed sometime around the 6th century BC) can still be seen by the theatre, but much of the wall is of newer construction. Namely, the 4th century BC.

For even more sweetness, take your sweetie down 'Girl-Kissing Alley'. Try the town's delicacy, Fichi Girotti (see Eating, p313). Locals vie with Narnians for the friendliest people in Italy and, knowing Umbria, they just might invent a festival testing that theory one day.

Orientation

The town is still a walled city, with several *porte* (doors) leading in and out. The main entrance is the Porta Romana. Just outside of it is the tourist office, parking facilities, the bus station and several cafés (some selling Fichi Girotti, an Amerino fig snack). Signs posted in front of monuments are all listed in Italian and English, so it's easy to get around.

Information

Tourist Office (☎ 0744 98 14 53; info@iat.amelia.tr.it; outside city walls at Porta Romana; ☺ 3.30-6.30pm Mon, 9am-12.30pm Tue-Sat 15 Sep-30 May, 9.30am-12.30pm & 3.30-6.30pm rest of year)

Sights

Amelia has some of the oldest fortification walls in Umbria. **Piazza Matteotti** was the site of an ancient Roman forum.

In 1783 Amelia's Theatrical Society (comprised of the middle class and bourgeoisie) decided that their hamlet needed some culture. They banded together and built the **Teatro Sociale** (☎ 0744 97 83 15; Via del Teatro; ☺ most concerts begin at 8pm), turning the theatre into the most important gathering spot in town. The moving wings still work on the original wood wheels. Domenico Bruschi frescoed the ceiling and booths in 1886. You can either visit as a tourist during the day or see a performance – Moliére, opera or the Rome orchestra, just to name a few – in the evening.

From the theatre, go to Via della Valle to get the best look at the **Mura Megalitiche**, stone walls built by the Etruscans in the 6th century BC. The rougher the texture, the older the stone. The builders didn't have mortar, but the walls were constructed well enough so that we can still see them.

If you're with your darling be sure to walk down from Piazza Matteotti past the Palazzo Municipale to **Vicolo Baciafemmine** (Girl-Kissing Alley), known as such because its narrowness has been known to

cause passers-by to get close enough to let their passions run amok.

An ancient **Roman cistern** (☎ 0744 97 84 36; ☺ 4.30-7.30pm Sat, 10.30am-12.30pm & 4.30-7.30 Sun Apr-Sep; 3-6pm Sat, 10.30am-12.30pm & 3-6pm Sun Oct-Mar) goes underneath Piazza Matteotti from what is now a private house to the youth hostel.

The **Chiesa di San Francesco** (☎ 0744 97 81 20; ☺ 10am-noon & 3-6.30) was originally built in the 13th century, but most of the architecture now is from the 15th and 20th century. The facade is from 1406, and is decorated in the Romanesque and Gothic style.

In the same building, don't miss the small but worthwhile **Museo Archeologico e Pinacoteca** (Archaeological Museum & Art Museum; Piazza Augusto Vera 10; ☎ 0744 97 81 20; www.sistemamuseo.it - Italian only; ☺ 10.30am-1pm & 3.30-6.30pm Fri-Sun Oct-Mar, 10.30-1pm & 4-7pm Tue-Sat Jun & Sep, 10.30am-1pm & 4.30-7.30pm Tue-Sun Jul-Aug), with some fine examples of Roman tombstones, a fascinating bronze statue of the Roman captain Germanico and a painting by one of Amelia's most famous residents, Piermatteo d'Amelia. Piermatteo was instrumental in securing Christopher Columbus the three ships used to discover America.

Since AD 872, there has been a religious institution on this sacred site. Currently, the **cathedral** (☺ 10am-noon & 3-6.30pm) holds this position. It has been rebuilt after several disasters, and is certainly not the most impressive in Umbria, but there are several paintings and sculptures of interest inside. Next to the cathedral is the **Torre Civica**, which was built in 1050. Like many towers that were constructed in the medieval period, it was constructed on a dodecagonal plan (12-sided) based on the symbolic importance of the number 12 (12 apostles, 12 signs of the zodiac).

Courses

If you're looking for somewhere easy-going to learn Italian, try **Eurolinks** (☎ 0744 98 18 60; info@eurolinkschool.com; www.eurolinkschool.com; Viale Rimembranze 48). It offers all sorts of language and cooking courses, and arranges a variety of accommodation options, from €660 per week for a double room in a farmhouse to €1232 for two weeks full-board staying with a local family. It also arranges completely inclusive wellness retreats (over €3000) at a popular health centre nearby.

Festivals & Events

Amelia knows how to throw a party during its medieval *manifestazione* (event), the **Palio dei Columbi**. Every August, teams comprised of neighbourhood residents vie against each other in competitions recorded in the municipal records from the 14th century. Knights and crossbowmen are paired up to attempt to shoot an arrow through a target, which then sets free a dove. Practically every resident of the town is in full costume. The wooden doors you see on the Porta Romana are closed on only this day once a year.

Sleeping

BUDGET

Ostello per la Gioventù Giustiniani (☎ 0744 97 86 73, mobile 348 764 56 64; ostello.giustiniani@tiscalinet.it; Piazza Mazzini 9; dm €12.45-16) This is a truly fabulous youth hostel, central and convenient, and built in a restored palace.

MID-RANGE

Il Piccolo Hotel del Carleni (☎ 0744 98 39 25; www.ilcarleni.com; Via Pellegrino Carleni 21; s/d €80/85; ste with kitchenette €105, meal supplement €28.50 per person; 😰) Like its surrounding village, this hotel is one of the sweetest places in Umbria. A vertical climb, it houses seven rooms on four floors. The building dates back to the 13th century, and the oasis-like garden has olive trees. Low brick-and-wood-beam ceilings give it a cosy feel.

Eating

Be sure to try the local sweet Fichi Girotti at any shop in town. It's kind of like eating the hardened insides of a fig biscuit mixed in with chocolate and nuts.

Hotel Ristorante Il Carleni (☎ 0744 98 39 25; Via Carleni; 😒 only lunch Sat & Sun; meals around €23) This small restaurant is run by the hospitable and warm owners of Il Piccolo Hotel. The menu is small and offers simple country cooking, but the ingredients and quality are superb.

Osteria dei Cansacchi (☎ 0744 97 85 57; Piazza Cansacchi 4; meals around €12) Set in a medieval atmosphere, this restaurant combines two excellent local delicacies by serving *bistecche di cinghiale e porcini* (wild boar with *porcini* mushrooms). Pizza is a good and inexpensive bet here.

La Gabelletta (☎ 0744 98 21 59; Str Tuderte Amerina 20) Its signature dish is *pappardelle al sugo di lepre* (pasta with wild hare sauce).

DETOUR: THE AMERINO

The area surrounding Amelia is known as the Amerino and has an untold amount of little treasures, natural and cultural. Holm-oak groves, ilex trees, and an ample amount of rivers and interesting geological terrain makes for a worthwhile drive through the Amerino. In nearby Alviano you'll find a country life museum and the **Lago di Alviano** (marshlands formed when Lago di Corbara was dammed, now a bird habitat). Nearby in Avigliano is the **Fossil Forest** (adult/reduced €5/3; 😒 9.30-11.30am & 3-5pm Sun & public holidays Apr-Sep, 9.30-11.30am & 2.30-4.30pm Sun & public holidays Oct-Mar), a natural archaeological site of importance with a fossilised forest.

Getting There & Away

Amelia is serviced by ATC Terni. Buses leave from in front of the main gate. From Amelia, nine buses travel daily to the centre of Narni, plus another 10 to Narni Scalo and the train station (€1.60, 30 minutes). Buses also travel to Orvieto (€4, one hour and 10 minutes, seven daily; check with the driver as to whether the bus stops at the train station or Piazza Cahen) and Terni (€2.40, one hour, 16 daily). To get to Perugia, switch in Terni.

Getting Around

There is some paid parking in the city centre. Note (this goes for all of Umbria): parking spaces outlined in blue are designated for paid parking. White or yellow outlines almost always indicate reserved parking or that residential permits are needed. You buy your ticket at a machine that's usually a few metres from wherever you've parked and display it in the front window.

ORVIETO

pop 20,709

The phalanxes of high-season tourists who crowd into Orvieto are drawn first and foremost by the magnificent cathedral, one of Italy's finest Gothic buildings. The town rests on top of a craggy tufaceous (volcanic) cliff, pretty much in the same spot as its precursor, the Etruscan League city of Velsina. Although medieval Orvieto is the magnet, Etruscan tombs and the city's underground chambers testify to the area's antiquity.

ORVIETO

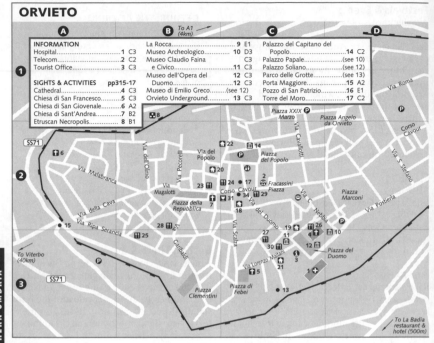

Orientation

Trains pull in at Orvieto Scalo, the modern, downhill extension of the town. From here you can catch bus No 1 up to the old town or board the cable car to Piazza Cahen. From the cable car and bus station, walk straight along Corso Cavour, turning left into Via del Duomo to reach the cathedral. There's plenty of parking space in Piazza Cahen and in several designated areas outside the old city walls.

Information

DISCOUNTS

Orvieto Unica Card (€12.50) If you plan to spend more than a day in Orvieto and want to see absolutely everything the town has to offer, consider buying this card, which entitles you to five hours' free car parking at the train station or a return trip on the cable car and city buses, and offers discounts at many shops and restaurants in town, plus admission (only once) to the Cappella di San Brizio in the cathedral, the Museo Claudio Faina e Civico, the Torre del Moro and Orvieto Underground in Parco delle Grotte. The card is valid for one year, and is available from the tourist office, see p315.

EMERGENCY

Police Station (☎ 0763 3 92 11; Piazza Cahen)

INTERNET ACCESS

Caffè Montanucci (☎ 0763 34 12 61; Corso Cavour 21; ⏰ closed Wed)

MEDICAL SERVICES

Hospital (☎ 0763 3071; Loc. Ciconia) Just beyond the train station.

MONEY

There are several banks, all with Visa- and MasterCard-friendly ATMs, on Piazza della Repubblica.

POST

Post Office (Via Cesare Nebbia, off Corso Cavour; ⏰ 8.10am-6pm Mon-Sat)

TELEPHONE

Telecom (Corso Cavour 119) Unstaffed.

TOILETS

Orvieto has several public toilets, including next to the post office and a wheelchair accessible toilet behind the cathedral halfway down a staircase (wheelchair users can use the mobility lift attached to the stairs).

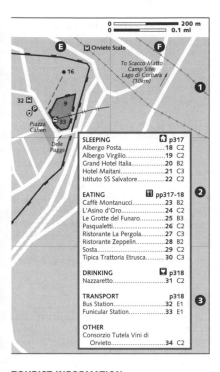

0 — 200 m
0 — 0.1 mi

Orvieto Scalo

To Scacco Matto
Camp Site;
Lago di Corbara
(10km)

Piazza
Cahen

Delle
Piagge

SLEEPING	🏠 p317
Albergo Posta	18 C2
Albergo Virgilio	19 C2
Grand Hotel Italia	20 B2
Hotel Maitani	21 C3
Istituto SS Salvatore	22 C2

EATING	🍴 pp317-18
Caffè Montanucci	23 B2
L'Asino d'Oro	24 C2
Le Grotte del Funaro	25 B3
Pasqualetti	26 C2
Ristorante La Pergola	27 C3
Ristorante Zeppelin	28 C2
Sosta	29 C2
Tipica Trattoria Etrusca	30 C3

| DRINKING | 🍷 p318 |
| Nazzaretto | 31 C2 |

TRANSPORT	p318
Bus Station	32 E1
Funicular Station	33 E1

OTHER	
Consorzio Tutela Vini di	
Orvieto	34 C2

TOURIST INFORMATION

Tourist Office (☎ 0763 34 17 72; info@ iat.orvieto.tr.it; Piazza del Duomo 24; ☉ 8.15am-1.50pm & 4-7pm Mon-Fri, 10am-1pm & 4-7pm Sat, 10am-noon & 4-6pm Sun)

Sights

At the tourist office you can purchase an Orvieto Unica Card (€12.50). See Discounts (p314) for details.

THE CATHEDRAL

Little can prepare you for the visual feast that is the **cathedral** (☎ 0763 34 11 67; Piazza del Duomo; admission free; ☉ 7.30am-12.45pm year-round, plus 2.30-7.15pm Apr-Sep, 2.30-6.15pm Mar & Oct, 2.30-5.15pm Nov-Feb). Originating in 1290, this remarkable edifice was originally planned in the Romanesque style but, as work proceeded and architects changed, Gothic features were incorporated into the structure. The black-and-white marble banding of the main body of the church, reminiscent of other great churches you may already have seen in Tuscan cities such as Siena and Pisa, is overshadowed by the rich rainbow colours of the facade. A harmonious blend

of mosaic and sculpture, plain stone and dazzling colour, it has been likened to a giant outdoor altar screen.

Pope Urban IV ordered that the cathedral be built, following the so-called Miracle of Bolsena in 1263. A Bohemian priest who was passing through the town of Bolsena (near Orvieto) had his doubts about transubstantiation dispelled when blood began to drip from the Host onto the altar linen while he celebrated mass. The linen was presented to Pope Urban IV, in Orvieto at the time, who declared the event a miracle and set the wheels in motion for the construction of the cathedral. He also declared the new feast day of Corpus Domini. The reliquary holding the blood-stained altar cloth now leads the Corpus Domini procession, held in June.

The building took 30 years to plan and three centuries to complete. It was probably started by Perugia's Fra Bevignate and continued over the years by Lorenzo Maitani (responsible for Florence's cathedral), Andrea Pisano, his son Nino Pisano, Andrea Orcagna and Michele Sanmicheli.

The **facade** appears almost unrelated to the main body of the church and has greatly benefited from meticulous restoration, completed in 1995. The three huge doorways are separated by fluted columns and the gables are decorated with mosaics that, although mostly reproductions, seem to come to life in the light of the setting sun and in the evening under spotlights. The areas between the doorways feature 14th-century bas-reliefs of scriptural scenes by Maitani and his pupils, while the rose window is by Andrea Orcagna. The great bronze doors, the work of Emilio Greco, were added in the 1960s.

Reopened in late 1996 after years of painstaking restoration, Luca Signorelli's fresco cycle *The Last Judgement* shimmers with life. Look for it to the right of the altar in the **Cappella di San Brizio** (admission €3; ☉ 10am-12.45pm year-round, plus 2.30-7.15pm Apr-Sep, 2.30-6.15pm Mar & Oct, 2.30-5.15pm Mon-Sat & 2.30-5.45pm public holidays Nov-Feb, closed during Mass). Signorelli began work on the series in 1499, and Michelangelo is said to have taken inspiration from it when he began the Sistine Chapel fresco of the same subject 40 years later. Indeed, to some, Michelangelo's masterpiece runs a close second to Signorelli's work. Not to be ignored in the chapel are ceiling frescoes by

SOUTHERN UMBRIA

Fra Angelico. To buy a ticket, go first to the tourist office in Piazza del Duomo.

The **Cappella del Corporale** (admission free; ☿ 7.30am-12.45pm & 2.30-7.15pm in summer, shorter hours in winter, closed during Mass) houses the blood-stained altar linen, preserved in a silver reliquary decorated by artists of the Sienese school. The walls feature frescoes depicting the miracle, painted by Ugolino di Prete Ilario. Mass is celebrated here daily at 9am (in Italian).

PIAZZA DEL DUOMO

An absolutely fantastic museum for ancient history is the **Museo Claudio Faina e Civico** (☎ 0763 34 12 16; www.museofaina.it; Palazzo Faina, Piazza del Duomo 29; adult/child €4.50/3; ☿ 9.30am-6pm daily Mar-Oct, 10am-5pm Tue-Sun Nov-Feb), opposite the cathedral. Much of the display here comes from the Etruscan Necropolis found on the outskirts of town (see the boxed text, p318). There are examples of Gorgons, an incredibly thorough collection of numismatics (coins, many of Roman emperors) and bronze figures from the 2nd and 3rd centuries BC. Kids will enjoy following the questions (in Italian and English) for developing little historians to ponder along the way.

Next to the cathedral is the **Museo dell'Opera del Duomo** (☎ 0763 34 24 77; Palazzo Soliano, Piazza del Duomo), which houses a clutter of religious relics from the cathedral, as well as Etruscan antiquities and works by artists such as Simone Martini and the three Pisanos: Andrea, Nino and Giovanni. The museum has been closed for restoration for ages; contact the tourist office to see if it has reopened.

Museo di Emilio Greco (☎ 0763 34 46 05; Palazzo Soliano, Piazza del Duomo; adult/child €2.50/1.50 single ticket; ☿ 10.30am-1pm & 2.30-6pm Tue-Sun Apr-Sep, 10.30am-1pm & 2-5.30pm Tue-Sun Oct-Mar) displays a collection of modern pieces donated by the creator of the cathedral's bronze doors. You can get a combined ticket (adult/child €4.50/3) for admission to the Pozzo di San Patrizio (see Out of Town, following).

Around the corner, you can see Etruscan antiquities in the **Museo Archeologico** (☎ 0763 34 10 39; Palazzo Papale, Piazza del Duomo; admission €2; ☿ 9am-8pm). It doesn't have information in English, so visit the Museo Claudio Faina e Civico first to get your bearings.

The coolest place – literally – in Orvieto is the **Orvieto Underground** (☎ 0763 34 48 91; Parco delle Grotte; admission €5.15; ☿ 11am-6pm),

six caves open to the public (there are 440 altogether). The caves were initially used as wells by the first inhabitants of Orvieto, the Etruscans, who needed water but couldn't risk leaving the hill, what with all the Romans milling about. During the Middle Ages, locals experiencing a high volume of pesky sieges used the caves again for protected sustenance, but this time they were trapping pigeons in dovecotes for food (pigeon is still found on menus to this day – look for *palomba*). During WWII, the caves were turned into bomb shelters, but luckily they never had to be used, as the tufaceous volcanic rock that makes up the Orvieto hill crumbles easily. Tours leave from in front of the tourist office on Piazza del Duomo at 11am, 12.15pm, 4pm and 5.15pm. Hint: the caves remain at 12° to 15°C year-round. Since many museums and shops close at noon, take the 12.15pm tour.

OUT OF TOWN

Head northwest along Via del Duomo to Corso Cavour and you'll see the stout **Torre del Moro** (Moor's Tower; ☎ 0763 34 45 67; Corso Cavour; adult/reduced €2.60/1.85; ☿ 10am-8pm May-Aug, 10am-7pm Mar, Apr, Sep & Oct, 10.30am-1pm & 2.30-5pm Nov-Feb). Climb all 250 steps (or take an elevator part way) for sweeping, pigeon-eye views of the city. Back on ground level, continue west to Piazza della Repubblica, where you'll stumble upon the 12th-century **Chiesa di Sant'Andrea** (Piazza della Repubblica; admission free; ☿ 8.30am-12.30pm & 3.30-7.30pm) and its curious decagonal bell tower. As with many Italian churches, it was built over a Roman structure, which itself incorporated an earlier Etruscan building. You can see the ancient foundations in the crypt. The piazza, once Orvieto's Roman forum, is at the heart of what remains of the medieval city.

North of Corso Cavour, the 12th-century Romanesque-Gothic **Palazzo del Capitano del Popolo** presides over the piazza of the same name. At the northwestern end of town is the 11th-century **Chiesa di San Giovenale** (Piazza Giovenale; admission free; open 8am-12.30pm & 3.30-6pm daily), its interior brightened by 13th- and 14th-century frescoes.

Standing watch at the town's eastern-most tip is the 14th-century **La Rocca**, part of which is now a public garden. To the north of the fortress, the **Pozzo di San Patrizio** (St Patrick's Well; ☎ 0763 34 37 68; Via Sangallo; adult/child €3.50/2.50;

10am-6.45pm Apr-Sep, 10am-5.45pm Oct-Mar) is a well, which was sunk in 1527 on the orders of Pope Clement VII. More than 60m deep, it is lined by two spiral staircases for water-bearing mules.

If you're planning on visiting the well, buy a combined ticket (€4.50/3 adult/child) to visit the Museo di Emilio Greco.

Sleeping

You should have no trouble getting a room in Orvieto during most of the year, but it is always a good idea to book ahead if you're planning to come during New Year, the Umbria Jazz festival, in summer or on a weekend.

BUDGET

Porziuncola (☎ 0763 34 13 87; Loc. Cappuccini 8; dm €10.32) Take bus No 5 to this small hostel. With only 16 beds in two rooms, you'll want to call ahead.

Istituto SS Salvatore (☎ /fax 0763 34 29 10; istituto sansalvatore@tiscalinet.it; Via del Popolo 1; s/d/t €41.32/51.65/72.30) Practice your Italian with these jovial nuns. There's a 10.30pm curfew, but the place is comfortable and clean, and has a beautiful garden. Singles don't have bathrooms.

Albergo Posta (☎ /fax 0763 34 19 09; Via L Signorelli 18; s/d without bathroom €31/43, s/d with bathroom €37/56) Rooms in this solid 16th-century building are simple but have a quirky edge, and the owners are friendly and helpful.

MID-RANGE

Albergo Virgilio (☎ 0763 34 18 82; fax 34 37 97; Piazza del Duomo 5; s/d with bathroom €62/85) This three-star hotel has an unrivalled position on Piazza del Duomo but we could have received a friendlier reception.

Grand Hotel Italia (☎ 0763 34 20 65; fax 34 29 02; www.bellaumbria.net/grand-hotel-italia/; Via dei Palazzo dei Popolo 13; s/d €52/88; P 🖳) Around the corner from Corso Cavour, this hotel is comfortable and quiet, with a decent breakfast included. A garage for parking is available, but ask for directions really, really carefully if you don't have the best sense of direction.

Hotel Maitani (☎ 0763 34 20 11; Via Lorenzo Maitani 5; s/d €75/124; P 🕮) Every detail is covered, from a travel-sized toothbrush and toothpaste in each room to chocolates (Perugino, of course) on your pillow. Several rooms have views of the cathedral or the countryside. Rooms are pin-drop quiet, as they come with not one but two double-pane windows.

TOP END

La Badia Hotel (☎ 0763 30 19 59; www.labadiahotel.it; Loc. La Badia 8; d €86-114 per person, ste up to €172 per person; P 🕮 🖳) Occupied 1200 years ago by Benedictine monks, this hotel – claimed to be the oldest in Italy – was once known as the Abbey of St Severo and Martirio. It's been a holiday retreat since the 15th century, with guests such as Pope Paul II, Borghese and Barberini. For the past century it's been under the ownership of a noble family who turned it into the hotel it is today. Twenty-one rooms and seven suites consist of modern comforts along with attractive antiques and furnishings.

Eating

Orvietan restaurants almost all feature the local delicacies, truffles and *porcini*.

La Badia Ristorante (☎ 0763 30 19 59; Loc. La Badia 8; meals around €35) The restaurant at La Badia is as refined as its hotel (see Sleeping, previous). The chef's speciality is suckling pig and *tagliolini* pasta with truffles. If you enjoy the Orvieto Classico here, tell the owner, Count Fiumi, as it's from his vineyards. Even if you don't stay or eat here, you can still see it; when you're in the Orvieto Underground, look for the 8th-century abbey in the fields below.

Sosta (☎ 0763 34 30 25; Corso Cavour 100a; meals around €8) This extremely simple self-service restaurant serves some really good pizza, as well as cafeteria-style pasta, and meat and vegetable dishes. Students get a discount.

Ristorante La Pergola (☎ 0763 34 30 65; Via dei Magoni 9b; meals around €18; closed Wed) The food here is typically Umbrian – good and filling – but the real draw is dining in the flower-filled back garden. Try the *cinghiale*.

L'Asino d'Oro (☎ 0763 34 44 06; Vicolo del Popolo 9; main courses around €8; Tue-Sun Apr–mid-Oct & during Umbria Jazz festival) Despite its modest appearance, the food is superb. Meals are served outside on wooden tables under an arbour, and the menu changes daily.

Tipica Trattoria Etrusca (☎ 0763 34 40 16; Via Lorenzo Maitani 10; meals around €16; closed Mon) This is a good trattoria just 100m from the cathedral. The chef's specialities include *coniglio all' Etrusca* (Etruscan-style rabbit

---

DETOUR: CROCIFISSO DEL TUFO ETRUSCAN NECROPOLIS

Besides the Hypogea di Volumni outside of Perugia, the **Crocifisso del Tufo Etruscan Necropolis** (☎ 0763 34 36 11; Loc. Le Conce, SS71, Km 1.6) is one of only two Etruscan necropolises that travellers can visit in Umbria. It dates back to the mid-6th century BC. Several series of burial chambers feature the etched names of their deceased residents. The manner in which the graves are laid out shows the preciseness of good ancient urban planning, albeit one whose residents couldn't quite appreciate it. Many of the furnishings from the Necropolis can be found at the Louvre, British Museum and various other museums, though some of the collection hasn't left: the Museo Claudio Faina e Civico in Orvieto still holds onto a good chunk.

---

cooked in aromatic herbs), broad beans, and local dishes made with *tartufo* and *porcini*.

Ristorante Zeppelin (☎ 0763 34 14 47; Via G Garibaldi 28; ☺ closed Sun) This natty place has a cool 1920s atmosphere, jazz on the stereo and a long wooden bar where Ingrid Bergman would have felt right at home. It serves creative Umbrian food, and has tasting menus for vegetarians (€25), children (€20), truffle lovers (€40) and traditionalists (€25).

Caffè Montanucci (☎ 0763 34 12 61; Corso Cavour 21; cafeteria-style meals around €5; ☺ closed Wed) This is a good place for a sandwich or pasta. It also make its own chocolate and sells brands from around the world. Internet access is available.

Nazzaretto (Corso Cavour 40) A wine bar offering *degustazione* (wine-tasting) and light snacks. It's a lovely place to sit outside during the summer and watch tourists, locals and teenagers walk by Corso Cavour.

Le Grotte del Funaro (☎ 0763 34 32 76; Via Ripa Serancia 41; meals around €22; ☺ closed Mon) Eating here, you'll think you have died and gone to...well, a funerary cave. This restaurant was created out of a cavern and drips with atmosphere. There's an amazing view through the narrow windows, antique agricultural objects and a piano bar.

SWEETS
Pasqualetti (☎ 0763 34 10 34; Piazza del Duomo 14) This *gelateria* serves mouth-watering ice-cream, and there are plenty of tables on the piazza for you to gaze at the magnificent cathedral while you gobble.

Getting There & Away
Buses depart from the bus station on Piazza Cahen and also make a stop at the train station to pick up passengers. COTRAL buses connect the city with Viterbo in Lazio (€2.80, 1½ hours, seven daily) and Bagnore-

gio (€1.55, one hour, seven daily). **ATC buses** (☎ 0763 34 22 65) run to Baschi (€1.75, 40 minutes, seven daily), Bolsena (€2.60, 40 minutes, twice daily), Perugia (€8.70, two hours, one daily at 5.45am) and Todi (€4.15, one hour, one daily at 1.55pm returning at 5.50am). **SIRA** (☎ 0763 417 30 053) travels daily to Rome at 8.10am, and at 7.10am on Sunday (€5.16, 1½ hours).

Trains run to Rome (€6.80, one hour 20 minutes, hourly) and Florence (€9.30, 2¼ hours, two hourly); change at Terontola for Perugia (€5.90, 1¼ hours, two hourly). The city is on the A1, and the S71 heads north to Lago di Trasimeno.

Getting Around
A century-old cable car connects Piazza Cahen with the train station, with carriages leaving every 10 minutes from 7.15am to 8.30pm daily (€0.80 or €0.90, including the bus from Piazza Cahen to Piazza del Duomo). Bus No 1 also runs up to the old town from the train station (€0.80). Once in Orvieto, the easiest way to get to know the city is by walking around, although ATC bus A connects Piazza Cahen with Piazza del Duomo and bus B runs all the way through town up to Piazza della Repubblica.

CIVITA DI BAGNOREGIO
Civita di Bagnoregio is a tiny, ancient island of a village resting atop cliffs that rise from the valley floor. Accessible only by a 300m-long footbridge, as you approach you'd swear that it couldn't possibly still be inhabited. Once you walk through the gate of Santa Maria and notice the flowers decorating the homes, you'll realise that the town is still occupied. Well, technically. Only about 20 residents live here year-round, which expands to a whopping 300 in the summer.

Civita dates back to Etruscan times and is notable as the birthplace of St Bonaventure, as well as three other Christian saints. DH Lawrence mentioned Civita in his short story *Etruscan Places*.

Once a thriving and important commercial and agricultural centre, Civita has been steadily disintegrating for centuries. Built on unstable clay and volcanic sediments, whole neighbourhoods have been lost to landslides, so what we see today is only the central and most ancient part of the city.

Orientation
The only way to get into the town is to walk across the footbridge from a car park in Bagnoregio. There's no other way to get to Civita than to walk over an enormous land bridge. Only two cars are allowed into Civita: a Fiat Panda for the elderly and physically disabled, and a mini-tractor that brings goods in or rubbish out. Watch as it precariously manoeuvres the vertical steps as it splutters its way towards Civita.

Information
The only public toilet on the island is...well, just try to go before you arrive. If you have to go, bring your own toilet paper and plug your nose. The better bet is to buy a quick meal at the *bruschetteria* and use their toilet.

Sights & Activities
Walking out of the east end of the city (opposite the main gate) you'll find a path that leads down some ancient steps to the right and along the base of the town. Ancient Etruscan tombs cut into the cliffs can be seen along the way. The path terminates at an **Etruscan tunnel** that runs north to south under the width of the town, and was used at various times as an access tunnel to the Etruscan necropolis, a water conduit and a footpath for farmers to reach their fields. If you look up from either side of the tunnel, you'll see first-hand the precarious nature of Civita's existence. Note: go back the way you came, as there is no other route back into town.

In town, the **bruschetteria** features a minimuseum that displays an ancient **frantoio** (olive-oil press) dating from the 1500s. The **Chiesa di San Donato** on the east side of Piazza Duomo Vecchio in the town centre houses the remains of St Victoria.

Festivals & Events
If you'd like to see grown men race jockeys through an ancient village, show up on the first Monday in June or the second Monday in September for **La Tonna**. In August, the local arts festival **Civit'arte** features all sorts of modern and traditional live arts performances.

Sleeping
BUDGET
Romantica Pucci (☎ 0761 79 21 21; lacasadipucci@libero.it; www.hotelromanticapucci.it; Piazza Cavour 1, Bagnoregio; s/d €39/65) The breakfast alone is worth a stay here. Pucci (the owner) makes homemade blood orange and kiwi jam. Special touches like cookies before bed, bottled water in the rooms and four-poster beds make this a truly Romantica spot.

Civita Bed & Breakfast (☎ 0761 76 00 16; main square; fsala@pelagus.it; www.civitadibagnoregio.it; s/d/t with bathroom €45/68/73, s/d without bathroom €40/62) Eleven very basic rooms, some with shared bathrooms and rather hard mattresses. Remember that you're staying here for the charm. It's just off the main square to the left.

AGRITURISMO
Agriturismo Le Corone (☎ 0761 79 31 79; info@agrilecorone.com; www.agrilecorone.com; Loc. Palombaro, Strada per Vaiano, Km 4; per person per night in high season €35, 2-night minimum) This *agriturismo* is extremely comfortable, authentic and in as remote a setting as you can find in central Italy (but still only an hour from Orvieto). The stone farmhouse holds up to a family of five. Owner Fabrizio Rocchi can trace his family's roots back to the 1500s, and he and his American-born wife now run an adjoining organic farm that grows wine and olive oil, and raises cattle. Be sure to take advantage of a guided tour of the area on horseback by Fabrizio and Heather. Civita is a short but steep climb up a well-marked path.

Eating
Trattoria Antico Forno (☎ 0761 76 00 16) This is the restaurant attached to Civita Bed & Breakfast. In fact, it's the only restaurant in town. The menu is good country food: tagliatelle with a 'medieval' sauce of tomatoes, red peppers and sausages; pesto gnocchi; *piciarello* pasta with truffles or asparagus and mushrooms; and a good array of bruschetta (also available at the *bruschetteria/frantoio* museum).

Hostaria del Ponte (☎ 0761 79 35 65; Contrada Mercatello; meals around €20) A favourite of locals, this restaurant is at the foot of the bridge on the Bagnoregio side of Civita. A covered outdoor patio allows you to eat here even in winter, with a spectacular view of Civita. Specialities are truffles and *cinghiale*.

Shopping
Le Cordelier (☎ 0761 79 29 81; Via della Fraticella; next to Civita Bed & Breakfast) This little shop sells English-language books on Civita and beautiful local products. The owner studies the history of Civita's own St Bonaventure, and has been compiling a history that she hopes to turn into a book soon. For now, she's got a written history along the shop's walls. It's in Italian, but she's more than willing to explain anything about Bonaventure – or Civita – in English or French.

Getting There & Away
Buses leave from Piazza Cahen in Orvieto about every hour or so (€1.60, 50 minutes), with a gap between 9.10am and 12.40pm. The bus makes a stop in Bagnoregio and a smaller shuttle bus runs between there and the parking lot for Civita. By car, take the S71 south from Orvieto and get off in the direction of Bagnoregio. The cost to park

in the car park in front of the footbridge is €1 per hour. Buy a parking ticket at any of the three businesses surrounding the car park.

STRADA DEI VINI
The Etruscans produced wine in the district, the Romans continued the tradition and today the Orvieto Classico wines are among the country's most popular. Although Umbria is a major wine-growing region, it doesn't have a traditional wine-tasting setup. In the main tourist map of wineries, *La Strada del Sagrantino*, only six allow tastings, and then only on certain days, and preferably in large quantities. If you want to taste wine, it's easier to do so in town at any number of *enoteche* (wine bars) or shops that offer *degustazione*. Plus, if you're staying in town, you can stumble back to your hotel.

Grab a copy of the free booklet *Strada dei Vini del Cantico* at any tourist office in Umbria. It's in Italian, but it has a handy list of all of the wineries that accept visitors, their opening hours, contact details and languages spoken. Pair this with *La Strada del Sagrantino* and create a bit of a wine tour. Also check out www.umbriadoc.com/stradevino/cantico.

DIRECTORY

CONTENTS

> **PRACTICALITIES**
>
> - Use the metric system for weights and measures.
> - Buy or watch videos on the PAL system.
> - Plugs have two or three round pins so bring an international adapter; the electric current is 220V, 50Hz but older buildings may still use 125V.
> - If your Italian's up to it, try the following national newspapers: *Corriere della Sera*, the country's leading daily; Turin's *La Stampa* or Rome's centre-left *La Repubblica*. Florence-based *La Nazione* is the main regional broadsheet.
> - Tune into state-Italian RAI-1 (1332 AM or 89.7 FM), RAI-2 (846 AM or 91.7 FM) and RAI-3 (93.7 FM) for classical and light music with news broadcasts; local stations Controradio on 93.6 AM and Nova Radio on 101.5 FM in Florence play contemporary music.
> - Turn on the TV to watch Italy's commercial stations Canale 5, Italia 1, Rete 4 and La 7, as well as state-run RAI-1, RAI-2 and RAI-3.

ACCOMMODATION

Prices for accommodation quoted in this book are intended as a guide only. Accommodation rates fluctuate wildly, depending on the season and whether hoteliers decide to raise prices when they have the opportunity. Occasionally prices remain fixed for years on end, and in some cases they even go down. More often than not, they rise by around 5% or 10% annually. Always check room charges before putting your bags down.

Peak tourist season occurs in July and August and clashes with the time that most Tuscans take their annual holiday. During this period, good quality accommodation can be hard to come by, particularly if you're looking for something close to the beach. During the summer months and other peak holiday times such as Easter and Christmas, you should book accommodation in advance. It is also advisable to ring up and confirm your arrival – especially if you have been delayed or are intending to arrive late.

January and February are the quietest months. During the off-peak season you should be able to bargain with hoteliers and secure lower rates.

In this book we've used the term budget to describe accommodation where a double costs less than €70 a night, mid-range for those places where a double costs between €70 and €150, and top end where a double costs over €150 a night.

Agriturismo

This is a holiday on a working farm and is particularly popular in Tuscany and

Umbria. Traditionally the idea was that families rented out rooms in their farmhouses, and it is still possible to find this type of accommodation. However, more commonly it is a restaurant in a restored farm complex, with rooms available for rent. It used to be the case that all *agriturismo* establishments were operating farms but with the recent boom, there's been a massive influx of smartly renovated country properties jumping on the 'agritourism' bandwagon. Tourist offices can supply listings or online try www.agriturismo.net or www.agriturist.com.

This is a good option for families or small groups who can share the cost between them. Generally you need to have your own transport to get to and from these places.

Camping

Camping is very popular in Tuscany but it can work out to be quite expensive once you add up combined costs. You will be expected to pay a charge for each person, the site for your tent or caravan and at some sites you have to pay to use the shower facilities. If you are travelling by car, you may have to pay for parking. Most camp sites are often located away from the town centre so, if you are relying on public transport, you'll also have to factor in the cost of your fares.

Independent camping is generally not permitted.

Touring Club Italiano (TCI) publishes an annual book, *Campeggi e Villaggi Turistici* (€20), which lists camp sites in Italy. Online try www.campeggitalia.com or www.camping.it for regional and provincial listings.

Convents & Monasteries

Many of the more than 50 convents and monasteries scattered about the region offer some form of accommodation to outsiders. The standard is usually quite good, but the rooms can be rather spartan and often single sex. You generally need to call ahead rather than just turn up. A handy book available in good travel bookshops in Tuscany is *Guida ai Monasteri d'Italia*, by Gian Maria Grasselli and Pietro Tarallo (around €10). To get the best out of it you really need to read Italian. In the worst case, you can at least make out the phone numbers and call to see whether you can get into your chosen monastery. Alternatively,

the provincial or local tourist office should be able to provide listings.

Hostels

Youth hostels in Tuscany and Umbria and are run by the AIG (Associazone Italiana Alberghi per la Gioventù), which is affiliated to Hostelling International (HI). You need to be a member but most places will let you join when you arrive. Accommodation is usually in segregated dormitories and beds cost around €12 per night. Some hostels offer family rooms at a higher price. In the summer months you should book in advance, especially in Florence and Perugia. It is usually necessary to pay before 9am on the day of your departure, otherwise you could be charged for an additional night.

Visit www.ostellionline.com for further information, including a list of hostels in the region, details on how to join HI and an online booking service.

Hotels

Prices quoted in this book are intended as a guide only. Hotels are strictly regulated in Italy and are classified on a scale of one to five stars. Hotels are known by many names including *albergo, locande, affittacamere* or *pensione*. A *pensione* is no longer officially recognised but if you do come across a place by this name you can assume that it is a one- or two-star hotel.

The quality of accommodation can vary a great deal. One-star hotels tend to be basic and usually do not have an ensuite bathroom. Standards at two-star places are often only slightly better, but rooms will generally have a private bathroom. Once you arrive at three stars you can assume that standards will be reasonable, although quality still varies dramatically. Four- and five-star hotels are sometimes part of a group of hotels and offer facilities such as room service, laundry and dry-cleaning.

You'll find that the prices are highest in Florence and on Elba (in July and August). Some hotels may impose a multi-night stay in high season.

A single room is called a *camera singola,* a double room with twin beds is a *camera doppia* and a double room with a double bed is called a *camera matrimoniale.*

The tourist board can provide extensive accommodation listings.

VILLAS AMONG THE VINES

If you want to get away from it all and relax in style, then renting a villa just may be the ticket for you. In recent years it has become a popular accommodation option and villas can be found in most corners of Tuscany, Umbria and surrounding areas.

People wanting to rent a villa in the countryside can seek information from specialist travel agencies in their own country, or contact an organisation in Italy directly. One major Italian company with villas in Tuscany is Cuendet. This reliable firm publishes a booklet listing all the villas in its files, many with photos. Prices for a villa for four to six people range from around €460 a week in winter up to €1300 week in August. For details contact **Cuendet & Cie spa** (☎ 0577 57 63 10; www.cuendet.com). Those following are in the UK:

Invitation to Tuscany (☎ 01481 72 72 98; www.invitationtotuscany.com) is another reputable purveyor of self-catering villas. Properties, many with a pool, can cost anything from UK£400 to UK£1200 per week for four to eight people. It has representatives in the UK, USA, Australia and New Zealand.

Cottages to Castles (☎ 01622 77 52 17; www.cottagestocastles.com) also has an enticing collection of properties to choose from. The company has agents in New Zealand, Australia and across Europe. Its website is packed full of information and online booking is available. Prices are comparable to those of Invitation to Tuscany.

Simply Travel (☎ 020 8541 2206; www.simplytravel.com) has over a hundred properties in Tuscany and Umbria. It also has a good selection of late availability deals for last-minute booking.

Traditional Tuscany (☎ 0700 4887 226; www.traditionaltuscany.co.uk) is a specialist company with a wide range of rural villas and converted farmhouses. Its website contains a wealth of information with each listing accompanied by a detailed description and lots of pictures.

CIT offices throughout the world also have lists of villas and apartments available for rent in Tuscany and Umbria.

Rental Accommodation

Finding rental accommodation in the cities can be difficult and time-consuming, but not impossible. Rental agencies will assist, for a fee. A one-room apartment with kitchenette in Florence's city centre will cost anything from €300 to €550 a month (long term). Renting in other towns can be considerably cheaper.

You can look for rental ads in the advert rags such as Florence's *La Pulce* and *Panorama*. However, if you're looking for ads for shared accommodation, you won't find many. Short-term rental is more expensive, but many locals are keen to rent to foreigners for brief periods.

Rifugi

If you are planning to hike in the Apuane Alps, first obtain some information on the network of *rifugi* (mountain huts). The most common are the ones run by the **Club Alpino Italiano** (CAI; www.cai.it) and accommodation is generally in bunk rooms sleeping anything from two to a dozen or more people. Half board (dinner, bed and breakfast) is often available.

In addition to CAI *rifugi* there are some private ones and the occasional *bivacchio*, a basic, unstaffed hut. In general, *rifugi* remain open from mid-June to mid-September, but some at lower altitudes may remain open longer.

If you are counting on staying in a *rifugo*, always call ahead of your arrival, or have someone do so for you, to check that it is open and has room for you. Where possible, let staff know approximately when you expect to arrive.

Student Accommodation

People planning to study in Italy can usually organise accommodation through the school or university they will be attending. Options include a room with an Italian family, or a share arrangement with other students in an independent apartment.

BUSINESS HOURS

Shops generally open 9am to 1pm and 3.30pm to 7.30pm (or 4pm to 8pm) Monday to Friday, but in main towns and cities it's increasingly popular for shops to remain open all day. Smaller shops often close on

Mondays. Bank hours are generally from 8.30am to 1.30pm and 3pm to 4pm (but times vary). They're closed at weekends but you should be able to find an exchange office if you need one. Post offices open 8.30am to 1.30pm Monday to Friday, but usually close at 11.45am on Saturday mornings. Pharmacies open 9am to 12.30pm and 3.30pm to 7pm Monday to Friday, but are closed on Saturday and Sunday afternoons. When closed they are obliged to display details of pharmacies in the area that are open.

Restaurants usually serve meals from 12pm to 3pm and 7.30pm to 11pm. Bars usually open at 8am and stay open until the early hours. Both types of establishment usually close one day a week. Nightclubs open their doors at about 10pm but don't usually start filling up until midnight.

CHILDREN

Your children will get a great reception in Tuscany and Umbria and most places will happily accommodate them. Discounts are available for children (usually under 12 years of age) on public transport and for admission to museums and galleries, etc.

Travelling with children can be extremely rewarding with the right planning. For more information see Lonely Planet's *Travel With Children*.

Practicalities

If possible, families should book accommodation in advance to avoid inconvenience. You might want to try a villa or other self-catering accommodation so you have your own kitchen facilities to prepare snacks and meals. If not, ask the tourist office for suggestions of hotels and guesthouses that cater specifically for children. Many hotels have kids-club options. Most places will have cots and high chairs available, if you request them in advance, although hotels will probably make you pay a supplement. Car seats can also be hired with rental cars but if you plan to do a lot of travelling you might be better off taking your own: if you are flying, remember to check your luggage allowance.

Farmacie (pharmacies) sell baby formula in powder or liquid form as well as sterilising solutions. Disposable nappies are widely available at supermarkets, pharmacies (where they are more expensive) and sometimes in larger stationery stores. Fresh cow's milk is sold in cartons in bars (which have a 'Latteria' sign) and in supermarkets. If it is essential that you have milk you should carry an emergency carton of UHT milk, since bars usually close at 8pm.

Stock up on sunscreen as the climate can be particularly harsh on young skin and try and schedule your day to fit in with the cooler periods (early morning and late afternoon).

Watch out for the amount of sugary sweets that are heaped upon them by well-meaning locals and be aware that most restaurants and bars do not uphold a nonsmoking policy.

CLIMATE CHARTS

Tuscany and Umbria both enjoy a typically Mediterranean climate with a mean annual temperature of around 15°C. Summertime can be oppressive and hot with temperatures reaching 35°C. For more information see p9.

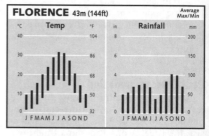

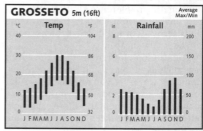

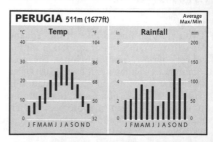

COURSES

Tuscany, and increasingly Umbria, are popular destinations for people who want to learn Italian. Universities and private schools all over the region offer tuition, although the two main magnets are Florence and Siena. It's a great way to get a feel for the place.

Individual schools and universities are listed under Information in the relevant towns throughout this book. The handy website www.it-schools.com lists a plethora of schools and courses. Accommodation can usually be arranged through the school.

Many schools also offer courses in painting, art history, sculpture, architecture and cooking; however, all these courses can be expensive (up to €1000). For cooking courses see the Food & Drink chapter (p64).

It is also possible to undertake serious academic study at a university, although obviously only if you have a solid command of the language.

Istituto Italiano di Cultura (www.italcult.net) is a government-sponsored organisation promoting Italian culture and language. It can provide information about where to study and has branches all over the world.

In the UK, **Vallicorte** (☎ /fax 020-7680 1377; www .vallicorte.com) organises small-group courses in art and architecture, painting, cooking and wine near Lucca and Florence. Courses run in spring and autumn and start at UK£685 for four days, including food and accommodation.

CUSTOMS

Duty-free sales within the EU no longer exist. Under the rules of the single market, goods bought in and exported within the EU incur no additional taxes, provided duty has been paid somewhere within the EU and the goods are for personal consumption.

Travellers who are coming from outside the EU, on the other hand, are permitted to import, duty free: 200 cigarettes, 1L of spirits, 2L of wine, 60mL of perfume, 250mL of eau de toilette, and other goods up to a total value of €175; anything over this limit must be declared on arrival and the appropriate duty paid (it is advisable to carry all receipts).

DANGERS & ANNOYANCES
Theft

Pickpockets and bag-snatchers operate in the more touristy parts of the bigger cities and some of the coastal resort towns. Invest in a money belt to keep your important items safe and pay attention to what's going on around you. In Florence especially you should also watch out for groups of dishevelled-looking women and children. They generally work in groups of four or five and carry paper or cardboard which they use to distract your attention while they swarm around and riffle through your pockets and bag. Never underestimate their skill – they are as fast as lightning and very adept.

Parked cars are also prime targets for thieves, particularly those with foreign number plates or rental-company stickers. Never leave valuables in your car and make sure you are adequately insured. See p343 for more details. In case of theft or loss, always report the incident to the police within 24 hours and ask for a statement, otherwise your travel insurance company may not pay out.

Traffic

Italian traffic can at best be described as chaotic, at worst downright dangerous, for the unprepared tourist. Drivers are not keen to stop for pedestrians, even at pedestrian crossings, and are more likely to swerve. Italians simply step off the footpath and walk through the (swerving) traffic with determination – it is a practice which seems to work, so if you feel uncertain about crossing a busy road, wait for the next Italian. In many cities, roads that appear to be for one-way traffic have special lanes for buses travelling in the opposite direction, and it's not uncommon to see cyclists peddling or motoring the wrong way on one-way streets – always look both ways before stepping out.

Driving in the Tuscan and Umbrian countryside is far less intense but be prepared to take it slowly. The winding roads can be narrow and difficult to navigate.

DISABLED TRAVELLERS

Tuscany and Umbria are not the easiest places for disabled travellers. Cobblestone streets, common in many towns in the region, can be a nuisance for those who are wheelchair-bound, and many buildings (including hotels) don't have lifts.

The Italian State Tourist Office in your country may be able to provide advice on Italian associations for the disabled and what help is available in the country. It may also carry a small brochure, *Services for Disabled People*, published by the Italian railways, which details facilities at stations and on trains. There's an airline directory that provides information on the facilities offered by various airlines on the disability-friendly website at www.everybody.co.uk.

Organisations

The UK-based **Royal Association for Disability & Rehabilitation** (Radar; ☎ 020-7250 3222; www .radar.org.uk; Unit 12, City Forum, 250 City Rd, London EC1V 8AF) publishes a useful Holiday Fact Pack, which provides a good overview of facilities available to disabled travellers throughout Europe.

Another organisation worth calling is **Holiday Care Service** (☎ 0845 124 9971; www .holidaycare.org.uk). It produces an information pack on Italy for the physically disabled and others with special needs and its website has lots of useful resources.

In Italy itself you may also be able to get help. **COIN** (Cooperative Integrate; ☎ 06 712 9011; www .sociale.it - Italian only, some English information available on www.coinsociale.it, turismo@coinsociale.it; Via Enrico Giglioli 54a, Rome) is a national voluntary group with links to the government and branches all over the country. They have information on accessible accommodation, transport and attractions.

Promotur – Accessible Italy (☎ 011 309 63 63; www.tour-web.com/accessibleitaly/index.html; Piazza Pitagora 9, 10137 Turin) is a private company that specialises in holiday services for the disabled, ranging from tours to the hiring of adapted transport.

DISCOUNT CARDS
Senior Cards

Seniors over 60 or 65 (depending on what they are seeking a discount for) can get many discounts simply by presenting their passport or ID card as proof of age.

Student & Youth Cards

These cards can get you worthwhile discounts on travel, and reduced prices at some museums, sights and entertainments. The **International Student Identity Card** (ISIC), for full-time students, and the **International Teacher Identity Card** (ITIC), for full-time teachers and professors, are issued by more than 5000 organisations around the world – mainly student travel–related, and often selling student air, train and bus tickets too. In Australia, the USA or the UK try STA Travel.

Anyone under 26 can get a **Euro26** card. This gives similar discounts to the ISIC and is issued by most of the same organisations. See www.euro26.org for details.

CTS (Centro Turistico Studentesco e Giovanile) youth and student travel organisation branches in Italy can issue ISIC, ITIC and Euro26 cards.

Note that many places in Italy give discounts according to age rather than student status. An ISIC card may not always be accepted without proof of age (eg, passport).

EMBASSIES & CONSULATES

It's important to realise what your own embassy – the embassy of the country of which you are a citizen – can and can't do to help you if you get into trouble. Generally speaking, it won't be much help in emergencies if the trouble you're in is remotely your own fault. Remember that you are bound by the laws of the country you are in. Your embassy will not be sympathetic if you end up in jail after committing a crime locally, even if such actions are legal in your own country.

In genuine emergencies you might get some assistance, but only if other channels have been exhausted. For example, if you need to get home urgently, a free ticket home is exceedingly unlikely – the embassy would expect you to have insurance. If you have all your money and documents stolen, it might assist with getting a new passport, but a loan for onward travel is out of the question.

Italian Embassies & Consulates

The following is a selection of Italian diplomatic missions abroad. As a rule, you will need to approach a consulate rather than an embassy (where both are present) on visa matters. Also bear in mind that in many of the countries listed below there are further consulates in other cities.

Australia Canberra (☎ 02-6273 3333; embassy@ambit alia.org.au; 12 Grey St, Deakin, Canberra, ACT 2600); Melbourne (☎ 03-9867 5744; itconmel@netlink.com.au; 509

St Kilda Rd, Melbourne, Vic 3004); Sydney (☎ 02-9392 7900; itconsydn@itconsyd.org; Level 45, The Gateway, 1 Macquarie Place, Sydney, NSW 2000)
Austria (☎ 01-712 51 21; ambitalviepress@via.at; Metternichgasse 13, Vienna 1030)
Canada Ottawa (☎ 613-232 2401; www.italyincanada .com; 21st floor, 275 Slater St, Ottawa, Ontario K1P 5H9); Montreal (☎ 514-849 8351; www.italconsul.montreal.qc .ca; 3489 Drummond St, Montreal, Quebec H3G 1X6); Toronto (☎ 416-977 1566; www.italconsulate.org; 136 Beverley St, Toronto, Ontario M5T 1Y5)
France Embassy (☎ 01 49 54 03 00; ambasciata@ amb-italie.fr; 47 rue de Varenne, Paris 75007) Consulate (☎ 01 44 30 47 00; fax 01 45 25 87 50; 5 blvd Emile Augier, Paris 75016)
Germany Berlin (☎ 030-25 44 00; www.botschaft-italien.de - German or Italian only; Dessauer Strasse 28-29, 10963 Berlin); Frankfurt (☎ 069-753 10; italia.consolato .francoforte@t-online.de; Beethovenstrasse, 17, D 60325 Frankfurt-am-Main)
Ireland (☎ 01-660 1744; info@italianembassy.ie; 63-65 Northumberland Rd, Dublin 4)
The Netherlands (☎ 070-302 1030; italemb@ worldonline.nl; Alexanderstraat 12, 2514 JL The Hague)
New Zealand (☎ 04-473 53 39; ambwell@xtra.co.nz; 34-38 Grant Rd, Thorndon, Wellington)
Slovenia (☎ 061-426 21 94; fax 061-425 33 02; Snezniska Ulica 8, Ljubljana 61000)
Spain Madrid (☎ 91 423 3300; segreamb@ambitalia madrid.org; Calle de Lagasca 98, Madrid 28006); Barcelona (☎ 93 467 7305; cqbarcconsolare@infonegocio.com; Calle Mallorca 270, Barcelona 08037)
Switzerland Bern (☎ 031-3500777; ambital.berna@spe ctraweb.ch; Elfenstrasse 14, Bern 3006); Geneva (☎ 022-839 67 44; fax 022-839 67 45; 14 rue Charles Galland, Geneva 1206)
UK Embassy (☎ 020-7312 2200; itconlond@btconnect .com; 14 Three Kings Yard, London W1Y 2EH); Consulate (☎ 020-7235 9371; fax 020-7823 1609; 38 Eaton Place, London SW1X 8AN)
USA Washington (☎ 202-612 4400; stampa@itwash.org; 1601 Fuller St, NW Washington, DC 20009); New York (☎ 212-737 9100; italconsulnyc@italconsulnyc.org; 690 Park Ave, New York, NY 10021-5044)

Embassies & Consulates in Italy
Most countries have an embassy (and often a consulate) in Rome, though there are a few consulates in Florence. Passport enquiries should be addressed to the offices below.

Australia Rome (☎ 06 85 27 21; Via Alessandria 215)
Austria Rome (☎ 06 844 01 41; Via G Pergolesi 3)
Canada Rome (☎ 06 44 59 81; Via G B de Rossi 27)

France Rome (☎ 06 68 60 11; Piazza Farnese 67); Florence (☎ 055 230 25 56; Piazza Ognissanti 2)
Germany Rome (☎ 06 49 21 31; Via San Martino della Battaglia 4); Florence (☎ 055 29 47 22; Lungarno Vespucci 30)
Ireland Rome (☎ 06 697 91 21; Piazza Campitelli 3)
The Netherlands Rome (☎ 06 322 11 41; Via Michele Mercati 8)
New Zealand Rome (☎ 06 441 71 71; Via Zara 28)
Slovenia Rome (☎ 06 809 14 310; Via Leonardo Pisano 10)
Spain Rome (☎ 06 684 04 01; Palazzo Borghese, Largo Fontanella Borghese 19)
Switzerland Rome (☎ 06 80 95 71; Via Barnarba Oriani 61); Florence (☎ 055 22 24 34; Piazzale Galileo 5)
UK Rome (☎ 06 422 00 001; Via XX Settembre 80a); Florence (☎ 055 28 41 33; Lungarno Corsini 2)
USA Rome (☎ 06 4 67 41; Via Vittorio Veneto 119a-121)

FESTIVALS & EVENTS
The calendar is full to bursting with events, ranging from colourful traditional celebrations with a religious and/or historical flavour, through to festivals of the performing arts, including opera, music and theatre. Occasionally celebrations are country wide (see below) but more often than not the events relate specifically to a city or town. Details of destination-specific festivals and events can be found in the regional chapters.

Carnevale
During the period before Ash Wednesday, many towns stage carnivals and enjoy their last opportunity to indulge before Lent. The popular carnival celebrations held at Viareggio are among the best known in all Italy, second only to the extravaganza of Venice.

Pasqua (Easter)
Holy Week is marked by solemn processions and passion plays. In Florence the Scoppio del Carro is staged in the Piazza del Duomo at noon on Easter Saturday. This event features the explosion of a cart full of fireworks – a tradition dating back to the Crusades and seen as a good omen for the city if the explosion works.

FOOD
In this book we've used the term budget to describe places where you can grab a meal for less than €15; mid-range places cost between €15 and €40, while the full works

at a top-end restaurant will cost over €40 a head.

For more on *what* to eat in Tuscany and Umbria, see the Food & Drink chapter on p56.

GAY & LESBIAN TRAVELLERS

Homosexuality is legal in Italy and well tolerated in the northern half of the country.

Gay-friendly bars and clubs can be tracked down through local gay organisations (see later) or the national monthly gay magazine *Pride* (€3.10). There's a website at www.gay.it/pinklily with lots of information on activities and places to go, but it was last updated in 1999.

International gay and lesbian guides worth tracking down are the *Spartacus Guide for Gay Men*, published by Bruno Gmünder Verlag, Mail Order, PO Box 61 01 04, 10921 Berlin; and *Places for Women*, published by Ferrari Publications, Phoenix, AZ, USA.

ArciGay (☎ 051 649 30 55, fax 528 22 26; www.arcigay.it - Italian only), the Italian gay association, is the main organisation campaigning for the rights of gays and lesbians in Italy. Its headquarters are located in Bologna. Other organisations include **Azione Gay e Lesbica Finisterrae** (☎ /fax 055 67 12 98; www.azionegayelesbica.it - Italian only) in Florence. Its website has lots of useful links.

Online, visit www.gay.it (Italian only) to get lots of general information on the gay and lesbian scene in Italy and access plenty of useful links.

Versilia and Torre del Lago have a lively and popular gay scene. In the latter you'll find 'La Lecciona', a gay-friendly beach with lots of bars and restaurants lining the waterfront. Five years ago the local gay community created **Friendly Versilia** (☎ 050 55 56 18 for tourist information; www.friendlyversilia.it) to promote the area as a gay holiday destination. Every August they hold the 'Friendly Versilia Mardi Gras', which attracts thousands of visitors. Their website has bar and restaurant listings as well as recommended accommodation.

HOLIDAYS

Most Tuscans take their annual holidays in August, deserting the cities for the cooler seaside or mountains. This means that many businesses and shops close for at least part of the month, particularly during the week around Ferragosto (Feast of the Assumption) on 15 August. Cities such as Florence are left to the tourists, who may be frustrated that many restaurants and shops are closed until early September. The Easter break (Settimana Santa) is another busy holiday period for Italians and many schools take pupils on cultural excursions during this time. Museums and places of interest may be more crowded than usual. Allow for long queues.

During the holidays, it may be difficult to secure accommodation. Families should definitely book in advance to avoid inconvenience.

Italian national public holidays include the following:

New Year's Day (Anno Nuovo) 1 January – the celebrating takes place on New Year's Eve (Capodanno)
Epiphany (Befana) 6 January
Good Friday (Venerdì Santo) March/April
Easter Monday (Pasquetta/Giorno dopo Pasqua) March/April
Liberation Day (Giorno della Liberazione) 25 April – marks the Allied victory in Italy and the end of the German presence and Mussolini
Labour Day (Giorno del Lavoro) 1 May
Feast of the Assumption (Ferragosto) 15 August
All Saints' Day (Ognissanti) 1 November
Feast of the Immaculate Conception (Concezione Immaculata) 8 December
Christmas Day (Natale) 25 December
St Stephen's Day (Boxing Day, Festa di Santo Stefano) 26 December

Individual towns also have public holidays to celebrate the feasts of their patron saints. Details can be found in the relevant chapters.

INSURANCE

Never leave home without travel insurance – it's just not worth the risk. Most policies will cover theft, loss and medical problems. Some policies offer lower and higher medical-expense options; the higher ones are chiefly for countries such as the USA, which have extremely high medical costs. There's a wide variety of policies available, so check the small print.

Some policies specifically exclude 'dangerous activities', which can include scuba diving, motorcycling, even trekking. Check your policy to be sure. A locally acquired motorcycle licence isn't valid under some policies.

You may prefer a policy that pays doctors or hospitals directly, rather than you having to pay on the spot and claim later. If you have to claim later make sure you keep all documentation. Some policies ask you to call back (reverse charges) to a centre in your home country, where an immediate assessment of your problem is made.

Check that the policy covers ambulances or an emergency flight home.

If you are planning to travel by car then insurance is not only recommended but legally required. See p343 for details.

INTERNET ACCESS
Travelling with a portable computer is a great way to stay in touch with life back home, but unless you know what you're doing it's fraught with potential problems. If you plan to carry your notebook or palmtop computer, remember that the power supply voltage in Italy may be different from that at home, risking damage to your equipment. The best investment is a universal AC adaptor for your appliance, which will enable you to plug it in anywhere without frying the innards. You'll also need a plug adaptor for each country you visit – often it's easiest to buy these before you leave home.

Also, your PC-card modem may or may not work once you leave your home country – and you won't know for sure until you try it out. The safest option is to buy a reputable 'global' modem before you leave home, or buy a local PC-card modem, if you're spending an extended time in any one country. Keep in mind that the telephone socket in each country you visit will probably be different from the one at home, so ensure that you have at least a US RJ-11 telephone adaptor that works the modem that you have. You can almost always find an adaptor that will convert from RJ-11 to the local variety. For some more information on travelling overseas with a notebook or laptop computer, see www.teleadapt .com.

Major Internet service providers such as AOL (www.aol.com) and CompuServe (www.compuserve.com) have dial-in nodes available in Italy – it's best to make sure you download a list of the dial-in numbers before you leave home.

Some Italian servers can provide short-term accounts for Internet access. **Agora** (☎ 800 304 999; www.agoratelematica.it) has English-speaking staff.

If you access your email account at home through a smaller ISP or your office or school network, your best option is either to open an account with a global ISP, such as those mentioned above, or to rely on cybercafés and other public-access points to collect your mail.

If you do intend to rely on cybercafés, you'll need to remember to carry three pieces of information with you to enable you to access your Internet mail account: your incoming (POP or IMAP) mail server name, your account name and your password. Your ISP or network supervisor will be able to give you these. Armed with this information, you should be able to access your email account from any Net-connected machine in the world, provided it runs some kind of email software (remember that Netscape and Internet Explorer both have mail modules). It pays to become familiar with the process for doing this before you leave home.

You'll find plenty of Internet cafés in Florence and most of the larger towns in Tuscany and Umbria will have some sort of Internet access available. See individual chapters for details.

LEGAL MATTERS
For many Italians, finding ways to get around the law (any law) is a way of life. They are likely to react with surprise, if not annoyance, if you point out that they might be breaking a law. Few people pay attention to speed limits and many motorcyclists and drivers don't stop at red lights – and certainly not at pedestrian crossings. No-one bats an eyelid about littering or dogs pooping in the middle of the footpath, even though many municipal governments have introduced laws against these things. But these are minor transgressions when measured up against the country's organised crime, the extraordinary levels of tax evasion and corruption in government and business.

The average tourist will probably have a brush with the law only if unfortunate enough to be robbed by a bag-snatcher or pickpocket.

DIRECTORY

Drugs

Italy's drug laws are lenient on users and heavy on pushers. If you're caught with drugs that the police determine are for your own personal use, you'll be let off with a warning (and, of course, the drugs will be confiscated). If, instead, it is determined that you intend to sell the drugs, you could find yourself in prison. It's up to the police to determine whether or not you're a pusher, since the law is not specific about quantities. The sensible option is to avoid illicit drugs altogether.

Drink Driving

The legal limit for blood-alcohol level is 0.05%. Random breath tests are carried out by the authorities and penalties can range from an on the spot fine to the confiscation of your licence.

Police

The police are a civil force and take their orders from the Ministry of the Interior, while the *carabinieri* fall under the Ministry of Defence. There is a considerable duplication of their roles, despite a 1981 reform intended to merge the two forces.

The *carabinieri* wear a dark-blue uniform with a red stripe and drive dark-blue cars that also have a red stripe. They are well trained and tend to be helpful. Their police station is called a *caserma* (barracks).

The police wear powder-blue trousers with a fuchsia stripe and a navy-blue jacket and drive light-blue cars with a white stripe and *'polizia'* written on the side. Tourists who want to report thefts, and people wanting to get a residence permit, will have to deal with them. Their headquarters are called the *questura*.

Other varieties of police in Italy include the *vigili urbani*, basically traffic police, who you will have to deal with if you get a parking ticket, or your car is towed away; and the *guardia di finanza*, who are responsible for fighting tax evasion and drug smuggling.

YOUR RIGHTS

Italy has some antiterrorism laws on its books that could make life difficult if you happen to be detained by the police. You can be held for 48 hours without a magistrate being informed and you can be interrogated without the presence of a lawyer. It is difficult to obtain bail and you can be held legally for up to three years without being brought to trial.

MAPS

If you are driving around Tuscany and Umbria, the AA's *Road Atlas – Italy* is available in the UK for £13.99. It uses large-scale mapping and includes 31 town maps. In Italy, de Agostini's *Atlante Turistico Stradale d'Italia* (1:250,000) contains city plans and sells for €20.50. TCI publishes an *Atlante Stradale d'Italia* (1:200,000), which is divided into three parts – Nord, Centro and Sud; each costs €18. TCI also produces a comprehensive edition including all three parts and a CD-ROM for €51.15.

Michelin's map No 430, *Italia Centro* (1:400,000), includes Tuscany and parts of surrounding regions. Michelin also produces a similar regional map specifically covering *Tuscany, Umbria, Marches, Lazio, Abruzzo and San Marino* (1:400,000).

One of the best maps of Umbria is the de Agostini 1:200,000 map, a greenish topological foldout paper map available for free at most tourist offices and many hotels. It marks many features that make it extremely helpful: tertiary/dirt roads, sites of interest – sanctuaries, Etruscan tombs, grottos, ruins, monasteries. (A note about the terrain: 94% of Umbria is hilly. Industrial complexes have taken advantage of the remaining flat 6%, so if you want attractive landscapes, don't go toward anything white on your map, i.e., the flat areas directly around Foligno or Terni.) On the reverse side is a list of every major town in Umbria (from Assisi to Monte Castello di Vibio) along with every hotel, camp site, *agriturismo*, youth hostel and religious house, and their addresses and phone numbers.

TCI produces regional maps of Tuscany and Umbria at a scale of 1:200,000 (€7),

LEGAL AGE	
Driving	18
Voting	18
Drinking	16
Heterosexual sex	14
Homosexual sex	14

while several other publishers do the region at 1:250,000. For greater scale detail, you have to revert to provincial maps (the region is divided up into 10 provinces). Edizioni Multigraphic Firenze publishes a series of provincial maps. Ask for the *Carta Stradale Provinciale* of the province(s) you want. They are scaled at 1:100,000. Various other publishers produce comparable maps.

City maps in this book, combined with tourist-office maps, are generally adequate. But more detailed maps are available at good bookshops (such as Feltrinelli) or newspaper stands.

The quality of city maps available commercially varies considerably, depending on the city. Most tourist offices stock free maps of the city they cover, and commercial maps of larger cities are available from newsstands and bookstores. Try Lonely Planet's city map for Florence. For suggestions on maps for the other main cities covered in this book, refer to each destination.

Tuscany and Umbria are great destinations for those who love the outdoors. Edizioni Multigraphic publishes a couple of series designed for walkers and mountain-bike riders are scaled at 1:50,000 and 1:250,000. Where possible you should go for the latter. Ask for the *Carta dei Sentieri e Rifugi* or *Carta Turistica e dei Sentieri.* Another publisher is Kompass, which produces 1:50,000 scale maps of Tuscany and the surrounding areas. Occasionally you will also come across useful maps put out by the Club Alpino Italiano (CAI). For cycling enthusiasts Verlag Esterbauer produces a *Cycling Atlas to Tuscany.* This spiral-bound book depicts 23 tours through the region.

Those planning a driving holiday should consult the AA's *Best Drives Series: Tuscany & Umbria,* which contains hand-picked car tours, essential motoring tips and specially designed maps.

MONEY

The unit of currency is the euro (€).The euro is divided into 100 cents. Coin denominations are one, two, five, 10, 20 and 50 cents, €1 and €2. The notes are €5, €10, €20, €50, €100, €200 and €500. All euro notes of each denomination are identical on both sides in all EU countries, and the coins are identical on the side showing their value, but there are also 12 different obverses, each repre-

senting one of the 12 euro-zone countries. For more information check out the website www.europa.eu.int/euro.

See the inside cover for a handy table to help you calculate the exchange rate. The Getting Started chapter (p10) has information on costs.

Money can be exchanged in banks, post offices and exchange offices. Banks generally offer the best rates but shop around as rates fluctuate considerably.

ATMs

You'll find ATMs in all big cities and towns in Tuscany and Umbria. It's not uncommon for Italian ATMs to reject foreign cards, so try a couple of machines before assuming that the problem lies with your card.

Cash

Smaller establishments will only accept cash so you'll need to carry a small amount of currency on your person for day-to-day transactions. Other than that, keep cash to a minimum and store it in an under-the-clothes money belt if possible. Try and keep it separate from your other valuables in case your credit cards or travellers cheques are stolen.

Credit & Debit Cards

The simplest way to organise your holiday funds is to carry plastic (whether a credit, debit or ATM card). You don't have large amounts of cash or cheques to lose, you can get money after hours and at weekends, and the exchange rate is sometimes better than that offered for travellers cheques or cash exchanges. By arranging for payments to be made into your card account while you are travelling, you can avoid paying interest.

Major credit/debit cards, for example Visa, MasterCard, Eurocard, Cirrus and Eurocheque cards, are accepted in Italy.

As well as making purchases and paying accommodation costs, credit cards can also be used in ATMs *(bancomat)* displaying the appropriate sign or (if you have no PIN number) to obtain cash advances over the counter in many banks – Visa and Master-Card are among the most widely recognised for such transactions. Check charges with your bank before departure. You should also check the procedure on what to do if you experience problems or your card is stolen. Most card suppliers will offer you an emergency number you can call free of charge for help and advice.

Travellers Cheques

Travellers cheques can be cashed at most banks and exchange offices. American Express (AmEx), Thomas Cook and Visa are widely accepted brands.

It may be preferable to buy travellers cheques in euros rather than another currency, as they are less likely to incur commission on exchange. AmEx and Thomas Cook don't charge commission, but other exchange places do have charges. Get most of the cheques in largish denominations to save on per-cheque exchange charges.

It's vital to keep your initial receipt, and a record of the cheque numbers you have used, separate from the cheques themselves. If your travellers cheques get stolen, you'll need these documents to get them replaced. You must take your passport with you when cashing travellers cheques.

PHOTOGRAPHY

Airports are all fully equipped with modern inspection systems that do not damage most film or other photographic material that is carried in hand luggage. Getting a roll of film developed (24 exposure) costs anywhere between €8 and €13. Photographic services are often cheaper in the main towns and cities such as Florence and Perugia.

Photography is not allowed in many churches, museums and galleries. Look out for signs with a crossed-out camera symbol as you go in.

For tips on how to make the most of your camera try Lonely Planet's *Travel Photography*.

POST

Italy's postal service is notoriously slow, unreliable and expensive.

Francobolli (stamps) are available at post offices and authorised tobacconists (look for the official *tabacchi* sign: a big 'T', often white on black). Main post offices in the bigger cities are generally open from around 8am to at least 5pm; many open on Saturday morning too. Tobacconists keep regular shop hours.

Postcards and letters up to 20g sent airmail cost €0.52 to Australia and New Zealand, €0.52 to the USA and €0.41 within Europe. You can also send express letters *(posta prioritaria)* and registered letters *(raccomandata)* at additional cost. Charges vary depending on type of post and weight of letter. Normal air-mail letters can take up to two weeks to reach the UK or the USA, while a letter to Australia will take between two and three weeks. The service within Italy is not much better: local letters take at least three days and up to a week to arrive in another city.

Poste restante is known as *fermo posta*. Letters marked thus will be held at the counter of the same name in the main post office in the relevant town. Poste restante mail should be addressed as follows:

John SMITH
Fermo Posta
Posta Centrale
50100 Florence
Italy

You will need to pick up your letters in person and present your passport as ID.

SOLO TRAVELLERS

Those travelling alone should experience few problems in Tuscany and Umbria. Although there are not large numbers of solo travellers, as in other places with an established backpacking culture, you should not feel out of place and you will certainly not be made to feel uncomfortable. You may, however, experience difficulties with accommodation. Many single rooms tend to be priced extortionately high when compared to twin or double rooms. If you are travelling to a tight budget you may want to consider hostel accommodation – it will work out cheaper and it's also a great way to meet fellow travellers.

In general, normal common-sense rules apply. Avoid unlit streets and parks at night and ensure your valuables are safely stored.

TELEPHONE

Privatised Telecom Italia is the largest phone company in the country and its orange public pay phones are liberally scattered all over the place. The most common accept only *carte/schede telefoniche* (telephone cards), although you will still find some that accept cards and coins.

Some card phones now also accept special Telecom credit cards and even commercial credit cards. Phones can be found in the streets, train stations and some big stores as well as in unstaffed Telecom centres. Most phones have clear instructions in English.

Telephone numbers change quickly in Italy so check the local directory for up-to-date information. For directory enquiries within Italy, dial ☎ 12.

Mobile Phones

Italy uses GSM 900/1800, which is compatible with the rest of Europe and Australia but not with the North American GSM 1900 or the totally different system in Japan (though some North Americans have GSM 1900/900 phones that do work here). If you have a GSM phone, check with your service provider about using it in Italy, and beware of calls being routed internationally (very expensive for a 'local' call).

Phone Codes

The international access code is ☎ 00 and the country code is ☎ 39.

Telephone area codes all begin with 0 and consist of up to four digits. The area code is followed by a telephone number of anything from four to eight digits.

Area codes are an integral part of all telephone numbers in Italy, even if you are calling within a single zone. For example, any number you ring in Florence will start with ☎ 055, even if it's next door. When making domestic and international calls you must always dial the full number including the initial zero.

Numeri verdi (freephone numbers) usually begin with ☎ 800 (some start with ☎ 199 and ☎ 848). Mobile-telephone numbers begin with a three-digit prefix such as ☎ 330, ☎ 335, ☎ 347, etc.

Phone Cards

You can buy phone cards at post offices, tobacconists, newspaper stands and from vending machines in Telecom offices. They come with a value of €1, €2.50, €5 and €7.50. Remember to snap off the perforated corner before using them.

TIME

Italy operates on a 24-hour clock. It is one hour ahead of GMT/UTC. Daylight-saving

time starts on the last Sunday in March, when clocks are put forward one hour. Clocks are put back an hour on the last Sunday in October.

There's a time-zone world map at the back of this book.

TOURIST INFORMATION
Local Tourist Offices

Tuscany's regional **tourist office** (☎ 055 438 51 35; www.regione.toscana.it - Italian only) can be found at Via di Novoli 26, Florence. Umbria's regional **tourist office** (☎ 075 575 951; www.umbria-turismo.it) is at Via Mazzini 21, Perugia. Azienda di Promozione Turistica (APT) offices, in all the provincial capitals, generally provide information only on that province, usually including the city itself, but little or nothing on the rest of the region. Since tourism isn't exactly new to Tuscany and Umbria you'll generally find English is spoken, and sometimes other languages as well.

The next rung down are local city or town tourist offices. These can operate under various names but most commonly are known as Pro Loco. They may deal with a town only, or in some cases the surrounding countryside.

Things you may want to ask for include: *pianta della città* (map); *elenco degli alberghi* (a list of hotels); and *informazioni sulle attrazioni turistiche* (information on the major sights). Many will help you find a hotel.

The bigger tourist offices will often respond to written and telephone requests – for example, information about hotels or apartments for rent.

The addresses and telephone numbers of offices are listed under the relevant towns and cities throughout this book.

TOURS

Options for organised travel to Tuscany abound. The **Italian State Tourist Office** (www.enit.it) can provide a list of tour operators and what each specialises in. Such tours can save you hassles but they rob you of independence and generally do not come cheap.

An established specialist in the UK is **Magic of Italy** (☎ 0870 888 0228; www.magictravelgroup.co.uk). It offers a wide range of Tuscan tours, city breaks and resort-based holidays.

In London, **Kirker Travel Ltd** (☎ 020-7231 3333; www.kirkerholidays.com; 3 New Concordia Wharf, Mill St, London SE1 2BB) specialises in short breaks.

DIRECTORY

The cost (higher in summer) usually includes accommodation, air fare, transfers and breakfast.

There are several companies offering organised walking tours in Tuscany – try the UK's **Explore Worldwide** (☎ 01252-760000; www.exploreworldwide.com) or **Headwater** (☎ 01606-720033; www.headwater.com). The latter also offers cycling tours around both Tuscany and Umbria.

Cultural tours are also very popular in the region. **Martin Randall** (☎ 020-8742 3355; www.martinrandall.com) offers several small-group holidays in Tuscany and Umbria, concentrating on art, music and architecture. **ACE Study Tours** (☎ 01223-835055; www.study -tours.org) not only provides specialist cultural tours around Tuscany and Umbria but each year the organisation makes charitable donations to all the regions that it covers.

Andante Travels (☎ 01722-713800; www.andante travels.co.uk) specialises in historical and archaeological tours. Their program includes an 8-day trip studying the archaeology of the hill towns of Umbria. The long established **Cox & Kings** (☎ 020-7872 5027; www.coxandkings.co.uk) offers escorted tours for art and music lovers. Destinations include Tuscany, Florence and Assisi. The **Italian Connection** (☎ 020-7520 0470; www.italian -connection.co.uk) offers tailor-made itineraries, useful for those who have limited time.

Naturetrek (☎ 01962-733051; www.naturetrek.co .uk) is ideal for travellers with an interest in natural history and crave a countryside environment. Try the eight-day tour of rural Umbria.

VISAS

The following information on visas was correct at the time of writing but restrictions and regulations can quickly change. Use the following as a guideline only and contact your embassy for the latest details. Travellers may also want to visit the Lonely Planet website, www.lonelyplanet.com, for useful links and up-to-date information.

Visas

Italy is one of 15 countries that have signed the Schengen Convention, an agreement whereby all EU member countries (except the UK and Ireland) plus Iceland and Norway have agreed to abolish checks at internal borders. The other EU countries are Austria, Belgium, Denmark, Finland, France, Germany, Greece, Luxembourg, the Netherlands, Portugal, Spain and Sweden. Legal residents of one Schengen country do not require a visa for another Schengen country. In addition, nationals of a number of other countries, including the UK, Canada, Ireland, Japan, New Zealand and Switzerland do not need visas for tourist visits of up to 90 days to any Schengen country.

Various other nationals not covered by the Schengen exemption can also spend up to 90 days in Italy without a visa. These include Australian, Israeli and US citizens. However all non-EU nationals entering Italy for any reason other than tourism (such as study or work) should contact an Italian consulate as they may need a specific visa. They should also insist on having their passport stamped on entry as, without a stamp, they could encounter problems when trying to obtain a *permesso di soggiorno* (see p335). If you are a citizen of a country not mentioned in this section, you should check with an Italian consulate as to whether you need a visa.

The standard tourist visa issued by Italian consulates is the Schengen visa, valid for up to 90 days. A Schengen visa issued by one Schengen country is generally valid for travel in all other Schengen countries. However individual Schengen countries may impose additional restrictions on certain nationalities. It is therefore worth checking visa regulations with the consulate of each Schengen country you plan to visit.

It's mandatory that you apply for a visa in your country of residence. You can apply for no more than two Schengen visas in any 12-month period and they are not renewable inside Italy.

STUDY VISAS

Non-EU citizens who want to study at a university or language school in Italy must have a study visa. These visas can be obtained from your nearest Italian embassy or consulate. You will normally need confirmation of your enrolment and payment of fees, as well as proof of adequate funds to be able to support yourself. The visa will then cover only the period of the enrolment. This type of visa is renewable within Italy but, again, only with confirmation of ongoing enrolment and proof that you are able to support yourself – bank statements are preferred.

Permits

EU citizens supposedly do not need any permits to live, work or start a business in Italy. They are, however, advised to register with a *questura*, if they take up residence – in accordance with an anti-Mafia law that aims at keeping a watch on everyone's whereabouts in the country. Failure to do so carries no consequences, although some landlords may be unwilling to rent out a flat to you if you cannot produce proof of registration. Those considering long-term residence will want to get a *permesso di soggiorno*, a necessary first step to acquiring a *carta d'identità*, or residence card (see below). While you're at it, you'll need a *codice fiscale* (tax-file number) if you wish to be paid for working in Italy.

WORK PERMITS

Non-EU citizens wishing to work in Italy will need to obtain a *permesso di lavoro* (work permit). If you intend to work for an Italian company and will be paid in euros, the company must organise the *permesso* and forward it to the Italian consulate in your country – only then will you be issued an appropriate visa.

If non-EU citizens intend to work for a non-Italian company or will be paid in foreign currency, or wish to go freelance, they must organise the visa and *permesso* in their country of residence through an Italian consulate. This process can take many months, so look into it early.

Some foreigners prefer simply to work 'black' in areas such as teaching English, bar work and seasonal jobs (see p336).

RESIDENCE PERMITS

Visitors are technically obliged to report to a *questura* if they plan to stay at the same address for more than one week (this does not apply to holiday-makers), to receive a *permesso di soggiorno* (residence permit). Tourists who are staying in hotels are not required to do this because hotelowners are required to register all guests with the police.

A *permesso di soggiorno* only becomes a necessity if you plan to study, work (legally) or live in Italy. Obtaining one is never a

---

COPIES

All important documents (passport data page and visa page, credit cards, travel insurance policy, air/bus/train tickets, driving licence etc) should be photocopied before you leave home. Leave one copy with someone at home and keep another with you, separate from the originals.

---

pleasant experience, although for EU citizens it is straightforward. Other nationals will find it involves enduring long queues, rude police officers and the frustration of arriving at the counter (after a two-hour wait) to find that you don't have all the necessary documents.

The exact requirements, such as documents and official stamps *(marche da bollo)*, vary from year to year. In general, you will need a valid passport, containing a visa stamp indicating your date of entry into Italy; a special visa issued in your own country if you are planning to study; four passport-style photographs; and proof of your ability to support yourself financially.

It is best to go to the *questura* to obtain precise information.

WOMEN

Tuscany is not a dangerous region for women, but women travelling alone will sometimes find themselves plagued by unwanted attention from men. This attention usually involves catcalls, hisses and whistles and, as such, is usually more annoying than threatening. In some cases the harassment may get more serious and we have had several readers report instances of men exposing themselves on public transport in Florence. Some travellers claim that the best way to handle these situations is to simply ignore the offender – others find it useful to point and laugh loudly, thus turning the embarrassment back onto the man. In all cases, if you feel threatened or at risk in any way, it is best to seek help.

As in many parts of Europe, lone women may at times also find it difficult to be left alone. It is not uncommon for Italian men to harass foreign women in the street, while drinking a coffee in a bar or trying to read a book in a park. Usually the best response is to just ignore them, but if that doesn't work, politely tell them that you are waiting for your *marito* (husband) or *fidanzato* (boyfriend) and, if necessary, walk away. Florence can be a pain in this way, especially in the bars. It can also be an issue in some of the coastal resorts and on Elba.

Avoid becoming aggressive as this almost always results in an unpleasant confrontation. If all else fails, approach the nearest member of the police or *carabinieri* (military police force).

Avoid walking alone on deserted and dark streets and look for centrally located hotels within easy walking distance of places where you can eat at night. Lonely Planet does not recommend hitchhiking, and women travelling alone should be particularly wary of doing so.

The *Handbook for Women Travellers*, by M and G Moss, is recommended reading.

WORK

It is illegal for non-EU citizens to work in Italy without a work permit, but trying to obtain one can be time consuming. EU citizens are allowed to work in Italy, but they still need to obtain a *permesso di soggiorno* from the main *questura* in the town where they have found work. See p335 for more information about these permits.

Babysitting and au pair work is possible if you organise it before you come to Italy.

A useful guide is *The Au Pair and Nanny's Guide to Working Abroad,* by S Griffith and S Legg.

The easiest source of work for foreigners is teaching English, but even with full qualifications a native English speaker might find it difficult to secure a permanent position. Most of the larger, more reputable schools will hire only people with a *permesso di lavoro*, but their attitude can become more flexible if demand for teachers is high and they come across someone with good qualifications. The more professional schools will require at least a TEFL (Teaching English as a Foreign Language) certificate. It is advisable to apply for work early in the year, in order to be considered for positions available in October (language-school years correspond roughly to the Italian school year: late September to the end of June).

Some people pick up private students by placing advertisements in shop windows and on university notice boards. Rates of pay vary according to experience. You can use other ads as a yardstick.

Some travellers are able to pick up kitchen and bar work in the more touristy restaurants, particularly in Florence.

Further reading resources include *Work Your Way Around the World*, by Susan Griffith and *Live and Work in Italy* by Victoria Pybus.

TRANSPORT

CONTENTS

> **WARNING**
>
> The information in this chapter is particularly vulnerable to change: prices for international travel are volatile, routes are introduced and cancelled, schedules change, special deals come and go, and rules and visa requirements are amended. You should check directly with the airline or a travel agent to make sure you understand how a fare (and ticket you may buy) works and be aware of the security requirements for international travel.
>
> The upshot of this is that you should get opinions, quotes and advice from as many airlines and travel agents as possible before you part with your hard-earned cash. The details given in this chapter should be regarded as pointers and are not a substitute for your own careful, up-to-date research.

GETTING THERE & AWAY

AIR
Airports & Airlines

Tuscany's main hub is Pisa's Galileo Galilei airport, which is where the bulk of European scheduled and charter flights for this area land. Intercontinental flights use Rome's Leonardo da Vinci (Fiumicino) airport, which is to the south of Tuscany. The small Amerigo Vespucci airport, just outside of Florence, does take some flights to other European countries. Both the Galileo Galilei and Amerigo Vespucci airports are used for domestic flights from other parts of Italy, as well as being used for international flights. The main airport in Umbria is Perugia's Sant'Egidio.

Note that, in response to the threat of terrorism, airport security is tighter than ever. Check with your airline how long you need to allow for check-in and what you can carry in hand luggage.

Rome Fiumicino (code FCO; www.adr.it)
Florence Amerigo Vespucci (code FLR; www.safnet.it)
Pisa Galileo Galilei (code PSA; www.pisa-airport.com)
Perugia Sant'Egidio (code PEG; www.airport.umbria.it)

Airlines flying into the region include:
Air Littoral (☎ 036 23 30 04; www.air-littoral.fr; airline code FU; hub Nice)

Alitalia (☎ 8488 6 56 42; www.alitalia.it; airline code AZ; hub Fiumicino, Rome)
bmi baby (☎ 02 7539 7253; www.bmibaby.com; airline code CWW; hub East Midlands)
British Airways (☎ 199 712 266; www.britishairways.com; airline code BA; hub Heathrow)
easyJet (☎ 848 88 77 66; www.easyjet.com; airline code U2; hub Luton)
Ryanair (☎ 899 712 266; www.ryanair.com; airline code FR; hub London Stansted)
Virgin Express (☎ 800 09 70 97; www.virgin-express.com; airline code TV; hub Brussels)

Tickets

Air travel is a competitive business and fares fluctuate wildly due to season, availability and current special offers. The secret to getting a good deal is to shop around and compare prices. Surfing the Internet is a good way to do your research. Most airline companies now have websites and there are an increasing number of online ticketing agencies that will compare the available fares for you and automatically generate the best options. Some of the better ones include www.travelocity.co.uk and www.deckchair.com. One of the pitfalls of online researching and booking is the limited amount of advice available – a super-fast fare generator is no substitute for a travel agent who knows all about special deals and can offer advice on everything from which airline has the most amount of legroom to which has the best facilities for children.

All applicable airport taxes are factored into the price of your ticket.

From Australia & New Zealand

Two agents that are well-known for offering cheap fares are **STA Travel** (☎ 1300 733 035; www.statravel.com.au) and **Flight Centre** (☎ 133 133; www.flightcentre.com.au). Both companies have offices throughout Australia.

Several travel offices specialise in discount air tickets and many agencies advertise cheap airfares in the travel sections of weekend newspapers.

For flights from Australia to Europe, there are a number of competing airlines and a wide variety of airfares. Most of the cheaper flights go via Southeast Asia, involving stopovers in Kuala Lumpur, Bangkok or Singapore. If a long stopover between connections is necessary, transit accommodation is sometimes included in the price of the ticket. If it's not included, it may be worth considering a more expensive ticket that does cover accommodation. Ask your agent for further details.

From New Zealand, round-the-world (RTW) tickets are generally good value as they can sometimes be cheaper than a normal return fare. Otherwise, you can fly from Auckland to pick up a connecting flight in Melbourne or Sydney.

Flight Centre (☎ 0800 24 35 44; www.flightcentre .co.nz) has a large central office in Auckland and many more branches across the country. **STA Travel** (☎ 09 366 6673; www.statravel.com.nz; 229 Queen St, Auckland) is also based in Auckland and has branches across New Zealand.

From Continental Europe

Air travel between the rest of Continental Europe and Italy is worth considering if you are pushed for time. Be flexible – the cheapest fares are often those that require you to fly late at night or early in the morning.

It's easy to fly to Tuscany or Umbria from France. Try **OTU Voyages** (☎ 08 25 00 40 27; www.otu.fr) for good student deals and cut-price travel. The company has offices

countrywide. **Air Littoral** (☎ 08 25 83 48 34; www.air-littoral.fr) operates flights between Nice and Florence and offers connections from other airports in France.

In Germany, **STA Travel** (☎ 01805 456 422; www.statravel.de) has branches across the country. There are also several reputable online agents: try www.lastminute.de and www.justtravel.de.

In the Netherlands, there are plenty of discount travel agents along Amsterdam's Rokin, but shop around to compare prices. One recommended travel agent, **Holland International** (☎ 070 361 4561), has branches in most cities. Online, try www.airfair.nl or visit www.budgettravel.com for a list of other agencies in the Netherlands.

In Belgium, it's worth trying **Connections** (☎ 02 55 00 100; www.connections.be) for student and youth travel. Alternatively, **Nouvelle Frontières** (☎ 02 547 44 22; www.nouvelles-frontieres.be) often has good deals available.

From the Rest of Italy

Travelling by plane is expensive within Italy and it generally makes much better sense to use the efficient and considerably cheaper train and bus services. In any case, only a few domestic airports offer flights to Florence. **Alitalia** (☎ 8488 6 56 41 from Italy; www.alitalia.it/en /home.asp) and **Meridiana** (☎ 199 11 13 33; www .meridiana.it) are the domestic airlines.

There are flights from Bari, Bergamo, Cagliari, Catania, Milan, Olbia, Palermo and Rome into Florence's Amerigo Vespucci Airport. You can get to Pisa from Alghero, Catania, Milan, Olbia, Palermo and Rome. Domestic flights can be booked through any travel agency or by contacting the airline direct.

It should be noted that very specific restrictions usually apply to special deals.

With Alitalia, you can fly to Florence or Pisa from pretty much anywhere in Italy if you are prepared to change flights. There are three or four daily flights to each airport from either Rome or Milan.

You may be able to find cheaper fares by buying internal flights at the same time as a flight into the country, or by booking while you are actually in Italy.

From the UK

Discount air travel is big business in London. Advertisements for many travel agencies appear in the travel pages of the weekend broadsheets, in *Time Out*, the *Evening Standard* and the free magazine *TNT*.

STA Travel (☎ 0870 160 0599; www.statravel.co.uk) has branches throughout the UK. It sells tickets to all travellers, but caters especially to young people and students.

Other recommended discount travel agents include **Trailfinders** (☎ 020-7937 1234; www.trailfinders.co.uk), **Bridge the World** (☎ 020-7734 7447; www.b-t-w.co.uk) and **Flightbookers** (☎ 0870 010 7000; www.ebookers.com).

No-frills airlines are continually increasing the number of routes available and there are now several options between the UK and Ireland and Italy. They generally serve minor airports and encourage you to book flights online. The best deals are usually to be had if you travel mid-week and book early.

Ryanair (☎ 0871 246 0000; www.ryanair.com) flies directly to Tuscany, with two flights daily to Pisa from London Stansted airport. With **bmi baby** (☎ 0870 264 2229; www.bmibaby.com) you can fly to Pisa from the East Midlands airport.

If you're happy to fly to Rome, Bologna or Milan and take the train or bus to Tuscany or Umbria from there, you can get good deals with other no-frills airlines such as **easyJet** (☎ 0870 600 0000; www.easyjet.com) and **Virgin Express** (☎ in the UK 020 7744 0004, in Italy 800 09 70 97; www.virgin-express.com). It should be noted that Ryanair also offers flights to Bologna, Rome and Milan and bmi baby flies direct to Milan.

The two principal full-service airlines linking the UK and Italy are **British Airways** (BA; ☎ 0845 773 3377; www.british-airways.com) and **Alitalia** (☎ 0870 544 82 59; www.alitalia.co.uk). Alitalia offers direct flights between London and Florence but to go to Pisa or Perugia you must fly via Rome or Milan. BA regularly flies direct to Pisa.

The **Charter Flight Centre** (☎ 020 7828 1090; www.charterflights.co.uk) also offers flights to Pisa, Perugia (via Rome) and Florence (via Rome).

Meridiana (☎ 020 7839 2222; www.meridiana.it) offers direct flights to Florence.

From the USA & Canada

The North Atlantic is the world's busiest long-haul air corridor and the flight options are bewildering. Flights from the USA to either Florence, Pisa or Perugia are possible with Alitalia and with other European airlines such as Lufthansa and Air France. Whichever you opt for, you will almost certainly have to change flights. You might also want to consider flying to Rome and taking the train from there. This will increase your flight options but be aware that often the difference in ticket prices is negligible.

Discount travel agencies in the USA are known as consolidators and good deals can be found in most big cities. Consolidators can be found through the *Yellow Pages* or the major daily newspapers. The *New York Times*, the *Los Angeles Times*, the *Chicago Tribune* and the *San Francisco Examiner* all produce weekly travel sections in which you will find a number of ads.

Two of the largest US student travel organisations have joined forces. Both **Council Travel** (☎ 1 800 2268 6245; www.counciltravel.com) and **STA Travel** (☎ 1 800 329 9537; www.statravel.com) have offices in most major cities.

Fares vary wildly depending on season, availability and a little luck. After March, prices begin to rise rapidly and availability declines.

Discount options from the USA include charter, stand-by and courier flights. Stand-by fares are often sold at 60% of the normal price for one-way tickets.

A courier flight from the USA to Italy can cost a third to two-thirds of the standard price. **Now Voyager** (☎ 212 431 1616; www.nowvoyagertravel.com) specialises in courier flights but you must pay an annual membership fee (around US$50) that entitles you to take as many courier flights as you like.

Also well worth considering are **Europe by Air** (☎ 1 888 387 2479; www.europebyair.com) coupons. You purchase the US$99 coupons before leaving North America and each coupon is valid for a one-way flight within the combined system of more than 30 participating regional airlines in Europe (exclusive of local taxes, which you will be charged when you make the flight). The coupons are valid for 120 days from the day you take your first flight. A few words of caution – using one of these coupons for a one-way flight won't always be better value than local alternatives, so check them out before committing yourself to any given flight. The same company also offers one-off airfares.

If you just can't find a particularly good deal, it's always worth considering a cheap trans-Atlantic hop to London to trawl through the bargains there.

Canadian discount air-ticket sellers are also known as consolidators and their fares tend to be higher than those available in the USA. Scan the budget travel agencies' ads in the *Toronto Star* and the *Vancouver Province*.

Travel CUTS (☎ 1 866 246 9762; www.travelcuts.com) is Canada's national student travel agency, with offices in all major cities. In Quebec it is known as Voyages Campus.

LAND

There are plenty of options to consider for reaching Tuscany and Umbria by train, bus or private vehicle. Bus is generally the cheapest, but services are usually less frequent and considerably less comfortable than the train.

Border Crossings

If you are travelling by bus, train or car to Italy, remember to check whether you require visas for any countries you intend to pass through.

The main points of entry to Italy by land are the Mont Blanc tunnel from France at Chamonix, which connects with the A5 for Turin and Milan; the Grand St Bernard tunnel from Switzerland, which also connects with the A5; and the Brenner Pass from Austria, which connects with the A22 to Bologna. Mountain passes in the Alps are often closed in winter and sometimes in autumn and spring, making the tunnels a less scenic but more reliable way to arrive in Italy (though there are safety concerns following the fires in the Mont Blanc and Gotthard tunnels). Make sure you have snow chains in winter.

Bus

BUS PASSES

The Eurolines Pass is a useful option for travellers touring Europe. It allows unlimited travel between over 30 European cities including Florence, Milan, Rome and Venice. Passes are valid for 15, 30 or 60 days and discounts are available for those under 26. For prices and restrictions see the Eurolines website.

A similar option is **Busabout** (☎ 020 7950 1661; www.busabout.com). This company offers passes of varying duration allowing travellers to use its hop-on hop-off bus network

in Western and Central Europe. For more information visit its website.

FROM CONTINENTAL EUROPE

Eurolines (www.eurolines.com), a consortium of European coach companies, operates international coach services across Europe. Details of offices, routes, fares and how to book can be found online.

FROM THE REST OF ITALY

Long-haul travel is generally more comfortably done by train, particularly if you're travelling around the north of Italy or coming from Rome and Naples. If you're travelling from the south, where train services are often non-existent or painfully slow, the bus is sometimes a sensible alternative.

Lazzi (☎ 055 36 30 41; www.lazzi.it) is responsible for long-haul bus services from other parts of Italy. **SITA** (☎ 800 37 37 60, 055 47 821; www.sita-on-line.it) also offers a handful of long-distance services, mostly to southern Italy.

In collaboration with SITA, Lazzi also operates a winter service called Alpi Bus, which runs extensive routes to the Alps. These buses depart from numerous cities and towns throughout Tuscany, Lazio, Umbria and Emilia-Romagna for most main resorts in the Alps. A brochure detailing the service is available from the Lazzi office.

The same company also operates the Freccia dell'Appennino (Apennine Arrow) service, with buses connecting Florence, Siena and Montecatini with destinations in Le Marche (such as Ascoli Piceno) and in Abruzzo (such as Chieto and Pescara). These services tend to stop in Perugia. For onward travel you may have to change bus.

See Lazzi's website for further details, or try calling ☎ 0577 28 32 03.

FROM THE UK

Eurolines (☎ 0870 514 32 19; www.nationalexpress.com) runs buses from London to Florence and Pisa. Avoid travelling during peak periods such as July, August and the second half of December, as fares increase and availability is limited. Discounts are available year round for seniors and travellers under 26. Buses leave from Victoria Coach Station.

Car & Motorcycle

From the UK, take your car across to France by ferry or via the Channel Tunnel car train,

Eurotunnel (☎ 0870 535 35 35; www.eurotunnel.com). The latter runs between terminals in Folkestone and Calais round the clock, with crossings lasting 35 minutes. You pay for the vehicle only and fares vary according to time of day and season.

Tuscany and Umbria are made for motorcycle touring – the winding, scenic roads are ideal to explore. Advantages include the fact that motorcyclists rarely have to book ahead for ferries and that you will be able to enter restricted traffic areas in Italian cities without any problems. Parking is also less of a headache for those on two wheels.

Roads are generally good throughout Italy and there is a great network of *autostrade* (motorways). The main north–south link, which skirts Florence, is the Autostrada del Sole, extending from Milan to Calabria (called the A1 from Milan to Naples and the A3 from Naples to Reggio di Calabria). The A11 heads west via Pistoia and Lucca towards Pisa and Livorno and meets the A12 to La Spezia and Genoa. As well as the A1, you can take the SS1 south from Livorno to Rome via Grosseto. Where there is a single carriageway it can be hairy, but progress on the parallel A12 extension continues.

Several back roads cross the Apennines from Emilia-Romagna in more picturesque style. One example is the SS302, or Via Faenza, from that town south to Borgo San Lorenzo in the Mugello. From there you are a fairly short drive from Florence. From Perugia (Umbria), the SS75b west along the north of Lago di Trasimeno puts you on the road to Siena, intersecting the A1 on the way.

Drivers usually travel at high speeds in the left-hand fast lane on the *autostrada*, so use that lane only to pass other cars. You have to pay a toll to use the *autostrada*, which generally can be paid by credit card (including Visa, MasterCard, American Express and Diners Club). Another way to pay is to buy a Viacard (available in €25, €50 and €75 denominations at toll booths and some service stations and tourist offices – check www.autostrade.it for details). You present it to the attendant as payment or insert it into the appropriate Viacard machine as you exit an *autostrada*. Left-over credit is not refundable on leaving Italy.

Travellers with time to spare could consider using the system of *strade statali* (state roads), which are sometimes multi-lane dual carriageways and are toll-free. They are represented on maps as 'S' or 'SS'. The *strade provinciali* (provincial roads) are sometimes little more than country lanes, but provide access to some of the more beautiful scenery and the many towns and villages. They are represented as 'SP' on maps.

An interesting website loaded with advice for people planning to drive in Europe is www.ideamerge.com/motoeuropa. If you want help with route planning, try out www.euroshell.com or www.rac.co.uk.

Proof of ownership of a private vehicle should always be carried (Vehicle Registration Document for UK registered cars) when driving through Europe. You should also display a sticker detailing the country of origin of your vehicle (for example GB if you have come from the UK).

For further information on driving in Italy, see p343.

Hitching

Hitching is never entirely safe in any country in the world, and we don't recommend it. Travellers who decide to hitch should understand that they are taking a small but potentially serious risk. People who do choose to hitch will be safer if they travel in pairs and let someone know where they are planning to go.

Train

FROM CONTINENTAL EUROPE

Florence is an important hub so it's easy to get to Tuscany and Umbria from numerous European destinations. The *Thomas Cook European Timetable* has an extensive listing of train schedules and is an invaluable resource for route planning. It is updated monthly and available from Thomas Cook offices and agents worldwide. Travellers should also consult their national train operator who will be able to provide information and advice on international train travel.

On overnight hauls you can book a *cuccetta* (couchette) for about €20 on most international trains. In 1st class there are four bunks per cabin and six in 2nd class.

It is always advisable, and sometimes compulsory, to book seats on international trains to and from Italy.

Some of the main international services include transport for private cars – an option worth examining to save wear and tear on your vehicle before it arrives in Italy.

FROM THE REST OF ITALY

Trenitalia (www.trenitalia.com) operates the entire Italian rail system. For information on trains visit the website or call ☎ 89 20 21 (in Italian) from anywhere in Italy. It is possible to get a timetable outside Italy as well. If you're in the UK, for instance, you can find it at **Italwings** (☎ 020 728 72 117;162/168 Regent St, London W1) for UK£9.

Main train timetables generally display *arrivi* (arrivals) on a white background and *partenze* (departures) on a yellow one. Imminent arrivals and departures also appear on electronic boards.

There are many types of train and many ticketing possibilities. Apart from the division between first and second class, you usually have to pay a supplement for travelling on a fast train. When enquiring about a route, check to see what type of train you are travelling on. Types to look out for include *regionali, inter-regionali, intercity* and *ETR*.

You can buy rail tickets for major destinations from most travel agents. If you choose to buy them at the station, there are automatic machines that accept cash.

When you buy a ticket you must stamp it in one of the yellow machines scattered about all stations (usually with a *convalida* sign on them). Failure to do so will be rewarded with an on-the-spot fine. This rule does not apply to tickets purchased outside Italy. If you buy a return ticket, you must stamp it each way (each end of the ticket). The ticket you buy is valid for two months until stamped. Once stamped it is valid for 24 hours if the journey distance (one-way) is greater than 200km, six hours if it is less. For a return ticket, the time is calculated separately for each one-way journey (that is, on a short return trip you get six hours from the time of stamping on the way out and the same on the way back).

Eurail (www.eurail.com), **InterRail** (www.inter-rail .co.uk), **Eurodomino** (www.eurodomino.it/eng) and the **Trenitalia Pass** (www.trenitalia.com) are valid on the national rail, all of which can be bought in Italy and abroad. They allow you unlimited rail travel for varying periods of time. The passes are only useful if you plan to travel extensively around Italy by train. Passes have their own validating

rules, which are generally written inside the pass cover.

People aged between 12 and 26 can acquire the Carta Verde and people aged 60 and over the Carta d'Argento. Both cost about €25, are valid for a year and entitle holders to 15% off ticket prices. Children aged between four and 12 years are automatically entitled to a 50% discount; those under four travel for free.

Special offers for families and group travel are also available. Check what reductions are available when booking your tickets.

FROM THE UK

Land travel between Britain and Continental Europe has been made possible by the Channel Tunnel. The **Eurostar** (☎ 0870 518 61 86; www.eurostar.com) passenger train service travels between London and Paris and London and Brussels. The **Eurotunnel** (☎ 0870 535 35 35; www.eurotunnel.com) vehicle service travels between Folkestone and Calais.

For information on international rail travel (including Eurostar services), contact **Rail Europe** (☎ 0870 584 8848; www.raileurope.co.uk).

SEA

Ferries connect Italy with countries all over the Mediterranean, but if you want to reach Tuscany directly by sea, the only options are the ferry crossings to Livorno from Sardinia and Corsica. See p173 for more details.

GETTING AROUND

AIR

There are no direct flights between Pisa, Florence and Perugia.

BICYCLE

If you plan to bring your own bike, check restrictions with the airline. It may have to be disassembled and packed for the journey.

Cycle touring across Tuscany and Umbria is becoming increasingly popular. UK-based cyclists planning to give it a try could contact the **Cyclists' Touring Club** (☎ 0870 873 00 60; www.ctc.org.uk; Cotterell House, 69 Meadrow, Godalming, Surrey GU7 3HS, UK). It supplies information to members on cycling conditions, itineraries and cheap insurance. Route and information sheets include: *Emilia-Romagna & Tuscany; Tuscany & Umbria; Circular Tour* *of Tuscany*; and *Day Rides from Sambuca*. Membership costs £28.50 per annum.

Once in Italy, it's possible to take your bike on many trains. Those marked on timetables with a bicycle symbol have a carriage set aside for the transport of bicycles. Otherwise you need to dismantle it and pack it. In all cases where you are allowed to take the bike, you will probably have to pay a supplement.

You can hire bicycles, including mountain bikes, from several outlets in Florence (p125) and other towns around the region (see regional chapters for details).

BOAT

Regular ferries connect Piombino with Elba. In summer, trips depart from Portoferraio on Elba for the island of Capraia, and from Porto Azzurro to the tiny island of Pianosa. From Livorno, ferries run to Capraia via the prison island of Gorgona. You can reach the islands of Giglio and Giannutri from Porto Santo Stefano. See the relevant chapters for more details. Travellers can also check www.traghetti.com for information on ferry companies, schedules, fares and availability.

BUS

Unless you have your own transport, bus is often the best way to get around Tuscany and Umbria. Where there is a train, you should probably take it, but there are some exceptions. One of them is the Florence–Siena run, which is much quicker and more convenient by rapid SITA bus.

Lazzi has buses from Florence to parts of Tuscany, mostly in the northwest, including Pisa, Lucca and Pistoia. The CAP and Copit companies serve towns in the northwest. In Umbria look out for the company ACT that serves southern Umbria and ASP which covers Perugia, Assisi and the north.

In general, the separate bus companies operate services in each province, radiating from the provincial capital. Frequently services overlap into neighbouring provinces.

Services can be frequent on weekdays, but between smaller towns often reduce to a few or even none on Sundays and public holidays. If you are depending on buses to get around, always keep this in mind, as it is easy to get stuck in smaller places at the weekend. The tourist office can provide schedules.

You should buy your ticket from the kiosk located at the bus stop or terminal before you board. All tickets should be validated in the machine inside the bus. Failure to do so may result in a fine.

CAR & MOTORCYCLE
Bringing Your Own Vehicle

Touring Tuscany and Umbria with your own wheels gives you maximum flexibility but make sure you check all the restrictions and regulations before you leave. Your motoring organisation can provide you with a list of requirements.

The main highways are good but busy. The traffic around Florence, on the *autostrade* (four- to six-lane motorways) and the superstrade (up to four-lane motorways) between Florence and Siena can be intense.

The most congested areas are in and around the towns of Florence, Prato, Pistoia, Lucca, Pisa and Viareggio and, although slightly less so, in Perugia and Spoleto. Road rules are intermittently obeyed and driving in Tuscany and Umbria can be quite overwhelming – don't be disheartened if it takes a while to feel confident.

When you get away from the main centres, the smaller back roads offer scenic drives, but be prepared to take your time. Progress around the winding hill country of Tuscany and Umbria can be slow. Signposts are generally easily understood and informative but locals will happily give you directions.

Parking can be a nightmare in urban areas and is often restricted. When visiting historical centres, try and park in designated parking areas outside the boundaries and walk the rest of the way. Wherever you park, never leave valuable items in your vehicle.

Driving Licence

All EU member states' driving licences are fully recognised throughout the union regardless of your stay. Those with a non-EU licence should obtain an International Driving Permit (IDP) to accompany their national licence. You can get an IDP from your national automobile association. UK citizens who still hold an old UK licence should contact the **Driver and Vehicle Licensing Agency** (☎ 0870 240 00 10) to obtain the updated version.

Insurance

Third-party motor insurance is a minimum requirement in Italy. The Green Card is an

TRANSPORT

Road Distances (km)

	Arezzo	Assisi	Carrara	Cortona	Florence	Livorno	Lucca	Orbetello	Orvieto	Perugia	Pisa	Pistoia	Prato	Siena	Spoleto	Viareggio	Volterra
Arezzo	---																
Assisi	96	---															
Carrara	198	317	---														
Cortona	28	72	237	---													
Florence	80	172	122	109	---												
Livorno	195	266	72	224	115	---											
Lucca	155	243	52	184	74	45	---										
Orbetello	175	222	247	215	180	175	216	---									
Orvieto	104	87	282	94	156	264	230	118	---								
Perugia	78	38	256	30	153	268	227	204	86	---							
Pisa	175	263	57	203	95	20	21	190	246	245	---						
Pistoia	115	208	92	143	35	85	45	215	204	190	65	---					
Prato	99	189	109	128	19	95	55	199	188	170	84	20	---				
Siena	65	124	153	99	70	130	140	116	134	109	110	105	81	---			
Spoleto	133	49	355	108	249	336	307	197	80	78	323	284	248	187	---		
Viareggio	180	266	30	206	97	41	25	195	250	247	21	69	89	123	325	---	
Volterra	111	175	135	151	75	69	74	168	186	161	65	108	88	52	239	86	---

internationally recognised proof of insurance obtainable from your insurer, and is mandatory. Ask your insurer for a European Accident Statement form, which can simplify matters in the event of an accident. Never sign statements you can't understand – insist on a translation and sign only if it's acceptable.

A European breakdown assistance policy is advisable. In the UK try the **AA** (☎ 0870 550 06 00) Five Star Service or the **RAC** (☎ 0800 55 00 55) Eurocover Motoring Assistance. Holders of these policies will usually be provided with an emergency assistance number to use while travelling. Alternatively, assistance can be obtained through the Automobile Club Italia (ACI) by dialling ☎ 116.

Contact the automobile association in your own country for more information.

Purchase

Visitors are unable to buy a car to use (and then sell) while staying in Tuscany and Umbria. In accordance with Italian regulations all vehicles must be registered and licensed. This cannot be done unless residency is established.

Rental

There's a confusing variety of special deals and conditions attached to car rental but with a bit of careful planning you can make sure you get the best deal.

Multinational agencies – Hertz, Avis, Budget and Europcar – will provide a reliable service and good standard of vehicle. However, if you walk into an office and ask for a car on the spot, you will always pay high rates. National and local firms can sometimes undercut the multinationals, but be sure to examine the rental agreement carefully.

Planning ahead and pre-booking a car through a multinational agency before leaving home will enable you to clinch a cheaper rate. If you don't know exactly when you will want to rent, you could call back home from Italy and reserve through an agency there. This way you get the benefits of booking from home. Fly/drive packages are also worth looking into – ask your travel agency for information or contact one of the major rental agencies.

Make sure you understand what is included in the price (unlimited kilometres, tax, insurance, collision damage waiver and so on) and what your liabilities are. Insurance can be a thorny issue but it is important that you are adequately covered for every eventuality.

The minimum rental age in Italy is 21.

Keep all the documents relating to your rental agreement as you may be asked to produce them by the authorities.

Holiday Autos (☎ 0870 400 44 47; www.holidayautos .co.uk) often has good rates for Italy; remember to book ahead. There's also a **French branch** (☎ 01 45 15 38 86; www.holidayautos.fr) and **German branch** (☎ 01805 17 91 91; www.holidayautos.de).

All the big car rental companies have outlets in the main cities and at the airports. The Internet may cough up cheaper deals so if you have time, do a bit of surfing. If you are looking to rent a motorbike, try **Alinari** (☎ 055 28 05 00) in Florence or **Bruno Bellini** (☎ 0577 94 02 01) in San Gimignano.

If you decide to rent a motorhome, try **Caravan Mec** (☎ 055 31 19 28; www.caravanmec.it). Based in Florence it is one of Italy's few caravan rental specialists.

Road Rules

European road rules apply: vehicles drive on the right; drinking and driving is not tolerated; and the blood alcohol limit is 0.05% (50mg). All passengers must wear seatbelts wherever fitted. Children under 12 must travel in the back seat and those under four must use child seats. Mobile phones may only be used with a hands-free kit or speakerphone. It is compulsory for motorcyclists and their passengers to wear crash helmets.

On three-lane roads, the middle lane is reserved for overtaking. At crossroads, give way to traffic from the right.

In built-up areas the speed limit is usually 50km/h, rising to 90km/h on secondary roads, 110km/h (caravans 80km/h) on main roads and up to 130km/h (caravans 100km/h) on *autostrade*. In some sections of three-lane roads the limit is 150km/h.

All vehicles must carry a warning triangle, spare bulbs and headlamp beam-converters.

LOCAL TRANSPORT

Most of the towns and cities have a reasonable bus service but you'll probably find that amenities and places of interest are usually

---

ROAD SIGNS

You can save yourself some grief in Tuscany and Umbria by learning what some of the many road signs mean:

- *entrata* – entrance (for example, onto an *autostrada*)
- *incrocio* – intersection/crossroads
- *lavori in corso* – roadworks ahead
- *parcheggio* – car park
- *passaggio a livello* – level crossing
- *rallentare* – slow down
- *senso unico* – one-way street
- *senso vietato* – no entry
- *sosta autorizzata* – parking permitted (during times displayed)
- *sosta vietata* – no stopping/parking
- *svolta* – bend
- *tutte le direzioni* – all directions (useful when looking for town exit)
- *uscita* – exit (for example, from an *autostrada*)

---

within walking distance. Bus tickets should be bought from newsagents, tobacconists or kiosks before boarding and validated in the machine once on board.

Buses and trains connect Pisa's Galileo Galilei airport with Pisa and Florence, while buses link Amerigo Vespucci airport with central Florence. An infrequent bus service connects Sant'Egidio to Perugia's centre.

Taxis are widely available. Travellers are advised to use only the official taxis, which are easily identifiable.

TRAIN

The regional train network is extensive and you can get around most towns and cities quite easily. Be aware that trains on the minor routes, known as *regionali*, can be limited and slow. For smaller towns and villages you may need to make a bus connection.

Note that all tickets must be validated before you board your train. Simply punch them in the yellow machines installed at the entrance to all train platforms. If you don't validate them, you risk a large fine. For more information on train travel, see p341.

Health

CONTENTS

BEFORE YOU GO

While Tuscany and Umbria have excellent health care, prevention is the key to staying healthy while abroad. A little planning before departure, particularly for pre-existing illnesses, will save trouble later. Bring medications in their original, clearly labelled, containers. A signed and dated letter from your physician describing your medical conditions and medications, including generic names, is also a good idea. If carrying syringes or needles, be sure to have a physician's letter documenting their medical necessity. If you are embarking on a long trip, make sure your teeth are OK (dental treatment is particularly expensive in Italy) and take your optical prescription with you.

INSURANCE

If you're an EU citizen, an E111 form, available from health centres (and post offices in the UK), covers you for most medical care but not emergency repatriation home or non-emergencies. Citizens from other countries should find out if there is a reciprocal arrangement for free medical care between their country and Italy. If you do need health insurance, make sure you get a policy that covers you for the worst possible

scenario, such as an accident requiring an emergency flight home. Find out in advance if your insurance plan will make payments directly to providers or reimburse you later for overseas health expenditures.

RECOMMENDED VACCINATIONS

No jabs are required to travel to Italy. The World Health Organization (WHO), however, recommends that all travellers should be covered for diphtheria, tetanus, measles, mumps, rubella and polio, as well as hepatitis B.

ONLINE RESOURCES

The WHO's publication *International Travel and Health* is revised annually and is available online at www.who.int/ith/. Other useful websites include www.mdtravelhealth.com (travel health recommendations for every country; updated daily), www.fitfortravel.scot.nhs.uk (general travel advice), www.ageconcern.org.uk (advice on travel for the elderly) and www.mariestopes.org.uk (information on women's health and contraception).

IN TRANSIT

DEEP VEIN THROMBOSIS (DVT)

Blood clots may form in the legs during plane flights, chiefly because of prolonged immobility; the longer the flight, the greater the risk. The chief symptom of DVT is swelling or pain of the foot, ankle, or calf, usually but not always on just one side. When a blood clot travels to the lungs, it may cause chest pain and breathing difficulties. Travellers with any of these symptoms should immediately seek medical attention. To prevent the development of DVT on long flights you should walk about the cabin, contract the leg muscles while sitting, drink plenty of fluids and avoid alcohol and tobacco.

JET LAG

To avoid jet lag try drinking plenty of nonalcoholic fluids and eating light meals. Upon arrival, get exposure to natural sunlight and readjust your schedule (for meals, sleep, etc) as soon as possible.

IN TUSCANY & UMBRIA

AVAILABILITY & COST OF HEALTH CARE

If you need an ambulance anywhere in Italy call ☎ 118. For emergency treatment, go straight to the *pronto soccorso* (casualty) section of a public hospital, where you can also get emergency dental treatment.

Excellent healthcare is readily available throughout Italy but standards can vary. Pharmacists can give valuable advice and sell over-the-counter medication for minor illnesses. They can also advise when more specialised help is required and point you in the right direction. In major cities you are likely to find English-speaking doctors or a translator service available.

TRAVELLERS' DIARRHOEA

If you develop diarrhoea, be sure to drink plenty of fluids, preferably in the form of an oral rehydration solution such as Dioralyte. If diarrhoea is bloody, persists for more than 72 hours or is accompanied by fever, shaking, chills or severe abdominal pain you should seek medical attention.

ENVIRONMENTAL HAZARDS
Heatstroke

Heatstroke occurs following excessive fluid loss with inadequate replacement of fluids and salt. Symptoms include headache, dizziness and tiredness. Dehydration is already happening by the time you feel thirsty – aim to drink sufficient water to produce pale, diluted urine. To treat heatstroke drink water and/or fruit juice, and cool the body with cold water and fans.

Hypothermia

Hypothermia occurs when the body loses heat faster than it can produce it. As ever, proper preparation will reduce the risks of getting it. Even on a hot day in the mountains, the weather can change rapidly, so carry waterproof garments, wear warm layers and a hat, and inform others of your route. Hypothermia starts with shivering, loss of judgment and clumsiness. Unless re-warming occurs, the sufferer deteriorates into apathy, confusion and coma. Prevent

further heat loss by seeking shelter, warm dry clothing, hot sweet drinks and shared body warmth.

Bites, Stings & Insect-Borne Diseases

Tuscan beaches are occasionally inundated with jellyfish. Their stings are painful but not dangerous. Dousing in vinegar will deactivate any stingers that have not fired. Calamine lotion, antihistamines and analgesics may reduce the reaction and relieve pain.

Italy's only dangerous snake, the viper, is found throughout Tuscany and Umbria. To minimise the possibilities of being bitten, always wear boots, socks and long trousers when walking through undergrowth where snakes may be present. Don't put your hands into holes and crevices, and be careful when collecting firewood. Viper bites do not cause instantaneous death and an antivenin is widely available in pharmacies. Keep the victim calm and still, wrap the bitten limb tightly, as you would for a sprained ankle, and attach a splint to immobilise it. Seek medical help, if possible with the dead snake for identification. Don't attempt to catch the snake if there is a possibility of being bitten again. Tourniquets and sucking out the poison are now comprehensively discredited.

Always check all over your body if you have been walking through a potentially tick-infested area as ticks can cause skin infections and other more serious diseases such as Lyme disease and tick-borne encephalitis. If a tick is found attached, press down around the tick's head with tweezers, grab the head and gently pull upwards. Avoid pulling the rear of the body as this may squeeze the tick's gut contents through the attached mouth parts into the skin, increasing the risk of infection and disease. Lyme disease begins with the spreading of a rash at the site of the bite, accompanied by fever, headache, extreme fatigue, aching joints and muscles and severe neck stiffness. If untreated, symptoms usually disappear but disorders of the nervous system, heart and joints can develop later. Treatment works best early in the illness – medical help should be sought. Symptoms of tick-borne encephalitis include blotches around the bite, which is sometimes pale in the middle, and headaches, stiffness and other flu-like symptoms (as well as extreme tiredness) appearing a week or two after the bite. Again, medical help must be sought.

Leishmaniasis is a group of parasitic diseases transmitted by sandflies and found in coastal parts of Tuscany. Cutaneous leishmaniasis affects the skin tissue and causes ulceration and disfigurement; visceral leishmaniasis affects the internal organs. Avoiding sandfly bites by covering up and using repellent is the best precaution against this disease.

TRAVELLING WITH CHILDREN

Make sure children are up to date with routine vaccinations and discuss possible travel vaccines well before departure as some vaccines are not suitable for children under a year old. Lonely Planet's *Travel with Children* includes travel health advice for younger children.

WOMEN'S HEALTH

Emotional stress, exhaustion and travelling through different time zones can all contribute to an upset in the menstrual pattern.

If using oral contraceptives, remember some antibiotics, diarrhoea and vomiting can stop the pill from working. Time zones, gastrointestinal upsets and antibiotics do not affect injectable contraception.

Travelling during pregnancy is usually possible but always consult your doctor before planning your trip. The most risky times for travel are during the first 12 weeks of pregnancy and after 30 weeks.

SEXUAL HEALTH

Condoms are readily available but emergency contraception is not so take the necessary precautions.

HEALTH

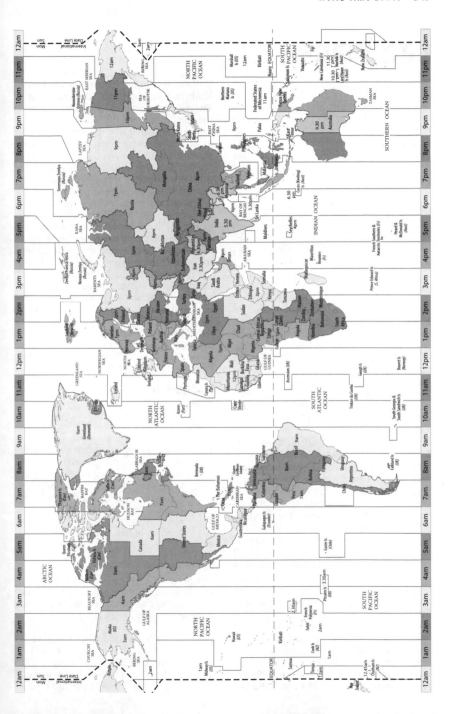

Language

CONTENTS

Italian is a Romance language related to French, Spanish, Portuguese and Romanian. The Romance languages belong to the Indo-European group of languages, which includes English. Indeed, as English and Italian share common roots in Latin, you will recognise many Italian words.

Modern literary Italian began to develop in the 13th and 14th centuries, predominantly through the works of Dante, Petrarch and Boccaccio, who wrote chiefly in the Florentine dialect. The language drew on its Latin heritage and many dialects to develop into the standard Italian of today. Although many dialects are spoken in everyday conversation, standard Italian is the national language of schools, media and literature, and is understood throughout the country.

While standard Italian was essentially born out of the Florentine dialect, anyone who has learned Italian sufficiently well will find many Florentines surprisingly hard to understand, at least at first. Whether or not they have their own localised non-standard vocabulary you could argue about at length, but no-one can deny the peculiarity of the local accent. Here, and in other parts of Tuscany, you are bound to hear the hard 'c' pronounced as a heavily aspirated 'h'. *Voglio una cannuccia per la Coca Cola* (I want a straw for my Coca Cola) in Florence sounds more like *voglio una hannuccia per*

la Hoha Hola! Over the regional border in Umbria, you'll be spared the anomalies of Tuscan pronunciation, and understanding the local accent should be a lot easier.

If you've managed to gain more than the most fundamental grasp of the language you'll need to be aware that many older Italians still expect to be addressed by the third person polite, that is, *lei* instead of *tu*. Also, it is not considered polite to use the greeting *ciao* when addressing strangers, unless they use it first; it's better to say *buon giorno* (or *buona sera*, as the case may be) and *arrivederci* (or the more polite form, *arrivederla*). We've used the polite address for most of the phrases in this guide. Use of the informal address is indicated by (inf). Italian also has both masculine and feminine forms (in the singular they often end in 'o' and 'a' respectively). Where both forms are given in this guide, they are separated by a slash, with the masculine form first.

If you'd like a more comprehensive guide to the language, pick up a copy of Lonely Planet's *Italian phrasebook*.

PRONUNCIATION
Vowels
Vowels are generally more clipped than in English:

a	as in 'art', eg *caro* (dear); sometimes short, eg *amico/a* (friend)
e	short, as in 'let', eg *mettere* (to put); long, as in 'there', eg *mela* (apple)
i	short, as in 'it', eg *inizio* (start); long, as in 'marine', eg *vino* (wine)
o	short, as in 'dot', eg *donna* (woman); long, as in 'port', eg *ora* (hour)
u	as the 'oo' in 'book', eg *puro* (pure)

Consonants
The pronunciation of many Italian consonants is similar to that of their English counterparts. Pronunciation of some consonants depends on certain rules:

c	as the 'k' in 'kit' before **a**, **o** and **u**; as the 'ch' in 'choose' before **e** and **i**
ch	as the 'k' in 'kit'
g	as the 'g' in 'get' before **a**, **o**, **u** and **h**; as the 'j' in 'jet' before **e** and **i**

gli	as the 'lli' in 'million'	
gn	as the 'ny' in 'canyon'	
h	always silent	
r	a rolled 'rr' sound	
sc	as the 'sh' in 'sheep' before **e** and **i**; as 'sk' before **a**, **o**, **u** and **h**	
z	as the 'ts' in 'lights', except at the beginning of a word, when it's as the 'ds' in 'suds'	

Note that when **ci**, **gi** and **sci** are followed by **a**, **o** or **u**, the 'i' is not pronounced unless the accent falls on the 'i'. Thus the name 'Giovanni' is pronounced joh-*vahn*-nee.

A double consonant is pronounced as a longer, more forceful sound than a single consonant.

Word Stress

Stress is indicated in our pronunciation guide by italics. Word stress generally falls on the second-last syllable, as in spa-*ghet*-ti, but when a word has an accent, the stress falls on that syllable, as in cit-*tà* (city).

ACCOMMODATION

I'm looking for a ...	Cerco ...	*cher*·ko ...
guesthouse	*una pensione*	oo·na pen·*syo*·ne
hotel	*un albergo*	oon al·*ber*·go
youth hostel	*un ostello per la gioventù*	oon os·*te*·lo per la jo·ven·*too*

Where is a cheap hotel?
Dov'è un albergo a buon prezzo? do·*ve* oon al·*ber*·go a bwon *pre*·tso

What is the address?
Qual'è l'indirizzo? kwa·*le* leen·dee·*ree*·tso

Could you write the address, please?
Può scrivere l'indirizzo, per favore? pwo *skree*·ve·re leen·dee·*ree*·tso per fa·*vo*·re

Do you have any rooms available?
Avete camere libere? a·*ve*·te *ka*·me·re *lee*·be·re

I'd like (a) ...	Vorrei ...	vo·*ray* ...
bed	*un letto*	oon *le*·to
single room	*una camera singola*	oo·na *ka*·me·ra *seen*·go·la
double room	*una camera matrimoniale*	oo·na *ka*·me·ra ma·tree·mo·*nya*·le
room with two beds	*una camera doppia*	oo·na *ka*·me·ra *do*·pya
room with a bathroom	*una camera con bagno*	oo·na *ka*·me·ra kon *ba*·nyo

MAKING A RESERVATION
(for inclusion in letters, faxes and emails)

To ...	*A ...*
From ...	*Da ...*
Date	*Data*
I'd like to book ...	*Vorrei prenotare ...* (see the list on this page for bed/room options)
in the name of ...	*nel nome di ...*
for the night/s of ...	*per la/le notte/i di ...*
credit card ...	*carta di credito ...*
number	*numero*
expiry date	*data di scadenza*
Please confirm availability and price.	*Vi prego di confirmare disponibilità e prezzo.*

to share a dorm	*un letto in dormitorio*	oon *le*·to een dor·mee·*to*·ryo

How much is it ...?	*Quanto costa ...?*	kwan·to *ko*·sta ...
per night	*per la notte*	per la *no*·te
per person	*per persona*	per per·*so*·na

May I see it?
Posso vederla? po·so ve·*der*·la

Where is the bathroom?
Dov'è il bagno? do·*ve* eel *ba*·nyo

I'm/We're leaving today.
Parto/Partiamo oggi. par·to/par·*tya*·mo o·jee

CONVERSATION & ESSENTIALS

Hello.	*Buon giorno.*	bwon *jor*·no
	Ciao. (inf)	chow
Goodbye.	*Arrivederci.*	a·ree·ve·*der*·chee
	Ciao. (inf)	chow
Yes.	*Sì.*	see
No.	*No.*	no
Please.	*Per favore/*	per fa·*vo*·re
	Per piacere.	per pya·*chay*·re
Thank you.	*Grazie.*	*gra*·tsye
That's fine/ You're welcome.	*Prego.*	*pre*·go
Excuse me.	*Mi scusi.*	mee *skoo*·zee
Sorry (forgive me).	*Mi scusi/ Mi perdoni.*	mee *skoo*·zee/ mee per·*do*·nee

What's your name?
Come si chiama?	ko·me see *kya*·ma
Come ti chiami? (inf)	ko·me tee *kya*·mee

My name is ...
Mi chiamo ... mee *kya*·mo ...
Where are you from?
Da dove viene? da *do*·ve vye·ne
Di dove sei? (inf) dee *do*·ve se·ee
I'm from ...
Vengo da ... *ven*·go da ...
I (don't) like ...
(Non) Mi piace ... (non) mee *pya*·che ...
Just a minute.
Un momento. oon mo·*men*·to

DIRECTIONS
Where is ...?
Dov'è ...? do·*ve* ...
Go straight ahead.
Si va sempre diritto. see va *sem*·pre dee·*ree*·to
Vai sempre diritto. (inf) va·ee *sem*·pre dee·*ree*·to
Turn left.
Giri a sinistra. *jee*·ree a see·*nee*·stra
Turn right.
Giri a destra. *jee*·ree a *de*·stra
at the next corner
al prossimo angolo al *pro*·see·mo *an*·go·lo
at the traffic lights
al semaforo al se·*ma*·fo·ro

SIGNS
Ingresso/Entrata	Entrance
Uscita	Exit
Informazione	Information
Aperto	Open
Chiuso	Closed
Proibito/Vietato	Prohibited
Camere Libere	Rooms Available
Completo	Full/No Vacancies
Polizia/Carabinieri	Police
Questura	Police Station
Gabinetti/Bagni	Toilets
Uomini	Men
Donne	Women

behind *dietro* *dye*·tro
in front of *davanti* da·*van*·tee
far (from) *lontano (da)* lon·*ta*·no (da)
near (to) *vicino (di)* vee·*chee*·no (dee)
opposite *di fronte a* dee *fron*·te a
beach *la spiaggia* la *spya*·ja
bridge *il ponte* eel *pon*·te
castle *il castello* eel kas·*te*·lo
cathedral *il duomo* eel *dwo*·mo
island *l'isola* *lee*·so·la
(main) square *la piazza (principale)* la *pya*·tsa (preen·chee·*pa*·le)

market *il mercato* eel mer·*ka*·to
old city *il centro storico* eel *chen*·tro *sto*·ree·ko
palace *il palazzo* eel pa·*la*·tso
ruins *le rovine* le ro·*vee*·ne
sea *il mare* eel *ma*·re
tower *la torre* la *to*·re

EMERGENCIES
Help!
Aiuto! a·*yoo*·to
There's been an accident!
C'è stato un incidente! che *sta*·to oon een·chee·*den*·te
I'm lost.
Mi sono perso/a. mee *so*·no *per*·so/a
Go away!
Lasciami in pace! *la*·sha·mi een *pa*·che
Vai via! (inf) va·ee *vee*·a

Call ...!
Chiami ...! kee·*ya*·mee ...
Chiama ...! (inf) kee·*ya*·ma ...
a doctor *un dottore/ un medico* oon do·*to*·re/ oon *me*·dee·ko
the police *la polizia* la po·lee·*tsee*·ya

HEALTH
I'm ill. *Mi sento male.* mee *sen*·to *ma*·le
It hurts here. *Mi fa male qui.* mee fa *ma*·le *kwee*

I'm ... *Sono ...* *so*·no ...
asthmatic *asmatico/a* az·*ma*·tee·ko/a
diabetic *diabetico/a* dee·a·*be*·tee·ko/a
epileptic *epilettico/a* e·pee·*le*·tee·ko/a

I'm allergic ... *Sono allergico/a ...* *so*·no a·*ler*·jee·ko/a ...
to antibiotics *agli antibiotici* a·lyee *an*·tee·bee·o·tee·chee
to aspirin *all'aspirina* a·*la*·spe·ree·na
to penicillin *alla penicillina* a·la pe·nee·see·*lee*·na
to nuts *ai noci* a·ee *no*·chee

antiseptic *antisettico* an·tee·*se*·tee·ko
aspirin *aspirina* as·pee·*ree*·na
condoms *preservativi* pre·zer·va·*tee*·vee
contraceptive *contraccetivo* kon·tra·che·*tee*·vo
diarrhoea *diarrea* dee·a·*re*·a
medicine *medicina* me·dee·*chee*·na
sunblock cream *crema solare* *kre*·ma so·*la*·re
tampons *tamponi* tam·*po*·nee

LANGUAGE DIFFICULTIES

Do you speak English?
Parla inglese?   par·la een-*gle*·ze
Does anyone here speak English?
C'è qualcuno che   che kwal-*koo*·no ke
parla inglese?   par·la een-*gle*·ze
How do you say ... in Italian?
Come si dice ...   ko·me see *dee*·che ...
in italiano?   een ee·ta-*lya*·no
What does ... mean?
Che vuol dire ...?   ke vwol *dee*·re ...
I understand.
Capisco.   ka·*pee*·sko
I don't understand.
Non capisco.   non ka·*pee*·sko
Please write it down.
Può scriverlo, per   pwo *skree*·ver·lo per
favore?   fa·*vo*·re
Can you show me (on the map)?
Può mostrarmelo   pwo mos·*trar*·me·lo
(sulla pianta)?   (soo·la *pyan*·ta)

NUMBERS

0	*zero*	*dze*·ro
1	*uno*	*oo*·no
2	*due*	*doo*·e
3	*tre*	tre
4	*quattro*	*kwa*·tro
5	*cinque*	*cheen*·kwe
6	*sei*	say
7	*sette*	*se*·te
8	*otto*	*o*·to
9	*nove*	*no*·ve
10	*dieci*	*dye*·chee
11	*undici*	oon-*dee*·chee
12	*dodici*	do-*dee*·chee
13	*tredici*	tre-*dee*·chee
14	*quattordici*	kwa-*tor*·dee·chee
15	*quindici*	*kween*·dee·chee
16	*sedici*	se-*dee*·chee
17	*diciassette*	dee·cha-*se*·te
18	*diciotto*	dee-*cho*·to
19	*diciannove*	dee·cha-*no*·ve
20	*venti*	*ven*·tee
21	*ventuno*	ven-*too*·no
22	*ventidue*	ven·tee-*doo*·e
30	*trenta*	*tren*·ta
40	*quaranta*	kwa-*ran*·ta
50	*cinquanta*	cheen-*kwan*·ta
60	*sessanta*	se-*san*·ta
70	*settanta*	se-*tan*·ta
80	*ottanta*	o-*tan*·ta
90	*novanta*	no-*van*·ta
100	*cento*	*chen*·to
1000	*mille*	*mee*·le

PAPERWORK

name	*nome*	*no*·me
nationality	*nazionalità*	na·tsyo·na·lee-*ta*
date of birth	*data di*	*da*·ta dee
	nascita	na-*shee*·ta
place of birth	*luogo di*	*lwo*·go dee
	nascita	na-*shee*·ta
sex (gender)	*sesso*	*se*·so
passport	*passaporto*	pa·sa·*por*·to
visa	*visto*	*vee*·sto

QUESTION WORDS

Who?	*Chi?*	kee
What?	*Che?*	ke
When?	*Quando?*	*kwan*·do
Where?	*Dove?*	*do*·ve
How?	*Come?*	*ko*·me

SHOPPING & SERVICES

I'd like to buy ...
Vorrei comprare ...   vo·*ray* kom·*pra*·re ...
How much is it?
Quanto costa?   *kwan*·to *ko*·sta
I don't like it.
Non mi piace.   non mee *pya*·che
May I look at it?
Posso dare   *po*·so *da*·re
un'occhiata?   oo·no·*kya*·ta
I'm just looking.
Sto solo guardando.   sto *so*·lo gwar-*dan*·do
It's cheap.
Non è caro/cara.   non e *ka*·ro/*ka*·ra
It's too expensive.
È troppo caro/a.   e *tro*·po *ka*·ro/*ka*·ra
I'll take it.
Lo/La compro.   lo/la *kom*·pro

Do you accept credit cards?	*Accettate carte di credito?*	a·che-*ta*·te *kar*·te dee *kre*·dee·to
I want to change ...	*Voglio cambiare ...*	*vo*·lyo kam-*bya*·re ...
money	*del denaro*	del de-*na*·ro
travellers cheques	*assegni dee viaggio*	a·*se*·nyee dee vee·*a*·jo
more	*più*	pyoo
less	*meno*	*me*·no
smaller	*più piccolo/a*	pyoo *pee*·ko·lo/la
bigger	*più grande*	pyoo *gran*·de
I'm looking for ...	*Cerco ...*	*cher*·ko ...
a bank	*un banco*	oon *ban*·ko
the church	*la chiesa*	la *kye*·za

the city centre	*il centro*	eel *chen*·tro
the ... embassy	*l'ambasciata di ...*	lam·ba·*sha*·ta dee ...
my hotel	*il mio albergo*	eel *mee*·o al·*ber*·go
the market	*il mercato*	eel mer·*ka*·to
the museum	*il museo*	eel moo·*ze*·o
the post office	*la posta*	la *po*·sta
a public toilet	*un gabinetto*	oon ga·bee·*ne*·to
the telephone centre	*il centro telefonico*	eel *chen*·tro te·le·*fo*·nee·ko
the tourist office	*l'ufficio di turismo*	loo·*fee*·cho dee too·*reez*·mo

TIME & DATES

What time is it?	*Che ore sono?*	ke *o*·re *so*·no
It's (8 o'clock).	*Sono (le otto).*	*so*·no (le *o*·to)

in the morning	*di mattina*	dee ma·*tee*·na
in the afternoon	*di pomeriggio*	dee po·me·*ree*·jo
in the evening	*di sera*	dee *se*·ra
When?	*Quando?*	*kwan*·do
today	*oggi*	*o*·jee
tomorrow	*domani*	do·*ma*·nee
yesterday	*ieri*	*ye*·ree

Monday	*lunedì*	loo·ne·*dee*
Tuesday	*martedì*	mar·te·*dee*
Wednesday	*mercoledì*	mer·ko·le·*dee*
Thursday	*giovedì*	jo·ve·*dee*
Friday	*venerdì*	ve·ner·*dee*
Saturday	*sabato*	*sa*·ba·to
Sunday	*domenica*	do·*me*·nee·ka

January	*gennaio*	je·*na*·yo
February	*febbraio*	fe·*bra*·yo
March	*marzo*	*mar*·tso
April	*aprile*	a·*pree*·le
May	*maggio*	*ma*·jo
June	*giugno*	*joo*·nyo
July	*luglio*	*loo*·lyo
August	*agosto*	a·*gos*·to
September	*settembre*	se·*tem*·bre
October	*ottobre*	o·*to*·bre
November	*novembre*	no·*vem*·bre
December	*dicembre*	dee·*chem*·bre

TRANSPORT
Public Transport

What time does the ... leave/ arrive?	*A che ora parte/ arriva ...?*	a ke *o*·ra *par*·te/ a·*ree*·va ...
boat	*la nave*	la *na*·ve
(city) bus	*l'autobus*	*low*·to·boos
(intercity) bus	*il pullman*	eel *pool*·man
plane	*l'aereo*	la·*e*·re·o
train	*il treno*	eel *tre*·no

I'd like a ... ticket.	*Vorrei un biglietto ...*	vo·*ray* oon bee·*lye*·to ...
one-way	*di solo andata*	dee *so*·lo an·*da*·ta
return	*di andata e ritorno*	dee an·*da*·ta e ree·*toor*·no
1st class	*di prima classe*	dee *pree*·ma *kla*·se
2nd class	*di seconda classe*	dee se·*kon*·da *kla*·se

I want to go to ...		
Voglio andare a ...		*vo*·lyo an·*da*·re a ...
The train has been cancelled/delayed.		
Il treno è soppresso/ in ritardo.		eel *tre*·no e so·*pre*·so/ een ree·*tar*·do

the first	*il primo*	eel *pree*·mo
the last	*l'ultimo*	*lool*·tee·mo
platform (two)	*binario (due)*	bee·*na*·ryo (*doo*·e)
ticket office	*biglietteria*	bee·lye·te·*ree*·a
timetable	*orario*	o·*ra*·ryo
train station	*stazione*	sta·*tsyo*·ne

Private Transport

I'd like to hire a/an ...	*Vorrei noleggiare ...*	vo·*ray* no·le·*ja*·re ...
car	*una macchina*	oo·na *ma*·kee·na
4WD	*un fuoristrada*	oon fwo·ree·*stra*·da
motorbike	*una moto*	oo·na *mo*·to
bicycle	*una bici(cletta)*	oo·na bee·*chee*·(*kle*·ta)

Is this the road to ...?		
Questa strada porta a ...?		*kwe*·sta *stra*·da *por*·ta a ...

Where's a service station?		
Dov'è una stazione di servizio?		do·*ve* oo·na sta·*tsyo*·ne dee ser·*vee*·tsyo

ROAD SIGNS

Dare la Precedenza	Give Way
Deviazione	Detour
Divieto di Accesso	No Entry
Divieto di Sorpasso	No Overtaking
Divieto di Sosta	No Parking
Entrata	Entrance
Passo Carrabile	Keep Clear
Pedaggio	Toll
Pericolo	Danger
Rallentare	Slow Down
Senso Unico	One Way
Uscita	Exit

Please fill it up.
Il pieno, per favore.   eel *pye*·no per fa·*vo*·re
I'd like (30) litres.
Vorrei (trenta) litri.   vo·ray (*tren*·ta) *lee*·tree

diesel	*gasolio/diesel*	ga·*zo*·lyo/*dee*·zel
leaded petrol	*benzina con piombo*	ben·*dzee*·na kon *pyom*·bo
unleaded petrol	*benzina senza piombo*	ben·*dzee*·na *sen*·dza *pyom*·bo

(How long) Can I park here?
(Per quanto tempo)   (per *kwan*·to *tem*·po)
Posso parcheggiare qui? po·so par·ke·*ja*·re kwee
Where do I pay?
Dove si paga?   *do*·ve see *pa*·ga
I need a mechanic.
Ho bisogno di un   o bee·*zo*·nyo dee oon
meccanico.   me·*ka*·nee·ko
The car/motorbike has broken down (at ...).
La macchina/moto   la *ma*·kee·na/*mo*·to
si è guastata (a ...). see e gwas·*ta*·ta (a ...)
The car/motorbike won't start.
La macchina/moto   la *ma*·kee·na/*mo*·to
non parte.   non *par*·te
I have a flat tyre.
Ho una gomma bucata. o oo·na *go*·ma boo·*ka*·ta
I've run out of petrol.
Ho esaurito la benzina. o e·zo·*ree*·to la ben·*dzee*·na
I've had an accident.
Ho avuto un incidente. o a·*voo*·to oon een·chee·*den*·te

TRAVEL WITH CHILDREN

Is there a/an ...?	*C'è ...?*	che ...
I need a/an ...	*Ho bisogno di ...*	o bee·*zo*·nyo dee ...
baby change room	*un bagno con fasciatoio*	oon *ba*·nyo kon fa·sha·*to*·yo
car baby seat	*un seggiolino per bambini*	oon se·jo·*lee*·no per bam·*bee*·nee
child-minding service	*un servizio di babysitter*	oon ser·*vee*·tsyo dee be·bee·*see*·ter
children's menu	*un menù per bambini*	oon me·*noo* per bam·*bee*·nee
(disposable) nappies/diapers	*pannolini (usa e getta)*	pa·no·*lee*·nee· (*oo*·sa e *je*·ta)
formula (milk)	*latte in polvere*	*la*·te in *pol*·ve·re
(English-speaking) babysitter	*un/una babysitter (che parli inglese)*	oon/*oo*·na be·bee·*see*·ter (ke *par*·lee een·*gle*·ze)
highchair	*un seggiolone*	oon se·jo·*lo*·ne
potty	*un vasino*	oon va·*zee*·no
stroller	*un passeggino*	oon pa·se·*jee*·no

Do you mind if I breastfeed here?
Le dispiace se allatto le dees·*pya*·che se a·*la*·to
il/la bimbo/a qui?   eel/la *beem*·bo/a kwee
Are children allowed?
I bambini sono   ee bam·*bee*·nee so·no
ammessi?   a·*me*·see

Also available from Lonely Planet:
Italian phrasebook

Glossary

A

abbazia – abbey
aeroporto – airport
affittacamere – rooms for rent (relatively inexpensive and not part of the classification system)
agriturismo – tourist accommodation on farms or country inns
albergo – hotel (up to five stars)
alimentare – grocery shop
alloggio – lodging (relatively inexpensive and not part of the classification system)
alto – high
ambulanza – ambulance
anfiteatro – amphitheatre
appartamento – apartment, flat
arco – arch
autobus – local bus
autostazione – bus station/terminal
autostop – hitching
autostrada – motorway, highway

B

baldacchino – canopy supported by columns over the altar in a church
basilica – a Christian church with a rectangular hall, aisles and an apse at the end
battistero – baptistry
benzina – petrol
biblioteca – library
bicicletta – bicycle
biglietteria – ticket office
biglietto – ticket
binario – platform
borgo – ancient town or village

C

cabinovia – two-seater cable car
calcio – football
camera doppia – room with twin beds
camera matrimoniale – double room with a double bed
camera singola – single room
campanile – bell tower
campeggio – camping
campo – field
cappella – chapel
carabinieri – military police
carnevale – carnival period between Epiphany and Lent
carta d'identità – identity card

carta telefonica – phonecard (also *scheda telefonica*)
cartolina (postale) – postcard
casa – house, home
castello – castle
cattedrale – cathedral
cava – quarry
cena – evening meal
centro – city centre
centro storico – (literally, historical centre) old town
chiaroscuro – (literally, light-dark) the artistic distribution of light and dark areas in a painting
chiesa – church
chiostro – cloister; a covered walkway, which is usually enclosed by columns, around a quadrangle
circo – oval or circular arena
codice fiscale – tax number
colonna – column
comune – equivalent to a municipality or county; town or city council; historically, a commune (self-governing town or city)
contado – district around a major town (the area surrounding Florence was once known as the *contado di Firenze*)
contrada – town district
convalida – ticket stamping machine
coperto – cover charge
corso – main street, avenue
cortile – courtyard
cupola – dome

D

deposito bagagli – left luggage
distributore di benzina – petrol pump (see *stazione di servizio*)
duomo – cathedral

F

ferrovia – train station
festa – festival
fiume – river
fontana – fountain
foro – forum
francobollo – postage stamp
fresco – the painting method in which watercolour paint is applied to wet plaster
funicolare – funicular railway
funivia – cable car

G
gabinetto – toilet, WC
golfo – gulf
grisaille – technique of monochrome painting in shades of grey
grotta – cave
guardia di finanza – fiscal police

H
HI – Hostelling International

I
intarsio – inlaid wood, marble or metal
isola – island

L
lago – lake
largo – (small) square
lavanderia – laundrette
lavasecco – dry-cleaning
lettera – letter
libreria – bookshop
lido – beach
locanda – inn, small hotel (relatively inexpensive and not part of the classification system)
loggia – covered area on the side of a building; porch
lungomare – seafront road; promenade

M
macchia – scrub, bush
mare – sea
mercato – market
monte – mountain, mount
motorino – moped
municipio – town hall

N
navata centrale – nave; central part of a church
navata laterale – aisle of a church
nave – ship
necropoli – (ancient) cemetery, burial site

O
oggetti smarriti – lost property
ostello per la gioventù – youth hostel

P
palazzo – palace; a large building of any type, including an apartment block
parco – park
passaggio ponte – deck class
passeggiata – traditional evening stroll

permesso di lavoro – work permit
permesso di soggiorno – residence permit
piazza – square
piazzale – (large) open square
pietà – (literally, pity or compassion) sculpture, drawing or painting of the dead Christ supported by the Madonna
pinacoteca – art gallery
piscina – pool
poltrona – (literally, armchair) airline-type chair on a ferry
polyptych – altarpiece consisting of more than three panels (see also *triptych*)
ponte – bridge
portico – covered walkway, usually attached to the outside of buildings
porto – port
presepio – nativity scene
profumeria – perfumery
pronto soccorso – first aid
pullman – long distance bus

Q
questura – police station

R
rifugio – mountain hut, Alpine refuge
rocca – fort

S
sagra – festival (usually dedicated to one culinary item or theme)
sala – room in a museum or a gallery
santuario – sanctuary
scalinata – flight of stairs
scavi – excavations
scheda telefonica – see *carta telefonica*
servizio – service fee
spiaggia – beach
spiaggia libera – public beach
stazione – station
stazione di servizio – service/petrol station
stazione marittima – ferry terminal
strada – street, road
superstrada – expressway; highway with divided lanes (but no tolls)

T
tabaccheria/tabaccaio – tobacconist's shop/tobacconist
teatro – theatre
tempio – temple
terme – thermal baths
tesoro – treasury
torre – tower

torrente – stream
traghetto – ferry
triptych – painting or carving over three panels, hinged so that the outer panels fold over the middle one, often used as an altarpiece (see *polyptych*)

U

ufficio postale – post office
ufficio stranieri – (police) foreigners' bureau
uffizi – offices

V

via – street, road
via aerea – air mail
via ferrata – a path with a climbing trail with permanent steel cables to aid walkers, usually in a hilly area
vicoli – alley, alleyway
vigili urbani – traffic police, local police

Behind the Scenes

THE LONELY PLANET STORY

The story begins with a classic travel adventure: Tony and Maureen Wheeler's 1972 journey across Europe and Asia to Australia. There was no useful information about the overland trail then, so Tony and Maureen published the first Lonely Planet guidebook to meet a growing need.

From a kitchen table, Lonely Planet has grown to become the largest independent travel publisher in the world, with offices in Melbourne (Australia), Oakland (USA), London (UK) and Paris (France).

Today Lonely Planet guidebooks cover the globe. There is an ever-growing list of books and information in a variety of media. Some things haven't changed. The main aim is still to make it possible for adventurous travellers to get out there – to explore and better understand the world.

At Lonely Planet we believe travellers can make a positive contribution to the countries they visit – if they respect their host communities and spend their money wisely. Since 1986 a percentage of the income from each book has been donated to aid projects and human rights campaigns, and, more recently, to wildlife conservation.

THIS BOOK

The 1st edition of *Tuscany* was researched and written by Damien Simonis, and the 2nd edition was updated by Neal Bedford with help from Damien Simonis and Imogen Franks. This edition of *Tuscany & Umbria* was written by Josephine Quintero, Rachel Suddart and Richard Watkins. Alex Leviton wrote the chapters on Umbria, a new regional addition to the guide, and also wrote The Arts in Tuscany & Umbria. The Food & Drink chapter was based on Lonely Planet's *World Food Italy* by Matthew Evans and adapted for this title by Michala Green. The boxed text 'Fiestas for Foodies' in the Food & Drink chapter was written by Josephine Quintero and the Health chapter was written by Dr Caroline Evans.

THANKS from the authors

Alex Leviton Many people lent their support to create these chapters. Above all, I want to thank my travelling partners/drivers Cliff Leviton (aka Dad) and Len Amaral (aka Il Muffino) for their company and hill-town manoeuvering abilities, and also Fabiano and Katya for their never-ending helpfulness. My appreciation also goes out to Friar John Kapenda and Stefania in Assisi, Ricci in Spello and Jasmine in Spoleto. Thanks to all the locals that helped me navigate my way around: Adele Bevilacqua, Lois Martin, Pietro Flori, Jane Karnac, Rob Backhouse and Luciano Lucantoni (and thanks to Gene for the gardens). Back home, I couldn't have done this without the support of Jeanette Stokes and the Studio, Betty Fingold, Peter Lynch, Dave Barnes, Daniele Armaleo, Rob Womack and Amy Elliott. And, of course, thanks to Katy Longshore for starting it all.

Josephine Quintero Firstly many thanks to Robin Chapman for his sense of humour, map reading and sharing his expertise in photography and Italian wines. Also a mega-thank you to my Italy-based daughter, Isabel, for the crash-course in Italian and some insiders' tips. Also thanks to the staff of all

the tourist offices, particularly the helpful ladies in Siena, Pisa and Volterra. Thanks also to Michala Green for her compassion and understanding when an early family emergency threatened to throw me off course and for her troop-rallying emails during research.

Rachel Suddart I would like to thank Alessandra Smith from the Italian Tourist Board, Paul Gowen (RAC) for all things road related, Bianca Spiezia from Trenitalia, Loris Servirni from the Italian Embassy in London, Simona Prete from the British Embassy, Enrico Maricanola, Larzia Lo Guzzo, Alex Leviton and Josephine Quintero for taking time out of their busy schedules to add a touch of personal insight. Thanks also to Michala Green for her superb editing skills and all the travellers who took the time to write to LP with tips and suggestions. M, J and P – cheers one and all.

Richard Watkins Many thanks to Alessandra and Lorenzo Gatteschi and Monica Bernardoni, who went out of their way to share their boundless enthusiasm for their home patch of Chianti with me, making my stay there such a memorable one.

Thanks also go to Giuseppe Mazzocchi in Nievole, who introduced me to the simple wonders of Tuscan cuisine, and to Maria Pia Bracali and Dr Andrea Giuliani in Montecatini Terme for their kind hospitality and insight. The Cialde di Montecatini *biscotti* were delicious. I'm also grateful to Giovannella Stianti Mascheroni and her family in Volpaia for a very civilised lunch in pleasant company, not to mention the wonderful wine. Thanks also to Guido Stucchi Prinetti, for taking the time to show me around his family wine cellars in Coltibuono, followed, of course, by the obligatory tasting. Finally, a big thank you goes to staff at tourist offices across Tuscany, especially those in Sansepolcro, Pistoia, Prato, Bibbiana, Florence and Arezzo.

CREDITS

Tuscany & Umbria 3 was commissioned and developed in the UK office by Michala Green and Imogen Franks and the project was managed in Melbourne by Bridget Blair. Series Publishing Manager Susan Rimerman oversaw the redevelopment of the regional guides series and Regional Publishing Manager Katrina Browning steered the development of this title. The editing of the guide was coordinated by Stefanie Di Trocchio with assistance from John Hinman, Kristin Odijk, Fionnuala Twomey, Stephanie Pearson, Michelle Coxall, Tom Smallman, Victoria Harrison, Elizabeth Swan and Meaghan Amor, and the cartography was coordinated by Helen Rowley with assistance from Birgit Jordan, Tony Fankhauser, Simon Tillema and Ray Thomson. Invaluable cartographic assistance was provided by Lachlan Ross, Paul Piaia and Chris LeeAck. Many thanks to Bruce Evans and Mark Griffiths for their support and guidance throughout, and also to Michelle Glynn for compiling the index. The book was laid out by Steven Cann with assistance from David Kemp, the cover designed by Pepi Bluck and the cover artwork prepared by James Hardy. The Language chapter was compiled by Quentin Frayne.

THANKS from Lonely Planet

Many thanks to the travellers who used the last edition and contacted us with helpful hints, advice and interesting anecdotes:

Anja Wolf, Anne-Lyse Tardiva, BJ Chippendale, Bruce Doy, E Thobe, Eleanor May, Fabiola Menchetti, Frances Neal, Frank Barendregt, Geoff Collins, Juergen Klaus, Kathleen Epeldi, Keela Shackell, Kenneth Fan, Kiri Brokenshire, Laura Dias, Libby Crothers, Matthew Knight, Michael Nielsen, Paul Taylor, Peter Roissetter, Reinier Zegwaard, Robert Davis, Timo Kaartinen.

SEND US YOUR FEEDBACK

We love to hear from travellers – your comments keep us on our toes and help make our books better. Our well-travelled team reads every word on what you loved or loathed about this book. Although we cannot reply individually to postal submissions, we always guarantee that your feedback goes straight to the appropriate authors, in time for the next edition. Each person who sends us information is thanked in the next edition – and the most useful submissions are rewarded with a free book.

To send us your updates – and find out about LP events, newsletters and travel news – visit our award-winning website: **www.lonelyplanet.com**.

Note: We may edit, reproduce and incorporate your comments in Lonely Planet products such as guidebooks, websites and digital products, so let us know if you don't want your comments reproduced or your name acknowledged. For a copy of our privacy policy, email privacy@lonelyplanet.com.au.

Index

INDEX

INDEX

000 Map pages
000 Location of colour photographs

000 Map pages
000 Location of colour photographs

INDEX

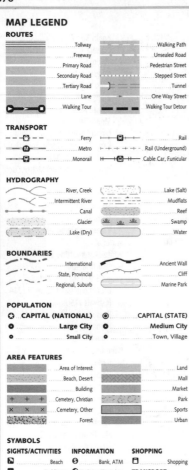

MAP LEGEND

ROUTES

- Tollway
- Freeway
- Primary Road
- Secondary Road
- Tertiary Road
- Lane
- Walking Tour
- Walking Path
- Unsealed Road
- Pedestrian Street
- Stepped Street
- Tunnel
- One Way Street
- Walking Tour Detour

TRANSPORT

- Ferry
- Metro
- Monorail
- Rail
- Rail (Underground)
- Cable Car, Funicular

HYDROGRAPHY

- River, Creek
- Intermittent River
- Canal
- Glacier
- Lake (Dry)
- Lake (Salt)
- Mudflats
- Reef
- Swamp
- Water

BOUNDARIES

- International
- State, Provincial
- Regional, Suburb
- Ancient Wall
- Cliff
- Marine Park

POPULATION

- ⊕ CAPITAL (NATIONAL)
- ● Large City
- ● Small City
- ◉ CAPITAL (STATE)
- ● Medium City
- ● Town, Village

AREA FEATURES

- Area of Interest
- Beach, Desert
- Building
- Cemetery, Christian
- Cemetery, Other
- Forest
- Land
- Mall
- Market
- Park
- Sports
- Urban

SYMBOLS

SIGHTS/ACTIVITIES
- Beach
- Buddhist
- Castle, Fortress
- Christian
- Confucian
- Diving, Snorkeling
- Hindu
- Islamic
- Jain
- Jewish
- Monument
- Museum, Gallery
- Picnic Area
- Point of Interest
- Ruin
- Shinto
- Sikh
- Skiing
- Taoist
- Winery, Vineyard
- Zoo, Bird Sanctuary

INFORMATION
- Bank, ATM
- Embassy/Consulate
- Hospital, Medical
- Information
- Internet Facilities
- Parking Area
- Petrol Station
- Police Station
- Post Office, GPO
- Telephone
- Toilets

SLEEPING
- Sleeping
- Camping

EATING
- Eating

DRINKING
- Drinking
- Café

ENTERTAINMENT
- Entertainment

SHOPPING
- Shopping

TRANSPORT
- Airport, Airfield
- Border Crossing
- Bus Station
- Cycling, Bicycle Path
- General Transport
- Taxi Rank
- Trail Head

GEOGRAPHIC
- Hazard
- Lighthouse
- Lookout
- Mountain, Volcano
- National Park
- Oasis
- Pass, Canyon
- River Flow
- Shelter, Hut
- Spot Height
- Waterfall

NOTE: Not all symbols displayed above appear in this guide.

LONELY PLANET OFFICES

Australia
Head Office
Locked Bag 1, Footscray, Victoria 3011
☎ 03 8379 8000, fax 03 8379 8111
talk2us@lonelyplanet.com.au

USA
150 Linden St, Oakland, CA 94607
☎ 510 893 8555, toll free 800 275 8555
fax 510 893 8572, info@lonelyplanet.com

UK
72–82 Rosebery Ave,
Clerkenwell, London EC1R 4RW
☎ 020 7841 9000, fax 020 7841 9001
go@lonelyplanet.co.uk

France
1 rue du Dahomey, 75011 Paris
☎ 01 55 25 33 00, fax 01 55 25 33 01
bip@lonelyplanet.fr, www.lonelyplanet.fr

Published by Lonely Planet Publications Pty Ltd
ABN 36 005 607 983

© Lonely Planet 2004

© photographers as indicated 2004

Cover photographs by Zefa Images and Lonely Planet Images: House surrounded by cypress trees, Tuscany, Wolfgang Meier (front); Wine cellar near Montalcino, Tuscany, Alan Benson (back). Many of the images in this guide are available for licensing from Lonely Planet Images: www.lonelyplanetimages.com.

All rights reserved. No part of this publication may be copied, stored in a retrieval system, or transmitted in any form by any means, electronic, mechanical, recording or otherwise, except brief extracts for the purpose of review, and no part of this publication may be sold or hired, without the written permission of the publisher.

Printed by SNP SPrint (M) Sdn Bhd
Printed in Malaysia

Lonely Planet and the Lonely Planet logo are trademarks of Lonely Planet and are registered in the US Patent and Trademark Office and in other countries.

Lonely Planet does not allow its name or logo to be appropriated by commercial establishments, such as retailers, restaurants or hotels. Please let us know of any misuses: www.lonelyplanet.com/ip.

Although the authors and Lonely Planet have taken all reasonable care in preparing this book, we make no warranty about the accuracy or completeness of its content and, to the maximum extent permitted, disclaim all liability arising from its use.